1 9 9 7
Guide to Literary Agents

EDITED BY
DONALD M. PRUES

WRITER'S DIGEST BOOKS
CINCINNATI, OHIO

Excerpts from the book *Literary Agents: What They Do, How They Do It, and How to Find and Work With the Right One for You*, by Michael Larsen are reprinted by permission from John Wiley & Sons, Inc. Copyright © 1996 by Michael Larsen.

Excerpts from the book *The Complete Book of Scriptwriting*, revised edition, by J. Michael Straczynski are reprinted by permission from Writer's Digest Books. Copyright © 1996 by J. Michael Straczynski.

Managing Editor, Annuals Department: Constance J. Achabal;
Supervisory Editor: Mark Garvey;
Production Editors: Chantelle Bentley and Tara A. Horton.

International Standard Serial Number
ISSN 1078-6945
International Standard Book Number
0-89879-766-7

Cover illustration: Brenda Grannan

Attention Booksellers: This is an annual directory of F&W Publications. Return deadline for this edition is April 30, 1998.

9. Do you issue an agent-author contract? May I review a specimen copy? And may I review the language of the agency clause that appears in contracts you negotiate for your clients?

10. What is your approach to providing editorial input and career guidance for your clients or for me specifically?

11. How do you keep your clients informed of your activities on their behalf? Do you regularly send them copies of publishers' rejection letters? Do you provide them with submission lists and rejection letters on request? Do you regularly, or upon request, send out updated activity reports?

12. Do you consult with your clients on any and all offers?

13. Some agencies sign subsidiary contracts on behalf of their clients to expedite processing. Do you?

Checklist continued on back endleaf

Contents

From the Editor

A running joke with this friend of mine comes from a slogan spray-painted on an overpass somewhere in Southern California: "Love is a risk. Risk it all." Loving is a major risk, but to reap love's benefits you must risk your all. So it is with securing representation. Think about it: Are you choosing the most suitable prospect? Will you get rejected? What if you initially like each other but have clashing visions for your future? Can you really trust this person? A risk indeed, but without risk there's no opportunity. Turning a risk into an opportunity requires smart decision-making.

This edition of the *Guide* enables you to make smart decisions. Our goal is fourfold: to provide listings with up-to-date information on over 500 agencies, to offer varying perspectives on agenting, to present how the electronic medium is affecting the industry, and to keep you abreast of the agent's evolving role.

We make our wisest decisions when we evaluate all options. Unsure whether to solicit a fee-charging or nonfee-charging agent? Richard Curtis makes a case against reading fees, while Cindy Laufenberg posits the grounds for them. Confused about how to be a good client? Michael Larsen outlines his dream client, while Elizabeth Pomada ruminates on her client from hell. Need advice about the author-agent relationship? Don Maass offers an agent's perspective on how to find (and keep) the right agent, while four authors give their takes on how they found and continue to work with their agents. What if you write scripts? Jack Scagnetti tells what an agent wants from a scriptwriter, while J. Michael Straczynski expands on what a scriptwriter should look for in an agent. Finally, new writers will learn plenty from Sheree Bykofsky's responses to common questions posed to agents, while seasoned scribes can check out Bert Holtje's piece on planning a nonfiction writing career.

Whether a certifiable cybernut or a card-carrying member of the Lead Pencil Club, you should see what Kelly Milner Halls has unearthed about how agents and publishers are handling electronic rights. Along the same electronic vein is Diana Gabaldon's testimonial about how going online helped her find representation and land a subsequent million dollar, three-book contract.

Since fewer publishers are accepting unagented submissions, the agent's status is improving. Jeff Herman and Stephen Pevner reveal how agents are redefining themselves. They're representing clients not just book projects, and relying on strong author support in promoting books. Writers Meredith Maran and Jim Kingston explain how their agents have helped develop their careers through hands-on editing and writer's workshops. Howard Jay Smith expounds upon the rising importance of packaging to script agents, and Janice Pieroni spells out writing assignments available in Hollywood.

It's not coincidental author-agent relationships have been likened to marriages. The best last a lifetime; the worst collapse before a sale is made. While there's no guarantee you'll find that perfect match, you can read away and take time to evaluate your options before plunging into your agent search. But don't spend too much time reading about getting representation without acting on making it happen. After all—as my friend said of that spray-painted slogan on love—why read about it when you can experience it.

Don Prues

Don Prues

How to Use Your *Guide to Literary Agents*

You bought this book because you want to find an agent. Whether you've written a science fiction novel, a midlist nonfiction book, a hardcover coffee table book, a mass market paperback, or the script for a half-hour sitcom or a blockbuster movie, you'll find agents who represent your type of work. The *Guide* is specifically designed to provide you with the information you need to locate the most suitable agent for your work and your writing career.

WHAT'S IN THIS BOOK

The book is divided into literary agents and script agents. Each section begins with feature articles that demystify the agent search by providing perspectives on the author/agent relationship, how an agent spends his time, and the agent's role in publishing. Written by agents and other industry professionals, these pieces come from years of experience and offer pointers to help you succeed in finding a good agent. Before you get to the agent listings, you'll find a brief introduction to each section with tips on approaching agents in that section, and an explanation of the ranking system we use to designate an agency's openness to submissions. Next come the listings, full of specific information from the agencies themselves on what they want and how they want you to present it. Scattered throughout the book are a few "Insider Reports," two- to three-page personalized articles providing tips from interviews with writers and agents.

LITERARY AGENTS

The Literary Agents section is divided into nonfee-charging and fee-charging literary agents. Nonfee-charging agents earn income from commissions made on manuscript sales. Their focus is selling books, and they typically do not offer editing services or promote books that have already been published. These agents tend to be more selective, often preferring to work with established writers and experts in specific fields. While most will accept queries from new writers, a few will not. Check the listing carefully to determine an agent's current needs.

Fee-charging agents charge writers for various services (e.g., reading, critiquing, editing, evaluation, consultation, marketing, etc.) in addition to taking a commission on sales. These agents tend to be more receptive to handling the work of new writers. Some of them charge a reading or handling fee only to cover the additional costs of this openness. Others offer services designed to improve your manuscript or script. But payment for any of these services rarely ensures representation. If you pay for a critique or edit, request references and sample critiques. If you do approach a fee-charging agent, know exactly what the fee will cover—what you'll be getting before any money changes hands.

SCRIPT AGENTS

Script agents are grouped in one section; those who charge fees are indicated with an open box (☐) symbol. Most agents listed are signatories to the Writer's Guild of America. The WGA prohibits its signatories from charging reading fees to WGA members, but most signatories do not charge reading fees as an across-the-board policy. They are, however, allowed to charge for other services, such as critiquing, editing, or marketing.

Many agents who handle books also accept some scripts, and vice versa. Those agents handling at least 10 to 15 percent in another area, and in the case of fee-charging agents either report a sale or are a signatory of the WGA, have a capsulized cross-reference listing in the secondary section as well as a complete listing in their primary area of representation. Those agents handling less than 10 to 15 percent in the secondary area are listed in the Additional Agents at the end of each section.

GETTING THE MOST FROM THIS BOOK

Now that you've got a copy of the book in hand, you're probably tempted to go directly to the listings and start sending out your queries. But if you've spent time writing and polishing your work until it's just right, you owe it to yourself to take the time to find the best agent.

First determine whether you want a nonfee-charging or fee-charging agent. Then narrow your search by either reading through the listings or using the Subject Index at the back of the book. Reading through the listings gives a comprehensive idea of who is out there and what they want, as well as an idea of relative practices from one agency to another. Going to the Subject Index allows you to concentrate only on those listings handling what you write. It is divided into separate sections for nonfee-charging and fee-charging literary agents and script agents. Literary agents are further divided by fiction and nonfiction subject categories, e.g. mainstream literary fiction or self-help nonfiction. Script subjects, such as biography or romantic comedy, are listed alphabetically.

Other indexes in the back of the book will expedite your search. A Geographic Index is for writers who prefer dealing with an agent in their vicinity. The Format Index for Script Agents will help you determine agencies interested in scripts for particular types of TV programs or movies. An Agents Index helps you locate individual agents, and in Client Acceptance Policies agencies are listed according to their policies of working with new or previously published writers.

TARGETING YOUR SUBMISSIONS

Once you have a list of agents who represent your subject matter, go to the individual listings to find those agencies most likely to take an interest in your work. First check the Roman numeral code after each listing to determine how receptive the agency is to submissions. If you are a new, unpublished writer, you might want to concentrate on agencies in the **I-II** range, because they're more receptive to you. Also notice how long the agency has been in business, whether it's a member of the Association of Authors' Representatives or any other organization, such as the Romance Writers of America. Knowing how many clients it represents will give you an idea of what your status might be in the agency, and seeing what percentage of books it represents helps you figure out how much time is spent selling books similar to yours. The beginning of the listing for Columbia Literary Associates offers the following:

COLUMBIA LITERARY ASSOCIATES, INC., (II, IV), 7902 Nottingham Way, Ellicott City MD 21043-6721. (410)465-1595. Fax: Call for number. Contact: Linda Hayes. Estab. 1980. Member of AAR, IACP, RWA, WRW. Represents 40 clients. 10% of clients are new/previously unpublished writers. Specializes in women's fiction (mainstream/genre), commercial nonfiction, especially cookbooks. Currently handles: 40% nonfiction books; 60% novels.

Check under the "Handles" subhead to make sure your agent is in fact interested in your subject matter, and to see how you should tailor your submissions. Does the agent want a query, the first three chapters, plus an outline and SASE? Remember that writing is not "one size fits all" when it comes to representation. Each agency has different submission requirements. Consider only those agents whose interests correspond with your work. You can also check to see the agency's estimated response time.

"Recent Sales" information is extremely helpful as well, as it provides clues to the caliber of publishing contacts the agent has developed. Ask for a list of sales when you query an agent, then check *Books in Print* for the titles. *Literary Market Place* contains thumbnail descriptions of publishers; look up some of the publishers who have bought manuscripts from the prospective agent to get a better idea of who the agent knows and sells to. It's also a good idea to go to your local bookstore or library to see if these titles are making it to the shelves.

A particularly important section in the listings is "Terms," which will let you know the agent's commission, whether a contract is offered and for how long, and what possible expenses you might have to pay (postage, photocopying, etc.). These considerations will be very important once your book is published. While a 15 percent commission is only five percent more than a ten percent commission, that five percent can be a lot of money if your book sells well. The expenses can add up, too, and can be costly if your manuscript never sells. So pay close attention. Consider these terms provided by Lowenstein Associates:

> **Terms:** Agent receives 15% commission on domestic and dramatic sales; 20% on foreign sales. Offers written contract, binding for 2 years, with 60 day cancellation clause. Charges for photocopying, foreign postage, messenger expenses.

"Writer's Conferences" will give you an idea of the agent's professional interests (if he attends a few mystery conferences, for example, he probably has a high interest in mystery writers) and lets you know where you could possibly meet your agent. While it is rude to visit an agent's office, introducing yourself and telling a bit about your work at a conference are expected. Agent Joyce Flaherty lets us know she attends a number of romance conferences:

> **Writer's Conferences:** Often attends Romance Writers of America; Virginia Romance Writers (Williamsburg VA); Moonlight & Magnolias (Atlanta GA).

"Tips" usually consists of direct quotes from agents about what they deem important for readers of the book. Read the comments carefully, because they can reveal even more specifics about what the agent wants, and a quote can tell a bit about the agent's personality. You probably want an agent with a disposition similar to yours. The Nancy Love Literary Agency supplies these tips:

> **Tips:** "Send query, synopsis and first 50 pages. If you don't hear from us, you didn't send SASE. We are looking for westerns and romance—women in jeopardy, suspense, contemporary, historical, some regency and any well-written fiction and nonfiction. Both agents are New York state certified teachers who have taught writing and are published authors."

Finally, when you are confident you have targeted the best agent for your work, submit your material according to the procedures outlined in the listing. For more specific information on approaching agents, see How to Find (and Keep) the Right Agent, in Literary Agents, and Finding a Hollywood Agent for Your Script or Screenplay, in Script Agents. Also check the introductions to each section.

Literary Agents

How to Find (and Keep) the Right Agent

BY DONALD MAASS

Any experienced author will tell you: A good agent can do wonders for your career; a bad agent can really screw it up.

Choosing and working with an agent—the right agent—is clearly important. So where are the courses on this subject? Not in any school I know about. Most authors learn by trial and error. Once that may have been safe enough but in the cold, numbers-driven marketplace of the 1990s early errors can be fatal. I know. My agency gets calls every week from authors whose careers have crashed.

These authors give many reasons for their trouble: low advances, no support, poor covers, orphaned books . . . and on and on. The thing is, these problems are routine. Every author faces them, if not sooner then later. They need not be fatal. One big help is a trusty Sherpa: a good agent. Here's how to find yours.

THE SEARCH AND HOW IT FEELS

If you are a new author, the first thing to realize is that you probably feel anxious. Oh, there may be good moments, particularly when you are writing; moments when you feel confident that your work is equal to—even better than—anything out there.

Then there are the bad moments when you remember what you've heard about the odds, slush piles, agents. Maybe you have heard that it is easier to get a publisher than to get an agent. Or that without an agent no decent publisher will touch you.

The truth, here, is that you have a choice. Of agents. You may not feel like it, but you do. Understanding that, believing it, is your first challenge. To help you, here are three common feelings that block the empowerment I am talking about. See if any apply to you:

1) *This book is my baby!* Sure it is. You conceived it, grew it, disciplined it. You don't want to let it go. You probably also fear that no one will ever fully appreciate its many qualities.

If this is you, you are sharing a common experience. A lingering emotional attachment to your novel is normal. So is its opposite: finishing it and finding that you hate it. Both are flip sides of the same coin. You've invested a lot in this. It matters.

But you can't sell a baby. You can't even be objective about it. And if you can't be

DONALD MAASS *is president of the Donald Maass Literary Agency in New York City. He is the author of 14 pseudonymous novels and of the book* The Career Novelist, *published by Heinemann in June 1996. He travels widely to writers' conferences, where he conducts seminars for new and mid-career authors called "Breaking In" and "Breaking Out."*

objective about your novel, then how will you be able to evaluate what you hear about it from agents?

2) *What does it matter? No one's going to want it anyway.* You know the score. You are no fool. If you are extremely lucky you might land a decent agent but the odds are against it, right?

If this describes you, you are also having a common experience. Offering your work in the marketplace is risky. The chances of getting hurt—even humiliated—are high. The easiest way to lessen the pain of rejection is to plan for it in advance. The problem with this defense mechanism is that it leads authors to feel that the process is out of their hands. Why discriminate? Why push? Why feel anything but shock and joy when some randomly-chosen agent finally says "yes." No reason. And so begins many a woeful and tragic publishing tale.

3) *I've got to get my book in front of publishers—fast!* My premise/setting/theme is hot right now. If I don't publish this book soon, then someone else may beat me to the punch. Worse, my moment may have passed. My window of opportunity will be closed.

If this is you, please relax. It is a rare book that is truly as hot as today's headlines. And in fact, being highly topical may not be a plus. One year is the average time it takes to go from edited manuscript to finished book. Do you recall what was on the front pages exactly one year ago? I don't, either. A truly topical book that seems hot today is likely to be ice cold when it finally hits the shelves in a year's time.

That is particularly true of fiction. Now, of course fiction can be *of* its time—certainly it can become dated—but if it is of the immediate moment then its chances of success are slim.

Where does this sense of urgency that I am talking about come from? Probably from the fear that goes with beginning a scary task. One way to cope with such a task is to put it off. Another is to rush. Quite often when I respond positively to a query letter, I get back a hurried note: "Disk crashed. I'll send the manuscript next week." Or: "Final revisions in progress. You'll have it in a month."

Final revisions? Probably that means "first draft." Either way, this author rushed. He wrote to me before his book was ready. Why? He was under-confident, anxious for validation. He could not wait to find out if I would be interested. As a result, the manuscript finally served up to me will probably be undercooked.

That's a shame, because all that stuff about the odds is correct. The odds *are* long. To calm these fears and avoid mistakes let's break the agent hunt into its components and find out what really works.

WHEN TO LOOK

First ask, "Do I need to look at all?" That is, as a new author do you really need an agent? Opinions differ. Most professional authors have agents, but it is often said that first timers will not get a noticeably better deal if they are represented.

That is true to a point. With few exceptions advances for first books are low. An agent may get you a few thousand dollars more up front, yes, but why pay a commission when royalties eventually close the gap anyway? What's the difference?

The difference shows in a couple of ways. First, because many major publishers will not read unagented manuscripts, an agent can open doors. Even more important, a savvy agent who knows individual editors' tastes and publishing houses' relative strengths can be an effective matchmaker, pairing your work with the company best able to make that work a success.

There are also contracts to consider: Advance levels, royalty rates, copyright, options and control of subsidiary rights are all vital issues in which a new author can benefit from an agent's expertise. Take, for instance, the right to publish your novel in German.

The unagented author typically cedes control to his publisher, who typically keeps 50 percent of the proceeds from licensing this right. On a first novel deal, most agents like to retain control. The cost to the author thus drops to 20 or 25 percent. More money for you.

How much more? Maybe not much but, hey, money is money. In addition, there's the matter of marketing. One first novel in a catalog of hundreds of books is not likely to get much help from its publisher. To an agent small subsidiary rights sales matter more.

Okay, let's assume you're convinced. When should you approach agents? Before you start to write? After you've sold a few articles or short stories? When you've finished your first manuscript? When you've got a publisher interested in it, perhaps even an offer on the table?

Beginning with the last of those options, it should be obvious that approaching agents with an offer in hand is going to produce powerful results. Agents are drawn to commissions like bears to honey. If this is your situation, expect to hear some highly flattering noise about your writing.

But how deep is that enthusiasm? To find out you will have to listen hard and cut through much self-serving PR. It is wise to begin this scenario with a strong idea of what you want in an agent.

Most authors do not wait so long. They want the security, ease and status of representation as soon as possible. How soon is realistic? Certainly not before there is a book to sell. Article and story sales help attract attention, but they are not in-and-of themselves a guarantee that a writer can produce a saleable manuscript.

For the first-time author, having a finished manuscript is nearly always essential. That is particularly true of first novels. Exceptions may occur in the case of celebrities (whose value to publishers, after all, is not their writing ability), or with acknowledged authorities whose nonfiction will sell because of their message, insight, advice or expert status.

So, finish your book. No problem, right? Then again, how do you know when your book is *really* finished? That's a tough call. Even experienced authors may find it difficult to decide.

I have no magic formula to offer, but I can say this: The anxious desire for an agent's validation is in no way connected to whether or not your book is finally ready. Believe me, too many authors contact me as soon as their first draft is near completion. And I will bet that you can guess the most common result of their premature queries. (Yeah, you got it.)

HOW TO CONNECT

How to approach an agent? How do you approach anyone? You can do it in person, on the phone, by letter, by fax, by e-mail. Books like this one tell you how individual agents prefer to be pitched, but really there are no absolute rules except common sense.

Speaking of common sense, consider how you introduce yourself to someone at a party: Unless you are uncommonly bold, or insensitive, I'll bet you do not march up to total strangers and announce, "Greetings! Here's why you are dying to be my friend. . . ."

A pushy manner is off-putting. Amazingly, it is also the most common tone in query letters. I'm not kidding! You'd be astonished how often I receive letters that sound something like this:

Dear Mr. Maass:
    This is your lucky day! I have carefully analyzed the techniques of such best-

selling authors such as Stephen King, Jeffrey Archer and John Grisham. As a result I can guarantee you that my terrifying apocalyptic thriller, *Gene Poolution*, is a slam-bang page turner that no reader will be able to put down.

In fact, 20 test readers have already confirmed *Gene Poolution* was the most frightening reading experience of their lives. Ripped right out of today's headlines, this novel cannot miss. Believe me, you will long remember the day when you rushed to the phone to request my manuscript, etc.

This hard sell disappoints most in that it insists upon making up my mind for me. Test readers? I am sure they genuinely loved his novel, but unless they work in publishing they are unlikely to be able to judge accurately its potential. (And frankly I already have my qualms: DNA-doom thrillers are quite difficult to pull off, Michael Crichton notwithstanding.)

So, if the hard sell is no fun at parties or in query letters, why do authors fall back on it? Insecurity is one big reason, I believe. Another is the advice that authors too often find in writers' magazines; articles that say things like: *You've got to sell yourself! You must show that you understand the market! Get their attention and don't let it go!*

Don't get me wrong: I like authors who know what they have got. Spelling that out for me briefly and knowledgeably is not pushy. It is a plus. But that is far different than the hard sell.

However you approach an agent—in person, by phone, by letter—a relaxed-but-business-like approach is probably the best. The most effective pitches I get start with an icebreaker: "I notice that you represent Anne Perry, whose mysteries I admire." Or, "My friend Dean Koontz gave me your name." Or even, "I believe that fans of Patrick O'Brien will enjoy my work, too."

It is easy to overdo comparisons like that last one, but you see my point: There's a real person on the other side of your pitch, and he is not a used-car salesman. He (or she) is a book person. Treat him like a sensitive, intelligent publishing professional and you will be far ahead of the game.

Now, let's get specific. *Should you drop by?* Common sense: Meetings take time, and besides what is there to talk about until I have read your writing? *Should you phone?* Common sense: There is not much point unless you have an "in," such as an introduction from a professional to use. *Should you fax?* Common sense: since a fax arrives without a reply envelope it is less likely to receive a response than a traditional snail-mail query with SASE. *Should you write?* Common sense: You are a writer. Do I really have to say more than that?

More specific still: *Should you send an outline with your query?* Common sense: If a listing suggests it, yes. If not then it depends on whether you can write an effective synopsis. If so, go for it. If not, stick with a tantalizing capsule description in your letter. *Should you go ahead and send the manuscript?* Common sense: It takes much longer to read a book than a letter. Do you really want your novel to languish on a slush pile, miles behind the manuscripts that were requested?

Protocol questions: *Is it okay to write/submit to more than one agent at a time?* Yes, but it is also polite to let your prospects know what you are doing. Besides, if they know the heat is on they may get back to you more quickly. *What if an agent demands to have my novel exclusively?* Well, it is up to you. Are you significantly more interested in that agent than in others? What if that agent says "yes?" Will you really keep looking?

SMART SHOPPERS

Are you the kind of shopper who reads *Consumer Reports?* Probably not when selecting shoelaces, but I'll bet you do a bit of research when buying a big-ticket item like a car. Well, guess what? Perhaps the most expensive service you will ever purchase will be provided by your literary agent. When your writing finally earns you a living, you will be paying that professional many thousands of dollars per year, probably more than your doctor or lawyer (unless you are very unlucky).

So, be a smart shopper. Do your homework. This book is a good place to start, but what criteria matter most? The answer will be slightly different for everyone, but there are a few factors that everyone should consider. Do your prospects have experience in your field? Heck, do they have experience, period? Start-up agents may not be bad—indeed, some are the stars of tomorrow—but many do not last, and some so-called agents are not really agents at all. A good indicator of experience and integrity is membership in the Association of Authors' Representatives (AAR).

Beyond that, you need to begin to discern whether your prospects would be a good match for you. Sourcebook entries are helpful here, but they do not necessarily convey an agent's strengths and weaknesses, or their background, approach to marketing, business style, negotiating tactics, total results for all clients, follow through . . . all the factors that will, over time, spell success or failure for this most important relationship.

If an agent is interested in representing you, ask for introductions to some of her clients, especially those who are at your stage of career. Of course, satisfied clients will generally sing their agents' praises. The most telling information you receive will, in the end, come from your own discussions with your prospective agents.

WHAT TO ASK AGENTS

I hope you enjoy your agent search. For me it is a fascinating dance. Eventually, though, all authors hope to hear the following: "I've read your manuscript and I love it. I want to represent you." The usual response is delirious joy. Nothing wrong with that, but do take a moment to ask some important questions.

Most urgent question? Not *"How much do you charge?"* but *"What do you think of my book?"* The answer to that one will tell you volumes about the experience you are about to have.

The first thing you want from the answer is enthusiasm. For agents, handling new authors often means taking a loss. Commissions will not necessarily cover the overhead involved in the first few books. Plus, it is a rough road. It can take years to swing that first sale. Even after that, problems may abound.

What sustains an agent through that? I will tell you: passion. By that I mean an irrational faith in a writer's future or at least the conviction that his writing is worthy, even brilliant. You must have that. Without it you are already sunk.

The second thing you need from the answer is a sense of your prospective agent's editorial vocabulary and approach. *Editorial?* Yes. In all likelihood, your agent is going to serve as your first and most long-standing editor. Surprised? I am, too. I used to think that editors edited and agents sold. That's still true, mostly, but as corporate demands sponge up more and more of editors' time the truth is that editorial functions are shifting increasingly to agents. Ask your fellow authors.

So, what is good editorial advice? That depends. If you are a facile, outline-handy, trend-watching sort of author then you probably want an agent to tell you how to tailor your writing to what's hot, what's selling. If, however, you are a slow, style-conscious, trend-ignoring type of author then you probably want an agent who nurtures your own unique voice.

After that comes another crucial question: *What plans do you have for marketing my work?* The answer had better be detailed and logical. Today there are many more strategies to choose from than in years past. For instance, once the best possible hardcover deal was always the top objective, not so anymore. Hard/soft deals with large commercial houses are far smarter for many authors. Certain others are best served by original paperback publication. What is the best plan for you? And why? Ask.

Okay, now you may ask *"How much do you charge?"* Fifteen percent on domestic revenues has become standard. A trickier issue is whether expenses are charged on top of that, and if so which? Certainly outside legal, public relations and accounting advice need not be covered by commissions. But policies vary widely on things like photocopying, messengers, phone charges, overseas postage and such. If charged, must you front some money or will the agent foot it? Do you get advance clearance?

Next vital question: *Are you a member of the AAR?* There is more information on that subject elsewhere in this book, read it.

Keep going: *How many people work at your company? How many are agents? Who will actually handle my work? How are overseas sales and movie/TV sales accomplished? Will you consult with me before closing every deal? Will you ever sign agreements (especially subsidiary rights agreements) on my behalf?*

Still more: *Are you incorporated? When you receive money for me, how quickly will you pay out my share? Will you issue a 1099 tax form at the end of the year? What happens if you die or are incapacitated? How will I receive monies due to me?*

Aren't you glad you are asking these questions now? There's one more biggie, so big that it deserves a section of its own.

THE AGENCY AGREEMENT

I use the simplest and most trusting form of contract between me and my clients: a handshake. I do this because unless there is a high level of mutual respect involved I do not feel that we have a useful working relationship. Also, if my clients are unhappy I feel they should be free to leave at any time.

Not everyone is comfortable with that, however. Most agencies have written agreements between themselves and their clients. Review yours before you sign it. What follows is a discussion of some of the most common provisions you will come across:

Commissions. Naturally commission rates are set out for domestic sales, movie/TV sales, overseas sales, special sales. Expenses to be charged and clearance procedures should also be spelled out.

Works covered. Will your agent handle everything you write, down to essays you dash off for your industry trade journal? Or will only specific work be handled? You may want representation only on a per-project basis. If so, establish that in writing.

Duration. Most agency agreements lock you in for a certain length of time. Two years is typical. After that, the agreement is renewed by mutual consent. A highly important aspect of duration is what happens to unsold rights after termination. Does your agent retain control? If so, for how long? Believe me, when agents and authors split, no issue causes more grief than this one. Work out something equitable in advance.

For contracts still in force upon termination (that is, for books still in print and earning) the agent generally continues to receive funds, and his commission, as long as earnings continue. The same holds true for ongoing subsidiary rights income, whether the rights were sold by the agent or by the publisher.

One situation that few agency agreements cover is this one: Your agent submits a project to a publisher, but while it is still under consideration you and your agent split. Now an offer appears but who negotiates the deal and collects the commission, your old agent or your new agent? That's a tricky one, huh?

Generally ad hoc arrangements are made in these cases. Perhaps the new agent approves the deal, but does not get a commission. Or perhaps the new agent does the deal and splits the commission with the old agent. Whatever the arrangement, be sure you feel comfortable with the way the deal will be handled.

WORKING WITH YOUR AGENT

Phew! You made it! Now you and your agent are off and running. What now? How much feedback can you expect? How often should you call?

If you have chosen well, you are probably paired with an agent whose experience, temperament and business style are well suited to your needs. But even author-agent relationships have a honeymoon; after that comes the bumpy breaking-in period.

The important thing here is to accurately identify what you need and communicate it clearly to your agent. That is not always easy. It can be tough to separate, say, a need for reporting on submissions from feelings of anxiety if a novel is not selling. Here you must know yourself and your agent. Be patient.

One thing that helps, I find, is a career plan. You know that old job interview ploy, "Where do you want to be in five years?" That is a good question for you and your agent to ask. What are your career goals? How will you get there? What specific steps are needed?

A career plan is especially important if you intend to, or already, write more than one type of book. Maintaining momentum and growing an audience can be tricky when one's focus is split. On the other hand, career planning can be difficult for organic writers—those whose do not closely outline their work in advance, but instead discover its shape and substance as they write. For such writers, the best plan may simply be to find a supportive publisher and stick with that house.

Whatever its particulars, I find that a career plan gives both me and my clients a way to measure progress. In fact, recently I have begun making up advance *marketing* plans for individual projects. Together with new clients I choose potential publishers. We then follow our progress through the list, adjusting as circumstances change. A sense of participation is healthy.

About calling . . . no one likes to be a pest, but at the same time waiting for news can be depressing. How often should you call? I advise my clients to phone any time they feel a need for information. Some call every few days. A few call twice a year.

As you go forward, you will probably come to rely more and more on your agent for advice and counsel. Some of this is mere "hand-holding" while waiting for offers, contracts, checks. However, some of the comments you hear may change the way you write. Some may even change the entire direction of your career.

Given clear goals, hard work, good communication and a bit of luck, the author-agent relationship is usually happy and mutually profitable. Sometimes, though, it does not work out so well. I hate to drop clients. On occasion they leave, and that hurts too.

MOVING ON

How do you know when it is time to leave your agent? Boy, that is a tough one. Having taken over many authors from other agencies I can tell you that the level of problems authors experience varies. Some problems are slight, but of long standing. Others are so sudden and big that it boggles the mind.

One factor that remains constant, though, is this: Leaving your agent sheds light on your own shortcomings as well as your agent's. Smart authors use this opportunity to examine themselves and their writing.

But back to the first question: How do you know? Breakdown of communication is one warning sign. Do your calls go unreturned? Is there no follow-through on routine requests? If so, examine the situation. Are you being unreasonable? Are there differences or disagreements causing bad feelings?

Lack of progress is another worry, but again it is wise to study the situation before making any moves. Say that your advances have hit a plateau: Is this your agent's fault or yours? Maybe your *writing* has hit a plateau. If your sales are not growing either and your publisher is not at fault, well . . . perhaps it is time to take an objective look at your work.

Certainly there are problems for which only your agent is to blame. Blown deals. Lost manuscripts. Misunderstandings with your publisher. That kind of thing is just bad business. Even here, though, I advise caution: Are there mitigating circumstances? Did your agent's spouse recently die? Is he facing surgery?

Once you do decide to move on, try to maintain a business-like demeanor. You will thank yourself later. Dignity is a precious possession.

And when you hook up with your new agent? Well, you begin a new honeymoon. And soon thereafter, the bumpy part. But if you have taken my advice you will have learned a lot about yourself during the divorce. And that self-knowledge should serve you well as you stride toward new levels of success.

THE ULTIMATE TRANSACTION

I hope that all this talk of agents has left you feeling empowered. There is, however, one relationship that is more important to an author's career than any other: His relationship with his readers.

When you publish a book you invite readers into your world. If you have written it well, they will probably return. Think of it as opening a store: Your readers are your repeat customers. They are the foundation under your career. Give them good value, reopen your store on a reliable schedule, and they will eventually make you successful beyond your dreams.

So, how much effort should you put into your search for an agent? Plenty, but think about this: Your query letter gets you, perhaps, one minute of an agent's attention. The cover on your book gets, maybe, a few seconds from a buyer for a bookstore chain. But once that book is sold to a customer, taken home and opened . . . ah! You have hours upon hours in which to lure that reader into your world, then take him on a ride he will never forget.

The Seven Most Common Questions Posed To Agents

BY SHEREE BYKOFSKY

1. What is a typical agent's day like? (or Why shouldn't I call an agent on the phone?)

On a typical day, I receive a filled mail bag, which might include 50 queries, several requested manuscripts, rejections from publishers, forms to fill out, contracts, royalty statements and, thankfully, a check or two. Each of these transmissions must be read, dealt with in some way, or delegated. Which queries do I wish to pursue? Which requested manuscripts do I think I can sell? Which forms must be dealt with today? Which contracts negotiated? Which authors must I communicate with? Should I write them letters or call?

Meanwhile, I must make several phone calls. I must call publishers to excite them about the book I am selling today. Then I must write to them and send them the proposal or manuscript. Many publishers I call are not immediately available, and so I leave a message for them to return my call. I also need to speak with certain authors. One of them did not get the proper promotional support from the publisher. Another has a question about a royalty statement. Another saw books in the store before getting his author copies. Another is excited about her review in *The New York Times*. Another has a question about the contract. I have to speak to all of them. Sometimes I must take action as a result of these calls—such as calling or writing to their publishers—and then get back to them.

Also, I am busy developing proposals with authors who have projects I wish to represent. It's necessary to do some bookkeeping, to oversee workers, to go to the bank, and almost every day I have a lunch with a publisher and a professional meeting at night. Sometimes one of my out-of-town authors is in New York and wants to come by for a quick visit. At the same time, the phone is ringing constantly with people returning my calls and calling with reasons of their own.

Once you assimilate this vision, you'll understand that it is impossible to be a good agent and still take calls from prospective authors who call to say, "I met you at a conference six months ago and am terribly sorry that I waited this long to send you my manuscript, a heart-wrenching autobiography called WHY IS IT SO HARD TO GET PUBLISHED? I know that you've been eagerly expecting it, but I caught the flu from my cousin Doris, and it was pretty nasty. Anyway, I'm sending it tomorrow by Express Mail and you should have it by Wednesday. It was only seen by Joe Smith of St. Martin's who is my cousin's brother-in-law (actually, he's only in the mailroom), but he says that St. Martin's will only consider agented manuscripts, so please let me know

For over five years **SHEREE BYKOFSKY** *has led her own New York-based literary agency, Sheree Bykofsky Associates, Inc., which represents adult commercial and literary fiction and all areas of nonfiction. She is the author of seven books and a member of both the American Society of Journalists and Authors and the Association of Authors' Representatives.*

when you receive it, and if you don't like it, I want to know why. I'll call you on Thursday to make sure you received it, and I'll call you on Friday to find out what you thought of it."

Please forgive the sarcasm, but every day brings several calls that are not very different from this composite, and because I believe in niceness in business, I answer my own phone whenever possible and take and return nearly every call. That's why you can usually make the best impression by sending a professional query with a self-addressed stamped envelope concisely stating everything that needs stating. A good agent is equipped to deal with your query by mail in a timely manner.

Once an agent has expressed interest in representing you, and certainly after the agent sends you a contract, you should expect to have reasonable phone access.

2. Can I send my manuscript to more than one agent at a time?

After researching qualified agents whom you think might be compatible with your material, it is reasonable to send a short query letter and SASE to any number of agents. Although, everyone likes to feel special, and so when you tell an agent that she is the only one seeing a particular query, you are very likely to get special attention. It is when you are sending a large volume of material such as a long proposal or an entire manuscript that many agents, like myself, require an exclusive period to decide whether they wish to represent you. Some agents do not require that your long manuscript be exclusive, but this is not necessarily to your advantage. Often such nonexclusive submissions will sit for months or forever on such agents' over-piled desktops.

I, on the other hand, feel I have devised a fair solution that works for me and the author. When I see a query I like, I call the author and ask for an exclusive three- or four-week period to decide about representation. This way authors know that if it is with me alone for three weeks, they will have an answer—and sometimes I can provide an answer even sooner. Because I make this promise and am devoted to keeping it, I'm very selective about the number of manuscripts I request. I understand that if it turns out that I am incompatible with the author, we may not actually end up working together, and that would be fine, albeit a pity (and unlikely). The only situation I wish to avoid is reading the entire manuscript, loving it, telling the author I want to represent her and having her tell me she is going with another qualified agent. I want authors to choose me first; then I'll choose them back.

Incidentally, when I request an exclusive, I also request that the author tell me in writing if the manuscript has been to publishers, and if it has, to whom and what they said. Furthermore, I always request a SASE with which to respond.

3. Do I need to write a book proposal and what goes into a good one?

You usually need to write a book proposal to sell a nonfiction book in progress or completed manuscript. Sometimes there are exceptions such as in the case of creative narrative nonfiction, which is sometimes treated more like fiction in that you usually need to have written the entire book before selling it.

All good nonfiction book proposals should contain the following, and query letters should contain (concisely) the main points and the most compelling highlights:

    I. COVER PAGE WITH GREAT TITLE, AUTHOR, AGENT'S NAME AND ADDRESS (in most cases, professional authors don't register the copyright or state name; they know it is not beneficial to appear paranoid).

    II. THREE- TO FIVE-PAGE PITCH

        1) Repeat title.

        2) Describe your book in one sentence.

        3) Elaborate on that in a paragraph or two. Describe the contents of your book

enticingly and thoroughly.

4) Who is the audience? How big is the audience? Who will actually walk into the bookstore or library and request this book?

5) Where will they buy it besides bookstores? Catalogs? Gift stores? Hospitals? Hardware stores?

6) What important, enticing and special points and features does this book have?

7) What will the book look like as you see it, ideally? Size? Number of pages? Number of entries? Number of essays?

8) What are your sources? How do you intend to do your research?

9) Do you consider the book humorous, touching, poignant? Attribute some descriptive adjectives.

10) Why are you the perfect author to write this book? Include your writing experience, educational experience, and any other special experience that makes you uniquely qualified to write this book.

11) Take on the competition. Visit a bookstore and imagine where on the shelf your book will go (or could go). Mention some titles that your book will go near. How is your book different? How is your book better? Ask the bookstore owner or manager how these other books are selling and work that information into the proposal in a way that will cast your book in the best light.

12) Try to find statistics to support your arguments.

13) Are there special times of the year when this book can be promoted in a special way?

14) Are you a promotable author? Do you and can you tour or speak in public? Would it help to promote the book on tour (i.e., wouldn't be relevant if you're writing a dictionary, for example)? Do you have other promotion ideas (that are not outlandish)? Do you have famous friends who will read and supply a quote for your book? Have you been on television or radio? Do you have contacts who will help sell your book?

15) What is your style? Work it in somewhere. What famous authors, if any, do you think your style can be compared to?

16) Anything else you think is relevant?

III. TABLE OF CONTENTS

IV. REPRESENTATIVE AND INTERESTING SAMPLE CHAPTER/S OR ENTRIES

V. ATTACHMENTS, IF ANY, SUCH AS RECENT MAJOR MAGAZINE ARTICLES ABOUT THE TOPIC OR BY THE AUTHOR

There is an excellent book about writing proposals. I highly recommend Michael Larsen's *How to Write a Book Proposal.*

4. What can I expect from my agent in terms of correspondence, phone calls and information?

Agents appreciate authors who respect their time and do not call when it is completely unnecessary or when a note or fax will do. That said, I believe strongly that it is an author's right to receive copies of all correspondence between the agent and the publisher pertaining to the book—and in a timely fashion. When I receive a rejection letter from a publisher, I immediately have it copied and sent to the author. This not only keeps the author informed about who is seeing his manuscript but it also allows the author to see if the rejections have a common theme, which might mean the proposal or manuscript needs further work. When an editor calls to express interest or make an offer, I immediately call the author. When an editor sends a contract, the author sees it before I negotiate so I can answer any questions and present a united front to the publisher. When royalty statements and other correspondence arrive, they are immediately examined and copied and sent to authors.

I remain available to the author to answer all questions and to troubleshoot in case there are problems between the publisher and the author. I also try to lend moral support and offer publicity and marketing suggestions to both the author and the publisher. Sometimes the author has a favorite publisher to whom she wants the manuscript sent. I always make every effort to comply with such requests.

5. How do agents sell books? or What happens after I have given you an acceptable proposal or manuscript?

When I am ready to start submitting a proposal or a manuscript to a publisher, the first thing I do is write a compelling submission letter and think about a concise but irresistible phone pitch. Then I make a list of all the publishers I think would like the project. Next, I call them all and pitch the pitch. I then send the material, telling each publisher that it is with other publishers, and I ask for a response by a particular date, approximately three or four weeks in the future. If several publishers are interested, I set an auction date and hold an auction. If only one publisher is interested, I try to negotiate a fair contract, which includes a reasonable advance against royalties.

6. Is it important to have a New York agent?

As a New York agent, I would like to say yes, but the answer is no. It is true that New York agents benefit from easy access to New York publishers, but with faxes and phones and e-mail, and frequent visits, out-of-town agents have found ways to maintain close ties with publishers in New York and all over the world. I am friends with some of the best agents in the world who are in California, and I can tell you that I see them more frequently than I do some of my neighbors. Just be sure to thoroughly research your potential agents, no matter where they're located.

7. Is it common for agencies to refer potential clients (or anyone, for that matter) to editing companies, and do editing companies normally charge fees into the thousands to do a critique or line-by-line edit?

It does happen that agents refer writers to independent editors when the book shows promise but is not representable in its current form. When I make such a referral, I make it clear that I make no representations about the editors, and I do not receive any commission from them. In fact, I don't have a clue what they charge and want to remain in the dark about it. If and when the author and editor put together a revised proposal they are satisfied with, I hope they will ask me again to consider it for representation, but no one is under any obligation. It is just a courtesy. If other agents make arrangements other than what I have just described, I am unaware of it, and I can't say whether I would approve of them unless I studied the situation.

Writer to Writer: The Author-Agent Alliance

BY DON PRUES

Whenever we approach something new we typically find ourselves both brimming with curiosity and shaken by anxiety. Because we are uncertain about what we are getting into, we try to uncover as much as possible about this new endeavor. We gather information from a variety of sources—newspapers, magazines, books, the Internet—hoping to learn all we can before immersing ourselves in this foreign world. Checking these sources helps, of course, but what we really want to do is talk with those who've gone through it—ask them what it's like, what to expect, and a myriad of other related questions.

The following writers have obtained what you desire: a good agent. They also have their names attached to at least one dustjacket—because they found agents who have successfully sold their manuscripts to publishers. So how did they find their agents? What does the author-agent relationship demand? What do writers expect from agents? What do agents expect from writers? Listen in as four writers detail the ins and outs of their experiences with their agents, providing you some inkling of what you might encounter as you verge upon your own author-agent alliance.

Anna Tuttle Villegas has been writing and publishing short stories since her graduation from Stanford over 20 years ago. She teaches literature and composition in the Central Valley of California, where she lives with her 16-year-old daughter. Her first novel, *All We Know of Heaven*, was published by St. Martin's Press in 1995. Her agent is Doris Michaels of the Doris S. Michaels Literary Agency, Inc.

Carol Turkington is a freelance writer specializing in psychology, medicine, and women's issues. She's published in numerous national magazines and her books include *No Holds Barred: The Strange Life of John E. du Pont* (Turner, 1996); *Reflections of Working Women* (McGraw Hill, 1996); *Making the Prozac Decision: A Guide to Antidepressants* (coauthor) (Lowell House, 1995), and a dozen other titles. She is also a nonfiction instructor for the Writer's Digest School. Her agent is Bert Holtje of James Peter Associates, Inc.

Photo by Larry Laszlo

Terry Bisson is a bestselling science fiction author and contributor to *Playboy*. His short story collection *Bears Discover Fire and Other Stories* (Tor, 1993) won both Hugo and Nebula Awards. His most recent novel, *Pirates of the Universe*, is available from Tor Books. He also recently completed *St. Liebowitz and the Wild Horse Woman* (Bantam, Fall 1997), the long-awaited sequel to Walter M. Miller's *Canticle for Liebowitz*. His agent is Susan Protter of the Susan Ann Protter Literary Agent agency.

Photo by Shale Aaron

Antonya Nelson is the author of three short story collections and two novels. Her novel *Talking in Bed* (Houghton Mifflin, 1996) won the 1996 Heartland Award and *Nobody's Girl* was just published by Scribner. She teaches at New Mexico State University and in the Warren Wilson MFA program. She is married to the writer Robert Boswell. Her agent is Bonnie Nadell of Frederick Hill Associates.

How did you come to writing and what do you write?

Villegas: I've been teaching English at the college level for 20 years, publishing short stories and essays in literary magazines and journals. In 1994, inspired by the spectacular success of Robert Waller's book (*The Bridges of Madison County*), I told myself that if I ever wanted to earn the freedom to write fulltime, I'd better get working on a novel. *All We Know of Heaven* is the result of some serious midlife decision-making, a bit of risk-taking, and a lot of love.

Nelson: I'd always been an avid reader and knew I wanted to write fiction. So I went to graduate school to get my MFA in Creative Writing, during which time I had a story accepted and published by *Mademoiselle*. That's really when things started for me.

Turkington: I graduated with a degree in journalism from Penn State, worked in newspapers for three years and didn't like it, so I went to Duke Medical Center where I was a medical writer for three years. Then I went to the American Psychological Association Newsletter and covered clinical and developmental psychology for five years. I loved medical writing and psychology and made a lot of contacts, so I decided to freelance in those areas.

Bisson: I worked for ten years in and around publishing as an editor and copywriter. And I worked in the magazine business. I do a lot of book doctoring and editing and promotional and publicity stuff for publishers, in addition to writing my own fiction.

How did you find your agent?

Turkington: I was freelancing and found it very frustrating. After three or four years I heard about Bert Holtje. I sent him a note to see if we could work together. I was particularly interested in him because he had an advanced degree in psychology. And because he belonged to the APA (American Psychological Association), he was familiar with my work. He brought a project to me and I've been working with him ever since. That was seven years ago.

Nelson: Bonnie is actually my second agent. When I was in graduate school, a professor gave me the name of her agent and he agreed to take me on to sell my thesis. It wasn't a really strong book, and I wasn't high on the agent's list of priorities. Later, when I finally had a strong collection of stories, I turned to Bonnie. I found her through a friend of mine from graduate school, David Foster Wallace, who was a client of hers and spoke highly of her. She liked my stories and began sending them out to commercial publishers. That year I won the Flannery O'Connor Award for my collection called *The Expendables*. Bonnie sold Avon the paperback rights to it and then Morrow had the first refusal on my next book, *In the Land of Men*, which they bought. When I finished my third book, we decided to go for a two-book deal. So Bonnie held an auction and I ended up with Houghton Mifflin.

Villegas: As I was writing my novel, I wanted to know if it was market-worthy. I sent out probably 30 letters in a 6-month period, getting some interest from agents asking for chapters. Although none of these first queries got me a contract, I did get a solid sense that the novel's concept was appealing. One agent wrote back saying "no thanks," but she offered me the name and address of a new agency: the Doris S. Michaels Literary Agency in New York. I queried Doris, who asked for sample chapters and then the whole manuscript. The day she finished reading it, she called me—absolutely passionate about the story—and said yes, she would represent me. My methodical plan and the intervention of fate brought me an agent.

Bisson: Well, I sold my first book without an agent and the editor told me I needed an agent and he gave me a few names. So I spoke with them and ended up going with Susan Protter. This was about 20 years ago.

What do you expect from your agent?

Villegas: I expect her to represent my project with total enthusiasm, to have faith in what I'm doing. I expect her to work hard to sell my book, which she did: She sold it to St. Martin's Press in less than six weeks! I expect her to keep me up-to-date on what's going on with the publishing process and with the publisher's sales to other venues. I expect her to deal with incoming moneys in a timely manner. She's been wonderful in meeting and exceeding all of these expectations.

Turkington: I hope he will bring projects to me. Certainly he has in the past, and it's great to have an agent out there mentioning my name. What I really expect of him is to negotiate on my behalf. I'm terrible at negotiating and I hate it. I just let him handle all those issues. In particular, if there's a problem with payment, I don't have to pick up the phone and deal with it. He does it for me, and that is an enormous burden off my shoulders. Finally, it can be isolating to be a writer on your own. If I get frustrated or have a problem I can call him and talk about it. I can't imagine doing my job without Bert, and after all this time he's become not just a good agent but a good friend. Editors like and respect him a lot. He's just a wonderful, honest and kind person.

Bisson: Different agents do different things for different people. I'm a writer who lives in New York, who is known and knows people in the publishing business. So my agent does not really have to do a lot to sell my stuff. Mostly for me, she looks after contracts and makes sure all the paperwork is in order. She pays close attention to foreign rights, subrights, film options, things like that. But she doesn't really have to send my manuscripts out, because usually when I complete a novel—or even start it—it's already placed with a publisher.

Nelson: I don't know whether other writers expect this, but I expect my agent—because we've been together a while now—to give me and my work continuing attention and support. She's certainly done that for me. The role of the agent is a peculiar one in that it's a little bit like a friend, a little bit like an editor, and a little like a business partner. I can send her work and she might not seem totally enthusiastic about it, but in some important ways she goes out and promotes me with a kind of unconditional support. She's very steadfast. She's been my ally. She's the person I call when I really need to let down my guard. I'll tell her that my work seems weak, or that I'm afraid to call some editor. She will act as my spokesperson, my advocate. She's very loyal and I appreciate that so much.

Is there anything you initially expected from your agent that has changed?

Bisson: Not really. A lot of agents have to spend some time explaining the ropes of the business to authors and explain to them their role. I didn't need any of that because I was already in the business.

Nelson: I never expected to have a sort of friendship with my agent. My husband says he feels like she's a friend of the family and that he could call her and ask her about things very easily. This closeness I never anticipated. My dealings with my first agent were very business-like and I was very intimidated by him. I did not feel comfortable calling him. Part of what was so attractive about Bonnie is that she's my age and I feel comfortable with her. She's very open to talking on the phone with me and she returns calls very promptly. I've come to feel that she's one of the people really pushing for me. I feel like a priority to her. What struck me at first was that she had no problem sending out a collection of short stories. I've come to learn that most agents won't do that.

Turkington: Certainly I rely on him more now than I ever could have imagined in the past. But there weren't any rude awakenings. And I've been overwhelmed by all the book projects he's sent my way. Much of what I've published would not have been written if Bert hadn't come to me and said, "I need somebody to do this book on this topic. Would you like to do it?" So he's proven to be more than just a person who sells my books. He also brings book projects to me.

Villegas: Naively, I thought that a book agent would also peddle stories and essays. Very few agents do that, I've learned. On the other hand, I didn't expect Doris to fly to the Frankfurt Book Fair and return with a slew of overseas sales, several of which have since been completed. But she did. I didn't expect her to connect me with a Hollywood producer, resulting in my writing a screenplay (something she knew I was dying to do!). But she did. I didn't expect her to fire up readers from New York City to Hollywood about the story. But she did. She continually surprises me with her imagination and chutzpah in promoting the book.

What does your agent expect from you?

Turkington: I think Bert expects me to handle myself in a professional manner, to meet my deadlines, deliver work of acceptable caliber, because that's really a reflection on both of us. If he recommends me and then I turn out to be a really bad experience for an editor, that reflects badly on the agent as well as on me. I've got to make sure I do a good job for both of us and he expects that I will.

Nelson: I know she hopes that every book I write will get a little better and be more commercially appealing, but I don't know if she expects that necessarily. But I know she wants me to produce books that she can sell. She expects that I'm committed to her for the long haul, and I've felt for a long time we've both understood this.

Villegas: She expects me to respond quickly, responsibly, when issues come up. If she needs something in writing, she expects me to have it done in a timely manner. If the publisher tells her such-and-such is going on, she expects me to handle my part. I had a heck of a time gathering permissions for the use of Emily Dickinson's work in my book, and Doris clearly said to me, "This is your job." It was, and I did it.

Bisson: Fifteen percent. She also needs me to deliver a lot of material. Agents can't do much with somebody who doesn't produce a lot regularly. You can't just do a book every eight or ten years and expect an agent to be happy with that. So Sue really counts on me to stay busy and to let her handle the business end of it, which is what I do. She also sends projects my way and expects I'll do them and do them well.

What fosters a healthy author-agent relationship?

Villegas: Above all, to understand each other and communicate clearly. A writer ought to be able to trust the agent to understand what a book's trying to accomplish, to have the book's best interest at heart. The agent works for the writer, but the writer in some sense needs to support the agent, too, with continuing good work, with devotion to the task. And although the modern agent isn't, obviously, a shrink, there are things she can do to protect a writer from the underbelly of the business. I don't need to know the infinitesimal details of the most virulent rejections; Doris protects me from that, an important consideration, I think.

Nelson: I think my relationship with Bonnie epitomizes what's healthy. We've established a kind of mutual respect and a mutual confidence that are pretty far-reaching and deep. She's been very willing to go with my need to have a book more than my need to have money or New York approval. So she's been good about accepting something so small as 15 percent of a $500 check, which is what I got for the first sale. Actually, I don't even think she took that. But she's been faithful that way, and I think that suggests she has faith and things will continue to escalate and get better.

Turkington: We both have to be open and receptive to what each other wants. I think it's important for the author and the agent to really like and trust each other. I have to trust my agent will do what's best for me. I try not to pester him too much. I know I'm not the only author he has, and that he's very busy. He gets many, many unsolicited queries a week. So I try not to call him everyday, but I feel comfortable about calling when I need to. I try to respect his time and he does the same with me. What helps our relationship is that Bert has great relationships with editors, a sense for what editors want right now, for what's out there, what the industry situation is. I never feel like I have to concede to mass-market pressure. And he's good at modifying ideas and coming up with really good titles, something I'm not good at.

Bisson: An agent has to be honest, diligent, and like and respect the author's work.

Some agents are nudges and some are laid back. It depends on what the writer is looking for. My agent just handles the business end of my writing and nothing else. What I write she takes, and she doesn't try to change it. But some writers need somebody to direct them on how to write for this or that part of the market, somebody to hold their hand a little bit. I don't expect any of that from Sue. I just want her to be diligent with negotiating deals and keeping the business end in order.

Have you been surprised at how much your agent has helped you, whether it be practically, emotionally, financially?

Bisson: I still get surprised at how much more she knows about what I have to offer than I do. We recently just had this incident where a production company wanted to option a story of mine for film, and so we went through a long process in which they wanted to just option it. I told Sue, "you should just sell the thing, because nobody else is looking for it." She disagreed and we ended up doing it her way and got a lot more money and a much better deal.

Turkington: I have ten books out now. Three other books in press. Two are forthcoming. And I have three book proposals. All have been with Bert, and more than half of these books he brought to me. He would either bring the idea or an unfinished project that needed completion. If a project falls through with another writer, the editor at the publishing company will call Bert to find a qualified writer to get the book written. So Bert keeps steering projects my way, whether he wants me to write the entire book myself, co-author it with someone else, or finish where another has left off. I didn't expect ten years ago that I'd have all this published material.

Villegas: Yes, yes, yes. First, I didn't realize the scope of the agent's job. From the beginning, Doris has served as broker, publicist, buffer, negotiator, and head cheerleader. She likes to talk about the roller-coaster ride my book has taken us on, and she has never failed to tackle new challenges as the project evolves. My gosh, she flew from New York to Lodi, California, with me and the Hollywood producer—that is real hand-holding!

Nelson: I didn't realize how important Bonnie would become to me. Each of my five books has had a different editor, but Bonnie has been there for me through all of them. And I didn't expect that she'd teach me so much about the publishing industry. I'm so out of the publishing loop and she keeps me apprised of what's going on. She has become a mainstay for me, and I never realized how important her investment in me would become to my career and to me personally.

How often do you communicate with your agent? How should an author conduct himself with an agent?

Nelson: In the initial process of finding an agent, do not make phone calls. Agents would much rather be reached by mail, and a phone call is useless in the beginning. Bonnie and I go for months without contact—then suddenly we'll exchange a flurry of phone calls. It's casual business, at this point.

Villegas: It depends on what phase your book is in. If you've sent your agent a manuscript and it's being shopped around, I think you should hear from your agent every couple of weeks with a status check, even just a quick fax, phone call or letter. After my book was sold, things moved so quickly we spoke several times a week: about Hollywood, about overseas sales, about the status of revisions. There were periods during some option negotiating when we spoke several times a day. I think a writer needs to ask the agent: "At what point should I hear from you on such and such an issue?" That way, because the date was agreed upon, the writer can contact the agent on the deadline without ever feeling like a pest. No agent appreciates a whiner.

Bisson: Sue and I have become pretty good friends and I talk to her on the phone a few days a week, but that's because I live in New York, we're old friends, we've both been working so long in the business, and I have a lot of different projects going on. If I were a writer just starting out and living in Kentucky or Indiana or somewhere, the agent would be horrified if I called everyday. So early on the relationship has to have some distance until you both get comfortable with each other.

Turkington: I talk to Bert several times a week, keeping track of current projects and trying out new ideas.

Any other advice for authors seeking representation?

Nelson: Know that it's necessary for an agent to be enthusiastic about your work. A person can't fake enthusiasm very well, and it is so necessary for the success of the book. I think the agent can also pass that enthusiasm on to a publisher. And a good agent has to give the writer some sort of priority. But I don't think the role of the agent is to perform as mentor or editor even. I think if you're a fiction writer you ought to write the best book you can before you even try to get an agent. An agent is the second step in the process. Coming up with a solid book is the first. It could be a real waste of time to try to find an agent before you're finished with a book, and the wasted time could have been spent improving that unfinished book.

Villegas: It's really important to have an agent who reads your book the way you would hope your best reader would. From then on out it's the agent's business to get it to those readers, so you want someone whose sensibility is close to yours and that of your imagined reader. Ideally, your agent should be someone who understands your longterm goals and who also works with you to define and achieve the writing life you're after. Your agent should advise you of the marketability of your work, even if this means telling you something is a long shot.

Bisson: I think authors need to figure out what they want from the relationship. I also think authors need to not shop around for approval from lots of different sources. That's the biggest weakness I see in most authors. Every author wants feedback. Sometimes you get that from agents, sometimes you don't. If you continually search for it, however, it can be damaging and pretty unprofessional. You should understand that you need it and you should take it when you can get it, but don't go around barking for biscuits. The big thing an author needs to do is write. Agents want authors not books. So if you really want an agent you've got to convince them you're going to be worth the agent's time, that you'll keep writing material they can sell.

Turkington: I would recommend that writers not jump into an agent relationship without learning quite a bit about the person. I've heard some amazing stories about agents who charge for every stamp they put on an envelope. Do not feel uncomfortable about looking for an agent you can really get along with because when you have a good fit it makes your job so much easier. Think about it as a long-term relationship, because you have to deal with this person for more than just one day or one week. Good relationships continue year after year, book after book.

Explaining AAR's Ban on Reading Fees

BY RICHARD CURTIS

Charging "reading fees"—the practice by which literary agents and others charge authors for reading and evaluating their material—has long been controversial among authors and agents. Effective January 1, 1996, the Association of Authors' Representatives (AAR)—the major national organization of literary agents—added a provision to its Canon of Ethics that completely prohibits its members from engaging in that practice. Indeed, the Canon now provides that members may not even benefit indirectly from the practice, such as by accepting payments or other benefits for referring authors to fee-charging reading services.

A BRIEF HISTORY

The AAR was formed in 1991 as a result of the merger of the Society of Authors' Representatives (SAR) and the Independent Literary Agents Association (ILAA). At that time, SAR prohibited reading fees, while ILAA had no official position on them. A handful of ILAA members charged fees, most did not. As part of the merger agreement, AAR adopted a policy that prohibited new members from charging reading fees but permitted those ILAA members who previously charged them to continue to do so, subject to compliance with stringent disclosure and other ethical regulations. The new organization was also committed to reviewing the whole subject in two years.

EXPLORING THE ISSUES

At first glance, it would not appear that reading fees are a bad thing. After all, many—perhaps most—authors need (or at least can benefit from) a professional evaluation of their work, and experienced literary agents are presumably well qualified to provide such evaluations. Also, reading and evaluating written material requires time, talent, and sometimes actual out-of-pocket expense, for which compensation would seem to be justified. And with more and more publishers refusing even to read unsolicited manuscripts, agents have become in effect the slush-pile readers for the publishing industry. Many agents believe that if they don't read the work of unrepresented authors, the risk is great that important—or at least saleable—work will go unrecognized and unsold.

Several years ago I wrote an article in which I wondered why, if the procedure was handled ethically and honorably, agents should not be able to charge authors for their time (or for the time of those they hire to evaluate work for them) if asked by authors to provide evaluations of their work? I answered my own question when I realized that it is impossible to define and enforce "ethically and honorably." For legal and other

RICHARD CURTIS *is president of the Association of Authors' Representatives and Richard Curtis Associates, Inc. He has been a literary agent for nearly 30 years and is the author of* Beyond the Bestseller: A Literary Agent Takes You Inside the Book Business *and* How to Be Your Own Literary Agent.

reasons, trade organizations like AAR cannot set or regulate the fees charged by their members. Also, it would be impossible to effectively regulate the quality/sufficiency of any given evaluation.

Further, history documents that charging reading fees is subject to a variety of deceptive practices, including inducing the author to believe that as a result of the evaluation the work will be rendered saleable and/or that the reader will agree to represent the work. History also shows that some "agents" who charge reading fees are primarily in the reading-for-hire business, with little or no agent capability.

Thus, although no AAR member who was permitted to charge fees was ever found to have violated AAR's guidelines, the AAR in 1994 concluded that because the practice of charging reading fees is capable of serious abuse and is impossible to regulate effectively, and because the publishing community generally sees it as shady and unethical, the practice should be banned for all its members.

THE FINAL PROVISION

The AAR Board of Directors therefore ruled that the remaining fee-charging agents who had been "grandfathered" into the organization in 1991 would have to discontinue the practice or leave the organization. Of the half-dozen or so agents charging fees at that time, most agreed to discontinue the practice. A couple resigned from the organization.

Moreover, when the AAR learned that some fee-charging services were soliciting referrals from its members, offering compensation for the referrals, the AAR added to its Canon of Ethics a prohibition against members benefiting even indirectly from reading fees, thus raising the level of integrity yet another notch.

The AAR regularly receives complaints from authors claiming that they have been victimized by persons or companies whom they paid for reading services. Unfortunately, the AAR is not able to police nonmembers. But we can and do refer all authors to our prohibition against reading fees, which expresses our view on the practice and which separates our members from any taint associated with the abuse of the practice by others.

Authors who ask prospective agents whether they are AAR members can at least know that an affirmative answer will mean that those agents are ethically prohibited from charging reading fees. Considering AAR's policy against reading fees, its stringent membership standards, its requirement of prompt remittance of client monies, its insistance on segregation of author funds from agent's funds, and its active Ethics Committee capable of enforcing the organization's Canon of Ethics, membership in the AAR would appear to offer a reliable standard by which the honesty and integrity of literary agents can be measured.

A Rationale for Reading Fees

BY CINDY LAUFENBERG

Some agents charge a reading fee because they feel they should be compensated for their work. Unlike most people in publishing, agents receive no salary but work on commission. Income from reading fees can help justify time spent reading manuscripts by unpublished writers. The volume of phone calls, unsolicited queries and manuscripts an agent gets in one week can be overwhelming. To keep up with such a large amount of material, an agent does most of her reading in her spare time—during the evening at home, and on the weekends. Fee-charging agents see reading fees as a small payment for the extra time they spend reading sample chapters and manuscripts.

SOME BENEFITS OF PAYING A FEE

The Association of Authors' Representatives (AAR) forbids its members from charging reading fees, and avoiding agents who charge reading fees may protect you from possible abuses by unprincipled fee-charging agents, but working with a legitimate fee-charging agent can get you a reading for your manuscript that you might not get with a nonfee-charging agent. Nonfee-charging agents may start to read your manuscript but feel no obligation to continue. With fee-charging agents, you are paying for their time and for them to read your manuscript. Moreover, when you pay a reading fee your manuscript is more likely to be read by the agent rather than by an intern or an assistant. Many fee-charging agents will critique and edit your work (sometimes for an additional fee), which is something most nonfee-charging agents will not do unless they really want to represent you.

REASONS AGENTS CHARGE A FEE

Toni Lopopolo, an agent from Manhattan Beach, CA who does not charge reading fees but offers an editing service, understands why charging fees is so prevalent in the fiction market. "Now that so many people have computers, everybody thinks they can write fiction," she says, which results in agents being inundated with unsolicited manuscripts. "I think it's perfectly legitimate to pay an agent to read three chapters and a synopsis, especially if that agent's specialty is fiction. I don't charge reading fees, but I understand why a lot of agents do—legitimate agents, that is. I can see why agents would charge $35-45 for a reading because they do not do it during office time, they do it during free time. A lot of people who work in publishing condemn reading fees, but they forget something. They get a salary."

Agent Gerry Wallerstein charges a reading fee for unpublished writers that includes a critique of the work as well. "I resent the attitude that because you charge a fee there's something dishonest about you," says Wallerstein. "I'm giving important help to new writers. My time is my money, and I can't afford to give my time to someone who has no track record. One reason I charge a fee is that I may have to wait six months to a year before I get any income from a client. I can't afford to coast along on nothing."

CINDY LAUFENBERG *is editor of Writer's Digest Books'* Songwriter's Market *and a frequent contributor to other Writer's Digest books.*

UNDERSTAND WHAT YOU'RE GETTING INTO

Writers wanting to work with a fee-charging agent need to find out exactly what the agent's fees are and just what the agent will do for those fees. Is the agent offering simply to read a few chapters of your book to decide whether she's interested in representing you? Is she offering to critique your work, letting you know where your manuscript is weak and where the strengths lie? Or is she willing to edit your manuscript in preparation to send it to publishers? Many writers assume that if they pay an agent a fee, they're guaranteed representation and will emerge with a book that is ready to be presented to publishers. But this is hardly ever the case. You're paying the agent to *consider* acquiring you as a client.

You must understand the difference between reading fees, critiques and editing services to make an informed decision on what you'll be getting for your money. (See the introduction to the Fee-charging Agents section of this book for detailed definitions of the different kinds of services for which an agent may charge.) Fees vary from agency to agency, so weigh what you're paying against what you're gaining. Be wary of unreasonable fees. Sometimes agents will require additional fees for editing or reading any revisions you might make after the initial critique. Sometimes an agent will refund your fee if she decides to take you on as a client. And some agents offer to refund fees after a sale is made. Find out these things before you agree to pay anything.

ASK THE RIGHT QUESTIONS

If you are required to pay a reading fee, there are several questions you should ask the prospective agent. First, what is the fee? Ask for a fee schedule and find out exactly what you can expect for this fee. Will the agent be reading the manuscript with the intent of perhaps representing you if she likes your work? How long will it take for a response? Also be sure to ask for examples of work sold in the past year, how many manuscripts she takes on each month and how many new clients she represents each year. This will help you gauge how much time an agent is likely to spend on your manuscript. If an agent is offering a critique for a fee, ask the same kinds of questions. How extensive is the critique; is it a paragraph summary of the strengths and weaknesses of the manuscript, or is it an actual page by page critique? Find out who will read the manuscript, the agent herself or an assistant. Who will write the critique? Ask for a sample critique so you can see the type of work she has done for other clients. How long will it take for you to get your critique back?

RESEARCH YOUR AGENT, PROCEED WITH CAUTION

Along with finding out what an agent is offering for a fee, it's also important to find out as much as you can about the agent's reputation in the publishing field. Wallerstein emphasizes the importance of looking into an agent's background when seeking representation. "What does she know about judging literary material, and what does she know about the business of publishing? Find out the agent's background, where she worked and what she did there. You should feel comfortable with the agent you're going to work with. Each person has to trust the other and each person has to be willing to help the other." Lopopolo advises writers to "watch out for brand new agents who have never worked in publishing. Check out each agent to determine if that person is legitimate. Anyone can set themselves up as a book agent because there's no licensing."

If you do the proper research and know what an agent is offering and whether that will help you in your quest for representation, there should be no surprises as to what you can expect from a fee-charging agent. Then it's up to you to make an informed decision about who will represent you.

My Dream Client

BY MICHAEL LARSEN

Congratulations! You have found an agent who has taken you on and is trying to sell your book. You both are reveling in the honeymoon, with all the feelings of confidence, enthusiasm, goodwill, and anticipation that follow the consummation of your working marriage.

As with any relationship, the challenge now is to make your working marriage with your agent as fruitful and rewarding as possible. The best way to accomplish this is to be a dream client.

Who are dream clients? Dream clients are writers who:
- Know as much as possible about agents and approach them in a professional way with fresh ideas, impeccable writing and enthusiasm
- Are patient with our busy schedule, faithful to the project, grateful for our services, loyal, conscientious about writing and rewriting, and tireless in promoting
- Understand that our working marriage is a collaboration and provide whatever support and ideas they can to help us
- Are totally committed to developing their craft and career
- Deliver a book a year, on time, each book better than the last
- Understand that we want them to be satisfied with our efforts
- Call when they need us
- Mention us in their dedications or acknowledgments
- Become lifelong friends (we need friends more than clients)
- Inspire us to be dream agents

So how can you become a dream client?

Write Well

Make your books as good as they can be. Make your agent, your editor, and your readers eager to see your next book. Also remember that your agent's credibility is on the line with every submission.

A writer sent the manuscript for his novel to a publisher, and on the envelope he wrote, "FISH INSIDE. DELIVER IN FIVE DAYS OR NEVER MIND." He got this message back: "PACKAGE DELIVERED IN FIVE DAYS BUT HAD TO OPEN THE WINDOW ANYWAY."

Deliver Your Books on Time

There are enough challenges in publishing a book. Don't add to them and risk a rejection by being late with your manuscript.

With wife Elizabeth Pomada, **MICHAEL LARSEN** *runs Michael Larsen/Elizabeth Pomada Literary Agents in San Francisco. He is the author of* Literary Agents: What They Do, How They Do It and How to Find and Work with the Right One for You, How to Write a Book Proposal, *and coauthor with Hal Bennett of* How to Write with a Collaborator.

Communicate Only When Necessary

One point to settle when your agent starts to submit your work is when you can expect to hear from him. Let the agent make calls to you. Unless it's for personal or social reasons such as suggesting an evening out, call or write your agent and expect contact only when necessary.

Regardless of how popular an author you become, your agent can't devote all his time to you. You may have only one agent, but you are not your agent's only client. Calling your agent about every small frustration will damage your relationship.

However, if you have a serious concern, tell your agent about it immediately. Agents are not mind readers. If a problem arises that you can't handle—either with your book, your editor, or your publisher—contact your agent. Never assume your agent knows about the problem, and don't delay, hoping it will go away by itself.

Don't beat your head against a wall trying to solve a problem by yourself. Part of an agent's value is his or her experience. Your agent may have dealt with a similar problem before and may know how to solve it. He may be able to show you why it really isn't a problem or why it's an opportunity in work clothes. Don't be defensive in your relationship with your agent. Remember: You don't work for your agent; your agent works for you.

But, keep in mind that until your agent sells your book, he or she is working for free. When you do contact your agent, be cheerful and optimistic. Ask if there's any way you can help.

Live and Help Live

When you start working with an agent, agree on how he or she will go about sending out your work and whether one or more copies will be submitted at a time. Once you establish a mutually satisfactory way of working together, be patient. If it stops working, change it.

Try to Forget About Your Manuscript

Bay Area children's agent Kendra Marcus once faxed a children's book manuscript to an editor on a Friday morning and sold it that afternoon. Your book will probably take longer.

Once your agent begins submitting your manuscript, try to put it out of your mind. Publishing is a slow business, and the movement of paper through the labyrinths of the publishing behemoths is slowing down even more. Contracts and advances from large houses used to take one month to arrive, but now they take two months or more.

You and your agent both want to sell your book as quickly as possible, and your agent will be delighted to call you with good news the moment there is any to report. What can you do while you're waiting?

- If you have a brainstorm on how to improve your manuscript and your agent agrees with you, revise it and get it back to the agent quickly.
- If your book isn't finished and you have faith that it will sell, continue to work on it.
- Start your next book.
- Go on vacation.

Celebrate When Your Book Is Sold

When your agent sells your book, show your appreciation. A bottle of champagne or a celebratory meal at a favorite restaurant will do nicely. Publishing people appreciate a simple, relevant gift.

Crown Senior Editor Peter Ginna feels that personal letters are more meaningful than gifts. The goal isn't to make a grand gesture, just to express your gratitude. For agent Martha Jane Casselman, the best gifts are a simple thank you and recommendations to other writers.

Acknowledge Your Agent

Like most people, agents like to see their name in print. Thanking your agent in your dedication or acknowledgments will bring added pride and pleasure every time your agent thinks about your book. Your book is your baby, but it's also part of your agent's extended literary family.

Use Your Agent Reflex

If an editor approaches you and wants to buy your book or wants you to write one, talk about the book but not about the money. Memorize and use this line: "Gee, that sounds great, but if you want to talk about money, you'd better call my agent." Even if your book is sold, don't talk to your editor about money without asking your agent. Otherwise, you may do yourself more harm than good.

Trust Your Agent

Trust your agent to work well on your behalf. You will have the final say about selling your book. Esther Newberg, a senior vice-president at International Creative Management, believes that "it's passion that makes a book work." You might, for example, fare best at a small house or with a small advance but with a passionate editor. Have faith in your agent's instincts as well as your own.

Be Loyal to Your Agent

Agents take on new writers in the hope that they will become better at their craft and more profitable clients as time goes by. If your agent gives you a reason to leave, do so without hesitation. However, to leave an agent who is doing an effective job is to deprive the agent of future commissions earned partly because of the commitment to you and your career.

Every book is different, a unique combination of author, subject, timing, agent, editor, and publisher. Harmonizing these elements to make a book as successful as it can be is a creative challenge for everyone involved. Agents who help their authors do it well earn the right to a lasting relationship.

Mae West once quipped, "Marriage is a great institution, but I'm not ready for an institution." If you are ready, be prepared to enter into this secular state with the belief that marriage is not a 50-50 proposition. Make it a 100-100 proposition by doing all you can to help it survive and thrive. You and your agent have to be equally committed to doing whatever it takes to create and sustain an enduring relationship.

My Client From Hell

BY ELIZABETH POMADA

In every life, rain must fall. But in every agent's life are writers who create thunderstorms. Here are nine kinds of writers who make agents want to take up ditch-digging:

The Nag

The most common answer agents have, when asked who their "client from hell" would be is The Nag. This is the writer who wants to know every time his manuscript is mailed, and to whom, or rejected, and by whom. Who wants to know what's happening often, much too often, and calls constantly just to nag. Agents have a hard enough time handling all the telephone calls to and from publishers.

We once received three faxes the same day from a client, asking why he hadn't received an amendment to his contract. He had made a side-deal with his publisher and wanted us to be sure the language was correct. I knew nothing about this and called the publisher. She was astonished, because she had agreed to everything that very morning. Neither one of us could figure out how anything could have been written up and sent to me, for him, all on the same day. Unless you are the agent's only client, an agent can't afford to be in constant contact with you.

The Prevaricator

AAR member Andrea Brown, who specializes in children's books, had a client who was late with her manuscript. She assured Andrea that it was finished, just being typed up. Weeks went by. The author assured the editor the book was in the mail. Two more weeks went by. The editor started a trace for the missing manuscript. Andrea was finally told that the book was only half done. She had to apologize on the author's behalf and try to keep the editor from canceling the contract.

The Procrastinator

Late manuscripts are a problem for publishers because publishers want to start earning their advances back as soon as possible. If you're writing a self-help book, publishers may plan to publish in early spring, when consumers are still trying to live up to their New Year's resolutions and get off to a fresh start. If you are six months late, the book might be published at an inopportune selling-time. You wouldn't want a diet book, for example, published just before Christmas. But don't just keep saying, "it's ready, it's on the way." By the time your book is finally delivered, competitive books may have been published or your editor's enthusiasm may have waned.

The Nervous Nellie

This is the person who calls to make sure the manuscript has arrived at an agent's office. If you want to be sure something has arrived, send it "return receipt requested"

With husband Michael Larsen, **ELIZABETH POMADA** *runs Michael Larsen/Elizabeth Pomada Literary Agents in San Francisco. She also collaborates with him on the* Painted Ladies *series and is the author of* Places to Go With Children in Northern California, *now in its seventh edition.*

or enclose a filled-out postcard, clipped to the top of your letter so it's the first thing the assistant sees. Don't waste the agent's time with unnecessary calls.

One reason publishers like to work with agents is that in the past publishers were bedeviled by authors asking for advances on their advances. Now when publishers pay the agent, who pays the client, they can be sure that they won't have authors claiming, as they had in the past, that they never got their checks.

The Announcer

"I'm putting my manuscript in the mail" is one message an agent can live without. Of course you're excited about shipping your baby off, but time is precious, and agents don't need to know when something is coming their way. Nor do agents welcome "I'm-sorry-I'm-late-sending-you-my-submission-because . . ." calls. Agents aren't sitting at their desks looking at the clock waiting for manuscripts.

The Know-It-All

Agents appreciate clients who have learned about the publishing business and know how to focus and market their books. But you have hired a professional to represent you. Would you interrupt your dentist while he's drilling to tell him to use another size bit? Whatever your agent says and does on your behalf should make sense to you. If it doesn't, ask about it. But when it comes to negotiating contracts, trust your agent to know more than you do.

The I'll-Push-It-Myselfer

An agent friend told us about the client she just decided to stop working with because the client had a habit of calling the editor trying to pitch the book while the editor was still considering her proposal. That's a sure way to turn off editors—and agents.

The Ingrate

There are some authors who seem bent on squeezing every drop of humanity out of their agents. Agent Pat Teal told us of a client of hers whose response to the news that Pat had just received a $400,000 offer on a good-but-not-earth-shattering book was "Why isn't it a million? That's what everyone else gets."

The reason you read about seven- and eight-figure deals is that they're rare. Agents would love to make every deal newsworthy, but they are not magicians.

Another agent complained to us about a writer she'd worked with for years, selling five mysteries but not the literary novel. The author decided she needed a new couch, so she found an agent who charged 10% instead of 15%.

The Insecure One

An agent must believe in an author's work. But an agent is not a psychiatrist. Agents do reassure clients about their work and their future. We always tell our clients not to start worrying until we say so. But constant questioning about "Is it all right?" "Can I do this?" "Am I a good writer?" will only make an agent dread your calls.

An author can become "The Client From Hell" in many ways, but you're much better off making yourself a dream client, which boils down to two virtues: courtesy and consideration. If you are courteous with your agent, your calls will be welcome and your needs will be met. If you are considerate with your agent, your agent will be considerate with you. Good luck!

Electronic Rights—Managing the Digital Revolution

BY KELLY MILNER HALLS

More and more professionals within the publishing world see the Internet and the concept of electronic publishing as a New Age Pandora's Box—an electronic vision of promise and far reaching consequences still half buried somewhere along the information highway. And while the potential impact of the 'net'—a medium used worldwide by as many as a billion computer-savvy consumers—is impossible to ignore, most agents, authors and publishers aren't quite sure how to effectively employ the resource.

Literary agents seem to be watching the cyber beast, studying it with a guarded resolve. They admit the Internet will likely play an important part in future literary game plans. But only a few virtual pioneers have begun to explore what it could mean in terms of electronic rights and author royalties.

THE COMPLEXITY OF ELECTRONIC RIGHTS

"In terms of print versus electronic rights, electronics are obviously much more complicated," says 20-year William Morris veteran Robert Gottlieb, who negotiated what has been called a ground-breaking book/CD-ROM/online deal with Simon & Schuster and Putnam for Tom Clancy. "With print rights, there is a much narrower spectrum in terms of what a publisher can do with a manuscript. But when you're selling electronics, the applications are varied and ever evolving. I think the business model for a CD-ROM deal like Tom's is much closer to a motion picture negotiation involving the sale of rights."

Gottlieb believes because most literary agencies are expert in print-based contracts, they recruit special outside forces to handle electronic negotiations when the need arises. "But William Morris is a media-based company so the agents here are exposed to a wide variety of multimedia contacts and businesses. Because we're a conduit of sorts, our agents learn a great deal about all facets of the entertainment industry." According to Gottlieb, that is what makes William Morris uniquely qualified to blaze the electronic trail.

WHAT AGENTS MUST CONSIDER

But for many of New York's top agencies, caution is a practical consideration. Investing the time and money to research Internet implications simply doesn't seem cost effective at this point. "We don't have the manpower or capabilities to handle electronic rights," says Sheri Holman, personal assistant to Aaron Priest-super-agent Molly Friedrich (Aaron Priest represents such authors as George Dawes Green, John Gilstrap, Sue Grafton and Terry McMillan). "We'd have to hire a whole other person just to handle

---

KELLY MILNER HALLS *is a freelance writer specializing in nonfiction for national family and children's magazines. She has two nonfiction books published,* Dino-Trekking *and* Kids Go Denver, *and two more are scheduled for release later this year.*

it. And most of our projects are novels. They are not necessarily well-suited for CD-ROM or multimedia purposes. If we represented nonfiction or medical references, even historical material, maybe it would be different. We are careful to protect film rights, but for the time being we tend to give electronic rights away."

When it comes to novel-length fiction, "almost no one sells electronic rights," according to Elizabeth Ziemska, an agent at Nicholas Ellison, Inc. (Nicholas Ellison represents Nelson DeMille, Lee Grunfeld, Richard Montanari and Janis Weber among others). "William Morris is adamant about reserving them, but they don't do anything with them. No one knows what to do with them. We try to retain electronic rights whenever possible here at Nicholas Ellison. But I would never do what William Morris has done—for example refusing to do business with Random House over an electronic rights dispute. Simply put, I will not hold up a writer's career waiting for something that doesn't exist at this point.

"Until that changes, as far as I'm concerned, the publisher can have them, unless the author I represent has special Internet connections. If he or she does, I will reserve the electronic rights for the author's specific purposes. But it's more a personal option than a contractual consideration."

EMBRACING THE REVOLUTION

Lawyer and agent Gay Young understands the dilemma some top level literary agencies face in the wake of a multimedia revolution. "Publishing is filled with people who are intimidated by electronic media," she says. But she insists it's not just a matter of resistance to change. "First of all, most novels will never find their way into digital format. So if you have a thriving agency that specializes in that kind of work, you don't have time to study electronics."

Young has made it her business to bridge the electronic gaps. She says, "I field dozens of calls everyday from agents and authors who need information on electronic rights but don't have the time or resources to research the fast-paced realm for themselves.

"The fact is, we are in the midst of a revolution," Young says. "But it's going to take a long time before we actually see what the implications are. And it's not very lucrative yet. We are just beginning to see the potential in this new media. People are just learning how to create. We forget the practical format of the book took time to evolve. Even movies didn't take off until people realized making a film wasn't the same as producing a play. Eventually, there will be money to be made in electronic applications beyond CD-ROMs."

Young tries to help publishers and authors prepare for the shift. "I suppose I am a pioneer with more than a few arrows in my back to prove it," she says. "But I believe there will be an alternative revenue stream via electronic rights." By keeping her clients informed, she believes they are at least poised to take advantage of every dream-like possibility.

FILM RIGHTS, CD-ROMS AND THE INTERNET

However, the focus on electronics can shift from dream state to rock hard reality when film rights are involved, says Sanford-Greenburger agent Theresa Park. But the heart of the dispute is primarily between publishers and film production companies. "One of my worst legal battles was with the movie company that bought the rights to Nicholas Sparks's book, *The Notebook* (Warner). The most contentious action of the negotiation revolved around who would retain multimedia rights."

Park says film companies try to gobble up electronic rights to guarantee they'll be compensated for the multimedia use of motion picture film clips and musical treatments.

Publishers are determined to keep them as leverage to help maximize their own profit margins. After all, she says, the entertainment industry is a very serious business. But the real problem with electronic rights is the unknown quality of the Internet.

"Obviously, not all books are made into films. And not all works are suitable for CD-ROM applications. But nobody really knows what form Internet-uses are going to take. Publishers try to cover their bases by drafting wide-sweeping contracts. They essentially try to grab as many rights as they can.

"It's my job as an agent to pare back, to protect the future rights of my authors. I try to make sure every new evolution of a project will be subject to further negotiation. I try to make sure each step is subject to author approval. That's especially important on the net, because there is a lot of debate as to what form compensation is going to take. How writers will be compensated and how providers will be charged are pretty much up for grabs when it comes to the Internet. So the best I can do is to keep my authors' options open."

Nicholas Ellison agent and Internet guru Dan Mandel agrees. "CD-ROMs are so 1995. They've become less and less important. They are more a form of information storage and retrieval than anything else." Mandel says the real debate will begin when publishing discovers the World Wide Web. "I believe electronic rights as we know them will eventually become almost totally web-based. And on the Web, content is king. Internet service providers are always looking for outstanding content that will draw people (new members) in. I think we will eventually see the online serial run of novels, even in advance of their print release. When that happens, electronic rights will shift from subsidiary to primary rights." And as it becomes easier to calculate what material is most appealing to cyber citizens, real financial considerations will be at stake.

Writers House electronics expert Liza Landsman agrees that past CD-ROM projects face extinction. "Sure, some forms of CD-ROMs are dead. Original from start to finish entertainment titles are definitely a thing of the past. Because frankly, there are much better platforms for gaming. But don't underestimate reference and educational products—particularly K-12 focused titles." And she says more and more of those products will move toward branded content.

"Developers are saying, rather than create completely original products, let's do a deal with, say, Nickelodeon. It's expensive enough to market and distribute an electronic title. There are a lot of titles competing for shelf space and consumer attention. In order to break out from the pack, a lot of publishers are going for name recognition."

But Landsman has her doubts about the Internet and novel serialization. While she admits some adult publications have hit pay dirt on the Internet using a turnstile, pay-per-view approach, she is quick to note there is a huge difference between looking and reading online. "We've all heard the jokes about people only reading 'those' magazines for the articles. Well, trust me—people spending money to get onto the *Penthouse* website are not reading the articles. The Internet is just not a good medium for reading. Nobody is going to read a novel online, so I don't see a huge potential for profit. The market focus will have to mature before money can be made."

Until then, these literary mavericks of electronic rights will do their best to predict the future. And, Landsman says, "It won't be easy. But the good news is a lot of extremely bright, focused people are investing a lot of time and energy trying to figure this out. Publishing is in the business of creating copyrights. If that's your primary business, you'd better be looking hard at the Internet and the whole issue of electronic rights."

Career Planning for Nonfiction Writers

BY BERT HOLTJE

Let's assume you can write. You know a noun from a verb, and you know something of style. You've read the best writers and you've read the others. You know why a book on a dull subject by a great writer is often much more enjoyable than a book on an exciting subject by a pedestrian writer. And you are seriously considering making a living as a nonfiction writer. Is there a future for you? Can you make a decent income from your writing? You can if you are realistic, flexible, and plan your career as carefully as any other professional plans his or her career.

Career planning for nonfiction writers is a lifetime pursuit, a never-ending process. You must keep your finger in the wind at all times, knowing not only what sells now but anticipating what will sell in two years—when that book you are writing will be published. It's also knowing when to abandon a project and when to exploit one. And it's understanding the many ways nonfiction writers can succeed.

A career nonfiction writer needs to find a good agent early in his or her career, for a good agent does more than get the best advance for your book. He also knows the editors who should know you. This agent will not only respond to your ideas but will suggest projects, help you shape them, and then get you the best possible deal. When you have a good agent, you think of him as your partner, not just the person who gets you extensions when you are late with a manuscript or takes 15 percent.

WHAT A WRITING CAREER ENTAILS

Many authors I represent do not write fulltime but consider writing an integral part of their careers. Some are physicians. Some are historians, political scientists, psychologists and others whose main source of income is teaching. Some are in politics and business, and many are editors. But all are, in my view, career writers because they have more than one book in them. Regardless of whatever else they do, they write. And they treat their writing careers as seriously as they do their other careers.

Today, most professional nonfiction writers are generalists as well as specialists. That is, they secure a reputation by writing their own books in well-defined fields, and they do books in other fields either as ghost writers or collaborators. One of my clients has made an enviable reputation writing popular history under his own name, but when collaborating or writing on other topics (biographies, self-help books, business books, reference books), he will use a pseudonym. Another client made a name for herself writing popular health books. She writes these books under her own name and collaborates with health care professionals on others. She also writes for a business audience, and recently did an "instant" book for a major publisher about a celebrity murderer.

BERT HOLTJE *is president of James Peter Associates, Inc., a literary agency in Tenafly, New Jersey, which represents only writers of nonfiction books. A division within the agency, Ghosts & Collaborators International, represents authors who provide ghosting and collaboration services to publishers. Mr. Holtje is the author of 27 published nonfiction books.*

Both of these writers have planned their careers carefully. They recognize that it's important to publish in their field of interest and to do other projects as well.

Many agents read a wide range of periodicals searching for authors who have the spark they want. In fact, writing for periodicals is probably one of the best ways to attract attention to yourself and your writing. New York agent Dan Bial says that although he is seldom looking for new clients, he reads widely in publications that interest him. "I look for people who write well and who have something interesting to say. If I think there might be potential, I'll contact the writer to see if he or she might be thinking of writing a book."

STAYING ON TOP OF THE INDUSTRY

At the moment, advances for nonfiction books are generally good. Major publishers are offering strong advances for books they anticipate will sell well. Publishers large and small are, in general, offering fair advances for other nonfiction books. The midlist, which used to be proving ground for first-time writers, is not what it used to be, because publishers are a lot less willing to take risks with unknown midlist authors. Most publishers have first-year sales goals of at least 10,000 copies for nonfiction. If a proposed book won't meet this goal, many publishers will not consider it. Ten years ago, most publishers were willing to take a chance on an unknown author, to promote the author, to make the book work. Today, it's different.

How much can you expect to earn writing nonfiction books? There is no limit, but your earning potential will depend on many factors. If you write that one big book that gets a staggering advance, you will, obviously, make a lot of money. And your chances of repeating the act are probably pretty good. Publishers like to go with a winner. But if you look at your nonfiction writing as steady work (writing your own books, ghosting and collaborating with others, taking on occasional projects such as speech writing), your income will only be limited by your ability to get contracts and produce the work. Rather than tell you how much—or little—some writers make, let me give you some figures. An advance for a midlist book with a typical large publisher can bring you anywhere from $15,000 to $50,000. A publisher might offer you between $7,500 and $15,000 for a less ambitious book.

THE BEST STRATEGY

If you can make it for a few years receiving middling advances writing books with backlist potential, your chances of earning a significant income for a lifetime are good. A backlist book is a book that publishers keep on their list for years. Many of these books are popular reference books or books on health-related subjects. They are often revised every few years, a job for which the author is usually paid again by the publisher. The backlist is the bread and butter for many authors, because royalties from these titles keep coming in. However, career planning is critical for the author contemplating this route. He will need enough money to survive until royalties on the published book start accumulating.

Because we are talking about career planning, and not the lucky hit with one big book, I have to say the plan I just described is probably the best strategy for those wanting to make a living writing nonfiction. You and your agent can fine-tune it to your needs and abilities. If you write fast and can turn out a lot of work, you can make a lot of money doing it. If you are not so fast, you can still do well. And if writing is a part-time activity for you, it's an ideal way to augment your income and satisfy your creative urges. Just don't forget to have a plan.

KEY TO SYMBOLS AND ABBREVIATIONS

‡ A listing new to this edition
* Agents who charge fees to previously unpublished writers only
☐ Script agents who charge reading or other fees
● Comment from the editor of *Guide to Literary Agents*
ms—manuscript; mss—manuscripts
SASE—self-addressed, stamped envelope
SAE—self-addressed envelope
IRC—International Reply Coupon, for use on reply mail in countries other than your own.
The Glossary contains definitions of words and expressions used throughout the book. The Table of Acronyms translates acronyms of organizations connected with agenting or writing.

LISTING POLICY AND COMPLAINT PROCEDURE

Listings in *Guide to Literary Agents* are compiled from detailed questionnaires, phone interviews and information provided by agents. The industry is volatile and agencies change addresses, needs and policies frequently. We rely on our readers for information on their dealings with agents and changes in policies or fees that differ from what has been reported to the editor. Write to us if you have new information, questions about agents or if you have any problems dealing with the agencies listed or suggestions on how to improve our listings.

Listings are published free of charge and are not advertisements. Although the information is as accurate as possible, the listings are *not* endorsed or guaranteed by the editor or publisher of *Guide to Literary Agents*. If you feel you have not been treated fairly by an agent or representative listed in *Guide to Literary Agents* we advise you to take the following steps:

● First try to contact the listing. Sometimes one phone call or a letter can quickly clear up the matter.
● Document all your correspondence with the listing. When you write to us with a complaint, provide the name of your manuscript, the date of your first contact with the agency and the nature of your subsequent correspondence.
● We will enter your letter into our files and attempt to contact the agency.
● The number, frequency and severity of complaints will be considered in our decision whether or not to delete the listing from the next edition.

Guide to Literary Agents reserves the right to exclude any listing for any reason.

Literary Agents: Nonfee-charging

Agents listed in this section generate from 98 to 100 percent of their income from commission on sales. They do not charge for reading, critiquing, editing, marketing or other editorial services. They make their living solely from their contacts and experience, with time their most limited commodity.

For you as a writer looking for an agent, this can cut two ways. On one hand, it will cost you no more than postage to have your work considered by an agent with an imperative to find saleable manuscripts: Her income depends on her clients' incomes. Her job is to know the market, who is buying what and when. Effective agents generally know a large number of editors who specialize in a variety of work, and know how to present a work to producers and studios interested in TV and movie rights. They capitalize on that knowledge and devote their time to selling.

On the other hand, these agents must be selective, offering representation to writers whose work is outstanding and requires minimal shaping and editing. They often prefer to work with established authors, celebrities or those with professional credentials in a particular field. These agents simply don't have the time to nurture a beginning writer through many stages of development before a work is saleable.

STANDARD OPERATING PROCEDURES

Most agents open to submissions prefer initially to receive a query letter that briefly describes your work. Some agents (particularly those dealing largely in fiction) ask for an outline and a number of sample chapters, but you should send these only if you are requested to do so in an agent's listing. It takes time for agents to answer the detailed questionnaires we use to compile the listings. If an agent specifies what to send her, follow it to the letter. She is telling you exactly what she needs to judge your abilities and extend an offer of representation.

Always send a self-addressed stamped envelope (SASE) or postcard for reply. If you have not heard back from an agent within the approximate reporting time given (allowing for holidays and summer vacations) a quick, polite phone call to ask when it will be reviewed would be in order. Never fax or e-mail a query letter, outline or sample chapters to an agent without permission to do so. Due to the volume of material they receive, it may take a long time to receive a reply, so you may want to query several agents at a time. It is best, however, to have the complete manuscript considered by only one agent at a time.

Commissions range from 10 to 15 percent for domestic sales and usually are higher for foreign or dramatic sales, often 20 to 25 percent. The difference goes to the subagent who places the work.

Many agents in this section charge for ordinary business expenses in addition to the commission. Expenses can include foreign postage, fax charges, long distance phone calls, messenger and express mail services and photocopying. Some charge only for what they consider "extraordinary" expenses. Make sure you have a clear understanding of what these are before signing an agency agreement. Most agents will agree to discuss these expenses as they arise.

While most agents deduct expenses from the advance or royalties before passing them on to the author, a few agents included here charge a low ($100 or less) one-time only expense fee upfront. Sometimes these are called "marketing" or "handling" fees. Agents charging more than $100 in marketing fees are included in the Literary Agents: Fee-charging section.

Please note that on January 1, 1996, the Association of Authors' Representatives (AAR) implemented a mandate prohibiting member agents from charging reading or evaluation fees.

SPECIAL INDEXES AND ADDITIONAL HELP

To help you with your search, we've included a number of special indexes in the back of the book. The Subject Index is divided into sections for nonfee-charging and fee-charging literary agents and script agents. Each of these sections in the index is then divided by nonfiction and fiction subject categories. Some agencies indicated that they were open to all nonfiction or fiction topics. These have been grouped in the subject heading "open" in each section. Many agents have also provided additional areas of interest in their listings this year.

We've included an Agent Index as well. Often you will read about an agent who is an employee of a larger agency and you may not be able to locate her business phone or address. We asked agencies to list the agents on staff, then we've listed the agents' names in alphabetical order along with the name of the agency they work for. Find the name of the person you would like to contact and then check the agency listing. You will find the page number for the agency's listing in the Listings Index.

A Geographic Index lists agents state by state for those who are looking for an agent close to home. A Client Acceptance Policies index lists agencies according to their openness to new clients.

Many literary agents are also interested in scripts; many script agents will also consider book manuscripts. Nonfee-charging script agents who primarily sell scripts but also handle at least 10 to 15 percent book manuscripts appear among the listings in this section, with the contact information, breakdown of work currently handled and a note to check the full listing in the script section. Those nonfee-charging script agencies that sell scripts and less than 10 to 15 percent book manuscripts appear in "Additional Nonfee-charging Agents" at the end of this section. Complete listings for these agents also appear in the Script Agent section.

Before contacting any agency, check the listing to make sure it is open to new clients. Those designated (**V**) are currently not interested in expanding their rosters.

For more information on approaching agents and the specifics of the listings, read How to Use Your Guide to Literary Agents and How to Find (and Keep) The Right Agent. Also see the various articles at the beginning of the book for explorations of different aspects of the author/agent relationship.

We've ranked the agencies listed in this section according to their openness to submissions. Below is our ranking system:

I Newer agency actively seeking clients.

II Agency seeking both new and established writers.

III Agency prefers to work with established writers, mostly obtains new clients through referrals.

IV Agency handling only certain types of work or work by writers under certain circumstances.

V Agency not currently seeking new clients. We have included mention of agencies rated **V** to let you know they are currently not open to new clients. In addition to those ranked **V**, we have included a few well-known agencies' names who have declined the opportunity to receive full listings at this time. *Unless you have a strong recommendation from someone well respected in the field, our advice is to approach only those agents ranked I-IV.*

ADLER & ROBIN BOOKS INC., (II), 3000 Connecticut Ave. NW, Suite 317, Washington DC 20008. (202)986-9275. Fax: (202)986-9485. E-mail: adlerbooks@earthlink.net. Contact: Lisa M. Swayne. Estab. 1986. Represents 100 clients. 10% of clients are new/previously unpublished writers. Currently handles: 60% nonfiction books; 20% fiction; 20% technology related topics. Member agents: Bill Adler, Jr. (commercial nonfiction, biographies, pop culture books); Lisa M. Swayne (fiction, particularly mysteries and first novels; women's health, pop culture books, computer books).
Handles: Nonfiction books. Considers these nonfiction areas: biography/autobiography; business; child guidance/parenting; computers/electronics; cooking/food/nutrition; current affairs; ethnic/cultural interests; gay/lesbian issues; government/politics/law; health/medicine; history; how-to; money/finance/economics; nature/environment; popular culture; true crime/investigative; women's issues/women's studies. Considers these fiction areas: contemporary issues; detective/police/crime; literary; mainstream; mystery/suspense; thriller/espionage. Query with outline/proposal. Reports in 2 months on queries.
Recent Sales: *Fatal Gift*, by A. Michael Frase (Carroll & Graf); *The Prophet of Rage: A Biography of Louis Farrakhan*, by Arthur Magida (Basic Books).
Terms: Agent receives 15% commission on domestic; 20% on foreign sales. Offers written contract.
Tips: Obtains new clients through recommendations.

AGENCY CHICAGO, (II), 601 S. LaSalle St. #600A, Chicago IL 60605. Contact: Ernest Santucci. Estab. 1990. 50% of clients are new/previously unpublished writers. Specializes in corporate histories, stories, biographies. Art (American), and stage plays.
Handles: Nonfiction books. Considers these nonfiction areas: travel, fitness; gambling; sports; crime. Considers these fiction areas: erotica; experimental. Send query letter only.
Terms: Agent receives 10-15% commission on domestic sales; 15% on foreign sales. Offers written contract.
Writers' Conferences: Midwest Writers Conference; International Writers and Translators Conference; ABA.
Tips: Obtains new clients through recommendations. "Do not send dot matrix printed manuscripts. Manuscripts and letters should have a clean professional look, with correct grammar and punctuation." Include SASE or material will be confidentially recycled. No phone calls.

AGENTS INC. FOR MEDICAL AND MENTAL HEALTH PROFESSIONALS, (II), P.O. Box 4956, Fresno CA 93744. Phone/fax: (209)438-1883. Director: Sydney H. Harriet, Ph.D. Estab. 1987. Member of APA. Represents 55 clients. 40% of clients are new/previously unpublished writers. Specializes in "writers who have education and experience in the medical, mental health and legal professions. It is helpful if the writer is licensed, but not necessary. Prior book publication not necessary." Currently handles: 95% nonfiction books; 5% novels.
Handles: Nonfiction books, novels. Considers these nonfiction areas: cooking/food/nutrition; psychology; reference; science/technology; self-help/personal improvement; sociology; sports medicine/psychology; mind-body healing. Considers these fiction areas: detective/police/crime; mystery/suspense; science fiction; thriller. Currently representing only previously published novelists. Query with vita and SASE. Reports in 2-3 weeks on queries; 6 weeks on mss. "Craft is crucial since 99% of fiction mss are rejected."
Recent Sales: *Profound Life/Simple Life*, by Christopher McCullough, Ph.D. (Clarkson Potter); *Life After Fifty*, by Othneil Seiden, M.D. (Taylor); *A Guide for Golfers Past 40*, by Sol Grazi, M.D. with Mike Henderson (Brassey's, Inc.); and *The Alternative Medicine Source Book*, by Steve Bratman M.D. (Lowell House).

THE PUBLISHING FIELD is constantly changing! If you're still using this book and it is 1998 or later, buy the newest edition of *Guide to Literary Agents* at your favorite bookstore or order directly from Writer's Digest Books.

Terms: Agent receives 15% commission on domestic sales; 20% on foreign sales. Offers written contract, binding for 6-12 months (negotiable).

Writers' Conferences: Scheduled at a number of conferences across the country in 1997-98. Available for conferences by request.

Tips: "Study *Writer's Guide to Software Developers, Electronic Publishers, and Agents* (Prima) for tips on how to submit manuscripts. Please, please, ask yourself why someone would be compelled to buy your book. If you think the idea is unique, spend the time to create a proposal where every word counts. Please avoid calling to pitch an idea. The only way we can judge the quality of your idea is to see it in writing. We are much in need of business-oriented proposals. Unfortunately, we cannot respond to queries or proposals without receiving a return envelope and sufficient postage."

THE JOSEPH S. AJLOUNY AGENCY, (II), 29205 Greening Blvd., Farmington Hills MI 48334-2945. (810)932-0090. Fax: (810)932-8763. E-mail: agencyajl@aol.com. Contact: Joseph S. Ajlouny. Estab. 1987. Signatory of WGA. "Represents humor and comedy writers, humorous illustrators, cartoonists." Member agents: Joe Ajlouny (original humor, how-to); Elena Pantel (music, popular culture); Gwen Foss (general nonfiction).

Handles: "In addition to humor and titles concerning American popular culture, we will consider general nonfiction in the areas of 'how-to' books, history, joke books, cookbooks, popular reference, trivia, biography and memoirs." Query first with SASE. Reports in 4-6 weeks.

Recent Sales: *Tell Me All That You Know: Unofficial Grateful Dead Trivia Book*, by Brian Folker (Pinnacle); *The Confused Quote Book*, by Gwen Foss (Random House/Gramercy); *The Universal Crossword Index*, by Diane Spino (Berkley).

Terms: Agent receives 15% commission on domestic sales. Charges for postage, photocopying and phone expenses. Foreign and subsidiary rights commission fees established on per-sale basis.

Writers' Conferences ABA (Chicago); Mid-America Publishers Assoc. (Grand Rapids MI, September) Book Fair (Frankfurt, Germany, October).

Tips: Obtains new clients "typically from referrals and by some advertising and public relations projects. We also frequently speak at seminars for writers on the process of being published. Just make sure your project is clever, marketable and professionally prepared. We see too much material that is limited in scope and appeal. It helps immeasurably to have credentials in the field or topic being written about. Please do not submit material that is not within our areas of specialization."

LEE ALLAN AGENCY, (II), 7464 N. 107 St., Milwaukee WI 53224-3706. (414)357-7708. Contact: Lee Matthias. Estab. 1983. Signatory of WGA. Represents 15 clients. 50% of clients are new/previously unpublished writers. Specializes in suspense fiction. Currently handles: 90% novels; 5% movie scripts; 5% TV scripts. Member agents: Lee A. Matthias (all types of genre fiction and screenplays); Andrea Knickerbocker (fantasy, science fiction, romance); (Mr.) Chris Hill (fantasy).

Handles: Novels. Considers these fiction areas: action/adventure; contemporary issues; detective/police/crime; fantasy; feminist; historical; horror; mystery/suspense; psychic/supernatural; romance (contemporary, historical); science fiction; thriller/espionage. "No children's material, young adult, academic, textbooks, self-help, New Age, health, humor books."

Also Handles: Movie scripts (feature film); TV scripts (TV mow, episodeic drama). Considers these script subject areas: action/adventure; comedy; contemporary issues; detective/police/crime; horror; mystery/suspense; psychic/supernatural; romantic comedy and drama; science fiction; thriller; westerns/frontier.

● This agency reports that it is closed to queries and submissions for books and scripts through June 1997.

Terms: Agent receives 15% commission on domestic sales, except where commissions set by WGA; foreign higher. Offers written contract. Charges for photocopying, international telephone calls and/or excessive long-distance telephone calls, or international and/or mass submission shipping.

Tips: Obtains new clients mainly through recommendations and solicitations. If interested in agency representation, "read agency listings carefully and query the most compatible. Always query by letter with SASE or IRC with return-addressed envelope. A very brief, straightforward letter (one-two pages, maximum) introducing yourself, describing or summarizing your material will suffice. Avoid patronizing or 'cute' approaches. We *do not reply* to queries *without* SASE; we *do not* consider unsolicited submissions, and we *will not* hold them for later retrieval. Do not expect an agent to sell a manuscript that you know is not a likely sale if nonagented. Agents are not magicians; they serve best to find better and more of the likeliest publishers or producers. And they really do their work after an offer by way of negotiating contracts, selling subsidiary rights, administrating the account(s), advising the writer with objectivity, and acting as the buffer between writer and editor."

LINDA ALLEN LITERARY AGENCY, (II), 1949 Green St., Suite 5, San Francisco CA 94123. (415)921-6437. Contact: Linda Allen or Amy Kossow. Estab. 1982. Represents 35-40 clients. Specializes in "good books and nice people."

Handles: Nonfiction, novels (adult). Considers these nonfiction areas: anthropology/archaeology; art/ architecture/design; biography/autobiography; business; child guidance/parenting; computers/electronics; ethnic/cultural interests; gay/lesbian issues; government/politics/law; history; music/dance/theater/ film; nature/environment; New Age/metaphysics; popular culture; psychology; sociology; true crime/ investigative; women's issues/women's studies. Considers these fiction areas: action/adventure; contemporary issues; detective/police/crime; ethnic; feminist; gay; glitz; horror; lesbian; literary; mainstream; mystery/suspense; psychic/supernatural; regional; romance (regency); thriller/espionage. Query with SASE. Reports in 2-3 weeks on queries.
Terms: Agent receives 15% commission. Charges for photocopying.
Tips: Obtains new clients "by referral mostly."

MARCIA AMSTERDAM AGENCY, (II), 41 W. 82nd St., New York NY 10024-5613. (212)873-4945. Contact: Marcia Amsterdam. Estab. 1970. Signatory of WGA. Currently handles: 10% nonfiction books; 75% novels; 10% movie scripts; 5% TV scripts.
Handles: Novels. Considers these fiction areas: action/adventure; detective; glitz; historical; horror; humor; mainstream; mystery/suspense; romance (contemporary, historical); science fiction; thriller/ espionage; westerns/frontier; young adult. Send outline plus first 3 sample chapters and SASE. Reports in 1 month on queries.
Recent Sales: *Patrick Stewart: The Unauthorized Biography*, by James Hatfield and George Burt (Kensington); *Dark Morning*, by William H. Lovejoy (Kensington); *Moses Goes a Concert*, by Isaac Millman (Farrar, Straus & Giroux).
Also Handles: Movie scripts (feature film), TV scripts (TV mow, sitcom).
Terms: Agent receives 15% commission on domestic sales; 20% on foreign sales. Offers written contract, binding for 1 year, "renewable." Charges for extra office expenses, foreign postage, copying, legal fees (when agreed upon).
Tips: "We are always looking for interesting literary voices."

BART ANDREWS & ASSOCIATES INC., (III), 7510 Sunset Blvd., Suite 100, Los Angeles CA 90046. (213)851-8158. Contact: Bart Andrews. Estab. 1982. Member of AAR. Represents 25 clients. 25% of clients are new/previously unpublished authors. Specializes in nonfiction only, and in the general category of entertainment (movies, TV, biographies, autobiographies). Currently handles: 100% nonfiction books.
Handles: Nonfiction books. Considers these nonfiction areas: biography/autobiography; music/dance/ theater/film; TV. Query. Reports in 1 week on queries; 1 month on mss.
Recent Sales: *Roseanne*, by J. Randy Taraborrelli (G.P. Putnam's Sons); *Out of the Madness*, by Rose Books (packaging firm) (HarperCollins).
Terms: Agent receives 15% commission on domestic sales; 15% on foreign sales (after subagent takes his 10%). Offers written contract, "binding on a project-by-project basis." Author/client is charged for all photocopying, mailing, phone calls, postage, etc.
Writers' Conferences: Frequently lectures at UCLA in Los Angeles.
Tips: "Recommendations from existing clients or professionals are best, although I find a lot of new clients by seeking them out myself. I rarely find a new client through the mail. Spend time writing a query letter. Sell yourself like a product. The bottom line is writing ability, and then the idea itself. It takes a lot to convince me. I've seen it all! I hear from too many first-time authors who don't do their homework. They're trying to get a book published and they haven't the faintest idea what is required of them. There are plenty of good books on the subject and, in my opinion, it's their responsibility— not mine—to educate themselves before they try to find an agent to represent their work. When I ask an author to see a manuscript or even a partial manuscript, I really must be convinced I want to read it—based on a strong query letter—because I have no intention of wasting my time reading just for the fun of it."

APOLLO ENTERTAINMENT, (II), 1646 W. Julian, Unit C, Chicago IL 60622. (312)862-7864. Fax: (312)862-7974. Contact: Bruce Harrington. Estab. 1993. Signatory of WGA. Represents 8 clients. 20% of clients are new/previously unpublished writers. Specializes in feature screenplays of unordinary topics. Currently handles: 10% nonfiction books; 80% movie scripts, 10% TV scripts. Member agent: Nancy Lombardo (V.P. of Acquisitions).
● See the expanded listing for this agency in Script Agents.

APPLESEEDS MANAGEMENT, (II), 200 E. 30th St., Suite 302, San Bernardino CA 92404. (909)882-1667. For screenplays and teleplays only, send to 1870 N. Vermont, Suite 560, Hollywood CA 90027. Executive Manager: S. James Foiles. Estab. 1988. Signatory of WGA, licensed by state of California. 40% of clients are new/previously unpublished writers. Currently handles: 25% nonfiction books; 60% novels; 10% movie scripts; 5% teleplays (mow).
● This agency reports that it is not accepting unsolicited screenplays and teleplays at this time.

Handles: Nonfiction books, novels. Considers these nonfiction areas: business; health/medicine; money/finance/economics; music/dance/theater/film; psychology; self-help/personal improvement; true crime/investigative. Considers these fiction areas: detective/police/crime; fantasy; horror; mystery/suspense; psychic/supernatural; science fiction; true crime/investigative. Query. Reports in 2 weeks on queries; 2 months on mss.
Also Handles: Movie scripts. Specializes in materials that could be adapted from book to screen; and in screenplays and teleplays. TV scripts (TV mow, no episodic).
Terms: Agent receives 10-15% commission on domestic sales; 20% on foreign sales. Offers written contract, binding for 1-7 years.
Tips: "In your query, please describe your intended target audience and distinguish your book/script from similar works."

THE AUTHOR'S AGENCY, (I, II), 3355 N. Five Mile Rd., Suite 332, Boise ID 83713-3925. (208)376-5477. Contact: R.J. Winchell. Estab. 1995. Represents 30 clients. 35% of clients are new/previously unpublished writers. "We specialize in high concepts which have a dramatic impact." Currently handles: 30% nonfiction books; 40% novels; 30% movie scripts.
Handles: Nonfiction books, novels, movie scripts, TV scripts. Considers these nonfiction areas: animals; anthropology/archaeology; biography/autobiography; business; child guidance/parenting; cooking/food/nutrition; crafts/hobbies; current affairs; education; ethnic/cultural interests; government/politics/law; health/medicine; history; how-to; humor; interior design/decorating; language/literature/criticism; military/war; money/finance/economics; music/dance/theater/film; nature/environment; New Age/metaphysics; photography; popular culture; psychology; religious/inspirational; science/technology; self-help/personal improvement; sociology; sports; translations; true crime/investigative; women's issues/women's studies. Considers "any fiction supported by the author's endeavor to tell a story with excellent writing." Query or send entire ms with SASE. Reports in 1 month on mss.
Recent Sales: *Stargazer* (Warner); *The Quotable Vampire* (Kensington); *New Year's Eve, 1999* (BluStar).
Terms: Agent receives 15% commission on domestic sales; 15% on foreign sales. Offers written contract on project-by-project basis.
Also Handles: Movie scripts (feature film, animation); TV scripts (TV mow, miniseries, episodic drama, animation). "We consider all types of scripts." Query or send synopsis and 3 chapters with SASE. Reports in 1 month on mss.
Recent Sales: *Movie script(s) optioned/sold: New Year's Eve, 1999.*
Terms: Agent receives 10% commission on domestic sales; 10% on foreign sales. Charges for expenses (photocopying, etc.). 100% of business is derived from commissions on sales.
Tips: "We obtain writers through speaking engagements, and referrals such as this book. We believe that writers make a valuable contribution to society. As such, we offer encouragement and support to writers, whether we represent them or not."

‡AUTHORS ALLIANCE INC., (II), 45 Park Terrace West, Suite 3G, New York NY 10034. (212)942-7634. Fax: (212)942-7634. E-mail: camp544@aol.com. Contact: Chris Cane. Represents 15 clients. 10% of clients are new/previously unpublished writers. Currently handles: 40% nonfiction books; 30% movie scripts; 30% novels.
Handles: Nonfiction books, movie scripts, scholarly books, novels. Considers these nonfiction areas: biography/autobiography; business; child guidance/parenting; computers/electronics; cooking/food/nutrition; crafts/hobbies; current affairs; education; government/politics/law; health/medicine; history; how-to; humor; language/literature/criticism; military/war; money/finance/economics; music/dance/theater/film; nature/environment; New Age/metaphysics; psychology; religious/inspirational; self-help/personal improvement; sports; true crime/investigative. Considers these fiction areas: contemporary issues; detective/police/crime; erotica; fantasy; glitz; historical; literary; mainstream; mystery/suspense; romance (contemporary, gothic, historical); science fiction; thriller/espionage. Send outline and 3 sample chapters. Reports in 2 weeks on queries; 1 month on mss.
Terms: Agent receives 15% commission on domestic sales; 10% on foreign sales. Offers a written contract. Charges for postage, photocopying. Usually obtains clients through recommendations and queries.

AUTHORS' LITERARY AGENCY, (III), P.O. Box 610582, DFW Airport TX 75261-0582. (817)267-1078. Fax: (817)267-4368. E-mail: authorsliterary@juno.com. Contact: Dick Smith. Estab. 1992. Represents 25 clients. 70% of clients are new/previously unpublished writers. Currently handles: 60% nonfiction books; 40% novels.
Handles: Nonfiction books, novels. Considers most nonfiction areas, especially how-to; psychology; spiritual; self-help/personal improvement; true crime/investigative; women's issues/women's studies. Considers these fiction areas: detective/police/crime; fantasy; historical; horror; mystery/suspense; romance; science fiction; thriller/espionage; westerns/frontier; young adult. Query first always. Reports in 1 month on queries; 2 months on mss.

Recent Sales: *Fourth and Long: The Kent Waldrep Story*, by Kent Waldrep and Susan Malone (Crossroad); *Sessions: A Self-Help Guide Through Psychotherapy*, by Dr. Ann P. Wildemann, Ph.D. (Crossroad).

Terms: Agent receives 15% commission on domestic sales; 25% on foreign sales. Offers written contract.

Tips: "For fiction, always send query letter first with: 1) a synopsis or outline of your work, 2) an author's bio, 3) the first three chapters of your work, and 4) SASE. *Do not send entire manuscript* until the agency requests it. For nonfiction, submit a query letter first with 1) a bio stating your experience and credentials to write the work, 2) a book proposal (we suggest using Michael Larsen's *How To Write A Book Proposal* as a guideline), and 3) SASE. Always send SASE with all queries. We can neither consider nor respond to work submitted without SASE and adequate postage for return to you."

THE AXELROD AGENCY, (III), 54 Church St., Lenox MA 01240. (413)637-2000. Fax: (413)637-4725. Contact: Steven Axelrod. Estab. 1983. Member of AAR. Represents 30 clients. Specializes in commercial fiction, nonfiction. Currently handles: 40% nonfiction books; 60% fiction.
 • Prior to opening his agency, Mr. Axelrod served as an associate editor with The Literary Guild.

Handles: Considers these nonfiction areas: art; business; computers; government/politics/law; health/medicine; history; money/finance/economics; music/dance/theater/film; nature/environment; science/technology. Considers these fiction areas: cartoon/comic; detective/police/crime; family saga; glitz; historical; literary; mainstream; mystery/suspense; picture book; romance (contemporary, historical, regency); thriller/espionage. Query. Reports in 10 days on queries; 2-3 weeks on mss.

Terms: Agent receives 10% commission on domestic sales; 20% on foreign sales. Charges for photocopying.

Writers' Conferences: Romance Writers of America, Novelists, Inc.

Tips: Obtains new clients through referrals.

MALAGA BALDI LITERARY AGENCY, (II), 2112 Broadway, Suite 403, New York NY 10023. (212)579-5075. Contact: Malaga Baldi. Estab. 1985. Represents 40-50 clients. 80% of clients are new/previously unpublished writers. Specializes in quality literary fiction and nonfiction. Currently handles: 60% nonfiction books; 40% novels.

Handles: Nonfiction books, novels, novellas, short story collections. Considers any well-written nonfiction, but do *not* send child guidance, crafts, juvenile nonfiction, New Age/metaphysics, religious/inspirational or sports material. Considers any well-written fiction, but do *not* send confessional, family saga, fantasy, glitz, juvenile, picture book, psychic/supernatural, religious/inspirational, romance, science fiction, western or young adult. Query first, but prefers entire ms for fiction. Reports within a minimum of 10 weeks. "Please enclose self-addressed stamped jiffy bag or padded envelope with submission. If a self-addressed stamped postcard is included with the submission, it will be returned with notification of the arrival of the manuscript."

Recent Sales: *Like People in History*, by Felice Picano (Viking/Penguin); *What Jane Austen Ate and Charles Dickens Knew*, by Daniel Pool (Simon & Schuster).

Terms: Agent receives 15% commission on domestic sales; 20% on foreign sales. Offers written contract. Charges "initial $50 fee to cover photocopying expenses. If the manuscript is lengthy, I prefer the author to cover expense of photocopying."

Tips: "From the day I agree to represent the author, my role is to serve as his or her advocate in contract negotiations and publicity efforts. Along the way, I wear many different hats. To one author I may serve as a nudge, to another a confidante, and to many simply as a supportive friend. I am also a critic, researcher, legal expert, messenger, diplomat, listener, counselor and source of publishing information and gossip. I work with writers on developing a presentable submission and make myself available during all aspects of a book's publication."

BALKIN AGENCY, INC., (III), P.O. Box 222, Amherst MA 01004. (413)548-9835. Fax: (413)548-9836. President: Rick Balkin. Estab. 1972. Member of AAR. Represents 50 clients. 10% of clients are new/previously unpublished writers. Specializes in adult nonfiction. Currently handles: 85% nonfiction books; 5% scholarly books; 5% reference books; 5% textbooks.

AGENTS RANKED I AND II are most open to both established and new writers. Agents ranked **III** are open to established writers with publishing-industry references.

• Prior to opening his agency, Mr. Balkin served as executive editor with Bobbs-Merrill Company.

Handles: Nonfiction books, textbooks, reference, scholarly books. Considers these nonfiction areas: animals; anthropology/archaeology; biography; current affairs; health/medicine; history; how-to; language/literature/criticism; music/dance/theater/film; nature/environment; pop culture; science/technology; social science; translations; travel; true crime/investigative. Query with outline/proposal. Reports in 2 weeks on queries; 3 weeks on mss.

Recent Sales: *A Natural History of Glacier National Park*, by David Rockwell (Houghton-Mifflin); *Hiroshima: Why We Dropped The A-Bomb*, by Takaki (Little-Brown); *Consumer's Guide to Generic Drugs*, by D. Sullivan (Putnam/Berkley); *The Spirits Speak: One Woman's Mystical Journey Into the African Spirit World*, by Nicky Arden (Holt).

Terms: Agent receives 15% commission on domestic sales; 20% on foreign sales. Offers written contract, binding for 1 year. Charges for photocopying, trans-Atlantic long-distance calls or faxes and express mail.

Writers' Conferences: Jackson Hole Writers Conference (WY, July).

Tips: Obtains new clients through referrals. "I do not take on books described as bestsellers or potential bestsellers. Any nonfiction work that is either unique, paradigmatic, a contribution, truly witty or a labor of love is grist for my mill."

VIRGINIA BARBER LITERARY AGENCY, INC., 101 Fifth Ave., New York NY 10003. This agency did not respond to our request for information. Query before submitting.

LORETTA BARRETT BOOKS INC., (II), 101 Fifth Ave., New York NY 10003. (212)242-3420. Fax: (212)691-9418. President: Loretta A. Barrett. Associate: Karen Gerwin-Stoopack. Estab. 1990. Represents 70 clients. Specializes in general interest books. Currently handles: 25% fiction; 75% nonfiction.

Handles: Considers all areas of nonfiction. Considers these fiction areas: action/adventure; cartoon/comic; confessional; contemporary issues; detective/police/crime; erotica; ethnic; experimental; family saga; fantasy; feminist; gay; glitz; historical; horror; humor/satire; juvenile; lesbian; literary; mainstream; mystery/suspense; picture book; psychic/supernatural; regional; religious/inspirational; romance; sports; thriller/espionage; westerns/frontier; young adult. Query first, then send partial ms and synopsis. Reports in 4-6 weeks on queries and mss.

Terms: Agent receives 15% commission on domestic sales; 20% on foreign sales. Offers written contract.

THE WENDY BECKER LITERARY AGENCY, (I), 530-F Grand St., #11-H, New York NY 10002. Phone/fax: (212)228-5940. Estab. 1994. Specializes in business/investment/finance, due to agent's background as acquisitions editor in these areas. Currently handles: 90% nonfiction books; 10% novels (genre fiction: romance, mystery/thriller, science fiction).

Handles: Nonfiction books, novels (genre fiction only). Considers these nonfiction areas: art/architecture/design; biography/autobiography; business; child guidance/parenting; cooking/food/nutrition; crafts/hobbies; current affairs; government/politics/law; history; how-to; humor; interior design/decorating; military/war; money/finance/economics; music/dance/theater/film; nature/environment; photography; popular culture; psychology; science/technology; sociology; sports; women's issues/women's studies. Considers these fiction areas: fantasy; mystery/suspense; romance (gothic, historical, regency); science fiction; thriller/espionage. For nonfiction, send outline/proposal and résumé. For fiction, send outline and up to 3 sample chapters. Reports in 6 weeks on queries and partial mss.

Terms: Agent receives 15% commission on domestic sales; 20% on foreign sales. Offers written contract, with 90 day cancellation clause. 100% of business is derived from commissions on sales.

Writers' Conferences: RWA; ABA.

Tips: Obtains new clients through referrals and recommendations from editors, existing clients, meeting at conferences, unsolicited submittals. "Do your homework. Understand as much as you can (before contacting an agent) of the relationship between authors and agents, and the role an agent plays in the publishing process."

‡THE BEDFORD BOOK WORKS, INC., (I, III), 194 Katonah Ave., Katonah NY 10536. (914)242-6262. Fax: (914)242-5232. Contact: Joel E. Fishman (president), Lucy Herring Chambers (agent). Estab. 1993. Represents 30 clients. 50% of clients are new/previously unpublished writers. Currently handles: 80% nonfiction books, 20% novels. Member agents: Joel E. Fishman (narrative nonfiction, category nonfiction and commercial fiction); Lucy H. Chambers (literary fiction and women's issues).

Handles: Nonfiction books, novels. Considers these nonfiction areas: biography/autobiography; business; current affairs; health/medicine; history; how-to; humor; money/finance/economics; popular culture; psychology; science/technology; sports; women's issues/women's studies. Considers these fiction

areas: contemporary issues; literary; mainstream; mystery/suspense; thriller/espionage. Query. Reports in 2 weeks on queries; 2 months on mss.
Recent Sales: *Circle of Simplicity*, by Cecile Andrews (HarperCollins); *Winning's Only Part of the Game*, by Bobby Bowden et.al. (Warner); *Comedy Comes Clean*, by Adam Christing (Crown); *No Free Ride*, by Kweisi Mfume (Ballantine).
Terms: Agent receives 15% commission on domestic sales; 20% on foreign sales. Offers written contract, binding for 1 year with 60 day cancellation clause. Charges for postage and photocopying.
Tips: Obtains new clients through recommendations and solicitation. "Grab my attention right away with your query—not with gimmicks, but with excellent writing."

JOSH BEHAR LITERARY AGENCY, (I), Empire State Bldg., 350 Fifth Ave., Suite 3304, New York NY 10118. (212)826-4386. Contact: Josh Behar. Estab. 1993. Represents 12 clients. 90% of clients are new/previously unpublished writers. "I specialize in new and unpublished authors." Currently handles: 10% nonfiction books; 90% novels.
Handles: Nonfiction books, novels. Considers these nonfiction areas: biography/autobiography; business; money/finance/economics; New Age/metaphysics; self-help/personal improvement; women's issues/women's studies. Considers these fiction areas: action/adventure; detective/police/crime; fantasy; literary; psychic/supernatural; romance (contemporary, gothic, historical, regency); science fiction; thriller/espionage. Query. Reports in 1 week on queries; 1 month on mss.
Terms: Agent receives 15% commission on domestic sales; 20% on foreign sales. Offers written contract "only after sale has been made."
Writers' Conferences: RWA (NYC); MWA (NY); SciFi (TBA).
Tips: Obtains new clients through "conferences, editors and former agent I worked for. Tell me a good story."

PAM BERNSTEIN, (II), 790 Madison Ave., Suite 310, New York NY 10021. (212)288-1700. Fax: (212)288-3054. Contact: Pam Bernstein or Donna Dever. Estab. 1992. Member of AAR. Represents 50 clients. 20% of clients are new/previously unpublished writers. Specializes in commercial fiction and nonfiction. Currently handles: 60% nonfiction books; 40% fiction.
Handles: Considers these nonfiction areas: biography/autobiography; child guidance/parenting; cooking/food/nutrition; current affairs; government/politics/law; health/medicine; how-to; New Age/metaphysics; popular culture; psychology; religious/inspirational; science/technology; self-help/personal improvement; sociology; true crime/investigative; women's issues/women's studies. Considers these fiction areas: action/adventure; contemporary issues; detective/police/crime; ethnic; historical; mainstream; mystery/suspense; romance (contemporary); thriller/espionage. Query. Reports in 2 weeks on queries; 1 month on mss. Include postage for return of ms.
Terms: Agent receives 15% commission on domestic sales; 20% on foreign sales. Offers written contract, binding for 3 years, with 30 day cancellation clause. 100% of business is derived from commissions on sales.
Tips: Obtains new clients through referrals from published authors.

MEREDITH BERNSTEIN LITERARY AGENCY, (II), 2112 Broadway, Suite 503 A, New York NY 10023. (212)799-1007. Fax: (212)799-1145. Contact: Elizabeth Cavanaugh. Estab. 1981. Member of AAR. Represents approximately 85 clients. 20% of clients are new/previously unpublished writers. Does not specialize, "very eclectic." Currently handles: 50% nonfiction books; 50% fiction. Member agents: Meredith Bernstein, Elizabeth Cavanaugh.
  • Prior to opening her agency, Ms. Bernstein served in another agency for five years.
Handles: Fiction and nonfiction books. Query first.
Recent Sales: *Saving the Kingdom*, by Dr. Marty Goldstein (Knopf); *Optimum Health*, by Dr. Stephen Sinatra (Bantam); *Good Girls Guide to Great Sex*, by Debbie Peterson and Thom King (Harmony); *Pregnant Fathers*, by Jack Heinowitz (Andrews and McMeel).
Terms: Agent receives 15% commission on domestic sales; 20% on foreign sales. Charges $75 disbursement fee per year.
Writer's Conferences: Southwest Writers Conference (Albuquerque, August); Rocky Mountain Writers Conference (Denver, September); Beaumont (TX, October); Pacific Northwest Writers Conference; Austin League Writers Conference.
Tips: Obtains new clients through recommendations from others, queries and at conferences; also develops and packages own ideas.

‡DANIEL BIAL AGENCY, (II), 41 W. 83rd St., Suite 5-C, New York NY 10024. (212)721-1786. Contact: Daniel Bial. Estab. 1992. Represents under 50 clients. 15% of clients are new/previously unpublished writers. Currently handles: 90% nonfiction books; 10% novels.
Handles: Nonfiction books, novels. Considers these nonfiction areas: animals; anthropology/archaeology; biography/autobiography; business; child guidance/parenting; cooking/food/nutrition; current affairs; ethnic/cultural interests; gay/lesbian issues; government/politics/law; history; how-to; humor;

language/literature/criticism; military/war; money/finance/economics; music/dance/theater/film; nature/environment; New Age/metaphysics; popular culture; psychology; religious/inspirational; science/technology; self-help/personal improvement; sociology; sports; true crime/investigative; women's issues/women's studies. Considers these fiction areas: action/adventure; cartoon/comic; contemporary issues; detective/police/crime; erotica; ethnic; feminist; gay; humor/satire; literary. Send outline/proposal. Reports in 2 weeks on queries.

Recent Sales: *Encyclopedia of UFOs*, by Lewis (Contemporary Books); *PC Bible Stories*, by Moser (Crown); *Gay Guides*, by Collins (Fodors); *Econoguides*, by Sandler (Contemporary Books); *Encyclopedia of Modern Wicca*, by Louis/Kelly (Harper San Francisco).

Terms: Agent receives 15% commission on domestic sales; 20% on foreign sales. Offers written contract, binding for 1 year with 6 week cancellation clause. Charges for overseas calls, overnight mailing, photocopying.

Tips: Obtains new clients through recommendations, solicitation, "good Rolodex, over the transom. Good marketing is a key to success at all stages of publishing—successful authors know how to market themselves as well as their writing."

DAVID BLACK LITERARY AGENCY, INC. (II), 156 Fifth Ave., New York NY 10001. (212)242-5080. Fax: (212)924-6609. Contact: David Black, owner. Estab. 1990. Member of AAR. Represents 150 clients. Specializes in sports, politics, novels. Currently handles: 80% nonfiction; 20% novels. Member agent, Susan Raihofer, Gary Morris.

Handles: Nonfiction books, literary and commercial fiction. Considers these nonfiction areas: politics; sports. Query with outline and SASE. Reports in 2 months on queries.

Recent Sales: *The Temple Bombing*, by Melissa Fay Greene (Addison-Wesley); *Like Judgement Day*, by Michael D'orso (Grosset); *Turning Stones*, by Marc Parent (Harcourt Brace).

Terms: Agent receives 15% commission. Charges for photocopying and books purchased for sale of foreign rights.

BLASSINGAME SPECTRUM CORP., (II), 111 Eighth Ave., Suite 1501, New York NY 10011. (212)691-7556. Contact: Eleanor Wood, president. Represents 50 clients. Currently handles: 95% fiction; 5% nonfiction books. Member agent: Lucienne Diver.

Handles: Considers these fiction areas: contemporary issues; fantasy; historical; literary; mainstream; mystery/suspense; science fiction. Considers select nonfiction. Query with SASE. Reports in 2 months on queries.

Terms: Agent receives 10% commission on domestic sales.

Tips: Obtains new clients through recommendations from authors and others.

REID BOATES LITERARY AGENCY, (II), P.O. Box 328, 69 Cooks Crossroad, Pittstown NJ 08867. (908)730-8523. Fax: (908)730-8931. Contact: Reid Boates. Estab. 1985. Represents 45 clients. 15% of clients are new/previously unpublished writers. Specializes in general fiction and nonfiction, investigative journalism/current affairs; bios and autobiographies; serious self-help; literary humor; issue-oriented business; popular science; "no category fiction." Currently handles: 85% nonfiction books; 15% novels; "very rarely accept short story collections."

Handles: Nonfiction books, novels. Considers these nonfiction areas: animals; anthropology/archaeology; art/architecture/design; biography/autobiography; business; child guidance/parenting; current affairs; ethnic/cultural interests; government/politics/law; health/medicine; history; language/literature/criticism; nature/environment; psychology; science/technology; self-help/personal improvement; sports; true crime/investigative; women's issues/women's studies. Considers these fiction areas: contemporary issues; crime; family saga; mainstream; mystery/suspense; thriller/espionage. Query. Reports in 2 weeks on queries; 6 weeks on mss.

Terms: Agent receives 15% commission on domestic sales; 20% on foreign sales. Offers written contract, binding "until terminated by either party." Charges for photocopying costs above $50.

Tips: Obtain new clients through recommendations from others.

‡BOOK DEALS, INC., (I), 65 E. Scott St., Suite 16N, Chicago IL 60610. (312)664-4502. Contact: Caroline Carney. Estab. 1996. Represents 30 clients. 25% of clients are new/previously unpublished writers. Specializes in general interest adult fiction and nonfiction. Currently handles: 70% nonfiction books, 30% novels. Member agent: Andrew Seagre, associate agent.

Handles: Nonfiction books, novels, short story collections. Considers these nonfiction areas: animals; art/architecture/design; biography/autobiography; business; cooking/food/nutrition; current affairs; ethnic/cultural interests; government/politics/law; health/medicine; history; money/finance/economics; nature/environment; popular culture; science/technology; sports; translations. Considers these fiction areas: contemporary issues; ethnic; feminist; historical; humor/satire; literary; mainstream; science fiction; sports; white collar crime stories; urban literature. Send outline/proposal with SASE. Reports in 1-2 weeks on queries; 3-4 weeks on mss.

Terms: Agent receives 15% commission on domestic sales; 20% on foreign sales. Offers a written contract. Charges for professional expenses.

GEORGES BORCHARDT INC., (III), 136 E. 57th St., New York NY 10022. (212)753-5785. Fax: (212)838-6518. Estab. 1967. Member of AAR. Represents 200 clients. 10% of clients are new/previously unpublished writers. Specializes in literary fiction and outstanding nonfiction. Currently handles: 60% nonfiction books; 1% juvenile books; 37% novels; 1% novellas; 1% poetry books. Member agents: Denise Shannon, Anne Borchardt, Georges Borchardt.
Handles: Nonfiction books, novels. Considers these nonfiction areas: anthropology/archaeology; biography/autobiography; current affairs; history; women's issues/women's studies. Considers literary fiction. "Must be recommended by someone we know." Reports in 1 week on queries; 3-4 weeks on mss.
Recent Sales: *Snow Falling on Cedars*, by David Guterson (Harcourt Brace, Vintage, rights sold in England, France, Germany, Italy, Holland, Sweden, Denmark, Norway, Brazil, Greece); *John's Wife*, by Robert Coover (Simon & Schuster); *The Here and Now*, by Robert Cohen (Scribner). Also new books by John Lahr, Stanley Crouch, Richard Rodriguez, Ned Rorem, George Steiner and first novels by Pearl Abraham, Michael Jaffe and Kate Phillips.
Terms: Agent receives 15% commission on domestic and British sales; 20% on foreign sales (translation). Offers written contract. "We charge cost of (outside) photocopying and shipping mss or books overseas."
Tips: Obtains new clients through recommendations from others.

THE BARBARA BOVA LITERARY AGENCY, (II), 3951 Gulfshore Blvd., PH1-B, Still Naples FL 34103. (941)649-7237. Fax: (941)649-0757. Estab. 1974. Represents 35 clients. Specializes in fiction and nonfiction hard and soft science. Currently handles: 35% nonfiction books; 65% novels.
Handles: Considers these nonfiction areas: biography; business; cooking/food/nutrition; how-to; money/finance/economics; self-help/personal improvement; social sciences; true crimes/investigative; women's issues/women's studies. Considers these fiction areas: action/adventure; contemporary issues; detective/police/crime; family saga; glitz; mainstream; mystery/suspense; regional; romance (contemporary); science fiction; thrillers/espionage. Query with SASE. Reports in 1 month on queries.
Recent Sales: *Gray Matter*, by Shirley Kennett (Kensington); *Treasure Box*, by Orson Scott Card (HarperCollins); *Riding Towards Home*, by Borto Milan (Bantam); *Outside Agencies*, by Conor Daly (Kensington); *Moon Rise*, Ben Bova (Avon).
Terms: Agent receives 15% commission on domestic sales; handles foreign rights, movies, television, CDs.
Tips: Obtains new clients through recommendations from others.

‡BRADY LITERARY MANAGEMENT, (III), P.O. Box 64, Hartland Four Corners VT 05049. Contact: Sally Brady. Estab. 1986. Represents 100 clients.
Handles: Nonfiction books, literary and commercial fiction. Query with SASE. For fiction submit first 50 pages; for nonfiction submit outline and 2 sample chapters. Reports in 6-8 weeks on queries.
Terms: Agent receives 15% commission on domestic sales; 15% on foreign sales. Charges for extensive international postage and photocopying.

BRANDENBURGH & ASSOCIATES LITERARY AGENCY, (III), 24555 Corte Jaramillo, Murrieta CA 92562. (909)698-5200. Contact: Don Brandenburgh. Estab. 1986. Represents 10 clients. "We prefer previously published authors, but will evaluate submissions on their own merits." Works with a small number of new/unpublished authors. Specializes in adult nonfiction for the religious market; limited fiction for religious market. Currently handles: 70% nonfiction books; 20% novels.
● Prior to opening his agency, Mr. Brandenburgh served as executive director of the Evangelical Christian Publishers Association.
Handles: Nonfiction books, novels. Query with outline. Reports in 2 weeks on queries. No response without SASE.
Recent Sales: *Downsizing the U.S.A.*, by Thomas Naylor and Will Willimon (William B. Eerdmans); *What to Do With Wishes That Don't Come True*, by Maribeth Ekey (Servant Publications).

AGENTS WHO SPECIALIZE in a specific subject area such as computer books or in handling the work of certain writers such as gay or lesbian writers are ranked **IV**.

Terms: Agent receives 10% commission on domestic sales; 20% on dramatic sales; 20% on foreign sales. Charges $35 mailing/materials fee with signed agency agreement.

THE JOAN BRANDT AGENCY, (II), 788 Wesley Dr. NW, Atlanta GA 30305-3933. (404)351-8877. Contact: Joan Brandt or Alan Schwartz. Estab. 1990. Represents 100 clients. Also handles movie rights for other agents.

● Prior to opening her agency, Ms. Brandt served as an agent with Sterling Lord Literistic in New York for 18 years.

Handles: Novels, nonfiction books. Considers these fiction areas: contemporary issues; detective/police/crime; literary; mainstream; mystery/suspense; thriller/espionage; "also will consider popular, topical nonfiction." Query with SASE. Reports in 2 weeks on queries.

Terms: Agent receives 15% commission on domestic sales; 20% on foreign sales (co-agents in all major marketplaces). Charges for photocopying and submission postage.

Tips: "Query letter and synopsis only: no writing samples, no telephone or fax queries. A well-written query/synopsis with professional presentation may result in a Joan Brandt Agency request to see a partial or whole manuscript. Most new clients are recommended by other agents, editors or current clients."

Hochman

BRANDT & ~~BRANDT~~ LITERARY AGENTS INC., (III), 1501 Broadway, New York NY 10036. (212)840-5760. Fax: (212)840-5776. Contact: Carl Brandt, Gail Hochman, Marianne Merola, Charles Schlessiger. Estab. 1913. Member of AAR. Represents 200 clients.

Handles: Nonfiction books, scholarly books, juvenile books, novels, novellas, short story collections. Considers these nonfiction areas: agriculture/horticulture; animals; anthropology/archaeology; art/architecture/design; biography/autobiography; business; child guidance/parenting; cooking/food/nutrition; crafts/hobbies; current affairs; ethnic/cultural interests; gay/lesbian issues; government/politics/law; health/medicine; history; interior design/decorating; juvenile nonfiction; language/literature/criticism; military/war; money/finance/economics; music/dance/theater/film; nature/environment; psychology; science/technology; self-help/personal improvement; sociology; sports; true crime/investigative; women's issues/women's studies. Considers these fiction areas: action/adventure; contemporary issues; detective/police/crime; erotica; ethnic; experimental; family saga; feminist; gay; historical; humor/satire; lesbian; literary; mainstream; mystery/suspense; psychic/supernatural; regional; romance; science fiction; sports; thriller/espionage; westerns/frontier; young adult. Query. Reports in 1 month on queries.

Terms: Agent receives 15% commission on domestic sales; 20% on foreign sales. Charges for "manuscript duplication or other special expenses agreed to in advance."

Tips: Obtains new clients through recommendations from others or "upon occasion, a really good letter. Write a letter which will give the agent a sense of you as a professional writer, your long-term interests as well as a short description of the work at hand."

‡BROCK GANNON LITERARY AGENCY, (I), 172 Fairview Ave., Cocoa FL 32927. (407)633-6217. Contact: Louise Peters. Estab. 1996. Represents 12 clients. "We are a new agency open to all writers with marketable writing skills." Currently handles: 100% novels. Member agents: Deborah Hudak (young adult, children); James D. Roaché (fiction); Louise Peters.

Handles: Nonfiction books, juvenile books, novels, poetry books, short story collections. Considers these nonfiction areas: animals; anthropology/archaeology; biography/autobiography; business; child guidance/parenting; cooking/food/nutrition; current affairs; ethnic/cultural interests; gay/lesbian issues; government/politics/law; health/medicine; how-to; humor; juvenile nonfiction; language/literature/criticism; military/war; money/finance/economics; music/dance/theater/film; nature/environment; New Age/metaphysics; popular culture; religious/inspirational; self-help/personal improvement; sports; true crime/investigative; women's issues/women's studies. Considers these fiction areas: action/adventure; confessional; contemporary issues; detective/police/crime; erotica; ethnic; family saga; fantasy; feminist; gay; historical; horror; humor/satire; juvenile; lesbian; literary; mainstream; mystery/suspense; psychic/supernatural; regional; religious/inspirational; romance (contemporary, gothic, historical, regency); sports; thriller/espionage; young adult. Query. Reports in 3 weeks on queries; 4-6 weeks on ms.

Terms: Agent receives 10% commission on domestic sales; 20% on foreign sales. Offers written contract, binding for 6 months, with 30 day cancellation clause. Charges for postage, photocopying, long-distance calls.

Also Handles: Movie scripts (feature film); TV scripts (TV mow, miniseries, episodic drama). Considers these script subject areas: action/adventure; comedy; contemporary issues; detective/police/crime; ethnic; experimental; family saga; fantasy; feminist; gay; glitz; horror; humor; juvenile; lesbian; mainstream; mystery/suspense; psychic/supernatural; religious/inspirational; romantic; science fiction; teen; thriller; western/frontier. Send outline/proposal with SASE. Reports in 1-2 weeks on queries; 2-4 weeks on mss.

Writers' Conferences: Space Coast Writers Guild (Cocoa Beach, FL, first weekend in November).
Tips: Obtains new clients through recommendations, solicitation (short-term, to establish an initial client list) and at conferences.

MARIE BROWN ASSOCIATES INC., (II, III), 625 Broadway, New York NY 10012. (212)533-5534. Fax: (212)533-0849. Contact: Marie Brown. Estab. 1984. Represents 100 clients. Specializes in multicultural African-American writers. Currently handles: 50% nonfiction books; 25% juvenile books; 25% other. Associate agents: Joanna Blankson, Lesley Ann Brown, Janell Walden Agyeman.
Handles: Considers these nonfiction areas: art; biography; business; ethnic/cultural interests; gay/lesbian issues; history; juvenile nonfiction; money/finance/economics; music/dance/theater/film; psychology; religious/inspirational; self-help/personal improvement; sociology; women's issues/women's studies. Considers these fiction areas: contemporary issues; ethnic; feminist; gay; historical; juvenile; literary; mainstream. Query with SASE. Reports in 10 weeks on queries.
Recent Sales: *Slim Brown Face at the Table*, by Gwendolyn Parker (Houghton Mifflin); *Lessons in Living*, by Susan Taylor (Doubleday); *Brother Man*, by Boyd & Allen (Ballantine).
Terms: Agent receives 15% commission on domestic sales; 25% on foreign sales. Offers written contract.
Tips: Obtains new clients through recommendations from others.

CURTIS BROWN LTD., (II), 10 Astor Place, New York NY 10003-6935. (212)473-5400. Member of AAR; signatory of WGA. Perry Knowlton, Chairman & CEO. Peter L. Ginsberg, President. Member agents: Laura J. Blake; Ellen Geiger; Emilie Jacobson, Vice President; Virginia Knowlton; Timothy Knowlton, COO (film, screenplays, plays); Marilyn Marlow, Executive Vice President; Jess Taylor (film, screenplays, plays); Maureen Walters, Queries to Laura J. Blake.
Handles: Nonfiction books, juvenile books, novels, novellas, short story collections, poetry books. All categories of nonfiction and fiction considered. Query. Reports in 3 weeks on queries; 3-5 weeks on mss (only if requested).
Terms: Offers written contract. Charges for photocopying, some postage.
Also Handles: Movie scripts (feature film), TV scripts (TV mow), stage plays. Considers these script subject areas: action/adventure; comedy; detective/police/crime; ethnic; feminist; gay; historical; horror; lesbian; mainstream; mystery/suspense; psychic/supernatural; romantic comedy and drama; thriller; westerns/frontier.
Tips: Obtains new clients through recommendations from others, solicitation, at conferences and query letters.

ANDREA BROWN LITERARY AGENCY, INC., (III, IV), P.O. Box 429, El Granada CA 94018-0429. (415)728-1783. Contact: Andrea Brown. Estab. 1981. Member of AAR, WNBA. 10% of clients are new/previously unpublished writers. Specializes in "all kinds of children's books—illustrators and authors including multimedia writers and designers." Currently handles: 98% juvenile books; 2% novels. Member agent: Andrea Brown (president).
 • Prior to opening her agency, Ms. Brown served as an editorial assistant at Random House and Dell Publishing and as an editor with Alfred A. Knopf.
Handles: Juvenile books and multimedia projects. Considers these juvenile nonfiction areas: animals; anthropology/archaeology; art/architecture/design; biography/autobiography; current affairs; ethnic/cultural interests; history; how-to; juvenile nonfiction; nature/environment; photography; popular culture; science/technology; sociology; sports. Considers these fiction areas: historical; juvenile; picture book; romance (historical); science fiction; young adult. Query. Reports in 1-3 weeks on queries; 1-3 months on mss.
Recent Sales: *X-Files Novelization*, by Eric Elfman (HarperCollins); *Barf and Booger Book*, by Shirley Gross (Berkley); *Tiger, Tiger Burn Bright*, by Mel Glenn (Dutton/Lodestar); *Beyond the Five Senses*, by Caroline Arnold (Charlesbridge).
Terms: Agent receives 15% commission on domestic sales; 20% on foreign sales. Written contract.
Writers' Conferences: Austin Writers League; SCBWI, Orange County Conferences; Mills College Childrens Literature Conference (Oakland CA); Asilomar (Pacific Grove CA); Maui Writers Conference, Southwest Writers Conference.
Tips: Mostly obtains new clients through recommendations, editors, clients and agents. "Taking on very few picture books. Must be unique—no rhyme, no anthropomorphism. Do not fax queries or manuscripts."

PEMA BROWNE LTD., (II), HCR Box 104B, Pine Rd., Neversink NY 12765-9603. (914)985-2936. Contact: Perry Browne or Pema Browne. Estab. 1966. Member of SCBWI, RWA. Represents 50 clients. Handles any commercial fiction, nonfiction, romance, juvenile and children's picture books. Currently handles: 25% nonfiction books; 25% juvenile books; 45% novels; 5% movie scripts. Member agents: Pema Browne (juvenile, nonfiction); Perry Browne (romance, nonfiction, literary fiction).

INSIDER REPORT

From mega bytes to mega bucks: Online exchange leads to multi-book deal

Landing a spot on the *New York Times* bestseller list was the farthest thing from Diana Gabaldon's mind when she began writing and posting bits of her writing on CompuServe. An assistant ecology professor at Arizona State University and a freelance writer specializing in computers, Gabaldon decided nearly ten years ago to write a novel, just to see if she could get from beginning to end. Now she's authored four books: *Outlander, Voyager, Dragonfly in Amber* and *Drums of Autumn.*

Diana Gabaldon

Photo by Carl Shumacher

"I knew from doing a little research that writing was a very uncertain career. Most people don't even finish their books, and most who do, don't get published. Those who do get published—for the most part—don't make a living off their writing," says Gabaldon. "I think the Writers Guild of America said that its average member makes $7,000 a year from writing. If you have Danielle Steel and Stephen King at one end, you have a whole lot of people at the other end to get that as an average. So I was not counting on writing as a career. But at the same time, I always wanted to do it. Finally, I said, 'I don't want to be 65 and think I should have tried this when I was younger. So I'm going to try. And I don't care whether I succeed. I just want to see if I can write a book. I just want to know if I can get from one end to the other.' "

She began writing, but kept quiet about it. She didn't even tell those she chatted with regularly online in CompuServe's Literary Forum. The forum was designed for writers and readers, and was full of some impressive company. "I know way too many people who say, 'Oh yes, I'm writing a book,' and then you never hear anymore about it," says Gabaldon, who did not want to be one of those people. "And I was certainly not going to mention my writing a book in front of any of the published authors who were there, those godlike beings."

She probably wouldn't have either, if not for a certain e-mail conversation. "I was having a discussion with a gentleman online, and he was telling me that he knew all about what it felt like to be pregnant because his wife had three children. I just laughed electronically. I said, 'Yeah, buster, I've had three children,' " and, coincidentally, she had just finished writing a chapter in which character Jenny Murray—born Janet Fraser—tells her brother Jamie what pregnancy is like. When pressed, Gabaldon posted the chapter in the electronic library where it was read

INSIDER REPORT, *Gabaldon*

by several Literary Forum regulars. They wanted more.

"They said, 'This is great. What is it?' And I said, 'I don't know.' They said, 'Where's the beginning?' And I said, 'I haven't written that yet.' And they said, 'Well, put up some more!' So whenever I had a chunk that would stand by itself I would put it in the library, one every two to three months. And people kept getting more and more interested in it, and they began talking about the pieces I posted."

Her Literary Forum followers also encouraged her to try to publish her work. She asked them how, and was advised first to find an agent. Eventually, one of her online friends, author John Stith, offered to write to his agent Perry Knowlton, of Curtis Brown Ltd., on her behalf. "So I followed this up with my own query, explaining to Perry the various things that I had done, but that now I was undertaking fiction for the first time and I understood that I really needed a literary agent," Gabaldon says. "He very kindly called me back a couple of weeks later and said yes, he'd be happy to read my excerpts. So I sent him the chunks I had and sort of a crude synopsis so that he could tell where they fit. And he took me on, on the basis of an unfinished first novel, which is unusual."

Gabaldon says she's glad he did. Four days after Gabaldon met with Knowlton in New York, four editors were bidding for the chance to publish her now-finished book. She eventually ended up with a contract for three books worth just a little more than $1 million. "I was sandbagged, thinking 'this is not real, this has not happened,' " Gabaldon says. Not only was she impressed by the size of the contract, but the speed with which everything happened. That is, she says, an advantage of a good agent. "They may have offered so much because it was a good book, but they read it in four days because it came from Perry."

Gabaldon doesn't believe any of this success would have happened without her agent. "I've seen quite a lot of writers by now, and I know several without agents. Those without agents do not do nearly as well as those with agents. The inexperienced ones—these are especially romance writers, where it is possible to make a sale without an agent—tend to be taken advantage of, scandalously, by their publishers. They're offered very low advances, poor royalty arrangements, and often have their subsidiary rights virtually stolen."

Agents also offer contract advice, Gabaldon says. When the bidding battle narrowed to two, Knowlton suggested Gabaldon sign with Delacorte Press because their offer came from editor Jackie Cantor. He said she was not only an excellent editor but this was her first week on the job. "You'd be her first acquisition and she'd make you a star," he told Gabaldon. Considering the contract she received, Knowlton's speculation wasn't far off. A good agent anticipates how an editor will respond to a manuscript.

Although going online has proven beneficial for her, Gabaldon wants to make it clear that Knowlton was not roaming around online soliciting writers. Keep in mind that she pursued him because other authors she met online had recommended him to her. She did her own research to make sure he was with a reputable firm, and that he handled her sort of book, before she entrusted him with her work.

Gabaldon stresses that you must always research your prospective agents, regardless of where or how you meet them. "What I usually recommend is that

---

INSIDER REPORT, *continued*

writers either check out the literary agent reference guides or join one of the very large writers organizations like the Romance Writers of America or the Western Writers of America, many of whom keep a list of solid agents," she says. "Another option is to write to the Association of Authors' Representatives and ask if this agent is a member. While there are many good agents who are not AAR members, knowing the agent is a member tells you two things. One, they have been in the business for at least two years, because that's a requirement for membership; and two, they subscribe to the canon of ethics the AAR upholds."

One final suggestion Gabaldon offers is that once you get to the point of talking with agents, ask them for a client list. "If there isn't much on that list, or if the agent won't show you his list, you should steer clear," she says. "But if there are authors and publishers you recognize on that list, that's a good sign."

—*Mary Jennings*

Handles: Nonfiction books, scholarly books, juvenile books, novels. Considers these nonfiction areas: anthropology/archaeology; art/architecture/design; biography/autobiography; business; child guidance/ parenting; cooking/food/nutrition; current affairs; education; ethnic/cultural interests; gay/lesbian issues; government/politics/law; health/medicine; how-to; juvenile nonfiction; military/war; money/finance/economics; nature/environment; New Age/metaphysics; popular culture; psychology; religious/ inspirational; science/technology; self-help/personal improvement; sports; true crime/investigative; women's issues/women's studies. Considers these fiction areas: action/adventure, contemporary issues; detective/police/crime; ethnic; feminist; gay; glitz; historical; humor/satire; juvenile; lesbian; literary; mainstream; mystery/suspense; picture book; psychic/supernatural; religious/inspirational; romance (contemporary, gothic, historical, regency); science fiction; thriller/espionage; westerns/frontier; young adult. Query with SASE. Reports in 2 weeks on queries; within 1 month on mss.
Recent Sales: *Old Games New Rules*, by Gary Grappo (Berkley); *Forever In My Heart*, by Joanne Goodman (Historical/Kensington); *The Kwanzaa Contest*, by Moore/Taylor (Hyperion Children's Books); *The Little Ghost Who Couldn't Say Boo*, by Lynda Graham Barber (Candlewick); *Deadbeat*, by Linda Cargill (Cora Verlag).
Terms: Agent receives 15% commission on domestic sales; 20% on foreign sales.
Tips: Obtains new clients through "editors, authors, *LMP*, *Guide to Literary Agents* and as a result of longevity! If writing romance, be sure to receive guidelines from various romance publishers. In nonfiction, one must have credentials to lend credence to a proposal. Make sure of margins, double-space and use clean, dark type."

HOWARD BUCK AGENCY, (II), 80 Eighth Ave., Suite 1107, New York NY 10011. (212)807-7855. Contact: Howard Buck or Mark Frisk. Estab. 1981. Represents 75 clients. "All-around agency." Currently handles: 75% nonfiction books; 25% novels.
Handles: Nonfiction, novels. Considers all nonfiction and fiction areas except children's, juvenile, picture book, young adult or science fiction/fantasy. Query with SASE. Reports in 6 weeks on queries. "We do not read original screenplays."
Terms: Agent receives 15% commission on domestic sales. Offers written contract. Charges for office expenses, postage and photocopying.
Tips: Obtains new clients through recommendations from others.

SHEREE BYKOFSKY ASSOCIATES, INC., (IV), 11 E. 47th St., Box WD, New York NY 10017. Estab. 1984. Incorporated 1991. Member of AAR, ASJA, WNBA. Represents "a limited number of" clients. Specializes in popular reference nonfiction. Currently handles: 80% nonfiction; 20% fiction.
• Prior to opening her agency, Ms. Bykofsky served as the manager of Chiron Press. She is also the author of six books. See Ms. Bykofsky's article, The Seven Most Common Questions Posed to Agents, in this edition of the *Guide*.
Handles: Nonfiction and commercial and literary fiction. Considers all nonfiction areas, especially biography/autobiography; business; child guidance/parenting; cooking/foods/nutrition; current affairs;

ethnic/cultural interests; gay/lesbian issues; health/medicine; history; how-to; humor; music/dance/ theater/film; popular culture; psychology; inspirational; self-help/personal improvement; true crime/ investigative; women's issues/women's studies. "I have wide-ranging interests, but it really depends on quality of writing, originality, and how a particular project appeals to me (or not). I take on very little fiction unless I completely love it—it doesn't matter what area or genre." Query with SASE. No unsolicited mss or phone calls. Reports in 1 week on short queries; 1 month on solicited mss.

Recent Sales: *Handbook for the Soul*, by Richard Carlson and Benjamin Shield (Little Brown); *Give Me a Moment and I'll Change Your Life*, by Alan Lakein (Kodansha); *No Human Involved*, by Barbara Seranella (St. Martin's); *Talking With Confidence for the Painfully Shy*, by Don Gabor (Crown); *Life's Little Frustration Book*, by G. Gaynor McTigue (St. Martin's); *Jimmy Carter: American Moralist*, by Kenneth Morris (University of Georgia); *Movie Time*, by Gene Brown (Macmillan); and *Debt Free*, by John and James Caher (Holt).

Terms: Agent receives 15% commission on domestic sales; 15% on foreign sales. Offers written contract, binding for 1 year "usually." Charges for postage, photocopying and fax.

Writers' Conferences: ASJA (NYC); Asilomar (Pacific Grove CA); Kent State; Southwestern Writers; Dorothy Canfield Fisher (San Diego); Writers Union (Maui); Pacific NW; ASJA (New York); IWWG; and many others.

Tips: Obtains new clients through recommendations from others. "Read the agent listing carefully and comply with guidelines."

CANTRELL-COLAS INC., LITERARY AGENCY, (II), 229 E. 79th St., New York NY 10021. (212)737-8503. Estab. 1980. Represents 80 clients. Currently handles: 45% nonfiction books; 10% juvenile books; 45% mainstream.

Handles: Considers these nonfiction areas: anthropology; art; biography; child guidance/parenting; cooking/food/nutrition; current affairs; ethnic/cultural interests; government/politics/law; health/medicine; history; juvenile nonfiction; language/literature/criticism; military/war; money/finance/economics; nature/environment; New Age/metaphysics; psychology; science/technology; self-help/personal improvement; sociology; true crime/investigative; women's issues/women's studies. Considers these fiction areas: contemporary issues; detective/police/crime; experimental; family saga; feminist; historical; humor/satire; juvenile; literary; mainstream; mystery/suspense; psychic/supernatural; science fiction; thriller/espionage; young adult. Query with outline, 2 sample chapters, SASE and "something about author also." Reports in 2 months on queries.

Recent Sales: *Escapade*, by Kasey Michaels (Pocket Books); *Roosevelt and De Gaulle*, by Raoul Aglion; *Miami: A Saga*, by Evelyn Wilde-Mayerson (Viking); *Bride of the Unicorn*, by Kasey Michaels (Pocket Books).

Terms: Agent receives 15% commission on domestic sales; commission varies on foreign sales. Offers written contract. Charges for foreign postage and photocopying.

Tips: Obtains new clients through recommendations from others. "Make sure your manuscript is in excellent condition both grammatically and cosmetically. Check for spelling, typing errors and legibility."

MARIA CARVAINIS AGENCY, INC., (II), 235 West End Ave., New York NY 10023. (212)580-1559. Fax: (212)877-3486. Contact: Maria Carvainis. Estab. 1977. Member of AAR, Authors Guild, signatory of WGA. Represents 35 clients. 10% of clients are new/previously unpublished writers. Currently handles: 25% nonfiction books; 15% juvenile books; 55% novels; 5% poetry books.

● Maria Carvainis is a member of the AAR Board of Directors, AAR Treasurer and Board Liaison to the AAR Contracts Commmittee.

Handles: Nonfiction books, scholarly books, novels, poetry books. Considers these nonfiction areas: biography/autobiography; business; current affairs; government/politics/law; health/medicine; history; military/war; money/finance/economics; psychology; true crime/investigative; women's issues/women's studies; popular science. Considers these fiction areas: action/adventure; detective/police/crime; family saga; fantasy; glitz; historical; humor/satire; juvenile; literary; mainstream; mystery/suspense; romance; thriller/espionage; westerns/frontier; children's; young adult. Query first with SASE. Reports within 2-3 weeks on queries; within 3 months on solicited mss.

Terms: Agent receives 15% commission on domestic sales; 20% on foreign sales. Offers written contract, binding for 2 years "on a book-by-book basis." Charges for foreign postage and bulk copying.

Tips: "75% of new clients derived from recommendations or conferences. 25% of new clients derived from letters of query."

MARTHA CASSELMAN LITERARY AGENT, (III), P.O. Box 342, Calistoga CA 94515-0342. (707)942-4341. Contact: Martha Casselman or Judith Armenta. Estab. 1978. Member of AAR, IACP. Represents 30 clients. Specializes in "nonfiction, especially food books. Do not send any submission without query." Member agent: Judith Armenta (New Age and alternative medicine nonfiction, general nonfiction).

Handles: Nonfiction proposals only, food-related proposals and cookbooks. Considers these nonfiction areas: agriculture/horticulture; anthropology/archaeology; biography/autobiography; cooking/food/nutrition; health/medicine; women's issues/women's studies. Send proposal with outline, SASE, plus 3 sample chapters. "Don't send mss!" Reports in 3 weeks on queries.
Terms: Agent receives 15% commission on domestic sales; 20% on foreign sales (if using subagent). Offers contract review for hourly fee, on consultation with author. Charges for photocopying, overnight and overseas mailings.
Writers' Conferences: IACP (Chicago, April 1997), other food-writers' conferences.
Tips: Obtains new clients through referrals. "No tricky letters; no gimmicks; *always* include SASE or mailer."

CASTIGLIA LITERARY AGENCY, (II), 1155 Camino Del Mar, Suite 510, Del Mar CA 92014. (619)753-4361. Fax: (619)753-5094. Contact: Julie Castiglia. Estab. 1993. Member of AAR, PEN. Represents 50 clients. Currently handles: 60% nonfiction books; 35% novels.
  • Prior to opening her agency, Ms. Castiglia served as an agent with Waterside Productions, as well as working as a freelance editor and published writer of three books.
Handles: Nonfiction books, novels. Considers these nonfiction areas: animals; anthropology/archaeology; biography/autobiography; business; child guidance/parenting; cooking/food/nutrition; current affairs; ethnic/cultural interests; finance; health/medicine; history; language/literature/criticism; nature/environment; New Age/metaphysics; psychology; religious/inspirational; science/technology; self-help/personal improvement; sociology; women's issues/women's studies. Considers these fiction areas: contemporary issues; ethnic; glitz; literary; mainstream; mystery/suspense; women's fiction especially. Send outline/proposal plus 2 sample chapters; send synopsis with 2 chapters for fiction. Reports in 6-8 weeks on mss.
Recent Sales: *Old Mac Donald*, by John Peak (St. Martin's Press); *The Way is Within*, by Ron Rathbun (Berkeley Press); *Growing Something Besides Old*, by Laurie Beth Jones (Simon & Schuster); *The Quotable Mark Twain*, by Kent Rasmussen (Contemporary); *Living with Your Genes*, by Dean Hamer and Peter Copeland (Doubleday); *Remember the Time*, by Annette Reynolds (Bantam).
Terms: Agent receives 15% commission on domestic sales; 20% on foreign sales. Offers written contract, 6 week termination. Charges for excessive postage and copying.
Writers' Conferences: Southwestern Writers Conference (Albuquerque NM August). National Writers Conference; Willamette Writers Conference (OR); San Diego State University (CA).
Tips: Obtains new clients through solicitations, conferences, referrals. "Be professional with submissions. Attend workshops and conferences before you approach an agent."

CHARISMA COMMUNICATIONS, LTD., (IV), 210 E. 39th St., New York NY 10016. (212)832-3020. Fax: (212)772-0393. Contact: James W. Grau. Estab. 1972. Represents 10 clients. 20% of clients are new/previously unpublished writers. Specializes in organized crime, Indian casinos, FBI, CIA, secret service, NSA, corporate and private security, casino gaming, KGB. Currently handles: 50% nonfiction books; 20% movie scripts; 20% TV scripts; 10% other. Member agent: Phil Howart; Rena Delduca (reader).
Handles: Nonfiction books, novels, movie scripts, TV scripts. Considers these nonfiction areas: biography/autobiography; current affairs; government/politics/law; military/war; true crime/investigative. Considers these fiction areas: contemporary issues; detective/police/crime; mystery/suspense; religious/inspirational; sports; cult issues. Considers these script areas: movie scripts (feature film, documentary); TV scripts (TV mow, miniseries). Send outline/proposal. Reports in 1 month on queries; 2 months on mss.
Recent Sales: Untitled documentary (Scripps Howard).
Terms: Agent receives 10% commission on domestic sales; variable commission on foreign sales. Offers variable written contract. 100% of business is derived from commissions on sales.
Tips: New clients are established writers.

JAMES CHARLTON ASSOCIATES, (II), 680 Washington St., #2A, New York NY 10014. (212)691-4951. Fax: (212)691-4952. Contact: Lisa Friedman: Estab. 1983. Specializes in military history, sports. Currently handles: 100% nonfiction books.
Handles: Nonfiction books. Considers these nonfiction areas: child guidance/parenting; cooking/food/nutrition; health/medicine; how-to; humor; military/war; popular culture; self-help/personal improvement; sports. Query with SASE for response. Reports in 2 weeks on queries.
Recent Sales: *The Safe Child Book*, by Kraizer (Simon & Schuster); *West Point Atlas of American Wars, Vol. II*, compiled by West Point (Holt); *Terrible Moms*, by Greg Daugherty (Simon & Schuster).
Terms: Agent receives 15% commission on domestic sales. Offers written contract, with 60 day cancellation clause.
Tips: Obtains new clients through recommendations from others.

CIRCLE OF CONFUSION LTD., (II), 666 Fifth Ave., Suite 303J, New York NY 10103. (212)969-0653. Fax: (212)975-7748. Contact: Rajeev K. Agarwal, Lawrence Mattis. Estab. 1990. Signatory of WGA. Represents 60 clients. 60% of clients are new/previously unpublished writers. Specializes in screenplays for film and TV. Currently handles: 15% novels; 5% novellas; 80% movie scripts. Member agents: Rageev Agarwal, Lawrence Mattis, Annmarie Negretti.

• See the expanded listing for this agency in Script Agents.

CISKE & DIETZ LITERARY AGENCY, (II), P.O. Box 555, Neenah WI 54957. (414)722-5944. Contact: Fran Ciske. Also: 10605 W. Wabash Ave., Milwaukee WI 53224. (414)355-8915. Contact: Andrea Boeshaar. Represents 20 clients. Estab. 1993. Member of RWA. Specializes in romance, women's fiction. Currently handles: 80% fiction; 20% nonfiction. Member agents: Patricia Dietz (action/adventure, thrillers, young adult); Fran Ciske (romance, mystery/suspense, action/adventure, fiction, nonfiction); Andrea Boeshaar (primarily Christian).
Handles: Considers these nonfiction areas: cooking/food/nutrition; religious/inspirational; self-help/personal improvement; true crime; women's issues/women's studies. Considers these fiction areas: mystery/suspense; religious/inspiration; romance (contemporary, historical, regency, time travel); thriller; westerns/frontier. Query. No unsolicited mss. Reports in 2 weeks on queries; 2 months on mss.
Terms: Agent receives 15% commission on domestic sales; 20% on foreign sales. Offers non-binding terms agreement. Expenses for photocopying will be agreed upon in advance.
Writers' Conferences: RWA National conference, Wisconsin RWA conferences and workshops.
Tips: Obtains new clients through recommendation, solicitation and conferences. No phone queries, please. "Agency handles religious/inspirationals for the Evangelical Christian market. No New Age or occult. No reply without SASE. Target a market."

CONNIE CLAUSEN ASSOCIATES, (II), 250 E. 87th St., New York NY 10128. (212)427-6135. Fax: (212)996-7111. Contact: Connie Clausen or Stedman Mays. Estab. 1976. 10% of clients are new/previously unpublished writers. Specializes in nonfiction with a strong backlist. Member agent: Stedman Mays.
Handles: Considers these nonfiction areas: academic works with mass-market potential; biography/autobiography; cooking/food/nutrition; fashion/beauty; gardening; health/medicine; how-to; humor; money/finance/economics; psychology; spirituality; true crime/investigative; women's issues/women's stories. Considers literary fiction. Send outline/proposal with return postage. Reports in 3 weeks on queries; 1-2 months on mss.
Recent Sales: *Looking for the Other Side: A Skeptic's Odyssey*, by Sherry Suib Cohen (Clarkson Potter); *Resident Alien: The New York Diaries*, by Quentin Crisp (Alyson); *Permanent Remissions: Life Extending Diet Strategies*, by Robert Haas (Pocket Books); *The Pocket Doctor*, by Michael LaCombe, M.D. (Andrews & McMeel); *The Pocket Pediatrician*, by Michael LaCombe, M.D. (Andrews & McMeel); *Drawing Angels Near: Children Tell of Angels in Words and Pictures*, by Mimi Doe and Garland Waller (Pocket Books); *Nurturing Your Child's Soul: Ten Rules for Spiritual Parenting*, by Mimi Doe and Marsha Walch, Ph.D. (HarperCollins).
Terms: Agent receives 15% commission on domestic sales; 20% of foreign sales. Send query or outline/proposal with return postage.
Tips: "Research proposal writing and the publishing process; always study your book's competition; send a proposal and outline instead of complete manuscript for faster response; always pitch books in writing, not over the phone."

‡THE COHEN AGENCY, (III), 331 W. 57th St. #176, New York NY 10019. (212)399-9079. Contact: Rob Cohen. Estab. 1994. Member of AAR, signatory of WGA. Represents 35 clients. 10% of clients are new/previously unpublished writers. Specializes in historical romance. Currently handles: 5% nonfiction books; 1% movie scripts; 90% novels; 4% novellas. Member agents: Rob Cohen (women's fiction).
Handles: Nonfiction books, novels. Considers these nonfiction areas: biography/autobiography; child guidance/parenting; education; ethnic/cultural interests; government/politics/law; language/literature/criticism; music/dance/theater/film; women's issues/women's studies. Considers these fiction areas: contemporary issues; detective/police/crime; erotica; ethnic; fantasy; feminist; historical; horror; humor/satire; literary; mainstream; mystery/suspense; regional; romance (contemporary, historical, regency); science fiction. Send outline and 3 sample chapters. Reports in 6 weeks on queries.
Recent Sales: *Scare Tactics*, by Elizabeth Manz (St. Martin's Press); *Tin Lizzy*, by Margaret Brownley (New American Library); and *Nowhere to Turn*, by Rachel Gibson (Avon Books).
Terms: Agent receives 15% commission on domestic sales; 20% on foreign sales. No written contract.
Writers' Conferences: Romance Writers of America National Conference (July).
Tips: Obtains new clients through recommendations from others, solicitation and conferences.

RUTH COHEN, INC. LITERARY AGENCY, (II), P.O. Box 7626, Menlo Park CA 94025. (415)854-2054. Contact: Ruth Cohen or associates. Estab. 1982. Member of AAR, Authors Guild,

Romance Writers of America, SCBWI. Represents 75 clients. 20% of clients are new/previously unpublished writers. Specializes in "quality writing in juvenile fiction; mysteries; adult women's fiction, historical romances." Currently handles: 15% nonfiction books; 40% juvenile books; 45% novels.

- Prior to opening her agency, Ms. Cohen served as directing editor at Scott Foresman & Company (now HarperCollins).

Handles: Adult novels, juvenile books. Considers these nonfiction areas: ethnic/cultural interests; juvenile nonfiction; women's issues/women's studies. Considers these fiction areas: detective/police; ethnic; historical; juvenile; literary; mainstream; mystery/suspense; picture books; romance (historical, long contemporary); young adult. *No unsolicited mss.* Send outline plus 2 sample chapters. Must include SASE. Reports in 1 month on queries.

Terms: Agent receives 15% commission on domestic sales; 20% on foreign sales, "if a foreign agent is involved." Offers written contract, binding for 1 year "continuing to next." Charges for foreign postage and photocopying for submissions.

Tips: Obtains new clients through recommendations from others. "A good writer cares about the words he/she uses—so do I. Also, if no SASE is included, material will not be read."

HY COHEN LITERARY AGENCY LTD., (II), P.O. Box 43770, Upper Montclair NJ 07043. (201)783-4627. Contact: Hy Cohen. Estab. 1975. Represents 25 clients. 50% of clients are new/previously unpublished writers. Currently handles: 20% nonfiction books; 5% juvenile books; 75% novels.

Handles: Nonfiction books, novels. All categories of nonfiction and fiction considered. Send 100 pages with SASE. Reports in about 2 weeks (on 100-page submission).

Terms: Agent receives 10% commission.

Tips: Obtains new clients through recommendations from others and unsolicited submissions. "Send double-spaced, legible scripts and SASE. Good writing helps."

FRANCES COLLIN LITERARY AGENT, (III), P.O. Box 33, Wayne PA 19087-0033. (610)254-0555. Estab. 1948. Member of AAR. Represents 90 clients. 1% of clients are new/previously unpublished writers. Currently handles: 50% nonfiction books; 1% textbooks; 48% novels; 1% poetry books.

Handles: Nonfiction books, novels. Considers these nonfiction areas: anthropology/archaeology; biography/autobiography; health/medicine; history; nature/environment; true crime/investigative. Considers these fiction areas: detective/police/crime; ethnic; family saga; fantasy; historical; literary; mainstream; mystery/suspense; psychic/supernatural; regional; romance (historical); science fiction. Query with SASE. Reports in 1 week on queries; 2 months on mss.

Terms: Agent charges 15% commission on domestic sales; 20% on foreign sales. Offers written contract. Charges for overseas postage for books mailed to foreign agents; photocopying of mss, books, proposals; copyright registration fees; registered mail fees; passes along cost of any books purchased.

Tips: Obtains new clients through recommendations from others.

COLUMBIA LITERARY ASSOCIATES, INC., (II, IV), 7902 Nottingham Way, Ellicott City MD 21043-6721. (410)465-1595. Fax: Call for number. Contact: Linda Hayes. Estab. 1980. Member of AAR, IACP, RWA, WRW. Represents 40 clients. 10% of clients are new/previously unpublished writers. Specializes in women's fiction (mainstream/genre), commercial nonfiction, especially cookbooks. Currently handles: 40% nonfiction books; 60% novels.

Handles: Nonfiction books, novels. Considers these nonfiction areas: cooking/food/nutrition; health/medicine; self-help. Considers these fiction areas: mainstream; commercial women's fiction; suspense; contemporary romance; psychological/medical thrillers. Reports in 2-4 weeks on queries; 6-8 weeks on mss; "rejections faster."

Recent Sales: *Cold White Fury*, by Beth Amos (HarperPaperbacks); *Face to Face*, by Rebecca York (Harlequin Intrigue); *Asian Cooking*, by Alexandra Greeley (Macmillan); *Shanghaied*, by Metsy Hingle (Silhouette Desire); *What Love Sees (The Movie)*, by Susan Vreeland (Rosemont Productions).

Terms: Agent receives 15% commission on domestic sales. Offers single- or multiple-book written contract, binding for 6-month terms. "Standard expenses are billed against book income (e.g., books for subrights exploitation, toll calls, UPS)."

Writers' Conferences: Romance Writers of America; International Association of Culinary Professionals; Novelists, Inc.

Tips: "CLA's list is very full; we're able to accept only a rare few top-notch projects." Submission requirements: "For fiction, send a query letter with author credits, narrative synopsis, first chapter or two, manuscript word count and submission history (publishers/agents); self-addressed, stamped mailer mandatory for response/ms return. (When submitting romances, note whether manuscript is mainstream or category—if category, say which line(s) manuscript is targeted to.) Same for nonfiction, plus include table of contents and note audience, how project is different and better than competition (specify competing books with publisher and publishing date.) Please note that we do *not* handle: historical or literary fiction, westerns, science fiction/fantasy, military books, poetry, short stories or screenplays."

DON CONGDON ASSOCIATES INC., (III), 156 Fifth Ave., Suite 625, New York NY 10010-7002. (212)645-1229. Fax: (212)727-2688. E-mail: doncongdon@aol.com. Contact: Don Congdon, Michael Congdon, Susan Ramer. Estab. 1983. Member of AAR. Represents approximately 100 clients. Currently handles: 50% fiction; 50% nonfiction books.
Handles: Nonfiction books, novels. Considers all nonfiction and fiction areas, especially literary fiction. Query. "If interested, we ask for sample chapters and outline." Reports in 1 week on queries; 1 month on mss.
Recent Sales: *The Courts of Love*, by Ellen Gilchrist (Little, Brown); *Quicker Than the Eye*, by Ray Bradbury (Avon Books); and *Act of Betrayal*, by Edna Buchanan (Hyperion).
Terms: Agent receives 10% commission on domestic sales.
Tips: Obtains new clients through referrals from other authors. "Writing a query letter is a must."

CONNOR LITERARY AGENCY, (III, IV), 2911 West 71st St., Richfield MN 55423. (612)866-1486. Fax: (612)869-4074. Contact: Marlene Connor Lynch. Estab. 1985. Represents 50 clients. 30% of clients are new/previously unpublished writers. Specializes in popular fiction and nonfiction. Currently handles: 50% nonfiction books; 50% novels. Member agents: Deborah Connor Coker (children's books); Richard Zanders (general fiction and nonfiction)..
  ● Prior to opening her agency, Ms. Lynch served at the Literary Guild of America, Simon and Schuster and Random House. She is also the author of *What is Cool? Understanding Black Manhood in America* (Crown).
Handles: Nonfiction books, novels, illustrated books, children's books (especially with a minority slant). Considers these nonfiction areas: business; child guidance/parenting; cooking/food/nutrition; crafts/hobbies; current affairs; ethnic/cultural interests; government/politics/law; health/medicine; how-to; humor; interior decorating; language/literature/criticism; money/finance/economics; photography; popular culture; self-help/personal improvement; sports; true crime/investigative; women's issues/women's studies. Considers these fiction areas: contemporary issues; detective/police/crime; ethnic; experimental; family saga; horror; mystery/suspense; thriller/espionage. Query with outline/proposal. Reports in 1 month on queries; 6 weeks on mss.
Recent Sales: *Essence: 25 Years of Celebrating the Black Woman* (Abrams); *The Marital Compatibility Test*, by Susan Adams (Carol Publishing Group); *We Are Overcome*, by Bonnie Allen (Crown); *Choices*, by Maria Corley (Kensington); *Grandmother's Gift of Memories*, by Danita Green (Broadway); *How to Love a Black Man*, by Ronn Elmore (Warner); *Simplicity Book of Home Decorating*, by Simplicity (Simon & Schuster).
Terms: Agent receives 15% commission on domestic sales; 25% on foreign sales. Offers a written contract, binding for 1 year.
Writers' Conferences: Howard University Publishing Institute; ABA; Oklahoma Writer's Federation.
Tips: Obtains new clients through queries, recommendations, conferences, grapevine, etc. "Seeking previously published writers with good sales records and new writers with real talent."

THE DOE COOVER AGENCY, (II), P.O. Box 668, Winchester MA 01890. (617)488-3937. Fax: (617)488-3153. President: Doe Coover. Agent: Colleen Mohyde. Estab. 1985. Represents 60 clients. Specializes in serious nonfiction and fiction. Currently handles: 80% nonfiction; 20% fiction. Member agents: Doe Coover (cooking, general nonfiction); Colleen Mohyde (fiction, general nonfiction).
Handles: Nonfiction books, fiction. Considers these nonfiction areas: anthropology; biography/autobiography; business; child guidance/parenting; cooking/food; ethnic/cultural interests; finance/economics; health/medicine; history; language/literature/criticism; nature/environment; psychology; religious/inspirational; science/technology; sociology; true crime; women's issues/women's studies. Query with outline. All queries must include SASE and should be addressed to Ms. Mohyde. Reporting time varies on queries.
Recent Sales: *Drinking: A Love Story*, by Caroline Knapp (Dial); *Novena*, by Sandra Shea (Houghton Mifflin); *LifeLines: Creating Your Financial Life Story*, by Ginger Applegarth (Viking).

AGENTS RANKED I-IV are actively seeking new clients. Those ranked **V** prefer not to be listed but have been included to inform you they are not currently looking for new clients.

Terms: Agent receives 15% commission on domestic sales; 15% on foreign sales.
Writers' Conferences: ABA (Chicago).
Tips: Obtains new clients through recommendations from others and solicitation.

ROBERT CORNFIELD LITERARY AGENCY, (II), 145 W. 79th St., New York NY 10024-6468. (212)874-2465. Fax: (212)874-2641. Contact: Robert Cornfield. Estab. 1979. Member of AAR. Represents 60 clients. 20% of clients are new/previously unpublished writers. Specializes in film, art, literary, music criticism, food, fiction. Currently handles: 60% nonfiction books; 20% scholarly books; 20% novels.
Handles: Nonfiction books, novels. Considers these nonfiction areas: animals; anthropology/archaeology; art/architecture/ design; biography/autobiography; cooking/food/nutrition; history; language/literature/criticism/ music/dance/theater/film. Considers literary fiction. Query. Reports in 2-3 weeks on queries.
Recent Sales: *Arthur Evans & The Minoans*, by J.A. Mae Gillivray (HarperCollins); *Disney's Sketchbooks*, by John Canemaker (Hyperion); *Sunday Dinners*, by Barbara Scott-Goodman (Chronicle); *Parenting Cookbook*, by Kathy Gunst & *Parenting* magazine (Holt); *Bean Cookbook*, by Melanie Barnard (Harper); *Adam's Task*, by Vicki Hearne (Harper).
Terms: Agent receives 10% commission on domestic sales; 20% on foreign sales. No written contract. Charges for postage, excessive photocopying.
Tips: Obtains new clients through recommendations.

CRAWFORD LITERARY AGENCY, (III), 94 Evans Rd., Barnstead NH 03218. (603)269-5851. Fax: (603)269-2533. Contact: Susan Crawford. Estab. 1988. Represents 40 clients. 10% of clients are new/previously unpublished writers. Currently handles: 50% nonfiction books; 50% novels. Member agents: Lorne Crawford, Scott Neister, Kristen Hales (cooking/food/nutrition).
Handles: Nonfiction books. Considers these nonfiction areas: biography/autobiography; business; child guidance/parenting; cooking/food/nutrition; how-to; true crime/investigative; women's issues/women's studies. Query with SASE. Reports in 3 weeks on queries. Send SASE for details on fiction needs.
Recent Sales: Untitled Autobiography, by Ruby Dee and Ossie Davis (William Morrow & Co.); *Elegant Irish Cooking*, by Noel Cullen (Van Nostrand Reinhold); *Walk On Water For Me*, by Lorian Hemingway (Simon & Schuster); *Secret of the House of Usher*, by Robert Bruce Poe (Tor/Forge).
Terms: Agent receives 15% commission on domestic sales; 20% on foreign sales. Offers written contract, binding for 90 days. 100% of business is derived from commissions on sales.
Also Handles: Movie scripts; TV scripts. Considers these script subject areas: action/adventure; contemporary issues; detective/police/crime; ethnic; experimental; family saga; fantasy; feminist; glitz; historical; mainstream; mystery/suspense; psychic/supernatural; religious/inspirational; romantic (drama); science fiction; thriller; western/frontier. Query. Reports in 3 weeks on queries; 6 weeks on mss.
Recent Sales: *Movie script optioned: The Huntress*, by Christopher Keane with Dottie Thorson (Citadel Entertainment). *TV script optioned: Doc Holliday's Woman*, by Jane Candia Coleman (Benchmark Productions).
Writers' Conferences: Hemingway Festival/Writers' Conference (Key West FL); International Film & Writers Workshop (Rockport ME); Southwest Florida Writers Conference (Ft. Myers FL).
Tips: Obtains new clients through recommendations and at conferences.

BONNIE R. CROWN INTERNATIONAL LITERATURE AND ARTS AGENCY, (II, IV), 50 E. Tenth St., New York NY 10003-6221. (212)475-1999. Contact: Bonnie Crown. Estab. 1976. Member of Association of Asian Studies. Represents 14 clients. 10% of clients are previously unpublished writers. Specializes in Asian cross-cultural and translations of Asian literary works, American writers influenced by one or more Asian cultures. Currently handles: 5% scholarly books; 80% novels; 10% short story collectors; 5% poetry.
Handles: Nonfiction books, novels, short story collections (if first published in literary magazines). Considers these nonfiction areas: ethnic/cultural interests; nature/environment; translations from Asian languages; women's issues/women's studies. Considers these fiction areas: ethnic; experimental; family saga; historical; humor/satire; literary. Query with SASE. Reports in 2 weeks on queries; 2-4 weeks on mss.
Terms: Agent receives 15% commission on domestic sales; 20% on foreign sales. Charges for processing, usually $35, on submission of ms.
Tips: Obtains new clients through "referrals from other authors and listings in reference works. If interested in agency representation, send brief query with SASE."

RICHARD CURTIS ASSOCIATES, INC., (III), 171 E. 74th St., New York NY 10021. (212)772-7363. E-mail: curtisagency.com. Website: http://www.curtisagency.com. Contact: Richard Curtis. Estab. 1969. Member of AAR, signatory of WGA. Represents 100 clients. 5% of clients are new/previously unpublished writers. Specializes in general and literary fiction and nonfiction, as well as genre fiction such as science fiction, women's romance, horror, fantasy, action-adventure. Currently handles: 49% nonfiction books; 1% juvenile books; 50% novels. Member agents: Amy Victoria Meo, Laura Tucker.

• Mr. Curtis is the current President of the AAR. See Mr. Curtis's article, Explaining AAR's Ban on Reading Fees, in this edition of the *Guide*.

Handles: Nonfiction books, novels. Considers these nonfiction areas: biography/autobiography; business; child guidance/parenting; history; military/war; money/finance/economics; music/dance/theater/film; science/technology; self-help/personal improvement; sports; true crime/investigative. Considers these fiction areas: action/adventure; detective/police/crime; family saga; fantasy; feminist; historical; horror; mainstream; mystery/suspense; romance; science fiction; thriller/espionage; westerns/frontier. "We do not accept fax or e-mail queries, conventional queries must be accompanied by SASE." Reports in 1 month on queries.

Recent Sales: *Anti-Aging Bible*, by Earl Mindell (Simon & Schuster); *Americans No More*, by Georgie Ann Geyer (Atlantic Monthly Press); *Hidden Latitudes*, by Alison Anderson (Scribner Press); *Tigress*, by Jennifer Blake (Fawcett); *The Waterborn*, by Gregory Keyes (Del Rey).

Terms: Agent receives 15% commission on domestic sales; 20% on foreign sales. Charges for photocopying, express, fax, international postage, book orders.

Writers' Conferences: World Fantasy (Baltimore MD); Romance Writers of America (Dallas TX); Nebula Science Fiction Conference (San Diego CA).

Tips: Obtains new clients through recommendations from others.

JAMES R. CYPHER, AUTHOR'S REPRESENTATIVE, (II), 616 Wolcott Ave., Beacon NY 12508-4247. (914)831-5677. E-mail: jimcypher@aol.com. Contact: James R. Cypher. Estab. 1993. Represents 48 clients. 71% of clients are new/previously unpublished writers. Currently handles: 43% nonfiction book; 57% novels.

• Mr. Cypher is a special contributor to Prodigy Service Books and Writing Bulletin Board.

Handles: Nonfiction books, novels. Considers these nonfiction areas: biography/autobiography; business; computers/electronics; current affairs; ethnic/cultural interests; gay/lesbian issues; government/politics/law; health/medicine; history; how-to; humor; language/literature/criticism; military/war; money/finance/economics; music/dance/theater/film; nature/environment; popular culture; psychology; science/technology; self-help/personal improvement; sociology; sports; true crime/investigative; women's issues/women's studies; travel memoirs. Considers these fiction areas: action/adventure; contemporary issues; detective/police/crime; ethnic; family saga; feminist; gay; historical; horror; humor/satire; lesbian; literary; mainstream; mystery/suspense; sports; thriller/espionage. For nonfiction, send outline proposal, 2 sample chapters and SASE. For fiction, send synopsis, 3 sample chapters and SASE. Reports in 2 weeks on queries; 6 weeks on mss.

Recent Sales: *The Heart Disease Sourcebook*, by Roger Cicala, M.D. (Lowell House); *They Tasted Glory: Among the Missing in Baseball's Hall of Fame*, by Wil A. Linkugel and Edward J. Pappas (MacFarland & Company).

Terms: Agent receives 15% commission on domestic sales; 20% on foreign sales. Offers written contract, with 30 day cancellation clause. Charges for postage, photocopying, overseas phone calls and faxes. 100% of business is derived from commissions on sales.

Tips: Obtains new clients through referrals from others and networking on online computer services. "I especially enjoy character-driven fiction. Make me, acquiring editors and, ultimately, your readers, really care about your protagonist and his or her adventures or misadventures. Horror, thriller or suspense novels *must* be genuine 'page turners.' "

DARHANSOFF & VERRILL LITERARY AGENTS, (II), 179 Franklin St., 4th Floor, New York NY 10013. (212)334-5980. Estab. 1975. Member of AAR. Represents 100 clients. 10% of clients are new/previously unpublished writers. Specializes in literary fiction. Currently handles: 25% nonfiction books; 60% novels; 15% short story collections. Member agents: Liz Darhansoff, Charles Verrill, Leigh Feldman.

Handles: Nonfiction books, novels, short story collections. Considers these nonfiction areas: anthropology/archaeology; biography/autobiography; current affairs; health/medicine; history; language/literature/criticism; nature/environment; science/technology. Considers literary and thriller fiction. Query letter only. Reports in 2 weeks on queries.

Recent Sales: *Water From the Well*, by Myra McLarey (Atlantic Monthly Press); *Sahara Unveiled*, by William Langewiesche (Pantheon).

Tips: Obtains new clients through recommendations from others.

JOAN DAVES AGENCY, (II), 21 W. 26th St., New York NY 10010. (212)685-2663. Fax: (212)685-1781. Contact: Jennifer Lyons, director. Estab. 1960. Member of AAR. Represents 100 clients. 10% of clients are new/previously unpublished writers. Specializes in literary fiction and nonfiction, also commercial fiction.

Handles: Nonfiction books, novels. Considers these nonfiction areas: biography/autobiography; gay/ lesbian issues; popular culture; translations; women's issues/women's studies. Considers these fiction areas: ethnic, family saga; gay; literary; mainstream; thriller/espionage. Query. Reports in 3 weeks on queries; 6 weeks on mss.

Recent Sales: *Fire on the Mountain*, by John Maclean (William Morrow); Bruno Bettelhelm biography, by Nina Sutton (Basic Books); *Entertaining Angels*, by Marita Van der Vyr (Dutton); *Ruby Tear*, by Suzy Charnas (TOR/St. Martin's).

Terms: Agent receives 15% commission on domestic sales; 20% on foreign sales. Offers written contract, on a per book basis. Charges for office expenses. 100% of business is derived from commissions on sales.

Tips: Obtains new clients through editors' and author clients' recommendations. "A few queries translate into representation."

THE LOIS DE LA HABA AGENCY INC., (III), 1133 Broadway, Suite 810, New York NY 10010. (212)929-4838. Fax: (212)924-3885. Contact: Lois de la Haba. Estab. 1978. Represents 100 clients. Currently handles: 50% nonfiction books; 3% scholarly books; ½% textbooks; 10% juvenile books; 21% novels; ½% poetry; ½% short story collections; 10% movie scripts; 2% stage plays; 2% TV scripts; ½% syndicated material. Member agents: Laura de la Haba, associate.

Handles: Nonfiction books, scholarly books, juvenile books, novels, movie scripts, TV scripts, stage plays. Considers these nonfiction areas: anthropology/archaeology; art/architecture/design; biography/ autobiography; business; cooking/food/nutrition; current affairs; ethnic/cultural interests; gay/lesbian issues; government/politics/law; health/medicine; history; juvenile nonfiction; money/finance/economics; music/theater/dance/film; nature/environment; New Age/metaphysics; popular culture; psychology/healing; religious/inspirational; self-help/personal improvement; women's issues/women's studies. Considers these fiction areas: contemporary issues; detective/police/crime; ethnic; family saga; fantasy; feminist; gay; historical; humor/satire; juvenile; literary; mainstream; mystery/suspense; religious/inspirational; young adult. Query with outline/proposal. "We will contact if interested." Reports in 5 weeks on queries; 2 months on mss.

Recent Sales: *Out of the Blue*, by Mark Hansen (HarperCollins).

Terms: Agent receives 15% commission on domestic sales; 25% on foreign sales. Offers written contract. Charges for office expenses.

Writers' Conferences: Mystery Writers of America.

Tips: Obtains new clients through recommendations from others.

DH LITERARY, INC., (I, II), P.O. Box 990, Nyack NY 10960-0990. (212)753-7942. E-mail: dhendin@aol.com. Contact: David Hendin. Estab. 1993. Represents 50 clients. 50% of clients are new/ previously unpublished writers. Specializes in trade fiction, nonfiction and newspaper syndication of columns or comic strips. Currently handles: 60% nonfiction books; 10% scholarly books; 20% novels; 10% syndicated material.

• Prior to opening his agency, Mr. Hendin served as president and publisher for Pharos Books/ World Almanac as well as senior vp and COO at sister company United Feature Syndicate.

Handles: Nonfiction books, scholarly books, novels, syndicated material. Considers these nonfiction areas: animals; anthropology/archaeology; biography/autobiography; business; child guidance/parenting; cooking/food/nutrition; current affairs; education; ethnic/cultural interests; gay/lesbian issues; government/politics/law; health/medicine; history; how-to; humor; language/literature/criticism; military/ war; money/finance/economics; music/dance/theater/film; nature/environment; New Age/metaphysics; popular culture; psychology; religious/inspirational; science/technology; self-help/personal improvement; sociology; sports; true crime/investigative; women's issues/women's studies. Considers these fiction areas: action/adventure; cartoon/comic; contemporary issues; detective/police/crime; ethnic; feminist; glitz; historical; humor/satire; literary; mainstream; psychic/supernatural; thriller/espionage. Reports in 2-4 weeks on queries.

Recent Sales: *Nobody's Angels*, by Leslie Haynesworth and David Toomey (William Morrow); *Catmassage*, by Maryjean Ballner (St. Martin's Press); *Eating the Bear*, by Carole Fungaroli (Farrar, Straus & Giroux); *Miss Manners Rescues Civilization*, by Judith Martin (Crown); *Do Unto Others*, by Abraham Twerski, M.D. (Andrews & McMeel).

Terms: Agent receives 15% commission on domestic sales; 20% on foreign sales. Offers written contract, binding for 1 year. Charges for out of pocket expenses for postage, photocopying manuscript, and overseas phone calls specifically related to a book.

Tips: Obtains new clients through referrals from others (clients, writers, publishers). "Have your project in mind and on paper before you submit. Too many writers/cartoonists say 'I'm good . . . get me a project.' Publishers want writers with their own great ideas and their own unique voice. No faxed submissions."

DHS LITERARY, INC., (II, IV), 6060 N. Central Expwy., Suite 624, Dallas TX 75206. (214)363-4422. Fax: (214)363-4423. E-mail: dhslit@computek.net. Contact: V. Michele Lewis, submissions

director. Estab. 1994. Represents 35 clients. 50% of clients are new/previously unpublished writers. Specializes in commercial fiction and nonfiction for adult trade market. Currently handles: 50% nonfiction books; 50% novels.
Handles: Nonfiction books, novels. Considers these nonfiction areas: biography/autobiography; business; child guidance/parenting; computers/electronics; cooking/food/nutrition; current affairs; ethnic/cultural interests; gay/lesbian issues; popular culture; sports; true crime/investigative. Considers these fiction areas: action/adventure; detective/police/crime; erotica; ethnic; feminist; gay; historical; horror; literary; mainstream; mystery/suspense; sports; thriller/espionage; westerns/frontier. Query for fiction; send outline/proposal and sample chapters for nonfiction. Reports in 2 weeks on queries; 10 weeks on mss.
Recent Sales: *Firebirds* (reprint), by Chuck Carlock (Bantam); *The Vitality Factor*, by Elizabeth Somer (Morrow); *Could You Love Me Like My Cat?*, by Beth Fowler (Simon & Schuster).
Terms: Agent receives 15% commission on domestic sales; 25% on foreign sales. Offers written contract, with 30 day cancellation clause or upon mutual consent. Charges for client expenses, i.e., postage, photocopying. 100% of business is derived from commissions on sales.
Writers' Conferences: University of Texas-Dallas "Craft of Writing" (Dallas TX, September); University of Oklahoma "Short Course on Professional Writing" (Norman OK, June).
Tips: Obtains new clients through referrals from other clients, editors and agents, presentations at writers conferences and via unsolicited submissions. "Remember to be courteous and professional, and to treat marketing your work and approaching an agent as you would any formal business matter. When in doubt, always query first—in writing—with SASE."

ANITA DIAMANT LITERARY AGENCY, THE WRITER'S WORKSHOP, INC., (II), 310 Madison Ave., New York NY 10017-6009. (212)687-1122. Contact: Robin Rue. Estab. 1917. Member of AAR. Represents 125 clients. 25% of clients are new/previously unpublished writers. Currently handles: 20% nonfiction books; 80% novels. Member agents: Robin Rue (fiction and nonfiction); John Talbott (agent); Mark Chelius (associate).
Handles: Nonfiction books, young adult, novels. Considers these nonfiction areas: animals; art/architecture/design; biography/autobiography; business; child guidance/parenting; cooking/food/nutrition; crafts/hobbies; current affairs; government/politics/law; health/medicine; history; juvenile nonfiction; money/finance/economics; nature/environment; New Age/metaphysics; psychology; religious/inspirational; science/technology; self-help/personal improvement; sports; true crime/investigative; women's issues/women's studies. Considers these fiction areas: action/adventure; contemporary issues; detective/police/crime; experimental; family saga; feminist; gay; historical; juvenile; literary; mainstream; mystery/suspense; psychic/supernatural; religious/inspirational; romance; thriller/espionage; westerns/frontier; young adult. Query with SASE. Reports "at once" on queries; 2 months on mss.
Recent Sales: *All That Glitters*, by V.C. Andrews (Pocket); *Why Smart People Do Dumb Things*, by John Tarrand (Fireside); *Jacqueline Kennedy Onassis*, by Lester David (Carol); *Old Ways in the New World*, by Richard Conroy (St. Martin's); *Death of Love*, by Bartholomew Gill (Morrow).
Terms: Agent receives 15% commission on domestic sales; 20% on foreign sales. Offers written contract.
Writers' Conferences: RWA; ABA.
Tips: Obtains new clients through "recommendations from publishers and clients, appearances at writers' conferences, and through readers of my written articles."

DIAMOND LITERARY AGENCY, INC., (III), P.O. Box 24805, Denver CO 80224. (303)759-0291. President: Pat Dalton. Contact: Jean Patrick. Estab. 1982. Represents 20 clients. 10% of clients are new/previously unpublished writers. Specializes in romance, romantic suspense, women's fiction, thrillers, mysteries. Currently handles: 20% nonfiction books; 80% novels.
Handles: Nonfiction books, novels. Considers these nonfiction areas with mass market appeal: business; health/medicine; money/finance/economics; psychology; self-help/personal improvement. Considers these fiction areas: detective/police/crime; family saga; glitz; historical; mainstream; mystery/suspense; romance; thriller/espionage. Send SASE for agency information and submission procedures. Reports in 1 month on mss (partials).
Recent Sales: Specializes in romance, including sales to Harlequin and Silhouette. Specifics on request if representation offered.
Terms: Agent receives 15% commission on domestic sales; 20% on foreign sales. Offers written contract, binding for 2 years "unless author is well established." Charges a "$15 submission fee for writers who have not previously published the same type of book." Charges for express and foreign postage. "Writers provide the necessary photostat copies."
Tips: Obtains new clients through "referrals from writers, or someone's submitting saleable material. We represent only clients who are professionals in writing quality, presentation, conduct and attitudes—whether published or unpublished. People who are not yet clients should not telephone. We consider query letters a waste of time—most of all the writer's, secondly the agent's. Submit approximately the first 50 pages and a complete synopsis for books, along with SASE and standard-sized audiocassette

tape for possible agent comments. Non-clients who haven't sold the SAME TYPE of book or script within five years must include a $15 submission fee by money order or cashier's check. Material not accompanied by SASE is not returned. Until mid-1997 only considering new clients who are previously published and romance suspense or contemporary romance writers (series or single title). Previously unpublished writers with completed romance suspense or contemporary romance manuscripts must have a letter of recommendation from a client, editor or other published author personally known to us."

SANDRA DIJKSTRA LITERARY AGENCY, (II), 1155 Camino del Mar, #515, Del Mar CA 92014. (619)755-3115. Contact: Debra Ginsberg. Estab. 1981. Member of AAR, Authors Guild, PEN West, Poets and Editors, MWA. Represents 100 clients. 30% of clients are new/previously unpublished writers. "We specialize in a number of fields." Currently handles: 60% nonfiction books; 5% juvenile books; 35% novels. Member agent: Sandra Dijkstra.
Handles: Nonfiction books, novels. Considers these nonfiction areas: anthropology; biography/autobiography; business; child guidance/parenting; nutrition; current affairs; ethnic/cultural interests; government/politics; health/medicine; history; literary studies (trade only); military/war (trade only); money/finance/economics; nature/environment; psychology; science/technology; self-help/personal improvement; sociology; sports; true crime/investigative; women's issues/women's studies. Considers these fiction areas: contemporary issues; detective/police/crime; ethnic; family saga; feminist; literary; mainstream; mystery/suspense; thriller/espionage. Send "outline/proposal with sample chapters for nonfiction, synopsis and first 50 pages for fiction and SASE." Reports in 2-4 weeks on queries; 1-6 weeks on mss.
Recent Sales: *The Mistress of Spices*, by Chitra Divakaruni (Anchor Books); *The Flower Net*, by Lisa See (HarperCollins); *Outsmarting the Menopausal Fat Cell*, by Debra Waterhouse (Hyperion); *Verdi*, by Janell Cannon (children's, Harcourt Brace); *The Nine Secrets of Women Who Get Everything They Want*, by Kate White (Harmony).
Terms: Agent receives 15% commission on domestic sales; 20% on foreign sales. Offers written contract, binding for 1 year. Charges for expenses from years we are *active* on author's behalf to cover domestic costs so that we can spend time selling books instead of accounting expenses. We also charge for the photocopying of the full manuscript or nonfiction proposal and for foreign postage."
Writers' Conferences: "Have attended Squaw Valley, Santa Barbara, Asilomar, Southern California Writers Conference, Rocky Mountain Fiction Writers, to name a few. We also speak regularly for writers groups such as PEN West and the Independent Writers Association."
Tips: Obtains new clients "primarily through referrals/recommendations, but also through queries and conferences and often by solicitation. Be professional and learn the standard procedures for submitting your work. Give full biographical information on yourself, especially for a nonfiction project. Always include SASE with correct return postage for your own protection of your work. Query with a 1 or 2 page letter first and always include postage. Nine page letters telling us your life story, or your book's, are unprofessional and usually not read. Tell us about your book and write your query well. It's our first introduction to who you are and what you can do! Call if you don't hear within a reasonable period of time. Be a regular patron of bookstores and study what kind of books are being published. READ. Check out your local library and bookstores—you'll find lots of books on writing and the publishing industry that will help you! At conferences, ask published writers about their agents. Don't believe the myth that an agent has to be in New York to be successful—we've already disproved it!"

THE JONATHAN DOLGER AGENCY, (II), 49 E. 96th St., Suite 9B, New York NY 10128. (212)427-1853. President: Jonathan Dolger. Contact: Dee Ratterree. Estab. 1980. Member of AAR. Represents 70 clients. 25% of clients are new/unpublished writers. Writer must have been previously published if submitting fiction. Prefers to work with published/established authors; works with a small number of new/unpublished writers. Specializes in adult trade fiction and nonfiction, and illustrated books.
Handles: Nonfiction books, novels, illustrated books. Query with outline and SASE.
Terms: Agent receives 15% commission on domestic and dramatic sales; 25% on foreign sales. Charges for "standard expenses."

DONADIO AND ASHWORTH, INC., (II), 121 W. 27th St., Suite 704, New York NY 10001. (212)691-8077. Fax: (212)633-2837. Contact: Neil Olson. Estab. 1970. Member of AAR. Represents

CHECK THE SUBJECT INDEX to find the agents who are interested in your nonfiction or fiction subject area.

100 clients. Specializes in literary fiction and nonfiction. Currently handles: 40% nonfiction; 50% novels; 10% short story collections. Member agent: Edward Hibbert (literary fiction).
Handles: Nonfiction books, novels, short story collections. Query with 50 pages and SASE.
Terms: Agent receives 15% commission on domestic sales; 20% on foreign sales.

DOYEN LITERARY SERVICES, INC., (II), 1931 660th St., Newell IA 50568-7613. (712)272-3300. President: (Ms.) B.J. Doyen. Estab. 1988. Member of RWA, SCBA. Represents 50 clients. 20% of clients are new/previously unpublished writers. Specializes in nonfiction and handles genre and mainstream fiction mainly for adults (some children's). Currently handles: 90% nonfiction books; 2% juvenile books; 8% novels. No poetry books.
Handles: Nonfiction books, juvenile books, novels. Considers most nonfiction areas. Considers these fiction areas: action/adventure; contemporary issues; detective/police/crime; ethnic; family saga; fantasy; glitz; historical; horror; literary; mainstream; mystery/suspense; psychic/supernatural; thriller/espionage. Query first with SASE. Reports immediately on queries; 6-8 weeks on mss.
Recent Sales: *Homemade Money*, by Barbara Brabec (Betterway); *Megahealth*, by Sorenson (Evans); *The Family Guide to Financial Aid for Higher Education*, by Black (Putnam/Perigee).
Terms: Agent receives 15% commission on domestic sales; 20% commission on foreign sales. Offers written contract, binding for 1 year.
Tips: "We are very interested in nonfiction book ideas at this time; will consider most topics. Many writers come to us from referrals, but we also get quite a few who initially approach us with query letters. Do *not* use phone queries unless you are successfully published or a celebrity. It is best if you do not collect editorial rejections prior to seeking an agent, but if you do, be up-front and honest about it. Do not submit your manuscript to more than one agent at a time—querying first can save you (and us) much time. We're open to established or beginning writers—just send us a terrific letter with SASE!"

ROBERT DUCAS, (II), 350 Hudson St., New York NY 10014. (212)924-8120. Fax: (212)924-8079. Contact: R. Ducas. Estab. 1981. Represents 55 clients. 15% of clients are new/previously unpublished writers. Specializes in nonfiction, journalistic exposé, biography, history. Currently handles: 70% nonfiction books; 2% scholarly books; 28% novels.
Handles: Nonfiction books, novels, novellas. Considers these nonfiction areas: animals; biography/autobiography; business; current affairs; gay/lesbian issues; government/politics/law; health/medicine; history; military/war; money/finance/economics; nature/environment; science/technology; sports; true crime/investigative. Considers these fiction areas: action/adventure; contemporary issues; detective/police/crime; family saga; literary; mainstream; mystery/suspense; sports; thriller/espionage. Send outline/proposal and SASE. Reports in 2 weeks on queries; 2 months on mss.
Terms: Agent receives 15% commission on domestic sales; 20% on foreign sales. Charges for photocopying and postage. "I also charge for messengers and overseas couriers to subagents."
Tips: Obtains new clients through recommendations.

DUPREE/MILLER AND ASSOCIATES INC. LITERARY, (II), 100 Highland Park Village, Suite 350, Dallas TX 75205. (214)559-BOOK. Fax: (214)559-PAGE. E-mail: dmabook@aol.com. President: Jan Miller. Contact: Submissions Department. Estab. 1984. member of ABA. Represents 100 clients. 20% of clients are new/previously unpublished writers. Specializes in commercial fiction, nonfiction. Currently handles: 75% nonfiction books; 25% novels. Member agents: Jan Miller; Ashley Carroll (agent); Elisabeth Grant (office manager).
Handles: Nonfiction books, scholarly books, novels, syndicated material. Considers all nonfiction areas. Considers these fiction areas: action/adventure; cartoon/comic; contemporary issues; detective/police/crime; ethnic; experimental; family saga; fantasy; feminist; gay; glitz; historical; horror; humor/satire; lesbian; literary; mainstream; mystery/suspense; picture book; psychic/supernatural; religious/inspirational; romance (contemporary, historical); science fiction; sports; thriller/espionage; westerns/frontier. Send outline plus 3 sample chapters. Reports in 1 week on queries; 2-3 months on mss.
Recent Sales: *Will The Real Women Please Stand Up*, by Ella Patterson (Simon & Schuster); *Notes From A Friend*, by Tony Robbins (Simon & Schuster); *Come on America Let's Eat*, by Susan Powter (Simon & Schuster).
Terms: Agent receives 15% commission on domestic sales. Offers written contract, binding for "no set amount of time. The contract can be cancelled by either agent or client, effective 30 days after cancellation." Charges $20 processing fee and express mail charges.
Writers' Conferences: Southwest Writers (Albuqurque NM); Brazos Writers (College Station TX).
Tips: Obtains new clients through conferences, lectures, other clients and "very frequently through publisher's referrals." If interested in agency representation "it is vital to have the material in the proper working format. As agents' policies differ, it is important to follow their guidelines. The best advice I can give is to work on establishing a strong proposal that provides sample chapters, an overall synopsis (fairly detailed) and some bio information on yourself. Do not send your proposal in pieces;

it should be complete upon submission. Remember you are trying to sell your work and it should be in its best condition."

JANE DYSTEL LITERARY MANAGEMENT, (I, II), One Union Square West, New York NY 10003. (212)627-9100. Fax: (212)627-9313. Contact: Miriam Goderich. Estab. 1994. Member of AAR. Presently represents 200 clients. 50% of clients are new/previously unpublished writers. Specializes in commercial and literary fiction and nonfiction plus cookbooks. Currently handles: 65% nonfiction books; 25% novels; 10% cookbooks.
  • Prior to opening her agency, Ms. Dystel was a principal agent in Acton, Dystel, Leone and Jaffe.
Handles: Nonfiction books, novels, cookbooks. Considers these nonfiction areas: animals; anthropology/archaeology; biography/autobiography; business; child guidance/parenting; cooking/food/nutrition; current affairs; education; ethnic/cultural interests; gay/lesbian issues; government/politics/law; health/medicine; history; humor; military/war; money/finance/economics; New Age/metaphysics; popular cultures; psychology; religious/inspirational; science/technology; true crime/investigative; women's issues/women's studies. Considers these fiction areas: action/adventure; contemporary issues; detective/police/crime; ethnic; family saga; gay; lesbian; literary; mainstream; thriller/espionage. Query. Reports in 3 weeks on queries; 6 weeks on mss.
Recent Sales: *What the Deaf Mute Heard*, by Dan Gearino (Simon & Schuster). *Tiger's Tail*, by Gus Lee (Knopf); *I Never Forget A Meal*, by Michael Tucker (Little Brown); *The Sparrow*, by Mary Russell (Villard); *A Tavola Con Lidia*, by Lidia Bastianich (William Morrow); *Simplify Your Life*, by Elaine St. James (Hyperion).
Terms: Agent receives 15% commission on domestic sales; 19% of foreign sales. Offers written contract on a book to book basis. Charges for photocopying. Galley charges and book charges from the publisher are passed on to the author.
Writers' Conferences: West Coast Writers Conference (Whidbey Island WA, Columbus Day weekend); University of Iowa Writers' Conference; Pike's Peak Writer's Conference; Santa Barbara Writer's Conference.
Tips: Obtains new clients through recommendations from others, solicitation, at conferences.

EDUCATIONAL DESIGN SERVICES, INC., (II, IV), P.O. Box 253, Wantagh NY 11793-0253. (718)539-4107 or (516)221-0995. President: Bertram L. Linder. Vice President: Edwin Selzer. Estab. 1979. Represents 17 clients. 70% of clients are new/previously unpublished writers. Specializes in textual material for educational market. Currently handles: 100% textbooks.
Handles: Textbooks, scholarly books. Considers these nonfiction areas: anthropology/archaeology; business; child guidance/parenting; current affairs; ethnic/cultural interests; government/politics/law; history; juvenile nonfiction; language/literature/criticism; military/war; money/finance/economics; science/technology; sociology; women's issues/women's studies. Query with outline/proposal or outline plus 1-2 sample chapters. Reports in 1 month on queries; 4-6 weeks on mss.
Recent Sales: *New York and The Nation*, by McCarthy & Wattman (Amsco); *American History Worktext*, by Shakofsky (Minerva); *Nueva Historia de Los Estados Unidos (Teachers Guide)*, (Minerva).
Terms: Agent receives 15% commission on domestic sales; 25% on foreign sales. Offers written contract. Charges for photocopying.
Tips: Obtains new clients through recommendations, at conferences and through queries.

PETER ELEK ASSOCIATES, (II, IV), Box 223, Canal Street Station, New York NY 10013-2610. (212)431-9368. Fax: (212)966-5768. E-mail: 73174.2515@CompuServe.com. Contact: Debbie Miketta. Estab. 1979. Represents 20 clients. Specializes in children's picture books, adult nonfiction. Currently handles: 30% juvenile books. Staff includes Gerardo Greco (Director of Project Development/Multimedia); Josh Feder (curriculum specialist).
Handles: Juvenile books (nonfiction, picture books). Considers anthropology; parenting; juvenile nonfiction; nature/environment; popular culture; science; true crime/investigative. Considers juvenile picture books. Query with outline/proposal and SASE. Reports in 3 weeks on queries; 5 weeks on mss.
Recent Sales: *Anastasia's Album*, by Hugh Brewster (Hyperion); *Tell Me Again*, by Laura Cornell (HarperCollins); *I Was There* series, by various authors (Hyperion); *Parts*, by Tedd Arnold (Dial Books).
Terms: Agent receives 15% commission on domestic sales; 20% on foreign sales. If required, charges for photocopying, typing, courier charges.
Writers' Conferences: Internet (Atlanta GA); Frankfurt Book Fair (Frankfurt Germany, October); Milia (Cannes France); Bologna Children's Book Fair (Italy); Seybold (Boston, September).
Tips: Obtains new clients through recommendations and studying bylines in consumer and trade magazines and in regional and local newspapers. "No work returned unless appropriate packing and postage is remitted. Actively seeking intellectual property/content, text and images for strategic partner-

ing for multimedia. We are currently licensing series and single projects (juvenile, YA and adult) for electronic platforms such as CD-ROM, CD-I and WWW. Our subsidiary company for this is The Content Company Inc.—contact Gerardo Greco, at the same address."

ETHAN ELLENBERG LITERARY AGENCY, (II), 548 Broadway, #5-E, New York NY 10012. (212)431-4554. Fax: (212)941-4652. Contact: Ethan Ellenberg. Estab. 1983. Represents 70 clients. 10% of clients are new/previously unpublished writers. Specializes in commercial and literary fiction, fantasy, including first novels, thrillers, mysteries, science fiction, all categories of romance fiction, quality nonfiction, including biography, history, health, spirituality, business and popular science. Currently handles: 25% nonfiction books; 75% novels.
Handles: Nonfiction books, novels. Considers these nonfiction areas: biography/autobiography; business; child guidance/parenting; cooking/food/nutrition; current affairs; health/medicine; history; juvenile nonfiction; New Age/metaphysics; psychology; religious/inspirational; science/technology; self-help/personal improvement; true crime/investigative. Considers these fiction areas: detective/police/crime; family saga; fantasy; historical; humor; juvenile; literary; mainstream; mystery/suspense; picture book; romance; science fiction; thriller/espionage; westerns/frontier; young adult. Send outline plus 3 sample chapters. Reports in 10 days on queries; 3-4 weeks on mss.
Recent Sales: 2 untitled science thrillers by Bob Mayer (Dell); 2 untitled romances by Dallas Schulze (Mira Books); *The Glenkirk Chronicles* (2 books), by Beatrice Small (Zebra); 2 untitled suspense novels by Leonard Scott (Ballantine); untitled thriller by Tom Wilson (Dutton); 2 contemporary romance novels by Curtiss Ann Matlock (Avon); *Big Mama* (children's book), by Tony Crunk (Farrar, Straus and Giroux); illustrations by Julia Noonan for *The Bundle Book* (HarperCollins).
Terms: Agent receives 15% on domestic sales; 10% on foreign sales. Offers written contract, "flexible." Charges for "direct expenses only: photocopying, postage."
Writers' Conferences: Attends many RWA conferences (including Hawaii) and Novelists, Inc.
Tips: "We do consider new material from unsolicited authors. Write a good clear letter with a succinct description of your book. We prefer the first three chapters when we consider fiction. For all submissions you must include SASE for return or the material is discarded. It's always hard to break in, but talent will find a home. We continue to see natural storytellers and nonfiction writers with important books."

ELLIOTT AGENCY, (I, II), 130 Garth Rd., Suite 506, Scarsdale NY 10583. (914)793-4954. Contact: Elaine Elliott. Estab. 1995. Represents 15 clients. 40% of clients are new/previously unpublished writers. Currently handles: 10% nonfiction books; 80% novels; 10% short story collections.
Handles: Nonfiction books, novels, short story collections. Considers these nonfiction areas: humor; nature/environment; popular culture; science/technology; true crime/investigative. Considers these fiction areas: action/adventure; contemporary issues; detective/police/crime; horror; humor/satire; literary; mainstream. Query. Reports in 2 weeks on queries; 2 months on mss.
Terms: Agent receives 15% commission on domestic sales. No written contract. Agreement may be terminated by either party, at any time, for any reason. 100% of business is derived from commissions on sales.
Writers' Conferences: ABA (Chicago, June).
Tips: Obtains new clients through recommendations from editors and other agents and also from CompuServe writers forums. "No calls please."

NICHOLAS ELLISON, INC., (II), 55 Fifth Ave., 15th Floor, New York NY 10003. (212)206-6050. Affiliated with Sanford J. Greenburger Associates. Contact: Elizabeth Ziemska. Estab. 1983. Represents 70 clients. Currently handles: 25% nonfiction books; 75% novels. Member agent: Chritaina Harcar (foreign rights).
Handles: Nonfiction, novels. Considers most nonfiction areas. No biography, gay/lesbian issues or self-help. Considers literary and mainstream fiction. Query with SASE. Reporting time varies on queries.
Recent Sales: *Plum Island*, by Nelson DeMille (Warner); *The Violet Hour*, by Richard Montanari (Avon).
Terms: Agent receives 15% commission on domestic sales; 20% commission on foreign sales.
Tips: Usually obtains new clients from word-of-mouth referrals.

ANN ELMO AGENCY INC., (III), 60 E. 42nd St., New York NY 10165. (212)661-2880, 2881. Fax: (212)661-2883. Contact: Lettie Lee. Estab. 1961. Member of AAR, MWA, Authors Guild. Member agents: Lettie Lee, Mari Cronin (plays); A.L. Abecassis.
Handles: Nonfiction, novels. Considers these nonfiction areas: anthropology/archaeology; art/architecture/design; biography/autobiography; business; child guidance/parenting; computers/electronics; cooking/food/nutrition; crafts/hobbies; current affairs; education; health/medicine; history; how-to; juvenile nonfiction; money/finance/economics; music/dance/theater/film; photography; popular culture; psychology; self-help/personal improvement; true crime/investigative; women's issues. Considers

these fiction areas: action/adventure; contemporary issues; detective/police/crime; ethnic; family saga; feminist; glitz; historical; juvenile; literary; mainstream; mystery/suspense; psychic/supernatural; regional; romance (contemporary, gothic, historical, regency); thriller/espionage; young adult. Query with outline/proposal. Reports in 10-12 weeks "average" on queries.

Terms: Agent receives 15% commission on domestic sales; 20% on foreign sales. Offers written contract (standard AAR contract).

Tips: Obtains new clients through referrals. "Query first, and when asked please send properly prepared manuscript. A double-spaced, readable manuscript is the best recommendation. Include SASE, of course."

EMERALD LITERARY AGENCY, (I, II), 1212 N. Angelo Dr., Beverly Hills CA 90210. (310)247-0488. (310)247-0885. Contact: Debra Rodman. Estab. 1994. Represents 20 clients. 50% of clients are new/previously unpublished writers. Currently handles: 75% nonfiction books; 25% novels.

Handles: Nonfiction books, novels. Considers these nonfiction areas: biography; business; current affairs; finance/economics; literature/criticism; politics; popular culture; psychology; religious/inspirational; self-help/personal improvement; women's and men's issues. Considers these fiction areas: literary. Query with 3 sample chapters and SASE. Does not report on queries; 3 weeks on mss.

Recent Sales: *My Life With Elvis*, by Jim Dickerson and Scotty Moore, ed. by Richard Carlin (Schirmer Books, Simon & Schuster); *Story*, by Robert McKee, ed. by Judith Regan (Regan Books, HarperCollins Publishers); *Licking Our Wounds*, by Elise D'L laene (The Permanent Press); *Jack and Charlie*, by Howard Shanks (Commonwealth Publications, Canada).

Terms: Agent receives 15% commission on domestic sales; 10% on dramatic sales; 20% on foreign sales. Offers written contract. Charges for postage, photocopying.

Writers' Conferences: Maui; San Diego.

Tips: Obtains new clients through referrals, luck, conferences and listings in *LMP* and *Hollywood Directory*.

ESQ. LITERARY PRODUCTIONS, (II), 1492 Cottontail Lane, La Jolla CA 92037-7427. (619)551-9383. Fax: (619)551-9382. E-mail: fdh161@aol.com. Contact: Sherrie Dixon, Esq. Estab. 1993. Represents 15 clients. 50% of clients are new/previously unpublished writers. Currently handles: 25% nonfiction books; 75% novels. Agency specializes in adult mainstream fiction and nonfiction. Member agent: D.S. Lada (mainstream fiction.)

Handles: Fiction and nonfiction. Considers these nonfiction areas: cooking/food/nutrition; health/medicine; "and other topics if written by experts in their field." Considers these fiction areas: action/adventure; contemporary issues; detective/police/crime; mainstream; mystery/suspense; thriller/espionage. Send outline, SASE and 3 sample chapters for fiction; query for nonfiction. Reports in 1-2 weeks on queries; 1 month on mss.

Recent Sales: *Pure Fitness*, by Lori Fetnick and Dr. Robert Epstein (Masters Press); *Deadly Rescue*, by Jodie Larsen (Onyx); *Rock and Roll Cookbook*, by John D. Crisafulli, Sean Fisher and Teresa Villa (Dove Books); *Emperor Jones* (Dunhill Publishing Company).

Terms: Agent receives 15% commission on domestic sales; 20% on foreign sales. Offers written contract.

FELICIA ETH LITERARY REPRESENTATION, (II), 555 Bryant St., Suite 350, Palo Alto CA 94301-1700. (415)375-1276. Fax: (415)375-1277. Contact: Felicia Eth. Estab. 1988. Member of AAR. Represents 25-35 clients. Works with established and new writers; "for nonfiction, established expertise is certainly a plus, as is magazine publication—though not a prerequisite. I specialize in provocative, intelligent, thoughtful nonfiction on a wide array of subjects which are commercial and high-quality fiction; preferably mainstream and contemporary. I am highly selective, but also highly dedicated to those projects I represent." Currently handles: 85% nonfiction; 15% adult novels.

Handles: Nonfiction books, novels. Considers these nonfiction areas: animals; anthropology; biography/autobiography; business; child guidance/parenting; current affairs; ethnic/cultural interests; gay/lesbian issues; government/politics/law; health/medicine; history; nature/environment; popular culture; psychology; science/technology; sociology; true crime/investigative; women's issues/women's studies. Considers these fiction areas: ethnic; feminist; gay; lesbian; literary; mainstream; thriller/espionage. Query with outline. Reports in 3 weeks on queries; 1 month on proposals and sample pages.

Recent Sales: *Caught Up In the Rapture*, by Sheneska Jackson (Simon & Schuster/Scribners Paperback); *Courage to Complete; Competition and Intimacy in Women's Lives*, by Mariah Nelson (William Morrow); *The Whole Kitty "CAT"alog*, by Reed Huegel Southern California (Crown).

Terms: Agent receives 15% commission on domestic sales; 20% on dramatic sales; 20% on foreign sales. Charges for photocopying, express mail service—extraordinary expenses.

Writers' Conferences: Independent Writers of (LA); Conference of National Coalition of Independent Scholars (Berkeley CA); Writers Guild.

FARBER LITERARY AGENCY INC., (II), 14 E. 75th St., #2E, New York NY 10021. (212)861-7075. Fax: (212)861-7076. Contact: Ann Farber. Estab. 1989. Represents 30 clients. 84% of clients are new/previously unpublished writers. Currently handles: 65% fiction; 5% scholarly books; 20% stage plays.
Handles: Nonfiction books, textbooks, juvenile books, novels, stage plays. Considers these nonfiction areas: child guidance/parenting; cooking/food/nutrition; music/dance/theater/film; psychology. Considers these fiction areas: action/adventure; contemporary issues; humor/satire; juvenile; literary; mainstream; mystery/suspense; thriller/espionage; young adult. Send outline/proposal, 3 sample chapters and SASE. Reports in 1 week on queries; 1 month on mss.
Recent Sales: *Live A Little*, by Colin Neenan (Harcourt Brace); several books by Gloria Houston with various publishers.
Terms: Agent receives 15% commission on domestic sales; 20% on foreign sales. Offers written contract, binding for 2 years.
Tips: Obtains new clients through recommendations from others. Client must furnish copies of ms. "Our attorney, Donald C. Farber, is the author of many books. His services are available to the clients of the agency as part of the agency service."

‡BRENDA FEIGEN LITERARY AGENCY, (II), 10158 Hollow Glen Circle, Bel Air CA 90077. (310)271-0606. Fax: (310)274-0503. E-Mail: 104063.3247@compuserve.com. Contact: Brenda Feigen. Estab. 1995. Represents 25-35 clients. 85% of clients are new/previously unpublished writers. Currently handles: 15% nonfiction books, 2% juvenile books, 20% movie scripts, 60% novels, 2% TV scripts, 1% poetry. Member agent: Joanne Parrent (screenplays).
Handles: Nonfiction books, movie scripts, scholarly books, novels, TV scripts. Considers these nonfiction areas: art/architecture/design; biography/autobiography; child guidance/parenting; current affairs; ethnic/cultural interests; gay/lesbian issues; government/politics/law; health/medicine; language/literature/criticism; music/dance/theater/film; psychology; self-help/personal improvement; women's issues/women's studies. Considers these fiction areas: action/adventure; confessional; contemporary issues; detective/police/crime; family saga; feminist; gay; lesbian; literary; mainstream; mystery/suspense; thriller/espionage. Query with entire ms plus 2-page synopsis and author bio with SASE. Reports in 1-2 weeks on queries; 3-4 weeks on mss.
Recent Sales: *You'll Never Make Love in This Town Again*, by Joanne Parrent (Dove); *Life After Johnnie Cochran*, by Barbara Cochran Berry and Joanne Parrent (Basic Books); *The Tragic Kingdom*, by Kathy Harley Smith (Dove).
Terms: Agent receives 15% commission on domestic sales; 20% on foreign sales. Offers a written contract, binding for 1 year. Charges for postage, long distance calls, and photocopying.
Tips: Usually obtains clients through recommendations from other clients and publishers, through the Internet and listings in LMP.

FLORENCE FEILER LITERARY AGENCY, (III), 1524 Sunset Plaza Dr., Los Angeles CA 90069. (213)652-6920. Fax: (213)652-0945. Associate: Joyce Boorn. Estab. 1976. Member of PEN American Center, Women in Film, California Writers Club, MWA. Represents 40 clients. No unpublished writers. "Quality is the criterion." Specializes in fiction, nonfiction, screenplays, TV. No short stories.
 • See the expanded listing for this agency in Script Agents.

FIRST BOOKS, (II), 2040 N. Milwaukee Ave., Chicago IL 60647. (773)276-5911. Estab. 1988. Represents 70 clients. 50% of clients are new/previously unpublished writers. Specializes in book-length fiction and nonfiction for the adult and juvenile markets. No romance novels. Member agent: Jeremy Solomon.
Handles: Nonfiction books, juvenile books, novels. Query. Reports in 2-4 weeks on queries.
Recent Sales: *Polish Your Furniture With Panty Hose*, by Joey Green (Hyperion); *Bless This House*, by Ann Wall Frank (Contemporary); *Abracadabra*, by Jean MacCleod (St. Martin's Press); *Djuna: The Life and Work of Djuna Barnes*, by Phillip Herring (Viking).
Terms: Agent receives 15% commission on domestic sales; 20% on foreign sales. Offers written contract, with cancellation on demand by either party.
Tips: Obtains new clients through recommendations from others.

JOYCE A. FLAHERTY, LITERARY AGENT, (II, III), 816 Lynda Court, St. Louis MO 63122-5531. (314)966-3057. Contact: Joyce or John Flaherty. Estab. 1980. Member of AAR, RWA, MWA, Author's Guild. Represents 50 clients. "At this time we are adding only currently published authors." Currently handles: 15% nonfiction books; 85% novels. Member agents: Joyce A. Flaherty (women's fiction, romance, mystery and suspense, general fiction and nonfiction); John Flaherty (thrillers, male-oriented mysteries and espionage novels; also military fiction and nonfiction).
Handles: Nonfiction books, novels. Considers these nonfiction areas: Americana; animals; biography/autobiography (celebrity); child guidance/parenting; collectibles; crafts/hobbies; health/medicine; how-to; nature; popular culture; psychology; self-help/personal improvement; sociology; true crime/investi-

INSIDER REPORT

Having a third set of eyes: Agent as editor

The third time's the charm. After two book propos-als and two different agents, Meredith Maran and her agent, Felicia Eth, were brought together by a mutual friend to propel an article-writing career to the heights of book authorship.

What It's Like to Live Now, Maran's first solo book, contains personal anecdotes and observations that explore the diverse trials and triumphs of living today. Maran's politics, ethics and feelings are in-tertwined to create a funny, moving and intellectual read. This compilation of journal entries wasn't born that way; it wouldn't be such a tightly woven book without some editing.

Editing is a fact of life for any writer. The author edits, the editor edits, the agent edits. The agent edits? Yes, in some form or another, an agent has a hand in the final manuscript, whether an overall observation ("We might sell this better if you focused more on the irony") or a specific critique ("In chapter three, the plot begins to drag. Re-work it by including the villain in the carnival scene"). Some authors benefit from having an agent who edits. Maran didn't know she wanted one or could have one until she found Eth.

Eth worked with Maran chapter by chapter to create the best possible book. Because Eth sold the manuscript before the book was complete, she edited it as it was written. Within two or three days of receiving a batch of the manuscript from Maran, Eth would give her feedback. Maran made these revisions and then sent three chapters at a time to her editor in New York. "I found out pretty early that my editor always agreed with [Felicia], so it was like getting my editor's feedback without having to do the scary thing of showing my editor an unedited manuscript," says Maran.

This extra set of eyes was a definite boon to the project, both in the long and short runs. Having the manuscript evaluated and edited as it was put together taught Maran lessons she could apply to future projects as well as to the coming chapters. "All the individual responses I got from [Felicia and my editor] would start to have a more long-lasting effect on my writing," she says. "And after a while I could incorporate these critiques into the work as I was doing it instead of waiting for them to tell me at the end."

With all this critiquing and editing from an agent, one might expect Maran to question or even doubt her project. Not so. "Sometimes [Eth] caused me to have doubts for good reasons," says Maran. "She would question the politics of what

INSIDER REPORT, *Maran*

I was saying or whether I was saying what I meant to say. And so it would be a good kind of questioning. She never made me feel insecure."

An agent questions the politics? The usage? An agent edits? Maran found by knocking on the right door that indeed some do. When searching for an agent she didn't specifically ask about editorial capabilities or even the willingness to edit. Thus, she did not know how much editorial assistance she'd get or should expect. Luckily she was introduced to an agent with both editorial talent and the ambition to invest it. It wasn't until she started talking to other writers that she discovered many agents don't do aggressive editing.

If she had to do it over again, Maran would conduct her search differently. She would know to ask what part the agent takes in the editing process. On finding an agent who offers intensive editorial help, Maran would understand her next step would be to speak with other clients and ask them how the agent works editorially. Specifically, Maran would look for three services the agent must provide. "One is selling the book—there's not much point in having an agent if she can't do that." Second for Maran is contributing editorial feedback, which betters the project and the author, and the third is offering career guidance. Eth surpassed these standards and has now helped put a second Meredith Maran book on the shelves.

Having an agent with strong editorial skills and the drive to apply them can make all the difference—and it has. Maran appreciates the benefits of her partnership with Eth. "It's a huge luxury to be edited. It's like getting constant feedback on your work, which most people don't get. I think the opportunity to write a book and be edited twice, first by Felicia and then by my editor in New York, is like a training process. It's an apprenticeship."

—Tara A. Horton

gative; women's issues/women's studies. Considers these fiction areas: contemporary issues; crime; family saga; feminist; frontier; historical; mainstream; military; mystery/suspense; women's genre fiction. Send outline plus 1 sample chapter and SASE. No unsolicited mss. Reports in 1 month on queries; 2 months on mss unless otherwise agreed on.

Recent Sales: *In Roared Flynn*, by Jan Hudson (Silhouette-Desire); *Prairie Rose, As The Lily Grows, When Lilacs Bloom* (series), by Susan Kirby (Avon); *101 Things A College Girl Should Know*, by Stephanie Edwards (Andrews & McMee); *To Love A Dark Stranger*, by Colleen Faulkner (Kensington); *Gypsy Dance*, by Patt Bucheister (Bantam); *Firehawk's Bride*, by Judith E. French (Avon).

Terms: Agent receives 15% commission on domestic sales; 30% on foreign sales. Charges $75 marketing fee for new clients unless currently published book authors.

Writers' Conferences: Often attends Romance Writers of America; Virginia Romance Writers (Williamsburg VA); Moonlight & Magnolias (Atlanta GA).

Tips: Obtains new clients through recommendations from editors and clients, writers' conferences and from queries. "Be concise in a letter or by phone and well focused. Always include a SASE as well as your phone number. If a query is a multiple submission, be sure to say so and mail them all at the same time so that everyone has the same chance. Know something about the agent beforehand so that you're not wasting each other's time. Be specific about word length of project and when it will be completed if not completed at the time of contact. Be brief!"

FLAMING STAR LITERARY ENTERPRISES, (II), 320 Riverside Dr., New York NY 10025. Contact: Joseph B. Vallely or Janis C. Vallely. Estab. 1985. Represents 100 clients. 25% of clients are new/previously unpublished writers. Specializes in upscale commercial fiction and nonfiction. Currently handles: 90% nonfiction books; 10% novels.

• Prior to opening his agency, Mr. Vallely served as national sales manager for Dell.

Handles: Nonfiction books, novels. Considers these nonfiction areas: current affairs; government/politics/law; health/medicine; nature/environment; New Age/metaphysics; science/technology; self-help/personal improvement; sports. Considers only upscale commercial fiction. Query with SASE. Reports in 1 week on queries.
Terms: Agent receives 15% commission on domestic sales; 20% on foreign sales. Offers written contract. Charges for photocopying, postage, long distance phone calls only.
Tips: Obtains new clients over the transom and through referrals.

FLANNERY LITERARY, (II), 34-36 28th St., #5, Long Island City NY 11106-3516. (718)472-0523. Fax: (718)482-0718. Contact: Jennifer Flannery. Estab. 1992. Represents 33 clients. 90% of clients are new/previously unpublished writers. Specializes in children's and young adult, juvenile fiction and nonfiction. Currently handles: 5% nonfiction books; 95% juvenile books.
Handles: Nonfiction books, juvenile books. Considers these nonfiction areas: child guidance/parenting; juvenile nonfiction. Considers these fiction areas: action/adventure; contemporary issues; ethnic; experimental; family saga; historical; humor/satire; juvenile; literary; mainstream; mystery/suspense; picture book; sports; western/frontier; young adult. Query. Reports in 2-4 weeks on queries; 6-8 weeks on mss.
Also Handles: Movie scripts (feature film, animation), TV scripts (TV mow, miniseries, animation). Considers these script subject areas: action/adventure; cartoon/animation; comedy; contemporary issues; ethnic; family saga; historical; humor; juvenile; mainstream; mystery/suspense; sports; teen; western/frontier. Query. Reports in 2-4 weeks on queries; 6-8 weeks on scripts.
Terms: Agent receives 15% commission on domestic sales; 20% on foreign sales. Offers written contract, binding for life of book in print, with 30 day cancellation clause. 100% of business is derived from commissions on sales.
Writers' Conferences: SCBWI Fall Conference.
Tips: Obtains new clients through referrals. "Write an engrossing succinct query describing your work."

PETER FLEMING AGENCY, (IV), P.O. Box 458, Pacific Palisades CA 90272. (310)454-1373. Contact: Peter Fleming. Estab. 1962. Specializes in "nonfiction books: innovative, helpful, contrarian, individualistic, pro-free market . . . with bestseller big market potential." Currently handles: 100% nonfiction books.
Handles: Nonfiction books. Considers "any nonfiction area with a positive, innovative, helpful, professional, successful approach to improving the world (and abandoning special interests, corruption and patronage)." Query with SASE.
Recent Sales: *Launching Your Child In Show Biz*, by Dick Van Patten (General Publishing Group); *The Living Trust* (3rd edition), by Henry Abts (Contemporary).
Terms: Agent receives 15% commission on domestic sales; 25% on foreign sales. Offers written contract, binding for 1 year. Charges "only those fees agreed to *in writing*, i.e., NY-ABA expenses shared. We may ask for a TV contract, too."
Tips: Obtains new clients "through a *sensational*, different, one of a kind idea for a book usually backed by the writer's experience in that area of expertise. If you give seminars, you can begin by self-publishing, test marketing with direct sales. One of my clients sold 100,000 copies through his speeches and travels, and another writing duo sold over 30,000 copies of their self-published book before we offered it to trade bookstore publishers."

‡ARTHUR FLEMING ASSOCIATES, (II), P.O. Box 420024, San Diego CA 92124. (619)565-8484. Contact: Arthur Fleming. Estab. 1961. Represents 355 clients. 25% of clients are new/previously unpublished writers. Currently handles: 40% nonfiction books; 12% juvenile books; 6% short story collections; 4% scholarly books; 35% novels; 3% textbooks. Member agents: Rita Kahn (general agent, foreign rights); Arthur Fleming (family parenting, women's issues, health food, cooking).
Handles: Nonfiction books, juvenile books, movie scripts, scholarly books, novels, TV scripts, textbooks, poetry books, short story collections. Considers these nonfiction areas: agriculture/horticulture; animals; art/architecture/design; biography/autobiography; business; child guidance/parenting; cooking/food/nutrition; gay/lesbian issues; how-to; humor; juvenile nonfiction; military/war; money/finance/economics; New Age/metaphysics; photography; psychology; religious/inspirational; self-help/personal improvement; sociology; sports; women's issues/women's studies. Considers these fiction areas: action/adventure; contemporary issues; detective/police/crime; ethnic; family saga; fantasy; feminist; gay; historical; horror; humor/satire; juvenile; lesbian; mainstream; mystery/suspense; picture book; psychic/supernatural; religious/inspirational; romance; science fiction; sports; westerns/frontier. Send outline and 3 sample chapters. Reports in 1 week on queries; 2-3 weeks on mss.
Terms: Agent receives 15% commission on domestic sales; 15% on foreign sales. Offers written contract, binding for 8 months. Sometimes charges for postage and photocopying when book requires mass marketing.

Tips: Obtains new clients through recommendations "from authors we represent. Never solicitation of any kind."

B.R. FLEURY AGENCY, (I, II), 1228 E. Colonial Dr., Orlando FL 32803. (407)896-4976. Contact: Blanche or Margaret. Estab. 1994. Signatory of WGA. Currently handles: 50% books; 50% scripts.
• See the expanded listing for this agency in Script Agents.

THE FOLEY LITERARY AGENCY, (III), 34 E. 38th St., New York NY 10016. (212)686-6930. Contact: Joan or Joseph Foley. Estab. 1956. Represents 15 clients. 5% of clients are new/previously unpublished writers. Currently handles: 75% nonfiction books; 25% novels.
Handles: Nonfiction books, novels. Query with letter, brief outline and SASE. Reports in 2 weeks on queries.
Terms: Agent receives 10% commission on domestic sales; 20% on foreign sales. Charges for photocopying, messenger service and unusual expenses (international phone, etc.). 100% of business is derived from commissions on sales.
Tips: Obtains new clients through recommendations from others "and agency's reputation." Desires *brevity* in querying.

LYNN C. FRANKLIN ASSOCIATES, LTD., (II), 386 Park Ave. S., #1102, New York NY 10016. (212)689-1842. Fax: (212)213-0649. Contact: Candace Rondeaux. Estab. 1987. Member of PEN America. Represents 30-35 clients. 50% of clients are new/previously unpublished writers. Specializes in general nonfiction with a special interest in health, biography, international affairs and spirituality. Currently handles: 90% nonfiction books; 10% novels.
Handles: Nonfiction books. Considers these nonfiction areas: biography/autobiography; current affairs; health/medicine; history; New Age/metaphysics; psychology; religious/inspirational; self-help/personal improvement. Considers literary and mainstream commercial ficton. Query with SASE. No unsolicited mss. Reports in 2 weeks on queries; 6 weeks on mss.
Recent Sales: *At The Still Point*, by Carol Buckley (Simon & Schuster); *Stalin*, by Edvard Radzinsky (Nan A. Talese Books).
Terms: Agent receives 15% commission on domestic sales; 20% on foreign sales. Offers written contract, with 60 day cancellation clause. Charges for postage, photocopying, long distance telephone if significant. 100% of business is derived from commissions on sales.
Tips: Obtains new clients through recommendations from others and from solicitation.

‡**THE FRUSTRATED WRITER'S LTD., (II)**, P.O. Box 31579, Phoenix AZ 85046-1579. (602)996-8099. Fax: (602)996-8099. Contact: Wayne Fontenot. Estab. 1993. Represents 25 clients. 50% of clients are new/previously unpublished writers. Currently handles: 25% nonfiction books; 25% juvenile books; 50% novels. Member agents: Kathy McPherson, Mickey Fontenot, Tony Urdiales.
Handles: Nonfiction books, juvenile books, movie scripts, novels, TV scripts. Considers these nonfiction areas: child guidance/parenting; how-to; juvenile nonfiction; military/war; psychology; sociology; sports; true crime/investigative. Considers all fiction areas. Send outline/proposal with query. Reports in 2-3 weeks on queries; 2-3 months on mss.
Terms: Agent receives 15% commission on domestic sales; 15% on foreign sales. Offers written contract, binding for 3 years, with 1 month cancellation clause.
Writers' Conference: Annual Fall Conference (Durham, NC, November); Southeastern Writers Conference (St. Simon, GA, June); Southwest Christian Writers (Farmington, NM, September); Southwest Writer Workshop (Albuquerque, NM, September).
Tips: Obtains new clients through recommendations from others, solicitation, at conferences. "Never take 'No!' for an answer. Keep in mind that the literary business is very competitive. An author who goes the extra mile to make a professional presentation deserves *our* attention and time."

‡**SHERYL B. FULLERTON ASSOCIATES, (II)**, 1010 Church St., San Francisco CA 94114. (415)824-8460. Fax: (415)824-3037. E-Mail: sfullerton@aol.com. Contact: Sheryl Fullerton. Estab. 1994. Represents 20 clients. 80% of clients are new/previously unpublished writers. Specializes in nonfiction. Currently handles: 93% nonfiction books; 3% scholarly books, 1% novels, 3% textbooks.
Handles: Nonfiction books, scholarly books, textbooks, novels. Considers these nonfiction areas: anthropology/archaeology; business; current affairs; education; ethnic/cultural interests; health/medicine; how-to; humor; money/finance/economics; New Age/metaphysics; popular culture; psychology; religious/inspirational; self-help/personal improvement; sociology; women's issues/women's studies. Considers these fiction areas: feminist; gay; lesbian. Query with outline/proposal. Reports in 2 weeks on queries; 4 weeks on mss.
Terms: Agent receives 15% commission on domestic sales; 20% on foreign sales. Offers a written contract binding for 1 year, then renewable. Must give 60 days notice to terminate contract. Charges for phone calls, postage, photocopies. Usually obtains clients through recommendations, referrals and through previous contacts.

Tips: "With SASE, I will provide guidelines for writing a book proposal."

JAY GARON-BROOKE ASSOC. INC., (II), 101 W. 55th St., Suite 5K, New York NY 10019-5348. (212)581-8300. Vice President: Jean Free. Estab. 1952. Member of AAR, signatory of WGA. Represents 80 clients. 10% of clients are new/previously unpublished writers. Specializes in mainstream fiction and nonfiction. Currently handles: 15% nonfiction books; 75% novels; 5% movie scripts; 3% TV scripts; 2% stage plays. Member agents: Nancy Coffey, Dick Duane, Robert Thixton.
 • Mr. Garon passed away in 1995.
Handles: Nonfiction books, novels, movie scripts, TV scripts. Considers these nonfiction areas: biography/autobiography; child guidance/parenting; gay/lesbian issues; health/medicine; history; military/war; music/dance/theater/film; psychology; self-help/personal improvement; true crime/investigative. Considers these fiction areas: contemporary issues; detective/police/crime; family saga; fantasy; gay; literary; mainstream; mystery/suspense; romance; science fiction. Query with SASE. Reports in 3 weeks on queries; 2 months on mss.
Recent Sales: *The Run Away Jury,* by John Grisham (Doubleday-Dell); *Threshold,* by Ben Mezrich (HarperCollins); *The Plaza Wedding Book,* by Lawrence Harvey (Villard); *Society of the Mind,* by Eric Harry (HarperCollins).
Terms: Agent receives 15% on domestic sales; 30% on foreign sales. Offers written contract, binding for 3-5 years.
Tips: Obtains new clients through referrals and from queries. "Send query letter first giving the essence of the manuscript and a personal or career bio with SASE."

2 9 2 - 4 3 5 4

MAX GARTENBERG, LITERARY AGENT, (II, III), 521 Fifth Ave., Suite 1700, New York NY 10175-0105. (212)860-8451. Contact: Max Gartenberg. Estab. 1954. Represents 30 clients. 5% of clients are new writers. Currently handles: 90% nonfiction books; 10% novels.
Handles: Nonfiction books. Considers these nonfiction areas: agriculture/horticulture; animals; art/architecture/design; biography/autobiography; child guidance/parenting; current affairs; health/medicine; history; military/war; money/finance/economics; music/dance/theater/film; nature/environment; psychology; science/technology; self-help/personal improvement; sports; true crime/investigative; women's issues/women's studies. Query. Reports in 2 weeks on queries; 6 weeks on mss.
Recent Sales: *The Complete Art of War,* by Ralph D. Sawyer (Westview Press); *The Measured Man,* by Howard Owen (HarperCollins); *Sea Turtles,* by Anne and Jack Rudloe (Crown Publishers).
Terms: Agent receives 15% commission on first domestic sale, 10% commission on subsequent domestic sales; 15-20% on foreign sales.
Tips: Obtains new clients "primarily by recommendations from others, but often enough by following up on good query letters. However, this is a small agency serving established writers, and new writers whose work it is able to handle are few and far between. Nonfiction is more likely to be of interest here than fiction, and category fiction not at all."

RICHARD GAUTHREAUX—A LITERARY AGENCY (II), 2742 Jasper St., Kenner LA 70062. (504)466-6741. Contact: Jay Richards. Estab. 1985. Represents 11 clients. 75% of clients are new/previously unpublished writers. Currently handles: 45% novels; 25% movie scripts; 20% TV scripts; 5% short story collections.
 • See the expanded listing for this agency in Script Agents.

‡GHOSTS & COLLABORATORS INTERNATIONAL, Division of James Peter Associates, Inc., (IV), P.O. Box 772, Tenafly NJ 07670. (201)568-0760. Fax: (201)568-2959. E-mail: bholtje @attmail.com. Contact: Bert Holtje. Parent agency established 1971. Parent agency is a member of AAR. Represents 84 clients. Specializes in representing only published ghost writers and collaborators, nonfiction only. Currently handles: 100% nonfiction books. Member agent: Bert Holtje.
 • See Mr. Holtje's article, Career Planning for Nonfiction Writers, in this edition of the *Guide.*
Handles: Nonfiction collaborations and ghost writing assignments.
Terms: Agent receives 15% commission on domestic sales; 20% on foreign sales. Offers written contract.
Tips: "We would like to hear from professional writers who are looking for ghosting and collaboration projects. We invite inquiries from book publishers who are seeking writers to develop house-generated ideas, and to work with their authors who need professional assistance."

THE SEBASTIAN GIBSON AGENCY, (I), 125 Tahquitz Canyon Way, Suite 200, Palm Springs CA 92262. (619)322-2200. Fax: (619)322-3857. Contact: Sebastian Gibson. Estab. 1995. Member of the California Bar Association and Desert Bar Association. 100% of clients are new/previously unpublished writers. Specializes in fiction. Currently handles: 100% novels.
Handles: Nonfiction books, novels. Considers these nonfiction areas: animals; anthropology/archaeology; art/architecture/design; biography/autobiography; business; cooking/food/nutrition; current affairs; ethnic/cultural interests; government/politics/law; health/medicine; history; humor; military/war;

money/finance/economics; music/dance/theater/film; nature/environment; New Age/metaphysics; photography; popular culture; psychology; religious/inspirational; science/technology; self-help/personal improvement; sociology; sports; translations; true crime/investigative; women's issues/women's studies. Considers these fiction areas: action/adventure; cartoon/comic; contemporary issues; detective/police/crime; ethnic; family saga; fantasy; feminist; glitz; historical; horror; humor/satire; juvenile; literary; mainstream; picture book; psychic/supernatural; regional; religious/inspirational; romance (contemporary, gothic, historical, regency); science fiction; sports; thriller/espionage; westerns/frontier; young adult. Send outline and 3 sample chapters; $7.50 handling charge requested but not mandatory. SASE required for a response. Reports in 3 weeks.

Terms: Agent receives 10% commission on domestic sales; 20% on foreign sales. Offers written contract, with 30 day cancellation notice. Charges for postage, photocopying and express mail fees charged only against sales.

Writers' Conference: ABA (Chicago, June); Book Fair (Frankfurt); London Int'l Book Fair (London).

Tips: Obtains new clients through advertising, queries and book proposals, and through the representation of entertainment clients. "Consider hiring a freelance editor to make corrections and assist you in preparing book proposals. Try to develop unusual characters in your novels, and novel approaches to nonfiction. Manuscripts should be clean and professional looking and without errors. Do not send unsolicited manuscripts or disks. Save your money and effort for redrafts. Don't give up. We want to help you become published. But your work must be very readable without plot problems or grammatical errors. Do not send sample chapters or book proposals until you've completed at least your fourth draft. Unless you're famous, don't send autobiographies. We are looking primarily for all categories of fiction with unusual characters, new settings and well-woven plots. Please no more books involving housewives who find true love with their husbands, reincarnation of the Third Reich, or travel memoirs of trips to Orlando or Tijuana."

GODDARD BOOK GROUP (II), 203 N. Wabash Ave., Chicago IL 60601-2415. (312)759-5822. Contact: Connie Goddard. Estab. 1992. Represents 25 clients. 20% of clients are new/previously unpublished writers. Specializes in Chicago-area writers and projects with Midwest origins. Currently handles: 95% nonfiction books; 5% novels.
   • Prior to opening her agency, Ms. Goddard served as an editor and writer for various publishing houses and as a correspondent for *Publishers Weekly*. She currently directs the Center for Writing and Publishing at Columbia College in Chicago and is senior editor for *Chicago Books in Review*.
Handles: Nonfiction books, novels. Considers these nonfiction areas: agriculture/horticulture; animals; art/architecture/design; biography/autobiography; business; child guidance/parenting; cooking/food/nutrition; ethnic/cultural interests; government/politics/law; health/medicine; history; interior design/decorating; money/finance/economics; nature/environment; psychology; science/technology; self-help/personal improvement; sociology; women's issues/women's studies. Query with letter before sending ms or proposal. Always include SASE. Reports in 1 month.
Recent Sales: *The Great Chicago Trivia and Fact Book*, by Connie Goddard and Bruce Boyer (Cumberland House); *Brave New Girls*, by Jeanette Gadeberg (Fairview Press).
Terms: Agent receives 10-20% commission on domestic sales. Offers written contract. Charges for express postage, long distance phone calls, and photocopying.
Writers Conferernces: Printer's Row Book Fair (Chicago); Dark and Stormy Nights (Chicago).
Tips: Obtains new clients mainly by referral. "I want to work with people who want to work; writing books is a business as well as all the other fine things it might be."

GOLDFARB & GRAYBILL, ATTORNEYS AT LAW, (II), 918 16th St. NW, Washington DC 20006-2902. (202)466-3030. Contact: Nina Graybill. Estab. 1966. Represents "hundreds" of clients. "Minority" of clients are new/previously unpublished writers. Specializes primarily in nonfiction but has a growing interest in well-written fiction. Currently handles: 80% nonfiction books; 20% fiction. Member agents: Ronald Goldfarb, Esq. (nonfiction); Nina Graybill, Esq. (fiction, nonfiction); and Jenny Bent (fiction).
   • Both principals of this agency are published authors. Ron Goldfarb's latest book (his tenth), *Perfect Villains, Imperfect Heroes*, was published by Random House. Nina Graybill's sixth

IF YOU'RE LOOKING for a particular agent, check the Agents Index to find at which agency the agent works. Then check the listing for that agency in the appropriate section.

book, *Pasta Salad Light*, was published by Farragut Publishing Co.

Handles: Nonfiction books, fiction. Considers all nonfiction areas except children's books. No poetry. Considers these fiction areas: action/adventure; contemporary issues; detective/police/crime; ethnic; feminist; gay; glitz; literary; mainstream; mystery/suspense; thriller/espionage; especially interested in commercial women's fiction. Send outline or synopsis plus 1-2 sample chapters. Reports in 1 month on queries; 2 months on mss.

Recent Sales: *Elijah Mohammad* (biography), by Karl Eranzz (Pantheon); *The Search for the Golden Submarine*, by Paul Tidwell and Dick Billings (Judith Regan Books); *Mrs. Ike*, by Susan Eisenhower (Knopf); *The Leap of Death*, by Delal Baer (Norton).

Writers' Conferences: Attends Washington Independent Writers Conference (May); Medical Writers Conference; ABA (June); VCCA.

Tips: Obtains new clients mostly through recommendations from others. "We are a law firm which can help writers with related problems, Freedom of Information Act requests, libel, copyright, contracts, etc. As published authors ourselves, we understand the creative process, editor/author relationships, deadlines, and the like."

‡**GOODMAN ASSOCIATES, (III)**, 500 West End Ave., New York NY 10024-4317. (212)873-4806. Contact: Elise Simon Goodman. Estab. 1976. Member of AAR. Represents 100 clients. "Presently accepting new clients on a very selective basis."
 • Arnold Goodman is current chair of the AAR Ethics Committee.

Handles: Nonfiction, novels. Considers most adult nonfiction and fiction areas. No "poetry, articles, individual stories, children's or YA material." Query with SASE. Reports in 10 days on queries; 1 month on mss.

Terms: Agent receives 15% commission on domestic sales; 20% on foreign sales. Charges for certain expenses: faxes, toll calls, overseas postage, photocopying, book purchases.

‡**GOODMAN-ANDREW-AGENCY, INC., (II)**, 11225 Goodwin Way NE, Seattle WA 98125. (206)367-4052. Fax: (206)367-1991. Contact: David M. Andrew and Sasha Goodman. Estab. 1992. Represents 25 clients. 50% of clients are new/previously unpublished writers. Currently handles: 50% nonfiction books; 50% novels.

Handles: Nonfiction books, novels. Considers these nonfiction areas: agriculture/horticulture; anthropology/archaeology; art/architecture/design; biography/autobiography; business; child guidance/parenting; cooking/food/nutrition; current affairs; education; ethnic/cultural interests; gay/lesbian issues; government/politics/law; health/medicine; history; how-to; humor; language/literature/criticism; music/dance/theater/film; nature/environment; popular culture; psychology; self-help/personal improvement; sociology; sports; true crime/investigative; women's issues/women's studies. Considers these fiction areas: contemporary issues; ethnic; gay; lesbian; literary; mainstream. "Not big on genre fiction." Send outline and 2 sample chapters. Reports in 3 weeks on queries; 3 months on mss.

Terms: Agent receives 15% commission. Offers written contract. Charges for postage. 100% of business is derived from commission on domestic sales.

Writer's Conferences: Pacific Northwest (Seattle, July).

Tips: "Query with 1-page letter, brief synopsis and 2 chapters. Patience, patience, patience. Always enclose return postage/SASE if you want your material returned. Otherwise, say you do not. Remember the agent is receiving dozens of submissions per week so try to understand this and be patient and courteous."

CHARLOTTE GORDON AGENCY, (II), 235 E. 22nd St., New York NY 10010-4633. (212)679-5363. Contact: Charlotte Gordon. Estab. 1986. Represents 30 clients. 10% of clients are new/unpublished writers. "I'll work with writers whose work is interesting to me. Specializes in books (not magazine material, except for my writers, and then only in special situations). My taste is eclectic." Currently handles: 50% nonfiction; 30% novels; 20% juvenile.
 • Prior to opening her agency, Ms. Gordon served as an editor with Harper, Fawcett and Grossett.

Handles: Nonfiction books, novels; juvenile fiction and nonfiction. Considers these nonfiction areas: anthropology/archaeology; business; health/medicine; history; juvenile nonfiction; money/finance/economics; nature/environment; psychology; sociology; women's issues/women's studies. Considers these fiction areas: contemporary issues; family saga; gay; juvenile; lesbian; literary; mystery/suspense; romance (regency); young adult. Must query with first chapter. No unsolicited mss. Reports in 2 weeks on queries. SASE essential.

Terms: Agent receives 15% commission on domestic sales; 10% on dramatic sales; 10% on foreign sales, if another agent involved.

GRAHAM LITERARY AGENCY, INC., (II, IV), P.O. Box 1051, Alpharetta GA 30239-1051. (770)569-9755. E-mail: slgraham@atl.mindspring.com. Contact: Susan L. Graham. Estab. 1994. Represents 30 clients. 70% of clients are new/previously unpublished writers. Specializes in science fiction,

fantasy, mystery, thrillers, computer, political expose, business, popular science, CD-ROMs. Currently handles: 13% nonfiction books; 83% novels; 1% movie scripts; 1% CD-ROM.
Handles: Nonfiction books, novels, CD-ROM. Considers these nonfiction subjects: computers/electronics; government/politics/law; nature/environment; science/technology; true crime/investigative. Considers these fiction areas: detective/police/crime; fantasy; mystery/suspense; science fiction; thriller/espionage. Send outline and 3 sample chapters. Reports in 2 months on queries; 3 months on mss. "No phone calls, please."
Recent Sales: *Trouble No More*, by Anthony Grooms (La Questa Press; *Kingmaker's Sword*, by Ann Marston (HarperPrism); *Ladylord*, by Sasha Miller (TOR Books); *Living Real*, by James C. Bassett (HarperPrism); *The Western King*, by Ann Marston; *Broken Blade*, by Ann Marston (HarperPrism).
Terms: Agent receives 15% commission on domestic sales; 20% on foreign sales. Offers written contract, with 30 day cancellation clause. 100% of business is derived from commission on sales.
Writers' Conferences: Magic Carpet Con (Chattanooga TN, May); Dragon Con (Atlanta, July); World Con (August); World Fantasy Con (October).
Tips: Obtains new clients through recommendations, publicity, conferences and online. "Finish your book first, make sure to follow all of the formatting rules, then send the agency what they ask for. Be polite, and expect delays, but follow up."

SANFORD J. GREENBURGER ASSOCIATES, INC., (II), 55 Fifth Ave., New York NY 10003. (212)206-5600. Fax: (212)463-8718. Contact: Heide Lange. Estab. 1945. Member of AAR. Represents 500 clients. Member agents: Heide Lange, Faith Hamlin, Beth Vesel, Theresa Park, Elyse Cheney.
Handles: Nonfiction books, novels. Considers all nonfiction areas. Considers these fiction areas: action/adventure; contemporary issues, detective/police/crime; ethnic; family saga; feminist; gay; glitz; historical; humor/satire; juvenile; lesbian; literary; mainstream; mystery/suspense; psychic/supernatural; regional; sports; thriller/espionage. Query first. Reports in 3 weeks on queries; 2 months on mss.
Recent Sales: *Let Me Hear Your Voice*, by Catherine Maurice (Knopf); *The Beast: A Reckoning With Depression*, by Tracy Thompson (Putnam); *The Notebook*, by Nicholas Sparks (Warner).
Terms: Agent receives 15% commission on domestic sales; 20% on foreign sales. Charges for photocopying, books for foreign and subsidiary rights submissions.

ARTHUR B. GREENE, (III), 101 Park Ave., 43rd Floor, New York NY 10178. (212)661-8200. Fax: (212)370-7884. Contact: Arthur Greene. Estab. 1980. Represents 20 clients. 10% of clients are new/previously unpublished writers. Specializes in movies, TV and fiction. Currently handles: 25% novels; 10% novellas; 10% short story collections; 25% movie scripts; 10% TV scripts; 10% stage plays; 10% other.
• See the expanded listing for this agency in Script Agents.

RANDALL ELISHA GREENE, LITERARY AGENT, (II), 620 S. Broadway, Suite 210, Lexington KY 40508-3140. (606)225-1388. Contact: Randall Elisha Greene. Estab. 1987. Represents 20 clients. 30% of clients are new/previously unpublished writers. Specializes in adult fiction and nonfiction only. No juvenile or children's books. Currently handles: 50% nonfiction books; 50% novels.
• Prior to opening his agency, Mr. Greene worked at Doubleday & Co. as an editor.
Handles: Nonfiction books, novels. Considers these nonfiction areas: agriculture/horticulture; biography/autobiography; business; current affairs; government/politics/law; history; how-to; language/literature/criticism; psychology; religious/inspirational; true crime/investigative. Considers these fiction areas: action/adventure; contemporary issues; detective/police/crime; family saga; humor/satire; literary; mainstream; regional; romance (contemporary); thriller/espionage. Query with SASE only. No unsolicited mss. Reports in 1 month on queries; 2 months on mss.
Terms: Agent receives 15% commission on domestic sales; 20% on foreign sales and performance rights. Charges for extraordinary expenses such as photocopying and foreign postage.

‡BLANCHE C. GREGORY INC., (III, V), 2 Tudor City Place., New York NY 10017. (212)697-0828. Estab. 1930 Represents 5-10 clients. 10% of clients are new/previously unpublished writers.
Handles: Nonfiction, fiction. Query first. Does not accept unsolicited mss. Reports in 2 weeks on queries.
Terms: Agent receives 15% commission on domestic sales. 20% on foreign sales.
Tips: Usually obtains clients through referrals only.

LEW GRIMES LITERARY AGENCY, (II), 250 W. 54th St., Suite 800, New York NY 10019-5586. (212)974-9505. Fax: (212)974-9525. Contact: Lew Grimes. Estab. 1991. 25% of clients are new/previously unpublished writers. Currently handles: 50% nonfiction books; 5% scholarly books; 1% textbooks; 43½% novels; ½% poetry books.
Handles: Nonfiction books, novels. Query. Reports in 2 months on queries; 3 months on mss.
Terms: Agent receives 15% commission on domestic sales; 20% on foreign sales. Offers written contract. Charges $15 postage and handling for return of ms. "Expenses are reimbursed for unpublished authors and for non-commercial projects."

Tips: Obtains new clients through referral and by query. "Provide brief query and resume showing publishing history clearly. Always put phone number and address on correspondence and enclose SASE. No faxed queries."

MAXINE GROFFSKY LITERARY AGENCY, 2 Fifth Ave., New York NY 10011. This agency did not respond to our request for information. Query before submitting.

‡DEBORAH GROSVENOR LITERARY AGENCY, (II, III), 5515 Grosvenor Lane, Bethesda MD 20814. (301)564-6231. Fax: (301)530-8201. E-mail: dcgrosveno@aol.com. Contact: Deborah C. Grosvenor. Estab. 1995. Represents 24 clients. 20% of clients are new/previously unpublished writers. Currently handles: 80% nonfiction books, 20% novels.
Handles: Nonfiction books, novels. Considers these nonfiction areas: animals; anthropology/archaeology; art/architecture/design; biography/autobiography; business; child guidance/parenting; cooking/food/nutrition; current affairs; gay/lesbian issues; government/politics/law; health/medicine; history; how-to; humor; language/literature/criticism; military/war; money/finance/economics; music/dance/theater/film; nature/environment; New Age/metaphysics; photography; popular culture; psychology; religious/inspirational; science/technology; self-help/personal improvement; sociology; sports; translations; true crime/investigative; women's issues/women's studies. Considers these fiction areas: action/adventure; contemporary issues; detective/police/crime; ethnic; family saga; gay; glitz; historical; humor/satire; lesbian; literary; mainstream; mystery/suspense; romance (contemporary, gothic, historical); sports; thriller/espionage. Send outline/proposal for nonfiction; send outline and 3 sample chapters for fiction. Reports in 1 month on queries; 2 months on mss.
Recent Sales: *Angel of Secrets*, by Nina Burleigh (Bantam); *Life and Times of Alexander Graham Bell*, by Grosvenor and Wesson (Abrams); *I'm From National Geographic*, by Thomas Canby (Shearwater); *By the Numbers: Tales of a Gen-X Drunk*, by Mark Judge (Hazelden).
Terms: Agent receives 15% commission on domestic sales; 20% on foreign sales. Offers a written contract with a 10 day cancellation clause.
Tips: Obtains new clients from recommendations from others.

THE CHARLOTTE GUSAY LITERARY AGENCY, (II, IV), 10532 Blythe, Suite 211, Los Angeles CA 90064-3312. (310)559-0831. Fax: (310)559-2639. Contact: Charlotte Gusay. Estab. 1988. Member of SPAR, signatory of WGA. Represents 30 clients. 50% of clients are new/previously unpublished writers. Specializes in fiction, nonfiction, children's (multicultural, nonsexist), children's illustrators, screenplays, books to film. "Percentage breakdown of the manuscripts different at different times."
Handles: Nonfiction books, scholarly books, juvenile books, travel books, novels. Considers all nonfiction and fiction areas. No romance, short stories, science fiction or horror. SASE always required for response. "Queries only, *no* unsolicited manuscripts. Initial query should be 1- to 2-page synopsis with SASE. Also, enclose a processing fee of $25 (not a reading fee)." Reports in 4-6 weeks on queries; 6-10 weeks on mss.
Recent Sales: *A Garden Story*, by Leon Whiteson (Faber & Faber); *Bukowski In the Bathtub: An Oral History of Charles Bukowski and John Thomas*, by Philomene Long (Lou Brown); *This Nervous Breakdown is Driving Me Crazy*, by Annie Reiner (Dove Books).
Terms: Agent receives 15% commission on domestic sales; 10% on dramatic sales; 25% on foreign sales. Offers written contract, binding for "usually 1 year." Charges for out-of-pocket expenses for long distance phone, fax, express mail, postage, etc.
Also Handles: Movie scripts (feature film). Considers these script subject areas: action/adventure; comedy; detective/police/crime; ethnic; experimental; family saga; feminist; gay; historical; humor; lesbian; mainstream; mystery/suspense; romantic (comedy, drama); sports; thriller; western/frontier. Query or send outline/proposal with SASE. Reports in 3 weeks on queries; 10 weeks on mss.
Writers' Conferences: Attends Writers Connection, in San Jose, California; Scriptwriters Connection, in Studio City, California; National Women's Book Association, in Los Angeles.
Tips: Usually obtains new clients through referrals, queries. "Please be professional."

THE MITCHELL J. HAMILBURG AGENCY, (II), 292 S. La Cienega Blvd., Suite 312, Beverly Hills CA 90211. (310)657-1501. Contact: Michael Hamilburg. Estab. 1937. Signatory of WGA. Represents 70 clients. Currently handles: 70% nonfiction books; 30% novels.
Handles: Nonfiction, novels. Considers all nonfiction areas and most fiction areas. No romance. Send outline, 2 sample chapters and SASE. Reports in 3-4 weeks on mss.
Recent Sales: *A Biography of the Leakey Family*, by Virginia Morrell (Simon & Schuster); *A Biography of Agnes De Mille*, by Carol Easton (Little, Brown).
Terms: Agent receives 10-15% commission on domestic sales.
Tips: Usually obtains new clients through recommendations from others, at conferences or personal search. "Good luck! Keep writing!"

THE HARDY AGENCY, (II), 3020 Bridgeway, Suite 204, Sausalito CA 94965. (415)380-9985. Contact: Anne Sheldon, Michael Vidor. Estab. 1990. Represents 30 clients. 75% of clients are new/ previously unpublished writers. Specializes in literary fiction and nonfiction. Currently handles: 30% nonfiction books; 70% novels. Member agents: Anne Sheldon (fiction); Michael Vidor (nonfiction, media, marketing and PR).
Handles: Nonfiction books, novels. Considers these nonfiction areas: biography/autobiography; current affairs; government/politics/law; health/medicine; New Age/metaphysics. Considers these fiction areas: contemporary; literary. Send query and/or 2 sample chapters. Reports in 1 month on queries and mss.
Recent Sales: *The Donkey Man*, by Robert Petro (HarperCollins).
Terms: Agent receives 15% commission on domestic sales; 20% on foreign sales. Offers written contract, binding for 1 year. Charges for postage, copying. 100% of business is derived from commissions on sales.
Tips: Obtains new clients from recommendations. Welcomes new authors.

‡CHADWICK ALLEN HARP, (II), 119 Lincoln Terrace, Jeffersonville PA 19403. (610)631-9795. Fax: (610)631-9793. E-mail: wickmode@aol.com. Contact: Chadwick Allen Harp. Estab. 1995. 50% of clients are new/previously unpublished writers. Currently handles: 30% nonfiction books; 20% juvenile books; 30% novels; 20% textbooks. Member agents: Chadwick Allen Harp.
Handles: Nonfiction books, juvenile books, movie scripts, syndicated material, scholarly books, novels, TV scripts, textbooks, novellas, stage plays, poetry books, short story collections. Considers all nonfiction areas. Considers all fiction areas. Send a query packet containing "a 1- to 2-page cover letter describing your project, ideas, and the status of the project; résumé, biography, or other document about your background; the first 20-30 pages of the project and, if appropriate, the table of contents or a 1- to 2-page synopsis. Initial contact is requested by mail only. Always enclose a SASE." Reports in 4-6 weeks on queries.
Terms: Agent receives 10% commission on domestic sales; 10% on foreign sales. Offers written contract.
Tips: "A professionally prepared query packet is the beginning of all my professional relationships. The most costly mistake a writer can make is a poor first impression. Here are some helpful hints: Purchase good quality letterhead for your cover letters. Send a polished, professionally prepared cover letter and manuscript. Make sure all your printing is of laser quality. I will recycle all query packets if they are prepared unprofessionally."

JOHN HAWKINS & ASSOCIATES, INC., (II), 71 W. 23rd St., Suite 1600, New York NY 10010. (212)807-7040. Fax: (212)807-9555. Contact: John Hawkins, William Reiss. Estab. 1893. Member of AAR. Represents over 100 clients. 5-10% of clients are new/previously unpublished writers. Currently handles: 40% nonfiction books; 20% juvenile books; 40% novels. Member Agents: Warren Frazier, Elinor Sidel, Anne Hawkins, Moses Cardona.
Handles: Nonfiction books, juvenile books, novels. Considers all nonfiction areas except computers/ electronics; religion/inspirational; translations. Considers all fiction areas except confessional; erotica; romance. Query with outline/proposal. Reports in 1 month on queries.
Recent Sales: *We were the Mulvaneys*, by Joyce Carol Oates (Dutton); *And This Too Shall Pass*, by E. Lynn Harris (Doubleday).
Terms: Agent receives 15% commission on domestic sales; 20% on foreign sales. Charges for photocopying.
Tips: Obtains new clients through recommendations from others.

HEACOCK LITERARY AGENCY, INC., (II), 1523 Sixth St., Suite #14, Santa Monica CA 90401-2514. (310)393-6227. Contact: Rosalie Heacock. Estab. 1978. Member of AAR, Author's Guild, ATA, SCBWI; signatory of WGA. Represents 60 clients. 10% of clients are new/previously unpublished writers. Currently handles: 90% nonfiction books; 10% novels. Member agents: Rosalie Heacock (psychology, philosophy, women's studies, alternative health, new technology, futurism, new idea books, art and artists); Ms. Robin Henning (fiction and nonfiction).
Handles: Adult nonfiction and fiction books, children's picture books. Considers these nonfiction areas: anthropology; art/architecture/design; biography (contemporary celebrity); business; child guidance/parenting; cooking/food/nutrition; crafts/hobbies; ethnic/cultural interests; health/medicine (including alternative health); history; how-to; language/literature/criticism; money/finance/economics; music; nature/environment; popular culture; psychology; religious/inspirational; science/technology; self-help/personal improvement; sociology; spirituality/metaphysics; women's issues/women's studies. Considers limited selection of top children's book authors; no beginners. Query with sample chapters. Reports in 3 weeks on queries; 2 months on mss.
Terms: Agent receives 15% commission on domestic sales; 25% on foreign sales, "if foreign agent used; if sold directly, 15%." Offers written contract, binding for 1 year. Charges for actual expense for telephone, postage, packing, photocopying. We provide copies of each publisher submission letter

and the publisher's response." 95% of business is derived from commission on ms sales.
Writers' Conferences: Santa Barbara City College Annual Writer's Workshop; Pasadena City College Writer's Forum; UCLA Symposiums on Writing Nonfiction Books; Society of Children's Book Writers and Illustrators.
Tips: Obtains new clients through "referrals from present clients and industry sources as well as mail queries. Take time to write an informative query letter expressing your book idea, the market for it, your qualifications to write the book, the 'hook' that would make a potential reader buy the book. Always enclose SASE; we cannot respond to queries without return postage. Our primary focus is upon books which make a contribution."

HENDERSON LITERARY REPRESENTATION, (I, II), P.O. Box 476, Sicklerville NJ 08081. Contact: Rita Elizabeth Henderson. Estab. 1994. Specializes in autobiography and biography, especially celebrity bios. Currently handles: 100% nonfiction books.
Handles: Nonfiction books. Considers these nonfiction areas: art/architecture/design; biography/autobiography; biography (celebrity); business; child guidance/parenting; computers/electronics; cooking/food/nutrition; current affairs; education; ethnic/cultural interests; gay/lesbian issues; government/politics/law; health/medicine; history; how-to; humor; interior design/decorating; juvenile nonfiction; money/finance/economics; music/dance/theater/film; photography; popular culture; psychology; religious/inspirational; science/technology; self-help/personal improvement; sociology; sports; true crime/investigative; women's issues/women's studies. Query by mail with outline/proposal and 3 sample chapters. Reports in 1 month.
Recent Sales: *The Boyz II Men Success Story: Defying the Odds*, by Rita Elizabeth Henderson (Anderson Press Publishing).
Terms: Agent receives 10% commission on domestic sales; 20% on foreign sales. Offers written contract, binding for life of book or until mutually terminated. 100% of business derived from commissions on book sales.
Writers' Conferences: Meet the Agents (New York City, October).
Tips: Obtains new clients through conferences, solicitation and referrals from others. "Please be organized in your proposal. If you think you have a good manuscript, and know that there is a marketplace for it, continue to work diligently to get it sold and don't give up. Have patience because some books sell quickly and others can take more time. In preparing your manuscript, please follow the Chicago Manual of Style."

RICHARD HENSHAW GROUP, (II, III), 264 W. 73rd St., New York NY 10023. (212)721-4721. Fax: (212)721-4208. E-mail: rhgagents@aol.com. Contact: Rich Henshaw. Estab. 1995. Member of AAR, SinC, MWA, HWA, SFWA. Represents 35 clients. 20% of clients are new/previously unpublished writers. Specializes in thrillers, mysteries, science fiction, fantasy and horror. Currently handles: 20% nonfiction books; 10% juvenile books; 70% novels.
   • Prior to opening his agency, Mr. Henshaw served as an agent with Richard Curtis Associates, Inc.
Handles: Nonfiction books, juvenile books, novels. Considers these nonfiction areas: animals; biography/autobiography; business; child guidance/parenting; computers/electronics; cooking/food/nutrition; current affairs; gay/lesbian issues; government/politics/law; health/medicine; how-to; humor; juvenile nonfiction; military/war; money/finance/economics; music/dance/theater/film; nature/enrironment; New Age/metaphysics; popular culture; psychology; science/technology; self-help/personal improvement; sociology; sports; true crime/investigative; women's issues/women's studies. Considers these fiction areas: action/adventure; detective/police/crime; ethnic; family saga; fantasy; glitz; historical; horror; humor/satire; juvenile; literary; mainstream; psychic/supernatural; science fiction; sports; thriller/espionage; young adult. Query. Reports in 3 weeks on queries; 6 weeks on mss.
Recent Sales: *Blood Will Tell*, by Dana Stabenow (Putnam); *Dropshot*, by Harlan Coben (Dell); *The Lost Guardian*, by Ronald Anthony Cross (TOR); *Trick Me Twice*, by Stephen Solamita (Bantam).
Terms: Agent receives 15% commission on domestic sales; 20% on foreign sales. No written contract. Charges for photocopying manuscripts and book orders. 100% of business is derived from commission on sales.
Tips: Obtains new clients through recommendations from others, solicitation, at conferences and query letters. "Always include SASE with correct return postage."

THE JEFF HERMAN AGENCY INC., (II), 140 Charles St., Suite 15A, New York NY 10014. (212)941-0540. Contact: Jeffrey H. Herman. Estab. 1985. Member of AAR. Represents 100 clients. 10% of clients are new/previously unpublished writers. Specializes in adult nonfiction. Currently handles: 85% nonfiction books; 5% scholarly books; 5% textbooks; 5% novels. Member agents: Deborah Adams (vice president, nonfiction book doctor); Jamie Forbes (fiction).
   • Prior to opening his agency, Mr. Herman served as a public relations executive.

Handles: Considers these nonfiction areas: business; computers; health; history; how-to; politics; popular psychology; popular reference; recovery; self-help; spirituality. Query. Reports in 2 weeks on queries; 1 month on mss.

Recent Sales: *Joe Montana On The Magic of Making Quarterback*, by Joe Montana (Henry Holt); *The Aladdin Factor*, by Jack Canfield and Mark Victor Hansen (Putnam); *The I.Q. Myth*, by Bob Sternberg (Simon & Schuster); *All You Need to Know About the Movie and TV Business*, by Gail Resnick and Scott Trost (Fireside/Simon & Schuster).

Terms: Agent receives 15% commission on domestic sales. Offers written contract.

SUSAN HERNER RIGHTS AGENCY, (II), P.O. Box 303, Scarsdale NY 10583-0303. (914)725-8967. Fax: (914)725-8969. Contact: Susan Herner or Sue Yuen. Estab. 1987. Represents 100 clients. 30% of clients are new/unpublished writers. Eager to work with new/unpublished writers. Currently handles: 60% nonfiction books; 40% novels. Member agent: Sue Yuen (commercial genre fiction, especially romance and fantasy).

Handles: Adult nonfiction books, novels. Consider these nonfiction areas: anthropology/archaeology; biography/autobiography; business; child guidance/parenting; cooking/food/nutrition; current affairs; ethnic/cultural interests; gay/lesbian issues; government/politics/law; health/medicine; history; how-to; language/literature/criticism; nature/environment; New Age/metaphysics; popular culture; psychology; religious/inspirational; science/technology; self-help/personal improvement; sociology; true crime/investigative; women's issues/women's studies. "I'm particularly interested in women's issues, popular science, and feminist spirituality." Considers these fiction areas: action/adventure; contemporary issues; detective/police/crime; ethnic; family/saga; fantasy; feminist; glitz; historical; horror; literary; mainstream; mystery; romance (contemporary, gothic, historical, regency); science fiction; thriller; "I'm particularly looking for strong women's fiction." Query with outline, sample chapters and SASE. Reports in 1 month on queries.

Recent Sales: *Mangos, Bananas & Coconuts*, by Himilce Novas (Arte Publico and Riverhead Press); *Faith of Our Fathers*, by Andre Willis, ed. (Dutton); *Prince of Cups*, by Gayle Feyrer (Dell).

Terms: Agent receives 15% commission on domestic sales; 20% on dramatic sales; 20% on foreign sales. Charges for extraordinary postage, handling and photocopying. "Agency has two divisions: one represents writers on a commission-only basis; the other represents the rights for small publishers and packagers who do not have inhouse subsidiary rights representation. Percentage of income derived from each division is currently 80-20."

Writers' Conferences: Vermont League of Writers (Burlington, Vt); Gulf States Authors League (Mobile, AL).

FREDERICK HILL ASSOCIATES, (II), 1842 Union St., San Francisco CA 94123. (415)921-2910. Fax: (415)921-2802. Contact: Irene Moore. Estab. 1979. Represents 100 clients. 50% of clients are new/unpublished writers. Specializes in general nonfiction, fiction.

Handles: Nonfiction books, novels. Considers these nonfiction areas: biography/autobiography; current affairs; government/politics/law; language/literature/criticism; women's issues/women's studies. Considers literary and mainstream fiction.

Recent Sales: *Infinite Jest*, by David Foster Wallace (Little, Brown); *Silent Witness*, by Richard North Patterson (Knopf); *Gender Shock*, by Phyllis Burke (Anchor Books).

Terms: Agent receives 15% commission on domestic sales; 15% on dramatic sales; 20% on foreign sales. Charges for photocopying.

JOHN L. HOCHMANN BOOKS, (III, IV), 320 E. 58th St., New York NY 10022-2220. (212)319-0505. Director: John L. Hochmann. Contact: Theodora Eagle. Estab. 1976. Represents 23 clients. Member of AAR, PEN. Specializes in nonfiction books. Writers must have demonstrable eminence in field or previous publications. Prefers to work with published/established authors. Currently handles: 80% nonfiction; 20% textbooks. Member agent: Theodora Eagle (popular medical and nutrition books).

Handles: Nonfiction trade books, college textbooks. Considers these nonfiction areas: anthropology/archaeology; art/architecture/design; biography/autobiography; cooking/food/nutrition; current affairs; gay/lesbian issues; government/politics/law; health/medicine; history; military/war; music/dance/theater/film; sociology. Query first with outline, titles and sample reviews of previous books and SASE. Reports in 1 week on queries; 1 month on solicited mss.

Recent Sales: *The Low Fat African-American Cookbook*, by Ruby Banks-Payne (Contemporary); *Manuel Puig: A Biography*, by Suzanne Jill Levine (Farrar Straus).

Terms: Agent receives 15% commission on domestic sales; 25% on foreign sales.

Tips: Obtains new clients through recommendations from authors and editors. "Detailed outlines are read carefully; letters and proposals written like flap copy get chucked. We make multiple submissions to editors, but we do not accept multiple submissions from authors. Why? Editors are on salary, but we work for commission, and do not have time to read manuscripts on spec."

Present a package, not just another proposal

Nontraditional books by nontraditional publishers have been scaling the bestseller walls in recent years. Take the now bestselling *Chicken Soup for the Soul*, which was published by a small house in Florida—because nobody in New York wanted it. "I shopped the manuscript to almost every major New York house and was rejected by them all," says agent Herman. Finally, authors Canfield and Hansen picked up on an earlier offer and sold the book to Health Communications, a tiny outfit on the verge of bankruptcy. Herman assisted with the contract. "*Chicken Soup* only received a $1,000 advance with a 20% royalty on net profits, but that was the only game in town and the authors didn't want to self-publish. It was a risky last resort."

A last resort it might have been, but the book clearly has benefited its authors. A key reason: Canfield and Hansen went beyond the call of duty. "These guys didn't just have a proposal. They created a package. They had no books published at the time, but they were successful businessmen and speakers. They made a very strong presentation outlining everything they would do to build sales. They had a super promotional plan to create a bestseller, and the plan worked this time." Herman has helped them capitalize on their success. In his first sale for them, he negotiated a six figure advance from Putnam for *The Aladdin Factor*, which has sold over 250,000 copies. So what began as a small venture with a low advance from a publisher outside New York mushroomed into a hefty money-making deal with a major publisher.

Although agents have feared treading the publishing waters outside of New York, they now are beginning to find it worthwhile. "Publishing is institutional," says Herman. "An editor has to propose books that are going to be accepted, and the institutionalized way of doing things becomes inbred and then it becomes generational, what's known as bureaucratic inertia. Big publishers won't take many risks. But agents are becoming risk-takers, so it's up to them to take a chance with something that won't sell to New York houses. Sometimes that means finding a publisher you never would have imagined working with, especially if it's a project that's been untested in the marketplace. But taking the risk can pay off."

It certainly has "paid off" for Herman. Today he has established a solid reputation both in and out of New York as an agent masterful in finding saleable nonfiction books with immense author support. Earning this reputation has been most timely for Herman because "publishers are becoming more dependent upon strong author support as opposed to strong inhouse support. An author worth representing is not just one who will be available but who will actually bring their own marketing department with them."

INSIDER REPORT, *Herman*

That's just what Canfield and Hansen did. *"Chicken Soup for the Soul* did not become a bestseller overnight," says Herman. "It took many months for the book to start to show up on the lists. And, yes, it got there because Canfield and Hansen went on the road and hustled it." Combined, the pair did more than a hundred tour dates that first year after the book came out, and a lot of those dates had large audiences. They also took the initiative and hired their own publicist to book them on radio and TV shows and to arrange for a local bookstore to attend each event. "They'd promote the book right on the podium," says Herman. "They're great salesmen. They were selling 300 books a night."

Because few large advances are offered to writers without name recognition, many authors do what they can to increase sales so they can earn money from the royalties. That's the only way to go if you're not offered a big advance. Says Herman: "Some really enormous advances are being paid for books, and people don't understand why. Sure, some agents are cashing in on these big hits but that's hurting the average writer, because it dries up the pool. A $2 million dollar advance for one book could have paid a lot of $25,000 advances for midlist nonfiction book writers. A publisher only has so much capital, and if they're going to consolidate a lot of it into these one shot massive deals, there's just not much left for the smaller deals, which is what most writers count on."

Despite this seemingly gloomy reality of the industry, writers seeking representation should not be discouraged. Publishing is an agent's market. And agents have more influence and power today than they've ever had, because publishers have become dependent upon agents to give them a solid deal that's structured and packaged. "The agent's role is very strong today," says Herman. "More than a few agencies are thriving from selling books to publishers. Publishers are learning to trust the agent. They're using agents as a screen also, because they don't really have inhouse screening. And they don't want to be annoyed with the slush pile. Publishers know a bona fide agent has screened the manuscript thoroughly and considered its marketability before approaching them. It's qualified in effect. So to a certain extent the agent is becoming a traffic cop."

Herman insists that to keep the publishing crosswalk free of accidents, writers need to respect the agent's position in the industry. Writers can do this by concentrating on writing books, not sending hate mail to tardy or unresponsive agents. "When writers send unsolicited material to agencies, they must remember that it's like sending junk mail," says Herman. "It's not that the material is junk. But I get 100 submissions a week and don't have the people-power to make sure every manuscript is accounted for. That's why there are hundreds of agents out there. If you don't hear from one agent soon after you send the submission, go to another. There's stuff other agents miss that I'm going to get and stuff that I miss that other agents are going to get. Writers can't think they're being treated like crap. There's nothing personal about it, it's just someone trying to get through a day. Our days are best spent reading worthwhile manuscripts, not angry letters."

—*Don Prues*

BERENICE HOFFMAN LITERARY AGENCY, (III), 215 W. 75th St., New York NY 10023. (212)580-0951. Fax: (212)721-8916. Contact: Berenice Hoffman. Estab. 1978. Member of AAR. Represents 55 clients.
Handles: Nonfiction, novels. Considers all nonfiction areas and most fiction areas. No romance. Query with SASE. Reports in 3-4 weeks on queries.
Terms: Agent receives 15% on domestic sales. Sometimes offers written contract. Charges for out of the ordinary postage, photocopying.
Tips: Usually obtains new clients through referrals from people she knows.

BARBARA HOGENSON AGENCY, (III), 19 W. 44th St., Suite 1000, New York NY 10036. (212)730-7306. Fax: (212)730-8970. Contact: Barbara Hogenson. Estab. 1994. Member of AAR, signatory of WGA. Represents 60 clients. 5% of clients are new/previously unpublished writers. Currently handles: 35% nonfiction books; 15% novels; 15% movie scripts; 35% stage plays.
   • See the expanded listing for this agency in Script Agents.

HULL HOUSE LITERARY AGENCY, (II), 240 E. 82nd St., New York NY 10028-2714. (212)988-0725. Fax: (212)794-8758. President: David Stewart Hull. Associate: Lydia Mortimer. Estab. 1987. Represents 38 clients. 15% of clients are new/previously unpublished writers. Specializes in military and general history, true crime, mystery fiction, general commercial fiction. Currently handles: 60% nonfiction books; 40% novels. Member agents: David Stewart Hull (history, biography, military books, true crime, mystery fiction, commercial fiction by published authors); Lydia Mortimer (new fiction by unpublished writers, nonfiction of general nature including women's studies).
Handles: Nonfiction books, novels. Considers these nonfiction areas: anthropology/archaeology; art/architecture/design; biography/autobiography; business; current affairs; ethnic/cultural interests; government/politics/law; history; military/war; money/finance/economics; music/dance/theater/film; sociology; true crime/investigative. Considers these fiction areas: detective/police/crime; literary; mainstream; mystery/suspense. Query with SASE. Reports in 1 week on queries; 1 month on mss.
Recent Sales: *Midnight Hags*, by Mary Willis Walker (Doubleday/Bantam); *The Time of the Wolf*, by William D. Blankenship (Donald I. Fine, Inc.).
Terms: Agent receives 15% commission on domestic sales; 10% on foreign sales. Written contract is optional, "at mutual agreement between author and agency." Charges for photocopying, express mail, extensive overseas telephone expenses.
Tips: Obtains new clients through "referrals from clients, listings in various standard publications such as *LMP*, *Guide to Literary Agents*, etc. If interested in agency representation, send a single-page letter outlining your project, always accompanied by an SASE. If nonfiction, sample chapter(s) are often valuable. A record of past publications is a big plus."

IMG LITERARY, (II), (formerly IMG-Julian Bach Literary Agency), 22 E. 71st St., New York NY 10021. (212)772-8900. Fax: (212)772-2617. Contact: Meghan Sercombe. Estab. 1956. Member of AAR. Represents 150 clients. Currently handles: 60% nonfiction books; 5% juvenile books; 35% novels. Member agents: Julian Bach, David Chalfant, Carolyn Krupp, Ann Torrago.
Handles: Nonfiction books, novels. Considers these nonfiction areas: biography; business; current affairs; ethnic/cultural interests; gay/lesbian issues; government/politics; health/medicine; history; money/finance/economics; popular culture; sports; true crime/investigative; women's issues/women's studies. Considers these fiction areas: contemporary issues; detective/police/crime; literary; mainstream; thriller/espionage. Query with SASE. Reports in 2 weeks on queries; 6 weeks on mss.
Terms: Agent receives 15% commission on domestic sales; 20% on foreign sales. Offers written contract.
Tips: Obtains new clients through solicitation by the agent and referrals from existing clients.

INTERNATIONAL CREATIVE MANAGEMENT, (III), 40 W. 57th St., New York NY 10019. (212)556-5600. Fax: (212)556-5665. West Coast office: 8942 Wilshire Blvd., Beverly Hills CA 90211. (310)550-4000. Contact: Literary Department. Member of AAR, signatory of WGA. Member agents: Esther Newberg and Amanda Urban, department heads; Lisa Bankoff; Kristine Dahl; Mitch Douglas; Suzanne Gluck; Sloan Harris; Heather Schroder.
Terms: Agent receives 10% commission on domestic sales; 15% on UK sales; 20% on translations.

TO FIND AN AGENT near you, check the Geographic Index.

INTERNATIONAL PUBLISHER ASSOCIATES INC., (II), 304 Guido Ave., Lady Lake FL 32159-9014. Contact: Joseph De Rogatis. Estab. 1983. Represents 15 clients. Currently handles: 60% nonfiction books; 40% fiction.

• Prior to opening his agency, Mr. De Rogatis served for 18 years with New American Library and has held various management positions in publishing for the past 25 years.

Handles: Nonfiction books. Considers all nonfiction areas. Considers "mostly" mainstream fiction. Query with full ms, outline and SASE. Reports in 3 weeks on queries.

Recent Sales: *The Pocket Pediatrician*, by Dr. David Ziggelman (Doubleday).

Terms: Agent receives 15% commission on domestic sales; 20% on foreign sales. Offers written contract, binding for life of book. Charges for postage and photocopying.

Tips: Obtains new clients through word of mouth and *Guide to Literary Agents*. "We do read unsolicited queries, encourage new writers and read material from unpublished authors. We are seeking fiction and nonfiction in the centres and categories. No poetry."

J DE S ASSOCIATES INC., (II), 9 Shagbark Rd., Wilson Point, South Norwalk CT 06854. (203)838-7571. Contact: Jacques de Spoelberch. Estab. 1975. Represents 50 clients. Currently handles: 50% nonfiction books; 50% novels.

Handles: Nonfiction books, novels. Considers these nonfiction areas: biography/autobiography; business; current affairs; ethnic/cultural interests; government/politics/law; health/medicine; history; military/war; New Age; self-help/personal improvement; sociology; sports; translations. Considers these fiction areas: detective/police/crime; historical; juvenile; literary; mainstream; mystery/suspense; New Age; westerns/frontier; young adult. Query with SASE. Reports in 2 months on queries.

Terms: Agent receives 15% commission on domestic sales; 20% on foreign sales. Charges for foreign postage and photocopying.

Tips: Obtains new clients through recommendations from others, authors and other clients.

JABBERWOCKY LITERARY AGENCY, (II), P.O. Box 4558, Sunnyside NY 11104-0558. (718)392-5985. Contact: Joshua Bilmes. Estab. 1994. Represents 40 clients. 25% of clients are new/previously unpublished writers. "Agency represents quite a lot of genre fiction and is actively seeking to increase amount of nonfiction projects." Currently handles: 25% nonfiction books; 5% scholarly books; 5% juvenile books; 60% novels; 5% short story collections.

Handles: Nonfiction books, scholarly books, juvenile books, novels. Considers these nonfiction areas: biography/autobiography; business; cooking/food/nutrition; current affairs; gay/lesbian issues; government/politics/law; health/medicine; history; humor; language/literature/criticism; military/war; money/finance/economics; music/dance/theater/film; nature/environment; popular culture; science/technology; sociology; sports; true crime/investigative; women's issues/women's studies. Considers these fiction areas: action/adventure; cartoon/comic; contemporary issues; detective/police/crime; ethnic; family saga; fantasy; gay; glitz; historical; horror; humor/satire; juvenile; lesbian; literary; mainstream; picture book; psychic/supernatural; regional; romance; science fiction; sports; thriller/espionage; young adult. Query. Reports in 2 weeks on queries.

Recent Sales: *Dead Over Heels*, by Charlaine Harris (Scribner); *Anatomy Of A Miracle*, by Mickey Eisenberg (Oxford University Press); *Once a Hero*, by Elizabeth Moon (Baen); *Hot Blood 8: Kiss and Kill*, ed. by Jeff Gelb and Michael Garrett (Pocket).

Terms: Agent receives 10% commission on domestic sales; 20% on foreign sales. Offers written contract, binding for 1 year. Charges for book purchases, ms photocopying, international book/ms mailing, international long distance.

Writers' Conferences: Malice Domestic (Bethesda MD, April); World SF Convention (San Antonio, August).

Tips: Obtains new clients through recommendation by current clients, solicitation, "and through intriguing queries by new authors. In approaching with a query, the most important things to me are your credits and your biographical background to the extent its relevant to your work. I (and most agents I believe) will ignore the adjectives you may choose to describe your own work."

JAMES PETER ASSOCIATES, INC., (II), P.O. Box 772, Tenafly NJ 07670-0751. (201)568-0760. Contact: Bert Holtje. Estab. 1971. Member of AAR. Represents 84 clients. 15% of clients are new/previously unpublished writers. Specializes in nonfiction, all categories. "We are especially interested in trade and general reference projects." Currently handles: 100% nonfiction books.

• Prior to opening his agency, Mr. Holtje was a book packager, and before that, president of an advertising agency with book publishing clients. See Mr. Holtje's article, Career Planning for Nonfiction Writers, in this edition of the *Guide*.

Handles: Nonfiction books. Considers these nonfiction areas: anthropology/archaeology; art/architecture/design; biography/autobiography; business; child guidance/parenting; current affairs; ethnic/cultural interests; gay/lesbian issues; government/politics/law; health/medicine; history; language/literature/criticism; military/war; money/finance/economics; music/dance/theater/film; popular culture;

psychology; self-help/personal improvement; women's issues/women's studies. Send outline/proposal and SASE. Reports in 3-4 weeks on queries.

Recent Sales: *Dictionary of American Mythology*, by Dr. Harry Oster (Viking); *Passion and Penance: A Guide to Lesbian Pulp Fiction*, by Dr. Dawn Sova (Faber & Faber); *No Holds Barred: The Strange Life of John DuPont*, by Carol Turkington (Turner Publishing); *The Art & Skill of Dealing With People*, by Brandon Toropov (Simon & Schuster).

Terms: Agent receives 15% commission on domestic sales; 20% on foreign sales. Offers written contract on a per book basis. Charges for foreign postage.

Tips: Obtains new clients through recommendations from other clients and editors, contact with people who are doing interesting things, and over-the-transom queries. "Phone me! I'm happy to discuss book ideas any time."

JANKLOW & NESBIT ASSOCIATES, 598 Madison Ave., New York NY 10022. This agency did not respond to our request for information. Query before submitting.

‡JET LITERARY ASSOCIATES, INC., (III), 124 E. 84th St., New York NY 10028-0915. (212)879-2578. President: Jim Trupin. Estab. 1976. Represents 85 clients. 5% of clients are new/unpublished writers. Writers must have published articles or books. Prefers to work with published/established authors. Specializes in nonfiction. Currently handles: 50% nonfiction books; 50% novels.

Handles: Nonfiction books, novels. No unsolicited mss. Reports in 2 weeks on queries; 1 month on mss.

Recent Sales: *Fuzzy Memories*, by Jack Handey (Andrews & McMeel); *How Do Astronauts Scratch an Itch?*, by David Feldman (Putnam).

Terms: Agent receives 15% commission on domestic sales; 15% on dramatic sales; 25% on foreign sales. Charges for international phone and postage expenses.

LAWRENCE JORDAN LITERARY AGENCY, (II), A Division of Morning Star Rising, Inc., 250 W. 57th St., Suite 1517, New York NY 10107-1599. (212)662-7871. Fax: (212)662-8138. President: Lawrence Jordan. Estab. 1978. Represents 50 clients. 25% of clients are new/unpublished writers. Works with a small number of new/unpublished authors. Specializes in general adult fiction and nonfiction. Currently handles: 60% nonfiction; 25% novels; 3% textbooks; 5% movie scripts; 7% stage plays.

● Prior to opening his agency, Mr. Jordan served as an editor with Doubleday & Co.

Handles: Nonfiction books, novels, textbooks, juvenile books, movie scripts, stage plays. Handles these nonfiction areas: autobiography; business; computer manuals; health; religion; science; self-help; sports. Query with outline. Reports in 3 weeks on queries; 6 weeks on mss.

Recent Sales: *An Easy Burden*, by Andrew Young (HarperCollins); *Southern Journey: A Return to the Civil Rights Movement*, by Tom Dent (William Morrow); *A Once Perfect Place: A Jake Eaton Mystery*, by Larry Maness (Lyford Books).

Terms: Agent receives 15% commission on domestic sales; 20% on dramatic sales; 20% on foreign sales. Charges long-distance calls, photocopying, foreign submission costs, postage, cables and messengers. Makes 99% of income from commissions.

Writers' Conferences: ABA (Chicago, June); Frankfurt (Germany, October).

‡JUST WRITE AGENCY, INC., (I, II), P.O. Box 760263, Lathrup Village MI 48076. Phone/fax: (313)863-7036. Contact: Darrell Jerome Banks. Estab. 1996. Represents 2 clients. 100% of clients are new/previously unpublished writers. Specializes in nonfiction, plays. Currently handles: 50% nonfiction books, 50% stage plays.

Handles: Nonfiction books, novels, stage plays. Considers these nonfiction areas: business; history; true crime/investigative. Considers these fiction areas: detective/police/crime; historical; science fiction; thriller/espionage. Query. Reports in 1 week on queries; 3-4 weeks on mss.

Terms: Agent receives 15% commission on domestic sales; 15% on foreign sales. Offers written contract, binding for 5 years with a review at 2½ years, and a 90 day cancellation clause. Charges for all marketing costs including but not limited to postage, photocopying, faxing, e-mail.

Tips: Obtains new clients through referrals and advertising.

---

‡   THE DOUBLE DAGGER before a listing indicates the listing is new in this edition.

THE KELLOCK COMPANY INC., (III), Lakeview Center, 1440 Coral Ridge Dr. #322, Coral Springs FL 33071-5433. (954)255-0336. Fax: (954)255-0362. E-mail: alkellock@aol.com or 73313.23 02@compuserve.com. Contact: Alan C. Kellock. Estab. 1990. Represents 75 clients. 25% of clients are new/previously unpublished writers. Specializes in a broad range of practical and informational nonfiction, including illustrated works. Represents authors, packagers, and smaller publishers to larger print and electronic publishers and third party sponsors. Currently handles: 100% nonfiction books. Member agents: Loren Kellock (licensing).

- Prior to opening his agency, Mr. Kellock served as director of Sales & Marketing with Harcourt Brace, vice president of Marketing with Waldenbooks and president and publisher for Viking Penguin.

Handles: Nonfiction books. Considers these nonfiction areas: anthropology/archaeology, art/architecture/design, biography/autobiography, business, child guidance/parenting, computers/electronics, cooking/food/nutrition; crafts/hobbies, current affairs, education; ethnic/cultural interests, government/politics/law, health/medicine, history, how-to; humor, interior design/decorating, military/war, money/finance/economics, music/dance/theater/film, nature/environment, photography, popular culture; psychology; religious/inspirational; science/technology; self-help/personal improvement; sociology; sports; women's issues/women's studies. Query. Reports in 1 week on queries, 2 weeks on mss.

Recent Sales: *Computer Creations for Kids*, by Peggy Steinhauser (Ten Speed Press); *First Home*, by Leslie Linsley (Morrow); *Parenting A to Z*, by David Brownstone and Irene Franck (HarperCollins and AOL); *The Air Traveler's Atlas*, by James Sutton (Macmillan).

Terms: Agent receives 15% commission on domestic sales; 25% on foreign and multimedia sales. Offers written contract. Charges for postage, photocopying.

Worker's Conferences ABA (Chicago, May); Frankfurt (Germany, October).

Tips: Obtains most new clients through referrals, but all queries are carefully considered.

NATASHA KERN LITERARY AGENCY, (II), P.O. Box 2908, Portland OR 97208-2908. (503)297-6190. Contact: Natasha Kern. Estab. 1986. Member of AAR, RWA, MWA, SinC. Specializes in literary and commercial fiction and nonfiction.

Handles: Nonfiction books, novels. Considers these nonfiction areas: agriculture/horticulture; animals; anthropology/archaeology; art/architecture/design; biography/autobiography; business; child guidance/parenting; cooking/food/nutrition; current affairs; education; ethnic/cultural interests; gay/lesbian issues; health/medicine; how-to; language/literature/criticism; money/finance/economics; nature/environment; New Age/metaphysics; popular culture; psychology; science/technology; self-help/personal improvement; true crime/investigative; women's issues/women's studies; women's spirituality. Considers these fiction areas: detective/police/crime; ethnic; feminist; historical; mainstream; mystery/suspense; romance (contemporary, historical); thriller/espionage; westerns/frontier. "Send a detailed, one-page query with a SASE, including the submission history, writing credits and information about how complete the project is. If requested, for fiction send a two- to three-page synopsis, in addition to the first three chapters; for nonfiction, submit a proposal consisting of an outline, two chapters, SASE, and a note describing market and how project is different or better than similar works. Also send a blurb about the author and information about the length of the manuscript. For category fiction, a five- to ten-page synopsis should be sent with the chapters." Reports in 2 weeks on queries.

Recent Sales: *Herbal Prescriptions for Better Health*, by Don Brown (Prima); *Fertile Ground*, by Charles Wilson (St. Martin's); *Kiss Me, Katie*, by Robin Hatcher (HarperCollins); *Mortal Fear*, by Greg Iles (Dutton/Signet); *Aphrodite's Daughters*, by Jalaja Bonheim (Simon & Schuster).

Terms: Agent receives 15% commission on domestic sales; 20% on foreign sales.

Writers' Conference: RWA National Conference; Santa Barbara Writer's Conference; Golden Triangle Writer's Conference.

LOUISE B. KETZ AGENCY, (II), 1485 First Ave., Suite 4B, New York NY 10021-1363. (212)535-9259. Fax: (212)535-7719. Contact: Louise B. Ketz. Estab. 1983. Represents 25 clients. 15% of clients are new/previously unpublished writers. Specializes in science, business, sports, history and reference. Currently handles: 100% nonfiction books.

Handles: Nonfiction books only. Considers these nonfiction areas: biography/autobiography; business; current affairs; history; military/war; money/finance/economics; science/technology; sports. Send outline and 2 sample chapters plus author curriculum vitae. Reports in 6 weeks.

Recent Sales: *The Five Greatest Ideas of Science*, by Sidney Harris, Charles Wym and Art Wiggins (Wiley).

Terms: Agent receives 10-15% commission on domestic sales; 10% on foreign sales. Offers written contract.

Tips: Obtains new clients through recommendations, idea development.

KIDDE, HOYT & PICARD, (III), 335 E. 51st St., New York NY 10022. (212)755-9461. Contact: Katharine Kidde, Laura Langlie. Estab. 1980. Member of AAR. Represents 50 clients. Specializes in mainstream fiction and nonfiction. Currently handles: 15% nonfiction books; 5% juvenile books; 80%

novels. Member agents: Kay Kidde (mainstream fiction, romances, mysteries, suspense, literary fiction, general nonfiction); Laura Langlie (mainstream fiction, romances, mysteries, literary fiction, trade nonfiction).

Handles: Nonfiction books, novels. Considers these nonfiction areas: African studies; the arts; biography; current events; ethnic/cultural interests; gay/lesbian issues; history; language/literature/criticism; popular culture; psychology; self-help/personal improvement; sociology; women's issues. Considers these fiction areas: contemporary issues; detective/police/crime; feminist; gay; glitz; historical; humor; lesbian; literary; mainstream; mystery/suspense; regional; romance (contemporary, historical, regency); thriller. Query. Reports in a few weeks on queries; 3-4 weeks on mss.

Recent Sales: *The Kindness of Strangers*, by Mike McIntyre (Boulevard/Berkley); *The Judas Glass*, by Michael Cadnum (Carroll & Graf); *Mind Games*, by C.J. Koehler (Carroll & Graf); *See How They Run*, by Bethany Campbell (Bantam).

Terms: Agent receives 15% commission on domestic sales; 15% on foreign sales. Charges for photocopying.

Tips: Obtains new clients through query letters, recommendations from others, "former authors from when I was an editor at NAL, Harcourt, etc.; listings in *LMP*, writers' guides."

KIRCHOFF/WOHLBERG, INC., AUTHORS' REPRESENTATION DIVISION, (II), 866 United Nations Plaza, #525, New York NY 10017. (212)644-2020. Fax: (212)223-4387. Director of Operations: John R. Whitman. Estab. 1930s. Member of AAR, AAP, Society of Illustrators, SPAR, Bookbuilders of Boston, New York Bookbinders' Guild, AIGA. Represents 50 authors. 10% of clients are new/previously unpublished writers. Specializes in juvenile through young adult trade books and textbooks. Currently handles: 5% nonfiction books; 80% juvenile books; 5% novels; 5% novellas; 5% young adult. Member agent: Elizabeth Pulitzer-Voges (juvenile and young adult authors).

Handles: "We are interested in any original projects of quality that are appropriate to the juvenile and young adult trade book markets. Send a query that includes an outline and a sample; SASE required." Reports in 1 month on queries; 6 weeks on mss. Please send queries to the attention of Liza Pulitzer-Voges.

Recent Sales: *Snowballs*, by Lois Ehlert (Harcourt Brace); *Chicka Chicka Sticka Sticka*, by John Archambault & Bill Martin Jr. (Simon & Schuster); *From The Notebooks Of Melanin Sun*, by Jacqueline Woodson (Scholastic); *A Baby's Journal: A Book Of Firsts*, by Lizi Boyd (Chronicle); *Taking Flight: My Story, By Vicki Van Meter*, by Dan Gutman (Viking);' *Hold Fast To Dreams*, by Andrea Davis Pinkney (Morrow Junior Books).

Terms: Agent receives standard commission "depending upon whether it is an author only, illustrator only, or an author/illustrator book." Offers written contract, binding for not less than 1 year.

Writers' Conferences: International Children's Books Fair (Bologna Italy, Spring); International Reading Association (New Orleans); American Booksellers Association (Chicago, June).

Tips: "Usually obtains new clients through recommendations from authors, illustrators and editors. Kirchoff/Wohlberg has been in business for over 50 years."

HARVEY KLINGER, INC., (III), 301 W. 53rd St., New York NY 10019. (212)581-7068. Fax: (212)315-3823. Contact: Harvey Klinger. Estab. 1977. Member of AAR. Represents 100 clients. 25% of clients are new/previously unpublished writers. Specializes in "big, mainstream contemporary fiction and nonfiction." Currently handles: 50% nonfiction books; 50% novels. Member agents: Carol McCleary (mysteries, science fiction, fantasy, category fiction, all general categories); Laurie Liss (politics, women's issues).

Handles: Nonfiction books, novels. Considers these nonfiction areas: biography/autobiography; cooking/food/nutrition; health/medicine; psychology; science/technology; self-help/personal improvement; sports; true crime/investigative; women's issues/women's studies. Considers these fiction areas: action/adventure; detective/police/crime; family saga; glitz; horror (dark); literary; mainstream; mystery/suspense; romance (contemporary); science fiction; thriller/espionage; western. Query. "We do not accept queries by fax." Reports in 2 weeks on queries; 2 months on mss.

Recent Sales: *Timepiece*, a Richard Paul Evans (Simon & Schuster); *Eye Contact*, by Stephen Collins (Bantam); *Run with the Hunted*, by Charles Bukowski (HarperCollins); *Runaway Child*, by Terry Kay (Morrow); *39 Forever*, by Dr. Karlis Ullis (Simon & Schuster).

Terms: Agent receives 15% commission on domestic sales; 25% on foreign sales. Offers written contract. Charges for photocopying manuscripts, overseas postage for mss.

Tips: Obtains new clients through recommendations from others.

BARBARA S. KOUTS, LITERARY AGENT, (II), P.O. Box 560, Bellport NY 11713. (516)286-1278. Contact: Barbara Kouts. Estab. 1980. Member of AAR. Represent 50 clients. 10% of clients are new/previously unpublished writers. Specializes in adult fiction and nonfiction and children's books. Currently handles: 20% nonfiction books; 60% juvenile books; 20% novels.

Handles: Nonfiction books, juvenile books, novels. Considers these nonfiction areas: biography/ autobiography; child guidance/parenting; current affairs; ethnic/cultural interests; health/medicine; history; juvenile nonfiction; music/dance/theater/film; nature/environment; psychology; self-help/personal improvement; women's issues/women's studies. Considers these fiction areas: contemporary issues; family saga; feminist; historical; juvenile; literary; mainstream; mystery/suspense; picture book; young adult. Query. Reports in 2-3 days on queries; 4-6 weeks on mss.

Recent Sales: *Voice Lessons*, by Nancy Mairs (Beacon); *The Faithful Friend*, by Robert San Souci (Simon & Schuster).

Terms: Agent receives 10% commission on domestic sales; 20% on foreign sales. Charges for photocopying.

Tips: Obtains new clients through recommendations from others, solicitation, at conferences, etc. "Write, do not call. Be professional in your writing."

EDITE KROLL LITERARY AGENCY, (II), 12 Grayhurst Park, Portland ME 04102. (207)773-4922. Fax: (207)773-3936. Contact: Edite Kroll. Estab. 1981. Represents 40 clients. Currently handles: 60% adult books; 40% juvenile books.

Handles: Nonfiction, juvenile books, humor. Considers these nonfiction areas: social and political issues (especially feminist). Considers these fiction areas: juvenile; picture books by author/artists. Query in writing only with SASE; no phone or fax. For nonfiction, send outline and proposal. For fiction, send outline and 1 sample chapter. For picture books, send dummy. Reports in 1 month on queries; 6-8 weeks on mss.

THE CANDACE LAKE AGENCY, (II, IV), 822 S. Robertson Blvd., #200, Los Angeles CA 90035. (310)289-0600. Fax: (310)289-0619. Contact: Elizabeth Thomas. Estab. 1977. Signatory of WGA, member of DGA. 50% of clients are new/previously unpublished writers. Specializes in screenplay and teleplay writers. Currently handles: 20% novels; 40% movie scripts; 40% TV scripts.

• See the expanded listing for this agency in Script Agents.

PETER LAMPACK AGENCY, INC., (II), 551 Fifth Ave., Suite 1613, New York NY 10176-0187. (212)687-9106. Fax: (212)687-9109. Contact: Loren G. Soeiro. Estab. 1977. Represents 50 clients. 10% of clients are new/previously unpublished writers. Specializes in commercial fiction, male-oriented action/adventure, contemporary relationships, distinguished literary fiction, nonfiction by a recognized expert in a given field. Currently handles: 15% nonfiction books; 85% novels. Member agents: Peter Lampack (psychological suspense, action/adventure, literary fiction, nonfiction, contemporary relationships); Sandra Blanton (contemporary relationships, psychological thrillers, mysteries, literary fiction, nonfiction including literary and theatrical biography); Deborah Brown (literary and commercial fiction, mystery, suspense, journalistic nonfiction, high-concept medical, legal and science thrillers).

Handles: Nonfiction books, novels. Considers these nonfiction areas: anthropology/archaeology; art/architecture/design; biography/autobiography; business; current affairs; government/politics/law; health/medicine; history; money/finance/economics; music/dance/theater/film; popular culture; high profile true crime/investigative; women's issues. Considers these fiction areas: action/adventure; contemporary relationships; detective/police/crime; family saga; glitz; historical; literary; mainstream; mystery/suspense; thriller/espionage. Query. *No unsolicited mss.* Do not fax queries. Reports in 3 weeks on queries; 2 months on mss.

Recent Sales: *The Sea Hunters*, by Clive Cussler (Simon & Schuster); *Fly Away Home*, by Judith Kelman (Bantam); *Hotel Paradise*, by Martha Grimes (Knopf); *Not Much Fun: The Lost Poems of Dorothy Parker*, ed. by Stuart Y. Silverstein (Scribner); *The Young Savages*, by Fred Mustard Stewart (TOR Books); *True Colors*, by Doris Mortman (Crown/Ballantine); *Making of a Country Lawyer*, by Gerry Spence, Esq. (St. Martin's Press); *The Master of Petersburg*, by J.M. Coeztee (Viking/Penguin); *The Living Trust Workbook*, by Robert A. Esperti, Esq. and Renno L. Peterson, Esq. (Viking/Penguin).

Terms: Agent receives 15% commission on domestic sales; 20% on foreign sales. "Writer is required to furnish copies of his/her work for submission purposes."

Writers' Conferences: ABA (Chicago, June).

Tips: Obtains new clients from referrals made by clients. "Submit only your best work for consideration. Have a very specific agenda of goals you wish your prospective agent to accomplish for you. Provide the agent with a comprehensive statement of your credentials—educational and professional."

THE ROBERT LANTZ-JOY HARRIS LITERARY AGENCY INC., (II), 156 Fifth Ave., Suite 617, New York NY 10010. (212)924-6269. Fax: (212)924-6609. Contact: Joy Harris or Paul Chung. Member of AAR. Represents 150 clients. Currently handles: 50% nonfiction books; 50% novels.

Handles: Considers "adult-type books, not juvenile." Considers all fiction areas except fantasy; juvenile; science fiction; westerns/frontier. Query with outline/proposal and SASE. Reports in 2 months on queries.

Recent Sales: *The Magic Bullet*, by Harry Stein (Delacorte, film rights to Ruddy-Morgan Productions).

Terms: Agent receives 15% commission on domestic sales; 20% on foreign sales. Charges for extra expenses.
Tips: Obtains new clients through recommendations from clients and editors. "No unsolicited manuscripts, just query letters."

MICHAEL LARSEN/ELIZABETH POMADA LITERARY AGENTS, (II), 1029 Jones St., San Francisco CA 94109-5023. (415)673-0939. Contact: Mike Larsen or Elizabeth Pomada. Estab. 1972. Members of AAR, Authors Guild, ASJA, NWA, PEN, WNBA, California Writers Club. Represents 100 clients. 40-45% of clients are new/unpublished writers. Eager to work with new/unpublished writers. "We have very diverse tastes. We look for fresh voices and new ideas. We handle literary, commercial and genre fiction, and the full range of nonfiction books." Currently handles: 70% nonfiction books; 30% novels. Member agents: Michael Larsen (nonfiction), Elizabeth Pomada (fiction, books of interest to women).

  • Prior to opening their agency, both Mr. Larsen and Ms. Pomada were promotion executives for major publishing houses. Mr. Larsen worked for Morrow, Bantam and Pyramid (now part of Berkley); Ms. Pomada worked at Holt, David McKay, and The Dial Press. See Mr. Larsen's article, My Dream Client, and Ms. Pomada's article, My Client From Hell, in this edition of the *Guide*.

Handles: Adult nonfiction books, novels. Considers these nonfiction areas: anthropology/archaeology; art/architecture/design; biography/autobiography; business; cooking/food/nutrition; crafts/hobbies; current affairs; ethnic/cultural interests; futurism; gay/lesbian issues; government/politics/law; health/ medicine; history; how-to; humor; interior design/decorating; language/literature/criticism; money/ finance/economics; music/dance/theater/film; nature/environment; New Age/metaphysics; parenting; photography; popular culture; psychology; religious/inspirational; science/technology; self-help/personal improvement; sociology; sports; true crime/investigative; women's issues/women's studies. Considers these fiction areas: action/adventure; contemporary issues; detective/police/crime; ethnic; experimental; family saga; fantasy; feminist; gay; glitz; historical; horror; humor/satire; lesbian; literary; mainstream; mystery/suspense; psychic/supernatural; religious/inspirational; romance (contemporary, gothic, historical, regency). Query with synopsis and first 30 pages of completed novel. Reports in 2 months on queries. For nonfiction, "please read Michael's book *How to Write a Book Proposal* (Writer's Digest) and then call or write him with the title of your book and the list of things that you will do to promote the book nationally." Always include SASE. Send SASE for brochure.
Recent Sales: *Armor of Lies*, by Katharine Kerr (Tor); *A Crack In Forever*, by Jeannie Brewer (S & S); *Haunted Places: The National Directory*, by Dennis William Hauck (Penguin); *How High Can You Bounce? The 9 Keys to Personal Resilience*, by Roger Crawford (Bantam); *I'm Not As Old As I Used to Be*, by Frances Weaver (Hyperion); *Learning to Write Fiction From the Masters*, by Barnaby Conrad (Plume); *Making Documentary and Reality Videos*, by Barry Hampe (Holt).
Terms: Agent receives 15% commission on domestic sales; 15% on dramatic sales; 20% on foreign sales. May charge writer for printing, postage for multiple submissions, foreign mail, foreign phone calls, galleys, books, and legal fees.
Writers' Conferences: ABA (Chicago); Santa Barbara Writers Conference (Santa Barbara); Maui Writers Conference (Maui); ASJA (Los Angeles, February).

THE MAUREEN LASHER AGENCY, (II, III), P.O. Box 888, Pacific Palisades CA 90272-0888. (310)459-8415. Contact: Ann Cashman. Estab. 1980.
Handles: Nonfiction books, novels. Considers these nonfiction areas: animals; anthropology/archaeology; art/architecture/design; biography/autobiography; business; child guidance/parenting; cooking/ food/nutrition; current affairs; ethnic/cultural interests; government/politics/law; health/medicine; history; how-to; nature/environment; popular culture; psychology; science/technology; self-help/personal improvement; sociology; sports; true crime/investigative; women's issues/women's studies. Considers these fiction areas: action/adventure; contemporary issues; detective/police/crime; family saga; feminist; historical; literary; mainstream; sports; thriller/espionage. Send outline/proposal and 1 sample chapter.
Recent Sales: *Ten Greatest Closing Arguments*, by Bycel (Scribner); *Life Stone of Singing Bird*, by Stevenson (Faber & Faber); *Nancy's Healthy Kitchen*, by Fox (Macmillan); *Survivor Personality*, by Siebert (Putnam).
Terms: No information provided. Does not charge a reading fee or offer criticism service.

LAZEAR AGENCY INCORPORATED, (II), 430 First Ave., Suite 416, Minneapolis MN 55401. (612)332-8640. Fax: (612)332-4648. Contact: Editorial Board. Estab. 1984. Represents 250 clients. Currently handles: 50% nonfiction books; 10% juvenile books; 29% novels; 1% short story collections; 5% movie scripts; 2.5% TV scripts; 2.5% syndicated material. Member agents: Jonathon Lazear (agent); Christi Cardenas-Roen (agent); Dennis Cass (agent); Susie Moncur (agent).
Handles: Nonfiction books, juvenile books, novels, movie scripts, TV scripts, syndicated material, new media with connection to book project. Considers all nonfiction areas. Considers all fiction areas.

Query with outline/proposal and SASE. Reports in 3 weeks on queries; 2 months on ms. Highly selective. No phone calls or faxes.

Recent Sales: *Rush Limbaugh is a Big Fat Idiot & Other Observations*, by Al Franken (Dell); *Mother*, by Judy Olausen (Penguin Studio); *Sleeping at the Starlite Motel*, by Bailey White (Vintage); *Piano Lessons*, by Noah Adams (Delacorte/Dell).

Terms: Agent receives 15% commission on domestic sales; 20% on foreign sales. Offers written contract, binding "for term of copyright." Charges for "photocopying, international express mail."

Also Handles: Movie scripts (feature film); TV scripts (TV mow). Query with SASE. Reports in 3 weeks on queries; 2 months on ms.

Tips: Obtains new clients through recommendations from others, "through the bestseller lists, word-of-mouth. The writer should first view himself as a salesperson in order to obtain an agent. Sell yourself, your idea, your concept. Do your homework. Notice what is in the marketplace. Be sophisticated about the arena in which you are writing."

‡LEAP FIRST, (II), P.O. Box 0872, Planetarium Station, New York NY 10024. (212)465-3984. E-mail: leapfirst@aol.com. Contact: Lynn Rosen. Estab. 1991. Represents 40 clients.
Handles: Nonfiction books. Considers these nonfiction areas: ethnic/cultural interests; health/medicine; history; popular culture; psychology; sociology; sports; women's issues/women's studies. Considers these fiction areas: literary; feminist. Query by mail with cover letter, outline and 1 sample chapter. No phone queries. Reports in 1 month on queries.
Terms: Agent receives 15% commission on domestic sales; commission on foreign sales varies. Charges for office expenses such as postage and photocopying.

LESCHER & LESCHER LTD., (II), 67 Irving Place, New York NY 10003. (212)529-1790. Fax: (212)529-2716. Contact: Robert or Susan Lescher. Estab. 1966. Member of AAR. Represents 150 clients. Currently handles: 75% nonfiction books; 25% novels.
Handles: Nonfiction books, novels. Query with SASE.
Terms: Agent receives 15% commission on domestic sales; 20-25% on foreign sales.
Tips: Usually obtains new clients through recommendations from others.

LEVANT & WALES, LITERARY AGENCY, INC., (II, IV), 108 Hayes St., Seattle WA 98109-2808. (206)284-7114. Fax: (206)284-0190. E-mail: bizziew@aol.com. Contact: Elizabeth Wales or Adrienne Reed. Estab. 1988. Member of AAR, Pacific Northwest Writers' Conference, Book Publishers' Northwest. Represents 50 clients. We are interested in published and not-yet-published writers. Especially encourages writers living in the Pacific Northwest, West Coast, Alaska and Pacific Rim countries. Specializes in nonfiction and mainstream fiction. Currently handles: 75% nonfiction books; 25% novels.
Handles: Nonfiction books, novels. Considers these nonfiction areas: animals; anthropology/archaeology; art/architecture/design; biography/autobiography; business; child guidance/parenting; current affairs; education; ethnic/cultural interests; gardening; gay/lesbian issues; health; language/literature/criticism; lifestyle; memoir; nature; New Age/metaphysics; popular culture; psychology; science; self-help/personal improvement; sports; women's issues/women's studies—open to creative or serious treatments of almost any nonfiction subject. Considers these fiction areas: cartoon/comic/women's; ethnic; experimental; feminist; gay; lesbian; literary; mainstream (no genre fiction). Query first. Reports in 3 weeks on queries; 6 weeks on mss.
Recent Sales: *Embracing The Fire: Black Women & Sexuality*, by Julia A. Boyd (Dutton); *Callous Hands: Searching For A Grandfather*, by David Mas Masumoto (W.W. Norton); *A Long Way From St. Louie*, by Colleen J. McElroy (Coffee House Press).
Terms: Agent receives 15% commission on domestic sales. "We make all our income from commissions. We offer editorial help for some of our clients and help some clients with the development of a proposal, but we do not charge for these services. We do charge, after a sale, for express mail, manuscript photocopying costs, foreign postage and outside USA telephone costs."
Writers' Conferences: Pacific NW Writers Conference (Seattle, July); *The African-American Yellow Pages*, by Stanton F. Biddle, Ph.D. (Holt).

JAMES LEVINE COMMUNICATIONS, INC., (II), 330 Seventh Ave., 14th Floor, New York NY 10001. (212)268-4846. Fax: (212)465-8637. E-mail: levineja@aol.com. Estab. 1989. Represents 65 clients. 33⅓% of clients are new/previously unpublished writers. Specializes in business, psychology, parenting, health/medicine, narrative nonfiction. Currently handles: 90% nonfiction books; 10% fiction. Member agents: James Levine; Daniel Greenberg, associate agent, (sports, history, fiction); Arielle Eckstut (narrative nonfiction, psychology, spirituality, religion, women's issues).
• Prior to opening his agency, Mr. Levine served as vice president of the Bank Street College of Education.
Handles: Nonfiction books, novels. Considers these nonfiction areas: animals; art/architecture/design; biography/autobiography; business; child guidance/parenting; computers/electronics; cooking/food/

nutrition; gardening; gay/lesbian issues; health/medicine; juvenile nonfiction; money/finance/economics; nature/environment; New Age/metaphysics; psychology; religious/inspirational; science/technology; self-help/personal improvement; sociology; sports; women's issues/women's studies. Considers these fiction areas: contemporary issues; literary; mainstream. Send outline/proposal plus 1 sample chapter. Reports in 2 weeks on queries; 1 month on mss.

Recent Sales: *Undercurrents: A Therapist Recovering with Her Own Depression*, by Martha Manning (Harper San Francisco); *Catherine, Called Birdy*, by Karen Cushman (Clarion); *The Genesis of Ethics*, by Barton Visotzky (Crown); *Chasing Grace*, by Martha Manning (Harper San Francisco); *Awakening the Spirit*, by Bradford Keeney (Riverheard, Putnam).

Terms: Agent receives 15% commission on domestic sales; 20% on foreign sales. Offers written contract; length of time varies per project. Does not charge reading fee. Charges for out-of-pocket expenses—telephone, fax, postage and photocopying—directly connected to the project.

Writers' Conferences: ASJA Annual Conference (New York City, May); ABA (Chicago, June).

Tips: Obtains new clients through client referrals. "We work closely with clients on editorial development and promotion. We work to place our clients as magazine columnists and have created columnists for *McCall's* and *Child*. We work with clients to develop their projects across various media—video, software, and audio."

ELLEN LEVINE LITERARY AGENCY, INC., (II, III), 15 E. 26th St., Suite 1801, New York NY 10010. (212)889-0620. Fax: (212)725-4501. Contact: Ellen Levine, Elizabeth Kaplan, Diana Finch, Louise Quayle. Estab. 1980. Member of AAR. Represents over 100 clients. 20% of clients are new/previously unpublished writers. "My three younger colleagues at the agency (Louise Quayle, Diana Finch and Elizabeth Kaplan) are seeking both new and established writers. I prefer to work with established writers, mostly through referrals." Currently handles: 60% nonfiction books; 8% juvenile books; 30% novels; 2% short story collections.

Handles: Nonfiction books, juvenile books, novels, short story collections. Considers these nonfiction areas: anthropology; biography; current affairs; health; popular culture; psychology; science; women's issues/women's studies; books by journalists. Considers these fiction areas: literary; mystery; women's thrillers. Query. Reports in 3 weeks on queries, if SASE provided; 6 weeks on mss, if submission requested.

Recent Sales: *Cloudsplitter*, by Russell Banks (HarperCollins); *The Aguero Sisters*, by Cristina Garcia (Knopf); *Shaking the Money Tree: Women's Hidden Fear of Supporting Themselves*, by Colette Dowling (Little, Brown).

Terms: Agent receives 15% commission on domestic sales; 20% on foreign sales. Charges for overseas postage, photocopying, messenger fees, overseas telephone and fax, books ordered for use in rights submissions.

Tips: Obtains new clients through recommendations from others.

KAREN LEWIS & COMPANY, (I, II), P.O. Box 741623, Dallas TX 75374. (214)342-3885. Fax: (214)340-8875. Contact: Karen Lewis. Estab. 1995. Represents 20 clients. 25% of clients are new/previously unpublished writers. Currently handles: 50% nonfiction books; 50% novels.

Handles: Nonfiction books, juvenile books, novels. Considers these nonfiction areas: ethnic/cultural interests; gay/lesbian issues; juvenile nonfiction; New Age/metaphysics; self-help/personal improvement; women's issues/women's studies. Considers these fiction areas: action/adventure; detective/police/crime; erotica; ethnic; literary; mainstream; mystery/suspense; science fiction; thriller/espionage. Query. Reports in 2 weeks on queries; 1 month on mss.

Terms: Agent receives 15% commission on domestic sales; 20% on foreign sales. Offers written contract, binding for 1 year, with 30 day cancellation clause. Charges $35 processing fee. 100% of business is derived from commissions on sales.

Writers' Conferences: Southwest Writers (Albuquerque NM), Romance Writer's of America.

Tips: Obtains new clients through "conferences and referrals from people I know. Write a clear letter succinctly describing your book. Be sure to include a SASE. If you receive rejection notices, don't despair. Keep writing! A good book will always find a home."

‡LICHTMAN, TRISTER, SINGER, & ROSS, (III), 1666 Connecticut Ave. NW, #500, Washington DC 20009. (202)328-1666. Fax: (202)328-9162. Contact: Gail Ross, Howard Yoon. Estab. 1988. Member of AAR. Represents 200 clients. 75% of clients are new/previously unpublished writers. Specializes in adult trade nonfiction. Currently handles: 90% nonfiction books; 10% novels. Member agents: Gail Ross (nonfiction); Howard Yoon.

Handles: Nonfiction books, novels. Considers these nonfiction areas: anthropology/archaeology; biography/autobiography; business; cooking/food/nutrition; education; ethnic/cultural interests; gay/lesbian issues; government/politics/law; humor; money/finance/economics; nature/environment; psychology; religious/inspirational; science/technology; self-help/personal improvement; sociology; sports; true crime/investigative. Considers these fiction areas: ethnic; feminist; gay; literary. Query. Reports in 1 month.

Terms: Agent receives 15% commission on domestic sales; 25% on foreign sales. Charges for office expenses (i.e., postage, copying).
Tips: Obtains new clients through referrals.

ROBERT LIEBERMAN ASSOCIATES, (II), 400 Nelson Rd., Ithaca NY 14850. (607)273-8801. E-mail: rhl10@cornell.edu. Contact: Robert Lieberman. Estab. 1993. Represents 30 clients. 50% of clients are new/previously unpublished writers. Specializes in university/college level textbooks and popular tradebooks in science, math, engineering, economics and others. Currently handles: 20% nonfiction books; 80% textbooks.
Handles: Scholarly books, textbooks. Considers these nonfiction areas: agriculture/horticulture; anthropology/archaeology; art/architecture/design; business; computers/electronics; education; health/medicine; money/finance/economics; music/dance/theater/film; nature/environment; psychology; science/technology; sociology; college, high school and middle school level textbooks. Query with outline/proposal. Reports in 2 weeks on queries; 1 month on mss.
Recent Sales: *College Physics*, by Giambattista and Richardson (McGraw Hill); *Geology*, by Chimet (Addison-Wesley); *Pre-Calculus CD-ROM*, by Confrey (Addison-Wesley Interactive); *Student Guide to the Internet*, by Pejsa (Houghton-Mifflin).
Terms: Agent receives 15% commission on domestic sales; 20% on foreign sales. Offers written contract, binding for open-ended length of time, with 30 day cancellation clause. "Fees are changed only when special reviewers are required." 100% of business is derived from commissions on sales.
Tips: Obtains new clients through referrals. Send initial inquiries by mail with SASE or via e-mail. "E-mail preferred."

RAY LINCOLN LITERARY AGENCY, (II), Elkins Park House, Suite 107-B, 7900 Old York Rd., Elkins Park PA 19027. (215)635-0827. Contact: Mrs. Ray Lincoln. Estab. 1974. Represents 34 clients. 35% of clients are new/previously unpublished writers. Specializes in biography, nature, the sciences, fiction in both adult and children's categories. Currently handles: 30% nonfiction books; 20% juvenile books; 50% novels. Member agent: Jerome A. Lincoln.
Handles: Nonfiction books, scholarly books, juvenile books, novels. Considers these nonfiction areas: animals; anthropology/archaeology; art/architecture/design; biography/autobiography; business; child guidance/parenting; cooking/food/nutrition; crafts/hobbies; current affairs; ethnic/cultural interests; gay/lesbian issues; government/politics/law; health/medicine; history; horticulture; interior design/decorating; juvenile nonfiction; language/literature/criticism; money/finance/economics; music/dance/theater/film; nature/environment; psychology; science/technology; self-help/personal improvement; sociology; sports; women's issues/women's studies. Considers these fiction areas: action/adventure; contemporary issues; detective/police/crime; ethnic; family saga; fantasy; feminist; gay; historical; humor/satire; juvenile; lesbian; literary; mainstream; mystery/suspense; psychic/supernatural; regional; romance (contemporary, gothic, historical); science fiction; sports; thriller/espionage; young adult. Query first, then send outline, 2 sample chapters and SASE. "I send for balance of manuscript if it is a likely project." Reports in 2 weeks on queries; 1 month on mss.
Recent Sales: *Lizzie Borden Gets Married*, by Eileen Spinelli (Simon & Schuster); *Veritas*, by William Lashner (HarperCollins), *Charity*, by Paulette Callen (Simon & Schuster).
Terms: Agent receives 15% commission on domestic sales; 20% on foreign sales. Offers written contract, binding "but with notice, may be cancelled. Charges only for overseas telephone calls. I request authors to do manuscript photocopying themselves. Postage, or shipping charge, on manuscripts accepted for representation by agency."
Tips: Obtains new clients usually from recommendations. "I always look for polished writing style, fresh points of view and professional attitudes."

LINDSTROM LITERARY GROUP, (I), 871 N. Greenbrier St., Arlington VA 22205-1220. (703)522-4730. Fax: (703)527-7624. E-mail: lindlitgrp@aol.com. Contact: Kristin Lindstrom. Estab. 1994. Represents 22 clients. 40% of clients are new/previously unpublished writers. Currently handles: 20% nonfiction books; 70% novels; 10% movie scripts/TV scripts. Member agent: Perry Lindstrom (nonfiction, film/TV scripts).
Handles: Nonfiction books; novels. Considers these nonfiction areas: biography/autobiography; current affairs; ethnic/cultural interests; history; popular culture; psychology; science/technology. Considers these fiction areas: action/adventure; contemporary issues; detective/police/crime; ethnic; family saga; fantasy; historical; mainstream; science fiction; thriller/espionage. For fiction, send 3 chapters and outline with SASE to cover return of ms if desired. For nonfiction, send outline/proposal with SASE. Reports in 1 month on queries; 6 weeks on mss.
Recent Sales: *The Down Dogs*, by John Ramsey Miller (Bantam Books); *Genellan III: Outpost*, by Scott Grier (Ballantine Del Rey); *Trick Question*, by Tony Dunbar (G.P. Putnam & Sons).
Also Handles: Movie scripts (feature film), TV scripts (TV mow, miniseries). Considers these script subject areas: action/adventure; comedy; detective/police/crime; ethnic; family saga; historical; horror; mainstream; mystery/suspense; romantic comedy and drama; thriller.

Terms: Agent receives 15% commission on domestic sales; 20% on foreign sales; 20% on performance rights sales. Offers written contract. Charges for marketing and mailing expense, express mail, UPS, etc.

Tips: Obtains new clients through references, advertising, electronic mail. "Include biography of writer. Send enough material for an overall review of project scope."

WENDY LIPKIND AGENCY, (II), 165 E. 66th St., New York NY 10021. (212)628-9653. Fax: (212)628-2693. Contact: Wendy Lipkind. Estab. 1977. Member of AAR. Represents 60 clients. Specializes in adult nonfiction. Currently handles: 80% nonfiction books; 20% novels.

Handles: Nonfiction, novels. Considers these nonfiction areas: biography; current affairs; health/medicine; history; science; social history, women's issues/women's studies. Considers mainstream fiction. No mass market originals. For nonfiction, query with outline/proposal. For fiction, query with SASE only. Reports in 1 month on queries.

Recent Sales: *Where's The Baby* and *Animal's Lullaby*, both by Tom Paxton (Morrow Junior Books); *Methyl Magic*, by Dr. Craig Cooney and AJS Rayl (Andrews-McMeel).

Terms: Agent receives 15% commission on domestic sales; 20% on foreign sales. Sometimes offers written contract. Charges for foreign postage and messenger service.

Tips: Usually obtains new clients through recommendations from others. "Send intelligent query letter first. Let me know if you sent to other agents."

LITERARY AND CREATIVE ARTISTS AGENCY INC., (III), 3543 Albemarle St. NW, Washington DC 20008. (202)362-4688. Fax: (202)362-8875. Contact: Muriel Nellis, Jane Roberts, Elizabeth Pokempner. Estab. 1982. Member of Authors Guild, associate member of American Bar Association. Represents over 75 clients. "While we prefer published writers, it is not required if the proposed work has great merit." Requires exclusive review of material; no simultaneous submissions. Currently handles: 70% nonfiction books; 15% novels; 10% audio/video; 5% film/TV.

Handles: Nonfiction, novels, audio, film/TV rights. Considers these nonfiction areas: business; cooking; health; how-to; human drama; lifestyle; memoir; philosophy; politics. Query with outline, bio and SASE. No unsolicited mss. Reports in 3 weeks on queries.

Recent Sales: *The Path to Love*, by Deepak Chopra (Harmony); *Putting America on the Couch*, by Pythia Peay (Riverhead); *Emotional Resilience*, by David Viscott M.D. (Harmony); *Molecules of Emotion*, by Candace Pert Ph.D. (Scribner).

Terms: Agent receives 15% commission on domestic sales; 20% on dramatic sales; 25% on foreign sales. Charges for long-distance phone and fax, photocopying and shipping.

THE LITERARY GROUP, (II), 270 Lafayette St., #1505, New York NY 10012. (212)274-1616. Fax: (212)274-9876. E-mail: litgrp@aol.com. Contact: Frank Weimann. Estab. 1985. Represents 90 clients. 75% of clients are new/previously unpublished writers. Specializes in nonfiction (true crime; biography; sports; how-to). Currently handles: 80% nonfiction books; 20% novels. Member agents: Frank Weimann (thrillers, mysteries, nonfiction in all areas); Jim Hornfischer (all areas of nonfiction); Jessica Wainwright (women's issues, romance, how-to); Scott Waxman (sports, politics, inspirational); Cathy McCornacle (how-to's, cookbooks).

Handles: Nonfiction books, novels. Considers these nonfiction areas: animals; anthropology/archaeology; biography/autobiography; business; child guidance/parenting; cookbooks; crafts/hobbies; current affairs; education; ethnic/cultural interests; gay/lesbian issues; government/politics/law; health/medicine; history; how-to; humor; juvenile nonfiction; language/literature/criticism; military/war; money/finance/economics; music/dance/theater/film; nature/environment; New Age/metaphysics; popular culture; psychology; religious/inspirational; science/technology; self-help/personal improvement; sociology; sports; true crime/investigative; women's issues/women's studies. Considers these fiction areas: action/adventure; cartoon/comic; contemporary issues; detective/police/crime; ethnic; family saga; fantasy; feminist; gay; historical; horror; humor/satire; lesbian; mystery/suspense; psychic/supernatural; romance (contemporary, gothic, historical, regency); science fiction; sports; thriller/espionage; westerns/frontier; young adult. Query with outline plus 3 sample chapters. Reports in 1 week on queries; 1 month on mss.

Recent Sales: *Legally Correct Fairy Tales*, by David Fisher (Warner); *The Grand Ole Opry Christmas Book* (Doubleday); *Satisfied With Nothin*, by Ernest Hill (Simon & Schuster); *The Secret Diary of Scarlett O'Hara*, by Cathy Crimmins (Dove).

Terms: Agent receives 15% commission on domestic sales; 20% on foreign sales. Offers written contract, which can be cancelled after 30 days.

Writers' Conferences: Detroit Women's Writers (MI); Kent State University (OH); San Diego Writers Conference (CA).

Tips: Obtains new clients through referrals, writers conferences, query letters.

STERLING LORD LITERISTIC, INC., (III), 65 Bleecker St., New York NY 10012. (212)780-6050. Fax: (212)780-6095. Contact: Peter Matson. Estab. 1952. Signatory of WGA. Represents 500 clients. Specializes in "nonfiction and fiction." Currently handles: 50% nonfiction books, 50% novels. Member agents: Peter Matson, Sterling Lord; Joseph Hotchkiss (film scripts); Philippa Brophy; Elizabeth Grossman, Chris Calhoun; Jennifer Hengen, Charlotte Sheedy.
Handles: Nonfiction books, novels. Considers "mainstream nonfiction and fiction." Query. Reports in 1 month on mss.
Recent Sales: *Come To Grief*, by Dick Francis (Putnam); *In Retrospect*, by Robert MacNamara (Times Books); *King of Hearts*, by Susan Moody (Scribner).
Terms: Agent receives 15% commission on domestic sales; 20% on foreign sales. Offers written contract. Charges for photocopying.
Tips: Obtains new clients through recommendations from others.

NANCY LOVE LITERARY AGENCY, (III), 250 E. 65th St., New York NY 10021-6614. (212)980-3499. Fax: (212)308-6405. Contact: Nancy Love. Estab. 1984. Member of AAR. Represents 60-80 clients. Specializes in adult nonfiction. Currently handles: 90% nonfiction books; 10% novels.
Handles: Nonfiction books, novels. Considers these nonfiction areas: animals, biography/autobiography; child guidance/parenting; cooking/food/nutrition; current affairs; ethnic/cultural interests; gay/lesbian issues; government/politics/law; health/medicine; history; how-to; nature/environment; New Age/metaphysics; popular culture; psychology; science/technology; self-help/personal improvement; sociology; true crime/investigative; women's issues/women's studies. Considers these fiction areas: detective/police/crime; ethnic; mystery/suspense; thriller/espionage. "For nonfiction, send a proposal, chapter summary and sample chapter. For fiction, send the first 40-50 pages plus summary of the rest (will consider only *completed* novels)." Reports in 3 weeks on queries; 1 month on mss.
Recent Sales: *The Language of Fertility*, by Niravi Payne (Villard, Crown); *Understanding Your Child's Temperament*, by William Grey, M.D. (Macmillan); *Deadspin*, by Gregory M. MacGregor (Bantam).
Terms: Agent receives 15% commission on domestic sales; 20% on foreign sales. Offers written contract. Charges for photocopying, "if it runs over $20."
Tips: Obtains new clients through recommendations and solicitation. Needs an exclusive on fiction. Nonfiction author and/or collaborator must be an authority in subject area. Submissions will be returned only if accompanied by a SASE.

LOWENSTEIN ASSOCIATES, INC., (II), 121 W. 27th St., Suite 601, New York NY 10001. (212)206-1630. Fax: (212)727-0280. President: Barbara Lowenstein. Estab. 1976. Member of AAR. Represents 150 clients. 20% of clients are new/unpublished writers. Specializes in multicultural books (fiction and nonfiction), medical experts, commercial fiction, especially suspense, crime and women's issues. Currently handles: 60% nonfiction books; 40% novels. Member agents: Barbara Lowenstein (serious nonfiction, multicultural issues); Nancy Yost (commercial fiction, light nonfiction); Eileen Lope, associate (spirituality, serious fiction and nonfiction); Elise Proulx (literary and commercial fiction, general nonfiction).
Handles: Nonfiction books, novels. Considers these nonfiction areas: animals; anthropology/archaeology; art/architecture/design; biography/autobiography; business; child guidance/parenting; craft/hobbies; current affairs; education; ethnic/cultural interests; gay/lesbian issues; government/politics/law; health/medicine; history; how-to; humor; language/literature/criticism/, money/finance/economics; music/dance/theater/film; nature/environment; New Age/metaphysics, popular culture; psychology; religious/inspirational; science/technology; self-help/personal improvement; sociology; sports; true crime/investigative; women's issues/women's studies. Considers these fiction areas: contemporary issues; detective/police/crime; erotica; ethnic; feminist; gay; historical; humor/satire; lesbian; mainstream; mystery/suspense; romance (contemporary, historical, regency); medical thrillers. Send query with SASE, "otherwise will not respond." For fiction, send outline and 1st chapter. No unsolicited mss. Reports in 6 weeks on queries.

[handwritten:] www. lowensteinyost. com
[handwritten:] — Should go live end of Oct '02

FOR EXPLANATION OF SYMBOLS, see the Key to Symbols and Abbreviations. For translation of an organization's acronym, see the Table of Acronyms. For unfamiliar words, check the Glossary.

Recent Sales: *The Melatonin Miracle*, by Dr. Walter Pierpaooi and Dr. William Regelson (Simon & Schuster); *Invasion of Privacy*, by Perri O'Shaughnessy (Delacorte); *What the Animals Tell Me*, by Sonya Fitzpatrick (Hyperion).
Terms: Agent receives 15% commission on domestic and dramatic sales; 20% on foreign sales. Offers written contract, binding for 2 years, with 60 day cancellation clause. Charges for photocopying, foreign postage, messenger expenses.
Writers' Conference: Malice Domestic (Bethesda, Spring); Novelists, Inc.; RWA.
Tips: Obtains new clients through recommendations from others. "Know the genre you are working in and READ!"

‡LUKEMAN LITERARY MANAGEMENT LTD., (III), 205 W. 80 St., Suite 4C, New York NY 10024. (212)874-5959. Fax: (212)874-2538. Contact: Noah Lukeman. Estab. 1996. Represents 30 clients. 10% of clients are new/previously unpublished writers. Currently handles: 50% nonfiction books; 10% short story collections; 40% novels.
Handles: Nonfiction books, novels, novellas, short story collections. Considers these nonfiction areas: animals; anthropology/archaeology; art/architecture/design; biography/autobiography; business; child guidance/parenting; cooking/food/nutrition; current affairs; health/medicine; language/literature/criticism; military/war; money/finance/economics; music/dance/theater/film; nature/environment; New Age/metaphysics; photography; popular culture; psychology; religious/inspirational; self-help/personal improvement; translations; true crime/investigative; women's issues/women's studies. Considers these fiction areas: action/adventure; contemporary issues; experimental; horror; literary; mainstream; thriller/espionage. Send outline/proposal and 1 sample chapter. Reports in 2 weeks on queries; 2 months on mss.
Terms: Agent receives 15% commission on domestic sales; 20% on foreign sales. Offers written contract.
Tips: "Include SASE. Be patient."

DONALD MAASS LITERARY AGENCY, (III), 157 West 57th St., Suite 703, New York NY 10019. (212)757-7755. Contact: Donald Maass. Estab. 1980. Member of AAR, SFWA, MWA. Represents 75 clients. 5% of clients are new/previously unpublished writers. Specializes in commercial fiction, especially science fiction, fantasy, mystery, suspense. Currently handles: 100% novels. Member agent: Jennifer Jackson.
• Prior to opening his agency, Mr. Maass served as an editor at Dell Publishing and as an agent with The Scott Meredith Literary Agency. See Mr. Maass's article, How to Find (and Keep) the Right Agent, in this edition of the *Guide*.
Handles: Novels. Considers these fiction areas: detective/police/crime; family saga; fantasy; historical; horror; literary; mainstream; mystery/suspense; psychic/supernatural; romance (historical, paranormal, time travel); science fiction; thriller/espionage. Query with SASE. Reports in 2 weeks on queries, 3 months on mss (if requested following query).
Recent Sales: *Weighed in the Balance*, by Anne Perry (Fawcett Columbine); *Ashworth House*, by Anne Perry (Fawcett Columbine); *Voices of Hope*, by David Feintuch (Warner/Aspect); *God's Fires*, by Patricia Anthony (Berkley/Ace); *The Players*, by Stephanie Cowell (W.W. Norton).
Terms: Agent receives 15% commission on domestic sales; 20% on foreign sales. "Manuscript copying for auction charged separately."
Writers' Conferences: World Science Fiction Convention (San Antonio); Bouchercon.
Tips: "Most new clients are established authors referred by clients, publishers and other writers. We are fiction specialists. Few new clients are accepted, but interested authors should query with SASE. Subagents in all principle foreign countries and Hollywood. No nonfiction or juvenile works considered."

MARGRET MCBRIDE LITERARY AGENCY, (II), 7744 Fay Ave., Suite 201, La Jolla CA 92037. (619)454-1550. Fax: (619)454-2156. Contact: Mindy Riesenberg. Estab. 1980. Member of AAR, Authors Guild. Represents 50 clients. 15% of clients are new/unpublished writers. Specializes in mainstream fiction and nonfiction. Member agents: Winifred Golden (associate agent); Kim Sauer (submissions manager); Stacy Horne.
• Prior to opening her agency, Ms. McBride served in the marketing departments of Random House and Ballantine Books and the publicity departments of Warner Books and Pinnacle Books.
Handles: Nonfiction books, novels, audio, video film rights. Considers these nonfiction areas: biography/autobiography; business; child guidance/parenting; cooking/food/nutrition; current affairs; ethnic/cultural interests; gay/lesbian issues; government/politics/law; health/medicine; history; how-to; money/finance/economics; music/dance/theater/film; popular culture; psychology; religious/inspirational; science/technology; self-help/personal improvement; sociology; sports; true crime/investigative; women's issues/women's studies. Considers these fiction areas: action/adventure; detective/police/crime; ethnic; historical; literary; mainstream; mystery/suspense; thriller/espionage; westerns/frontier.

Query with synopsis or outline. No unsolicited mss. Reports in 6 weeks on queries.
Recent Sales: *Freeing Fauziya*, by Fauziya Kasinga with Layli Miller Bashir; *The Unimaginable Life*, by Kenny and Julia Loggins; *The Golden Door Cookbook*, by Michele Stroot.
Terms: Agent receives 15% commission on domestic sales; 10% on dramatic sales; 25% on foreign sales.

GINA MACCOBY LITERARY AGENCY, (II), P.O. Box 60, Chappaqua NY 10514. (914)238-5630. Contact: Gina Maccoby. Estab. 1986. Represents 35 clients. Currently handles: 33% nonfiction books; 33% juvenile books; 33% novels. Represents illustrators of children's books.
Handles: Nonfiction, juvenile books, novels. Considers these nonfiction areas: biography; current affairs; ethnic/cultural interests; juvenile nonfiction; women's issues/women's studies. Considers these fiction areas: juvenile; literary; mainstream; mystery/suspense; thriller/espionage; young adult. Query with SASE. "Please, no unsolicited mss." Reports in 2 months.
Recent Sales: *City of the Century*, by Donald Miller (Simon & Schuster); *Snapshot*, by Linda Barnes (Delacorte); *The Old Woman & Her Pig*, by Rosanne Litzinger (Harcourt Brace Jovanovich).
Terms: Agent receives 15% commission on domestic sales; 25% on foreign sales. May recover certain costs such as airmail postage to Europe or Japan or legal fees.
Tips: Usually obtains new clients through recommendations from own clients.

RICHARD P. MCDONOUGH, LITERARY AGENT, (II), 551 Franklin St., Cambridge MA 02139. Contact: Richard P. McDonough. Estab. 1986. Represents 30 clients. 50% of clients are new/unpublished writers. Works with unpublished and published writers "whose work I think has merit and requires a committed advocate." Specializes in nonfiction for general contract and fiction. Currently handles: 80% nonfiction books; 20% novels.
Handles: Nonfiction books, novels. Query with outline and SASE or send 3 chapters and SASE. Reports in 2 weeks on queries; 2 months on mss.
Recent Sales: *Love Warps the Mind a Little*, by John Dufresne (Norton); *Secret of the Incas*, by William Sullivan (Crown); *Nine Myths of Aging*, by Douglas Powell (Freeman).
Terms: Agent receives 15% commission on domestic sales; 15% on dramatic sales; 15% on foreign sales. Charges for photocopying, phone beyond 300 miles; postage for sold work only.

HELEN MCGRATH, (III), 1406 Idaho Ct., Concord CA 94521. (510)672-6211. Contact: Helen McGrath. Estab. 1977. Currently handles: 50% nonfiction books; 50% novels. Member agent: Doris Johnson.
Handles: Nonfiction books, novels. Considers these nonfiction areas: biography; business; current affairs; health/medicine; history; how-to; military/war; psychology; self-help/personal improvement; sports; women's issues/women's studies. Considers these fiction areas: contemporary issues; detective/police/crime; family saga; literary; mainstream; mystery/suspense; psychic/supernatural; romance; science fiction; thriller/espionage. Query with proposal and SASE. No unsolicited mss. Reports in 2 months on queries.
Terms: Agent receives 15% commission on domestic sales. Sometimes offers written contract. Charges for photocopying.
Tips: Usually obtains new clients through recommendations from others.

ROBERT MADSEN AGENCY, (II), 1331 E. 34th St., Suite #1, Oakland CA 94602. (510)223-2090. Agent: Robert Madsen. Senior Editor: Kim Van Nguyen. Estab. 1992. Represents 5 clients. 100% of clients are new/previously unpublished writers. Currently handles: 25% nonfiction books; 25% fiction books; 25% movie scripts; 25% TV scripts.
Handles: Nonfiction books, fiction, movie scripts, TV scripts, radio scripts, video, stage plays. Considers all nonfiction and fiction areas. Considers all script subject areas. "Willing to look at subject matter that is specialized, controversial, even unpopular, esoteric and outright bizarre. However, it is strongly suggested that authors query first, to save themselves and this agency time, trouble and expense." Query. Reports in 1 month on queries; 2-3 months on mss.
Terms: Agent receives 10% commission on domestic sales; 20% on foreign sales. Offers written contract, binding for 3 years.
Tips: Obtains new clients through recommendations, or by query. "Be certain to take care of business basics in appearance, ease of reading and understanding proper presentation and focus. Be sure to include sufficient postage and SASE with all submissions."

RICIA MAINHARDT AGENCY, (II), 612 Argyle Rd., #L5, Brooklyn NY 11230. (718)434-1893. Fax: (718)434-2157. Contact: Ricia. Estab. 1987. 40% of clients are new/previously unpublished writers. Currently handles: 20% nonfiction books; 30% juvenile books; 50% novels. Considers these nonfiction areas: agriculture/horticulture; animals; anthropology/archaeology; biography/autobiography; business; child guidance/parenting; cooking/food/nutrition; crafts/hobbies; current affairs; ethnic/cultural interests; government/

politics/law; health/medicine; history; how-to; humor; interior design/decorating; juvenile nonfiction; money/finance/economics; nature/environment; New Age/metaphysics; popular culture; psychology; science/technology; self-help/personal improvement; sociology; sports; true crime/investigative; women's issues/women's studies. Considers these fiction areas: action/adventure; contemporary issues; detective/police/crime; erotica; ethnic; family saga; fantasy; feminist; glitz; historical; horror; humor/satire; juvenile; literary; mainstream; picture book; psychic/supernatural; romance (contemporary, gothic, historical, regency); science fiction; sports; thriller/espionage; westerns/frontier; young adult. Send outline and first chapter with SASE. Reports in 1 month on queries; 2-3 months on mss.
Terms: Agent receives 15% commission on domestic sales; 20% on foreign sales. No written contract. Charges new writers $20 to cover postage and handling of initial submission. Charges for photocopying mss.
Writers' Conferences: "I attend the major genre conferences—World Fantasy, Bouchercon, Malice Domestic, Romance Writers, World Science Fiction, RT and one or two general writing conferences."
Tips: Obtains most new clients through recommendations of established writers and editors.

CAROL MANN AGENCY, (II, III), 55 Fifth Ave., New York NY 10003. (212)206-5635. Fax: (212)463-8718. Contact: Carol Mann. Estab. 1977. Member of AAR. Represents over 100 clients. 25% of clients are new/previously unpublished writers. Specializes in current affairs; self-help; psychology; parenting; history. Currently handles: 80% nonfiction books; 15% scholarly books; 5% novels. Member agent: Gareth Esersky (contemporary nonfiction).
Handles: Nonfiction books. Considers these nonfiction areas: anthropology/archaeology; art/architecture/design; biography/autobiography; business; child guidance/parenting; current affairs; ethnic/cultural interests; government/politics/law; health/medicine; history; interior design/decorating; money/finance/economics; psychology; self-help/personal improvement; sociology; true crime/investigative; women's issues/women's studies. Considers literary fiction. Query with outline/proposal and SASE. Reports in 3 weeks on queries.
Recent Sales: *The Good Marriage*, by Dr. Judith Wallerstein and Sandra Blakeslee (Houghton-Mifflin); *All God's Children*, by Fox Butterfield (Knopf); *What Your Boss Doesn't Tell You Until It's Too Late*, by Robert Bramson, Ph.D. (Fireside/Simon & Schuster); *Mockery of Justice: The True Story of the Sheppard Murder Case*, by Cynthia L. Cooper and Sam Reese Sheppard (Northeastern University Press).
Terms: Agent receives 15% commission on domestic sales; 20% on foreign sales. Offers written contract.

MANUS & ASSOCIATES LITERARY AGENCY, INC., (II), 417 E. 57th St., Suite 5D, New York NY 10022. (212)644-8020. Fax: (212)644-3374. Contact: Janet Wilkens Manus. Also: 430 Cowper St., Palo Alto CA 94301. (415)617-4556. Fax: (415)617-4546. Contact: Jillian Manus. Estab. 1985. Member of AAR. Represents 75 clients. 15% of clients are new/previously unpublished writers. Specializes in quality fiction, mysteries, thrillers, true crime, health, pop psychology. Currently handles: 60% nonfiction books; 10% juvenile books; 20% novels; 25% film rights, TV and feature films.
Handles: Nonfiction books, novels. Considers these nonfiction areas: biography/autobiography; business; child guidance/parenting; current affairs; ethnic/cultural interests; health/medicine; how-to; nature/environment; popular culture; psychology; self-help/personal improvement; true crime/investigative; women's issues/women's studies. Considers these fiction areas: action/adventure; confessional; contemporary issues; detective/police/crime; ethnic; family saga; feminist; mainstream; mystery/suspense; thriller/espionage. Send outline and 2-3 sample chapters with SASE. Reports in 3 weeks on queries; 6 weeks on mss.
Recent Sales: *A Natural Death*, by Ruth Furie (Avon); *New Hope*, by Dr. Richard Marrs, etc. (Delacorte); *Pink & Blue Baby PP*, by Waldstein & Zinberg (Contemporary); *Requiem for Renee*, by Carlton Stowers (St. Martin's).
Also Handles: Movie scripts (feature film); TV scripts (TV mow). Considers these script subject areas: contemporary issues; detective/police/crime; family saga; feminist; mainstream; mystery/suspense; romantic comedy; thriller. Query with outline/proposal and 3 sample scenes. "Send movie scripts to West Coast office only." Reports in 3 weeks on queries; 1 month on scripts.
Terms: Agent receives 15% commission on domestic sales; 20% on foreign sales. Offers written contract, binding for 2 years, with 45-day cancellation clause. 100% of business is derived from commissions on sales.
Writers' Conferences Squaw Valley Community of Writers; San Diego State University Writers Conference; Writer's Connection/Agent's Day Conference; Maui Writers Conference; ABA (Chicago).
Tips: Obtains new clients through recommendations from others, at conferences, and from editors.

MARCH TENTH, INC., (III), 4 Myrtle St., Haworth NJ 07641-1740. (201)387-6551. Fax: (201)387-6552. President: Sandra Choron. Estab. 1982. Represents 40 clients. 30% of clients are new/unpublished writers. "Writers must have professional expertise in the field in which they are writing." Prefers to work with published writers. Currently handles: 75% nonfiction books; 25% fiction.

Handles: Nonfiction books, fiction. Considers these nonfiction areas: biography/autobiography; current affairs; health/medicine; history; humor; language/literature/criticism; music/dance/theater/film; popular culture. Considers these fiction areas: confessional; ethnic; family saga; historical; horror; humor/satire; literary; mainstream. Query. Does not read unsolicited mss. Reports in 1 month.
Recent Sales: *If: Questions for the Game of Life*, by Evelyn McFarlane and James Saywell (Villard); *All Area Access: A History of the Rock Concert Industry*, by Dave Marsh (Simon & Schuster); *Countdown*, by Ben Mikaelsen (Hyperion).
Terms: Agent receives 15% commission on domestic sales; 20% on dramatic sales; 20% on foreign sales. Charges writers for postage, photocopying, overseas phone expenses. *#9C*

THE DENISE MARCIL LITERARY AGENCY, INC., (II), 685 West End Ave., New York NY 10025. (212)932-3110. Contact: Denise Marcil. Estab. 1977. Member of AAR. Represents 70 clients. 40% of clients are new/previously unpublished authors. Specializes in women's commercial fiction, business books, popular reference, how-to and self-help. Currently handles: 30% nonfiction books; 70% novels.
 • Prior to opening her agency, Ms. Marcil served as an editorial assistant with Avon Books and as an editor with Simon & Schuster.
Handles: Nonfiction books, novels. Considers these nonfiction areas: business; child guidance/parenting; nutrition; health/medicine; how-to; inspirational; money/finance/economics; psychology; self-help/personal improvement; spirituality; women's issues/women's studies. Considers these fiction areas: romance (contemporary); suspense/thrillers. Query with SASE *only*! Reports in 3 weeks on queries. "Does not read unsolicited mss."
Recent Sales: *Lethal Practice*, by Peter Clement M.D. (Ballantine); *Making Waves*, by Catherine Todd (Avon); *Managing Your Inheritance*, by Emily Card Ph.D. and Adam Miller JD/MBA (Times Business Books).
Terms: Agent receives 15% commission on domestic sales; 20% on foreign sales. Offers written contract, binding for 2 years.
Fees: Charges $100/year for postage, photocopying, long-distance calls, etc. 99.9% of business is derived from commissions on ms sales; .1% is derived from reading fees and criticism.
Writers' Conferences: Maui Writers Conference (August); Pacific Northwest Writers Conference; RWA (Dallas, July).
Tips: Obtains new clients through recommendations from other authors and "35% of my list is from query letters! Only send a one-page query letter. I read them all and ask for plenty of material; I find many of my clients this way. *Always* send a SASE."

BARBARA MARKOWITZ LITERARY AGENCY, (II), 117 N. Mansfield Ave., Los Angeles CA 90036-3020. (213)939-5927. Literary Agent/President: Barbara Markowitz. Estab. 1980. Represents 14 clients. Works with a small number of new/unpublished authors. Specializes in mid-level and YA; contemporary fiction; adult trade fiction and nonfiction. Currently handles: 25% nonfiction books; 25% novels; 50% juvenile books. Member agent: Judith Rosenthal (psychology, current affairs, women's issues, biography).
 • Prior to opening her agency, Ms. Markowitz owned the well-known independent Barbara's Bookstores in Chicago.
Handles: Nonfiction books, novels, juvenile books. Considers these nonfiction areas: biography/autobiography; current affairs; juvenile nonfiction; music/dance/theater/film; nature/environment; popular culture; sports; women's issues/women's studies. Considers these fiction areas: contemporary issues; detective/police/crime; ethnic; humor/satire; juvenile; mainstream; mystery/suspense; sports; thriller/espionage; young adult. No illustrated books. Query with SASE and first 2-3 chapters. Reports in 3 weeks.
Recent Sales: *The Broken Blade*, by William Durbin (Bantam-children's); *Beethoven In Paradise*, by Barbara O'Connor (Farrar, Straus & Giroux-children's); *A Most Congenial Man*, by John Hutchinson (Atheneum).
Terms: Agent receives 15% commission on domestic sales; 15% on dramatic sales; 15% on foreign sales. Charges writers for mailing, postage.
Tips: "We do *not* agent pre-school or early reader books. Only mid-level and YA contemporary fiction and historical fiction. We receive an abundance of pre-school and early reader mss, which our agency returns if accompanied by SASE. No illustrated books. No sci-fi/fable/fantasy or fairy tales."

● **A BULLET** introduces comments by the editor of the *Guide* indicating special information about the listing.

ELAINE MARKSON LITERARY AGENCY, (II), 44 Greenwich Ave., New York NY 10011. (212)243-8480. Estab. 1972. Member of AAR. Represents 200 clients. 10% of clients are new/unpublished writers. Specializes in literary fiction, commercial fiction, trade nonfiction. Currently handles: 35% nonfiction books; 55% novels; 10% juvenile books. Member agents: Geri Thoma, Sally Wofford-Girand, Elaine Markson.
Handles: Quality fiction and nonfiction. Query with outline (must include SASE). SASE is required for the return of any material.
Recent Sales: *George Burns*, by Martin Gottfried (Simon & Schuster); *The Sword of General England*, by Donald Honig (Scribner); *Biography of Nelson Rockefeller*, by Carry Reich.
Terms: Agent receives 15% commission on domestic sales; 20% on foreign sales. Charges for postage, photocopying, foreign mailing, faxing, long-distance telephone and other special expenses. "Please make sure manuscript weighs no more than 1 lb."

THE MARTELL AGENCY, (III), 545 Fifth Ave., Suite 1900, New York NY 10017. (212)317-2672. Contact: Stephen Williamson or Alice Fried Martell. Estab. 1984. Represents 75 clients. Currently handles: 65% nonfiction books; 35% novels.
Handles: Nonfiction books, novels. Considers all nonfiction areas. Considers most fiction areas. No science fiction or poetry. Query with outline plus 2 sample chapters and SASE. Reports in 3 weeks on queries, only if interested. Does *not* return submitted material.
Recent Sales: Untitled history of the rise and fall of Schwinn, by Glenn Coleman and Judith Crown (Holt).
Terms: Agent receives 15% commission on domestic sales; 20% on foreign sales. Offers written contract, binding for 1 year. Charges for foreign postage, photocopying, messenger services.
Tips: Usually obtains new clients by recommendations from agents and editors.

HAROLD MATSON CO. INC., 276 Fifth Ave., New York NY 10001. This agency did not respond to our request for information. Query before submitting.

‡TONI MENDEZ INC., (III), 141 E. 56th St., New York NY 10022. (212)838-6740. Fax: (212)755-5170. Contact: Toni Mendez.
Handles: Nonfiction books, juvenile books, newspaper syndication cartoons and columns. Send query with SASE. No unsolicited manuscripts.
Terms: Charges for photocopying and postage.
Tips: Obtains new clients through referrals.

METROPOLITAN TALENT AGENCY, (III), 4526 Wilshire Blvd., Los Angeles CA 90010. (213)857-4500. Fax: (213)857-4599. Contact: Andy Howard. Estab. 1990. Signatory of WGA. 20% of clients are new/previously unpublished writers. Specializes in feature film, TV rights, novels, screenplays, stories for the big screen or TV. Currently handles: 10% nonfiction books; 10% novels; 10% novellas; 50% movie scripts; 10% TV scripts; 10% short story collections.
 ● See the expanded listing for this agency in Script Agents.

DORIS S. MICHAELS LITERARY AGENCY, INC., (I), One Lincoln Plaza, Suite 29R, New York NY 10023-7137. (212)769-2430. Contact: Doris S. Michaels. Estab. 1994. Member of WNBA. Represents 25 clients. 50% of clients are new/previously unpublished writers. Currently handles: 40% nonfiction books; 60% novels. Member agent: Dahlia Porter, assistant literary agent.
Handles: Nonfiction books, novels. Considers these nonfiction areas: biography/autobiography; business; current affairs; ethnic/cultural interests; health; history; how-to; money/finance/economics; music/dance/theater/film; nature/environment; self-help/personal improvement; sports; women's issues/women's studies. Considers these fiction areas: action/adventure; contemporary issues; family saga; feminist; historical; literary; mainstream. Query with SASE. No phone calls or unsolicited mss. Reports ASAP on queries with SASE; no answer without SASE.
Recent Sales: *The Dollar Bill Knows No Sex*, by Wendy Rue and Karin Abarbanel (McGraw-Hill, Inc.); *All We Know of Heaven*, by Anna Tuttle Villegas (St. Martin's Press); *The Neatest Little Guide to Mutual Fund Investing*, by Jason Kelly (Plume); *Memories of the Mick*, by Maury Allen (Taylor Publishing).
Terms: Agent receives 15% commission on domestic sales; 20% on foreign sales. Offers written contract, binding for 1 year, with 30 day cancellation clause. Charges for office expenses including postage, photocopying and fax. 100% of business is derived from commissions on sales.
Writers' Conferences: ABA (Chicago, June); Frankfurt Book Fair (Germany, October).
Tips: Obtains new clients through recommendations from others, solicitation and at conferences.

THE MILLER AGENCY, (III), ~~801 West End Ave., New York NY 10025.~~ *1650 Broadway #406 NY NY 10019* ~~(212)866-6110.~~ Fax: ~~(212)866-0068.~~ E-mail: 74123.726@compuserve.com. Contact: Angela Miller. Estab. 1990. Represents 100 clients. 5% of clients are new/previously unpublished writers. Specializes in nonfiction,

Tel (212)957-1933   fax(212)957-1953

multicultural arts, psychology, self-help, cookbooks, biography, travel, memoir, sports. Currently handles: 99% nonfiction books.

Handles: Nonfiction books. Considers these nonfiction areas: anthropology/archaeology; art/architecture/design; biography/autobiography; business; child guidance/parenting; cooking/food/nutrition; current affairs; ethnic/cultural interests; gay/lesbian issues; health/medicine; language/literature/criticism; New Age/metaphysics; psychology; self-help/personal improvement; sports; women's issues/women's studies. Send outline and sample chapters. Reports in 1 week on queries.

Recent Sales: *Sparring with Charlie*, by Christopher Hunt (Anchor/Doubleday); *A Boy Named Phyllis*, by Frank DeCass (Viking); *I.M. Pei: Mandarin of Modernism*, by Michael Cannell (Crown Publishers); *Mother of Immortal Bliss*, by Naomi Mann (Houghton Mifflin).

Terms: Agent receives 15% commission on domestic sales; 20-25% on foreign sales. Offers written contract, binding for 2-3 years, with 60 day cancellation clause. Charges for postage (express mail or messenger services) and photocopying. 100% of business is derived from commissions on fees.

Tips: Obtains new clients through referrals.

MOORE LITERARY AGENCY, (IV), 83 High St., Newburyport MA 01950. (508)465-9015. Contact: Claire Horne, Claudette Moore. Estab. 1989. 20% of clients are new/previously unpublished writers. Specializes in trade computer books. Currently handles: 100% computer-related books.

Handles: Computer books only. Send outline/proposal. Reports in 3 weeks on queries.

Recent Sales: *Systems Programming for Windows 95*, by Walt Oney; *Business Wisdom of the Electronic Elite*, by Geoffrey James.

Terms: Agent receives 15% commission on all sales. Offers written contract.

Writers' Conferences: ABA (Chicago); Comdex (Las Vegas).

Tips: Obtains new clients through recommendations/referrals and conferences.

MAUREEN MORAN AGENCY, (III), (formerly Donald MacCampbell, Inc.), Park West Station, P.O. Box 20191, New York NY 10025-1518. Phone/fax: (212)222-3838. E-mail: memoran@delphi.com. Contact: Maureen Moran. Estab. 1940. Represents 50 clients. "The agency does not handle unpublished writers." Specializes in women's book-length fiction in all categories. Currently handles: 100% novels.

Handles: Novels. Query with outline and SASE; does not read unsolicited mss. Reports in 1 week on queries.

Recent Sales: *Once More With Feeling*, by Emilie Richards (Avon); *Alpine Mysteries*, by Mary Daheim (Ballantine).

Terms: Agent receives 10% commission on domestic sales; 15-20% on foreign sales.

WILLIAM MORRIS AGENCY, (III), 1325 Avenue of the Americas, New York NY 10019. (212)586-5100. Estab. 1898. Contact: Literary Department. West Coast office: 151 El Camino Dr., Beverly Hills CA 90212. (310)274-7451. Member of AAR. Works with a small number of new/unpublished authors. Specializes in novels, nonfiction.

Terms: Agent receives 10% commission on domestic sales; 10% on dramatic sales; 20% on foreign sales.

HENRY MORRISON, INC., (II, III), 105 S. Bedford Rd., Suite 306A, Mt. Kisco NY 10549. (914)666-3500. Fax: (914)241-7846. Contact: Henry Morrison. Estab. 1965. Signatory of WGA. Represents 48 clients. 5% of clients are new/previously unpublished writers. Currently handles: 5% nonfiction books; 5% juvenile books; 85% novels; 5% movie scripts.

Handles: Nonfiction books, novels. Considers these nonfiction areas: anthropology/archaeology; biography; government/politics/law; history; juvenile nonfiction. Considers these fiction areas: action/adventure; detective/police/crime; family saga. Query. Reports in 2 weeks on queries; 3 months on mss.

Recent Sales: *The Apocalypse Watch*, by Robert Ludlum; *Extreme Denial*, by David Morrell; *Choosers of the Slain*, by James Cobb (G.P. Putnam's Sons); *Last Rights*, by Philip Shelby.

Terms: Agent receives 15% commission on domestic sales; 20% on foreign sales. Charges for ms copies, bound galleys and finished books for submission to publishers, movie producers, foreign publishers.

Tips: Obtains new clients through recommendations from others.

MULTIMEDIA PRODUCT DEVELOPMENT, INC., (III), 410 S. Michigan Ave., Suite 724, Chicago IL 60605-1465. (312)922-3063. President: Jane Jordan Browne. Estab. 1971. Member of AAR, RWA, MWA, SCBWI. Represents 175 clients. 5% of clients are new/previously unpublished writers. "We are generalists." Currently handles: 60% nonfiction books; 8% juvenile books; 30% novels; 1% scholarly books; 1% textbooks. Member agent: Danielle Egan-Miller.

• Prior to opening her agency Ms. Browne served as the managing editor, then as head of the juvenile department for Hawthorn Books, senior editor for Thomas Y. Crowell, adult trade department and general editorial and production manager for Macmillan Educational Services, Inc.

Handles: Nonfiction books, novels. Considers these nonfiction areas: agriculture/horticulture; animals; anthropology/archaeology; biography/autobiography; business; child guidance/parenting; cooking/food/nutrition; crafts/hobbies; current affairs; ethnic/cultural issues; health/medicine; how-to; humor; juvenile nonfiction; money/finance; nature; popular culture; psychology; religious/inspirational; science/technology; self-help/personal improvement; sociology; sports; true crime/investigative; women's issues/women's studies. Considers these fiction areas: contemporary issues; detective/police/crime; ethnic; family saga; glitz; historical; juvenile; literary; mainstream; mystery/suspense; picture book; religious/inspirational; romance (contemporary, gothic, historical, regency, western); sports; thriller/espionage. Query "by mail with SASE required." Reports within 1 week on queries; 6 weeks on mss.

Recent Sales: *The Atonement Child*, by Francine Rivers (Tyndale House); *Planet Baywatch: Unofficial Guide to the New World Order*, by Brendan Baber and Eric Spitznagel (Michael O'Mara Books [UK]/St. Martin's Press); *The Healing Power of Peppers*, by Dave DeWitt, Melissa T. Stock and Kellye Hunler (Clarkson Potter); *A Deadly Harvest*, by Leonard Goldberg (Dutton).

Terms: Agent receives 15% commission on domestic sales; 20% on foreign sales. Offers written contract, binding for 2 years. Charges for photocopying, overseas postage, faxes, phone calls.

Writers' Conferences: ABA (Chicago, June); Frankfurt Book Fair (Frankfurt, October); RWA (Anaheim CA, July).

Tips: Obtains new clients through "referrals, queries by professional, marketable authors. If interested in agency representation, be well informed."

DEE MURA ENTERPRISES, INC., (II), 269 West Shore Dr., Massapequa NY 11758-8225. (516)795-1616. Fax: (516)795-8797. E-mail: samurai5@ix.netcom.com. Contact: Dee Mura. Estab. 1987. Signatory of WGA. 50% of clients are new/previously unpublished writers. "We work on everything, but are especially interested in true life stories, true crime and women's stories and issues." Currently handles: 20% nonfiction books; 15% scholarly books; 15% juvenile books; 20% novels; 15% movie scripts; 15% TV scripts.

Handles: Nonfiction books, scholarly books, juvenile books. Considers these nonfiction areas: agriculture/horticulture; animals; anthropology/archaeology; biography/autobiography; business; child guidance/parenting; computers/electronics; current affairs; education; ethnic/cultural interests; gay/lesbian issues; government/politics/law; health/medicine; history; how-to; humor; juvenile nonfiction; military/war; money/finance/economics; nature/environment; science/technology; self-help/personal improvement; sociology; sports; true crime/investigative; women's issues/women's studies. Considers these fiction areas: action/adventure; contemporary issues; detective/police/crime; ethnic; experimental; family saga; fantasy; feminist; gay; glitz; historical; humor/satire; juvenile; lesbian; literary; mainstream; mystery/suspense; psychic/supernatural; regional; romance (contemporary, gothic, historical, regency); science fiction; sports; thriller/espionage; westerns/frontier; young adult. Query. Reports in approximately 2 weeks on queries.

Terms: Agent receives 15% commission on domestic sales; 20-25% on foreign sales. Offers written contract. Charges for photocopying and mailing expenses directly pertaining to writer.

Also Handles: Movie scripts (feature film, documentary, animation), TV scripts (TV mow, miniseries, episodic drama, sitcom, variety show, animation). Considers these script subject areas: action/adventure; cartoon/animation; comedy; contemporary issues; detective/police/crime; family saga; fantasy; feminist; gay; glitz; historical; horror; humor; juvenile; mainstream; mystery/suspense; psychic/supernatural; religious/inspirational; romantic comedy and drama; science fiction; sports; teen; thriller; western/frontier.

Tips: Obtains new clients through recommendations from others. Query solicitation. "Please include a paragraph on writer's background even if writer has no literacy background and a brief synopsis of the project. We enjoy well-written query letters that tell us about the project and the author."

JEAN V. NAGGAR LITERARY AGENCY, (III), 216 E. 75th St., Suite 1E, New York NY 10021. (212)794-1082. Contact: Jean Naggar. Estab. 1978. Member of AAR. Represents 100 clients. 20% of clients are new/previously unpublished writers. Currently handles: 35% general nonfiction books; 5% scholarly books; 15% juvenile books; 45% novels. Member agents: Frances Kuffel; agent-at-large: Anne Engel (nonfiction).

Handles: Nonfiction books, novels. Considers these nonfiction areas among others: biography/autobiography; child guidance/parenting; current affairs; government/politics/law; health/medicine; history; juvenile nonfiction; New Age/metaphysics; psychology; religious/inspirational; self-help/personal improvement; sociology; women's issues/women's studies. "We would, of course, consider a query regarding an exceptional mainstream manuscript touching on any area." Considers these fiction areas: action/adventure; contemporary issues; detective/police/crime; ethnic; family saga; feminist; historical; literary; mainstream; mystery/suspense; psychic/supernatural; thriller/espionage. Query. Reports in 24 hours on queries; approximately 2 months on mss.

Recent Sales: *The Return*, by Joe De Mers (Dutton/Signet); *Cheevey*, by Gerald de Pego (Little Brown) *Breach of Trust*, by Bonnie MacDougal (Pocket Books); *Virus, Ground Zero* (nonfiction) by Ed Regis (Warner).
Terms: Agent receives 15% commission on domestic sales; 20% on foreign sales. Offers written contract. Charges for overseas mailing; messenger services; book purchases; long-distance telephone; photocopying. "These are deductible from royalties received."
Writers' Conferences: Willamette Writers Conference; Pacific Northwest Writers Conference; Breadloaf Writers Conference; Virginia Women's Press Conference (Richmond VA).
Tips: Obtains new clients through "recommendations from publishers, editors, clients and others, and from writers' conferences. Use a professional presentation. Because of the avalanche of unsolicited queries that flood the agency every week, we have had to modify our policy. We will now only guarantee to read and respond to queries from writers who come recommended by someone we know. Our areas are general fiction and nonfiction, no children's books by unpublished writers, no multimedia, no screenplays, no formula fiction, no mysteries by unpublished writers."

RUTH NATHAN, (II), 80 Fifth Ave., Room 706, New York NY 10011. Phone/fax: (212)675-6063. Estab. 1980. Member of AAR. Represents 12 clients. 5% of clients are new/previously unpublished writers. Specializes in art, decorative arts, fine art; theater; film; show business. Currently handles: 90% nonfiction books; 10% novels.
Handles: Nonfiction books, novels. Considers these nonfiction areas: art/architecture/design; biography/autobiography; theater/film; true crime/investigative. Considers some historical fiction. Query. Reports in 2 weeks on queries; 1 month on mss.
Recent Sales: *A Book of Days*, by Stephen Risulle (Macmillan London); *A Dangerous Gift*, by Claudia Crawford (Dutton); *Faking It*, by K.J. Lane (Harry Abrams).
Terms: Agent receives 15% commission on domestic sales; 20% on foreign sales. Charges for office expenses, postage, photocopying, etc.
Tips: "Read carefully what my requirements are before wasting your time and mine."

‡NATIONAL WRITERS LITERARY AGENCY, a division of NWA, (II, IV), 1450 S. Havana St., Suite 424, Aurora CO 80012. (303)751-7844. Fax: (303)751-8593. E-mail: aajw iii@aol.com. Contact: Andrew J. Whelchel III (childrens, nonfiction), Sandy Whelchel (novels, nonfiction). Estab. 1987. Represents 16 clients. 50% of clients are new/previously unpublished writers. Currently handles: 18% nonfiction books; 32% juvenile books; 40% novels; 5% novellas; 5% poetry.
Handles: Nonfiction books, juvenile books, textbooks. Considers these nonfiction areas: animals; biography/autobiography (famous only); child guidance/parenting; education; government/politics/law; how-to; juvenile nonfiction; popular culture; science/technology; sports. Considers these fiction areas: action/adventure; juvenile; mainstream; picture book; science fiction; sports; young adult. Query with outline and 3 sample chapters. Reports in 1-2 weeks on queries; 1-2 months on mss.
Terms: Agent receives 12% commission on domestic sales; 15% on foreign sales. Offers written contract, binding for 1 year with 30-day termination notice. "We charge a maximum of $25 per quarter for postage and copies, irregardless of number of submissions (i.e., If it costs $3x30 sub per quarter we only charge $25.).
Writers' Conferences: National Writers Assn. (Denver, CO, 2nd weekend in June); Sandpiper (Miami, FL, 1st weekend in October); Pikes Peak Writers (Colorado Springs, CO, April).
Tips: Obtains new clients at conferences or over the transom. "Query letters should include a great hook just as if you only had a few seconds to impress us. A professional package gets professional attention. Always include return postage!"

KAREN NAZOR LITERARY AGENCY, (II, III), Opera Plaza, 601 Van Ness Ave., Suite E3124, San Francisco CA 94102. (415)648-2281. Fax: (415)648-2348. E-mail: agentnazor@aol.com (queries only). Contact: Karen Nazor. Estab. 1991. Represents 35 clients. 15% of clients are new/previously unpublished writers. Specializes in "good writers! Mostly nonfiction—arts, culture, politics, technology, civil rights, etc." Currently handles: 75% nonfiction books; 10% electronic; 10% fiction.
Handles: Nonfiction books, novels, novellas. Considers these nonfiction areas: biography; business; computers/electronics; cooking/food; current affairs; ethnic/cultural interests; gay/lesbian issues; government/politics/law; history; how-to; music/dance/theater/film; nature/environment; photography; popular culture; science/technology; sociology; sports; travel; women's issues/women's studies. Considers these fiction areas: action/adventure; cartoon/comic; contemporary issues; ethnic; feminist; literary; regional. Query (preferred) or send outline/proposal (accepted). Reports in 2 weeks on queries; up to 2 months on mss.
Recent Sales: *LA Bizarro*, by Matt Maranian and Tony Lovett (St. Martin's); *BOTS: The Origin of New Species*, by Andrew Leonard (Hardwired); *Ebets Field*, by Bob McGee (Norton); *Moving to San Francisco*, by Christina Guinot (Prima).
Terms: Agent receives 15% commission on domestic sales; 20% on foreign sales. Offers written contract. Charges for express mail services and photocopying costs.

Tips: Referrals from editors and writers; online; teaching classes on publishing; newspaper article on agency. "I'm interested in writers that want a long term, long haul relationship. Not a one-book writer, but a writer who has many ideas, is productive, professional, passionate and meets deadlines!"

NEW BRAND AGENCY GROUP, (I), (a division of Alter Entertainment LLC), 205 Wildberry Lane, Nashville TN 37209. (615)353-8829. Fax: (615)353-0372. E-mail: agentnb@aol.com. Contact: Eric Alterman. Estab. 1994. Represents 30 clients. 80% of clients are new/previously unpublished writers. "Focus is on mainstream and topical materials." Currently handles: 50% novels, 50% nonfiction.
Handles: Novels. Considers these nonfiction areas: biography/autobiography; education; how-to; humor; military/war; popular culture; religious/inspirational; sports. Considers these fiction areas: action/adventure; contemporary issues; detective/police/crime; fantasy; horror; humor/satire; literary; mainstream; mystery/suspense; religious/inspirational; romance; science fiction; sports; thriller/espionage. Query with outline, 3 sample chapters and SASE. Reports in 3 weeks.
Recent Sales: *The Complete Book of the Shelter Dog*, by Myrna Weibel, D.V.M. (Barron's Educational Series); *Hero*, by Susan L. Rottman (Peachtree Publishing).
Terms: Agent receives 15% commission on domestic sales; 15-20% on foreign sales. Offers written contract, binding for 4-12 months, with 30 day cancellation clause. 100% of business is derived from commissions on sales.
Tips: Obtains new clients from recommendations, online discussions and magazine advertisement. "Don't let negative experiences influence your new relationships, particularly with respect to agents."

NEW ENGLAND PUBLISHING ASSOCIATES, INC., (II), P.O. Box 5, Chester CT 06412-0645. (203)345-READ and (203)345-4976. Fax: (203)345-3660. E-mail: nepa@nepa.com. Contact: Elizabeth Frost Knappman, Edward W. Knappman. Estab. 1983. Member of AAR. Represents over 100 clients. 15% of clients are new/previously unpublished writers. Specializes in adult nonfiction books of serious purpose.
Handles: Nonfiction books. Considers these nonfiction areas: biography/autobiography; business; child guidance/parenting; government/politics/law; health/medicine; history; language/literature/criticism; military/war; money/finance/economics; nature/environment; psychology; science/technology; personal improvement; sociology; true crime/investigative; women's issues/women's studies. "Occasionally publish crime fiction." Send outline/proposal. Reports in 3 weeks on queries; 5 weeks on mss.
Recent Sales: *Eudora Welty*, by Ann Waldron (Doubleday); *The Importance of Being Different*, by Robert Sherril (Crown); *Dictionary of Art*, by Nancy Frazier (Penguin); *The Prettiest Feathers, A Golden Feather* (crime fiction) and *Stalemate* (true crime), by John Philpin (Bantam); *Susan Sontag*, by Carl Rollyson and Lisa Paddock.
Terms: Agent receives 15% commission on domestic sales; 20% foreign sales (split with overseas agent). Offers written contract, binding for 6 months.
Writers' Conferences: ABA (Chicago, June); ALA (San Antonio, January); ALA (New York, July).
Tips: "Send us a well-written proposal that clearly identifies your audience—who will buy this book and why."

NINE MUSES AND APOLLO INC., (II), 2 Charlton St., New York NY 10014-4909. (212)243-0065. Contact: Ling Lucas. Estab. 1991. Represents 100 clients. 50% of clients are new/previously unpublished writers. Specializes in nonfiction. Currently handles: 90% nonfiction books; 10% novels. Member agents: Ling Lucas, Ed Vesneske, Jr.
• Ms. Lucas formerly served as a vice president, sales & marketing director and associate publisher of Warner Books. Mr. Vesneske was formerly an independent editor.
Handles: Nonfiction books. Considers these nonfiction areas: animals; biography/autobiography; business; current affairs; ethnic/cultural interests; gay/lesbian issues; government/politics/law; health/medicine; history; humor/satire; language/literature/criticism; psychology; science/technology; spirituality; women's issues/women's studies. Considers these fiction areas: commercial; ethnic; literary; mainstream. Send outline, 3 sample chapters and SASE. Reports in 1 month on mss.
Recent Sales: *The Unofficial X-Files Companion*, by N.E. Genge (Crown Publishing); *Tracks in the Wilderness of Dreaming*, by Robert Bosnak (Delacorte).
Terms: Agent receives 15% commission on domestic sales; 20-25% on foreign sales. Offers written contract. Charges for photocopying proposals and mss.
Tips: "Your outline should already be well developed, cogent, and reveal clarity of thought about the general structure and direction of your project."

THE BETSY NOLAN LITERARY AGENCY, (II), 224 W. 29th St., 15th Floor, New York NY 10001. (212)967-8200. Fax: (212)967-7292. President: Betsy Nolan. Estab. 1980. Represents 200 clients. 10% of clients are new/unpublished writers. Works with a small number of new/unpublished

authors. Currently handles: 90% nonfiction books; 10% novels. Member agents: Donald Lehr, Carla Glasser, Ellen Morrissey.
Handles: Nonfiction books. Query with outline. Reports in 3 weeks on queries; 2 months on mss.
Recent Sales: *Why I Am A Democrat*, by Theodore Sorenson (Holt); *Cooking With Too Hot Tamales* (Morrow).
Terms: Agent receives 15% commission on domestic sales; 20% on foreign sales.

THE NORMA-LEWIS AGENCY, (II), 360 W. 53rd St., Suite B-A, New York NY 10019-5720. (212)664-0807. Contact: Norma Liebert. Estab. 1980. 50% of clients are new/previously unpublished writers. Specializes in juvenile books (pre-school-high school). Currently handles: 60% juvenile books; 40% adult books.
Handles: Juvenile and adult nonfiction and fiction, miniseries, documentaries, movie scripts, TV scripts, radio scripts, stage plays. Considers these nonfiction areas: art/architecture/design; biography/autobiography; child guidance/parenting; cooking/food/nutrition; crafts/hobbies; current affairs; ethnic/cultural interests; government/politics/law; health/medicine; history; juvenile nonfiction; music/dance/theater/film; nature/environment; photography; popular culture; self-help/personal improvement; true crime/investigative; women's issues/women's studies. Considers these fiction areas: action/adventure; contemporary issues; detective/police/crime; family saga; historical; horror; humor/satire; juvenile; mainstream; mystery/suspense; picture book; romance (contemporary, gothic, historical, regency); thriller/espionage; westerns/frontier; young adult. Reports in 6 weeks.
Recent Sales: *Viper Quarry* and *Pitchfork Hollow*, both by Dean Feldmayer (Pocket Books).
Terms: Agent receives 15% commission on domestic sales; 20% on foreign sales.

NUGENT LITERARY, (III), 170 Tenth St. N, Naples FL 34102. Phone/fax: (941)262-3683. Contact: Ray Nugent. Estab. 1976. Represents 15 clients. No new previously unpublished writers. Specializes in nonfiction. Currently handles: 90% nonfiction books, 10% fiction.
Handles: Nonfiction books. Considers these nonfiction areas: biography/autobiography; health/medicine; true crime/investigative. Query. Reports in 1 month on queries; 2 months on mss.
Recent Sales: *Evil Web*, by Jose (New Horizon); *Winning with Arthritis*, by Debbie Bruce (John Wiley).
Terms: Agent receives 20% commission on domestic sales; 25% on foreign sales. Offers written contract, binding for 1 year. 100% of business derived from commission on sales.
Tips: Obtains new clients through referrals.

‡THE OASIS LITERARY AGENCY, (V), 832 Echo Rd., Vestal NY 13850. E-mail: chapin@spectra.net. Contact: Julie E. Chapin. Estab. 1996. Represents 10 clients. 80% of clients are new/previously unpublished writers. Currently handles: 100% novels.
Handles: Novels. Considers these fiction areas: fantasy; historical; mystery/suspense; religious/inspirational (Christian fiction); romance (gothic, historical); science fiction. Not currently accepting new clients.
Terms: Agent receives 15% commission on domestic sales; 20% on foreign sales. Offers written contract with a 30 day cancellation clause.

HAROLD OBER ASSOCIATES, (III), 425 Madison Ave., New York NY 10017. (212)759-8600. Fax: (212)759-9428. Estab. 1929. Member of AAR. Represents 250 clients. 10% of clients are new/previously unpublished writers. Currently handles: 35% nonfiction books; 15% juvenile books; 50% novels. Member agents: Phyllis Westberg, Henry Dunow, Wendy Schmalz, Anne Edelstein.
Handles: Nonfiction books, juvenile books, novels. Considers all nonfiction and fiction subjects. Query letter *only*; faxed queries are not read. Reports in 1 week on queries; 3 weeks on mss.
Terms: Agent receives 15% commission on domestic sales; 20% on foreign sales. Charges for photocopying and express mail or package services.
Tips: Obtains new clients through recommendations from others.

FIFI OSCARD AGENCY INC., (II), 24 W. 40th St., New York NY 10018. (212)764-1100. Contact: Ivy Fischer Stone, Literary Department. Estab. 1956. Member of AAR, signatory of WGA. Represents 108 clients. 5% of clients are new/unpublished writers. "Writer must have published articles or books in major markets or have screen credits if movie scripts, etc." Specializes in literary novels, commercial novels, mysteries and nonfiction, especially celebrity biographies and autobiographies. Currently handles: 40% nonfiction books; 40% novels; 5% movie scripts; 5% stage plays; 10% TV scripts.
Handles: Nonfiction books, novels, movie scripts, stage plays. Query with outline. Reports in 1 week on queries if SASE enclosed.
Recent Sales: *The Return*, by William Shatner (Pocket Books); *Calendar of Wisdom*, by Leo Tolstoy, translated by Peter Sekirin (Scribner); *Autopsy On An Empire*, by Jack Matlock, Jr. (Random House).
Terms: Agent receives 15% commission on domestic sales; 10% on dramatic sales; 20% on foreign sales. Charges for photocopying expenses.

OTITIS MEDIA, (II), 1926 DuPont Ave. S., Minneapolis MN 55403. (612)377-4918. Fax: (612)377-3096. Contact: Hannibal Harris. Signatory of WGA. Currently handles: novels; movie scripts; stage plays; TV scripts. Member agents: Hannibal Harris (queries, evaluation of proposals, books); Greg Boylan (screenplays, TV scripts); Ingrid DiLeonardo (script and ms evaluation, story development); B.R. Boylan (novels, nonfiction, screenplays, stage plays).
● See the expanded listing for this agency in Script Agents.

THE PALMER & DODGE AGENCY, (III), One Beacon St., Boston MA 02108. (617)573-0100. Fax: (617)227-4420. E-mail: ssilva@palmerdodge.com. Contact: Sharon Silva-Hamberson. Estab. 1990. Represents 100 clients. 5% of clients are new/previously unpublished writers. Specializes in trade nonfiction and quality fiction for adults. No genre fiction. Dramatic rights for books and life story rights only. Currently handles: 80% nonfiction books; 20% novels. Member agents: John Taylor (Ike) Williams, director (books, film, TV); Jill Kneerim, managing director (books); Elaine Rogers, director of subsidiary rights (dramatic rights, foreign, audio); Sandy Missakian, Assistant Director Subsidiary Rights (dramatic rights, foreign, audio). Currently handles: nonfiction books; novels.
Handles: Nonfiction books, novels. Considers these nonfiction areas: anthropology/archaeology; biography/autobiography; business; child guidance/parenting; current affairs; education; ethnic/cultural interests; gay/lesbian issues; government/politics/law; health/medicine; history; language/literature/criticism; money/finance/economics; music/dance/theater/film; nature/environment; New Age/metaphysics; popular culture; psychology; religous/inspirational; science/technology; self-help/personal improvement; sociology; women's issues/women's studies. Considers these fiction areas: contemporary issues; ethnic; feminist; gay; literary; mainstream. Query with outline/proposal. Reports in 2 weeks on queries; 3 months on mss.
Terms: Agent receives 15% commission on domestic sales; 20% on foreign sales. Offers written contract, with 4 month cancellation clause. Charges for direct expenses (postage, phone, photocopying, messenger service). 100% of business is derived from commissions on sales.
Tips: Obtains new clients through recommendations from others. "We are taking very few new clients for representation."

PARAVIEW, INC., (II, III), 1674 Broadway, Suite 4B, New York NY 10019. E-mail: jfparaview@aol.com. Contact: Justin E. Fernandez. Estab. 1988. Represents 80 clients. 50% of clients are new/previously unpublished writers. Specializes in spiritual, New Age and paranormal. Currently handles: 80% nonfiction books; 10% scholarly books; 9% fiction; 1% poetry. Member agents: Sandra Martin; Justin Fernandez (general); Leonard Belzer (nonfiction); Julie Starke (general).
Handles: Nonfiction and fiction books. Considers all nonfiction areas. Considers these fiction areas: action/adventure; contemporary issues; erotica; ethnic; fantasy; feminist; gay; historical; literary; mainstream; psychic/supernatural; regional; romance; science fiction; thriller/espionage. Query with synopsis and an author bio. "Electronic queries and submissions reduce reporting time and are encouraged." Reports in 1 month on queries; 3 months on mss.
Recent Sales: *A Closer Walk*, by Dr. William McGary (ARE Press); *Sexy Hexes*, by Lexa Rosian (St. Martin's Press); *Psychic Warriors*, by David Morehouse, Ph.D. (St. Martin's Press); *Alien Agenda*, by Jim Marrs (HarperCollins); *Talking To Heaven*, by James Von Praagh (Penguin); *101 Places To Flirt*, by Susan Rabin (Dutton).
Terms: Agent receives 15% commission on domestic sales; 20% on foreign sales.
Also Handles: Movie scripts (feature film, documentary); TV scripts (sitcom, syndicated material). Considers all script areas. Considers "multimedia and Internet-related work in all subject areas."
Writers' Conferences: ABA (Chicago, June); E3—Electronic Entertainment Exposition.
Tips: Obtains new clients through recommendations from editors mostly. "New writers should have their work edited, critiqued and carefully reworked prior to submission. First contact should be via e-mail or regular mail."

THE RICHARD PARKS AGENCY, (III), 138 E. 16th St., 5th Floor, New York NY 10003. (212)254-9067. Contact: Richard Parks. Estab. 1988. Member of AAR. Currently handles: 50% nonfiction books; 5% young adult books; 40% novels; 5% short story collections.
● Prior to opening his agency, Mr. Parks served as an agent with Curtis Brown, Ltd.
Handles: Nonfiction books, novels. Considers these nonfiction areas: animals; anthropology/archaeology; art/architecture/design; biography/autobiography; business; child guidance/parenting; cooking/

ALWAYS INCLUDE a self-addressed, stamped envelope (SASE) for reply or return of your manuscript.

food/nutrition; crafts/hobbies; current affairs; ethnic/cultural interests; gay/lesbian issues; government/ politics; health/medicine; history; horticulture; how-to; humor; language/literature/criticism; military/ war; money/finance/economics; music/dance/theater/film; nature/environment; popular culture; psychology; science/technology; self-help/personal improvement; sociology; women's issues/women's studies. Considers fiction by referral only. Query with SASE. "We will not accept any unsolicited material." Reports in 2 weeks on queries.

Recent Sales: *As She Climbed Across the Table*, by Jonathan Lethem (Doubleday); *Seven Cats and the Art of Living*, by Jo Coudert (Warner Books); *The Guardian*, by Bill Eidson (Forge).

Terms: Agent receives 15% commission on domestic sales; 20% on foreign sales. Charges for photocopying or any unusual expense incurred at the writer's request.

Tips: Obtains new clients through recommendations and referrals.

KATHI J. PATON LITERARY AGENCY, (II), 19 W. 55th St., New York NY 10019-4907. (212)265-6586. Fax: call first. Contact: Kathi Paton. Estab. 1987. Specializes in adult nonfiction. Currently handles: 65% nonfiction books; 35% fiction.

Handles: Nonfiction, novels, short story collections. Considers these nonfiction areas: business; child guidance/parenting; how-to; nature/environment; psychology; sociology; women's issues/women's studies. Considers literary and mainstream fiction; short stories. For nonfiction, send proposal, sample chapter and SASE. For fiction, send first 40 pages and plot summary or 3 short stories.

Recent Sales: *Total Quality Corporation*, by McInereyx White (Dutton); *White Trash, Red Velvet*, by Donald Secreast (HarperCollins); *The Home Environmental Sourcebook*, by Andrew Davis and Paul Schuffman (Holt).

Terms: Agent receives 15% commission on domestic sales; 20% on foreign sales. Offers written contract. Charges for photocopying.

Writers' Conferences: Attends International Womens Writing Guild panels and the Pacific Northwest Writers Conference.

Tips: Usually obtains new clients through recommendations from other clients. "Write well."

THE RICHARD PAUL LITERATI, (IV), 58 Duke Ellington Blvd., Suite 1B, New York NY 10025-3855. (212)665-8316. Fax: (212)665-8317. E-mail: rpliterati@aol.com. Contact: Richard Aloia Jr. Estab. 1993. Represents 13 clients. 90% of clients are new/previously unpublished writers. "Must have advanced writing degree or referral." Specializes in aggressively written fiction. Currently handles: 15% nonfiction books; 85% novels.

● Prior to opening his agency, Mr. Aloia was an agent in the literary department of International Creative Management, Inc.

Handles: Nonfiction books, novels. Considers all nonfiction areas, "especially topics with commercial appeal." Considers these fiction areas: contemporary issues; erotica; ethnic; experimental; family saga; gay; humor/satire; lesbian; literary; mainstream; regional. Exclusive query with adequate SASE. Reports in 2 weeks on queries; 1 month on mss.

Terms: Agent receives 15% commission on domestic sales; 20% on foreign sales. Offers written contract. Charges for international postage and international phone expenses. 100% of business is derived from commissions on sales.

Tips: Obtains new clients through recommendations from clients, professional writing instructors, graduate writing program recruitment visits and queries. "This is a very small, highly selective agency, specializing in outstanding fiction."

PELHAM LITERARY AGENCY, (I), 2290 E. Fremont Ave., Suite C, Littleton CO 80122. (303)347-0623. Contact: Howard Pelham. Estab. 1994. Represents 10 clients. 50% of clients are new/ previously unpublished writers. Specializes in genre fiction. Owner has published 15 novels in these categories. Currently handles: 10% nonfiction books; 80% novels; 10% short story collections.

Handles: Novels, short story collections. Considers these fiction areas: action/adventure; detective/ police/crime; fantasy; horror; literary; mainstream; romance (contemporary, gothic, historical); science fiction; sports; thriller/espionage; westerns/frontier. Send outline and sample chapters or query with description of novel or manuscript. Reports in 3 weeks on queries; 2 months on mss.

Recent Sales: *Death of A Gun Slinger*, by Howard Pelham (Thomas E. Bourgy).

Terms: Agent receives 15% commission on domestic sales; 20% on foreign sales. Offers written contract, with 30 day cancellation clause. Charges $50 processing free for copying, postage. 100% of business is derived from commissions on sales.

Writers' Conferences: Rocky Mountain Book Fair.

Tips: "Most of my clients have been from recommendation by other writers. Don't submit a manuscript until the writer has written it as professionally as he can achieve."

RODNEY PELTER, (II), 129 E. 61st St., New York NY 10021. (212)838-3432. Contact: Rodney Pelter. Estab. 1978. Represents 10 clients. Currently handles: 25% nonfiction books; 75% novels.

Handles: Nonfiction books, novels. Considers all nonfiction areas. Considers most fiction areas. No juvenile, romance, science fiction. Query with SASE. No unsolicited mss. Reports in 3 months.
Terms: Agent receives 15% commission on domestic sales; 20% on foreign sales. Offers written contract. Charges for foreign postage, photocopying.
Tips: Usually obtains new clients through recommendations from others.

PERKINS ASSOCIATES, (IV), 5800 Arlington Ave., Riverdale NY 10471-1419. (718)543-5354 and (212)304-1607. Fax: (718)543-5355 and (212)569-8188. Contact: Lori Perkins, Peter Rubie. Estab. 1990. Member of AAR, HWA. Represents 100 clients. 15% of clients are new/previously unpublished writers. Perkins specializes in horror, dark thrillers, literary fiction, pop culture, Latino and gay issues (fiction and nonfiction). Rubie specializes in science fiction, fantasy, off-beat mysteries, history, literary fiction, dark thrillers, journalistic nonfiction. Currently handles: 60% nonfiction books; 40% novels.
  • Mr. Rubie is the author of *The Elements of Storytelling* (John Wiley).
Handles: Nonfiction books, novels. Considers these nonfiction areas: art/architecture/design; current affairs; ethnic/cultural interests; music/dance/theater/film; "subjects that fall under pop culture—TV, music, art, books and authors, film, current affairs etc." Considers these fiction areas: detective/police/crime; ethnic; fantasy; horror; literary; mainstream; mystery/suspense; psychic/supernatural; science fiction; dark thriller. Query with SASE. Reports immediately on queries with SASE; 10 weeks on mss.
Recent Sales: *Song of the Banshee*, by Greg Kihn (Forge); *Light & Shadow*, by K. Ramsland (Harper); *Godzilla; The Unofficial Biography*, by S. Ryfle (Delta); *Keeper*, by Gregory Rucka (Bantam); *Witchunter*, by C. Lyons (Avon); *How the Tiger Lost Its Stripes*, by C. Meacham (Harcourt Brace).
Terms: Agent receives 15% commission on domestic sales; 20% on foreign sales. Offers written contract, only "if requested." Charges for photocopying.
Writers' Conferences: Horror Writers of America Conference; World Fantasy Conference; Necon and Lunacon; Southwest Writers Conference; MidAtlantic Writers Conference; ABA; Cape Cod Writers Conference, Oklahoma short course (Norman OK); Midwest Writers (Muncie IN).
Tips: Obtains new clients through recommendations from others, solicitation, at conferences, etc. "Sometimes I come up with book ideas and find authors (*Coupon Queen*, for example). Be professional. Read *Publishers Weekly* and genre-related magazines. Join writers' organizations. Go to conferences. Know your market and learn your craft."

STEPHEN PEVNER, INC., (II), 248 W. 73rd St., 2nd Floor, New York NY 10023. (212)496-0474. Fax: (212)496-0796. E-mail: spevner@aol.com. Contact: Stephen Pevner. Estab. 1991. Member of AAR, signatory of WGA. Represents under 50 clients. 50% of clients are new/previously unpublished writers. Specializes in motion pictures, novels, humor, pop culture, urban fiction, independent filmmakers. Currently handles: 25% nonfiction books; 25% movie scripts; 25% novels; TV scripts; stage plays.
Handles: Nonfiction books, novels, movie scripts, TV scripts, stage plays. Considers these nonfiction areas: art/architecture/design; biography/autobiography; business; cooking/food/nutrition; current affairs; ethnic/cultural interests; gay/lesbian issues; government/politics/law; history; humor; language/literature/criticism; money/finance/economics; music/dance/theater/film; New Age/metaphysics; photography; popular culture; religious/inspirational; science/technology; sociology. Considers these fiction areas: action/adventure; cartoon/comic; contemporary issues; detective/police/crime; erotica; ethnic; experimental; gay; glitz; horror; humor/satire; lesbian; literary; mainstream; psychic/supernatural; science fiction; thriller/espionage; urban. Query with outline/proposal. Reports in 2 weeks on queries; 1 month on mss.
Recent Sales: *Welcome to the Dollhouse*, by Todd Solondz (Faber & Faber); *Noise From the Underground: The Secret History of Alternative Rock*, by Michael Lavine, Henry Rollins and Pat Blashill (Simon & Schuster); *The Cross-Referenced Guide to the Baby Buster Generations Collective Unconscious*, by Glenn Gaslin and Rick Porter (Putnam/Berkley); *The Lesbian Brain*, by The Five Lesbian Brothers (Simon & Schuster).
Terms: Agent receives 15% commission on domestic sales; 20% on foreign sales. Offers written contract, binding for 1 year, with 6 week cancellation clause. 100% of business is derived from commissions on sales.
Also Handles: Movie scripts (feature film, documentary, animation); TV scripts (TV mow, miniseries, episodic drama); theatrical stage plays. Considers these script subject areas: action/adventure; comedy; contemporary issues; detective/police/crime; gay; glitz; horror; humor; lesbian; mainstream; mystery/suspense; romantic comedy and drama; science fiction; teen; thriller. Query with outline/proposal and SASE. Reports in 2 week on queries; 1 month on mss.
Represents: Writer/directors: Richard Linklater (*Slacker, Dazed & Confused, Before Sunrise*); Gregg Araki (*The Living End, Doom Generation*); Tom DiCillo (*Living in Oblivion*); Genvieve Turner/Rose Troche (*Go Fish*); Todd Solondz (*Welcome to the Dollhouse*).
Terms: Agent receives 10% commission on domestic sales; 10% on foreign sales.
Writers' Conferences: Sundance Film Festival, Independent Feature Market.
Tips: Obtains new clients through recommendations from others. "Be persistent, but civilized."

INSIDER REPORT

On the cutting edge: How the agent's role is changing

Books can no longer afford to be perceived as a rarefied commodity, written and purchased by the literati. Along with movies, television, music, theater, sports and the Internet, books are becoming a popular form of entertainment in fierce competition for the consumer's leisure time (and money). And all these areas of entertainment—now overwhelmingly owned by media conglomerates—are cross-pollinating. Books are a fortunate by-product. Consider a recent blockbuster: Howard Stern, a radio disc jockey who gets a television series, writes a bestselling book and sells it to the movies. Rodman, Seinfield, Reiser, DeGeneres, Oprah, Rush—all media personalities, all bestselling authors. Think of the Madonna marketing machine and you have a sense of the vertical exploitation of intellectual property.

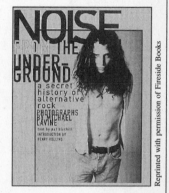

Because the media is growing and changing, the agent's role is changing: The traditional concept of a literary agent no longer applies. Now, agents must be savvy about the media industry at large, not just book publishing. It is that savvy, along with an ability to recognize talent, that makes an agent outstanding. A testimony to this evolution is Stephen Pevner, whose eclectic roster of clients epitomizes this new but necessary tendency in agenting. "I represent different artists," says Pevner. "Novelists, nonfiction authors, screenwriters, filmmakers, playwrights, journalists, photographers. What I do depends more on the property that is created and less on one area of specialization." He's not alone.

Hosts of literary agents are fast becoming utility agents, handling not just book deals but different aspects of a writer's career. The sphere of influence is expanding with the marketplace and agents can no longer be pigeonholed according to the types of books they represent. As Pevner notes, "We're seeing that an agent represents a client, not just one aspect of a client's work. The artist creates intellectual property and the agent exploits it in all the ancillary markets. What's happening is the agent is helping the client more fully realize his unique vision."

This is not to say agents are discarding personal interests as they sell out to make big money from clients with mass appeal. Instead, they are broadening who and what they'll represent. Many agents are still known for their expertise in specific areas, such as science fiction, mystery, self-help, etc., but others are emerging who do not crave a reputation for commanding expertise in one specific subject. They want to be perceived as acute agents who represent various types of books and authors. Pevner, for example, doesn't claim to have a traditional subject area of expertise. Nevertheless, he has managed to carve a niche for himself as a perceptive, cutting-edge New York agent with a knack for what strikes a chord on the emerging strings of non-mainstream culture.

Pevner's forté is anticipating which artists will have a powerful, sub-cultural impact and offering them the opportunity to bring that impact to the book world. "I do these books because I feel these artists are tapping into something in our society's social subtext that eventually will affect the larger culture. I'm equally interested in what and how something is being said, the voice, and the way it's executed. I ask myself: Can it be presented in a stronger way? I say to writers: 'Okay, you have an interesting and unique style, but why are you telling this story and why does it have to be told now? What is the urgency and why does it need to be published for a broader audience?' I address these questions before I am convinced something is worth representing."

Despite his appetite for a never-before-heard voice, Pevner is not simply looking for something "new." He wants something "fresh." And for him there is a clear distinction between the two: New is a category, whereas fresh is something independent of any category. As Pevner puts it: "New is simply a trend and fresh is its inspiration. I'm not interested in trends but personally inspired statements. I don't look for people who copy styles but for artists who have something to say. I'm looking for integrity and vision that you can't find anywhere else."

Considering his past projects and his criteria for taking on future projects, it's no wonder Pevner could easily be pinned "the cutting-edge agent," but he's uncomfortable with that label. "I might be perceived as cutting edge, but I'm simply responding to what I'm attracted to," he adamantly declares. "Everything today is 'cutting edge,' because everything has been declared 'hip.' I'm into what's totally original. That's what I'm looking for. If that's cutting edge, then sure, I want cutting-edge material."

With the industry ablaze in competition for the next "new" thing, Pevner feels it's his job to recognize artists who offer something real and fresh, and to help them to get into as broad a market as possible. "As a straightforward literary agent, I get people published who are worthy of publication. It doesn't matter to me if they're writing fiction, nonfiction, or something that's totally foreign to the marketplace. What matters is whether it will make a good, important book."

Although Pevner has had success turning scripts into books with movies such as *Welcome to the Dollhouse, Living in Oblivion, The Living End, Slacker, Dazed and Confused* and *Before Sunrise*, he's making strong efforts to turn other aspects of pop culture into books as well. One of Pevner's smartest and most timely forays is the recently published *Noise From the Underground: A Secret History of Alternative Rock* (Simon & Schuster/Fireside Books, 1996), a book juxtaposing striking photographic images with personalized prose that effectively chronicles the passage of the "alternative voice" in music to its current mainstream status.

Pevner's intuitive sense may lead him to unlikely pairings and seemingly unfamiliar places. But ultimately his success as an agent lies in recognizing trends before they have labels, unearthing what readers want before they know what they want, and forging the right connections to cast the material to the broadest audience possible—attributes every good agent must possess.

—*Don Prues*

ARTHUR PINE ASSOCIATES, INC., (III), 250 W. 57th St., New York NY 10019. (212)265-7330. Estab. 1966. Represents 100 clients. 25% of clients are new/previously unpublished writers. Specializes in fiction and nonfiction. Currently handles: 75% nonfiction; 25% novels. Member agents: Richard Pine; Arthur Pine; Lori Andiman; Sarah Piel.
Handles: Nonfiction books, novels. Considers these nonfiction areas: business; current affairs; health/medicine; money/finance/economics; psychology; self-help/personal improvement. Considers these fiction areas: action/adventure; detective/police/crime; family saga; literary; mainstream; romance; thriller/espionage. Send outline/proposal. Reports in 3 weeks on queries. "All correspondence must be accompanied by a SASE. Will not read manuscripts before receiving a letter of inquiry."
Recent Sales: *The Exchange Students*, by Marc Olden (Random House); *The Third Pandemic*, by Pierre Ouelette (Pocketbooks); *Kiss The Girls*, by James Patterson (Little, Brown & Warner Books); *The Optimistic Child*, by Dr. Martin Seligman (Houghton Mifflin).
Terms: Agency receives 15% commission on domestic sales; 25% on foreign sales. Offers written contract, which varies from book to book.
Tips: Obtains new clients through recommendations from others. "Our agency will only look at submissions that have not been submitted to any other agent or publisher simultaneously or at any time whatsoever and must be accompanied by a self-addressed, stamped envelope for return purposes . . . otherwise materials will not be returned."

POCONO LITERARY AGENCY, INC., (II), Box 759, Saylorsburg PA 18353-0069. (610)381-4152. Contact: Carolyn Hopwood Blick, president. Estab. 1993. Member of RWA. Represents 30 clients. 60% of clients are new/previously unpublished writers. Specializes in women's fiction and nonfiction. Currently handles: 25% juvenile; 75% women's fiction and nonfiction.
Handles: Nonfiction books, juvenile/young adult books, novels. Considers these nonfiction areas: biography; business; current affairs; education; gardening; government/politics/law; health/medicine; history; juvenile nonfiction; military/war; money/finance/economics; nature/environment; nutrition; psychology; self-help/personal improvement; sports; women's issues/women's studies. Considers these fiction areas: contemporary issues; detective/police/crime; ethnic; family saga; historical; horror; humor; juvenile; mainstream; mystery/suspense; picture book; psychic/supernatural; romance; thriller; young adult. Query with 1 page synopsis. Reports in 2 weeks on queries; 4-6 weeks on mss.
Terms: Agent receives 15% commission on domestic sales; 20% on foreign sales. Charges for photocopying, postage, long-distance telephone, UPS, and all other reasonable expenses.
Writer's Conferences: RWA conference (national); New Jersey Romance Writer's Conference.
Tips: Obtains clients through "referrals, writers' conferences, and through mailed submissions. We are especially interested in seeing romance novels. My background as an educator interests me in children's works and works which can be used as supplemental aids within the classroom. The children's market is fiercely competitive, and submissions must be truly exceptional. We do not accept responsibility for unsolicited manuscripts or manuscripts which are not accompanied by SASE."

POM INC., (II, III), 21 Vista Dr., Great Neck NY 11021. (212)522-6612. Fax: (212)522-4971. Contact: Simon Green. Estab. 1990. Represents 27 clients. 15% of clients are new/previously unpublished writers. Currently handles: 50% nonfiction books; 5% scholarly books; 35% novels; 10% syndicated material. Member agents: Dan Green; Simon Green.
Handles: Nonfiction books, novels, short story collections, syndicated material. Considers these nonfiction areas: biography/autobiography; business; cooking/food/nutrition; current affairs; ethnic/cultural interests; health/medicine; history; money/finance/economics; music/dance/theater/film; popular culture; sports; women's issues/women's studies. Considers these fiction areas: action/adventure; contemporary issues; detective/police/crime; erotica; fantasy; feminist; glitz; historical; horror; humor/satire; literary; mainstream; mystery/suspense; sports; thriller/espionage. Query. "Please no unsolicited manuscripts." Reports in 2 weeks on queries.
Terms: Agent receives 15% commission on domestic sales; 15% on foreign sales. No written contract. Charges "if a publishing entertainment electronic lawyer is needed to review a contract." 100% of business is derived from commissions on sales.
Tips: Obtains new clients through referrals.

JULIE POPKIN, (II), 15340 Albright St., #204, Pacific Palisades CA 90272-2520. (310)459-2834. Estab. 1989. Represents 26 clients. 40% of clients are new/unpublished writers. Specializes in selling book-length mss including fiction and nonfiction. Especially interested in social issues. Currently handles: 50% nonfiction books; 50% novels; some scripts. Member agents: Julie Popkin and Margaret McCord (fiction).
Handles: Nonfiction books, novels. Considers these nonfiction areas: art; criticism; feminist; history; politics. Considers these fiction areas: literary; mainstream; mystery. Reports in 1 month on queries; 2 months on mss.
Recent Sales: *Pre-Menstrual Syndrome*, by Dr. Michelle Harrison (Random House); *The Calling of Katie Makanya*, by Margaret McCord (John Wiley & Sons); *Terrible Teresa*, by Mittie Cuetara (Dut-

ton); *Peace Without Justice*, by Margaret Popkin (Penn State University Press); and *Patient* (translation of Soy Paciente), by Ana Marie Shua (Latin American Literary Review Press).

Terms: Agent receives 15% commission on domestic sales; 10% on dramatic sales; 25% on foreign sales.

Fees: Does not charge a reading fee. Charges $100/year for photocopying, mailing, long distance calls.

Writers' Conferences: Frankfurt (October); ABA (Chicago, June).

SIDNEY E. PORCELAIN, (II,III), 414 Leisure Loop, Milford PA 18337-9568. (717)296-6420. Manager: Sidney Porcelain. Estab. 1952. Represents 20 clients. 50% of clients are new/unpublished writers. Prefers to work with published/established authors; works with a small number of new/unpublished authors. Specializes in fiction (novels, mysteries and suspense) and nonfiction (celebrity and exposé). Currently handles: 2% magazine articles; 5% magazine fiction; 5% nonfiction books; 50% novels; 5% juvenile books; 2% movie scripts; 1% TV scripts; 30% "comments for new writers."
Recent Sales: *Steve McQueen*, by Marshall Terrill (Donald I. Fine).
Handles: Magazine articles, magazine fiction, nonfiction books, novels, juvenile books. Query with outline or entire ms. Reports in 2 weeks on queries; 3 weeks on mss.
Terms: Agent receives 15% commission on domestic sales; 15% on dramatic sales; 15% on foreign sales. Offers criticism service to new writers. 50% of income derived from commission on ms sales.

THE POTOMAC LITERARY AGENCY, (II), 19062 Mills Choice Rd., Suite 5, Gaithersburg MD 20879-2835. (301)208-0674. Fax: (301)869-7513. Contact: Thomas F. Epley. Estab. 1993. Represents 17 clients. 60% of clients are new/previously unpublished writers. Currently handles: 70% novels; 30% nonfiction. Currently seeking literary fiction, upscale commercial fiction and nonfiction.
 ● Prior to opening his agency, Mr. Epley was director of the Naval Institute Press.
Handles: Nonfiction books, literary and commercial fiction (novels, novellas). Considers these nonfiction areas: biography/autobiography; business; current affairs; ethnic/cultural interests; gay/lesbian issues; history; language/literature/criticism; military/war; money/finance/economics; nature/environment; psychology; science/technology; self-help/personal improvement; sports; true crime/investigative. Considers these fiction areas: action/adventure; contemporary issues; detective/police/crime; ethnic; experimental; family saga; feminist; gay; historical; humor/satire; lesbian; literary; mainstream; mysteries; sports; thriller/espionage; westerns/frontier. Query with brief synopsis (no more than 1 page), first 50 pages of ms and SASE. Reports in 2 weeks on queries; 6 weeks on mss.
Recent Sales: *Catherwood*, by Marly Youmans (Farrar, Straus & Giroux); *Divorce Mediation Handbook*, by Paula James (Jossey-Bass); *Manny*, by Isaac Rosen (Baskerville).
Terms: Agents receive 15% commission on domestic sales; 20% on foreign sales (if co-agent used). Offers written contract. Charges for photocopying, postage and telephone.
Tips: Obtains new clients through referrals and unsolicited submissions. "We want to increase the number of nonfiction projects."

AARON M. PRIEST LITERARY AGENCY, (II), 708 Third Ave., 23rd Floor, New York NY 10017. (212)818-0344. Contact: Aaron Priest or Molly Friedrich. Member of AAR. Currently handles: 25% nonfiction books; 75% fiction. Associate agents: Lisa Erbach Vance, Sheri Holman.
Handles: Nonfiction books, fiction. Query only (must be accompanied by SASE). Unsolicited mss will be returned unread.
Recent Sales: *Moo*, by Jane Smiley; *Absolute Power*, by David Baldacci; *Two for the Dough*, by Janet Evanovich (Scribner); *The Juror*, by George Green; *How Stella Got Her Groove Back*, by Terry McMillan; *Day After Tomorrow*, by Allan Folsom; *Angela's Ashes*, by Frank McCourt.
Terms: Agent receives 15% commission on domestic sales. Charges for photocopying, foreign postage expenses.

SUSAN ANN PROTTER LITERARY AGENT, (II), 110 W. 40th St., Suite 1408, New York NY 10018. (212)840-0480. Contact: Susan Protter. Estab. 1971. Member of AAR. Represents 40 clients. 10% of clients are new/unpublished writers. Writer must have book-length project or ms that is ready to be sold. Works with a very small number of new/unpublished authors. Currently handles: 40%

THE PUBLISHING FIELD is constantly changing! If you're still using this book and it is 1998 or later, buy the newest edition of *Guide to Literary Agents* at your favorite bookstore or order directly from Writer's Digest Books.

nonfiction books; 60% novels; occasional magazine article or short story (for established clients only).
Handles: Nonfiction books, novels. Considers these nonfiction areas: biography; child guidance/
parenting; health/medicine; psychology; science. Considers these fiction areas: detective/police/crime;
mystery; science fiction, thrillers. Send short query with brief description of project/novel, publishing
history and SASE. Reports in 3 weeks on queries; 2 months on solicited mss. "Please do not call;
mail queries only."
Recent Sales: *Freeware*, by Rudy Rucker (Morrow/AvoNova); *The Year's Best SF*, by David G.
Hartwell (HarperPrism); *Life Happens*, by Kathleen McCoy, Ph.D. and Charles Wibblesman, M.D.
(Perigee/Berkley); *20 Teachable Virtues*, by Barbara C. Unel and Jerry L. Wyckoff, Ph.D. (Perigee/
Berkley); *Shadowheart*, by Lynn Armistead McKee (Dutton Signet); *Pirates of the Universe*, by Terry
Bisson (TOR); *Door Number Three*, by Patrick O'Leary (TOR).
Terms: Agent receives 15% commission on domestic sales; 15% on TV, film and dramatic sales;
25% on foreign sales. Charges for long distance, photocopying, messenger, express mail, airmail
expenses.
Tips: "Please send neat and professionally organized queries. Make sure to include an SASE or we
cannot reply. We receive up to 100 queries a week and read them in the order they arrive. We usually
reply within two weeks to any query. Do not call. If you are sending a multiple query, make sure to
note that in your letter."

ROBERTA PRYOR, INC., (II), 288 Titicus Rd., N. Salem NY 10560. (914)669-5724. President:
Roberta Pryor. Estab. 1985. Member of AAR. Represents 50 clients. Prefers to work with published/
established authors; works with a small number of new/unpublished writers. Specializes in serious
nonfiction and (tends toward) literary fiction. Special interest in natural history, good cookbooks, media
studies. Currently handles: 80% nonfiction books; 20% novels.
  • Prior to opening her agency, Ms. Prior served as head of Subsidiary Rights for E.P. Dutton,
    editor with Trident Press (Simon & Schuster), and as an agent (VP) with International Creative
    Management.
Handles: Nonfiction books, novels, textbooks, juvenile books. Considers these nonfiction areas: animals; anthropology/archaeology; art/architecture/design; biography/autobiography; cooking/food; current affairs; ethnic/cultural interests; gay/lesbian issues; government/politics/law; history; juvenile nonfiction; literature/criticism; military/war; nature/environment; photography; popular culture; sociology;
theater/film; true crime/investigative; women's issues/women's studies. Considers these fiction areas:
contemporary issues; detective/police/crime; historical; literary; mainstream; mystery/suspense; young
adult. Query. SASE required for any correspondence. Reports in 10 weeks on queries.
Recent Sales: *Eagles of Fire* (techno-thriller), by Timothy Rizzi (Donald I. Fine); new vegetarian
cookbook, by Anna Thomas (Knopf); *Jerusalem*, (historical novel), by Cecelia Holland (TOR-Forge/
St. Martin's); *A Memoir*, by Paul Fussell (Little, Brown); *The Gulf War*, (media study), by Mark Crispin
Miller (WW Norton).
Terms: Charges 15% commission on domestic sales; 10% on film sales; 20% on foreign sales. Charges
for photocopying, and often express mail and messenger service.

PUBLISHING SERVICES, (II), 525 E. 86th St., New York NY 10028-7554. (212)535-6248. Fax:
(212)988-1073. Contact: Amy Goldberger. Estab. 1993. Represents 20 clients. 50% of clients are new/
previously unpublished writers. Currently handles: 75% nonfiction books; 25% novels.
Handles: Nonfiction books, novels. Considers these nonfiction areas: biography/autobiography; child
guidance/parenting; cooking/food/nutrition; education; ethnic/cultural interests; health/medicine; New
Age/metaphysics; popular culture; self-help/personal improvement; women's issues/women's studies.
Considers these fiction areas: contemporary issues; ethnic; feminist; historical; literary; mainstream.
Query with SASE. Reports in 2 weeks on queries.
Terms: Agent receives 15% commission on domestic sales; 20% on foreign sales. Offers written
contract. Charges for photocopying, postage, long distance calls.
Tips: Obtains new clients from queries and referrals. Query first and always include a SASE.

QUICKSILVER BOOKS-LITERARY AGENTS, (II), 50 Wilson St., Hartsdale NY 10530-2542.
(914)946-8748. Contact: Bob Silverstein. Estab. 1973 as packager; 1987 as literary agency. Represents
50 clients. 50% of clients are new/previously unpublished writers. Specializes in literary and commercial mainstream fiction and nonfiction (especially psychology, New Age, holistic healing, conscious-
ness, ecology, environment, spirituality). Currently handles: 75% nonfiction books; 25% novels.
  • Prior to opening his agency, Mr. Silverstein served as senior editor at Bantam Books and Dell
    Books/Delacorte Press.
Handles: Nonfiction books, novels. Considers these nonfiction areas: anthropology/archaeology; biography; business; child guidance/parenting; cooking/food/nutrition; current affairs; ethnic/cultural
interests; health/medicine; history; how-to; literature; nature/environment; New Age/metaphysics; popular culture; psychology; inspirational; science/technology; self-help/personal improvement; sociology; sports; true crime/investigative; women's issues/women's studies. Considers these fiction areas:

action/adventure; glitz; mystery/suspense. Query, "always include SASE." Reports in up to 2 weeks on queries; up to 1 month on mss.
Recent Sales: *Let Like Cure Like*, by Vinton McCabe (St. Martin's Press); *The National Public Radio Classical Music Desk Encyclopedia*, by Ted Libbey (Workman); *The Code of the Executive*, by Donald Schmincke (Tuttle).
Terms: Agent receives 15% commission on domestic sales; 20% on foreign sales. Offers written contract, "only if requested. It is open ended, unless author requests time frame." Charges for postage. Authors are expected to supply SASE for return of mss and for query letter responses.
Writers' Conferences: National Writers Union Conference (Dobbs Ferry NY, April).
Tips: Obtains new clients through recommendations, listings in sourcebooks, solicitations, workshop participation.

HELEN REES LITERARY AGENCY, (II, III), 308 Commonwealth Ave., Boston MA 02115-2415. (617)262-2401. Fax: (617)236-0133. Contact: Joan Mazmanian. Estab. 1981. Member of AAR. Represents 50 clients. 50% of clients are new/previously unpublished writers. Specializes in general nonfiction, health, business, world politics, autobiographies, psychology, women's issues. Currently handles: 60% nonfiction books; 40% novels.
Handles: Nonfiction books, novels. Considers these nonfiction areas: biography/autobiography; business; current affairs; government/politics/law; health/medicine; history; money/finance/economics; women's issues/women's studies. Considers these fiction areas: contemporary issues; detective/police/crime; glitz; historical; literary; mainstream; mystery/suspense; thriller/espionage. Query with outline plus 2 sample chapters. Reports in 2 weeks on queries; 3 weeks on mss.
Recent Sales: *Romeo*, by Elise Title (fiction); *Changing The Game*, by Adam M. Brandenburger (business) and Barry J. Nalebuff; *Thriving In Transition*, by Marcia Perleins-Reed (Fireside/Simon & Schuster).
Terms: Agent receives 15% commission on domestic sales; 20% on foreign sales.
Tips: Obtains new clients through recommendations from others, solicitation, at conferences, etc.

RENAISSANCE—H.N. SWANSON, (III), 8523 Sunset Blvd., Los Angeles CA 90069. (310)289-3636. Contact: Joel Gotler. Signatory of WGA; Member of SAG, AFTRA, DGA. Represents 150 clients. 10% of clients are new/previously unpublished writers. Currently handles: 60% novels; 40% movie and TV scripts. Specializes in selling movies and TV rights from books. Member agents: Irv Schwartz, partner (TV writers); Joel Gotler, partner (film rights); Allan Nevins, partner (book publishing); Brian Lipson, associate (motion picture writers); Steven Fisher.
Handles: Nonfiction books, novels. Considers these nonfiction areas: biography/autobiography; history; film; true crime/investigative. Considers these fiction areas: action/adventure; contemporary issue; detective/police/crime; ethnic; family saga; fantasy; historical; humor/satire; literary; mainstream; mystery/suspense; science fiction; thriller/espionage. Query with outline and SASE. Reports in 1 month on queries.
Recent Sales: *The Late Marilyn Monroe*, by Don Wolfe (Dutton); *I Was Amelia Earhart*, by Jane Mendohlson (New Line); *Heart of War*, by Lucian Truscott (Dutton); *Deadlock*, by Malcolm McPherson (Simon & Schuster).
Also Handles: Movie scripts (feature film); TV scripts (TV mow, episodic drama, sitcom, miniseries and animation). Considers these script subject areas: action/adventure; cartoon/animation; comedy; contemporary issues; detective/police/crime; erotica; ethnic; experimental; family saga; fantasy; feminist; gay; historical; horror; juvenile; lesbian; mainstream; mystery/suspense; psychic/supernatural; regiona; romantic comedy and drama; science fiction; sports; teen; thriller/espionage; westerns;frontier. Query with SASE. Reports in 2-6 weeks on queries; 1-2 months on mss.
Recent Sales: *Movie scripts optioned/sold:* *The Plague Season*, by James Ellroy (Universal); *Rockwood*, by Jere Cunningham (Imagine Ent.); *Leavenworth*, by Lucian Truscott (Mandalan); *TV scripts optioned/sold:* *Apocalypse Watch*, by Robert Ludlum (RHI); *Scripting assignments:* *Aftershock*, by David Stevens (RHI); *Moby Dick*, by Ben Fitzgerald (Hallmark).
Terms: Agent receives 15% commission on domestic books; 10% on film sales.
Tips: Obtains news clients through recommendations from others.

ANGELA RINALDI LITERARY AGENCY, (II), P.O. Box 7877, Beverly Hills CA 90212-2877. (310)287-0356. Contact: Angela Rinaldi. Estab. 1994. Represents 30 clients. Currently handles: 50% nonfiction books; 50% novels.
Handles: Nonfiction books, novels, TV and motion picture rights. Query first with SASE. For fiction, send the first 100 pages. For nonfiction, send outline/proposal. Considers these nonfiction areas: biography/autobiography; business; child guidance/parenting; food/nutrition; current affairs; health/medicine; money/finance/economics; popular culture; psychology; self-help/personal improvement; sociology; true crime/investigative; women's issues/women's studies. Considers these fiction areas: contemporary issues; detective/police/crime; ethnic; experimental; family saga; feminist; glitz; literary; mainstream; thriller/espionage. Reports in 3 weeks on proposals; 6 weeks on mss.

Recent Sales: *The Starlite Drive-In*, by Marjorie Reynolds (William Morrow & Co.); *Twins: From Fetal Development Through the First Years of Life*, by Agnew, Kleen and Ganon (HarperCollins); *If You're Writing, Let's Talk*, by Joel Saltzman (Prima); *The Book of Uncommon Prayer*, by Connie and Dan Pollock (Word Publishing).

Terms: Agent receives 15% commission on domestic sales; 20% on foreign sales. Offers written contract. Charges for marketing expenses.

‡**ANN RITTENBERG LITERARY AGENCY, INC., (V)**, 14 Montgomery Place, Brooklyn NY 11215. (718)857-1460. Fax: (718)857-1484. Contact: Ann Rittenberg. Estab. 1992. Member of AAR. Represents 35 clients. 70% of clients are new/previously unpublished writers. Specializes in literary fiction. Currently handles: 50% nonfiction books; 50% novels.

Handles: Considers these nonfiction areas: biography; gardening; memoir; social/cultural history; women's issues/women's studies. Considers these fiction areas: literary. Send outline and 3 sample chapters. Reports in 4-6 weeks on queries; 6-8 weeks on mss.

Recent Sales: *Every Day*, by Elizabeth Richards (Pocket Books); *The Poetry of Avis Berman* (Clarkson Potter); *Sight: Whistler & the Making of Modern Literature*, by Avis Berman (Clarkson Potter).

Terms: Agent receives 15% commission on domestic sales; 20% on foreign sales. Offers written contract. Charges for photocopying.

Tips: Obtains new clients only through referrals from established writers and editors.

RIVERSIDE LITERARY AGENCY, (III), Keets Brook Rd., Leyden MA 01337. (413)772-0840. Fax: (413)772-0969. Contact: Susan Lee Cohen. Estab. 1991. Represents 55 clients. 20% of clients are new/previously unpublished writers. Currently handles: 65% nonfiction books; 30% novels; 5% short story collections.

Handles: Nonfiction books, novels. Very selective. Query with outline and SASE. Reports in 2 months.

Terms: Agent receives 15% commission. Offers written contract at request of author.

Recent Sales: *Reviving Ophelia*, by Mary Pipher (Ballantine/Putnam); *Please Kill Me: An Uncensored Oral History of Punk*, by Legs McNeil and Gillian McCain (Grove Press); *What Every Woman Must Know About Heart Disease*, by Siegfried Kra, M.D. (Warner Books).

Tips: Mainly accepts new clients through referrals.

BJ ROBBINS LITERARY AGENCY, (II), 5130 Bellaire Ave., North Hollywood CA 91607-2908. (818)760-6602. Fax: (818)760-6616. Contact: (Ms.) B.J. Robbins. Estab. 1992. Represents 40 clients. 80% of clients are new/previously unpublished writers. Currently handles: 50% nonfiction books; 50% novels.

Handles: Nonfiction books, novels. Considers these nonfiction areas: biography/autobiography; child guidance/parenting; cooking/food/nutrition; current affairs; education; ethnic/cultural interests; gay/lesbian issues; government/politics/law; health/medicine; how-to; humor; music/dance/theater/film; nature/environment; popular culture; psychology; self-help/personal improvement; sociology; sports; true crime/investigative; women's issues/women's studies. Considers these fiction areas: contemporary issues; detective/police/crime; ethnic; family saga; gay; lesbian; literary; mainstream; mystery/suspense; sports; thriller/espionage. Send outline/proposal and 3 sample chapters. Reports in 2 weeks on queries; 6 weeks on mss.

Recent Sales: *Please, Please, Please*, by Reneé Swindle (The Dial Press); *Riding for a Fall*, by Lillian Roberts (Ballantine); *The Road to the Sundance*, by Manny Twofeathers (Hyperion).

Terms: Agent receives 15% commission on domestic sales; 20% on foreign sales. Offers written contract, with 3 months notice to terminate if project is out on submission. Charges for postage and photocopying only. 100% of business is derived from commissions on sales.

Writers' Conferences: Squaw Valley Fiction Writers Workshop (Squaw Valley CA, August); Art of the Wild (Squaw Valley CA, July); Palm Springs Writers Conference (Palm Springs CA, May).

Tips: Obtains new clients mostly through referrals, also at conferences.

THE ROBBINS OFFICE, INC., (II), 405 Park Ave., New York NY 10022. (212)223-0720. Fax: (212)223-2535. Contact: Kathy P. Robbins, owner; Bill Clegg, agent. Specializes in selling mainstream nonfiction, commercial and literary fiction.

AGENTS RANKED I AND II are most open to both established and new writers. Agents ranked **III** are open to established writers with publishing-industry references.

Handles: Nonfiction books, novels, magazine articles for book writers under contract. No unsolicited mss.

Recent Sales: *Primary Colors*, by Anonymous (Random House); *Great Books*, by David Derby (Simon & Schuster); *The Christmas Tree*, by Julie Salamon (Random House); *The Devil Problem & Other True Stories*, by David Remnick (Random House).

Terms: Agent receives 15% commission on all domestic, dramatic and foreign sales. Bills back specific expenses incurred in doing business for a client.

JANE ROTROSEN AGENCY, (II), 318 E. 51st St., New York NY 10022. (212)593-4330. Estab. 1974. Member of AAR. Works with published and unpublished writers. Specializes in trade fiction and nonfiction.
Handles: Adult fiction, nonfiction. Query with short outline. Reports in 2 weeks.
Terms: Receives 15% commission on domestic sales; 15% on dramatic sales; 20% on foreign sales. Charges writers for photocopying, long-distance/transoceanic telephone, telegraph, Telex, messenger service and foreign postage.

THE DAMARIS ROWLAND AGENCY, (I), RR #1, Box 513 A, Wallingford VT 05773. (802)446-3146. Fax: (802)446-3224. Contact: Damaris Rowland or Steve Axelrod. Estab. 1994. Member of AAR. Represents 40 clients. 10% of clients are new/previously unpublished writers. Specializes in women's fiction. Currently handles: 100% novels.
Handles: Nonfiction books, novels. Considers these nonfiction areas: animals; cooking/food/nutrition; health/medicine; nature/environment; New Age/metaphysics; religious/inspirational; women's issues/women's studies. Considers these fiction areas: detective/police/crime; historical; literary; mainstream; psychic/supernatural; romance (contemporary, gothic, historical, regency). Send outline/proposal. Reports in 6 weeks.
Recent Sales: *A Dangerous Man*, by Connie Brockway (Dell); *Captive*, by Heather Graham (NAL); *Shadows in Velvet*, by Haywood Smith (St. Martin's).
Terms: Agent receives 15% commission on domestic sales; 20% on foreign sales. Offers written contract, with 30 day cancellation clause. Charges only if extraordinary expenses have been incurred, e.g., Xeroxing and mailing 15 ms to Europe for a foreign sale. 100% of business is derived from commissions on sales.
Writers' Conferences: Novelists Inc. (Denver, October); RWA National (Texas, July).
Tips: Obtains new clients through recommendations from others, at conferences.

PESHA RUBINSTEIN LITERARY AGENCY, INC. (II), 1392 Rugby Rd., Teaneck NJ 07666. (201)862-1174. Fax: (201)862-1180. Contact: Pesha Rubinstein. Estab. 1990. Member of AAR, RWA, MWA, SCBWI. Represents 35 clients. 25% of clients are new/previously unpublished writers. Specializes in commercial fiction and children's books. Currently handles: 20% juvenile books; 80% novels.
● Prior to opening her agency, Ms. Rubenstein served as an editor at Zebra and Leisure Books.
Handles: Commercial fiction, juvenile books, picture book illustration. Considers these nonfiction areas: child guidance/parenting. Considers these fiction areas: detective/police/crime; ethnic; glitz; humor; juvenile; mainstream; mystery/suspense; picture book; psychic/supernatural; romance (contemporary, historical); spiritual adventures. "No westerns, fantasy or poetry." Send query, first 10 pages and SASE. Reports in 2 weeks on queries; 6 weeks on requested mss.
Recent Sales: *Subterranean*, by Jim Clemens (Avon); *Storyteller's Beads*, by Jane Kurtz (Harcourt Brace); *Fox Maiden*, illustrated by Tatsuno Kiuchi (Simon & Schuster).
Terms: Agent receives 15% commission on domestic sales; 20% on foreign sales. Offers written contract. Charges for photocopying. No weekend or collect calls accepted.
Tips: "Keep the query letter and synopsis short. Please send first ten pages of manuscript rather than selected chapters from the manuscript. The work speaks for itself better than any description can. Never send originals. A phone call after one month is acceptable. Always include a SASE covering return of the entire package with the material."

‡RUSSELL & VOLKENING, (II), 50 W. 29th St., #7E, New York NY 10001. (212)684-6050. Fax: (212)889-3026. Contact: Joseph Regal or Jennie Dunham. Estab. 1940. Member of AAR. Represents 140 clients. 10% of clients are new/previously unpublished writers. Specializes in literary fiction and narrative nonfiction. Currently handles: 40% nonfiction books; 15% juvenile books; 2% short story collections; 40% novels; 2% novellas; 1% poetry. Member agents: Timothy Seldes (nonfiction, literary fiction); Joseph Regal (literary fiction, thrillers, nonfiction); Jennie Dunham (children's books, literary fiction, nonfiction).
Handles: Nonfiction books, juvenile books, novels, novellas, short story collections. Considers these nonfiction areas: anthropology/archaeology; art/architecture/design; biography/autobiography; business; cooking/food/nutrition; current affairs; education; ethnic/cultural interests; gay/lesbian issues; government/politics/law; health/medicine; history; juvenile nonfiction; language/literature/criticism;

military/war; money/finance/economics; music/dance/theater/film; nature/environment; photography; popular culture; psychology; science/technology; sociology; sports; true crime/investigative; women's issues/women's studies. Considers these fiction areas: action/adventure; detective/police/crime; ethnic; juvenile; literary; mainstream; mystery/suspense; picture book; sports; thriller/espionage; young adult. Query. Reports in 1 week on queries; 1 month on mss.

Recent Sales: *Ladder of Years*, by Anne Tyler (Knopf); *Guide My Feet*, by Marian Wright Edelman (Beacon Press); *Writing & Being*, by Nadine Gordimer (Harvard University Press); *Breakheart Hill*, by Thomas H. Cook (Bantam); *Liliane*, by Ntozake Shange (St. Martin's); *The Last Debate*, by Jim Lehrer (Random House).

Terms: Agent receives 10% commission on domestic sales; 20% on foreign sales. Charges for "standard office expenses relating to the submission of materials of an author we represent, e.g., photocopying, postage."

Tips: Obtains new clients through "recommendations of writers we already represent. If the query is cogent, well-written, well-presented and is the type of book we'd represent, we'll ask to see the manuscript. From there, it depends purely on the quality of the work."

RUSSELL-SIMENAUER LITERARY AGENCY INC., (II), P.O. Box 43267, Upper Montclair NJ 07043-0267. (201)746-0539, (201)992-4198. Fax: (201)746-0754, (201)992-8062. Contact: Jacqueline Simenauer or Margaret Russell. Estab. 1990. Member of Authors Guild, Authors League, NASW. Represents 20-25 clients. 75% of clients are new/previously unpublished writers. Specializes in popular psychology, health/medicine, self-help/personal inprovement, women's issues, how-to. Currently handles: 95% nonfiction books; 5% novels. Member agents: Jacqueline Simenauer (popular psychology/psychiatry, popular health/medicine); Margaret Russell (fiction, women's issues, self-help/personal improvement).
   ● Prior to opening their agency, Ms. Russell served as associate director of publicity for Simon
   & Schuster and director of publicity for Basic Books, and Ms. Simenauer co-authored several
   books for Doubleday, Simon & Schuster and Times Books.

Handles: Nonfiction books, novels. Considers these nonfiction areas: child guidance/parenting; current affairs; education; health/medicine; how-to; money/finance; New Age/metaphysics; nutrition; popular culture; psychology; religious/inspirational; self-help/personal improvement; true crime/investigative; women's issues/women's studies. Considers these fiction areas: contemporary issues; family saga; feminist; gay; glitz; historical; literary; mainstream; mystery/suspense; psychic/supernatural; romance (contemporary); thriller/espionage. Query with outline/proposal. Reports in 4-6 weeks on queries; 2 months on mss.

Recent Sales: *The Thyroid Guide*, by Paul LoGerfo M.D. and Beth Ann Ditkoff, M.D. (HarperCollins); *The Joys of Fatherhood,* by Marcus Goldman, MD (Prime Publishing); *Till Death Do Us Part*, by Jamie Turndorf, Ph.D. (Bob Adams); *The Insider's Guide to Selling A Million Copies of Your Software*, by Herbert Kraft, Esq. (Bob Adams).

Terms: Agent receives 15% commission on domestic sales; 25% on foreign sales. "There are no reading fees. However, we have a special Breakthrough Program for the first-time author who would like an in-depth critique of his/her work by our freelance editorial staff. There is a charge of $2 per page for this service, and it is completely optional." Charges for postage, photocopying, phone, fax. 100% of business is derived from commissions on ms sales.

Worker's Conferences: The American Psychological Association (NYC, August).

Tips: Obtains new clients through recommendations from others; advertising in various journals, newsletters, publications, etc. and professional conferences.

‡THE SAGALYN AGENCY, 4825 Bethesda Ave., Suite 302, Bethesda MD 20814. (301)718-6440. Fax: (301)718-6444. Estab. 1980. Member of AAR. Currently handles: 50% nonfiction books; 25% scholarly books; 25% novels.

Handles: Send outline/proposal.

VICTORIA SANDERS LITERARY AGENCY, (II), 241 Avenue of the Americas, New York NY 10014-4822. (212)633-8811. Fax: (212)633-0525. Contact: Victoria Sanders and/or Diane Dickensheid. Estab. 1993. Member of AAR, signatory of WGA. Represents 50 clients. 25% of clients are new/previously unpublished writers. Currently handles: 50% nonfiction books; 50% novels.

Handles: Nonfiction, novels. Considers these nonfiction areas: biography/autobiography; current affairs; ethnic/cultural interests; gay/lesbian issues; govenment/politics/law; history; humor; language/literature/criticism; music/dance/theater/film; popular culture; psychology; translations; women's issues/women's studies. Considers these fiction areas: action/adventure; contemporary issues; ethnic; family saga; feminist; gay; lesbian; literary; thriller/espionage. Query and SASE. Reports in 1 week on queries; 1 month on mss.

Recent Sales: *Flight of the Blackbird*, by Faye McDonald Smith (Scribner); *He Say, She Say*, by Yolanda Joe (Doubleday); *Drew and the Bub Daddy Showdown*, by Robb Armstrong (HarperCollins); *So, You Want To Be A Lesbian*, by Liz Tracey (St. Martin's).

Terms: Agent receives 15% commission on domestic sales; 20% on foreign sales. Offers written contract binding at will. Charges for photocopy, messenger, express mail and extraordinary fees. If in excess of $100, client approval is required.

Also Handles: Movie scripts (feature film); TV scripts (TV mow, miniseries). Considers these script areas: action/adventure; comedy; contemporary issues; family saga; romantic comedy and drama; thriller. Query. Reports in 1 week on queries; 1 month on scripts.

Tips: Obtains new clients through recommendations, "or I find them through my reading and pursue. Limit query to letter, no calls and give it your best shot. A good query is going to get good responses."

SANDUM & ASSOCIATES, (II), 144 E. 84th St., New York NY 10028-2035. (212)737-2011. Fax number on request. Managing Director: Howard E. Sandum. Estab. 1987. Represents 35 clients. 20% of clients are new/unpublished writers. Specializes in general nonfiction. Currently handles: 80% nonfiction books; 20% novels.

Handles: Nonfiction books, literary novels. Query with proposal, sample pages and SASE. Do not send full ms unless requested. Reports in 2 weeks on queries.

Terms: Agent receives 15% commission. Agent fee adjustable on dramatic and foreign sales. Charges writers for photocopying, air express, long-distance telephone/fax.

‡BLANCHE SCHLESSINGER AGENCY, (III, V), 433 Old Gulph Rd., Penn Valley PA 19072. (610)664-5513. Fax: (610)664-5959. Contact: Blanche Schlessinger. Estab. 1984. Particular interests: mysteries, legal thrillers, true crime, cookbooks.

Handles: Nonfiction books, novels. Considers these nonfiction areas: biography/autobiography; cooking/food/nutrition; health/medicine; how-to; self-help/personal improvement; true crime/investigative. Considers these fiction areas: detective/police/crime; glitz; mainstream; mystery; thriller/espionage. No children's, horror or science fiction. Send outline and 2 sample chapters. Reports in 10 days on queries; 4-6 weeks on mss. SASE essential.

Recent Sales: *Superfoods For Life*, by Dolores Riccio (Perigee); *366 Healthful Ways to Cook Vegetables with Pasta*, by Dolores Riccio (Dutton); *Ruins of Civility*, by James Bradberry (St. Martin's); *America's Heirloom Vegetables*, by William Woys Weaver (Henry Holt).

Terms: Agent receives 15% commission on domestic sales; 20% on foreign sales. Offers written contract. Charges for office expenses (long distance telephone, UPS charges, copying and bound galleys).

Tips: Obtains new clients primarily through recommendations from others.

HAROLD SCHMIDT LITERARY AGENCY, (II), 343 W. 12th St., #1B, New York NY 10014. (212)727-7473. Fax: (212)807-6025. Contact: Harold Schmidt. Estab. 1983. Member of AAR. Represents 35 clients. 10% of clients are new/previously unpublished writers. Currently handles: 40% nonfiction books; 5% scholarly books; 55% novels.

Handles: Nonfiction books, scholarly books, novels, short story collections. Considers these nonfiction areas: anthropology/archaeology; art/architecture/design; biography/autobiography; business; current affairs; ethnic/cultural interests; gay/lesbian issues; government/politics/law; health/medicine; history; language/literature/criticism; military/war; money/finance/economics; music/dance/theater/film; nature/environment; New Age/metaphysics; psychology; science/technology; self-help/personal improvement; sociology; translations; true crime/investigative; women's issues/women's studies. Considers these fiction areas: action/adventure; contemporary issues; detective/police/crime; ethnic; family saga; feminist; gay; glitz; historical; horror; lesbian; literary; mainstream; mystery/suspense; psychic/supernatural; thriller/espionage. Query via regular mail before sending any material. Endeavors to report 2 weeks on queries; 4-6 weeks on mss.

Recent Sales: *The Gangster of Love*, by Jessica Hagedorn (Houghton Mifflin); *The King of Kings and I*, by Jaffe Cohen (Harper San Francisco); *What Keeps Me Here*, by Rebecca Brown (HarperCollins); *The Other World*, by John Wynne (City Lights Books); *Growing Your Own Business*, by Gregory and Patricia Kishel (Putnam).

Terms: Agent receives 15% commission on domestic sales; 20% commission on foreign sales. Offers written contract "on occasion—time frame always subject to consultation with author." Charges for "photocopying, long distance telephone calls and faxes, ms submission postage costs."

Tips: Obtains new clients through recommendations from others and solicitation. "I cannot stress enough how important it is for the new writer to present a clear, concise and professionally presented query letter. And, please, NEVER send material until requested. Also, please don't call to pitch your material. We cannot answer any phone queries and fax queries are not welcome. The information on how to acquire representation is clearly stated in this entry. Thanks."

SUSAN SCHULMAN, A LITERARY AGENCY, (III), 454 W. 44th St., New York NY 10036-5205. (212)713-1633/4/5. Fax: (212)581-8830. E-mail: schulman@aol.com. President: Susan Schulman. Estab. 1979. Member of AAR, Dramatists Guild, Women's Media Group, signatory of WGA. 10-15% of clients are new/unpublished writers. Prefers to work with published/established authors;

works with a small number of new/unpublished authors. Currently handles: 70% nonfiction books; 20% novels; 10% stage plays. Member agents: Clyde Kuemmerle (theater); Angel Butts (theater); Nicole Rajani (foreign rights).
Handles: Nonfiction, fiction, plays, emphasizing contemporary women's fiction and nonfiction books of interest to women. Considers these nonfiction areas: anthropology/archaeology; biography/autobiography; business; child guidance/parenting; current affairs; education; ethnic/cultural interests; gay/lesbian issues; government/politics/law; health/medicine; history; how-to; juvenile nonfiction; military/war; money/finance/economics; music/dance/theater/film; nature/environment; New Age/metaphysics; popular culture; psychology; religious/inspirational; self-help/personal improvement; sociology; translations; true crime/investigative; women's issues/women's studies. Considers these fiction areas: contemporary issues; detective/police/crime; historical; lesbian; literary; mainstream; mystery/suspense; young adult. Query with outline. Reports in 2 weeks on queries; 6 weeks on mss. SASE required.
Recent Sales: *The Vein of Gold*, by Julia Cameron (Putnam); *Your Heart's Desire*, by Sonia Choquette (Crown Publishing); *Preconceived: How to Get Pregnant*, by Amy Cross (Golden Entertain); *Skin: A Short Story Collection*, by Catherine Hiller (Carroll & Graf); *Memory Slips: A Memoir of Music*, by Linda Cutting (HarperCollins).
Terms: Agent receives 15% commission on domestic sales; 10-20% on dramatic sales; 7½-10% on foreign sales (plus 7½-10% to co-agent). Charges for special messenger or copying services, foreign mail and any other service requested by client.
Also Handles: Movie scripts (feature film), stage plays. Considers these script subject areas: comedy; contemporary issues; detective/police/crime; feminist; historical; mainstream; psychic/supernatural; religious/inspirational; mystery/suspense; teen. Query with outline/proposal and SASE. Reports in 1 week on queries; 6 weeks on mss.
Recent Sales: *Mockingbird*, by Walter Tevis (New Line); *The English Patient*, by Michael Ondaate (Saul Zaentz); *Voodoo Dreams*, by Jewell Parker Rhodes (Steve Tisch Co.); *Evelyn & the Polka King*, by John Olive (Amblin' Entertainment).

LAURENS R. SCHWARTZ AGENCY, (II), 5 E. 22nd St., Suite 15D, New York NY 10010-5315. (212)228-2614. Contact: Laurens R. Schwartz. Estab. 1984. Represents 100 clients. "General mix of nonfiction and fiction. Also handles movie and TV tie-ins, all licensing and merchandising. Works world-wide. *Very* selective about taking on new clients. Only takes on 2-3 new clients per year."
Handles: No unsolicited mss. Reports in 1 month.
Terms: Agent receives 15% commission on domestic sales; up to 25% on foreign sales. "No fees except for photocopying, and that fee is avoided by an author providing necessary copies or, in certain instances, transferring files on diskette—must be IBM compatible." Where necessary to bring a project into publishable form, editorial work and some rewriting provided as part of service. Works with authors on long-term career goals and promotion.
Tips: "Do not like receiving mass mailings sent to all agents. Be selective—do your homework. Do not send *everything* you have ever written. Choose *one* work and promote that. *Always* include an SASE. *Never* send your only copy. *Always* include a background sheet on yourself and a *one*-page synopsis of the work (too many summaries end up being as long as the work)."

‡SCOVIL CHICHAK GALEN LITERARY AGENCY, (IV), 381 Park Ave. South, Suite 1020, New York NY 10016. (212)679-8686. Fax: (212)679-6710. E-mail: rgalen@aol.com. Contact: Russell Galen. Estab. 1993. Member of AAR.
Recent Sales: *3001: The Final Odyssey*, by Arthur C. Clarke (Ballantine); *The Trial of Elizabeth Cree*, by Peter Ackroyd and Nan A. Talese (Doubleday); *Ember From The Sun*, by Mark Canter (Delacorte Press); *Kink*, by Kathe Koja (Holt); *The Lady of Avalon*, Marion Zimmer Bradley (Viking); *Princesses*, by Flora Fraser (Knopf); *Home From Nowhere*, by James Howard Kunstler (Simon & Schuster).

SEBASTIAN LITERARY AGENCY, (III), 333 Kearny St., Suite 708, San Francisco CA 94108. (415)391-2331. Fax: (415)391-2377. E-mail: harperlb@aol.com (query only—no attachments). Owner Agent: Laurie Harper. Estab. 1985. Member of AAR. Represents approximately 50 clients. Specializes in business, psychology and consumer reference. Taking new clients selectively; mainly by referral.

AGENTS WHO SPECIALIZE in a specific subject area such as computer books or in handling the work of certain writers such as gay or lesbian writers are ranked **IV**.

Handles: Nonfiction only at this time. "No children's or YA." Considers these nonfiction areas: biography; business; child guidance/parenting; consumer reference; current affairs; ethnic/cultural interests; government/politics/law; health/medicine; money/finance/economics; psychology; self-help/personal improvement; sociology; sports; women's issues/women's studies. Reports in 3 weeks on queries; 6 weeks on mss.

Recent Sales: *David Copperfield's "Beyond Imagination"*, edited by David Copperfield and Janet Boliner (HarperCollins); *The Little Book of Big Profit*, by William Buchsbaum (Macmillan); *Good Intentions: The 9 Unconscious Mistakes of Nice People*, by Duke Robinson (Warner); *365 Ways to Simplify Your Work Life*, by Odette Pollar (Dearborn Financial).

Terms: Agent receives 15% commission on domestic sales; 20% on foreign sales. Offers written contract.

Fees: No reading fees. Charges a $100 annual administration fee for clients and charges for photocopies of ms for submission to publisher.

Writers' Conferences: ASJA (Los Angeles, February).

Tips: Obtains new clients mostly through "referrals from authors and editors, but some at conferences and some from unsolicited queries from around the country.

LYNN SELIGMAN, LITERARY AGENT, (II), 400 Highland Ave., Upper Montclair NJ 07043. (201)783-3631. Contact: Lynn Seligman. Estab. 1985. Member of Women's Media Group. Represents 32 clients. 15% of clients are new/previously unpublished writers. Currently handles: 75% nonfiction books; 15% novels; 10% photography books.

- Prior to opening her agency, Ms. Seligman worked in the subsidiary rights department of Doubleday and Simon & Schuster and served as an agent with IMG-Julian Bach Literary Agency (now IMG Literary).

Handles: Nonfiction books, novels, photography books. Considers these nonfiction areas: anthropology/archaeology; art/architecture/design; biography/autobiography; business; child guidance/parenting; cooking/food/nutrition; current affairs; education, ethnic/cultural interests; government/politics/law; health/medicine; history; how-to; humor; interior design/decorating; language/literature/criticism; money/finance/economics; music/dance/theater/film; nature/environment; photography; popular culture; psychology; science/technology; self-help/personal improvement; sociology; translations; true crime/investigative; women's issues/women's studies. Considers these fiction areas: contemporary issues; detective/police/crime; ethnic; fantasy; feminist; gay; historical; horror; humor/satire; lesbian; literary; mainstream; mystery/suspense; romance (contemporary, gothic, historical, regency); science fiction. Query with letter or outline/proposal, 1 sample chapter and SASE. Reports in 2 weeks on queries; 2 months on mss.

Recent Sales: *Raising A Thinking Child Workbook*, by Myrna B. Shure & Theresa di Geronimo (Henry Holt); *Dry Water* and *Signal To Noise*, by Eric Nylund (Avon Books); *Take Action! 18 Proven Strategies For Advancing in Today's Changing Business World*, by Susan Bixler (Ballantine); *Vladimir's Story*, by Rick and Diana Stafford and Pamela Patrick Novotry (Dutton).

Terms: Agent receives 15% commission on domestic sales; 25% on foreign sales. Charges for photocopying, unusual postage or telephone expenses (checking first with the author), express mail.

Writers' Conferences: Attends Dorothy Canfield Fisher Conference.

Tips: Obtains new clients usually from other writers or from editors.

THE SEYMOUR AGENCY, (II), 475 Miner St. Rd., Canton NY 13617. (315)379-0235. Fax: (315)386-1037. Contact: Mike Seymour/Mary Sue Seymour. Estab. 1992. Member of RWA, New York State Outdoor Writers, OWAA. 50% of clients are new/previously unpublished writers. Specializes in women's fiction. Member agents: Mary Sue Seymour (fiction); Mike Seymour (nonfiction).

Handles: Considers these nonfiction areas: art/architecture/design; juvenile nonfiction; religious/inspirational. Considers these fiction areas: action/adventure; detective/police/crime; ethnic; glitz; historical; horror; humor/satire; mainstream; mystery/suspense; religious/inspirational; romance (contemporary, gothic, historical, medieval, regency); vampire; westerns/frontier. Will read any well thought out nonfiction proposals, and any good fiction in any genre. Query with first chapter and synopsis. Reports in 2 weeks on queries; 1 month on mss.

Recent Sales: *Code Alpha*, by Joseph Massucci (Leisure Books); *Silent Knight*, by Tori Phillips (Harlequin Historicals); *The Way Home*, by Jill Shalus (Bantam); *Color Me Loved*, by J. Sheldon (Robinson).

Terms: Agent receives 15% commission on domestic sales; 15% on foreign sales. Offers written contract, binding for 1 year. Offers criticism service for prospective clients only. 12½% commission for published authors.

Tips: "Send query, synopsis and first 50 pages. If you don't hear from us, you didn't send SASE. We are looking for westerns and romance—women in jeopardy, suspense, contemporary, historical, some regency and any well written fiction and nonfiction. Both agents are New York state certified teachers who have taught writing and are published authors."

THE SHEPARD AGENCY, (II), Pawling Savings Bank Bldg., Suite 3, Southeast Plaza, Brewster NY 10509. (914)279-2900 or (914)279-3236. Fax: (914)279-3239. Contact: Jean or Lance Shepard. Specializes in "some fiction; nonfiction: business, biography, homemaking; inspirational; self-help." Currently handles: 75% nonfiction books; 5% juvenile books; 20% novels.
Handles: Nonfiction books, scholarly books, novels. Considers these nonfiction areas: agriculture; horticulture; animals; biography/autobiography; business; child guidance/parenting; computers/electronics; cooking/food/nutrition; crafts/hobbies; current affairs; government/politics/law; health/medicine; history; interior design/decorating; juvenile nonfiction; language/literature/criticism; money/finance/economics; music/dance/theater/film; nature/environment; psychology; religious/inspirational; self-help/personal improvement; sociology; sports; women's issues/women's studies. Considers these fiction areas: contemporary issues; family saga; historical; humor/satire; literary; regional; sports; thriller/espionage. Query with outline, sample chapters and SASE. Reports in 6 weeks on queries; 2 months on mss.
Recent Sales: *Crane's Wedding Blue Book*, by Steven Feinberg (Simon & Schuster).
Terms: Agent receives 15% on domestic sales. Offers written contract. Charges for extraordinary postage, photocopying and long-distance phone calls.
Tips: Obtains new clients through referrals and listings in various directories for writers and publishers. "Provide info on those publishers who have already been contacted, seen work, accepted or rejected same. Provide complete bio and marketing info."

THE SHUKAT COMPANY LTD., (III), 340 W. 55th St., Suite 1A, New York NY 10019-3744. (212)582-7614. Fax: (212)315-3752. Estab. 1972. Member of AAR. Currently handles: literary and dramatic works. Query with outline/proposal or 30 pages and SASE.

ROSALIE SIEGEL, INTERNATIONAL LITERARY AGENCY, INC., (III), 1 Abey Dr., Pennington NJ 08534. (609)737-1007. Fax: (609)737-3708. Contact: Rosalie Siegel. Estab. 1977. Member of AAR. Represents 35 clients. 10% of clients are new/previously unpublished writers. Specializes in foreign authors, especially French, though diminishing. Currently handles: 45% nonfiction books; 45% novels; 10% juvenile books and short story collections for current clients.
Terms: Agent receives 15% commission on domestic sales; 20% on foreign sales. Offers written contract, with 60 day cancellation clause. Charges for photocopying. 100% of business is derived from commissions.
Tips: Obtains new clients through referrals from writers and friends. "I'm not looking for new authors in an active way."

EVELYN SINGER LITERARY AGENCY INC., (III), P.O. Box 594, White Plains NY 10602-0594. Contact: Evelyn Singer. Estab. 1951. Represents 30 clients. 25% of clients are new/previously unpublished writers. Specializes in nonfiction (adult/juvenile, adult suspense).
● Prior to opening her agency, Ms. Singer served as an associate in the Jeanne Hale Literary Agency.
Handles: Nonfiction books, juvenile books, novels. (No textbooks). Considers these nonfiction areas: anthropology/archaeology; biography; business; child guidance; current affairs; ethnic/cultural interests; government/politics/law; health/medicine; how-to; juvenile nonfiction; money/finance/economics; nature/environment; psychology; religious/inspirational; science; self-help/personal improvement; women's issues/women's studies. Considers these fiction areas: contemporary issues; detective/police/crime; ethnic; feminist; historical; literary; mainstream; mystery/suspense; regional; thriller/espionage. Query. Reports in 2 weeks on queries; 6-8 weeks on mss. "SASE must be enclosed for reply or return of manuscript."
Recent Sales: *Destiny*, by Nancy Covert Smith (Avon); *Homecoming For Murder*, by John Armistead (Carroll & Graf); *Indian Uprising on the Rio Grande*, by Franklin Fosom (Univ. of New Mexico Press).
Terms: Agent receives 15% commission on domestic sales; 20% on foreign sales. Offers written contract, binding for 3 years. Charges for long-distance phone calls, overseas postage ("authorized expenses only").
Tips: Obtains new clients through recommendations. "I am accepting writers who have earned at least $20,000 from freelance writing. SASE must accompany all queries and material for reply and or return of ms." Enclose biographical material and double-spaced book outline or chapter outline.

‡IRENE SKOLNICK, (II), 121 W. 27th St., Suite 601, New York NY 10001. (212)727-3648. Fax: (212)727-1024. Contact: Irene Skolnick. Estab. 1993. Member of AAR. Represents 45 clients. 75% of clients are new/previously unpublished writers.
Handles: Adult nonfiction books, adult fiction. Considers these nonfiction areas: biography/autobiography; current affairs. Considers these fiction areas: contemporary issues; historical; literary. Query with SASE, outline and sample chapter. No unsolicited mss. Reports in 2-4 weeks on queries.

Terms: Agent receives 15% commission on domestic sales; 20% on foreign sales. Sometimes offers criticism service; charges for service vary. Charges for international postage, photocopying over 20 pages.

‡BEVERLEY SLOPEN LITERARY AGENCY, (III), 131 Bloor St. W., Suite 711, Toronto, Ontario M5S 1S3 Canada. (416)964-9598. Fax: (416)921-7726. E-mail: slopen@inforamp.net. Contact: Beverley Slopen. Estab. 1974. Represents 52 clients. 70% of clients are new/previously unpublished writers. "Strong bent towards Canadian writers." Currently handles: 60% nonfiction books; 40% novels.
Handles: Nonfiction books, scholarly books, novels, textbooks. Considers these nonfiction areas: anthropology/archaeology; biography/autobiography; business; child guidance/parenting; cooking/food/nutrition; current affairs; psychology; sociology; true crime/investigative; women's issues/women's studies. Considers these fiction areas: detective/police/crime; literary; mystery/suspense. Query. Reports in 4-6 weeks.
Terms: Agent receives 15% commission on domestic sales; 10% on foreign sales. Offers written contract, binding for 2 years, 90 days notice to terminate contract.
Tips: "Please, no unsolicited manuscripts."

VALERIE SMITH, LITERARY AGENT, (III), 1746 Rt. 44/55, Modena NY 12548-5205. (914)883-5848. Contact: Valerie Smith. Estab. 1978. Represents 30 clients. 1% of clients are new/previously unpublished writers. Specializes in science fiction and fantasy. Currently handles: 2% nonfiction books; 96% novels; 1% novellas; 1% short story collections.
Handles: Novels. Considers these fiction areas: fantasy; literary; mainstream; science fiction; young adult. Query. Reports in 2 weeks on queries; 2 months on mss.
Recent Sales: *The Enchanted Forest*, by Patricia C. Wrede (Harcourt Brace); *Freedom and Necessity*, by Steven Brust & Emma Bull (TOR).
Terms: Agent receives 15% commission on domestic sales; 20% on foreign sales. Offers written contract. Charges for "extraordinary expenses by mutual consent."
Tips: Obtains new clients through recommendations from other clients, various respected contacts.

MICHAEL SNELL LITERARY AGENCY, (II), P.O. Box 1206, Truro MA 02666-1206. (508)349-3718. Contact: Michael Snell. Estab. 1980. Represents 200 clients. 25% of clients are new/previously unpublished authors. Specializes in how-to, self-help and all types of business and computer books, from low-level how-to to professional and reference. Currently handles: 90% nonfiction books; 10% novels. Member agents: Michael Snell (nonfiction); Patricia Smith (fiction and children's books).
   • Prior to opening his agency, Mr. Snell served as an editor at Wadsworth and Addison-Wesley for 13 years.
Handles: Nonfiction books. Open to all nonfiction categories, especially business, health, law, medicine, psychology, science, women's issues. Query with SASE. Reports in 1 week on queries; 2 weeks on mss.
Recent Sales: *The Joy of Horses*, by Joy Roberts (Contemporary); *60 Second Chronic Pain Relief*, by Peter Lehndorff (New Horizon); *11 Commandments of Wildly Successful Women*, by Pam Gilbert (Macmillan); *Bulletproofing Windows 95*, by Glenn Murdock (McGraw-Hill).
Terms: Agent receives 15% on domestic sales; 15% on foreign sales.
Tips: Obtains new clients through unsolicited mss, word-of-mouth, *LMP* and *Guide to Literary Agents*. "Send a half- to a full-page query, with SASE. Brochure 'How to Write a Book Proposal' available on request and SASE."

ELYSE SOMMER, INC., (II), P.O. Box 75113, Forest Hills NY 11375. (718)263-2668. President: Elyse Sommer. Estab. 1952. Member of AAR. Represents 20 clients. Works with a small number of new/unpublished authors. Specializes in nonfiction: reference books, dictionaries, popular culture.
Handles: Query with outline. Reports in 2 weeks on queries.
Terms: Agent receives 15% commission on domestic sales (when advance is under 5,000, 10% over); 5% on dramatic sales; 20% on foreign sales. Charges for photocopying, long distance, express mail, extraordinary expenses.

F. JOSEPH SPIELER, (II, III), 154 W. 57th St., 13th Floor, Room 135, New York NY 10019. (212)757-4439. Fax: (212)333-2019. Contact: Joe Spieler, Lisa Ross or John Thornton. West Coast office: contact Victoria Shoemaker, principal agent, 1328 Sixth Street, #3, Berkeley CA 94710. (510)528-2616. Fax: (510)528-8117. Estab. 1981. Represents 60 clients. 2% of clients are new/previously unpublished writers. Member agents: John Thornton (nonfiction); Lisa M. Ross (fiction/nonfiction); Emily Bloch.
Handles: Nonfiction books, novels. Considers these nonfiction areas: biography/autobiography; business; child guidance/parenting; cooking/food/nutrition; current affairs; ethnic/cultural interests; gay/lesbian issues; government/politics/law; history; money/finance/economics; sociology; women's issues/women's studies. Considers these fiction areas: ethnic; family saga; feminist; gay; humor/satire;

lesbian; literary; mainstream. Query. Reports in 2 weeks on queries; 5 weeks on mss.
Recent Sales: *The Fifth Discipline Fieldbook*, by Bryan Smith/Peter Senge (Doubleday); *Blindside*, by Eamonn Fingelton (Houghton Mifflin); *Where Are You?*, by George Constable; *Swimming the Channel*, by Sally Freedman.
Terms: Agent receives 15% commission on domestic sales. Charges for long distance phone/fax, photocopying, postage.
Writers' Conferences: Frankfurt Bookfair (October); ABA (Chicago, June).
Tips: Obtains new clients through recommendations and *Literary Marketplace* listing.

PHILIP G. SPITZER LITERARY AGENCY, (III), 50 Talmage Farm Lane, East Hampton NY 11937. (516)329-3650. Fax: (516)329-3651. Contact: Philip Spitzer. Estab. 1969. Member of AAR. Represents 60 clients. 10% of clients are new/previously unpublished writers. Specializes in mystery/suspense, literary fiction, sports, general nonfiction (no how-to). Currently handles: 50% nonfiction books; 50% novels.
  ● Prior to opening his agency, Mr. Spitzer served at New York University Press, McGraw Hill and the John Cushman Associates literary agency.
Handles: Nonfiction books, novels. Considers these nonfiction areas: biography/autobiography; business; current affairs; ethnic/cultural interests; government/politics/law; health/medicine; history; language/literature/criticism; military/war; music/dance/theater/film; nature/environment; popular culture; psychology; sociology; sports; true crime/investigative. Considers these fiction areas: contemporary issues; detective/police/crime; literary; mainstream; mystery/suspense; sports; thriller/espionage. Send outline plus 1 sample chapter and SASE. Reports in 1 week on queries; 6 weeks on mss.
Recent Sales: *Trunk Music*, by Michael Connelly (Little, Brown); *Cadillac Jukebox*, by James Lee Burke (Hyperion); *Eva Le Gallienne*, by Helen Sheehy (Knopf); *Dancing After Hours*, Andre Dubus (Knopf); *What We Know So Far: The Wisdom of Women*, by Beth Benatorich (St. Martin's Press); *The Game of Their Lives*, by Geoffrey Douglas (Holt).
Terms: Agent receives 15% commission on domestic sales; 20% on foreign sales. Charges for photocopying.
Writers' Conferences: ABA (Chicago).
Tips: Usually obtains new clients on referral.

NANCY STAUFFER ASSOCIATES, (II, III), 171 Newbury St., Boston MA 02116-2839. (617)247-0356. Fax: (617)267-2412. Contact: Nancy Stauffer Cahoon. Estab. 1989. Member of PEN Center USA West; Boston Literary Agents Society; Advisory Board Member, Writers At Work, and the Entrada Institute. 10% of clients are new/previously unpublished writers. Currently handles: 50% nonfiction books; 50% fiction.
Handles: Nonfiction books, literary fiction, short story collections. Considers these nonfiction areas: animals; biography/autobiography; business; current affairs; ethnic/cultural interests; nature/environment; popular culture; self-help/personal improvement; sociology; translations. Considers these fiction areas: contemporary issues; literary; mainstream; regional. No unsolicited queries.
Recent Sales: *Indian Killer*, by Sherman Alexie (Grove/Atlantic); *Hole In Our Soul*, by Martha Bayles (Univ. of Chicago Press); *Vendetta*, by Arthur Hailey (Crown).
Terms: Agent receives 15% commission on domestic sales; 20% on foreign sales. Charges for messenger and express delivery; photocopying."
Writers' Conferences: Authors of the Flathead (Whitefish MT, October); Writers At Work (Park City UT, July); and the Radcliffe Publishing Course.
Tips: Obtains new clients primarily through referrals from existing clients.

STEPPING STONE, (IV), 59 W. 71st St., New York NY 10023. (212)362-9277. Fax: (212)501-8240. Contact: Sarah Jane Freymann. Member of AAR. Represents 75 clients. 20% of clients are new/previously unpublished writers. Currently handles: 75% nonfiction books; 2% juvenile books; 23% novels.
Handles: Nonfiction books, novels, lifestyle-illustrated. Considers these nonfiction areas: animals; anthropology/archaeology; art/architecture/design; biography/autobiography; business; child guidance/parenting; cooking/food/nutrition; current affairs; ethnic/cultural interests; gay/lesbian issues; health/medicine; history; interior design/decorating; nature/environment; New Age/metaphysics; psychology; religious/inspirational; self-help/personal improvement; women's issues/women's studies. Considers these fiction areas: contemporary issues; ethnic; literary; mainstream; mystery/suspense; thriller/espionage. Query with SASE. Reports in 2 weeks on queries; 6 weeks on mss.
Recent Sales: *Just Listen*, by Nancy O'Hara (Broadway); *From the Earth to the Table*, by John Ash (Dutton); *Southern Exposure*, by Chef Marvin Woods (Clarks & Potter); *7 Deadly Sins*, by Steve Schwartz (McMillan).
Terms: Agent receives 15% commission on domestic sales; 20% on foreign sales. Offers written contract. Charges for long distance, overseas postage, photocopying. 100% of business is derived from commissions on ms sales.

Tips: Obtains new clients through recommendations from others. "I love fresh new passionate works by authors who love what they are doing and have both natural talent and carefully honed skills."

GLORIA STERN LITERARY AGENCY, (II, III, IV), 2929 Buffalo Speedway, Houston TX 77098-1707. (713)963-8360. Fax: (713)963-8460. Contact: Gloria Stern. Estab. 1976. Member of AAR. Represents 35 clients. 20% of clients are new/previously unpublished writers. Specializes in history, biography, women's studies, child guidance, parenting, business, cookbooks, health, cooking, finance, sociology, true crime. Currently handles: 80% nonfiction books; 5% scholarly books; 15% novels.

• This agency is not affiliated with the Gloria Stern Agency located in California.

Handles: Nonfiction books, scholarly books, novels. Considers these nonfiction areas: anthropology/archaeology; art/architecture/design; biography; business; child guidance/parenting; cooking/food/nutrition; current affairs; ethnic/cultural interests; government/politics/law; health/medicine; history; how-to; language/literature/criticism; money/finance/economics; psychology; science/technology; self-help/personal improvement; sociology; sports; true crime/investigative; women's issues/women's studies. Considers these fiction areas: contemporary issues; detective/police/crime; ethnic; experimental; family saga; feminist; literary; mainstream; mystery/suspense; thriller/espionage. Query with outline plus 2 sample chapters and SASE. No unsolicited mss. Reports in 1 week on queries; 1 month on mss.

Recent Sales: *Sexual Politics: The Legacy*, by Sheila Tobias (Westview/HarperCollins); *Stefan in Love*, by Joseph Machlis (W.W. Norton); *Breaking the Science Barrier*, by Sheila Tobias and Carl Tomizoka (College Board); *Big Noise from Winnetka*, by Jeanne N. Clark (biography of Harold Ikes).

Terms: Agent receives 15% commission on domestic sales; 20% on foreign sales (shared). Offers written contract, binding for 60 days.

Tips: Obtain new clients through editors, previous clients, listings. "I prefer fiction authors that have some published work such as short stories in either commercial or literary magazines or come recommended by an editor or writer. I need a short outline of less than a page, one or two chapters and SASE. For nonfiction, I need credentials, an outline, competitive books, one or two chapters and SASE."

‡EMMA SWEENEY LITERARY AGENCY, (II), 245 E. 80th St., 7E, New York NY 10021. (212)744-6503. Fax: (212)734-1874. Contact: Emma Sweeney. Estab. 1993. Member of AAR. Represents 30 clients. 10% of clients are new/previously unpublished writers. Currently handles: 40% nonfiction books; 5% scholarly books; 50% novels; 5% novellas.

Handles: Nonfiction books, scholarly books, novels. Considers these nonfiction areas: agriculture/horticulture; animals; anthropology/archaeology; art/architecture/design; biography/autobiography; ethnic/cultural interests; gay/lesbian issues; history; humor; interior design/decorating; language/literature/criticism; nature/environment; New Age/metaphysics; translations; women's issues/women's studies. Considers these fiction areas: ethnic; family saga; feminist; gay; historical; lesbian; literary. For fiction, query; for nonfiction, send outline and 1 sample chapter. Reports in 1 month on queries; 6 weeks on mss.

Terms: Agent receives 15% commission on domestic sales; 10% on foreign sales; 10% sub agents. Offers written contract. Charges for messengers and photocopying.

Tips: Obtains new clients through recommendations from others.

ROSLYN TARG LITERARY AGENCY, INC., (III), 105 W. 13th St., New York NY 10011. (212)206-9390. Fax: (212)989-6233. Contact: Roslyn Targ. Original agency estab. 1945; name changed to Roslyn Targ Literary Agency, Inc. in 1970. Member of AAR. Represents approximately 100 clients. Member agents: Lynn Polvino (assistant).

Handles: Nonfiction books, juvenile books, novels, self-help, genre fiction. No mss without queries first. Query with outline, proposal, curriculum vitae, and SASE.

Recent Sales: *Mercy of a Rude Stream* (Vol. 4), by Henry Roth (St. Martin's Press); *A Mythic Life*, by Jean Houston (Harper San Francisco); *Biggie & the Poisoned Politician*, by Nancy Bell (St. Martin's Press); *Scarlet Music: A Life of Hildegard of Bingen*, by Joan Ohanneson (Crossroad Publishing); *Listening In*, by Sorrell Ames (Dutton Signet).

AGENTS RANKED I-IV are actively seeking new clients. Those ranked **V** prefer not to be listed but have been included to inform you they are not currently looking for new clients.

Terms: Agent receives 10-15% commission on domestic sales; 20% on foreign sales. Charges standard agency fees (bank charges, long distance fax, postage, photocopying, shipping of books, etc.).
Tips: Obtains new clients through recommendations, solicitation, queries. "This agency reads on an exclusive basis only."

SANDRA TAYLOR LITERARY ENTERPRISES, (II), 38 Fairfield Rd., Hancock NH 03449. (603)525-4436. (603)525-4654. Contact: Sandra Taylor. Estab. 1992. Member of the Boston Literary Agents' Society. Represents 20 clients. 30% of clients are new/previously unpublished writers. Specializes in adult nonfiction. Currently handles: 100% nonfiction books.
Handles: Nonfiction books. Considers these nonfiction areas: cooking/food/nutrition; health/fitness; horticulture; how-to; nature/environment. Send outline/proposal with SASE. Reports in 4-6 weeks on queries; 6-8 weeks on mss.
Recent Sales: *366 Questions About Your Cosmic Dance*, by John Coleman (Hazelden); *Oddity Odyssey*, by James Chenoweth (Henry Holt & Co.); *Homespun Fun*, by The Mother Connection (St. Martin's); *Big Fish/Little Fish Knitwear*, by Jil Eaton (Clarkson Potter).
Terms: Agent receives 15% commission on domestic sales; 20% on foreign sales. Offers written contract. 100% of business is derived from commissions on sales.
Tips: Obtains new clients through recommendations from others, solicitation and at conferences.

PATRICIA TEAL LITERARY AGENCY, (III), 2036 Vista Del Rosa, Fullerton CA 92831-1336. (714)738-8333. Contact: Patricia Teal. Estab. 1978. Member of AAR, RWA, Authors Guild. Represents 60 clients. Published authors only. Specializes in category fiction and commercial, how-to and self-help nonfiction. Currently handles: 10% nonfiction books; 90% novels.
Handles: Nonfiction books, novels. Considers these nonfiction areas: animals; biography/autobiography; child guidance/parenting; health/medicine; how-to; psychology; self-help/personal improvement; true crime/investigative; women's issues. Considers these fiction areas: glitz, mainstream, mystery/suspense, romance (contemporary, historical, regency). Query. Reports in 10 days on queries; 6 weeks on requested mss.
Recent Sales: *Heartbreak Ranch*, by F. Michaels et.al. (Harlequin); *Regencies*, by Donna David (Kensington); *Surf City Dogs*, by Patricia Guiver (Berkley).
Terms: Agent receives 10-15% commission on domestic sales; 20% on foreign sales. Offers written contract, binding for 1 year. Charges for postage, photocopying.
Writers' Conferences: Romance Writers of America conferences; Asilomar (California Writers Club); Bouchercon; ABA (Chicago, June); California State University San Diego (January); Hawaii Writers Conference (Maui).
Tips: Usually obtains new clients through recommendations from authors and editors or at conferences. "Include SASE with all correspondence."

‡TENTH AVENUE EDITIONS, INC., (II), 625 Broadway, Suite 903, New York NY 10012. (212)529-8900. Fax: (212)529-7399. E-mail: cgiboire@panix.com. Contact: Suzanne Cobban. Estab. 1984. Represents 12 clients. 50% of clients are new/previously unpublished writers. Currently handles: 80% nonfiction books; 20% juvenile books.
Handles: Nonfiction books, juvenile books. Considers these nonfiction areas: art/architecture/design; biography/autobiography; business; child guidance/parenting; ethnic/cultural interests; juvenile nonfiction; language/literature/criticism; nature/environment; New Age/metaphysics; photography; popular culture. Query. SASE required for a reply. Reports in 2-3 weeks on queries; 1-2 months on mss.
Terms: Agent receives 15% commission on domestic sales; 25% on foreign sales. Offers written contract, binding for usually 1 year. Charges for photocopying and fax/phone/courier for foreign sales.
Tips: Obtains new clients through recommendations (70%) and solicitation (30%).

TOAD HALL, INC., (IV), RR 2, Box 16B, Laceyville PA 18623. (717)869-2942. Fax: (717)869-1031. E-mail: toad.hall@prodigy.com. Contact: Sharon Jarvis, Anne Pinzow. Estab. 1982. Member of AAR. Represents 20 clients. 10% of clients are new/previously unpublished writers. Specializes in popular nonfiction, some category fiction. Prefers New Age, paranormal, unusual but popular approaches. Currently handles: 50% nonfiction books; 40% novels; 5% movie scripts; 5% ancillary projects. Member agents: Anne Pinzow (TV, movies); Roxi LaRose (unpublished writers).
Handles: Nonfiction books. Considers these nonfiction areas: animals; anthropology/archaeology; business; child guidance/parenting; cooking/food/nutrition; crafts/hobbies; health/medicine; how-to; nature/environment; New Age/metaphysics; popular culture; religious/inspirational; self-help/personal improvement. Considers these fiction areas: historical; mystery/suspense; romance (contemporary, historical, regency); science fiction. Query. "No fax or e-mail submissions considered." Reports in 3 weeks on queries; 3 months on mss.
Recent Sales: *Ablaze!*, by Larry Arnold (M. Evans); *Daemons*, by Camille Bacon-Smith (DAW); UFO model kit, by McDonald, Randle & Schmitt (Testor).

Terms: Agent receives 15% commission on domestic sales; 15% on foreign sales. Offers written contract, binding for 1 year. Charges for photocopying and special postage (i.e., express mail). 100% of business is derived from commissions on sales.

Also Handles: Movie scripts (feature film); TV scripts (TV mow, episodic drama). Considers these script areas: action/adventure; comedy; contemporary issues; detective/police/crime; ethnic; family saga; fantasy; feminist; historical; horror; humor; juvenile; mainstream; mystery/suspense; romantic comedy; science fiction. Send outline/proposal with query. "We only handle scripts written by our clients who have published material agented by us." Reports in 3 weeks on queries; 3 months on mss.

Terms: Agent receives 10% commission on domestic sales; 20% on foreign sales.

Tips: Obtains new clients through recommendations from others, solicitation, at conferences. "Pay attention to what is getting published. Show the agent you've done your homework!"

SUSAN TRAVIS LITERARY AGENCY, (I), 1317 N. San Fernando Blvd., #175, Burbank CA 91504-4236. (818)557-6538. Fax: (818)557-6549. Contact: Susan Travis. Estab. 1995. Represents 10 clients. 60% of clients are new/previously unpublished writers. Specializes in mainstream fiction and nonfiction. Currently handles: 70% nonfiction books; 30% novels.

• Prior to opening her agency, Ms. Travis served as an agent with the McBride Agency.

Handles: Nonfiction books, novels. Considers these nonfiction areas: agriculture/horticulture; biography/autobiography; business; child guidance/parenting; cooking/food/nutrition; crafts/hobbies; ethnic/cultural interests; gay/lesbian issues; health/medicine; how-to; interior design/decorating; money/finance/economics; nature/environment; popular culture; psychology; religious/inspirational; self-help/personal improvement; women's issues/women's studies. Considers these fiction areas: action/adventure; contemporary issues; erotica; ethnic; feminist; gay; historical; lesbian; literary; mainstream; mystery/suspense; romance (historical); thriller/espionage. Query. Reports in 3 weeks on queries; 4-6 weeks on mss.

Terms: Agent receives 15% commission on domestic sales; 20% on foreign sales. Offers written contract, binding for 1 year, with 60 day cancellation clause. Charges for photocopying of mss and proposals if copies not provided by author. 100% of business is derived from commissions on sales.

Tips: Obtains new clients through referrals from existing clients, and mss requested from query letters.

2M COMMUNICATIONS LTD., (II), 121 W. 27 St., #601, New York NY 10001. (212)741-1509. Fax: (212)691-4460. Contact: Madeleine Morel. Estab. 1982. Represents 40 clients. 20% of clients are new/previously unpublished writers. Specializes in adult nonfiction. Currently handles: 100% nonfiction books.

Handles: Nonfiction books. Considers these nonfiction areas: biography/autobiography; child guidance/parenting; ethnic/cultural interests; gay/lesbian issues; health/medicine; music/dance/theater/film; self-help/personal improvement; women's issues/women's studies. Query. Reports in 1 week on queries.

Recent Sales: *Contemporary Catholicism*, by P. Ryan, Ph.D. (Henry Holt); *Passover Dessert Cookbook*, by Penny Eisenberg (Macmillan); *American Folk Remedies*, by Elena Oumano (Avon).

Terms: Agent receives 15% commission on domestic sales; 20% on foreign sales. Offers written contract, binding for 2 years. Charges for postage, photocopying, long distance calls and faxes.

Tips: Obtains new clients through recommendations from others, solicitation.

SUSAN P. URSTADT INC. AGENCY, (II), P.O. Box 1676, New Canaan CT 06840-4208. (203)966-6111 or (203)972-2226. Contact: Susan P. Urstadt. Estab. 1975. Member of AAR. Represents 55 clients. 10% of clients are new/previously unpublished authors. Specializes in history, biography, current affairs and journalism, natural history and environment, illustrated books, popular reference, art, antiques, decorative arts, gardening, travel, horses, armchair cookbooks, business, medical, self-help, crafts, hobbies, collectibles. Currently handles: 95% nonfiction books.

Handles: Nonfiction books and select quality commercial literary fiction. Considers these nonfiction areas: agriculture/horticulture; animals; anthropology/archaeology; art/architecture/design; biography/autobiography; business; child guidance/parenting; cooking/food/nutrition; crafts/hobbies; current affairs; education; ethnic/cultural interests; health/medicine; history; how-to; interior design/decorating; juvenile nonfiction; military/war; money/finance/economics; music/dance/theater/film; nature/environment; photography; popular culture; self-help/personal improvement; sports; women's issues/women's studies. "No unsolicited fiction please." Send outline, 2 sample writings, short author bio and SASE. "Tell us 'why this book'." Reports in 3 weeks on queries.

Recent Sales: *Book of Traditions*, by Emyl Jenkins (Crown); *New England Fish Tales*, by Martha Murphy (Holt); *Roses for Cold Climates*, by Doug Green (Chapters); *Riding the Dragon*, (business), by Donald Krause (Putnam); *Whole Healing*, by Elliot Dacher; *Edith Warton Encyclopedia*, by Sarah Bird Wright.

Terms: Agent receives 15% commission on domestic sales; 20% on foreign sales. Offers written contract.

Writers' Conferences: ABA (Chicago, June).
Tips: Obtains new clients through recommendations from others and from high quality proposals. "We are interested in building a writer's career through the long term and only want dedicated writers with special knowledge, which they share in a professional way."

THE RICHARD R. VALCOURT AGENCY, INC., (I, II), 177 E. 77th St., PHC, New York NY 10021. Phone/fax: (212)570-2340. Contact: Richard R. Valcourt. Estab. 1995. Represents 150 clients. 30% of clients are new/previously unpublished writers. Specializes in intelligence and other national security affairs; domestic and international politics; current events and biographies. Currently handles: 60% nonfiction books; 40% novels.
Handles: Nonfiction books, scholarly books, novels. Considers these nonfiction areas: biography; business; current affairs; education; ethnic/cultural interests; government/politics/law; health/medicine; history; Judaica; language/literature/criticism; military/war; money/finance/economics; sociology. Considers these fiction areas: contemporary issues; historical; thriller/espionage. Query with SASE. Reports in 1 week on queries; 1 month on mss.
Terms: Agent receives 15% commission on domestic sales; 20% on foreign sales. Offers written contract. Charges for photocopying, express mail and extensive overseas telephone expenses.
Tips: Obtains new clients through active recruitment and recommendations from others.

VAN DER LEUN & ASSOCIATES, (II), 22 Division St., Easton CT 06612. (203)259-4897. Contact: Patricia Van der Leun. Estab. 1984. Represents 30 clients. Specializes in fiction, science, biography. Currently handles: 60% nonfiction books; 40% novels.
Handles: Nonfiction books, novels. Considers all nonfiction areas. Considers these fiction areas: contemporary issues; ethnic; history; literary; mainstream. Query. Reports in 2 weeks on queries; 1 month on mss.
Recent Sales: *Zen Physics*, by David Darling (HarperCollins); *First Comes Love*, by Marion Winik (Pantheon); *Wherever You Go, There You Are*, by Jon Kabat-Zinn (Hyperion).
Terms: Agent receives 15% on domestic sales; 25% on foreign sales. Offers written contract.
Tips: "We are interested in high-quality, serious writers only."

ANNETTE VAN DUREN AGENCY, (III), 925 N. Sweetzer Ave., #12, Los Angeles CA 90069. (213)650-3643. Fax: (213)654-3893. Contact: Annette Van Duren or Patricia Murphy. Estab. 1985. Signatory of WGA. Represents 12 clients. No clients are new/previously unpublished writers. Currently handles: 10% novels; 50% movie scripts; 40% TV scripts.
  • See the expanded listing for this agency in Script Agents.

THE VINES AGENCY, INC. (II), 409 E. Sixth St., #4, New York NY 10009. (212)777-5522. Fax: (212)777-5978. Contact: James C. Vines or Gary Neuwirth. Estab. 1995. Represents 52 clients. 2% of clients are new/previously unpublished writers. Specializes in mystery, suspense, science fiction, mainstream novels, graphic novels, CD-ROMs, screenplays, teleplays. Currently handles: 10% nonfiction books; 2% scholarly books; 10% juvenile books; 50% novels; 15% movie scripts; 5% TV scripts; 1% stage plays; 5% short story collections; 2% syndicated material.
  • Prior to opening his agency, Mr. Vines served as an agent with the Literary Group.
Handles: Nonfiction books, juvenile books, novels. Considers these nonfiction areas: business; child guidance/parenting; how-to; humor; juvenile nonfiction; money/finance/economics; music/dance/theater/film; popular culture; psychology; true crime/investigative; women's issues/women's studies. Considers these fiction areas: action/adventure; cartoon/comic; contemporary issues; detective/police/crime; ethnic; fantasy; feminist; horror; humor/satire; juvenile; literary; mainstream; mystery/suspense; picture book; psychic/supernatural; regional; romance (contemporary, gothic, historical, regency); science fiction; sports; thriller/espionage; westerns/frontier; young adult. Send outline and first 3 chapters with SASE. Reports in 2 weeks on queries; 1 month on mss.
Recent Sales: *Pest Control*, by Bill Fitzhugh), film rights to Spring Creek Productions for Warner Bros.).
Terms: Agent receives 15% commission on domestic sales; 20% on foreign sales. Offers written contract, binding for 1 year, with 30 days cancellation clause. Charges for foreign postage and photocopying. 100% of business is derived from commissions on sales.
Also Handles: Movie scripts, TV scripts, stage plays.
Writers' Conferences: Kent State Writer's Conference (Kent State University OH).
Tips: Obtains new clients through recommendations from others, reading short stories in magazines and soliciting conferences. "Do not follow up on submissions with phone calls to the agency. The agency will read and respond by mail only. Do not pack your manuscript in plastic 'peanuts' that will make us have to vacuum the office after opening the package containing your manuscript. Always enclose return postage."

MARY JACK WALD ASSOCIATES, INC., (III), 111 E. 14th St., New York NY 10003. (212)254-7842. Contact: Danis Sher. Estab. 1985. Member of AAR, Authors Guild, SCBWI. Represents 55 clients. 5% of clients are new/previously unpublished writers. Specializes in literary works, juvenile. Currently handles: adult and juvenile fiction and nonfiction, including some original film/TV scripts. Member agents: Danis Sher, Lem Lloyd. Foreign rights representative: Lynne Rabinoff, Lynne Rabinoff Associates.
Handles: Nonfiction books, juvenile books, novels, novellas, short story collections, movie scripts, TV scripts. Considers these nonfiction areas: biography/autobiography; current affairs; ethnic/cultural interests; history; juvenile nonfiction; language/literature/criticism; music/dance/theater/film; nature/environment; photography; sociology; translations; true crime/investigative. Considers these fiction areas: action/adventure; contemporary issues; detective/police/crime; ethnic; experimental; family saga; feminist; gay; glitz; historical; juvenile; literary; mainstream; mystery/suspense; picture book; satire; thriller; young adult. Query with SASE. Reports in 2 months on with SASE. Will request more if interested.
Recent Sales: *Tombstones*, by John Peel (Pocket Book series/Simon & Schuster); *Cactus Tracks Cowboy Commentary*, by Baxter Black (Crown); *Sandy Dennis—A Personal Memoir* (Papier-Mache).
Terms: Agent receives 15% commission on domestic sales; 15-30% on foreign sales. Offers written contract, binding for 1 year.
Tips: Obtains new clients through recommendations from others.

WALLACE LITERARY AGENCY, INC., (III), 177 E. 70 St., New York NY 10021. (212)570-9090. Contact: Lois Wallace, Thomas C. Wallace. Estab. 1988. Member of AAR. Represents 125 clients. 5% of clients are new/previously unpublished writers. Specializes in fiction and nonfiction by good writers. Currently handles: 60% nonfiction books; 35% novels; 5% magazine articles and short stories.
Handles: Nonfiction books, novels. Considers these nonfiction areas: anthropology/archaeology, biography/autobiography, current affairs, history, literature, military/war, science; true crime/investigative. Considers these fiction areas: literary, mainstream, mystery/suspense. Send outline, 1-2 sample chapters, reviews of previously published books, curriculum vitae, return postage. Reports in 2 weeks on queries; 3 weeks on mss.
Terms: Agent receives 10-15% commission on domestic sales; 20% on foreign sales. Offers written contract; binding until terminated with notice. Charges for photocopying, book shipping (or ms shipping) overseas, legal fees (if needed, with writer's approval), galleys and books needed for representation and foreign sales.
Tips: Obtains new clients through "recommendations from editors and writers we respect."

JOHN A. WARE LITERARY AGENCY, (II), 392 Central Park West, New York NY 10025-5801. (212)866-4733. Fax: (212)866-4734. Contact: John Ware. Estab. 1978. Represents 60 clients. 40% of clients are new/previously unpublished writers. Currently handles: 75% nonfiction books; 25% novels.
   ● Prior to opening his agency, Mr. Ware served as a literary agent with James Brown Associates/Curtis Brown, Ltd. and as an editor for Doubleday & Company.
Handles: Nonfiction books, novels. Considers these nonfiction areas: animals; anthropology; biography/autobiography (memoirs); current affairs; gay/lesbian issues; government/politics/law; history (including oral history, Americana and folklore); investigative journalism; language; military/war; music; nature/environment; popular culture; psychology and health (academic credentials required); science; sports; true crime; women's issues/women's studies; 'bird's eye' views of phenomena. Considers these fiction areas: accessible literate noncategory fiction; detective/police/crime; mystery/suspense; thriller/espionage. Query by mail first, include SASE. Reports in 2 weeks on queries.
Recent Sales: *Into Thin Air*, by Jon Krakauer (Villard/Random House); *Booth*, by David Robertson (Anchor/Doubleday); *Hoops Nation*, by Chris Ballard (Henry Holt & Company); *Lay Low and Don't Make the Big Mistake*, by Rich Herschlag and Brian Harris (Simon & Schuster/Fireside).
Terms: Agent receives 15% commission on domestic sales; 15% on dramatic sales; 20% on foreign sales. Charges for messenger service, photocopying, extraordinary expenses.
Writers' Conferences: Golden Isles Writers' Conference (St. Simons Island, GA).
Tips: "Writers must have appropriate credentials for authorship of proposal (nonfiction) or manuscript (fiction); no publishing track record required. Open to good writing and interesting ideas by new or veteran writers."

HARRIET WASSERMAN LITERARY AGENCY, (III), 137 E. 36th St., New York NY 10016. (212)689-3257. Contact: Harriet Wasserman. Member of AAR. Specializes in fiction and nonfiction, some young adult and children's.
Handles: Nonfiction books, novels. Considers "mostly quality fiction (novels)." Referrals only. No unsolicited material.

Terms: Information not provided.

WATERSIDE PRODUCTIONS, INC., (II), 2191 San Elijo Ave., Cardiff-by-the-Sea CA 92007-1839. (619)632-9190. Fax: (619)632-9295. E-mail: 75720.410@CompuServe.com Website: http://www.waterside.com. President: Bill Gladstone. Contact: Matt Wagner, Margot Maley. Estab. 1982. Represents 300 clients. 20% of clients are new/previously unpublished writers. Currently handles: 100% nonfiction. Member agents: Bill Gladstone (trade computer titles, business); Margot Maley (women's issues, serious nonfiction, trade computer titles); Matthew Wagner (trade computer titles, nonfiction); Carole McClendon (trade computer titles); David Fugate (trade computer titles, business, sports books, humor, popular culture); Chris Van Buren (trade computer titles, spirituality, self-help); Pedro Casals (trade computer titles, foreign rights); Adrien Gordon (spirituality, self-help, metaphysical, New Age).
Handles: Nonfiction books. Considers these nonfiction areas: art/architecture/design; biography/autobiography; business; child guidance/parenting; computers/electronics; ethnic/cultural interests; health/medicine; humor; money/finance/economics; nature/environment; New Age/metaphysics; popular culture; psychology; sociology; sports; true crime/investigative; women's issues/women's studies. Query with outline/proposal and SASE. Reports in 2 weeks on queries; 2 months on mss.
Recent Sales: *24 Hours in Cyberspace*, by Rick Smolan (Que); *Profit From Experience*, by Gil Amelio and Bill Simon (Van Nostrand Reinhold); *Windows 95 for Dummies*, by Andy Rathbone (IDG); *Java Sourcebook*, by Ed Anuff (John Wiley).
Terms: Agent receives 15% commission on domestic sales; 25% on foreign sales. Offers written contract. Charges for photocopying and other unusual expenses.
Writers' Conferences: "We host the Waterside Publishing Conference each spring in San Diego."
Tips: Usually obtains new clients through recommendations from others. "For new writers, a quality proposal and a strong knowledge of the market you're writing for goes a long way towards helping us turn you into a published author."

WATKINS LOOMIS AGENCY, INC., (II), 133 E. 35th St., Suite 1, New York NY 10016. (212)532-0080. Fax: (212)889-0506. Contact: Lily Oei. Estab. 1908. Represents 150 clients. Specializes in literary fiction, London/UK translations. Member agent: Nicole Aragi; Gloria Loomis.
Handles: Nonfiction books, novels. Considers these nonfiction areas: art/architecture/design; biography/autobiography; cooking/food/nutrition; current affairs; ethnic/cultural interests; gay/lesbian issues; history; nature/environment; popular culture; science/technology; translations; true crime/investigative; women's issues/women's studies; journalism. Considers these fiction areas: contemporary issues; detective/police/crime; ethnic; gay; literary; mainstream; mystery/suspense; young adult. Query with SASE. Reports within 1 month on queries.
Recent Sales: *Drown*, by Junot Diaz (Riverhead); *Snake*, by Kate Jennings (Ecco); *Maybe One Is Enough*, by Bill McKibben (Villard).
Terms: Agent receives 15% commission on domestic sales; 20% on foreign sales.

*SANDRA WATT & ASSOCIATES, (II), 8033 Sunset Blvd., Suite 4053, Hollywood CA 90046-2427. (213)851-1021. Contact: Davida South. Estab. 1977. Signatory of WGA. Represents 55 clients. 15% of clients are new/previously unpublished writers. Specializes in scripts: film noir; family; romantic comedies; books: women's fiction, young adult, mystery, commercial nonfiction. Currently handles: 40% nonfiction books; 35% novels; 25% movie scripts. Member agents: Sandra Watt (scripts, nonfiction, novels); Davida South (scripts); Phyllis Sterling (young adult, fiction); Cecilia Flanagan (young adult, literary fiction).
Handles: Nonfiction books, novels. Considers these nonfiction areas: agriculture/horticulture; animals; anthropology/archaeology; art/architecture/design; crafts/hobbies; current affairs; how-to; humor; language/literature/criticism; nature/environment; New Age/metaphysics; popular culture; psychology; reference; religious/inspirational; self-help/personal improvement; sports; true crime/investigative; women's issues/women's studies. Considers these fiction areas: contemporary issues; detective/police/crime; family saga; mainstream; mystery/suspense; regional; religious/inspirational; thriller/espionage; women's mainstream novels. Query. Reports in 1 week on queries; 2 months on mss.
Recent Sales: *Gabberrock & Twang*, by Raymond Obstfeld (Henry Holt); *Greek and Roman Readers*, by Ken Atchity (Henry Holt); *Death by Rhubarb*, by Jane Temple (St. Martin's Press).

✱ AN ASTERISK indicates those agents who only charge fees to new or previously unpublished writers or to writers only under certain conditions.

Also Handles: Movie scripts (feature film, documentary, animation); TV scripts (TV mow). Considers these script subject areas: action/adventure; cartoon/animation; comedy; contemporary issues; detective/police/crime; family saga; humor; juvenile; mainstream; mystery/suspense; psychic/supernatural; religious/inspirational; romantic comedy and drama; teen; thriller/suspense. Query with SASE. Reports in 1 week on queries; 2 months on mss.

Recent Sales: *Movie scripts optioned/sold: Frog Prince,* by Robert Williams (Disney); *TV scripts optioned/sold: Not My Son,* by Karen Cooper (NBC).

Terms: Agent receives 15% commission on domestic sales; 25% on foreign sales. Offers written contract, binding for 1 year. Charges one-time nonrefundable marketing fee of $100 *for unpublished authors.*

Tips: Obtains new clients through recommendations from others, referrals and "from wonderful query letters. Don't forget the SASE!"

WECKSLER-INCOMCO, (II), 170 West End Ave., New York NY 10023. (212)787-2239. Fax: (212)496-7035. Contact: Sally Wecksler. Estab. 1971. Represents 20 clients. 50% of clients are new/previously unpublished writers. "However, I prefer writers who have had something in print." Specializes in nonfiction with illustrations (photos and art). Currently handles: 60% nonfiction books; 15% novels; 25% juvenile books. Member agents: Joann Amparan (general), S. Wecksler (foreign rights/co-editions).

Handles: Nonfiction books, novels, juvenile books. Considers these nonfiction areas: art/architecture design; biography/autobiography; business; current affairs; history; juvenile nonfiction; literary; music/dance/theater/film; nature/environment; photography. Considers these fiction areas: contemporary issues; historical; juvenile; literary; mainstream; picture book. Query with outline plus 3 sample chapters. Reports in 1 month on queries; 2 months on mss.

Recent Sales: *Do's & Taboos—Women in International Business,* by Roger Axtell (Wiley).

Terms: Agent receives 12-15% commission on domestic sales; 20% on foreign sales. Offers written contract, binding for 3 years.

Tips: Obtains new clients through recommendations from others and solicitations. "Make sure a SASE is enclosed. Send a clearly typed or word processed manuscript, double-spaced, written with punctuation and grammar in approved style. We do not like to receive presentations by fax."

THE WENDY WEIL AGENCY, INC. (V), 232 Madison Ave., Suite 1300, New York NY 10016. This agency did not respond to our request for information. Query before submitting.

CHERRY WEINER LITERARY AGENCY, (IV,V), 28 Kipling Way, Manalapan NJ 07726-3711. (908)446-2096. Fax: (908)792-0506. Contact: Cherry Weiner. Estab. 1977. Represents 40 clients. 10% of clients are new/previously unpublished writers. Specializes in science fiction, fantasy, westerns, all the genre romances. Currently handles: 2-3% nonfiction books; 97% novels.

● This agency is not currently looking for new clients except by referral or by contact at writers' conferences.

Handles: Nonfiction books, novels. Considers self-help/improvement, sociology nonfiction. Considers these fiction areas: action/adventure; contemporary issues; detective/police/crime; family saga; fantasy; glitz; historical; mainstream; mystery/suspense; psychic/supernatural; romance; science fiction; thriller/espionage; westerns/frontier. Query. Reports in 1 week on queries; 2 months on mss.

Recent Sales: *Strands of Strands* and two more, by Gael Boudino (ROC/NAL); *Lord Meren* series, by Lynda S. Robinson (Walker); *The White Abacus,* by Damien Broderick (Avon/Morrow); *Wyoming Renegade,* by Susan Amarillas (Harlequin); *The Hard Land,* by Jack Ballas (Berkley).

Terms: Agent receives 15% on domestic sales; 15% on foreign sales. Offers written contract. Charges for extra copies of mss "but would prefer author do it"; 1st class postage for author's copies of books; Express Mail for important document/manuscripts.

Writers' Conferences: Western Writers Convention (Albuquerque, June); Golden Triangle; Fantasy Convention.

Tips: "Meet agents and publishers at conferences. Establish a relationship, then get in touch with them reminding them of meetings and conference."

THE WEINGEL-FIDEL AGENCY, (III), 310 E. 46th St., 21E, New York NY 10017. (212)599-2959. Contact: Loretta Fidel. Estab. 1989. Specializes in commercial, literary fiction and nonfiction. Currently handles: 50% nonfiction books; 50% novels.

Handles: Nonfiction books, novels. Considers these nonfiction areas: art/architecture/design; biography/autobiography; investigative; music/dance/theater/film; psychology; science; sociology; women's issues/women's studies. Considers these fiction areas: contemporary issues; literary; mainstream. Referred writers only. No unsolicited mss.

Recent Sales: *Sleepers*, by Lorenzo Carcaterra (Ballantine, film rights to Propaganda Films);
Terms: Agent receives 15% on domestic sales; 20% on foreign sales. Offers written contract, binding for 1 year automatic renewal. Bills back to clients all reasonable expenses such as UPS, express mail, photocopying, etc.
Tips: Obtains new clients through referrals.

WEST COAST LITERARY ASSOCIATES, (II), 7960-B Soquel Dr., Suite 151, Aptos CA 95003-3945. (408)685-9548. E-mail: westlit@aol.com. Contact: Richard Van Der Beets. 1986. Member of Authors League of America, Authors Guild. Represents 50 clients. 75% of clients are new/previously unpublished clients. Currently handles: 20% nonfiction books; 80% novels.
● Prior to opening his agency, Mr. Van Der Beets served as a professor of English at San Jose State University.
Handles: Nonfiction books, novels. Considers these nonfiction areas: biography/autobiography; current affairs; ethnic/cultural interests; government/politics/law; history; language/literature/criticism; music/dance/theater/film; nature/environment; psychology; true crime/investigative; women's issues/women's studies. Considers these fiction areas: action/adventure; contemporary issues; detective/police/crime; experimental; historical; literary; mainstream; mystery/suspense; regional; romance (contemporary and historical); science fiction; thriller/espionage; westerns/frontier. Query first. Reports in 2 weeks on queries; 1 month on mss.
Terms: Agent receives 10% commission on domestic sales; 20% commission on foreign sales. Offers written contract, binding for 6 months.
Recent Sales: *Lorien Lost*, by Michael King (St. Martin's/A Wyatt Book); *Blues for the Buffalo*, by Manuel Ramos (St. Martin's); *The Tears of the Madonna*, by George Herman (Carroll & Graf).
Fees: Does not charge a reading fee. Charges $75-95 marketing and materials fee, depending on genre and length. Fees are refunded in full upon sale of the property.
Writers' Conferences: California Writer's Conference (Asilomar).
Tips: "Query with SASE for submission guidelines before sending material."

RHODA WEYR AGENCY, (II, III), 151 Bergen St., Brooklyn NY 11217. (718)522-0480. President: Rhoda A. Weyr. Estab. 1983. Member of AAR. Prefers to work with published/established authors; works with a small number of new/unpublished authors. Specializes in general nonfiction and fiction.
Handles: Nonfiction books, novels. Query with outline, sample chapters and SASE.
Terms: Agent receives 15% commission on domestic sales; 20% on foreign sales.

WIESER & WIESER, INC., (III), 118 E. 25th St., 7th Floor, New York NY 10010-2915. (212)260-0860. Contact: Olga Wieser. Estab. 1975. 30% of clients are new/previously unpublished writers. Specializes in mainstream fiction and nonfiction. Currently handles: 50% nonfiction books; 50% novels. Member agents: Jake Elwell (history, contemporary, sports, mysteries, romance); George Wieser (contemporary fiction, thrillers, current affairs); Olga Wieser (psychology, fiction, pop medical, translations, literary fiction).
Handles: Nonfiction books, novels. Considers these nonfiction areas: business; cooking/food/nutrition; current affairs; health/medicine; history; money/finance/economics; nature/environment; psychology; translations; true crime/investigative. Considers these fiction areas: contemporary issues; detective/police/crime; historical; literary; mainstream; mystery/suspense; romance; thriller/espionage. Query with outline/proposal. Reports in 1 week on queries.
Recent Sales: *Brightspun Destiny*, by Elizabeth Gregg (Topaz); *Medusa's Child*, by John J. Nance (Doubleday); *Virus*, by Bill Buchanan (Berkley); *The Good Cigar*, by H. Paul Jeffers (Lyons & Burford).
Terms: Agent receives 15% commission on domestic sales; 20% on foreign sales. Offers written contract. Offers criticism service. "No charge to our clients or potential clients." Charges for photocopying and overseas mailing.
Writers' Conferences: ABA; Frankfurt Book Fair.
Tips: Obtains new clients through queries, authors' recommendations and industry professionals.

WITHERSPOON & ASSOCIATES, INC., (II), 157 W. 57th St., Suite 700, New York NY 10019. (212)757-0567. Fax: (212)757-2982. Contact: Michele Geminder. Estab. 1990. Represents 100 clients. 20% of clients are new/previously unpublished writers. Currently handles: 50% nonfiction books; 45% novels; 5% short story collections. Member agent: Maria Massie (subsidiary rights).
Handles: Nonfiction books, novels. Considers these nonfiction areas: anthropology/archaeology; biography/autobiography; business; current affairs; ethnic/cultural interests; gay/lesbian issues; government/politics/law; health/medicine; history; money/finance/economics; music/dance/theater/film; science/technology; self-help/personal improvement; true crime/investigative; women's issues/women's studies. Considers these fiction areas: contemporary issues; detective/police/crime; ethnic; family saga; feminist; gay; glitz; historical; humor/satire; lesbian; literary; mainstream; mystery/suspense; romance

(contemporary); thriller/espionage. Query with SASE. Reports in 3 weeks on queries; 6-8 weeks on mss.

Recent Sales: *Tabloid Dreams*, by Robert Olen Butler (Holt); *The Story of B*, by Daniel Quinn (Bantam); *Eat Fat*, by Richard Klein (Pantheon); *Sex Crimes*, by Jennifer Shute (Doubleday).

Terms: Agent receives 15% commission on domestic sales; 20% on foreign sales. Offers written contract.

Writers' Conferences: ABA (Chicago, June); Frankfort (Germany, October).

Tips: Obtains new clients through recommendations from others, solicitation and conferences.

RUTH WRESCHNER, AUTHORS' REPRESENTATIVE, (II, III), 10 W. 74th St., New York NY 10023-2403. (212)877-2605. Fax: (212)595-5843. Contact: Ruth Wreschner. Estab. 1981. Represents 80 clients. 70% of clients are new/unpublished writers. "In fiction, if a client is not published yet, I prefer writers who have written for magazines; in nonfiction, a person well qualified in his field is acceptable." Prefers to work with published/established authors; works with new/unpublished authors. "I will always pay attention to a writer referred by another client." Specializes in popular medicine, health, how-to books and fiction (no pornography, screenplays or dramatic plays). Currently handles: 80% nonfiction books; 10% novels; 5% textbooks; 5% juvenile books.

● Prior to opening her agency, Ms. Wreschner served as an administrative assistant and associate editor at John Wiley & Sons for 17 years.

Handles: Nonfiction books, textbooks, adult and young adult fiction. Considers these nonfiction areas: biography/autobiography; business; child guidance/parenting; cooking/food/nutrition; crafts/hobbies; current affairs; ethnic/cultural interests; gay/lesbian issues; government/politics/law; health/medicine; history; how-to; juvenile nonfiction; money/finance/economics; popular culture; psychology; religious/inspirational; science/technology; self-help/personal improvement; true crime/investigative; women's issues/women's studies. Considers these fiction areas: action/adventure; contemporary issues; detective/police/crime; ethnic; family saga; gay; glitz; historical; horror; juvenile; lesbian; literary; mainstream; mystery/suspense; romance (contemporary, historical, regency); thriller/espionage; young adult. Particularly interested in literary, mainstream and mystery fiction. Query with outline. Reports in 2 weeks on queries.

Recent Sales: *Wall Street's Picks 1996* and *How To Buy Mutual Funds Free*, by Kirk Kazanjian (Dearborn); *The Seven Secrets of Successful Parents*, by Randy C. Rolfe (Contemporary); *Poised For Growth*, by Gabor Baumann/J.M. Weinstein (McGraw-Hill); *Eye Laser Surgery*, by Andrew Caster, M.D. (Ballantine/Random House).

Terms: Agent receives 15% commission on domestic sales; 20% on foreign sales. Charges for photocopying expenses. "Once a book is placed, I will retain some money from the second advance to cover airmail postage of books, long-distance calls, etc. on foreign sales. I may consider charging for reviewing contracts in future. In that case I will charge $50/hour plus long-distance calls, if any."

Writers' Conference: ABA (Chicago, June); New Jersey Romance Writer (September).

WRITERS HOUSE, (III), 21 W. 26th St., New York NY 10010. (212)685-2400. Fax: (212)685-1781. Estab. 1974. Member of AAR. Represents 280 clients. 50% of clients were new/unpublished writers. Specializes in all types of popular fiction and nonfiction, as well as the writing for multimedia projects such as "The Seventh Guest." No scholarly, professional, poetry or screenplays. Currently handles: 25% nonfiction books; 35% juvenile books; 40% novels. Member agents: Albert Zuckerman (major novels, thrillers, women's fiction, important nonfiction); Amy Berkower (major juvenile authors, women's fiction, art and decorating, psychology); Merrillee Heifetz (science fiction and fantasy, popular culture, literary fiction); Susan Cohen (juvenile and young adult fiction and nonfiction, Judaism, women's issues); Susan Ginsberg (serious and popular fiction, true crime, narrative nonfiction, personality books, cookbooks); Fran Lebowitz (juvenile and young adult, mysteries, computer-related books, popular culture); Michele Rubin (serious nonfiction); Liza Landsman (multimedia); Karen Solem (contemporary and historical romance, women's fiction, narrative nonfiction, horse and animal books).

Handles: Nonfiction books, juvenile books, novels, proposals for multimedia project. Considers these nonfiction areas: animals; art/architecture/design; biography/autobiography; business; child guidance/parenting; cooking/food/nutrition; health/medicine; history; interior design/decorating; juvenile nonfiction; military/war; money/finance/economics; music/dance/theater/film; nature/environment; psychology; science/technology; self-help/personal improvement; true crime/investigative; women's issues/

TO FIND AN AGENT near you, check the Geographic Index.

women's studies. Considers any fiction area. "Quality is everything." Query. Reports in 1 month on queries.

Recent Sales: *A Place Called Freedom*, by Ken Follett (Crown); *The Babysitters Club*, by Ann Martin, (Scholastic); *Born In Ice*, by Nora Roberts (Jove); *Writing The Blockbuster Novel*, by Albert Zuckerman (Writer's Digest Books).

Terms: Agent receives 15% commission on domestic sales; 20% on foreign sales. Offers written contract, binding for 1 year.

Tips: Obtain new clients through recommendations from others. "Do not send manuscripts. Write a compelling letter. If you do, we'll ask to see your work."

WRITERS' PRODUCTIONS, (II), P.O. Box 630, Westport CT 06881-0630. (203)227-8199. Contact: David L. Meth. Estab. 1982. Represents 25 clients. Specializes in literary-quality fiction and nonfiction, with a special interest in Asia. Currently handles: 40% nonfiction books; 60% novels.

Handles: Nonfiction books, novels. "Literary quality fiction. Especially interested in children's work that creates a whole new universe of characters and landscapes that goes across all media, i.e.—between Hobbits and Smurfs. Must be completely unique and original, carefully planned and developed." Send query letter only with SASE. Reports in 1 week on queries; 1 month on mss.

Terms: Agent receives 15% on domestic sales; 25% on foreign sales; 25% on dramatic sales; 25% on new media or multimedia sales. Offers written contract. Charges for electronic transmissions, long-distance calls, express or overnight mail, courier service, etc.

Tips: Obtain new clients through word of mouth. "Send only your best, most professionally prepared work. Do not send it before it is ready. We must have SASE for all correspondence and return of manuscripts. No telephone calls, please."

WRITERS' REPRESENTATIVES, INC., (II), 25 W. 19th St., New York NY 10011-4202. (212)620-9009. Contact: Glen Hartley or Lynn Chu. Estab. 1985. Represents 100 clients. 5% of clients are new/previously unpublished writers. Currently handles: 90% nonfiction books; 10% novels.

Handles: Nonfiction books, novels. Considers literary fiction. "Nonfiction submissions should include book proposal, detailed table of contents and sample chapter(s). For fiction submissions send sample chapters not synopses. All submissions should include author biography and publication list. SASE required." Does not accept unsolicited mss.

Recent Sales: *The Wealth of Cities*, by John Norquist (Addison-Wesley); *Tax Cut*, by Bob Dole (HarperCollins); *Roll Me Over*, by Raymond Gantler (Ballantine). *The Invention of the Human: Shakespeare's Characters*, by Harold Bloom (Riverhead); *It's Not My Fault*, by James Q. Wilson (HarperCollins).

Terms: Agent receives 15% commission on domestic sales; 20% on foreign sales. "We charge for out-of-house photocopying as well as messengers, courier services (e.g., Federal Express), etc."

Tips: Obtains new clients "mostly on the basis of recommendations from others. Always include a SASE that will ensure a response from the agent and the return of material submitted."

‡THE GAY YOUNG AGENCY, INC., (II), 700 Washington St., Suite 3 Upper, New York NY 10014. (212)691-3124. Fax: (212)807-9772. E-mail: gyagency@aol.com. Contact: Gay Young. Estab. 1993. Member of New York State Bar. Represents 20 clients. 35% of clients are new/previously unpublished writers. Specializes in new media, e.g., Internet, World Wide Web, CD-ROM, and electronic rights. Currently handles: 35% nonfiction books, 25% juvenile books, 10% novels, 30% electronic rights.

Handles: Nonfiction books, juvenile books. Considers these nonfiction areas: business; computers/electronics; cooking/food/nutrition; current affairs; ethnic/cultural interests; government/politics/law; health/medicine; history; humor; juvenile nonfiction; language/literature/criticism; money/finance/economics; music/dance/theater/film; popular culture; science/technology; women's issues/women's studies; new media. Considers these fiction areas: ethnic; feminist; juvenile; literary; mainstream; young adult. Query with outline/proposal. Reports in 1-2 weeks on queries; 2-3 weeks on mss.

Terms: Agent receives 15% commission on domestic sales. Offers written contract binding for 1 year with a 30 day cancellation clause. Charges for photocopying, courier or other overnight services.

Tips: Obtains new clients through recommendations. "Make your best effort (i.e., type query letter, check grammar, be professional) and be persistent."

KAREN GANTZ ZAHLER LITERARY AGENCY, (III), 860 Fifth Ave., New York NY 10021. Contact: Karen Gantz Zahler. Estab. 1990. Represents 40 clients. Specializes in nonfiction, cookbooks. Currently handles: 70% nonfiction books; 20% novels; 10% movie scripts.

● Ms. Gantz is also an entertainment lawyer.

Handles: Nonfiction books, novels, movie scripts. Considers all nonfiction and fiction areas; "anything great." Query. Reports in 2 months.

Recent Sales: *The Whole Truth: Kato Kaelin*, by Marc Elliot (HarperCollins); *Rosa Mexicano Cookbook*, by Josephina Howard (Penguin); *Faxes to God*, by Joyce Starr (Harper San Francisco).

Terms: Agent receives 15% commission on domestic sales; 20% commission on foreign sales. Offers written contract, binding for 1 year.

Writers' Conferences: ABA.

Tips: Obtains new clients through recommendations from others. "I'm a literary property lawyer and provide excellent negotiating services and exploitation of subsidiary rights."

SUSAN ZECKENDORF ASSOC. INC., (II), 171 W. 57th St., New York NY 10019. (212)245-2928. Contact: Susan Zeckendorf. Estab. 1979. Member of AAR. Represents 35 clients. 25% of clients are new/previously unpublished writers. Currently handles: 50% nonfiction books; 50% fiction.

Handles: Nonfiction books, novels. Considers these nonfiction areas: art/architecture/design; biography/autobiography; child guidance/parenting; health/medicine; history; music/dance/theater/film; psychology; science; sociology; true crime/investigative; women's issues/women's studies. Considers these fiction areas: action/adventure; contemporary issues; detective/police/crime; ethnic; family saga; glitz; historical; literary; mainstream; mystery/suspense; thriller/espionage. Query. Reports in 10 days on queries; 3 weeks mss.

Recent Sales: *The Best Address: A History of Fifth Avenue*, by Terry E. Patterson (Rizzuli); *Lethal Lessons*, by Karen Stryck (Berkley); *Fishing Sports for Women*, by Laurie Morrow (St. Martin's Press).

Terms: Agent receives 15% commission on domestic sales; 20% on foreign sales. Charges for photocopying, messenger services.

Writers' Conferences: Central Valley Writers Conference; the Tucson Publishers Association Conference; Writer's Connection; Frontiers in Writing Conference (Amarillo, TX); Golden Triangle Writers Conference (Beaumont TX); Oklahoma Festival of Books (Claremont OK).

Tips: Obtains new clients through recommendations, listings in writer's manuals.

‡BARBARA J. ZITWER AGENCY, (II), 525 West End Ave. #7H, New York NY 10024. (212)501-8426. Fax: (212)501-8462. Contact: Barbara J. Zitwer. Estab. 1994. Represents 20 clients. 99% of clients are new/previously unpublished writers. Specializes in literary/commercial fiction, nonfiction, pop culture. Currently handles: 35% nonfiction books, 65% novels. Member agent: Jakob Keel.

Handles: Nonfiction books, novels, TV scripts. Considers these nonfiction areas: biography/autobiography; current affairs; ethnic/cultural interests; gay/lesbian issues; humor; language/literature/criticism; music/dance/theater/film; nature/environment; New Age/metaphysics; popular culture; psychology; self-help/personal improvement; true crime/investigative. Considers these fiction areas: detective/police/crime; ethnic; gay; glitz; humor/satire; literary; mainstream; mystery/suspense; thriller/espionage. Send outline and 3 sample chapters with SASE. Reports in 2 weeks on queries; 4-6 weeks on mss.

Recent Sales: *Misbegotten*, by James Gabriel Berman (movie sale of book to American World Pictures); *Astronumerology*, by Pam Bell and Jordan Simon (Avon).

Terms: Agent receives 15% commission on domestic sales; 25% on foreign sales. Offers a written contract, binding for 6 months. Charges for postage, photocopying, long distance calls, legal fees for movie contracts.

Writer's Conferences: Newport Writer's Conference (Newport RI, September); Marymount Manhattan Writer's Conference (New York, May); New York University Publishing Program (New York, October).

Tips: Usually obtains clients through recommendations from other clients and editors. "1. Check your agent's reputation with editors and publishers. 2. Try to meet your potential agent. 3. Make sure you and the agent have the same goals. 4. Make sure you are given very specific updates on submissions and rejection letters. 5. Educate yourself—you need to be a part of your business too."

Additional Nonfee-charging Agents

The following nonfee-charging agencies have indicated they are *primarily* interested in handling the work of scriptwriters, but also handle less than ten to fifteen percent book manuscripts. After reading the main listing (find the page number in the Listings Index), send a query to obtain information on needs and manuscript submission policies. Note: Double daggers (‡) before titles indicate listings new to this edition.

Above the Line Agency
All-Star Talent Agency
Michael Amato Agency
‡Suzanna Camejo & Assoc.
Cinema Talent International
Communications and Entertainment, Inc.
Communications Management Associates
Dramatic Publishing

‡ES Talent Agency
The Susan Gurman Agency
‡HWA Talent Reps.
Legacies
Lenhoff/Robinson Talent and Literary Agency, Inc.
Montgomery-West Literary Agency
Panda Talent
‡Barry Perelman Agency

Premiere Artists Agency
Producers & Creatives Group
Stephanie Rogers And Associates
Jack Scagnetti Talent & Literary Agency
Ken Sherman & Associates
‡Lee Sobel Mgmt. Associates

Literary Agents:
Fee-charging

This section contains literary agencies that charge a fee to writers in addition to taking a commission on sales. The sales commissions are the same as those taken by nonfee-charging agents: 10 to 15 percent for domestic sales, 20 to 25 percent for foreign and dramatic sales, with the difference going to the subagent.

Several agencies charge fees only under certain circumstances, generally for previously unpublished writers. These agencies are indicated by an asterisk (*). Most agencies will consider you unpublished if you have subsidy publishing, local or small press publication credits only; check with a prospective agency before sending material to see if you fit its definition of published.

Agents who charge one-time marketing fees in excess of $100 are also included in this section. Those who charge less than $100 and do not charge for other services appear in the Literary Agents: Nonfee-charging section.

READING FEES AND CRITIQUE SERVICES

The issue of reading fees is as controversial for literary agents as for those looking for representation. While some agents dismiss the concept as inherently unethical and a scam, others see merit in the system, provided an author goes into it with his eyes open. Some writers spend hundreds of dollars for an "evaluation" that consists of a poorly written critique full of boilerplate language that says little, if anything, about their individual work. Others have received the helpful feedback they needed to get their manuscript in shape and have gone on to publish their work successfully.

Since January 1, 1996, however, all members of the AAR have been prohibited from directly charging reading fees. Until that time some members were allowed to continue to charge fees, provided they adhered to guidelines designed to protect the client. A copy of the AAR's Canon of Ethics may be obtained for $7 and a SASE. The address is listed in Professional Organizations toward the end of the book.

Be wary of an agent who recommends a specific book doctor. While the relationship may be that the agent trusts that professional editor's work, it is too hard to tell if there are other reasons the agent is working with him. As with the AAR, the Writers Guild of America, which franchises literary agencies dealing largely in scripts, prohibits their signatories from such recommendations simply because it is open to abuse.

In discussing consideration of a fee-charging agent, we must underscore the importance of research. Don't be bowled over by an impressive brochure or an authoritative manner. At the same time, overly aggressive skepticism may kill your chances with a legitimate agent. Business-like, professional behavior will help you gather the material you need to make an informed decision.
- Obtain a fee schedule and ask questions about the fees. Be sure you understand what the fees cover and what to expect for your money.
- Request a sample critique the agent has done for another person's manuscript. Are the suggestions helpful and specific? Do they offer advice you couldn't get elsewhere, such as in writing groups, conferences and seminars or reference books?
- Ask for recent sales an agent has made. Many agents have a pre-printed list of sales

they can send you. If there haven't been any sales made in the past two years, what is the agent living on? An agent's worth to you, initially, is who they know and work with. In the listings we provide information on the percentage of income an agency receives from commissions on sales, and the percentage from reading or critique fees.

• Verify a few of these sales. To verify that the publisher has a book by that title, check *Books in Print*. To verify that the agent made the sale, call the contracts department of the publisher and ask who the agent of record is for a particular title.

Recently, there has been a trend among a few agents to recommend contracts with subsidy publishers that ask the writer to pay from $3,500 to $6,000 toward the cost of publication. These deals are open to writers directly, without the intermediating "assistance" of an agent. Your best defense is to carefully examine the list of an agent's recent sales and investigate some of the publishers.

Don't hesitate to ask the questions that will help you decide. The more you know about an agent and her abilities, the fewer unpleasant surprises you'll receive.

Fees range from one agency to another in nomenclature, price and purpose. Here are some of the more frequent services and their generally-accepted definitions.

• *Reading fee*. This is charged for reading a manuscript (most agents do not charge to look at queries alone). Often the fee is paid to outside readers. It is generally a one-time, nonrefundable fee, but some agents will return the fee or credit it to your account if they decide to take you on as a client. Often an agent will offer to refund the fee upon sale of the book, but that isn't necessarily a sign of good faith. If the agency never markets your manuscript no sale would ever be made and the fee never refunded.

• *Evaluation fee*. Sometimes a reading fee includes a written evaluation, but many agents charge for this separately. An evaluation may be a one-paragraph report on the marketability of a manuscript or a several-page evaluation covering marketability along with flaws and strengths.

• *Marketing fees*. Usually a one-time charge to offset the costs of handling work, marketing fees cover a variety of expenses and may include initial reading or evaluation. Beware of agencies charging a monthly marketing fee; there is nothing to compel them to submit your work in a timely way if they are getting paid anyway.

• *Critiquing service*. Although "critique" and "evaluation" are sometimes used interchangeably, a critique is usually more extensive, with suggestions on ways to improve the manuscript. Many agents offer critiques as a separate service and have a standard fee scale, based on a per-page or word-length basis. Some agents charge fees based on the extent of the service required, ranging from overall review to line-by-line commentary.

• *Editing service*. While we do not list businesses whose primary source of income is from editing, we do list agencies who also offer this service. Many do not distinguish between critiques and edits, but we define editing services as critiques that include detailed suggestions on how to improve the work and reduce weaknesses. Editing services can be charged on similar bases as critiquing services.

• *Consultation services*. Some agents charge an hourly rate to act as a marketing consultant, a service usually offered to writers who are not clients and who just want advice on marketing. Some agents are also available on an hourly basis for advice on publishers' contracts.

• *Other services*. Depending on an agent's background and abilities, the agent may offer a variety of other services to writers including ghostwriting, typing, copyediting, proofreading, translating, book publicity, and legal advice.

Be forewarned that payment of a critique or editing fee does not ensure that an agent will take you on as a client. However, if you feel you need more than sales help and would not mind paying for an evaluation or critique from a professional, the agents listed in this section may interest you.

SPECIAL INDEXES AND ADDITIONAL HELP

To help you with your search, we've included a number of special indexes in the back of the book. The Subject Index is divided into sections for nonfee-charging and fee-charging literary agents and script agents. Each of these sections in the index is then divided by nonfiction and fiction subject categories. Some agencies indicated that they were open to all nonfiction or fiction topics. These have been grouped under the subject heading "open" in each section. Many agents have provided additional areas of interest that were not represented in their listings last year.

We've included an Agents Index as well. Often you will read about an agent who is an employee of a larger agency and may not be able to locate her business phone or address. We asked agencies to list the agents on staff, then listed the names in alphabetical order along with the name of the agency they work for. Find the name of the person you would like to contact and then check the agency listing. You will find the page number for the agency's listing in the Listing Index.

A Geographic Index lists agents state by state, for those authors looking for an agent close to home. A Client Acceptance Policies index ranks agencies according to their openness to new clients.

Many literary agents are also interested in scripts; many script agents will also consider book manuscripts. Fee-charging agents who primarily sell scripts but also handle at least 10 to 15 percent book manuscripts appear among the listings in this section, with the contact information, breakdown of work currently handled and a note to check the full listing in the script section, if they are a signatory of the WGA or report a sale. Those fee-charging script agencies that sell scripts and less than 10 to 15 percent book manuscripts appear in "Additional Fee-charging Agents" at the end of this section. Complete listings for these agents appear in the Script Agent section.

Before contacting any agency, check the listing to make sure it is open to new clients. Those designated (**V**) are currently not interested in expanding their rosters.

For more information on approaching agents and the specifics of the listings, read the articles How to Use Your Guide to Literary Agents and How to Find (and Keep) the Right Agent. Also see the various articles at the beginning of the book for explorations of different aspects of the author/agent relationship.

We've ranked the agencies listed in this section according to their openness to submissions. Below is our ranking system:

I Newer agency actively seeking clients.

II Agency seeking both new and established writers.

III Agency prefers to work with established writers, mostly obtains new clients through referrals.

IV Agency handling only certain types of work or work by writers under certain circumstances.

V Agency not currently seeking new clients. We have included mention of agencies rated **V** to let you know they are currently not open to new clients. *Unless you have a strong recommendation from someone well respected in the field, our advice is to approach only those agents ranked I-IV.*

‡***A.A. FAIR LITERARY AGENCY, (II)**, 3370 N. Hayden #123, Scottsdale AZ 85252. (606)967-4667. Contact: Lee Taylor. Estab. 1995. Member of Arizona Authors Association. Represents 26

clients. 80% of clients are new/previously unpublished writers. Currently handles: 30% nonfiction books, 30% juvenile books, 40% novels. Member agents: Betty Hatcher (how-to, romance); Chip Callahan (western, suspense); Lee Taylor (mystery, romance, historical).

Handles: Nonfiction books, juvenile books, movie scripts, novels, TV scripts. Considers these nonfiction areas: agriculture/horticulture; animals; anthropology/archaeology; child guidance/parenting; cooking/food/nutrition; crafts/hobbies; ethnic/cultural interests; history; how-to; juvenile nonfiction; military/war; New Age/metaphysics; popular culture; self-help/personal improvement; true crime/investigative; women's issues/women's studies. Considers these fiction areas: action/adventure; detective/police/crime; ethnic; family saga; fantasy; glitz; historical; humor/satire; juvenile; literary; mainstream; mystery/suspense; picture book; romance (contemporary, gothic, historical, regency); science fiction; thriller/espionage; westerns/frontier; children's books. Query. Reports in 2-3 weeks on queries; 4-6 weeks on mss.

Terms: Agent receives 15% commission on domestic sales; 20% on foreign sales. Offers written contract binding for 1 year.

Fees: Reading fee: $15 for new writers. 5% of business derived from reading fees.

Tips: Obtains new clients through phone book ads, Arizona Authors Association conference and word of mouth.

*ACACIA HOUSE PUBLISHING SERVICES LTD. (II, III), 51 Acacia Rd., Toronto, Ontario M4S 2K6 Canada. Phone/fax: (416)484-8356. Contact: (Ms.) Frances Hanna. Estab. 1985. Represents 30 clients. "I prefer that writers be previously published, with at least a few articles to their credit. Strongest consideration will be given to those with, say, three or more published books. However, I *would* take on an unpublished writer of outstanding talent." Works with a small number of new/unpublished authors. Specializes in contemporary fiction: literary or commercial (no horror, occult or science fiction); nonfiction: all categories but business/economics—in the trade, not textbook area; children's: very few picture books. Currently handles: 30% nonfiction books; 70% novels.

● Prior to opening her agency, Ms. Hanna had been in the publishing business for 25 years as a fiction editor with Barrie & Jenkins and Pan Books, and as a senior editor with a packager of mainly illustrated books. She was condensed books editor for 6 years for *Reader's Digest* in Montreal, senior editor and foreign rights manager for (the then) Wm. Collins & Sons (now HarperCollins) in Toronto.

Handles: Nonfiction books, novels. Considers these nonfiction areas: animals; biography/autobiography; cooking/food/nutrition; crafts/hobbies; current affairs; health/medicine; language/literature/criticism; military/war; music/dance/theater/film; nature/environment; popular culture; psychology. Considers these fiction areas: action/adventure; detective/police/crime; historical; literary; mainstream; mystery/suspense; romance (historical); thriller/espionage. Query with outline. No unsolicited mss. Reports in 3 weeks on queries.

Recent Sales: *Chicken Little Was Right* and sequel, *Whatever Happened to Jennifer Steele?*, (St. Martin's Press, USA); *Ghirlandaio's Daughter*, by John Spencer Hill (Constable, UK; St. Martin's, USA; McClelland & Stewart, Canada); *Sandman*, by J. Robert Janes (Constable, UK; Soho Press, USA); *Canada's Glory: Battles that forged a Nation*, by Arthur Bishop (McGraw-Hill Ryerson, Canada); *Goodbye Mom and Apple Pie*, by Robert Collins (McClelland & Stewart, Canada).

Terms: Agent receives 15% commission on English language sales; 20% on dramatic sales; 30% on foreign language sales.

Fees: Charges reading fee on mss over 200 pages (typed, double-spaced) in length; $200/200 pages. 4% of income derived from reading fees. "If a critique is wanted on a manuscript under 200 pages in length, then the charge is the same as the reading fee for a longer manuscript (which incorporates a critique)." 5% of income derived from criticism fees. Critique includes 2-3-page overall evaluation "which will contain any specific points that are thought important enough to detail. Marketing advice is not usually included, since most manuscripts evaluated in this way are not considered to be publishable." Charges writers for photocopying, courier, postage, telephone/fax "if these are excessive."

Writer's Conferences: LIBER (Spain); London International Book Fair (England); ABA (Chicago); Frankfurt Book Fair (Germany).

*AEI/ATCHITY EDITORIAL/ENTERTAINMENT INTERNATIONAL, Literary Management & Film Production, (I), 9601 Wilshire Blvd., Box 1202, Beverly Hills CA 90210. (213)932-0407. Fax: (213)932-0321. E-mail: aeikja@lainet.com. Website: http://www.lainet.com/~aeikja. Con-

---

● **A BULLET** introduces comments by the editor of the *Guide* indicating special information about the listing.

tact: Kenneth Atchity. Estab. 1994. Represents 30 clients. 75% of clients are new/previously unpublished writers. Specializes in novel-film tie-ins. Currently handles: 30% nonfiction books; 5% scholarly books; 30% novels; 25% movie scripts; 10% TV scripts. Member agents: Chi-Li Wong; Andrea McKeown; Monica Faulkner; David Angsten; Sidney Kiwitt (business affairs, NY).

Handles: Nonfiction books, novels, movie scripts, TV scripts. Considers these nonfiction areas: anthropology/archaeology; biography/autobiography; business; child guidance/parenting; computers/electronics; government/politics/law; health/medicine; how-to; humor; language/literature/criticism; money/finance/economics; music/dance/theater/film; nature/environment; New Age/metaphysics; popular culture; psychology; science/technology; self-help/personal improvement; translations; true crime/investigative; women's issues/women's studies. Considers these fiction areas: action/adventure; contemporary issues; erotica; historical; horror; literary; mainstream; mystery/suspense; science fiction; thriller/espionage. Send outline and 3 sample chapters. Reports in 2 weeks on queries; 1 month on mss.

Recent Sales: *Cash-Flow Reengineering*, by James Sagner (AMACOM); *Sins of the Mother, Telephone Tag, Moral Obligations*, by Cheryl Saban (Dove Books); *The Hong Kong Sanction*, by Mitch Rossi (Pinnacle); *The Cruelest Lie*, by Milt Lyles (Barclay House).

Terms: Agent receives 15% commission on domestic sales; 25% on foreign sales. Offers written contract, binding for 18 months, with 30 day cancellation clause.

Also Handles: Movie scripts (feature film); TV scripts (TV mow); no episodic. Considers these script subject areas: action/adventure; comedy; contemporary issues; detective/police/crime; erotica; horror; mainstream; mystery/suspense; psychic/supernatural; comedy and drama; science fiction; teen; thriller. Send outline and 25 sample pages with SASE. Reports in 2 weeks on queries; 1 month on mss.

Recent Sales: *TV script(s) optioned/sold:* Blood Witness, by Alexander Viespi (Susan Cooper [Saban Entertainment]); *Shadow of Obsession*, based on K.K. Beck's *Unwanted Attention* (NBC); *Amityville: The Evil Escapes*, based on John Jones' novel (NBC). ***Movie scripts sold:*** *180 Seconds at Willow Park*, by Rick Lynch (New Line Pictures); *Sign of the Watcher*, by Brett Bartlett (Propaganda Films); *Megalodon*, by Steve Allen (Walt Disney Pictures).

Terms: Agent receives 10% commission on domestic sales; (0% if we produce).

Fees: Offers criticism service through "AEI Writers' Lifeline." Charges $150 one-time signing fee for expenses for previously unpublished writers. 20% of business is derived from reading fees or criticism service. Payment of criticism or reading fee does not ensure representation.

Tips: Obtains new clients through referrals, directories. "No 'episodic' scripts, treatments, or ideas; no 'category' fiction of any kind. Please send a professional return envelope and sufficient postage. No: children's literature, category, poetry, religious literature. We are always looking for true, heroic, *contemporary* women's stories for both book and television. We perform the same function as a literary agent, but also produce films. Take writing seriously as a career, which requires disciplined time and full attention (as described in *The Mercury Transition* and *A Writer's Time* by Kenneth Atchity). Make your cover letter to the point and focused, your synopsis compelling and dramatic. Most submissions, whether fiction or nonfiction, are rejected because the writing is not at a commercially competitive dramatic level. We have a fondness for Louisiana subjects, and for thrillers (both screenplays and novels), as well as for mainstream nonfiction appealing to everyone today. We rarely do 'small audience' books. Our favorite client is one who has the desire and talent to develop both a novel and a film career and who is determined to learn everything possible about the business of writing, publishing, and producing. Dream big. Risk it. Never give up. Go for it!"

*THE AHEARN AGENCY, INC. (I), 2021 Pine St., New Orleans LA 70118-5456. (504)861-8395. Fax: (504)866-6434. E-mail: pahearn@aol.com. Contact: Pamela G. Ahearn. Estab. 1992. Member of RWA. Represents 25 clients. 20% of clients are new/previously unpublished writers. Specializes in historical romance; also very interested in mysteries and suspense fiction. Currently handles: 15% nonfiction books; 85% novels.

● Prior to opening her agency, Ms. Ahearn was an agent for eight years and an editor with Bantam Books.

Handles: Nonfiction books, juvenile books, novels, short story collections (if stories previously published), young adult (no picture books). Considers these nonfiction areas: animals; biography; business; child guidance/parenting; current affairs; ethnic/cultural interests; gay/lesbian issues; health/medicine; history; juvenile nonfiction; music/dance/theater/film; popular culture; self-help/personal improvement; true crime/investigative; women's issues/women's studies. Considers these fiction areas: action/adventure; contemporary issues; detective/police/crime; ethnic; family saga; fantasy; feminist; gay; glitz; historical; horror; humor/satire; juvenile; lesbian; literary; mainstream; mystery/suspense; psychic/supernatural; regional; romance (contemporary, gothic, historical, regency); science fiction; thriller/espionage; westerns/frontier; young adult. Query. Reports in 1 month on queries; 10 weeks on mss.

Recent Sales: *Dejima*, by Laura Joh Rowland (Villard/Random House); *Skin Deep, Blood Red*, by Robert Skinner (Kensington); *The Rose of Rowdene*, by Kate Moore (Avon Books); *Someone Like You*, by Susan Sawyer (Avon Books).

Terms: Agent receives 15% commission on domestic sales; 20% on foreign sales. Offers written contract, binding for 1 year; renewable by mutual consent.

Fees: "I charge a reading fee to previously unpublished authors, based on length of material. Fees range from $125-400 and are non-refundable. When authors pay a reading fee, they receive a three to five single-spaced-page critique of their work, addressing writing quality and marketability." Critiques written by Pamela G. Ahearn. Charges for photocopying. 90% of business derived from commissions; 10% derived from reading fees or criticism services. Payment of reading fee does not ensure representation.

Writers' Conferences: Attends Midwest Writers Workshop, Moonlight & Magnolias, RWA National conference (Dallas); Virginia Romance Writers (Williamsburg, VA); Florida Romance Writers (Ft. Lauderdale, FL), Golden Triangle Writers Conference; Bouchercon (Minneapolis, October).

Tips: Obtains new clients "usually through listings such as this one and client recommendations. Sometimes at conferences. Be professional! Always send in exactly what an agent/editor asks for, no more, no less. Keep query letters brief and to the point, giving your writing credentials and a very brief summary of your book. If one agent rejects you, keep trying—there are a lot of us out there!"

ALLEGRA LITERARY AGENCY, (V), 2806 Pine Hill Dr., NW, Kennesaw GA 30144. (770)795-8318. Fax: (770)795-8318. Contact: Cynthia Lambert. Estab. 1994. Represents 5 clients. 10% of clients are new/previously unpublished writers. Specializes in Christian fiction (mainstream, romance, mystery, science fiction); also some secular. Currently handles: 25% nonfiction books; 5% juvenile books; 70% novels.

• Agency does not anticipate adding new clients this year.

Handles: Nonfiction books, juvenile books, novels. Considers these nonfiction areas: religious/inspirational. Considers these fiction areas: detective/police/crime; juvenile; mainstream; mystery/suspense; religious/inspirational; romance. Query with 3 consecutive chapters. Reports in 2 weeks on queries; 2 months on mss.

Terms: Agent receives 12% commission on domestic sales; 16% on foreign sales. Offers written contract, binding for 1 year, with 60 day cancellation clause.

Fees: No reading fee. Charges $150 retainer, fully refundable upon the sale of the ms for postage, faxing, copying and long distance phone calls. Authors receive itemized monthly statements.

Tips: Obtains new clients through recommendations.

ALP ARTS CO., (I, II), 221 Fox Rd., Golden CO 80403-8517. Phone/fax: (303)582-5189. E-mail: sffuller@alparts.com. Contact: Ms. Sandy Ferguson Fuller. Estab. 1994. Represents 30 clients. 80% of clients are new/previously unpublished writers. "Specializes in children's books. Works with picture book authors and illustrators, also middle-grade and YA writers, nonfiction and fiction." Currently handles: 100% juvenile or young adult proposals. Member agents: Sandy Ferguson Fuller, director; Johnnie Greathouse, administrative assistant.

Handles: Juvenile and young adult books, all types. Considers juvenile nonfiction. Considers juvenile and young adult fiction, picture books. Query. For picture books and easy readers send entire ms. Reports in 3 weeks on queries; 8-10 weeks on mss.

Recent Sales: *Aspen*, by Huth (Dawn Publications); *First Day of School*, by Flood (Fairview Press).

Terms: 10-15% commission on domestic sales. Offers written contract, with 30 day cancellation clause.

Also Handles: Scripts. "Will co-agent." Considers these script areas: juvenile (all); teen (all). Query with SASE. Reports in 3 weeks on queries; 2 months on mss.

Recent Sales: *Movie scripts optioned: Secrets of Mount Jumbo*, by Cook (Eagle Vision).

Fees: Criticism service: $35/hour for critique and consulting session. Basic consultation is $35/submission. Contract custom to client's needs. Charges for postage, photocopying costs. Long-distance phone consultation at $35/hour plus phone bill. Receipts supplied to client for all of the above. 30% of business derived from criticism fees.

Writers' Conferences: PPWC (Colorado Springs, CO, April); ABA (Chicago, June); SCBWI (October).

Tips: Obtains new clients from referrals, solicitation and at conferences. "One mailing per year through advertising services, workshops and seminars. Referrals. Networking in publishing industry. Society of Children's Book Writers and Illustrators. Usually establish a working relationship via consulting or workshop prior to agenting. Agency representation is not for everyone. Some aspiring or published authors and/or illustrators have more confidence in their own abilities to target and market work. Others are 'territorial' or prefer to work directly with the publishers. The best agent/client relationships exist when complete trust is established prior to representation. I recommend at least one (or several) consultations via phone or in person with a prospective agent. References are important. Also, the author or illustrator should have a clear idea of the agent's role i.e., editorial/critiquing input, 'post-publication' responsibilities, exclusive or non-exclusive representation, fees, industry reputation, etc. Each author or illustrator should examine his or her objectives, talents, time constraints, and perhaps more important, personal rapport with an individual agent prior to representation."

‡**JOSEPH ANTHONY AGENCY, (II)**, 15 Locust Court, R.D. 20, Mays Landing NJ 08330. (609)625-7608. Contact: Joseph Anthony. Estab. 1964. Signatory of WGA. Represents 30 clients. 80% of clients are new/previously unpublished writers. "Specializes in general fiction and nonfiction. Always interested in screenplays." Currently handles: 5% juvenile books; 80% novellas; 5% short story collections; 2% stage plays; 10% TV scripts. Member agent: Lee Fortunato.
  • Prior to opening his agency, Mr. Anthony was a writer who sold nine books and four screenplays from 1964-1970.
Handles: Nonfiction books, juvenile books, novels. Considers these nonfiction areas: health/medicine; military/war; psychology; science/technology; self-help/personal improvement; true crime/investigative. Considers these fiction areas: action/adventure; confessional; detective/police/crime; erotica; fantasy; mystery/suspense; psychic/supernatural; romance (gothic, historical, regency); science fiction; thriller/espionage; young adult. Query, SASE required. Reports in 2 weeks on queries; 1 month on mss.
Also Handles: Movie scripts; TV scripts.
Recent Sales: Two romance novels to Silhouette Books.
Terms: Agent receives 15% commission on domestic sales; 20% on foreign sales.
Fees: Charges $85 reading fee for novels up to 100,000 words. "Fees are returned after a sale of $3,000 or more." Charges for postage and photocopying up to 3 copies. 10% of business is derived from commissions on ms sales; 90% is derived from reading fees ("because I work with new writers").
Tips: Obtains new clients through recommendations from others, solicitation. "If your script is saleable, I will try to sell it to the best possible markets. I will cover sales of additional rights through the world. If your material is unsaleable as it stands but can be rewritten and repaired, I will tell you why it has been turned down. After you have rewritten your script, you may return it for a second reading without *any additional fee*. But . . . if it is completely unsaleable in our evaluation for the markets, I will tell you why it has been turned down again and give you specific advice on how to avoid these errors in your future material. I do not write or edit or blue pencil your script. I am an *agent* and an agent is out to sell a script."

***AUTHOR AID ASSOCIATES, (II)**, 340 E. 52nd St., New York NY 10022. (212)758-4213; 980-9179. Editorial Director: Arthur Orrmont. Estab. 1967. Represents 150 clients. Specializes in aviation, war, biography, novels, autobiography. Currently handles: 3% magazine fiction; 2% adult fiction; 35% nonfiction books; 38% novels; 5% juvenile books; 5% movie scripts; 2% stage plays; 10% other. Member agent: Leonie Rosenstiel, vice president, "a musicologist and authority on New Age subjects and nutrition; Ed McCartan (military nonfiction, intelligence/espionage; Annette Bitterman (romance)."
  • Prior to opening his agency, Mr. Orrmont served in the editorial department with Farrar, Straus, and as senior editor for Popular Library and executive editor with Fawcett Books.
Handles: Magazine fiction, nonfiction books, novels, juvenile books, movie scripts, stage plays, TV scripts. Considers these nonfiction areas: animals; anthropology/archaeology; biography/autobiography; current affairs; ethnic/cultural interests; health/medicine; history; how-to; humor; juvenile nonfiction; language/literature/criticism; military/war; music/dance/theater/film; nature/environment; New Age/metaphysics; popular culture; psychology; religious/inspirational; science/technology; self-help/personal improvement; sociology; sports; translations; true crime/investigative; women's issues/women's studies. Considers these fiction areas: action/adventure; confessional; contemporary issues; detective/police/crime; erotica; ethnic; experimental; family saga; fantasy; glitz; historical; horror; humor/satire; juvenile; lesbian; literary; mainstream; mystery/suspense; picture book; psychic/supernatural; regional; religious/inspirational; romance (contemporary, gothic, historical, regency); science fiction; sports; thriller/espionage; westerns/frontier; young adult. Query with outline. No unsolicited mss. "Short queries answered by return mail." Reports within 6 weeks on mss.
Recent Sales: *World Series*, by John S. Snyder (Chronicle Books); *Rockies*, by Larry Ludmer (Hunter Publishers).
Terms: Agent receives 15% commission on domestic and dramatic sales; 20% on foreign sales.
Fees: Charges a reading fee to new, unpublished authors, refundable from commission on sale. Charges for cable, photocopying and messenger express. Offers consultation service through which writers not represented can get advice on a contract. 80% of income from commissions on sales; 20% of income derived from reading fees.
Tips: Publishers of *Literary Agents of North America* (5th edition).

---

‡ **THE DOUBLE DAGGER** before a listing indicates the listing is new in this edition.

‡*AUTHOR AUTHOR LITERARY AGENCY LTD., (II), P.O. Box 34051, 1200-37 St. SW, Calgary, Alberta T3C 3W2 Canada. Phone/fax: (403)242-0226. President: Joan Rickard. Associate Editor: Eileen McGaughey. Estab. 1992. Member of Writers' Guild of Alberta and CAA. Represents 40 clients. "Welcomes new writers." Currently handles: 20% nonfiction books; 5% scholarly books; 25% juvenile books; 45% novels; 5% short story collections.

Handles: Fiction and nonfiction, adult and juvenile, scholarly books, novels, novellas, short story collections. No poetry, screenplays or magazine short stories/articles. Considers these nonfiction areas: anthropology/archaeology; biography/autobiography; business; child guidance/parenting; cooking/food/nutrition; crafts/hobbies; education; ethnic/cultural interests; gay/lesbian issues; government/politics/law; health/medicine; history; how-to; humor; interior design/decorating; juvenile nonfiction; language/literature/criticism; military/war; money/finance/economics; nature/environment; New Age/metaphysics; photography; popular culture; psychology; self-help/personal improvement; sociology; sports; true crime/investigative; women's issues/women's studies. Considers these fiction areas: action/adventure; contemporary issues; detective/police/crime; erotica; experimental; family saga; fantasy; feminist; gay; historical; horror; humor/satire; juvenile; lesbian; literary; mainstream; mystery/suspense; picture book; psychic/supernatural; regional; romance (contemporary, gothic, historical, regency); science fiction; sports; thriller/espionage; westerns/frontier; young adult. "Responds to all letters of inquiry promptly." Reports in about 3 weeks on queries, ms outlines; 2 months on sample chapters; 4 months on complete mss.

Recent Sales: *Why Elephants and Fleas Don't Sweat*, by Gideon Louw, Ph.D. (Detselig/Temeron); *Past Anterior*, by Jacqueline Gerols, Ph.D.; *The Last Children of Eden*, by Gordon van Amsterdam (Commonwealth); *Groundsource I: The Pillars of Chilam Balam*, by Daniel Johnson (Commonwealth).

Terms: Agent receives 15% commission on domestic sales; 20% on foreign sales. Offers written contract.

Fees: "None for published authors (non-self-published books only). For unpublished writers: Will read at no charge unsolicited queries and outlines. Reads queries and evaluates outlines and partial manuscripts of up to three sample chapters (about 30 pages) for $75, which is applied toward entire fee if agency agrees to study complete work. Manuscript must be accompanied by handling fee: up to 65,000 words $350; up to 85,000 words $450; 85,000+ words flat rate $475 (certified check or money order, please). Due to publishers constraints, manuscripts should rarely exceed 100,000 words. Payment of partial or complete evaluation fee does not ensure representation. We discuss methods to improve and/or make the manuscripts marketable. Once we place an author's work, there are no further evaluating fees. Charges for additional photocopying of manuscripts submitted to publishers, long-distance telephone/fax to promote sales and express of manuscripts. Consults with and reports promptly to writers on all communications concerning handling and marketing of their manuscripts."

Tips: "We offer a complete package, assist with and discuss methods to improve your proposal's presentation and/or marketability. The key word is ASSIST. It is not the agents' or publishers' job to revise the mechanics of formatting, punctuation and literary content/context. It's a very tight, competitive market. Do the basics before submitting proposals. Study your chosen genre thoroughly to learn style/techniques and what book publishers/film producers are contracting. Submit professionally-presented proposals: properly typed and formatted; double-spaced throughout; standard print (11.5 to 12 point). Avoid dot matrix. When submitting to our agency always include a brief high-impact synopsis of your proposal (as seen on book jackets), and bio. Each may be shorter than, but not exceed 100 words (double-spaced). Always enclose SASEs or IRCs with inquiries and submissions. *A 'Crash Course' Kit in Business Letters, Basic Punctuation/Information Guidelines & Manuscript Formatting* is available upon request for $7.95, including postage/handling (free if required to clients)."

‡*AUTHORS' MARKETING SERVICES LTD., (II), 200 Simpson Ave., Toronto, Ontario M4K 1A6 Canada. (416)463-7200. Fax: (416)469-4494. E-Mail: 102047.1111@compuserve.com. Contact: Larry Hoffman. Estab. 1978. Represents 17 clients. 25% of clients are new/previously unpublished writers. Specializes in thrillers, romance, parenting and self-help. Currently handles: 65% nonfiction books; 10% juvenile books; 20% novels; 5% other. Member agents: Sharon DeWinter (romance, women's fiction); Bok Busboom (adventure).

● Prior to opening his agency, Mr. Hoffman worked at Coles for five years and was director of marketing for the book store chain.

Handles: Nonfiction books, novels. Considers these nonfiction areas: biography/autobiography; business; child guidance/parenting; cooking/food/nutrition; current affairs; education; health/medicine; history; how-to; military/war; money/finance/economics; nature/environment; popular culture; psychology; science/technology; self-help/personal improvement; sports; true crime/investigative. Considers these fiction areas: action/adventure; cartoon/comic; detective/police/crime; family saga; fantasy; historical; horror; humor/satire; literary; mainstream; mystery/suspense; psychic/supernatural; romance (contemporary, gothic, historical, regency); science fiction; thriller/espionage. Query. Reports in 1 week on queries; 2 months on mss.

Recent Sales: *Caring for the Disabled Child*, by Dr. M. Nagler (Stoddart); *So You Want to Be an O.T.!*, by Dr. D. Reid (Lugas); *Euromarket Electronic Day Finder*, by R. Lavers (Pitman); *Dark Shadow*, by Veronica Shaw (Ballantine).
Terms: Agent receives 15% commission on domestic sales; 20% on foreign sales. Offers written contract, binding for 6-9 months to complete first sale.
Fees: Charges $395 reading fee. "A reading/evaluation fee of $395 applies only to unpublished authors, and the fee must accompany the completed manuscript. Criticism service is included in the reading fee. The critique averages three to four pages in length, and discusses strengths and weaknesses of the execution, as well as advice aimed at eliminating weaknesses." 95% of business is derived from commissions on ms sales; 5% is derived from reading fees. Payment of criticism fee does not ensure representation.
Tips: Obtains new clients through recommendations from other writers and publishers, occasional solicitation. "Never submit first drafts. Prepare the manuscript as cleanly and as perfectly, in the writer's opinion, as possible."

‡AUTHOR'S SERVICES LITERARY AGENY (II), P.O. Box 2318, Pineland FL 33945-2318. (941)283-9562. Fax: (941)283-1839. E-mail: imagin-mas@worldnet.att.com. Contact: Edwina Berkman. Estab. 1995; editing and critiquing service established 1988. Represents 102 clients. 50% of clients are new/previously unpublished writers. "No erotica or porno please. All other genres accepted." Currently handles: 10% nonfiction books; 10% juvenile books; 2% movie scripts; 2% short story collections; 2% scholarly books; 44% novels; 10% syndicated material; 20% textbooks.
Handles: Nonfiction books, juvenile books, scholarly books, novels, textbooks, novellas. Considers these nonfiction areas: business; current affairs; gay/lesbian issues; government/politics/law; how-to; humor; military/war; money/finance/economics; psychology; religious/inspirational; true crime/investigative; women's issues/women's studies. Considers these fiction areas: action/adventure; contemporary issues; detective/police/crime; fantasy; feminist; gay; historical; horror; humor/satire; juvenile; lesbian; mainstream; mystery/suspense; picture book; psychic/supernatural; romance (contemporary, gothic, historical, regency); science fiction; thriller/espionage; westerns/frontier; young adult. Send outline and 3 sample chapters with SASE. Reports in 2 weeks on queries; 4-6 weeks on mss.
Recent Sales: *Dark Secrets; White Lies*, by Dana Reed (Commonwealth); *Traveling To Europe Like A Pro*, by Analu (Newjoy Press); *Code of Conduct* and *Jungle Bar & Grill*, by Gary Dent (STJ Publications); *The Flower of Death*, by Jim Shamblen (STJ Publications); *Tales of the Noot*, by Laurie Sutliff (STJ Publications).
Terms: Agent receives 10% commission on domestic sales; 10% on foreign sales; 15% movie sales. Offers written contract. To terminate a contract a certified letter must be issued after 90 days of effective date.
Fees: Criticism service: $65 (100 pp); $200 (up to 400 pp). "I write each critique personally. Clients receive a 3 page detailed letter plus line by line editing in addition to a 6 page detailed critique dealing with every facet of creative writing." Charges for photocopying; priority mail postage; overnight postage; handling fees ($30 flat rate). 5% of business derived from criticism fees. Payment of criticism does not always ensure representation. "If the novel is worthy and the writer is willing to work hard at correcting his errors, then the answer is 'yes.' "
Tips: Obtains new clients through recommendations, "but mostly online and web page advertising."

THE BLAKE GROUP LITERARY AGENCY, (II, III), 8609 Northwest Plaza Dr., Suite 300, Dallas TX 75225-4214. (214)373-2221. President: Albert H. Halff, D.Eng. Estab. 1979. Member of Texas Publishers Association (TPA) and Texas Booksellers Association (TBA). Works with published/established authors; works with a small number of new/unpublished authors. Currently handles: 30% fiction; 30% nonfiction; 10% juvenile; 30% poetry. Member agents: Mrs. Lee Halff (consulting editor); Hal Copeland (marketing/PR consultant).
Handles: Nonfiction books, novels, juvenile books. Query with synopsis and 2 sample chapters. Reports within 3 months. SASE must be included or mss will not be read.
Recent Sales: *Life on the King Ranch*, by Frank Goodwin (Texas A&M University Press); *A Patient's Guide to Surgery*, by Dr. Edward Bradley, MD (Consumer's Digest in conjunction with the University of Pennsylvania); *The Blue Cat*, by Pamela Sanchez (SRA).
Terms: Agent receives 15% commission on domestic sales; 20% on foreign sales.

THE BRINKE LITERARY AGENCY, (II), 4498 B Foothill Rd., Carpinteria CA 93013-3075. (805)684-9655. Contact: Jude Barvin. Estab. 1988. Represents 15 clients. Currently handles: 40% nonfiction books; 60% novels. Member agents: Allan Silberhartz (law, reader, advisor); Roger Engel (reader).
Handles: Considers these nonfiction areas: animals; anthropology/archaeology; biography/autobiography; meditation; history; New Age/metaphysics; religious/inspirational; self-help/personal improvement. Considers these fiction areas: action/adventure; fantasy; mystery/suspense; psychic/supernatural;

religious/inspirational; romance (contemporary); science fiction; thriller/espionage; New Age. Query with SASE.

Terms: Agent receives 15% commissions on domestic sales; 20% on foreign sales. Offers written contract, binding for 1 year.

Fees: Charges $125 reading fee for novel ms. No charges for office expenses, postage, photocopying.

Writers' Conferences: Santa Barbara Writers Conference; ABA (Chicago, June).

Tips: Obtains new clients through recommendations from others, queries, mail. Offers complete critique/evaluation or a contract.

ANTOINETTE BROWN, LITERARY AGENT, (II), P.O. Box 5048, Charlottesville VA 22905-5048. (804)295-9358. Contact: Antoinette Brown. Estab. 1991. Member of RWA. Represents 5 clients. 75% of clients are new/previously unpublished writers.

Handles: Nonfiction books, novels, short stories. Considers these nonfiction areas: business; ethnic/cultural interests; health/medicine; history; religious/inspirational (Buddhism); self-help/personal improvement; women's issues/women's studies. Considers these fiction areas: action/adventure; historical; mystery/suspense; romance (historical); thriller/espionage. Query with SASE. Reports in 2 weeks on queries; 2 months on mss.

Terms: Agent receives 15% commission on domestic sales; 20% on foreign sales. Offers written contract, with 60 day cancellation clause.

Fees: Charges reading fee: $25 (up to 250 pages); $35 (251-400 pages); $40 (401-500 pages); $50 (over 500 pages). Brief criticism of ms is offered in rejection letter.

Tips: Obtains new clients through recommendations, queries. "Unsolicited manuscripts will be returned unopened. No returns without SASE. The Dalai Lama says 'religion is kindness.' I am looking especially for writers who consider themselves secular humanists."

CAMBRIDGE LITERARY ASSOCIATES, (II), 7 Lincoln St., Suite 205, Wakefield MA 01880. (617)246-5011. E-mail: mrmv@aol.com. Contact: Michael Valentino. Estab. 1990. Represents 30 clients. 50% of clients are new/previously unpublished writers. Currently handles: 20% nonfiction books; 5% juvenile books; 60% novels; 15% short story collections. Member agent: Ralph Valentino (TV screenplays).

Handles: Nonfiction books, scholarly books, textbooks, juvenile books, novels, novellas, short story collections. Considers these nonfiction areas: biography/autobiography; business; current affairs; government/politics/law; history; how-to; humor; juvenile nonfiction; military/war; popular culture; religious/inspirational; sports; true crime/investigative. Considers these fiction areas: action/adventure; contemporary issues; detective/police/crime; erotica; family saga; fantasy; historical; horror; juvenile; literary; mainstream; mystery/suspense; regional; religious/inspirational; romance (contemporary, historical); science fiction; sports; thriller/espionage; westerns/frontier; young adult. Send outline and 3 sample chapters or send entire ms. Reports in 1 week on queries; 3 weeks on mss.

Also Handles: Movie scripts (feature film); TV scripts (TV mow).

Recent Sales: *Jitters*, by Linda Rentschlev (Victor TV Productions); *Five Centuries of Italian American History* (Executive Press).

Terms: Agent receives 15% commission on domestic sales; 20% on foreign sales. Offers written contract.

Fees: No reading fee. Offers criticism service. 30% of business is derived from criticism fees. Payment of criticism fee does not ensure representation.

Tips: Obtains new clients through advertising, networking and recommendations from others.

THE CATALOG™ LITERARY AGENCY, (II), P.O. Box 2964, Vancouver WA 98668-2964. (360)694-8531. Contact: Douglas Storey. Estab. 1986. Represents 70 clients. 50% of clients are new/previously unpublished writers. Specializes in business, health, psychology, money, science, how-to, self-help, technology, parenting, women's interest. Currently handles: 50% nonfiction books; 20% juvenile books; 30% novels.

Handles: Nonfiction books, textbooks, juvenile books, novels. Considers these nonfiction areas: agriculture/horticulture; animals; anthropology/archaeology; business; child guidance/parenting; computers/electronics; cooking/food/nutrition; crafts/hobbies; current affairs; education; ethnic/cultural interests; government/politics/law; health/medicine; how-to; juvenile nonfiction; military/war; money/finance/economics; nature/environment; photography; popular culture; psychology; science/technology; self-help/personal improvement; sociology; sports; women's issues/women's studies. Considers these fiction areas: action/adventure; family saga; horror; juvenile; mainstream; romance; science fiction; thriller/espionage; young adult. Query. Reports in 2 weeks on queries; 3 weeks on mss.

Recent Sales: *The Human Side of Human Resources*, by Richard Renckly (Barron's Educational Series).

Terms: Agent receives 15% on domestic sales; 20% on foreign sales. Offers written contract, binding for about 9 months.

Fees: Does not charge a reading fee. Charges an upfront handling fee from $85-250 that covers photocopying, telephone and postage expense.

‡*CDK TECHNICAL COMMUNICATIONS, INC., (V), 532 E. 58th St., Indianapolis IN 46220. (317)259-7390. E-mail: cdkatsaropoulos@msn.com. Contact: Chris Katsaropoulos. Estab. 1996. Represents 10 clients. "I specialize in computer book publishing, in which I was formerly an editor and publisher." Currently handles: 10% nonfiction books, 5% novels, 85% computer books.
   • This agency is no longer accepting queries or submissions of any sort.
Handles: Nonfiction books, novels, computer books. Considers these nonfiction areas: business; computers/electronics; how-to; money/finance/economics; science/technology; self-help/personal improvement. Considers these fiction areas: experimental; literary; mainstream; regional. Query or send outline and 3 sample chapters. Reports in 1 week on queries; 3 weeks on sample mss.
Terms: Agent receives 15% commission on domestic sales. 25% on foreign sales. Offers a written contract, binding for 1 year with annual renewal. Must give 30 days notice.
Fees: Charges $100/ms reading fee to new authors only. Refundable if represented. Charges for express mail, photocopying, fax and any "unusual" expenses. 95% of business is derived from commissions; 5% from reading or criticism fees.
Tips: Obtains new clients through recommendations from others. "Send a proposal that shows you know your target audience and have a unique vision for your book. Avoid the shotgun approach."

CHADD-STEVENS LITERARY AGENCY, (II), P.O. Box 2218, Granbury TX 76048. (817)326-4892. Fax: (817)326-3290. Contact: Lee F. Jordan. Estab. 1991. Represents 45 clients. Specializes in working with previously unpublished authors.
Handles: Novels, novellas, short story collections. Considers all nonfiction areas. Considers all fiction areas except feminist. Send entire ms or 3 sample chapters and SASE. Reports within 6 weeks on mss.
Recent Sales: *The Joy of Books*, by Eric Burns (Prometheus); *A Brief Education*, by Maren Sobar (Blue Moon); *The Cretaceous Paradox*, by Frank J. Carradine (Royal Fireworks).
Terms: Agent receives 15% commission on domestic sales; 15% on foreign sales. Offers written contract, binding for 3 months.
Fees: Charges $100 reading fee for entire ms only. Payment of handling fee does not ensure agency representation.
Writer's Conferences: Regional (Texas and Southwest) writers' conferences including Southwest Writers Conference (Houston, June).
Tips: "I prefer a query letter and I answer all of them with a personal note. My goal is to look at 80% of everything offered to me. I'm interested in working with people who have been turned down by other agents and publishers. I'm interested in first-time novelists—there's a market for your work if it's good. Don't give up. I think there is a world of good unpublished fiction out there and I'd like to see it."

*SJ CLARK LITERARY AGENCY, (IV), 56 Glenwood, Hercules CA 94547. (510)741-9826. Fax: (510)236-1052. Contact: Sue Clark. Estab. 1982. Represents 12 clients. 95% of clients are new/previously unpublished writers. Specializes in mysteries/suspense, children's books. Currently handles: 35% juvenile books; 65% novels.
Handles: Juvenile books, novels. Considers these nonfiction areas: New Age/metaphysics; true crime/investigative. Considers these fiction areas: detective/police/crime; juvenile; mystery/suspense; picture book; psychic/supernatural; thriller/espionage; young adult. Query with entire ms. Reports in 1 month on queries; 3 months on mss.
Recent Sales: *Six Feet Underground*, by D.B. Borton (Berkley); *Jeremy*, by Tatiana Strelkoff (Rebecca House).
Terms: Agent receives 20% commission on domestic sales. Offers written contract.
Fees: "I specialize in working with previously unpublished writers. If the writer is unpublished, I charge a reading fee of $50 which includes a detailed two to three page single-spaced critique. Fee is nonrefundable. If the writer is published, the reading fee is refundable from commission on sale if I agree to represent author. I also offer an editing service for unpublished or published authors. Payment of criticism fee does not ensure representation. Clients are asked to keep all agreed upon amounts in their account to cover postage, phone calls, fax, etc. (Note: Since February 1996, 60% of income from commissions, 40% from reading and critiquing fees from unpublished authors.)"

ALWAYS INCLUDE a self-addressed, stamped envelope (SASE) for reply or return of your manuscript.

Tips: Obtains new clients by word of mouth, listing in *Guide to Literary Agents* and *Mystery Writer's Sourcebook.*

COAST TO COAST TALENT AND LITERARY, (II), 4942 Vineland Ave., Suite 200, North Hollywood CA 91601. (818)762-6278. Fax: (818)762-7049. Estab. 1986. Signatory of WGA. Represents 25 clients. 35% of clients are new/previously unpublished writers. Specializes in one hour TV features. Currently handles: 10% nonfiction books; 60% movie scripts; 30% TV scripts.
  • See the expanded listing for this agency in Script Agents.

*COLLIER ASSOCIATES, (III), P.O. Box 21361, W. Palm Beach FL 33416-1361. (561)697-3541. Contact: Dianna Collier. Estab. 1967. Represents over 100 clients. 20% of clients are new/previously unpublished writers. Specializes in "adult fiction and nonfiction books only." Currently handles: 50% nonfiction books; 50% novels. Member agents: Dianna Collier (food, history, self help, women's issues, most fiction especially mystery, romance); Oscar Collier (financial, biography, autobiography, most fiction). "This is a small agency that rarely takes on new clients because of the many authors it represents already."
Handles: Nonfiction, novels. Considers these nonfiction areas: biography/autobiography; business; computers/electronics; cooking/food/nutrition; crafts/hobbies; history; how-to; self-help/personal improvement; true crime/investigative; women's issues/women's studies. Considers these fiction areas: action/adventure; detective/police/crime; fantasy; historical; mainstream; mystery/suspense; romance (contemporary, gothic, historical, regency); science fiction; thriller/espionage; westerns/frontier. Query with SASE. Reports in 2 months on queries; 4 months "or longer" on mss.
Recent Sales: *How I Found Freedom In An Unfree World*, by Harry Browne (Liam Works); *Leaving Missouri*, by Ellen Recknor (Berkley); *Down An Easy Florida River*, by Bernice Brooks Bergen and John Bergen (Gulf Publishing).
Terms: Agent receives 15% commission on domestic sales; 20% on foreign sales. Offers written contract.
Fees: Charges $50 reading fee for unpublished trade book authors. "Reserves the right to charge a reading fee on longer fiction of unpublished authors." Charges for mailing expenses, photocopying and express mail, "if requested, with author's consent, and for copies of author's published books used for rights sales."
Writer's Conferences: ABA (Chicago, June); Florida Mystery Writers (Ft. Lauderdale, March); Tallahassee Writer's Conference (October).
Tips: Obtains new clients through recommendations from others. Don't telephone. Send query with description of work plus biographical information. If you want material returned, send check or money order for exact amount of postage or send SASE.

‡*CS INTERNATIONAL LITERARY AGENCY, (I), 43 W. 39th St., New York NY 10018. (212)921-1610. Contact: Cynthia Neesemann. Estab. 1996. Represents 20 clients. Specializes in full-length fiction, nonfiction and screenplays (no pornography). Currently handles: 33% nonfiction books; 33% movie scripts; 33% novels; 1% TV scripts.
Handles: Nonfiction books, juvenile books, movie scripts, novels, TV scripts. Considers all nonfiction areas. Considers all fiction areas. Query. Reports in 1-2 weeks on queries; 2-3 weeks on mss.
Terms: Agent receives 15% commission on domestic sales; variable percentage on foreign sales. Sometimes offers written contract.
Fees: Charges reading fee for unestablished writers. Charges for marketing, office expenses, postage and photocopying depending on amount of work involved.
Tips: Obtains new clients through recommendations, solicitation and at conferences.

EXECUTIVE EXCELLENCE, (IV), 1344 East 1120 South, Provo UT 84606. (801)375-4060. Fax: (801)377-5960. President: Ken Shelton. Managing Agent: Trent O. Price. Estab. 1984. Represents 35-50 clients. Specializes in nonfiction trade books: business and personal development. Currently handles: 100% nonfiction. Member agents: Ken Shelton (president, editor); Trent Price (literary agent, acquisitions and sales).
Handles: Nonfiction books and audiotapes; some foreign and multimedia rights. Considers these nonfiction areas: business; health; psychology; self-help/personal improvement.
Recent Sales: *The Power Behind Positive Thinking*, by Eric Fellman (Harper San Francisco); *Personal Coaching for Results*, by Lou Tice (Thomas Nelson); *Surviving Your Boss*, by Ann Clark and Patt Perkins (Citadel); *The Complete Idiot's Guide to Handling Stress*, by Jeff Davidson (Alpha/Macmillan).
Terms: Agent receives 15% commission on domestic sales. 75% of business is derived from commissions on mss sales; 25% from book packaging/assisted self-publishing services.
Fees: $500 taken from initial advance to cover expenses (phone, mail, travel, etc.)
Writer's Conferences: ABA; ASTD; CBA.

*FRIEDA FISHBEIN LTD., (II), 2556 Hubbard St., Brooklyn NY 11235-6223. (212)247-4398. Contact: Janice Fishbein. Estab. 1928. Represents 32 clients. 50% of clients are new/previously unpublished writers. Currently handles: 10% nonfiction books; 5% young adult; 60% novels; 10% movie scripts; 10% stage plays; 5% TV scripts. Member agents: Heidi Carlson (literary and contemporary); Douglas Michael (play and screenplay scripts).
Handles: Nonfiction books, young adult books, novels. Considers these nonfiction areas: animals; biography/autobiography; cooking/food/nutrition; current affairs; juvenile nonfiction; military/war; nature/environment; self-help/personal improvement; true crime/investigative; women's issues/women's studies. Considers these fiction areas: action/adventure; contemporary issues; detective/police/crime; family saga; fantasy; feminist; historical; humor/satire; mainstream; mystery/suspense; romance (contemporary, historical, regency); science fiction; thriller/espionage; young adult. Query letter a must before sending ms. Reports in 2 months on queries; 2 months on mss accepted for evaluation.
Also Handles: Movie scripts, TV scripts ("not geared to a series"), stage plays.
Recent Sales: *Ghost in The Machine*, by David Gilman (play and screenplay).
Terms: Agent receives 10% commission on domestic sales; 15% on foreign sales. Offers written contract, binding for 30 days, cancellable by either party, except for properties being marketed or already sold.
Fees: Charges $80 reading fee up to 50,000 words, $1 per 1,000 words thereafter for new and published authors in a new genre; $80 for plays, TV, screenplays. Criticism service included in reading fee. Offers "an overall critique. Sometimes specific staff readers may refer to associates for no charge for additional readings if warranted." 60% of business is derived from commissions on ms sales; 40% is derived from reading fees or criticism services. Payment of criticism fee does not ensure representation.
Tips: Obtains new clients through recommendations from others. "*Always* submit a query letter first with an SASE. Manuscripts should be done in large type, double-spaced and one and one-half-inch margins, clean copy and edited for typos, etc."

‡FORT ROSS INC. RUSSIAN-AMERICAN PUBLISHING PROJECTS, (III), 269 W. 259 St., Riverdale NY 10471. (718)884-1042. Fax: (718)884-3373. Contact: Dr. Vladimir P. Kartsev. Estab. 1992. Represents 82 clients. 2% of clients are new/previously unpublished writers. Specializes in selling rights for Russian books and illustrations (covers) to American publishers and vice versa; also Russian-English and English-Russian translations. Currently handles: 48% nonfiction books; 10% juvenile books; 4% movie scripts; 2% short story collections; 30% novels; 2% novellas; 2% stage plays 2% poetry. Member agents: Ms. Olga Borodyanskaya; Ms. Svetlana Kolmanovskaya; Ms. Svetlana Dubovik.
Handles: Nonfiction books, juvenile books, novels. Considers these nonfiction areas: biography/autobiography; history; music/dance/theater/film; psychology; self-help/personal improvement; true crime/investigative. Considers these fiction areas: action/adventure; cartoon/comic; detective/police/crime; erotica; fantasy; horror; mystery/suspense; romance (contemporary, gothic, historical, regency); science fiction; thriller/espionage; young adult. Send published book or galleys.
Recent Sales: *Do's and Taboos Around the World*, by Wyley (translated to Meduza [Russia]); *Guru Papers*, by J. Cramer and D. Alstad (N. Atl. Press translated to "Transfers" [Russia]); *Christmas Origins Unriddled*, by J. Carmichael (translated to "Respublica" [Russia]); *Book of Bad Advice*, by Aster (translated to Byron Preis/Harry Abrams).
Terms: Agent receives 10% commission on domestic sales; 20% on foreign sales. Offers written contract, binding for 1 year with 2 month cancellation clause.
Fees: Charges $125 (up to 80,000 words); $195 (over 80,000 words), nonrefundable reading fee. Criticism service: $250 (critical overview); $750 (in-depth criticism). Critiqued by Russian book market analyst, offering 1-2 pp with the sales prognosis and what could be adjusted for better sales in Russia. Charges for regular office fees (postage, photocopying, handling). 10% of business derived from reading fees or criticism service. Payment of criticism fee ensures representation.
Tips: Obtains new clients through recommendations from others. "Book illustrators are welcome for the following genres: romance, fantasy, science fiction, mystery and adventure."

FORTHWRITE LITERARY AGENCY, (II), 3579 E. Foothill Blvd., Suite 327, Pasadena CA 91107. Phone: (818)798-0793. Fax: (818)798-5653. E-mail: literaryag@aol.com. Contact: Wendy L. Keller (formerly Zhorne). Estab. 1989. Member of Women's National Book Assn., National Speakers Association, Publisher's Marketing Association. Represents 150 clients. 10% of clients are new/previously unpublished writers. Specializes in nonfiction. Currently handles: 80% nonfiction books; 20% foreign; 80% nonfiction; foreign & other secondary rights. Member agents: Tom Hawkins (all categories plus political science, current affairs, social issues); Audrey LaVelle (relationships, film/TV/cinema-related books, others).
Handles: "We handle business books (sales, marketing and management especially); self-help and how-to books on many subjects." Considers commercial nonfiction in these areas: business computer sales, self-help and how-to on psychology, pop psychology, health, alternative health, business, child care/parenting, inspirational, spirituality, home maintenance and management, cooking, crafts, interior

design, art, biography, writing, film, consumer reference, ecology, coffee table and art books, current affairs, women's studies, economics and history. Query with SASE only. No unsolicited mss! Reports in 2 weeks on queries; 6 weeks on ms.

Recent Sales: *Timeless Face, Ageless Beauty*, by Ellae Elinwood (St. Martin's Press); *Heart At Work*, by Jack Canfield and Jacqueline Miller (McGraw-Hill); *NLP: The Key to Success*, by John Emerick (Prima Publishing); *Hiring Smart*, by Tom Winninger (Prima Publishing).

Also Handles: CD-& disk based rights; foreign, ancillary, upselling (selling a previously published book to a larger publisher) & other secondary & subsidiary rights.

Fees: Does not charge a reading fee.

Writers' Conferences: ABA, Frankfurt Booksellers' Convention, many regional conferences and regularly talks on finding an agent, how to write nonfiction proposals, query writing, creativity enhancement, persevering for creatives.

Tips: Obtains new clients through referrals, recommendations by editors, queries, satisfied authors, conferences etc. "Write only on a subject you know well and be prepared to show a need in the market for your book."

FRAN LITERARY AGENCY, (I, II), 7235 Split Creek, San Antonio TX 78238-3627. (210)684-1659. Contact: Fran Rathmann. Estab. 1993. Represents 32 clients. 55% of clients are new/previously unpublished writers. "Very interested in Star Trek novels/screenplays." Currently handles: 15% nonfiction books; 10% juvenile books; 30% novels; 5% novellas; 5% poetry books; 15% movie scripts; 20% TV scripts.

Handles: Nonfiction books, novels. Considers these nonfiction areas: agriculture/horticulture; animals; biography/autobiography; business; child guidance/parenting; cooking/food/nutrition; crafts/hobbies; ethnic/cultural interests; health/medicine; history; how-to; humor; interior design/decorating; juvenile nonfiction; military/war; nature/environment; religious/inspirational; self-help/personal improvement. Considers these fiction areas: action/adventure; cartoon/comic; contemporary issues; detective/police/crime; fantasy; historical; horror; humor/satire; juvenile; mainstream; mystery/suspense; picture book; regional; romance (contemporary, historical); science fiction; thriller/espionage; westerns/frontier; young adult. Send entire ms. Reports in 2 weeks on queries; 2 months on mss.

Recent Sales: *The Diary of Elena*, by David Sisler (Pocketbooks); *Mommies Nurse Their Babies*, by Fran Rathmann (Little, Brown).

Also Handles: Movie scripts (feature film, documentary, animation), TV scripts (TV mow, sitcom, miniseries, syndicated material, animation, episodic drama). Considers these script subject areas: action/adventure; cartoon/animation; comedy; contemporary issues; detective/police/crime; ethnic; family saga; historical; horror; humor; juvenile; mainstream; mystery/suspense; romantic comedy and drama; science fiction; thriller. Send entire ms.

Recent Sales: *TV Script*: *Family Tree* (Star Trek Deep Space 9), by Patricia Dahlin (Paramount).

Terms: Agent receives 15% commission on domestic sales; 20% on foreign sales. Needs "letter of authorization," usually binding for 2 years.

Fees: Charges $25 processing fee, nonrefundable. Written criticism service $100, average 4 pages. 90% of business is derived from commissions on mss sales; 10% from criticism services. Payment of fee does not ensure representation.

Writers' Conferences: SAWG (San Antonio, spring).

Tips: Obtains clients through recommendations, listing in telephone book. "Please send SASE or box!"

GELLES-COLE LITERARY ENTERPRISES, (II), 12 Turner Rd., Pearl River NY 10965. (914)735-1913. President: Sandi Gelles-Cole. Estab. 1983. Represents 50 clients. 25% of clients are new/unpublished writers. "We concentrate on published and unpublished, but we try to avoid writers who seem stuck in mid-list." Specializes in commercial fiction and nonfiction. Currently handles: 50% nonfiction books; 50% novels.

Handles: Nonfiction books, novels. "We're looking for more nonfiction—fiction has to be complete to submit—publishers buying fewer unfinished novels." No unsolicited mss. Reports in 3 weeks.

Terms: Agent receives 15% commission on domestic and dramatic sales; 20% on foreign sales.

Fees: Charges $100 reading fee for proposal; $150/ms under 250 pages; $250/ms over 250 pages. "Our reading fee is for evaluation. Writer receives total evaluation, what is right, what is wrong, is book 'playing' to market, general advice on how to fix." Charges writers for overseas calls, overnight mail, messenger. 5% of income derived from fees charged to writers. 50% of income derived from commissions on sales; 45% of income derived from editorial service.

GEM LITERARY SERVICES, (II), 4717 Poe Rd., Medina OH 44256. Contact: Darla Pfenninger. Estab. 1992. Represents 9 clients. 70% of clients are new/previously unpublished writers. Currently handles: 10% nonfiction books; 25% juvenile books; 65% novels.
Handles: Nonfiction books, scholarly books, textbooks, juvenile books, novels. Considers these non-fiction areas: biography/autobiography; business; child guidance/parenting; computers/electronics; cooking/food/nutrition; current affairs; gay/lesbian issues; government/politics/law; how-to; humor; juvenile nonfiction; money/finance/economics; music/dance/theater/film; New Age/metaphysics; religious/inspirational; science/technology; self-help/personal improvement; true crime/investigative; women's issues/women's studies. Considers these fiction areas: action/adventure; detective/police/crime; family saga; fantasy; feminist; historical; horror; humor/satire; juvenile; literary; mainstream; mystery; picture book; psychic/supernatural; regional; romance (gothic, historical); science fiction; thriller/espionage; westerns/frontier; young adult. Send outline/proposal with SASE for response. Reports in 2 weeks on queries; 1 month on mss.
Recent Sales: *Assassin's Destiny*, by Jim Shaw (Books-In-Motion); *Lannigan's Woods*, by Robert Clark (Books-In-Motion).
Terms: Agent receives 15% commission on domestic sales; 20% on foreign sales. Offers written contract, binding for 6 months, with 30 day cancellation clause.
Fees: Charges $175 for office expenses, refunded upon sale of property.
Writers' Conference: Midwest Writers Conference (Canton OH, September/October).
Tips: Obtains new clients through recommendations and solicitations. "Looking for well thought out plots, not run-of-the-mill story lines."

THE GISLASON AGENCY, (II), 219 Main St. SE, Suite 506, Minneapolis MN 55414-2160. (612)331-8033. Fax: (612)331-8115. Attorney/Agent: Barbara J. Gislason. Estab. 1992. Member of Minnesota State Bar Association, Art & Entertainment Law Section, MIPLA Copyright Committee, The Loft, Midwest Fiction Writers, UMBA. 70% of clients are new/previously unpublished writers. Specializes in fiction and nonfiction. Currently handles: 30% nonfiction books; 70% novels. Member agent: Wendy Valentine.
Handles: Nonfiction books, novels. Considers these nonfiction areas: how-to; law; self-help/personal improvement; true crime/investigative. Considers these fiction areas: fantasy; mystery/suspense; romance (contemporary, gothic, historical, regency); science fiction; law-related. Query with outline plus 3 sample chapters. Reports in 1 month on queries, 2 months on mss.
Terms: Agent receives 15% commission on domestic sales; 20% on foreign sales. Offers written contract, binding for 1 year with option to renew.
Fees: Client pays for all submission costs.
Writer's Conferences: Midwest Fiction Writers; ABA.
Tips: Obtains half of new clients through recommendations from others and half from *Guide to Literary Agents* and *Literary Market Place*. "Cover letter should be well written and include a detailed synopsis of the work, the first three chapters and author information. If the work was written with a specific publisher in mind, this should be communicated. In addition to owning an agency, Ms. Gislason practices law in the area of Art and Entertainment and has a broad spectrum of industry contacts."

GLADDEN UNLIMITED, (II), 3768 Curtis St., San Diego CA 92106. Contact: Carolan Gladden. Estab. 1987. Represents 20 clients. 91% of clients are new/previously unpublished writers. Currently handles: 10% nonfiction; 90% novels.
Handles: Novels, nonfiction. Considers these nonfiction areas: celebrity biography; business; how-to; self-help; true crime/investigative. Considers these fiction areas: action/adventure; detective/police/crime; ethnic; glitz; horror; mainstream; thriller. "No romance or children's." Query only with synopsis. Reports in 2 weeks on queries; 2 months on mss.
Terms: Agent receives 10% commission on domestic sales; 20% on foreign sales.
Fees: Does not charge a reading fee. Charges evaluation fee. Marketability evaluation: $100 (manuscript to 400 pages.) $200 (over 400 pages.) "Offers six to eight pages of diagnosis and specific recommendations to turn the project into a saleable commodity. Also includes a copy of the book 'Be a Successful Writer.' Dedicated to helping new authors achieve publication."

*ANDREW HAMILTON'S LITERARY AGENCY (II), P.O. Box 604118, Cleveland OH 44104-0118. (216)881-1032. E-mail: 103447.3175@compuserve.com. Contact: Andrew Hamilton. Estab. 1991. Represents 15 clients. 60% of clients are new/previously unpublished writers. Currently handles: 50% nonfiction books; 7% scholarly books; 3% juvenile books; 40% novels. Member agent: Andrew Hamilton (music, business, self-help, how-to, sports).
● Prior to opening his agency, Mr. Hamilton served as editor at several legal publications.

Handles: Nonfiction books, juvenile books, novels. Considers these nonfiction areas: animals; biography/autobiography; business; child guidance/parenting; cooking/food/nutrition; current affairs; government/politics/law; health/medicine; history; juvenile nonfiction; money/finance/economics; music/dance/theater/film; psychology; religious/inspirational; self-help/personal improvement; sociology; sports; true crime/investigative; women's issues/women's studies; minority concerns; pop music. Considers these fiction areas: action/adventure; confessional; contemporary issues; detective/police/crime; erotica; ethnic; family saga; humor/satire; juvenile; mystery/suspense; psychic/supernatural; religious/inspiration; romance (contemporary); sports; thriller/espionage; westerns/frontier; young adult. Send entire ms. Reports in 1 week on queries; 3 weeks on mss.
Recent Sales: *Outcast: My Journey From the White House to Homelessness,* by Michael Arthur Hobbs (Middle Passage Press).
Terms: Agent receives 15% commission on domestic sales; 20% on foreign sales. Offers written contract.
Also Handles: Movie scripts (feature film). Query with SASE. Reports in 1 week on queries; 3-4 weeks on mss.
Fees: "Reading fees are for new authors and are nonrefundable. My reading fee is $50 for 60,000 words or less; $100 for manuscripts over 60,000 words; and $150 for ms over 100,000 words. I charge a one time marketing fee of $250 for manuscripts." 70% of business derived from commissions on ms sales; 30% from reading fees or criticism services.
Tips: Obtains new clients through recommendations, solicitation and writing seminars. "Be patient: the wheels turn slowly in the publishing world."

*ALICE HILTON LITERARY AGENCY, (II), 13131 Welby Way, North Hollywood CA 91606-1041. (818)982-2546. Fax: (818)765-8207. Contact: Alice Hilton. Estab. 1986. Eager to work with new/unpublished writers. "Interested in any quality material, although agent's personal taste runs in the genre of 'Cheers.' 'L.A. Law,' 'American Playhouse,' 'Masterpiece Theatre' and Woody Allen vintage humor." Member agents: Marshall Severson; Denise Adams.
Handles: Nonfiction, fiction, juvenile. Considers these fiction areas: action/adventure; confessional; contemporary issues; detective/police/crime; erotica; ethnic; fantasy; historical; horror; humor/satire; juvenile; literary; mainstream; mystery/suspense; picture book; psychic/supernatural; romance (contemporary, gothic, historical, regency); science fiction; sports; thriller/espionage; westerns/frontier; young adult.
Recent Sales: *Raw Foods and Your Health,* by Boris Isaacson (Tomorrow Now Press); *Barnard's Star,* by Warren Shearer (New Saga Press).
Also Handles: Movie scripts (feature film); TV scripts (TV mow, sitcom, episodic drama). Considers all script subject areas. Query with SASE and outline/proposal or send entire ms. Reports in 2 weeks on queries; 1 month on mss.
Terms: Agent receives 10% commission. Brochure available with SASE. Preliminary phone call appreciated.
Fees: Charges evaluation fee of $3/1,000 words. Charges for phone, postage and photocopy expenses.

THE EDDY HOWARD AGENCY, (III), % 37 Bernard St., Eatontown NJ 07724-1906. (908)542-3525. Contact: Eddy Howard Pevovar, N.D., Ph.D. Estab. 1986. Signatory of WGA. Represents 20 clients. 1% of clients are new/previously unpublished writers. Specializes in film, sitcom and literary. Currently handles: 5% nonfiction books; 5% scholarly books; 5% juvenile books; 5% novels; 30% movie scripts; 30% TV scripts; 10% stage plays; 5% short story collections; 1% syndicated material; 4% other. Member agents: Eddy Howard Pevovar, N.D., Ph.D. (agency executive); Francine Gail (director of comedy development).
  ● See the expanded listing for this agency in Script/Agents.

*YVONNE TRUDEAU HUBBS AGENCY, (II), 32371 Alipaz, #101, San Juan Capistrano CA 92675-4147. (714)496-1970. Owner: Yvonne Hubbs. Estab. 1983. temporarily closed 1990, reopened 1993. Member of RWA. Represents 20 clients. 10% of clients are new/previously unpublished writers. Member agents: Thomas D. Hubbs, public relations; Yvonne Hubbs, agent, lecturer, writer.
Handles: Nonfiction books, novels. Considers these nonfiction areas: current affairs; history; women's issues/women's studies. Considers these fiction areas: action/adventure; contemporary issues; family

saga; fantasy; feminist; glitz; historical; mainstream; mystery/suspense; psychic/supernatural; romance (contemporary, gothic, historical, regency); science fiction; thriller/espionage. Query with outline/proposal plus 1 sample chapter. Reports in 2 weeks on queries, 6-8 weeks on mss.
Terms: Agent receives 15% commission on domestic sales; 20% on foreign sales. Offers written contract, binding for 1 year, with 30 day cancellation clause.
Fees: Charges $50 reading fee to new writers only; refundable if client is sold within 1 year. Criticism service included in reading fee. "I personally write the critiques after reviewing the manuscript." Charges for travel expenses (if approved), photocopying, telegraph/fax expenses, overseas phone calls. 60% of business is derived from commissions on ms sales; 40% derived from reading fees or criticism services. Payment of criticism fee does not ensure representation.
Writer's Conferences: RWA; Romantic Times.
Tips: Obtains new clients through recommendations, conferences. "Be professional in your query letter. Always include SASE with a query."

INDEPENDENT PUBLISHING AGENCY, (I), P.O. Box 176, Southport CT 06490-0176. Phone/fax: (203)332-7629. E-mail: henryberry@aol.com. Contact: Henry Berry. Estab. 1990. Represents 40 clients. 50% of clients are new/previously unpublished writers. Especially interested in topical nonfiction (historical, political, social topics, cultural studies, health, business) and literary and genre fiction. Currently handles: 70% nonfiction books; 10% juvenile books; 20% novels and short story collections.
Handles: Nonfiction books, juvenile books, novels, short story collections. Considers these nonfiction areas: anthropology/archaeology; art/architecture/design; biography/autobiography; business; child guidance/parenting; cooking/food/nutrition; crafts/hobbies; current affairs; ethnic/cultural interests; government/politics/law; history; juvenile nonfiction; language/literature/criticism; military/war; money/finance/economics; music/dance/theater/film; nature/environment; photography; popular culture; psychology; religious; science/technology; self-help/personal improvement; sociology; sports; true crime/investigative; women's issues/women's studies. Considers these fiction areas: action/adventure; cartoon/comic; confessional; contemporary issues; crime; erotica; ethnic; experimental; fantasy; feminist; historical; humor/satire; juvenile; literary; mainstream; mystery/suspense; picture book; psychic/supernatural; thriller/espionage; young adult. Send synopsis/outline plus 2 sample chapters. Reports in 2 weeks on queries; 6 weeks on mss.
Recent Sales: Available upon request by prospective clients.
Also Handles: Movie scripts (feature film, documentary); TV scripts (TV mow, miniseries, episodic drama, sitcom, syndicated material). Considers these subject areas: action/adventure; biography/autobiography; cartoon/comic; comedy; contemporary issues; erotica; experimental; fantasy; feminist; historical; juvenile; mainstream; mystery/suspense; psychic/supernatural; sports; thriller/espionage.
Terms: Agent receives 15% commission on domestic sales; 20% on foreign sales. Offers "agreement that spells out author-agent relationship."
Fees: No fee for queries w/sample chapters; $250 reading fee for evaluation/critique of complete ms. Offers criticism service if requested. Written critique averages 3 pages—includes critique of the material, suggestions on how to make it marketable and advice on marketing it. Charges $25/month for clients for marketing costs. 90% of business is derived from commissions on ms sales; 10% derived from criticism services.
Tips: Usually obtains new clients through referrals from clients, notices in writer's publications. Looks for "proposal or chapters professionally presented, with clarification of the distinctiveness of the project and grasp of intended readership."

‡JANUS LITERARY AGENCY, (V), 43 Lakeman's Lane, Ipswich MA 01938. (508)356-0909. Contact: Lenny Cavallaro or Eva Wax. Estab. 1980. Signatory of WGA. Represents 6 clients. 50% of clients are new/previously unpublished writers. Currently handles: 100% nonfiction books.
Handles: Nonfiction books. Considers these nonfiction areas: biography/autobiography; business; crafts/hobbies; current affairs; education; government/politics/law; health/medicine; history; how-to; money/finance/economics; New Age/metaphysics; self-help/personal improvement; sports; true crime/investigative. Call or write with SASE to query. Reports in 1 week on queries; 2 weeks on mss.
Terms: Agent receives 15% commission on domestic sales; 20% on foreign sales. Offers written contract, binding for "usually less than 1 year."
Fees: Charges handling fees, "usually $100-200 to defray costs."
Tips: Obtains new clients through LMP and/or referrals. "Not actively seeking clients, but will consider outstanding nonfiction proposals."

CAROLYN JENKS AGENCY, (II), 205 Walden St., Suite 1A, Cambridge MA 02140-3507. (617)876-6927. Contact: Carolyn Jenks. Reestab. 1990. 50% of clients are new/previously unpublished writers. Currently handles: 5% nonfiction books; 75% novels; 5% movie scripts; 10% stage plays; 5% TV scripts.
Handles: Fiction and nonfiction books. Considers these nonfiction areas: animals; biography/autobiography; gay/lesbian issues; health/medicine; history; inspirational; nature/environment; New Age/

metaphysics; psychology; theater/film; women's issues/women's studies. Considers these fiction areas: contemporary issues; feminist; historical; lesbian; literary; mystery/suspense; regional; westerns/frontier; young adult. Query. Reports in 2 weeks on queries; 6 weeks on mss.
Recent Sales: *White Wings*, by F. Daniel Montague (Penguin Inc.); *The Patient's Little Instruction Book* (Quality Medical Publishing).
Also Handles: Movie scripts (feature film); stage plays. Considers these script subject areas: comedy; contemporary issues; family saga; feminist; historical; humor; juvenile; mainstream; mystery/suspense; romantic comedy and drama; thriller; westerns/frontier. Query with bio and SASE. Reports in 2 weeks on queries; 6 weeks on mss.
Terms: Agent receives 15% commission on domestic sales; 10% on film and TV. Offers written contract.
Fees: Charges reading fee to non-WGA members: 120,000 words $150; screenplay $175. WGA members exempted.
Tips: Query first in writing with SASE.

‡**THE JETT LITERARY AGENCY (I)**, 7123 E. Jan Ave., Mesa AZ 85208. (602)985-9400. Contact: Dawn M. Snyder. Estab. 1996. Represents 3 clients. 100% of clients are new/previously unpublished writers. Currently handles: 50% nonfiction books; 10% movie scripts; 15% novels. Member agent: Dawn M. Snyder.
Handles: Nonfiction books, juvenile books, movie scripts, novels, TV scripts, textbooks, novellas, stage plays, poetry books, short story collections. Considers these nonfiction areas: animals; biography/autobiography; business; child guidance/parenting; cooking/food/nutrition; crafts/hobbies; current affairs; education; health/medicine; history; how-to; humor; interior design/decorating; juvenile nonfiction; language/literature/criticism; money/finance/economics; music/dance/theater/film; nature/environment; photography; psychology; self-help/personal improvement; sociology; sports; true crime/investigative; women's issues/women's studies. Considers these fiction areas: action/adventure; cartoon/comic; confessional; contemporary issues; detective/police/crime; family saga; fantasy; feminist; glitz; historical; horror; humor/satire; juvenile; literary; mainstream; mystery/suspense; picture book; regional; romance (contemporary, gothic, historical, regency); science fiction; sports; thriller/espionage; westerns/frontier; young adult. Send ms with reading fee or send SASE with a one-page query. Reports in 1-2 weeks; 1-2 months on mss.
Terms: Agent receives 15% commission on domestic sales; 20% on foreign sales. Offers written contract, binding for 1 year, with a 30 day cancellation clause.
Fees: Charges a reading fee of $50 (for children's and scripts); $75 (for all others). "Reading fee includes 2-page critique and is refundable with representation." Criticism service: varies depending upon work needed. Critiques written by Dawn M. Snyder. Charges $200 one time marketing fee. 10% of business derived from reading fees or criticism service.
Tips: Obtains new clients through recommendations from others, solicitation, at conferences. "If you are sending entire manuscript, include reading fee. The agency does not mind receiving unsolicited manuscripts as long as fee is enclosed. We read and respond to every manuscript."

*****JLM LITERARY AGENTS, (III)**, 5901 Warner Ave., Suite 92, Huntington Beach CA 92649. (714)547-4870. Fax: (714)840-5660. Contact: Judy Semler. Estab. 1985. Represents 25 clients. 5% of clients are new/previously unpublished writers. Agency is "generalist with an affinity for high-quality, spiritual self-help psychology and mystery/suspense." Currently handles: 90% nonfiction books; 10% novels.
Handles: Nonfiction books, novels. Considers these nonfiction areas: biography/autobiography; business (popular); current affairs; music/dance/theater/film; nature/environment; popular culture; psychology; religious/inspirational; self-help/personal improvement; sociology; true crime/investigative; women's issues/women's studies. Considers these fiction areas: glitz; mystery/suspense; psychic/supernatural; contemporary romance. For nonfiction, send outline with 2 sample chapters. For fiction, query with 3 chapters—except for mystery/suspense, send entire ms. "Accepting very few manuscripts in fiction." No faxed submissions. Reports in 1 month on queries; 10 weeks on mss.
Recent Sales: *The Blue Angel: The First 50 Years* (Motor Book). *The Breast Cancer Companion*, by Kathy LaTour (Morrow/Avon).
Terms: Agent receives 15% commission on domestic sales; 10% on foreign sales plus 15% to subagent. Offers written contract, binding for 1 year, with 30-day escape clause.
Fees: Does not charge a reading fee. Does not do critiques or editing, but will refer to freelancers. Charges retainer for marketing costs for unpublished authors or to authors changing genres. Charges for routine office expenses associated with the marketing. 100% of business is derived from commissions on ms sales.
Tips: "Most of my clients are referred to me by other clients or editors. If you want to be successful, learn all you can about proper submission and invest in the equipment or service to make your project *look* dazzling. Computers are available to everyone and the competition looks good. You must at least match that to even get noticed."

*J. KELLOCK & ASSOCIATES, LTD., (II), 11017 80th Ave., Edmonton, Alberta T6G 0R2 Canada. (403)433-0274. Contact: Joanne Kellock. Estab. 1981. Represents 50 clients. 10% of clients are new/previously unpublished writers. "I do very well with all works for children but do not specialize as such." Currently handles: 30% nonfiction books; 1% scholarly books; 50% juvenile books; 19% novels.

Handles: Nonfiction, juvenile, novels. Considers these nonfiction areas: animals; anthropology/archaeology; art/architecture/design; biography/autobiography; business; child guidance/parenting; cooking/food/nutrition; current affairs; health/medicine; history; juvenile nonfiction; language/literature/criticism; music/dance/theater/film; nature/environment; New Age/metaphysics; self-help/personal improvement; sports; true crime/investigative; women's issues/women's studies. Considers these fiction areas: action/adventure; contemporary issues; detective/police/crime; ethnic; experimental; family saga; fantasy; feminist; glitz; historical; horror; humor/satire; juvenile; literary; mystery/suspense; picture book; romance; science fiction; sports; thriller/espionage; westerns/frontier; young adult. Query with outline plus 3 sample chapters. Reports in 10 weeks on queries; 5 months on mss.

Recent Sales: *Song Bird* (picture book), by Tololwa M. Mollel (Clarion Books, New York); *Do You Want Fries with That?*, by Martyn Godfrey (Scholastic, Canada); *Satanic Ritual Abuse*, by Colin Ross, MD (University of Toronto Press).

Terms: Agent receives 15% commission on domestic sales (English language); 20% on foreign sales. Offers written contract, binding for 2 years.

Fees: Charges $150 reading fee. "Fee under no circumstances is refundable. *New writers only are charged.*" $140 (US) to read 3 chapters plus brief synopsis of any work; $100 for children's picture book material. "If style is working with subject, the balance is read free of charge. Criticism is also provided for the fee. If style is not working with the subject, I explain why not; if talent is obvious, I explain how to make the manuscript work. I either do critiques myself or my reader does them. Critiques concern themselves with use of language, theme, plotting—all the usual. Return postage is always required. I cannot mail to the US with US postage, so always enclose a SAE, plus either IRCs or cash. Canadian postage is more expensive, so double the amount for either international or cash. I do not return on-spec long-distance calls; if the writer chooses to telephone, please request that I return the call collect. However, a query letter is much more appropriate." 70% of business is derived from commissions on ms sales; 30% is derived from reading fees or criticism service. Payment of criticism fee does not ensure representation.

Tips: Obtains new clients through recommendations from others, solicitations. "Do not send first drafts. Always double space. Very brief outlines and synopsis are more likely to be read first. For the picture book writer, the toughest sale to make in the business, please study the market before putting pen to paper. All works written for children must fit into the proper age groups regarding length of story, vocabulary level. For writers of the genre novel, read hundreds of books in the genre you've chosen to write, first. In other words, know your competition. Follow the rules of the genre exactly. For writers of science fiction/fantasy and the mystery, it is important a new writer has many more than one such book in him/her. Publishers are not willing today to buy single books in most areas of genre. Publishers who buy science fiction/fantasy usually want a two/three book deal at the beginning. Do not put a monetary value on any manuscript material mailed to Canada, as Canada Post will open it and charge a considerable fee. I do not pay these fees on speculative material, and the parcel will be returned."

THE KIRKLAND LITERARY AGENCY, INC., (II), P.O. Box 50608, Amarillo TX 79159-0608. (806)356-0216. Fax: (806)356-0452. Contact: Dee Pace, submissions director. Estab. 1993. Member of Association of Authors' Representatives. Represents 60 clients. 50% of clients are new/previously unpublished writers. Specializes in romance and mainstream novels, but represents all categories of novel-length fiction. Currently handles: 15% nonfiction books; 5% juvenile books; 80% novels. Member agent: Jean Price (romance, mainstream).

Handles: Nonfiction books, juvenile books, novels. Considers these nonficton areas: current affairs; humor; self-help/personal improvement. Considers these fiction areas: action/adventure; contemporary issues; detective/police/crime; ethnic; family saga; fantasy; glitz; historical, horror (extremely selective); humor/satire; literary; mainstream; mystery/suspense; psychic/supernatural; romance (contemporary, gothic, historical, inspirational, regency); science fiction; thriller/espionage; westerns/frontier (extremely selective); young adult. Query with outline and 3 sample chapters. Reports in 6 weeks on queries; 3 months on mss.

Terms: Agent receives 15% commission on domestic sales; 20% on foreign sales. Offers written contract, binding for 1 year, with 30 day cancellation clause.

Fees: Does not charge a reading fee. Charges marketing fee to previously unpublished writers of $150 for postage, phone calls, photocopying, if necessary. Balance refunded upon first sale.

Tips: Obtains new clients through referrals and conferences. "Write toward publishers' guidelines, particularly concerning maximum and minimum word count."

‡*BERTHA KLAUSNER INTERNATIONAL LITERARY AGENCY, (II), 71 Park Ave., New York NY 10016. (212)685-2642. Fax: (212)532-8638. Contact: Bertha Klausner. Estab. 1938. Member of the Dramatists Guild. Represents 200 clients. 50% of clients are new/previously unpublished writers. Specializes in full-length fiction, nonfiction, plays and screenplays; no pornography.
Handles: Nonfiction books, juvenile books, movie scripts, syndicated material, scholarly books, novels, TV scripts, textbooks, novellas, stage plays. Considers all nonfiction areas. Considers all fiction areas. Query. Reports in 1-2 weeks on queries; 2-4 weeks on mss.
Recent Sales: *Murder, Inc.*, by Feder & Turkus (Gallimard [Paris]); *The Food We Eat*, by T.T. McCoy (Walker); *Christopher Park*, by Rosemary Clement (Delphineum); *Will Rogers & Wiley Post*, by B. Sterling (Evans); *A Guide to Classical Music*, by Anne Gray (Birch Lane).
Terms: Agent receives 15% commission on domestic sales; 20% on foreign sales. Offers written contract sometimes.
Fees: Charges reading fee for new authors. Criticism service: "Authors receive report from reader if they pay reading fee." Charges for office expenses and photocopying when applicable. Payment of criticism fee does not ensure representation.
Tips: Obtains new clients through queries and recommendations.

LAW OFFICES OF ROBERT L. FENTON PC, (II), 31800 Northwestern Hwy., #390, Farmington Hills MI 48334. (810)855-8780. Fax: (810)855-3302. Contact: Robert L. Fenton. Estab. 1960. Signatory of SAG. Represents 40 clients. 25% of clients are new/previously unpublished writers. Currently handles: 25% nonfiction books; 10% scholarly books; 10% textbooks; 10% juvenile books; 35% novels; 2½% poetry books; 2½% short story collections; 5% movie scripts. Member agents: Robert L. Fenton.
● Mr. Fenton has been an entertainment attorney for over 25 years, was a producer at 20th Century Fox and Universal Studios for several years and is a published author himself.
Handles: Nonfiction books, novels, short story collections, syndicated material. Considers these nonfiction areas: biography/autobiography; business; child guidance/parenting; computers/electronics; current affairs; government/politics/law; health/medicine; military/war; money/finance/economics; music/dance/theater/film; religious/inspirational; science/technology; self-help/personal improvement; sports; true crime/investigative; women's issues/women's studies. Considers these fiction areas: action/adventure; contemporary issues; detective/police/crime; ethnic; glitz; historical; humor/satire; mainstream; mystery/suspense; romance; science fiction; sports; thriller/espionage; westerns/frontier. Query with SASE. Send 3-4 sample chapters (approximately 75 pages). Reports in 1 month on queries; 2 months on mss.
Also Handles: Movie scripts (feature film); TV scripts (TV mow, episodic drama, syndicated material). Considers these script areas: action/adventure; comedy; detective/police/crime; family saga; glitz; mainstream; mystery/suspense; romantic comedy/drama; science fiction; sports; thriller/espionage; western/frontier.
Recent Sales: *Books: Audacious Stuff* and *Kishka Chronicles*, by Greta Lipson (Simon & Schuster); *23° North*, by Thomas Morrisey; *Shareholders Rebellion*, George P. Schwartz (Irwin Pub.); *Purification by Fire*, by Jeffrey Minor (Harper/Prism). *TV scripts sold: Woman on the Ledge*, by Hal Sitowitz (Robert Fenton, NBC).
Terms: Agent receives 15% on domestic sales. Offers written contract, binding for 1 year.
Fees: Charges reading fee. "To waive reading fee, author must have been published at least 3 times by a mainline New York publishing house." Criticism service: $350. Charges for office expenses, postage, photocopying, etc. 75% of business is derived from commissions on ms sales; 25% derived from reading fees or criticism service. Payment of criticism fee does not ensure representation.
Tips: Obtains new clients through recommendations from others, individual inquiry.

LAWYER'S LITERARY AGENCY, INC., (II), One America Plaza, 600 W. Broadway, San Diego CA 92101. (619)235-9228. Contact: H. Allen Etling and Ellen Shaw Tufts. Estab. 1994. Represents 10 clients. 50% of clients are new/previously unpublished writers. Specializes in true crime, including trial aspect written by attorneys, and lawyer biographies and autobiographies. Currently handles: 100% nonfiction books.
Handles: Nonfiction books, movie scripts, TV scripts. Considers these nonfiction areas: biography/autobiography (of lawyers); law; true crime/investigative. Query with outline and 3 sample chapters. Reports in 2 weeks.
Recent Sales: *Undying Love: A Key West Love Story*, by Ben Harrison (New Horizon Press).
Also Handles: Movie scripts (feature film); TV scripts (TV mow). Considers these script subject areas: detective/police/crime; mystery/suspense. Send outline and 3 sample scenes. Reports in 2 weeks.
Terms: Agent receives 15% commission on domestic sales; does not handle foreign rights. Offers written contract for 1 year, with 30 day cancellation clause.
Fees: Charges $500 for presentation design, printing, postage, fax and telephone.
Tips: Obtains new clients through recommendations from others and advertisements in attorney trade publications. "Both agents, former newspaper journalists, believe the best stories are real stories. And

many of the best real stories are true crime stories—including depiction of the crime, background of the participants, official investigation by authorities, defense/prosecution preparation and the trial. There are hundreds of intriguing cases that occur annually in the US and not all of them are handled by attorneys who are household names. We are looking for the most compelling of these stories where there is also a good chance of selling TV movie/feature movie rights. Manuscripts can entail one case or multiple cases. Those involving multiple cases would probably resemble an attorney's biography. The story or stories can be told by defense and prosecution attorneys alike. Our agency will also arrange for co-authors or ghost writers for those attorneys lacking the time or inclination to write the manuscripts."

L. HARRY LEE LITERARY AGENCY, (II), Box #203, Rocky Point NY 11778-0203. (516)744-1188. Contact: L. Harry Lee. Estab. 1979. member of Dramatists Guild. Represents 285 clients. 65% of clients are new/previously unpublished writers. Specializes in movie scripts. "Comedy is our strength, both features and sitcoms, also movie of the week, science fiction, novels and TV." Currently handles: 30% novels; 50% movie scripts; 5% stage plays; 15% TV scripts.
- See the expanded listing for this agency in Script Agents.

*LITERARY GROUP WEST, (II), 300 W. Shaw, Suite 453, Clovis CA 93612. (209)297-9409. Fax: (209)225-5606. Contact: Ray Johnson. Estab. 1993. Represents 5 clients. 50% of clients are new/previously unpublished writers. Specializes in novels. Currently handles: 20% nonfiction books; 70% novels; 10% novellas. Member agents: B.N. Johnson, Ph.D. (English literature).
Handles: Nonfiction books, novels. Considers these nonfiction areas: current affairs; ethnic/cultural interests; military/war; true crime/investigative. Considers these fiction areas: action/adventure; detective/police/crimes; historical; mainstream; thriller/espionage. Query. Reports in 1 week on queries; 1 months on mss.
Recent Sales: *In Vitro Madonna*, by Beverly White (European-Czech).
Terms: Agent receives 20% commission on domestic sales; 25% on foreign sales. Offers written contract.
Fees: Charges expense fees to unpublished authors. Deducts expenses from sales of published authors.
Writers' Conferences: Fresno County Writers Conference (Fresno CA, July).
Tips: Obtains new clients through queries. "Query first with strong letter. Please send SASE with query letter."

*TONI LOPOPOLO LITERARY AGENCY, (II), P.O. Box 1484-A, Manhattan Beach CA 90267-1484. (310)546-6690. Fax: (310)546-2930. Contact: Toni Lopopolo. Estab. 1990. Member of Sisters in Crime. Represents 40 clients. 85% of clients are new/previously unpublished writers. Specializes in true crime. Currently handles: 75% nonfiction books; 10% reference books; 15% novels. Member agent: Toni Lopopolo (mysteries, self-help/how-to); Nicole Ballard (science fiction, editorial evaluation).
- Prior to opening her agency, Ms. Lopopolo served for 20 years in the publishing industry, including as a marketing manager with Houghton Mifflin and as executive editor with Macmillan and St. Martin's Press.
Handles: Nonfiction books, novels. Considers these nonfiction areas: animals; anthropology/archaeology; art/architecture/design; biography/autobiography; business; child guidance/parenting; cooking/food/nutrition; ethnic/cultural interests; health/medicine; history; how-to; language/literature/criticism; money/finance/economics; nature/environment; New Age/metaphysics; popular culture; psychology; self-help/personal improvement; true crime/investigative; women's issues/women's studies. Considers these fiction areas: contemporary issues; detective/police/crime; erotica; ethnic; family saga; feminist; glitz; historical; literary; mainstream; mystery/suspense; psychic/supernatural; westerns/frontier. Query. Reports in 1 month on queries; 6 weeks on mss, "unless mail is overwhelming!!"
Recent Sales: *Leader of the Pack*, by Nancy Baer and Steve Duno (HarperCollins); *Coping with Chaos Culprits*, by Harriet Schechter (Crown); *Showbiz Tricks You Can Teach Your Cat*, by Steve Duno (Adams Publishing); *Terrific People: How to Attract & Keep People Who Bring Your Life Joy*, by Dr. Lillian Gloss.
Terms: Agent receives 15% commission on domestic sales; 10-15% on foreign sales. Offers written contract, binding for 2 years.

CHECK THE SUBJECT INDEX to find the agents who are interested in your nonfiction or fiction subject area.

Fees: Will work with first novelists through an optional editorial program. There is a fee only for this service. Entire fee refunded upon sale of novel. Offers criticism service: fee depends on length and genre of novel. Charges marketing fee to cover phone, fax, postage and photocopying only. 95% of business is derived from commissions on ms sales; 5% is derived from reading fees or criticism services. Payment of criticism fee does not ensure representation.

Writers' Conferences: San Diego Writers (San Diego, January); Pacific Northwest Writers (Seattle, July).

Tips: Obtains new clients through recommendations from clients, lectures, workshops, conferences, publishers.

M.H. INTERNATIONAL LITERARY AGENCY, (II), 706 S. Superior St., Albion MI 49224. (517)629-4919. Contact: Mellie Hanke. Estab. 1992. Represents 15 clients. 75% of clients are new/previously unpublished writers. Specializes in historical novels. Currently handles: 100% novels. Member agents: Jeff Anderson (detective/police/crime); Martha Kelly (historical/mystery); Costas Papadopoulos (suspense; espionage); Nikki Stogas (confession); Marisa Handaris (foreign language ms reviewer, Greek); Mellie Hanke (Spanish); Erin Jones Morgart (French).

Handles: Novels. Considers these fiction areas: confession; detective/police/crime; historical; mystery. "We also handle Greek and French manuscripts in the above categories, plus classics. No westerns." Send all material to the attention of Mellie Hanke. Reports in 6 weeks on mss.

Terms: Agent receives 10% commission on domestic sales; 15% on foreign sales.

Fees: Charges reading fee and general office expenses. Offers criticism service, translations from above foreign languages into English, editing, evaluation and typing of mss.

Tips: "We provide translation from Greek and French into English, editing and proofreading."

VIRGINIA C. MCKINLEY, LITERARY AGENCY, (I, II), 1830 Roosevelt Ave., #101, Racine WI 53406. (414)637-9590. Contact: Virginia C. McKinley. Estab. 1992. 100% of clients are new/previously unpublished writers. Currently handles: 30% nonfiction books; 20% juvenile books; 40% novels; 10% poetry books. Member agent: Virginia C. McKinley (religious books, biography/autobiography, fiction).

Handles: Nonfiction books, juvenile books, novels, short story collections, poetry books, movie scripts, stage plays, TV scripts. Considers these nonfiction areas: animals; biography/autobiography; business; child guidance/parenting; ethnic/cultural interests; health/medicine; juvenile nonfiction; military/war; money/finance/economics; music/dance/theater/film; nature/environment; psychology; religious/inspirational; self-help/personal improvement; sociology; sports; women's issues/women's studies. Considers these fiction areas: action/adventure; contemporary issues; detective/police/crime; ethnic; family saga; fantasy; feminist; humor/satire; juvenile; literary; mystery/suspense; religous/inspiration; romance (historical); westerns/frontier. Query with entire ms or 3 sample chapters. Reports in 4-6 weeks on queries; 1 month on mss.

Also Handles: Movie scripts (feature film); TV scripts (miniseries); theatrical stage plays. Considers these script subject areas: action/adventure; comedy; contemporary issues; detective/police/crime; ethnic; family saga; humor; juvenile; mainstream; mystery/suspense; religious/inspirational; romantic comedy; science fiction; sports; teen; thriller/espionage; western/frontier.

Terms: Agent receives 15% commission on domestic sales; 20% on foreign sales. Offers written contract.

Fees: Criticism service: $125 for 3-page critique. Reports within 2 months. Charges marketing fee—$100 per year for authors under contract, photocopying ms, postage, phone, any unusual expenses. 95% of business is derived from commissions on ms sales; 5% is derived from criticism services. Payment of criticism fee does not ensure representation.

Tips: Obtains new clients through solicitation. "No multiple submissions. We feel a dynamic relationship between author and agent is essential. SASE must be included with ms or 3 chapters; also query. Will work with writer to develop his full potential."

*McLEAN LITERARY AGENCY, (II), (formerly Follendore-McLean Literary Agency), 14206 110th Ave., Kirkland WA 93034. (206)487-1310. Fax: (206)487-2213. Contact: Nan deBrandt or Donna McClean. Estab. 1988. Represents 65 clients. 85% of clients are new/previously unpublished writers. Currently handles: 64% nonfiction books; 20% juvenile books; 15% novels; 1% poetry books. Member agents: Nan deBrandt (adult nonfiction/fiction); Donna McLean (children's books and adult fiction).

Handles: Fiction and nonfiction books, scholarly books, religious books, juvenile books, picture books, poetry, short story collections. Considers these nonfiction areas: agriculture/horticulture; animals; art/architecture/design; biography/autobiography; business; child guidance/parenting; crafts/hobbies; current affairs; education; ethnic/cultural interests; government/politics/law; health/medicine; history; how-to; humor; interior design/decorating; juvenile nonfiction; language/literature/criticism; military/war; money/finance/economics; nature/environment; New Age/metaphysics; popular culture; psychology; religious/inspirational; science/technology; self-help/personal improvement; sociology;

true crime/investigative; women's issues/women's studies. Considers all fiction areas. Query first. Reports in 1 week on queries.

Recent Sales: *Wings of Light,* by Herman (Belgium Publisher); *Coming Together: The Simultaneous Orgasm,* by Riskin & Risken (Hunter House); *How Your Body Works,* by Glen Langer MD (Harvard University Press); *The Collapse of Civilization,* by Christopher Humphrey, Ph.D. (University Press of America); *Wild Heart of Los Angeles,* by Margaret Huffman (Western Edge); *Economic Justice for All,* by Michael Murray, Ph.D. (Me Sharpe).

Terms: Agent receives 15% on domestic sales; 20% on foreign sales. Offers written contract.

Also Handles: Movie scripts (feature film); TV scripts (TV mow). Considers these script areas: detective/police/crime; mystery/suspense; psychic/supernatural; thriller/espionage. Query.

Terms: Agent receives 15% commission on domestic sales; 20% on foreign sales.

Fees: "No editing fee required for authors who've been published in the prior few years by a major house. Other authors are charged an evaluation fee and our editing service is offered. For nonfiction, we completely edit the proposal/outline and sample chapter; for fiction and children's, we need the entire manuscript. Editing includes book formats, questions, comments, suggestions for expansion, cutting and pasting, etc." Also offers other services: proofreading, rewriting, proposal development, authors' public relations, etc. Payment of fees does not ensure representation unless "revisions meet our standards."

Writer's Conferences: ABA (Chicago).

Tips: Obtains new clients through recommendations from others and personal contacts at literary functions. "Study and make your query as perfect and professional as you possibly can."

*THE EVAN MARSHALL AGENCY, (III), 6 Tristam Place, Pine Brook NJ 07058-9445. (201)882-1122. Fax: (201)882-3099. E-mail: esmarshall@aol.com. Contact: Evan Marshall. Estab. 1987. Currently handles: 48% nonfiction books; 48% novels; 2% movie scripts; 2% TV scripts.

● Prior to opening his agency, Mr. Marshall served as an editor with New American Library, Everest House, and Dodd, Mead & Co., and then worked as a literary agent at The Sterling Lord Agency.

Handles: Nonfiction books, novels. Considers these nonfiction areas: animals; biography/autobiography; business; child guidance/parenting; cooking/food/nutrition; crafts/hobbies; current affairs; government/politics/law; health/medicine; history; how-to; humor; interior design/decorating; language/literature/criticism; military/war; money/finance/economics; music/dance/theater/film; nature/environment; New Age/metaphysics; psychology; religious/inspirational; science/technology; self-help/personal improvement; true crime/investigative; women's issues/women's studies. Considers these fiction areas: action/adventure; contemporary issues; detective/police/crime; erotica; ethnic; family saga; glitz; historical; horror; humor/satire; literary; mainstream; mystery/suspense; psychic/supernatural; religious/inspirational; romance; (contemporary, gothic, historical, regency); science fiction; thriller/espionage; westerns/frontier. Query. Reports in 1 week on queries; 2 months on mss.

Recent Sales: *Another Spring,* by Joan Hohl (Kensington); *The Third Sister,* by Julia Barrett (Dutton); *Lady Deception,* by Bobbi Smith (Kensington); *Mourning Gloria,* by Joyce Christmas (Fawcett); *The Nun's Tale,* by Candace Robb (St. Martin's).

Also Handles: Movie scripts (feature film), TV scripts (TV mow, episodic drama, sitcom). Considers these script subject areas: action/adventure; comedy; contemporary issues; detective/police/crime; erotica; ethnic; family saga; fantasy; glitz; historical; horror; humor; mainstream; mystery/suspense; psychic/supernatural; religious/inspirational; romantic comedy and drama; science fiction; sports; teen; thriller; western/frontier.

Terms: Agent receives 15% on domestic sales; 20% on foreign sales. Offers written contract.

Fees: Charges a fee to consider for representation material by *writers who have not sold a book or script.* "Send SASE for fee schedule. There is no fee if referred by a client or an editor or if you are already published in the genre of your submission."

Tips: Obtains many new clients through referrals from clients and editors.

*MEWS BOOKS LTD., (II, III), 20 Bluewater Hill, Westport CT 06880. (203)227-1836. Fax: (203)227-1144. Contact: Sidney B. Kramer. Estab. 1972. Represents 35 clients. Prefers to work with published/established authors; works with small number of new/unpublished authors "producing professional work." Specializes in juvenile (preschool through young adult), cookery, self-help, adult nonfiction and fiction, technical and medical and electronic publishing. Currently handles: 20% nonfiction books; 10% novels; 20% juvenile books; 40% electronic; 10% miscellaneous. Member agent: Fran Pollak (assistant).

Handles: Nonfiction books, novels, juvenile books, character merchandising and video and TV use of illustrated published books. Query with precis, outline, character description, a few pages of sample writing and author's bio.

Recent Sales: *Dr. Susan Love's Breast Book*, 2nd edition, by Susan M. Love, MD, with Karen Lindsey (Addison-Wesley).

Terms: Agent receives 15% commission on domestic sales; 20% on foreign sales.

Fees: Does not charge a reading fee. "If material is accepted, agency asks for $350 circulation fee (4-5 publishers), which will be applied against commissions (waived for published authors)." Charges for photocopying, postage expenses, telephone calls and other direct costs.

Tips: "Principle agent is an attorney and former publisher. Offers consultation service through which writers can get advice on a contract or on publishing problems."

MONTGOMERY LITERARY AGENCY, (II), P.O. Box 8822, Silver Spring MD 20907-8822. (301)230-1807. Contact: M.E. Olsen. Estab. 1984. Signatory of WGA. 25% of clients are new/previously unpublished writers. Equal interest in scripts (films and TV mainly) and books. Currently handles: 12% nonfiction books; 2% poetry; 5% juvenile books; 25% novels; 30% movie scripts; 20% TV scripts; 1% short story collections; 2% syndicated material; 2% other (comics, etc.)
- See the expanded listing for this agency in Script Agents.

*BK NELSON LITERARY AGENCY & LECTURE BUREAU, (II, III), 84 Woodland Rd., Pleasantville NY 10570-1322. (914)741-1322. Fax: (914)741-1324. Contact: Bonita Nelson, John Benson or Erv Rosenfeld. Estab. 1980. Member of NACA, Author's Guild, NAFE, ABA. Represents 62 clients. 40% of clients are new/previously unpublished writers. Specializes in business, self-help, how-to, novels, biographies. Currently handles: 40% nonfiction books; 5% CD-ROM/electronic products; 40% novels; 5% movie scripts; 5% TV scripts; 5% stage plays. Member agents: Bonita Nelson (business books); John Benson (Director of Lecture Bureau); Erv Rosenfeld (novels and TV scripts); Dave Donnelly (videos); Geisel Ali (self-help); JW Benson (novels); Jean Rejaunier (biography, nonfiction).
- Prior to opening her agency, Ms. Nelson worked for a law firm specializing in entertainment law and at American Play Company, a literary agency.

Handles: Nonfiction books, CD ROM/electronic products, scholarly books, novels. Considers these nonfiction areas: agriculture; animals; anthropology/archaeology; art/architecture/design; biography/autobiography; business; child guidance/parenting; computers/electronics; cooking/food/nutrition; crafts/hobbies; current affairs; education; ethnic/cultural interests; government/politics/law; health/medicine; history; how-to; language/literature/criticism; military/war; money/finance/economics; music/dance/theater/film; nature/environment; popular culture; psychology; religious/inspirational; science/technology; self-help/personal improvement; sociology; sports; true crime/investigative; women's issues/women's studies. Considers these fiction areas: action/adventure; cartoon/comic; contemporary issues; detective/police/crime; family saga; fantasy; feminist; glitz; historical; horror; literary; mainstream; mystery/suspense; psychic/supernatural; romance (contemporary, historical); science fiction; sports; thriller/espionage; westerns/frontier. Query. Reports in 1 week on queries; 3 weeks on ms.

Recent Sales: *Runway Success*, by Jeanne Rejaunier (Barclay); *My Literary Agent*, by BK Nelson (Barclay); *Around The World in 72 Days*, by Jason Marks (Decca); *Why You Should Never Beam Down in a Red Shirt* (HarperCollins) and *Successful Telephone Sales* (Holt), both by Robert Bly; and *Sonya*, by Leon Katz (The Nelson PlayCompany).

Also Handles: Movie scripts (feature film, documentary, animation), TV scripts (TV mow, episodic drama, sitcom, variety show, miniseries, animation), stage plays. Considers these script subject areas: action/adventure; cartoon; comedy; contemporary issues; detective/police/crime; family saga; fantasy; historical; horror; mainstream; psychic/supernatural; romantic comedy and drama; thriller; westerns/frontier. Reports in 2 weeks.

Recent Sales: *Movie scripts optioned/sold: Mob Sisters*, by Jeanne Rejaunier (Paramount); *TV scripts optioned/sold: Sonya*, by Leon Katz (PBS); *Scripting assignments: Pinocchio*, by Leon Katz (GACT).

Terms: Agent receives 20% on domestic sales; 25% on foreign sales. Offers written contract, exclusive for 8-12 months.

Fees: Charges $350 reading fee for *new clients' material only.* "It is not refundable. We usually charge for the first reading only. The reason for charging in addition to time/expense is to determine if the writer is saleable and thus a potential client."

Writer's Conferences: Frankfurt Book Fair (Frankfurt, October); National NACA (Nashville TN, February); ABA (Chicago, June).

Tips: Obtains new clients through referrals and reputation with editors. "We handle the business aspect of the literary and lecture fields. We handle careers as well as individual book projects. If the author has the ability to write and we are harmonious, success is certain to follow with us handling the selling/business."

‡*NORDHAUS-WOLCOTT LITERARY AGENCY, (I),** P.O. Box 7493, Shawnee Mission KS 66207. Phone/fax: (816)767-1099. E-mail: nordwolc@oz.sunflower.org. Contact: David Nordhaus or Chris Wolcott. Estab. 1996. Member of Kansas City Professional Writer's Group and The Writer's Place. Represents a few clients. 90% of clients are new/previously unpublished writers. Specializes in mass-market genre fiction, science fiction, fantasy, horror, romance, erotica, etc. Currently handles: 10% movie scripts, 20% short story collections, 60% novels, 10% novellas. Member agents: David Nordhaus (science fiction, fantasy, horror, erotica); Chris Wolcott (mainstream, humor, mystery/suspense, screenplays, documentaries).

Handles: Movie scripts, novels, novellas, short story collections. Considers these nonfiction areas: documentary screenplays only. Considers these fiction areas: action/adventure; detective/police/crime; erotica; experimental; fantasy; historical; horror; humor/satire; literary; mainstream; mystery/suspense; psychic/supernatural; romance (gothic, historical); science fiction; thriller/espionage; westerns/frontier; young adult. Query with short explanation of storyline and SASE. "We accept e-mail queries for faster responses." Reports in 3 weeks on queries; 7 weeks on mss; 1-5 days on e-mail queries.

Terms: Agent receives 10% commission on domestic sales; 20% on foreign sales. Offers written contract, binding for 1 year, with a 30 day termination clause.

Fees: Reading fee: $150 for outline and full ms, refundable after sale of work; $50 for short stories to 10,000 words. Fee is for new writers only, includes a 3- to 6-page critique of all works they agree to review. Criticism service: all works reviewed receive a detailed critique. The critiques, written by the agents, focus on story flow, content and format, not necessarily punctuation and grammar, and advise as to the proper format for submissions. $50 monthly administration fee covering photocopying, postage, long distance phone calls, etc. "There are no hidden fees." 10% of business is derived from reading fees or criticism service.

Tips: Obtains new clients through recommendations from others, conferences, unsolicited queries and from their Internet site at http://www.sunflower.org/~nordwolc. "We form a strategy to help new authors get their name into the market so approaching the larger houses is made easier. The sales of short stories typically don't pay very much, but it's a way of getting credits under your belt for future references. We want you to succeed. It all starts with a simple query letter. Drop us a line, we'd like to hear from you."

*NORTHWEST LITERARY SERVICES, (II),** 2699 Decca Rd., Shawnigan Lake, British Columbia V0R 2W0 Canada. (604)743-8236. Contact: Brent Laughren or Jennifer Chapman. Estab. 1986. Represents 20 clients. 75% of clients are new/previously unpublished writers. Specializes in working with new writers. Currently handles: 45% nonfiction books; 10% juvenile books; 40% novels; 5% short story collections. Member agent: Jennifer Chapman (juvenile books). Send juvenile queries, etc., to Jennifer Chapman, 3420 Gardon Dr., Vancouver, British Columbia V5N 445 Canada.

Handles: Nonfiction books, juvenile books, novels. Considers these nonfiction areas: agriculture/ horticulture; animals; art/architecture/design; biography/autobiography; child guidance/parenting; cooking/food/nutrition; crafts/hobbies; ethnic/cultural interests; gay/lesbian issues; health/medicine; history; how-to; humor; juvenile nonfiction; language/literature/criticism; music/dance/theater/film; nature/environment; New Age/metaphysics; photography; popular culture; religious/inspirational; self-help/personal improvement; sports; translations; true crime/investigative; women's issues/women's studies. Considers these fiction areas: action/adventure; confessional; contemporary issues; detective/ police/crime; erotica; ethnic; experimental; family saga; fantasy; feminist; historical; humor/satire; juvenile; literary; mainstream; mystery/suspense; picture book; psychic/supernatural; romance; science fiction; sports; thriller/espionage; westerns/frontier; young adult. Query with outline/proposal. Reports in 1 month on queries; 2 months on mss.

Terms: Agent receives 15% on domestic sales; 20% on foreign sales. Offers written contract.

Fees: Charges reading fee for unpublished authors. Children's picture books $50; fiction/nonfiction synopsis and first 3 chapters $75. Reading fee includes short evaluation. Criticism service: $100 for book outline and sample chapters up to 20,000 words. Charges 75¢-$1/page for copyediting and content editing; $1/page for proofreading; $10-20/page for research. "Other related editorial services available at negotiated rates. Critiques are two to three page overall evaluations, with suggestions. All fees, if charged, are authorized by the writer in advance." 75% of business is derived from commissions on ms sales; 25% is derived from reading fees or criticism service. Payment of criticism fee does not ensure representation.

Tips: Obtains new clients through recommendations. "Northwest Literary Services is particularly interested in the development and marketing of new and unpublished writers. We are also interested in literary fiction."

*WILLIAM PELL AGENCY, (II), 5 Canterbury, Southampton NY 11968-5053 (516)287-7228. Contact: Susan Kelly. Estab. 1990. Represents 23 clients. 85% of clients are new/previously unpublished writers. Member agent: Susan Kelly (fiction); Clarissa Katz.
Handles: Novels. Considers these nonfiction areas: biography/autobiography; photography. Considers these fiction areas: action/adventure; detective/police/crime; humor/satire; thriller/espionage. Query with 2 sample chapters. Reports in 1 month on queries; 3 months on mss.
Recent Sales: *Mind-Set*, by Paul Dostor (Penguin USA); *Bewildering Beasties*, by Derek Pell (Dover); *Grown Men*, by Sheela Mauie (Avon).
Terms: Agent receives 15% commission on domestic sales; 20% on foreign sales. Offers written contract, binding for 1 year.
Fees: Charges $100 reading fee for new writers. 90% of business is derived from commission on ms sales; 10% is derived from reading fees or criticism services. Payment of criticism fees does not ensure representation.

PENMARIN BOOKS, (II), 504 Wexford Ct., Roseville CA 95661. (916)771-5869. Fax: (916)771-5879. President: Hal Lockwood. Estab. 1987. Represents 20 clients. 80% of clients are new/unpublished writers. "No previous publication is necessary. We do expect authoritative credentials in terms of history, politics, science and the like." Handles general trade nonfiction and illustrated books, as well as fiction.

  • Prior to opening his agency, Mr. Lockwood served as an editorial assistant at Stanford University Press, an editor with Painter/Hopkins Publishing and in editorial production with Presidio Publishing.

Handles: Nonfiction books, fiction. For nonfiction books, query with outline. For fiction, query with outline and sample chapters. Will read submissions at no charge, but may charge a criticism fee or service charge for work performed after the initial reading. Reports in 2 weeks on queries; 1 month on mss.
Recent Sales: *Compromised: Clinton, Bush and the C.I.A.*, by Terry Reed and John Cummings (Clandestine Pub.); *The Story the Soldiers Wouldn't Tell: Sex in the Civil War*, by Thomas Lowry (Stackpole Press); *Lamia: A Witch*, by Georgia Elizabeth Taylor (New American Library).
Terms: Agent receives 15% commission on domestic sales; 15% on dramatic sales; 15% on foreign sales.
Fees: "We normally do not provide extensive criticism as part of our reading but, for a fee, will prepare guidance for editorial development. Charges $200/300 pages. Our editorial director writes critiques. These may be two to ten pages long. They usually include an overall evaluation and then analysis and recommendations about specific sections, organization or style."

PMA LITERARY AND FILM MANAGEMENT, INC., 132 W. 22nd St., 12th Floor, New York NY 10011-1817. (212)929-1222. Fax: (212)206-0238. E-mail: pmalitfilm@aol.com. President: Peter Miller. Member agents: Jennifer Robinson (film and fiction); Yuri Skujins (fiction and nonfiction); Jody Saltzman. Estab. 1975. Represents 80 clients. 50% of clients are new/unpublished writers. Specializes in commercial fiction and nonfiction, thrillers, true crime and "fiction with *real* motion picture and television potential." Currently handles: 50% fiction; 25% nonfiction; 25% screenplays.
Handles: Fiction, nonfiction, film scripts. Considers these nonfiction areas: business; popular culture; true crime/investigative; women's issues/women's studies. Considers these fiction areas: action/adventure; contemporary issues; detective/police/crime; horror; literary; mainstream; mystery/suspense; thriller/espionage; young adult. Query with outline and/or sample chapters. Writer's guidelines for 5 × 8½ SASE with 2 first-class stamps. Reports in 3 weeks on queries; 6-8 weeks on ms. Submissions and queries without SASE will not be returned.
Recent Sales: *Head Case*, by Jay Bonansinga (Simon & Schuster); *Erotic Astrology*, by Olivia (Baccantine); *The Plague Tales*, by Ann Benson (Delacorte); *Slave Day*, by Rob Thomas (Simon & Schuster).
Also Handles: Movie scripts (feature film); TV scripts (TV mow, miniseries).
Terms: Agent receives 15% commission on domestic sales; 20-25% on foreign sales.
Fees: Does not charge a reading fee. Paid reading evaluation service available upon request. "The evaluation, usually five to ten pages in length, gives a detailed analysis of literary craft and commercial potential as well as further recommendations for improving the work." Charges for photocopying expenses.
Writer's Conferences: Maui Writer's Conference, Santa Fe Writer's Conference, New Orleans Writer's Conference.

*THE PORTMAN ORGANIZATION, (III), 7337 N. Lincoln Ave., Suite 283, Chicago IL 60076. (312)509-6421. Fax: (847)982-9386. Contact: Phyllis A. Emerman. Estab. 1972. Represents 33 clients. 10-15% of clients are new/previously unpublished writers. Currently handles: 50% nonfiction books; 10% movie scripts; 25% novels; 15% TV scripts. Member agents: Julien Portman (Hollywood); Ludmilla Dudin (novels); Joel Cohan (fiction); Capt. William Bradford (military).

Handles: Nonfiction books, novels. Considers these nonfiction areas: biography/autobiography; current affairs; history; military/war; music/dance/theater/film; sports; true crime/investigative; women's issues/women's studies. Considers these fiction areas: action/adventure; detective/police/crime; family saga; historical; romance (contemporary, historical); science fiction; sports; thriller/espionage; westerns/frontier. Query. Reports in 10 days on queries; 1 month on mss.

Recent Sales: *The Silver Bracelet*; *Camp Jupiter*; *The Understanding Candle*; *Ian Fleming: "Only" the War Years*.

Terms: Agent receives 15% commission on domestic sales; 25% on foreign sales. Offers written contract, binding for 1 year.

Fees: Charges reading fee for new writers only, $150 for 350 pages, $200 for 350- 600 pages. Fees refundable if representation offered. Less than 10% of business is derived from reading fees.

Also Hanels: Movie scripts (feature film); TV scripts (TV mows, miniseries). Considers these script subject areas: action/adventure; detective/police/crime; historical; mystery/suspense; science fiction. Query with SASE.

Writers' Conferences: "Rarely do we attend writers conferences, but do attend the yearly show, [ABA] which will be in Chicago for the next two years."

Tips: Obtains clients through referrals, recommendations and from referrals. "We have an excellent track record—we're very careful with solicitation. Reputation in the field of war, due to working with CIA for years. Spent time in Vietnam, and played the role in other areas: Australia, Hong Kong, Thailand, Japan and China. We, also, are involved with TV and motion picture projects. Our agent is William Morris Agency. Our office has been successful (modestly) through the years."

PUDDINGSTONE LITERARY AGENCY, (II), Affiliate of SBC Enterprises Inc., 11 Mabro Dr., Denville NJ 07834-9607. (201)366-3622. Contact: Alec Bernard or Eugenia Cohen. Estab. 1972. Represents 25 clients. 80% of clients are new/previously unpublished writers. Currently handles: 10% nonfiction books; 70% novels; 20% movie scripts.

Handles: Nonfiction books, novels, movie scripts. Considers these nonfiction areas: business; how-to; language/literature/criticism; military/war; true crime/investigative. Considers these fiction areas: action/adventure; detective/police/crime; horror; science fiction; thriller/espionage. Query first with SASE including $1 cash processing fee, "which controls the volume and eliminates dilettantism among the submissions." Reports immediately on queries; 1 month on mss "that are requested by us."

Recent Sales: *The Action-Step Plan to Owning And Operating A Small Business*, by E. Toncré (Prentice-Hall).

Terms: Agent receives 10-15% sliding scale (decreasing) on domestic sales; 20% on foreign sales. Offers written contract, binding for 1 year with renewals.

Fees: Reading fee charged for unsolicited mss over 20 pages. Negotiated fees for market analysis available. Charges for photocopying for foreign sales.

Tips: Obtains new clients through referrals and listings.

QCORP LITERARY AGENCY, (I), P.O. Box 8, Hillsboro OR 97123-0008. (800)775-6038. Contact: William C. Brown. Estab. 1990. Represents 14 clients. 75% of clients are new/previously unpublished writers. Currently handles: 40% nonfiction books; 60% fiction books. Member agent: William C. Brown.

Handles: Fiction and nonfiction books, including textbooks, scholarly books, novels, novellas, short story collections. Considers all nonfiction areas. Considers all areas of fiction, excluding cartoon/comic books. Query through critique service. Reports in 2 weeks on queries; 3 months on mss.

Recent Sales: *Good Girl, Bad Girl*, by Kevin Ammons with Nancy Bacon (Carol Publishing Group).

Terms: Agent receives 10% commission on domestic sales; 20% on foreign sales. Offers written contract, binding for 6 months, automatically renewed unless cancelled by author.

Fees: "No charges are made to agency authors if no sales are procured. If sales are generated, then charges are itemized and collected from proceeds up to a limit of $200, after which all expenses are absorbed by agency." Offers criticism service.

Tips: Obtains new clients through recommendations from others and from critique service. "New authors should use our critique service and its free, no obligation first chapter critique to introduce themselves. Call or write for details. Our critique service is serious business, line by line and comprehensive. Established writers should call or send résumé."

TO FIND AN AGENT near you, check the Geographic Index.

*DIANE RAINTREE AGENCY, (II), 360 W. 21st St., New York NY 10011-3305. (212)242-2387. Contact: Diane Raintree. Estab. 1977. Represents 6-8 clients. Specializes in novels, film and TV scripts, plays, poetry and children's books.

- Prior to opening her agency, Ms. Raintree was a a senior editor for Dial Press, copyeditor and proofreader for Zebra Books and Charter Books, and a reader for Avon Books.

Handles: Considers all fiction areas. Phone first.

Terms: Agent receives 10% on domestic sales.

Also Handles: Movie scripts (feature film); TV scripts (TV mow, sitcom). Considers these script areas: action/adventure; comedy; contemporary issues; detective/police/crime; ethnic; family saga; gay; historical; juvenile; lesbian; mainstream; mystery/suspense; psychic/supernatural; romance (romantic comedy, romantic drama); science fiction; teen; thriller/suspense. Phone first. Send entire script with SASE. Reports in 1 week on queries; 1-3 months on mss. Agent receives 5% commission. "Writer should engage an entertainment lawyer for negotiations of option and contract."

Fees: May charge reading fee. "Amount varies from year to year."

‡REMINGTON LITERARY ASSOC., INC. (I, II), 10131 Coors Rd. NW, Suite I 2-886, Albuquerque NM 87114. (505)898-8305. Fax: (505)890-0486. Contact: Kay Lewis Shaw. Estab. 1995. Member of Southwest Writers Workshop (SWW), RWA, LERA & National Writers Association & Four Corners Literary Alliance. Represents 35 clients. 80% of clients are new/previously unpublished writers. Specializes in adult genre fiction, "though we also represent selective commercial nonfiction." Currently handles: 10% nonfiction books; 50% novels; 40% children's. Member agents: Jeffrey A. Poston (westerns, science fiction, fantasy, nonfiction); Kay Lewis Shaw (mystery, romance, mainstream, historicals, young adult and children's books).

Handles: Nonfiction books, juvenile books, movie scripts, novels, TV scripts, textbooks. Considers these nonfiction areas: agriculture/horticulture; animals; anthropology/archaeology; art/architecture/design; biography/autobiography; business; child guidance/parenting; computers/electronics; cooking/food/nutrition; crafts/hobbies; current affairs; education; ethnic/cultural interests; government/politics/law; health/medicine; history; how-to; humor; interior design/decorating; juvenile nonfiction; language/literature/criticism; military/war; money/finance/economics; music/dance/theater/film; nature/environment; new age/metaphysics; photography; popular culture; psychology; religious/inspirational; science/technology; self-help/personal improvement; sociology; sports; true crime/investigative; women's issues/women's studies. Considers these fiction areas: action/adventure; cartoon/comic; contemporary issues; detective/police/crime; erotica; ethnic; family saga; fantasy; glitz; historical; horror; humor/satire; juvenile; mainstream; mystery/suspense; picture book; psychic/supernatural; regional; religious/inspirational; romance (contemporary, historical); science fiction; sports; thriller/espionage; westerns/frontier; young adult. Query. Reports in 2 weeks on queries; 2-4 months on mss.

Terms: Agent receives 15% commission on domestic sales; 20% on foreign sales. Offers written contract, binding for 1 year and can be renewed annually, with a 60 day cancellation clause.

Fees: Charges reading fee: "to authors that we have not met at conferences or have not been recommended either by a client, other agent, or editor. We charge $75 to look at 75 pages, which must include the synopsis or outline." Criticism service: "We rarely offer criticism service, but on occasion, if the person is being considered as a potential client, we will critique one book. Fees vary depending on the amount of work to be done. Usually, five dollars a page for critique only, and $3.50 for line-editing. Our agents write the critiques. They may be from 5 to 15 pages long." Charges "an annual marketing fee of $150, balance refundable if the book sells during that calendar year. Each client receives a balance sheet detailing amounts spent and for what, e.g., long distance calls, copying, postage, etc."

Writer's Conferences: Southwest Writers Workshop (Albuquerque, August '97).

Tips: "We are very selective. We want people who are willing to listen to criticism and who are willing to work hard." Obtains new clients at conferences, query letters, recommendations. "If your query letter is messy, unprofessionally written, or poorly photocopied, we know immediately that you aren't the client for us. Take classes. If you're writing novels, please study Jack Bickham's, Dwight Swain's, and Gary Provost's books on writing. Good ideas don't sell; good books do. Finally, learn to take criticism. Editors and agents are looking for professionals who realize that this is a business. If you are looking for pats on the back, have your family read your work. We want clients who will do whatever revisions are necessary to sell their work. Learning how to accept criticism early prepares you for the editorial requirements after you sell. Be professional, *always*, be professional."

‡RHODES LITERARY AGENCY, (II), P.O. Box 89133, Honolulu HI 96830-9133. (808)947-4689. Director: Fred C. Pugarelli. Estab. 1971. Signatory of WGA. Represents 50 clients. 85% of clients are new/previously unpublished writers. Currently handles: 10% nonfiction books; 1% juvenile books; 25% movie scripts; 1% short story collections; 1% scholarly books; 50% novels; 1% TV scripts; 1% textbooks; 5% stage plays; 5% poetry. Member agents: Fred C. Pugarelli; Angela Pugarelli.

Handles: Nonfiction books, juvenile books, movie scripts, syndicated material, scholarly books, novels, TV scripts, textbooks, stage plays, poetry books, short story collections. Considers these nonfiction areas: animals; anthropology/archaeology; art/architecture/design; biography/autobiography; business; child guidance/parenting; cooking/food/nutrition; crafts/hobbies; current affairs; education; ethnic/cultural interests; gay/lesbian issues; government/politics/law; health/medicine; history; how-to; humor; juvenile nonfiction; language/literature/criticism; military/war; money/finance/economics; music/dance/theater/film; nature/environment; new age/metaphysics; photography; popular culture; psychology; religious/inspirational; science/technology; self-help/personal improvement; sociology; sports; translations; true crime/investigative; women's issues/women's studies. Considers these fiction areas: action/adventure; confessional; contemporary issues; detective/police/crime; erotica; ethnic; experimental; family saga; fantasy; feminist; gay; glitz; historical; horror; humor/satire; juvenile; lesbian; literary; mainstream; mystery/suspense; psychic/supernatural; religious/inspirational; romance (contemporary, gothic, historical, regency); science fiction; sports; thriller/espionage; westerns/frontier; young adult. Send entire ms or query letter fully describing ms and author's bio. Include SASE. Reports in 2 weeks on queries; 4-6 weeks on mss.

Recent Sales: "Thus far this agency has sold over 120 manuscripts of various kinds to a wide variety of national markets. Sales have been made to Adams Publishing, *Travel & Leisure*, Signature, *The Saint Mystery Magazine*, *Fantastic Universe*, Camerarts Publishing, *Millionaire*, *Men's Digest*, *Rascal*, *Opinion*, *The Mendocino Robin*, *Mature Years*, *Hyacinths & Biscuits*, and other markets. We submit over 100 manuscripts a year to markets."

Terms: Agent receives 10% commission on domestic sales; 20% on foreign sales; 20% on electronic sales.

Fees: Charges reading fee: $165-175 (non refundable); 1-2 page report in return. 50% of business derived from reading fees.

Tips: Obtains new clients through recommendations from others, solicitation. "Send a good query letter fully describing your manuscript and including some biographical data about yourself and your writing background. Include sales so far, if any, and SASE for reply."

IRENE ROGERS LITERARY REPRESENTATION, (III), 9454 Wilshire Blvd., Suite 600, Beverly Hills CA 90212. (213)837-3511 or (310)276-7588. Estab. 1977. Currently represents 10 clients. 10% of clients are new/previously unpublished authors. "We are currently accepting new clients." Currently handles: 50% nonfiction; 50% novels.

Handles: Nonfiction, novels. Considers all nonfiction areas, especially medicine and self-help/personal improvement. Considers all areas of fiction. Query. Responds to queries in 6-8 weeks.

Terms: Agent receives 10% commission on domestic sales; 5% on foreign sales.

Fees: Charges $150 reading fees.

SLC ENTERPRISES, (II), 852 Highland Place, Highland Park IL 60035. (773)728-3997. Contact: Ms. Carole Golin. Estab. 1985. Represents 30 clients. 50% of clients are new/previously unpublished writers. Currently handles: 65% nonfiction books; 5% textbooks; 10% juvenile books; 20% novels. Member agents: Stephen Cogil (sports).

Handles: Nonfiction books, juvenile books, novels, short story collections. Considers these nonfiction areas: biography/autobiography, business, cooking/food/nutrition; current affairs; history; sports; women's issues/women's studies; Holocaust studies. Considers these fiction areas: detective/police/crime; feminist; historical; juvenile; literary; picture book; regional; romance (contemporary, historical); sports; young adult. Query with outline/proposal. Reports in 2 weeks on queries; 1 months on mss.

Recent Sales: *Eyeopeners II*, by Kubrin (Scholastic); *Will To Live*, by Adam Starkopt (SUNY); *The Enneagram Spectrum of Personality Styles*, by Dr. Jerome Wagner (Metamorphous Press).

Terms: Agent receives 15% commission on domestic sales. Offers written contract, binding for 9 months.

Fees: Charges $150 reading fee for entire ms; $75-150 for children's, depending on length and number of stories. Reading fee includes overall critique plus specifics. No line editing for grammar etc. Charges no other fees. 20% of business is derived from reading and criticism fees.

Tips: Obtains new clients through recommendations, listings in literary manuals.

*SOUTHERN LITERARY AGENCY, (III), 16411 Brookvilla Dr., Houston TX 77059. (713)480-6360. Contact: Michael Doran. Estab. 1980. Represents 58 clients. 20% of clients are new/previously unpublished writers. "We are most interested in popular financial, professional and technical books." Currently handles: 70% nonfiction books; 20% novels; 10% movie scripts. Member agents: Michael Doran (nonfiction); Patricia Coleman (fiction).

Handles: Nonfiction books, novels, movie scripts. Considers these nonfiction areas: anthropology/archaeology; biography/autobiography; business; child guidance/parenting; health/medicine; history; money/finance/economics; psychology; self-help/personal improvement. Considers these fiction areas: action/adventure; detective/police/crime; humor/satire; mainstream; mystery/suspense; thriller/espionage. Telephone query. Reports in 1 month on mss.

Recent Sales: *Fanfare for an Uncommon Man* and *The Life of Aaron Copland*, by Howard Pollack (Henry Holt); *Clean, Sweet Wind*, by Douglas Pyle (Texas A&M Press); *A Very Short War*, by John Guilmartin (Texas A&M Press).
Terms: Agent receives 15% commission on domestic sales; 20% on foreign sales. Offers written contract.
Fees: "There is a $350 fee on unpublished new novelists, returnable if their manuscript is publishable and we do the selling of it. Refund on first royalties. Offers multi-page critique on manuscripts which can be made marketable; 1-page remarks and suggestions for writing improvements otherwise. Charges cost-per on extraordinary costs, pre-agreed." 90% of business derived from commissions on ms sales; 10% from reading fees or criticism services.
Writers' Conferences: ABA; Texas and other Southern regional conferences.
Tips: Obtains new clients through conferences, Yellow Pages—mainly referrals. "Learn about the book business through conferences and reading before contacting the agent."

‡**STADLER LITERARY AGENCY, (I)**, P.O. Box 182, 3202 E. Greenway Rd., Suite #1307, Phoenix AZ 85032. (602)569-2481. Fax: (602)569-2265. E-mail: bookwoma@sprynet.com. Contact: Rose Stadler. Estab. 1995. Member of SCBWI, National Writer's Assoc., Az Author's Assoc. Represents 40 clients. 50% of clients are new/previously unpublished writers. Specializes in mystery/suspense, nonfiction social issues (for example, issues relating to foster care, adoption, etc.). Currently handles: 35% nonfiction books; 10% juvenile books; 50% novels; 1% textbooks.
Handles: Nonfiction books, juvenile books, novels. Considers these nonfiction areas: child guidance/parenting; current affairs; humor; juvenile nonfiction; new age/metaphysics; religious/inspirational; self-help/personal improvement; sociology; women's issues/women's studies. Considers these fiction areas: contemporary issues; detective/police/crime; family saga; feminist; humor/satire; juvenile; literary; mainstream; mystery/suspense; psychic/supernatural; thriller/espionage; young adult. Query with outline and 3 sample chapters. Reports in 3-6 weeks on queries; 3 months on mss.
Terms: Agent receives 15% commission on domestic sales; 20% on foreign sales. Offers written contract, binding for 2 years. 30 days notice to terminate contract.
Fees: Charges reading fee: $75 up to 350 pages; $100 over 350 pages; no fee for children's literature; no fee to evaluate first three chapters; no fee to non-profit associations or organizations. Offers criticism service. Price varies according to piece; standard fee. "I've taught fiction writing for 14+ years at local community colleges and have written a how-to guide for fiction writing. This is the area where a serious author will get the most help. Plotting, balance, dialogue, narrative, etc. For nonfiction, good writing counts. When and if publication takes place, the agency may be reimbursed for expenses such as postage, copying, typing services, etc."
Tips: Obtains new clients through queries and word of mouth. "Too many authors wear their egos on their sleeve and take rejection far too personally. Think of your work as a piece of real estate; if the house needs a new coat of paint, then paint it. Same with writing, if the manuscript needs to be edited, then the author needs to spend the time editing. It's best not to let emotions get in the way of the written word. I'm interested in social issues."

MICHAEL STEINBERG LITERARY AGENCY, (III), P.O. Box 274, Glencoe IL 60022. (847)835-8881. Contact: Michael Steinberg. Estab. 1980. Represents 27 clients. 5% of clients are new/previously unpublished writers. Specializes in business and general nonfiction, mysteries, science fiction. Currently handles: 75% nonfiction books; 25% novels.
Handles: Nonfiction books, novels. Considers these nonfiction areas: biography; business; computers; law; history; how-to; money/finance/economics; self-help/personal improvement. Considers these fiction areas: action/adventure; contemporary issues; detective/police/crime; erotica; mainstream; mystery/suspense; science fiction; thriller/espionage. Query for guidelines. Reports in 2 weeks on queries; 6 weeks on mss.
Recent Sales: *How to Buy Mutual Funds the Smart Way*, by Stephen Littauer (Dearborn Publishing); *The Complete Day Trader*, by Jake Bernstein (McGraw-Hill).
Terms: Agent receives 15% on domestic sales; 15-20% on foreign sales. Offers written contract, which is binding, "but at will."
Fees: Charges $75 reading fee for outline and chapters 1-3; $200 for a full ms to 100,000 words. Criticism included in reading fee. Charges actual phone and postage, which is billed back quarterly. 95% of business is derived from commissions on ms sales; 5% derived from reading fees or criticism services.
Writer's Conferences: ABA (Chicago).
Tips: Obtains new clients through unsolicited inquiries and referrals from editors and authors. "We do not solicit new clients. Do not send unsolicited material. Write for guidelines and include SASE. Do not send generically addressed, photocopied query letters."

GLORIA STERN AGENCY, (II), 1235 Chandler Blvd., #3, North Hollywood CA 91607-1934. Phone/fax: (818)508-6296. E-mail: af385@lafn.org. Contact: Gloria Stern. Estab. 1984. Member of

IWOSC, SCW. Represents 14 clients. 80% of clients are new/unpublished writers. Specializes in consultation, writer's services (ghost writing, editing, critiquing, etc.) and electronic media consultation. Currently handles: 79% fiction; 19% nonfiction books; 8% movie scripts; 2% reality based. Member agent: Gloria Stern (romance, detective, science fiction).

• This agency is not affiliated with the Gloria Stern Literary Agency in Texas.

Handles: Novels, short story collections. Considers these nonfiction areas: biography/autobiography; business; child guidance/parenting; computers/electronics; cooking; current affairs; education; ethnic/cultural interests; gay/lesbian issues; health/medicine; how-to; language/literature/criticism; money/finance/economics; music/dance/theater/film; New Age/metaphysical; popular culture; psychology (pop); self-help/personal improvement; sociology; true crime/investigative; women's issues/women's studies. Considers these fiction areas: action/adventure; contemporary issues; detective/police/crime; erotica; fantasy; feminist; glitz; horror; literary; mainstream; romance (contemporary, gothic, historical, regency); science fiction; thriller/espionage; western/frontier. Query with short bio, credits. Reports in 1 month on queries; 6 weeks on mss.

Also Handles: Movie scripts (feature film, TV mow). Considers these script subject areas: action/adventure; comedy; contemporary issues; detective/police/crime; erotica; ethnic; family saga; fantasy; feminist; gay; glitz; historical; horror; juvenile; mainstream; mystery/suspense; psychic/supernatural; romance (comedy, drama); science fiction; sports; thriller; westerns/frontier.

Recent Sales: *Create Your Own Web Page*, by Stern (Myriad).

Terms: Agent receives 12% commission on domestic sales; 20% on foreign sales. Offers written contract, binding for 1 year.

Fees: Charges reading fee, by project (by arrangement), $35/hour for unpublished writers. Criticism service: $35/hour. Critiques are "detailed analysis of all salient points regarding such elements as structure, style, pace, development, publisher's point of view and suggestions for rewrites if needed." Charges for long-distance, photocopying and postage. 38% of income derived from sales, 29% from reading fees, 26% from correspondence students, 7% from teaching. Payment of criticism fee does not ensure representation.

Writer's Conferences: ABA (Chicago, June); Show Biz Expo (Los Angeles, May); SigGraph (Los Angeles, August).

Tips: Obtains new clients from book (*Do the Write Thing: Making the Transition to Professional*), classes, lectures, listings, word of mouth and online column. "To a writer interested in representation: Be sure that you have researched your field and are aware of current publishing demands. Writing is the only field in which all the best is readily available to the beginning writer. Network, take classes, persevere and most of all, write, write and rewrite."

*MARIANNE STRONG LITERARY AGENCY, (III), 65 E. 96th St., New York NY 10128. (212)249-1000. Fax: (212)831-3241. Contact: Marianne Strong. Estab. 1978. Represents 15 clients. Specializes in biographies. Currently handles: 80% nonfiction books; 5% scholarly books; 5% novels; 10% TV scripts. Member agent: Craig Kayser (true crime).

Handles: Nonfiction books, novels, TV scripts, syndicated material. Considers these nonfiction areas: art/architecture/design; biography/autobiography; business; child guidance/parenting; cooking/food/nutrition; current affairs; education; health/medicine; history; how-to; interior design/decorating; juvenile nonfiction; military/war; money/finance/economics; religious/inspirational; self-help/personal improvement; true crime; women's issues/women's studies. Considers these fiction areas: action/adventure; contemporary issues; detective/police/crime; family saga; glitz; historical; literary; mainstream; religious/inspirational; romance (contemporary, gothic, historical, regency); thriller/espionage; western/frontier. Send complete outline plus 4-6 sample chapters. Reports "fairly soon" on queries; 2 months on mss.

Terms: Agent receives 15% commission on domestic sales; 20% on foreign sales. Offers written contract, binding for the life of book or play.

Fees: Charges a reading fee for new writers only, "refundable when manuscript sold." Offers criticism service. "Fee to read and service a manuscript to six to eight publishers $350. If using outside freelance writers and editors, entire fee goes to them. Critiques prepared by freelance writers and editors who receive entire fee." Charges for long distance calls for established clients, but not for unpublished writers as their fee covers these out-of-pocket expenses.

Tips: Obtains new clients through recommendations from others. "Submit a totally professional proposal with a story line that elucidates the story from A to Z plus several perfectly typed or word processed chapters. No disks, please. Also include background information on the author, especially literary or journalistic references."

‡*MARK SULLIVAN ASSOCIATES (II), 521 Fifth Ave., Suite 1700, New York NY 10175. (212)682-5844. Director: Mark Sullivan. Contact: Samantha Nicosia. Estab. 1989. 50% of clients are new/previously unpublished writers. Currently handles: 35% nonfiction books; 5% textbooks; 45% novels; 5% poetry books; 10% movie scripts. Specializes in science fiction, women's romance, detective/mystery/spy, but handles all genres. Member agents: Linda Tsai (romance); Jay Milligan (science fiction and nonfiction); Mark Sullivan; Diane Vadino (fiction); Samantha Nicosia (submissions); Oren Safdie (editor).

Handles: Nonfiction books, textbooks, scholarly books, novels, novellas, short story collections, poetry books. Considers these nonfiction areas: anthropology/archaeology; biography/autobiography; business; cooking/food/nutrition; crafts/hobbies; current affairs; health/medicine; interior design/decorating; language/literature/criticism; military/war; money/finance/economics; music/dance/theater/film; nature/environment; New Age/metaphysics; photography; psychology; religious/inspirational; science/technology; sports. Considers all fiction areas. Query or send query, outline and 3 sample chapters. Reports in 2 weeks on queries; 1 month on mss.

Recent Sales: *Metacosmos*, by Phillip Stahl (Barclay House); *Pantheon*, by T.J. Doyle (Decca); *Father's Secret Tapes*, by R. Zinn (Barclay House).

Terms: Agent receives 15% commission on domestic sales; 20% on foreign sales. Offers written contract.

Also Handles: Movie scripts (feature film). Considers all script subject areas.

Fees: Charges $95 reading fee for new writers. Critique included in reading fee. Charges for photocopying and long-distance telephone calls. 90% of business is derived from commissions on ms sales; 10% of business is derived from reading fees or criticism services. Payment of fee does not ensure representation.

Tips: Obtains new clients through "advertising, recommendations, conferences. Quality of presentation of query letter, sample chapters and manuscript is important. Completed manuscripts are preferred to works in progress."

DAWSON TAYLOR LITERARY AGENCY, (II), 4722 Holly Lake Dr., Lake Worth FL 33463-5372. (407)965-4150. Fax: (561)691-9763. Contact: Dawson Taylor, Attorney at Law. Estab. 1974. Represents 34 clients. 80% of clients are new/previously unpublished writers. Specializes in nonfiction, fiction, sports, military history. Currently handles: 80% nonfiction; 5% scholarly books; 15% novels.

• Mr. Taylor served as book editor at the *National Enquirer* from 1976-1983, and book editor at the *Globe* from 1984-1991.

Handles: Nonfiction books, textbooks, scholarly books, novels. Considers all nonfiction areas. Specializes in nonfiction on sports, especially golf. Considers these fiction areas: detective/police/crime; mystery/suspense; thriller/espionage. Query with outline. Reports in 5 days on queries; 10 days on mss.

Recent Sales: *I Remember Ben Hogan*, by D. Taylor (Contemporary Books).

Terms: Agent receives 15% or 20% commission "depending upon editorial help." Offers written contract, indefinite, but cancellable on 60 days notice by either party.

Fees: "Reading fees are subject to negotiation, usually $100 for normal length manuscript, more for lengthy ones. Reading fee includes critique and sample editing. Criticism service subject to negotiation, from $100. Critiques are on style and content, include editing of manuscript, and are written by myself." 90% of business is derived from commissions on ms sales; 10% is derived from reading fees or criticism services. Payment of reading or criticism fee does not ensure representation.

Tips: Obtains new clients through "recommendations from publishers and authors who are presently in my stable."

*JEANNE TOOMEY ASSOCIATES, (II), 95 Belden St., Falls Village CT 06031. (203)824-0831/5469. Fax: (203)824-5460. President: Jeanne Toomey. Assistant: Peter Terranovi. Estab. 1985. Represents 10 clients. 50% of clients are new/previously unpublished writers. Specializes in "nonfiction; biographies of famous men and women; history with a flair—murder and detection. No children's books, no poetry, no Harlequin-type romances." Currently handles: 45% nonfiction books; 20% novels; 35% movie scripts.

Handles: Nonfiction books, novels, short story collections, movie scripts. Considers these nonfiction areas: agriculture/horticulture; animals; anthropology/archaeology; art/architecture/design; biography/autobiography; government/politics/law; history; interior design/decorating; money/finance/economics; nature/environment; true crime/investigative. Considers these fiction areas: detective/police/crime; psychic/supernatural; thriller/espionage. Send outline plus 3 sample chapters. "Query first, please!" Reports in 1 month.

✝ **THE DOUBLE DAGGER** before a listing indicates the listing is new in this edition.

Recent Sales: *Silvio*, by Peter Lynch (Sunstone Books).
Terms: Agent receives 15% commission on domestic sales; 10% on foreign sales.
Fees: Charges $100 reading fee for unpublished authors; no fee for published authors. "The $100 covers marketing fee, office expenses, postage, photocopying. We absorb those costs in the case of published authors."

PHYLLIS TORNETTA AGENCY, (II), Box 423, Croton-on-Hudson NY 10521. (914)737-3464. President: Phyllis Tornetta. Estab. 1979. Represents 22 clients. 35% of clients are new/unpublished writers. Specializes in romance, contemporary, mystery. Currently handles: 90% novels and 10% juvenile.
Handles: Novels and juvenile. Query with outline. No unsolicited mss. Reports in 1 month.
Recent Sales: *Heart of the Wolf*, by Sally Dawson (Leisure); *Jennie's Castle*, by Elizabeth Sinclair (Silhouette).
Terms: Agent receives 15% commission on domestic sales and 20% on foreign sales.
Fees: Charges a reading fee for full mss, $100 for full ms.

A TOTAL ACTING EXPERIENCE, (II), Dept. N.W., 20501 Ventura Blvd., Suite 399, Woodland Hills CA 91364-2360. (818)340-9249. Contact: Dan A. Bellacicco. Estab. 1984. Signatory of WGA, SAG, AFTRA. Represents 30 clients. 50% of clients are new/previously unpublished writers. Specializes in "quality instead of quantity." Currently handles: 5% nonfiction books; 5% juvenile books; 10% novels; 5% novellas; 5% short story collections; 50% movie scripts; 10% TV scripts; 5% stage plays; 5% how-to books and videos.
  • See the expanded listing for this agency in Script Agents.

*VISIONS PRESS, (II), P.O. Box 4904, Valley Village CA 91617-0904. (805)285-8174. Contact: Allen Williams Brown. Estab. 1991. "We prefer to support writers who incorporate African-American issues in the storyline. We handle adult romance novels, children's books and consciousness-raising pieces." Currently handles: 50% novels; 50% magazine pieces.
Handles: Novels, magazine pieces. Considers these magazine areas: ethnic/cultural interests; gay/lesbian issues; religious/inspirational; self-help/personal improvement; women's issues/women's studies. Considers these fiction areas: confessional; contemporary issues; erotica; ethnic; gay; lesbian; mainstream; romance (contemporary); young adult. Send outline and 2 sample chapters and author bio or description of self. Reports in 2 weeks on queries; 1 month on mss.
Recent Sales: Available upon request.
Terms: Agent receives 10% commission on domestic sales; 15% on foreign sales. Offers written contract, specific length of time depends on type of work—novel or magazine piece.
Fees: Charges reading fee. "Reading fees are charged to new writers only. Fee is refunded if agency decides to represent author. Fees are based on length of manuscript ($100 for up to 300 pages; $150 for any length thereafter.)" Offers criticism service. "Same as for the reading fee. Both the reading fee and the criticism fee entitle the author to a critique of his/her work by one of our editors. We are interested in everyone who has a desire to be published . . . to hopefully realize their dream. To that end, we provide very honest and practical advice on what needs to be done to correct a manuscript." Additional fees "will be negotiated with the author on a project by project basis. Often there is a one-time fee charged that covers all office expenses associated with the marketing of a manuscript." 90% of business is derived from commissions on ms sales; 10% is derived from reading fees or criticism services. Payment of criticism fee does not ensure representation.
Writers' Conferences: "We do not usually attend writing conferences. Most of our contacts are made through associations with groups such as NAACP, Rainbow Coalition, Urban League and other such groups that promote consciousness-raising activities by African-Americans. We look for talent among African-American scholars and African-American 'common folk' who can usually be found sharing their opinions and visions at an issues-related conference and town hall type meeting."
Tips: Obtains new clients through recommendations from others and through inquiries. "We believe the greatest story ever told has yet to be written! For that reason we encourage every writer to uninhibitedly pursue his/her dream of becoming published. A no from us should simply be viewed as a temporary setback that can be overcome by another attempt to meet our high expectations. Discouraged, frustrated and demoralized are words we have deleted from our version of the dictionary. An aspiring writer must have the courage to press on and believe in his/her talent."

*THE GERRY B. WALLERSTEIN AGENCY, (II), 2315 Powell Ave., Suite 12, Erie PA 16506-1843. (814)833-5511. Fax: (814)833-6260 (queries only). Contact: Ms. Gerry B. Wallerstein. Estab. 1984. Member of Authors Guild, Inc., ASJA. Represents 40 clients. 25% of clients are new/previously unpublished writers. Specializes in nonfiction books and "personalized help for new novelists." Currently handles: 54% nonfiction books; 2% scholarly trade books; 2% juvenile books; 35% novels; 2% short story collections; 2% short material. (Note: juvenile books, scripts and short material marketed for *clients only!*)

• Prior to opening her agency, Ms. Wallerstein had worked as a writer, editor, publisher, and PR consultant.

Handles: Nonfiction books, scholarly trade books, novels, no textbooks. Considers these nonfiction areas for general trade: agriculture/horticulture; animals; anthropology/archaeology; art/architecture/design; biography/autobiography (celebrity only); business; child guidance/parenting; cooking/food/nutrition; crafts/hobbies; current affairs; education; ethnic/cultural interests; gay/lesbian issues; government/politics/law; health/medicine; history; how-to; humor; interior design/decorating; language/literature/criticism; military/war; money/finance/economics; music/dance/theater/film; nature/environment; photography; popular culture; psychology; science/technology; self-help/personal improvement; sociology; sports; true crime/investigative; women's issues/women's studies. Considers these fiction areas: action/adventure; contemporary issues; detective/police/crime; family saga; fantasy; glitz; historical; horror; humor/satire; literary; mainstream; mystery/suspense; romance (contemporary, historical); thriller/espionage; young adult. To query, send entire ms for fiction; proposal (including 3 chapters) for nonfiction books. "No manuscripts are reviewed until writer has received my brochure." Reports in 1 week on queries; 2 months on mss.

Recent Sales: *Thunder Along the Mississippi*, by Jack D. Coombe (Sarpendon Publishers); *Instant Expert/Collecting Glassware*, by Mark Pickvet (Alliance Pub.); *Guide to Antique Malls & Craft Malls*, by Jim Goodridge (Alliance Pub.).

Terms: Agent receives 15% on domestic sales; 20% on foreign sales. Offers written contract, which "can be cancelled by either party, with 60 days' notice of termination."

Fees: "To justify my investment of time, effort and expertise in working with newer or beginning writers, I charge a reading/critique fee based on length of manuscript, for example: $400 for each manuscript of 105,000-125,000 words." Critique included in reading fee. "Reports are 1-2 pages for proposals and short material; 2-4 pages for full-length mss; done by agent." Charges clients $25/month for postage, telephone and fax and if required, ms photocopying or typing, copyright fees, cables, attorney fees (if approved by author), travel expense (if approved by author). 50% of business is derived from commissions on ms sales; 50% is derived from reading fees and critique services. Payment of criticism fee does not ensure representation.

Writers' Conferences: Westminster College Conference; Midwest Writers' Conference; National Writers' Uplink; Writer's Center at Chautauqua; Midland Writers' Conference.

Tips: Obtains new clients through recommendations; listings in directories; referrals from clients and publishers/editors. "A query letter that tells me something about the writer and his/her work is more likely to get a personal response."

JAMES WARREN LITERARY AGENCY (II), 13131 Welby Way, North Hollywood CA 91606-1041. (818)982-5423. Fax: (818)765-8207. Contact: Mark Boothby. Estab. 1969. Represents 60 clients. 60% of clients are new/unpublished writers. "We are willing to work with select unpublished writers." Specializes in fiction, history, textbooks, professional books, craft books, how-to books, self-improvement books, health books and diet books. Currently handles: 40% nonfiction books; 20% novels; 10% textbooks; 5% juvenile books; 10% movie scripts; 15% TV scripts and teleplays. Member agents: Mark Boothby (teleplays/screenplays); Audrey Langer (fiction/nonfiction).

Handles: Juvenile books, historical romance novels. Query with outline. Does not read unsolicited mss. No reply without SASE. Brochure available for SASE. Reports in 1 week on queries; 1 month on mss.

Recent Sales: *The Cradled and the Called*, by Rodger Sargent (New Saga Press).

Also Handles: Movie scripts (especially drama and humor), TV scripts (drama, humor, documentary).

Terms: Agent receives 10% commission on domestic sales; 20% on foreign sales.

Fees: Charges reading fee of $3/1,000 words; refunds reading fee if material sells. 80% of income derived from commission on ms sales; 20% of income derived from fees. Payment of reading fee does not ensure representation.

‡THE WRITE THERAPIST, (II), 2000 N. Ivar, Suite 3, Hollywood CA 90068. (213)465-2630. Contact: Shyama Ross. Estab. 1980. Represents 6 clients. 90% of clients are new/previously unpublished writers. Specializes in contemporary fiction and nonfiction; pop psychology, philosophy, mysticism, Eastern religion, self-help, business, health, commerical novels. "No fantasy or SF." Currently handles: 40% nonfiction; 60% fiction (novels).

Terms: Agent receives 15% commission on domestic sales; 20% on foreign sales.

Fees: Does not charge a reading fee. Charges $125 critique fee for mss up to 300 pages, $10 each additional 50 pages. "Critique fees are 100% refundable if a sale is made." Critique consists of "detailed analysis of manuscript in terms of structure, style, characterizations, etc. and marketing potential, plus free guidesheets for fiction or nonfiction." Charges $85 one-time marketing fee. 50% of business is derived from commission on ms sales; 50% is derived from criticism and editing services. Payment of a criticism fee does not ensure agency representation. Offers editing on potentially publishable mss.

Tips: Obtains new clients through recommendations from others, solicitation and seminars. "We aggressively seek film rights/sales on all novels."

*WRITER'S CONSULTING GROUP, (II, III), P.O. Box 492, Burbank CA 91503-0492. (818)841-9294. Director: Jim Barmeier. Estab. 1983. Represents 10 clients. "We will work with established and unestablished writers. We welcome unsolicited queries." Currently handles: 40% nonfiction books; 20% novels; 40% movie scripts.
Handles: Nonfiction books, novels. Considers these nonfiction areas: biography/autobiography; business; current affairs; education; health/medicine; money/finance/economics; music/dance/theater/film; popular culture; psychology; science/technology; self-help/personal improvement; true crime/investigative. Considers these fiction areas: action/adventure; contemporary issues; detective police/crime; family saga; feminist; horror; mainstream; mystery/suspense; thriller/espionage. True stories (for which the author has legal rights) about women and families put in crisis situations overcoming adversities or challenges; finding unusual answers to problems (like tracking down a daughter's rapist when the legal system has failed); true stories of unusual survival and profiles in courage; show biz or celebrity stories; HBO-type stories involving controversial peole in the news (like Mike Tyson) or stories with controversial political overtones (like dramatic trial stories); stories about historical, famous or infamous women; unusual family stories; off-beat mother-daughter, wife-husband, sister-sister stories; death row or prison stories; true crime (especially if the villain is a female); true Christmas stories about family reunions or unusual miracles; little-known stories about the accomplishments of women; hot contemporary stories; Generation X; famous trial cases; health issues; novels (women's, mainstream, contemporary thrillers); movie scripts (comedies, love stories, thrillers, women's stories). Query or send proposal. Include SASE. Reports in 1 month on queries; 3 months on mss.
Recent Sales: *Moment to Moment* (Medical Consumers Publishing).
Also Handles: Movie scripts (feature film), TV scripts (TV mow). Considers these script subject areas: action/adventure; comedy; contemporary issues; detective/police/crime; family saga; feminist; horror; humor; mainstream; mystery/suspense; psychic/supernatural; romantic comedy and drama; thriller.
Recent Sales: "Witness Against My Mother" (Movie of the Week).
Terms: "We will explain our terms to clients when they wish to sign. We receive a 10% commission on domestic sales. We also work with other agencies in the sale of stories."
Fees: Sometimes charges reading fee. "Additionally, we offer ghostwriting and editorial services, as well as book publicity services for authors. Mr. Barmeier is a graduate of Stanford University's Master's Degree in Creative Writing Program."
Tips: "We will help an author from concept to final product—if need be, designing the proposal, creating the package, doing rewrites on the manuscript. We are on the lookout for controversial women's stories that can be turned into movies-of-the-week. These usually involve women who take risks, are involved in jeopardy or crisis situations, and have upbeat endings."

Additional Fee-charging Agents

The following fee-charging agencies have indicated they are *primarily* interested in handling the work of scriptwriters. However, they also handle less than ten to fifteen percent book manuscripts. After reading the listing (you can find the page number in the Listings Index), send them a query to obtain more information on their needs and manuscript submissions policies.

Agapé Productions	Haffey Agency	Earth Tracks Agency
Client First—A/K/A Leo P.	Dykeman Associates Inc.	Silver Screen Placements

---

FOR EXPLANATION OF SYMBOLS, see the Key to Symbols and Abbreviations. For translation of an organization's acronym, see the Table of Acronyms. For unfamiliar words, check the Glossary.

Script Agents
Finding a Hollywood Agent for Your Script or Screenplay

BY J. MICHAEL STRACZYNSKI

The trap of established cliché: It's impossible to get an agent until you've reached a point in your career when you no longer need one.

The truth: Agents make 10 percent of what their clients earn. If a writer is a little crazy to think she can make a living by typing out black-on-white figments of imagination, someone else has to be even crazier to think he can make a living off 10 percent of the other person's income. It's the joke of the psychiatrist talking to two patients brought in from Central Park.

"Where do you live?" he asks one.

"I live under the stars and the heavens and the sky above."

"And where do you live?" the doctor asks the other patient.

"Next door to him."

That's the agent.

It's an insane job description, and therefore you can't blame agents for trying to inject at least a little sanity into the situation by minimizing their degree of risk. Consequently, agents take on two kinds of clients: established writers who are changing agencies or have just made their first major sale and clients who they genuinely believe have the talent, drive and persistence to become successful scriptwriters. Agents do not accept charity cases. They are not a public service company. They don't want to hear your tales of a hard life. They're there because the client has made money or may reasonably make them money in the future. Period.

So there's no truth to the notion that agents aren't interested in acquiring new scriptwriters. Their interest may vary across different agencies and, over time, even within the same agency, depending on how many clients they are currently handling, but the interest is there because the roster of clients is always changing. Agents and writers share one characteristic with the shark: As soon as they stop moving, they die. Many writers start with one agent, enjoy some success, then at the expiration of the contract move on to a bigger agent or simply retire.

Some writers change agents like others change socks, and if an agent doesn't have at least a few new talents on tap to fill the gap, then the real estate profession will find itself with yet another practitioner.

It's the law of supply and demand: The writer supplies the scripts, and the agent

---

J. MICHAEL STRACZYNSKI *is executive producer of* Babylon 5. *He was a producer on* Murder, She Wrote, *as well as story editor on* The Twilight Zone, *among others. Nominated for WGA, Ace, Gemini and Bram Stoker Awards, he is also the author of* The Complete Book of Scriptwriting, *now in its second edition, published by Writer's Digest Books.*

demands whatever she humanly can without being run out of town on a rail.

UNDERSTANDING THE RELATIONSHIP

So agents need writers. Writers need agents. How do the two sides come together? The first step is to find an agent—a good, reliable, legitimate agent who does not happen to share any of the other characteristics of the shark except the need to keep moving. The problem is that there are literally hundreds of agents in the Los Angeles area alone. Some of them work out of lavish offices, some package stars and directors as well as writers, some are small but try very hard and some have offices built into the rear of a Ford station wagon or that go in and out with the tide in Santa Monica.

This may sound like exaggeration, but it isn't. My first agent had more or less retired from the business before I came into contact with him. He didn't choose to tell me this. I wrote sample scripts, sent them to him . . . and they sat fallow for the better part of a year. The second agent I engaged, whom I'll identify only as Carol, kept changing offices every month. She always had a reason for it, even made the reasons sound plausible enough for me to fall for the okeydoke. Never answered her phone, always let the machine get it. I would go by her office, which was often an apartment building, and she was never there ("out making deals" was her usual explanation). The day I found notices of eviction and a stack of bills in front of her door was the day I figured it was time to move on. Another wasted year.

My third agent was with a big agency but wasn't really into the kinds of projects I wanted to do, and I often found myself shunted into second position, with her other clients taking more time and attention. No career guidance, no sales, nothing.

Finally, I lucked out with a smaller boutique agency that was and is very selective in its roster of clients—they have about 60 or 70 clients. My specific agents within this agency are the two owners of the company, handling different aspects of my work. I've been with them for about ten years now, and it's been a terrific relationship.

And that word—*relationship*—is key to our discussion. There are many good agencies out there, but just as there are many good dating possibilities out there, not everyone is suited to your needs and tastes. Somewhere out there is the perfect marriage. And somewhere out there is the marriage from hell. Unfortunately, no one, and no book, can tell you which is which. The only way you're going to find out who's your ideal date is to plunge into the field and be very selective.

MINIMIZING RISKS

Agencies take certain steps to minimize their risk when selecting a client. Given the typical scenario above, how can you minimize your own risk in finding an agent?

First, you want an agent who's been around for a while, and be sure it's an agent who specializes in marketing scripts. There are a lot of good literary agents who can sell a book in two minutes but who simply don't or can't handle scripts. Sometimes they'll say they can, but the truth is usually a different situation. When you see a New York address for an agent, for instance, investigate further and determine if this is someone who actually handles scripts (probably for the soap-opera or movie business since that's what's available on the East Coast) or if he's primarily a book agent with a contact on the West Coast who handles scripts. If the latter, you might want to consider developing a relationship directly with a West Coast agent rather than have one more middleman between you and your potential buyers.

Any legitimate agency is bound to certain standards in terms of what it can charge a writer and the services it can provide in exchange. These regulations are specified in the Writers Guild of America Artists Managers' Basic Agreement, to which all of the major and minor agencies should be signatories. Not only does this protect you by guaranteeing the agency is reasonably legitimate, but it also has a long-term advantage. Let's say, for the moment, that you sign with a non-Guild signatory agent, and by gosh, she makes a sale for you. You then join the Writers Guild. The problem, though, is that writers can only be represented by Guild signatories after they join the Guild. Which simply means that the writer must now change agencies, a move that can be painful for both parties.

More important, though, the provisos of the WGA agent signatory contract are there to protect you against abuse. Under those provisos, an agent can only charge you 10 percent of any payments made to you while a client of that agency, and only in script areas. Some agencies will try to charge you anywhere from 12 to 15 percent. There are also rules about reading fees: No agency can charge a WGA member a reading fee of any sort.

If you're an absolutely new and uncredited writer, some agencies may ask you to contribute a percentage of their costs for copying and mailing your sample scripts. This, too, is frowned upon but is more of a grudgingly accepted practice. To make sure you're not taken, you can volunteer to make up script copies on your own (probably costing less than the agency's cost) or ask for hard-copy receipts and then contribute a percentage not to exceed 50 percent. You should not pay for agency phone calls. And if you're paying postage, you want to be sure to get complete reports on where the script has been sent and to whom.

Having a WGA signatory agent representing you will save you a great deal of time otherwise spent monitoring her behavior. It won't save you from all the drones out there (note that all of the agents I encountered earlier were WGA signatories), but it will at least help stack the odds more in your favor than would otherwise be the case; and if there should be a problem, the WGA can intervene on your behalf.

CONTACTING AN AGENCY

With this list in hand, the next step is to contact an agent. You may choose to wait until you've made your first sale, in which case it's much easier to find someone willing to represent you. You may also consider contacting an agent after you've had an offer but before concluding the sale, to provide additional inducement, since he'll be able to claim the 10 percent agency fee for handling the negotiation.

On the other hand, you may not want to wait until you've sold something. It's not a requirement. But you do have to have completed at least one, and preferably more, full-length film or television script. This is the only basis upon which an agent can determine whether to accept you as a client. If you approach an agent with the statement that you are interested in doing some scripts and that you will do one at some time in the future, or that you're considering one now but that you want to have an agent first, you'll get a rather rude response. Under those circumstances, an agent doesn't even want to know you exist.

"Nothing bugs me more than the person who calls and says, 'I'd like to be a scriptwriter, and I've got a lot of good ideas, but I'd really rather not bother actually writing the script until I've got an agent,' as though an agent were a guarantee of success," one agent told me. "The only guarantee of success is talent combined with persistence, and I can generally be certain that if someone comes at me with that kind of attitude, he hasn't got either of those qualities. Writing is work, just like anything else. There are no magic formulas, no miracles. If someone doesn't have the wherewithal to put together a script before I take him on as a client, the odds are good that he never will put together anything even remotely acceptable."

So let's start with the assumption that you have now written a couple of scripts. Your next step is to contact one of the agents and inquire about the possibility of representation. Explain that you have written one or more complete scripts that are available for examination by the agent and are ready to be marketed. If you have a background in other areas of writing, from playwriting to newspaper reporting, be sure to include that information. If not, the less said the better. Some agencies will indicate in their listings that they take new clients only on the basis of personal recommendation. If you have such a connection, use it. If not, apply elsewhere. Don't waste valuable time chasing down false or unproductive leads.

Briefly describe your goals as a writer and what kinds of scripts you are most interested in writing. This is important because not all agents handle the same areas. Some prefer to work only with feature films or television movies, while others work closely with the producers of episodic television. Many, though, do cover all of these areas. Describe the script itself in broad strokes in only a paragraph or so. State in closing that if the agent would be interested in looking at the script, you would be happy to send it along and that, should the agent find the script of interest, you will be ready to come to Los Angeles for a meeting at his or her convenience. If you're not ready to make this step and initiate a personal meeting, you lessen the chances the agent will choose to represent you.

MEETING AN AGENT

If the agency is not fully booked with clients, the odds are fair that you will eventually get a positive response. I use the word *eventually* for good reason. Agents can be maddeningly slow. Which is why you should send out your letters of inquiry in groups of ten to fifteen, not one at a time. Early on when I was still shopping, it took one agent literally a year and a half to get back to me. To simplify expenses, you should coordinate any positive responses so that you can hit Los Angeles and meet with all of them over a three- to four-day period, thus avoiding repeat trips. Prepare to be disappointed; this is a long and difficult process, and rejection can be painful. But if you stick with it, and the sample scripts have merit, you've got a fighting chance.

During the course of your meeting, the agent will again go over your goals, express any comments, praises, criticisms or reservations about the script, and then move the conversation into more casual areas. The agent will want to see how the two of you will get along, if you are open to advice and suggestions, how you react to criticism and so forth. Scriptwriting can be a temperamental business, so client-agent relationships are built upon mutual respect and trust. Consequently, you should never attempt to mislead your agent or do anything to endanger that mutual trust. Like any good relationship, once the bond of trust is shattered, it's almost impossible to reconstruct it.

If all the signs are right and each party understands exactly what is expected by the other, then a contract will be sent to you. Actually, you will get three separate contracts, all identical, each to be signed by yourself and the agent. One copy is for your records, a second copy stays with the agent and the third copy is filed with the Guild. Attached to the contract is a huge, bulky document called a "Rider W," which explains in detail the principles of the Basic Agreement so that both parties know precisely what their rights and responsibilities are. All contracts used by the Guild signatories are exactly the same.

LIFE AFTER SIGNING

Once you sign the contract and become a client, the agent will try to get your name and work known around town. Your scripts will be sent to producers doing projects along the lines of your submitted samples. You should not take this period to stop writing and wait for Hollywood to come knocking. Keep writing. Turn out more samples. The more your agent has to work with, the more diverse the samples, the greater your chance of hitting the right person. In addition, if a script is submitted to a major studio, it's "covered," meaning it's read and synopsized by a studio reader. That coverage stays inhouse forever. Consequently, even though studio personnel change rather rapidly, if a reader gives your script a black mark, that's known the instant your script comes in and someone checks the logs. (Yes, this is unfair; many good scripts get a bad rap because one reader thought it was crummy.) Scripts can thus become old very quickly; they can't be sent back again to some places. All the more reason to continue to provide new samples.

During this time, your agent should be trying to steer you in the right direction with additional samples. A good agent gives gentle career advice without trying to move you into areas you really don't want to explore. Your agent should also be setting up whatever meetings are possible, which in the beginning will be few and far between. Many of them will be simple "get to know you" meetings. Remember, Hollywood is to some extent personality driven. Producers like to know they can work with someone. So even though a meeting may not end with an assignment, if the producer comes away from the meeting impressed and intrigued, you stand a good chance of being called in later for a more serious meeting.

ONE LAST THING

Embarking on the search for an agent can be a long, slow, discouraging process. As you slog through it, remember that it's this way for everyone in the beginning. Just keep telling yourself this: At one time in his history, every selling writer went through a period where he didn't have any credits and didn't have an agent. Nonetheless, he persisted. And that is the key.

What Your Script Demands Before an Agent Sees It

BY JACK SCAGNETTI

After nearly two decades as a Hollywood agent I've seen a wide variety of scripts from a myriad of writers, and I must say it's still refreshing to receive a script that has all the ingredients most agents demand today. Despite the growing number of books and classes or seminars on screenwriting, a good percentage of writers who submit scripts fail to follow basic guidelines that make a script appealing to both an agent and a film or television production company.

A PROFESSIONAL LOOK ATTRACTS MY ATTENTION

Let's take a look at the checklist that my readers and I use before we decide to represent a script. Physical appearance is the first thing we notice. The presentation immediately tells me if this material comes from an experienced writer who knows the importance of professionalism or from a novice who hasn't taken the time to learn what a professional-looking script demands. Preferred is a pale blue cover of card stock, not too thick, perhaps 28- to 32-lb. weight, with no picture or artwork on it—only the title and the author's name. The pages should be bound in brads, short enough so they don't cut through an envelope when mailed, or with "Chicago" screws. Never use spiral or other machine-type bindings. Only two holes, top and bottom, are necessary.

The typeface should be 12-point and the printing laser-quality. There should be no sloppy corrections, such as crossed out or inserted words. The title page should include only the title and the author's and agent's names. There should be no copyright or Writers Guild registration dates or notations or draft numbers. Never date a script. Including any superfluous information on the title page is the mark of an amateur. And before mailing your script to an agent, check closely for typographical errors, misspelled words, improper grammar and punctuation, missing pages and pages out of numerical order.

Your feature film script should not be more than 120 pages or less than 100 (although some low budget film scripts can run 90-100 pages). Length of television scripts depends, of course, on whether the program is a half hour (28-50 pages), one hour (48-52 pages) or two hours (102-106 pages).

Several standard computerized script programs available today make proper formatting simple. Your script should not include camera directions, casting suggestions on characters introduced, or soundtrack recommendations. Numbering scenes is not necessary, either. Although you might have seen scripts with numbered scenes, they most likely are shooting-director's scripts that detail the camera directions for the production crew.

A professional-looking script attracts attention and will likely be read before others

---

JACK SCAGNETTI, *a former newspaper magazine editor and freelance writer of hundreds of magazine articles, author and coauthor of 15 books, has been operating The Jack Scagnetti Talent Agency for nearly two decades.*

that arrived earlier in an agent's office. Like most agents, I receive a lot of queries by telephone and mail. Therefore, I appreciate being reminded of the storyline or logline and genre of your script in a cover letter if it's sent a few days later.

PLUNGE ME INTO A WELL-STRUCTURED STORY

The first 20 pages of your script are crucial. They alone can decide your fate. If the story is weak up to that point and a major plot point pushing the story forward isn't revealed, you're in deep trouble. Due to the great number of scripts received, and the limited time available, most agents and their readers do what many studios do—they don't read any further. Your script goes into the reject pile.

Most agencies and studios have a form for a story analyst's report that rates and evaluates your premise, storyline, characters, dialogue and structure. A poor grading on any of those story ingredients is enough to make an agent or studio pass on your script.

Special attention is given to the plot. Make sure the conflict/problem is started early in the script and developed in the three-act structure, with a beginning (set-up), middle (confrontation) and end (resolution). Carefully noted, too, is whether the conflict builds between the protagonist and antagonist, with each crisis more serious than the last and each scene propelling the story. An inciting incident should push forward the central character's problem, preferably in the first 10 pages, with a major plot point by pages 20-25, a major twist by page 60, and another important plot point by pages 90-95, followed by the denouement.

Cary Solomon and Chuck Konzelman, of Numenorean Films, who have read hundreds of scripts and are themselves writers of several feature film scripts, emphasize that "the plot—man vs. self, man vs. man, or man vs. the environment—should make the character achieve something more than he or she was looking for, and should reveal that characters are as important as the story and vice versa." Be sure they complement each other.

LET YOUR CHARACTERS SPEAK—AND ACT—FOR THEMSELVES

A script may have a great plot, but if the characters' personalities aren't fully developed and consistent, the script is not going to attract an agent's interest. The characters' motivation, point of view and attitude must become clear. There must be sufficient contrast between each character—and the characterization should serve an obvious purpose as it's woven into the plot. We must care about the characters and there should be a strong first impression of them. The characters' needs must be developed and expressed.

Dialogue, of course, will play a key role in the development of each character and should reveal the character's traits. One of the biggest flaws found in inexperienced writers' scripts is the lack of a different voice for each character. The dialogue must fit the characters and be realistic while also revealing their emotions.

Dialogue must heighten the drama and amplify the relationships of the characters. Keep dialogue short. Get to the point. If the line doesn't move the story forward or develop the character, drop it. Dialogue needs to be threaded into the story and contribute to the story's pace and rhythm. Avoid long speeches. They really turn an agent off. And don't chitchat by using words such as "you know," "I think," or "well." It's unwise to write words in dialect, particularly for Southern people. For example, there's no need to drop the g's in "coming" or "going" even though many people do when speaking. Let the actors take care of dialect. Refrain from parenthetical direction on dialogue, because the actors will also take care of experimenting with the effects of emphasizing a particular word or phrase. The same goes for underscoring words or lines for emphasis. Don't do it; it only clutters the script.

Inexperienced screenwriters tend to overuse ellipses—a series of three dots after dialogue. They are not needed. Let the actors work out their pauses in their speech.

In writing dialogue, avoid "talking heads"—dialogue without any action. Film is a visual medium. Your characters should be doing something physical that hopefully adds to their character and pushes the story forward.

Subtext is good in dialogue. Think of another way, for example, to have a character say "I'm going to kill him" while getting the objective across. The subtext could be something like "He's not going to be a problem anymore," or "It'll be taken care of."

Avoid repeating dialogue as much as possible. Sometimes repeating key words or lines can be done for emphasis or irony, but seldom is it necessary. Pacing and rhythm are essential. Find the right places for a change from light to heavy moods.

A mistake quite often made by scriptwriting novices (and some book writers with limited scriptwriting experience) is trying to tell the story through dialogue. Such writers aren't viewing the story cinematically. A screenplay is not a novel. In film, much can be told without a word of dialogue. The image, action and music can reveal much about the scene and the characters. Again, keep in mind that dialogue should be included only to develop characters or advance the plot.

OTHER CONSIDERATIONS

Having graded your script on proper format, plot, structure and dialogue, an agent or reader still must consider other important factors before giving a script the green light. Does the script present visual excitement? Do scenes, particularly the opening ones, grab attention? Is there enough significant action? Is the action presented without getting in the way of the characters? Do the characters, setting and place interest the reader?

Above all, does the script hold interest throughout? No agent, reader or film production company will read the entire script if it doesn't. They can stop reading just as fast as they can change channels on a television set. A script that is easy to read, not overloaded with words, but wrought with precise and clear descriptions will hold an agent's interest.

BE REALISTIC ABOUT THE MARKET

There are times when we find a script that has all the necessary ingredients of a very professional work with a compelling, well-told story, but we may turn it down. The reason could be that a similar story has been told too many times before and perhaps too recently, or that a similar genre has not done well at the box office. Or it could be the budget is way too high. How many $80 million blockbuster films can the studios do a year? Period pieces with casts of thousands and many locations can shoot a film's budget sky high. Always consider the production cost.

Finally, understand your place in the market. Out of every 100 scripts we read at my agency, we might decide to represent only four or five. More than 30,000 scripts are registered each year with the Writers Guild of America; only a small portion of them is optioned and an even smaller number produced. Many scripts never find their way into an agent's hands and even those that do might never be read completely for reasons we've discussed. So if you want your script to be read by an agent, make sure it contains all the aforementioned ingredients. Take your time and do it right.

Understanding Your Contract: A View From the Other Side of the Table

BY JANICE PIERONI

"Make a good deal, but don't blow it," was a favorite directive at Universal Studios, where I was a business affairs executive.

Business affairs executives represent studios, production companies, networks and other film and television producers in negotiations with agents about writers. Agents protect writers' interests during such negotiations.

Becoming familiar with the agent-business affairs "tap dance," or knowing a little about how business affairs executives and agents interact while negotiating, can go a long way toward making writers feel in control during the nerve-wracking deal-making process. It may also help keep them focused on what they should be doing: developing new projects.

HOW THE DEAL-MAKING PROCESS BEGINS

Writers submit written material (usually through agents) or verbally "pitch" their ideas to producers, creative affairs executives or development executives in a position to buy material. If producers or executives like the material and decide to proceed, the deal is assigned to a business affairs executive.

The business affairs executive reads the project, finds out whatever she can about the writer and agent, and calls the agent to ask for "quotes"—the amounts of money a writer has earned on previous deals. The business affairs executive then calls the agent with a first offer, the agent reacts with outrage, and negotiations are officially underway.

The following are the major deal points business affairs executives and agents representing newer writers hash out with respect to movie and television deals.

MOVIE DEALS

Options

A friend recently complained that a major magazine had reported he'd just made a six figure deal with an Oscar-winning producer-director, while he was running around with a check for $1,500 in his pocket.

Welcome to the world of options.

An option is a payment made in exchange for a promise that the producer has the

JANICE PIERONI *worked as a business affairs attorney for Universal Studios, where she negotiated deals with agents representing writers, producers, directors and actors. She has also written screenplays, television episodes and articles. She broke into the film industry by working in various production and development capacities, including assistant to Martin Scorsese.*

exclusive right to purchase a property at a set price before the expiration of the option period. An option allows a producer time to assess a project's viability with minimal financial risk. He'll approach studios, production companies, directors and actors in an attempt to interest them in making a movie from the script under option.

The general rule of thumb is that option money is 10 percent of the purchase price, but options can be granted for as little as $100. Writers are entitled to keep any option money even if the project is not purchased. Option periods can run for six to twelve months, and are often renewable for another six to twelve months.

"Many are called but few are chosen" is the rule with options. Option money is often the only money a writer will see for a particular project.

Purchase Money

Naturally, producers try to minimize risks whenever possible. Consequently they purchase projects only when necessary. This can happen in one of three circumstances: the project is "greenlighted" and is about to go into production; the option period is about to run out and the project is in active development; or the project has received several bids and the only way to beat out the competition is to purchase the property.

Purchasing a project represents a substantial commitment. After purchasing a property, a company is entitled, but not required, to use it to create a film. Some writers considered successful may have optioned or sold a number of projects but have yet to see a single original project produced.

This can happen for many reasons. There is often a long gap between when a movie is sold and when it is produced. Or, a writer's work might be so controversial or unusual that it takes a long time to persuade studios or production companies to back it. Also, movie regimes are distinctly unstable. When new regimes enter, they often bring in their own pet projects and throw the others, no matter how worthwhile, into "turnaround"—another word for releasing them.

Production Bonus

Few scripts are optioned, fewer are purchased and even fewer are produced.

To reward writers of scripts that actually get produced, agents frequently negotiate for production bonuses. The amount varies and is often payable ⅓ upon start of principal photography (meaning filming involving the main characters); ⅓ upon completion of principal photography; and ⅓ upon distribution.

Writing Services

The WGA requires that writers of original screenplays be offered at least a first rewrite. Unless a scriptwriter is a true novice, the screenplay contains a great idea but terrible execution, or the development pace for the script is greatly accelerated, most studios, production companies or networks also prefer that writers rewrite their own scripts.

Securing at least a first rewrite helps protect writers' screen credits (which has important monetary and other consequences). It also gives writers a chance to work with and learn from top professionals, providing exposure and a chance to build contacts.

Screen Credit

Screen credit is not negotiable—the WGA determines this after the producer submits proposed screen credit. The WGA seeks to protect the original writer. More than 50% of original material has to be rewritten before a writer is required to share credit and is guaranteed a minimum of shared story credit.

Consulting Services

Agents representing writers with specialized knowledge or training who have written on their area of expertise can often negotiate a consulting deal for their client.

Consulting typically allows producers, directors and actors to draw on writers' expertise to aid with filming a movie story. Consulting is valuable to writers because it assists them in developing relationships with producers and directors who might hire them again. Moreover, consulting provides writers with additional compensation.

Producing

Producing is the least defined of all movie roles. Generally there are two types of producers, with some overlap. Line producers handle the nuts and bolts of everyday production. Creative producers work with writers to develop and sell ideas, raise financing and the like. Sometimes there may be four, five or more producers on a film.

Unless a writer can make a meaningful producing contribution, agents should not drive up costs by negotiating producing credits and fees, particularly for new writers. A producing credit and fee might be appropriate, for example, where the writer secured the rights to a newsworthy nonfiction story.

First-time producers will most often receive a co-producer or associate producer credit.

Profits and Merchandising

Most agents ask for and receive at least some profit participation. Writers will typically be entitled to between one and five percent of 100 percent of net (as opposed to gross). For newer writers the amount will probably be ½ to 2½ percent. However, chances are overwhelming that writers will never see profits even if their projects become hits. Net profits are an industry joke; studio accounting procedures rarely show any profit at all.

Remakes, Sequels and Spin-offs

A remake is where a movie is remade into another movie, using substantially the same story line and typically the same name. Remakes are often made to update good stories for contemporary audiences. Recent remakes include *Sabrina* and *Little Women*.

A sequel is a continuation of a movie story that was popular, using elements common to both movies, which might but will not necessarily include the same actors, characters, setting or themes. Recent sequels include *D3: The Mighty Ducks* and *A Very Brady Sequel*. The general rule is that writers receive half of what they originally were paid when a sequel is made, and a third for a remake.

A spin-off is when a writer's movie is adapted for a television series or one television series begets another. An example of a TV spin-off is *Dangerous Minds*. The WGA requires royalties be paid to a writer in these cases; agents representing experienced writers can generally negotiate higher royalties. Additionally, if a writer winds up working on the series, as often happens, she will receive additional compensation.

Step Deals

Producers frequently hire writers to write original scripts on a "step deal" basis. A step deal gives them the option of terminating the project at each successive step (treatment, first draft, etc.), thus minimizing their financial exposure. The WGA provides for minimum payments for each step. Total payments cannot be less than if the writer had been hired at the outset to write a complete script.

TELEVISION DEALS

Television Movies

Television movies are substantially similar to feature movie deals, with many of the same deal points. First-time television screenplay writers are often paid WGA minimum or close to it. They will receive additional sums for reruns.

Episodic Television

This is the land of television writing assignments—sitcoms and dramas. Assignments for existing shows are known in the industry as "one-shots."

Writers hired to write television episodes first write a story in prose instead of script form. Producers have the option of paying the writer for the story and either abandoning it or assigning it to another writer.

If they decide to proceed, they assign a first draft teleplay. A writer is also paid for a second draft, although it is sometimes not required. If the first draft was either very strong or very weak the producers might, under pressure of shooting dates, assign it right away to a staff member for revisions.

The WGA mandates minimum payments for each step. In addition, writers are also entitled to residual, or rerun, payments.

Staffing Deals

For writers talented enough to land on or create a hit series, it can be an endless gravy train. Even if the writer has trouble finding work or finds herself unable to work during, for example, a WGA strike, residuals and series royalties alone can often carry her through lean times.

In many ways, writing a television episode for a television series is an audition for a staff position. If you write several good episodes for a show on a freelance basis, you're surely in line for such a position.

Staff writers generally move on to become story editors. After that, they progress to co-producer, producer, supervising producer and, for the lucky few, executive producer (there may be two or three executive producers on any one show). Staff writers generally are paid WGA minimum. Sometimes they are also guaranteed one or two scripts, which can be credited against the staffer's weekly salary.

Staff writing is a tremendous training ground because it gives writers an opportunity to work closely with and learn from a show's story editors and producers. In addition, it also teaches writers to write quickly under the pressure of shooting and air dates.

Much to the chagrin of agents and writers, producers often require a trial period, typically around 14 weeks, at the end of which they have the option of firing writers. Naturally writers (who often sacrifice fulltime day jobs to come aboard) and agents (who are only human and like the steady stream of income staff writing generates) resist such trial periods. Nevertheless, their use is commonplace in the industry.

Producers also require options on writers' services for subsequent years—generally one additional year and up to three or four—that guarantee they will be able to bring needed writers back onto a show at a fixed salary that has been agreed to in advance.

New writers are often dismayed when they learn they will be contractually bound to optional years. Sometimes, writers even think at the outset that it is *they* who have the option of coming back onto the series—not the producers who get to choose whether to bring them on. Producers require options to hold a creative team in place. The ability to point to a stable creative team can be very persuasive to a network on the fence about picking up an option on a show.

However, effective agents work with business affairs executives to make sure staff writing deals do not become unduly burdensome. Concessions agents might ask for include keeping the option years to the minimum necessary, making sure that writers can only be assigned to a particular show, and demanding built-in raises that at least somewhat reflect writers' typical rise in their market worth once they gain experience.

Most importantly, agents can request guaranteed promotions to story editor followed by producer in subsequent years. Staff writers' writing assignments are credited against their salaries. Story editors and producers, in addition to having more prestigious positions, earn higher WGA minimum salaries plus are paid independently over and above their salaries for whatever scripts they write.

CAVEAT

Be forewarned.

Writers should be prepared to live with whatever deals they make. Most producers will not renegotiate, particularly with someone who is not yet a major player. If you refuse to perform under the terms of your contract, they might seek an injunction against you. They can't force you to work for them, but they can prevent you from working for any other company for the duration of your contract with them.

TIGHTWADS AND TENDERNESS

A colleague used to describe those who became agents and business affairs executives as the ones who, growing up, were "the bullies on the back of the bus." It's true, in a way.

But it's also true that they're much more well-educated, respectable and even, on occasion, more thoughtful than you might expect.

My department at Universal included law degrees from Stanford and NYU and MBAs from Harvard and UCLA. We all had, if not a true feel for the industry, at least a healthy awe with respect to it. "Graduates" of my department include Sid Sheinberg, who, until very recently was the number two person at powerhouse MCA/Universal Studios, and Wendy Wasserman, producer of the blockbuster, *Forrest Gump*. With that level of opportunity looming, we had a lot to lose. We all aimed to be tough, but in the end, we also wanted to be fair.

Attaching the Elements: When Agents Create a Package

BY HOWARD JAY SMITH

As the lights fade in the theater, you settle into your seat, munch a little popcorn and watch the preview trailers roll: a couple of action flicks, a comedy or two, and maybe a blockbuster with a team of mega-stars . . .

Or dinner's over, the kids are in bed, and you curl up in front of the tube. There's a new sitcom, a hot episode of your favorite drama, or a thriller of a TV movie unspooling that night . . .

And you wonder . . . How did those shows get made? After all, didn't you have the same idea, a similar script or an even better story to sell?

So how did they get made? Chances are it was part of a "package" assembled by one of the major Hollywood agencies. In a business where nothing is safe or secure, smart executives try to raise the odds of success as much as possible. That's where the concept of packaging comes in. Ideally you get the best writer, the best director, the biggest star. Put them together and you've assembled a package, an undeniable force in Hollywood. It has the power to turn a "No" script into a "Yes" one.

But to understand the dynamics of packaging in Hollywood—and thus how packaging can help or hurt your career as a writer—you need first to comprehend the "business" half of the expression "show business."

SHOW BUSINESS AS A MARKETPLACE

Despite the glitter and hype, the bottom line for all movies and television shows is that they are products, simple commodities to be bought and sold to generate a profit. For theatrical feature movies, the goal is to have consumers buy theater tickets, rent the video or purchase such ancillary merchandise as action figures, CD-ROM games, coffee cups, T-shirts or anything that's emblazoned with the logo of your favorite flick.

In TV the goal is less direct, but no less critical. Even the best network shows exist solely to deliver you, the viewing audience, into the hands of advertisers. Network television programs, the shows you love to watch, are in truth merely the fillers between commercials and not the other way around, as is more commonly supposed. The higher the viewership of a given sitcom or drama, the more the networks can charge advertisers for ad spots. With the cost of ads running in the hundreds of thousands of dollars, the payoffs and risks are steep.

Annual budgets for 22 episodes of your favorite sitcom may approach 15-20 million dollars; for an hour drama, 25-35 million. The typical cost of a theatrical movie exceeds 30 million dollars. Blockbuster action pictures may go from 70 or 80 million to close to 200 million. The risks of failure are high, very high. Just ask Kevin Costner and the *Waterworld* crew. In fact, most movies lose money, and most television shows are

HOWARD JAY SMITH *is a screenwriter and producer as well as a former executive with ABC-TV and Columbia-Embassy TV. He is also the co-author of* Opening the Doors to Hollywood: How to Sell Your Idea, Story, Book or Screenplay.

dropped off the schedule before they can generate enough episodes to recoup their costs through syndication. It's the few hits that carry the rest of the load.

If studio or network executives say "yes" to a project (hopefully your project), they are gambling that the millions of dollars thrown into the fray will be well spent with major profits accruing back to their company.

As artists, we believe our stories should be made because they're important, wonderful and enriching. On a personal level Hollywood producers and executives may feel the same way, but when it comes to business, their final decision usually rests on a single criterion: Is this project strong enough to turn a profit?

Imagine then that every script submitted for sale is like a cry in the dark that says, "I'm worth the risk. I'm worth the gamble. Because with me, you're going to make back millions more." If you can deliver that script, you too will have a successful career in Hollywood.

But are you good enough? No one knows. When executives throw the dice on your script as the one to be made, they're ultimately putting their careers on the line. Given the high stakes atmosphere that pervades this business, it's little wonder that the natural instinct of every producer and executive in this town is to say, "No, I'm not going to put myself in jeopardy by taking on this project."

Before you submit that next script, take a long, hard, cold look at it and ask yourself one question: Would you gamble your job, your livelihood, your career on the pages you've written? If the answer is "no," why should anyone else?

If the answer is "yes," read on.

ASSEMBLING PACKAGES

Agencies evaluate scripts for potential packages, which means they attach elements to a project, such as stars, director, writer or producer—all to enhance its saleability. If an agent then submits that script to a studio with a major element attached, it's designated a package.

We've already said a package is an undeniable force. In a world where it's much safer for executives and producers to be negative, the goal of a packaging agent is to present them an assembly that's so powerful it can't be ignored.

Packages most commonly originate at the major agencies, which have the depth and breadth of clients necessary to assemble all the needed elements.

In Hollywood there are hundreds of agents and agencies involved in movie and TV development. You'll find that agencies come in many shapes and sizes, from the sole entrepreneur, to the giants, such as Creative Artists Agency (CAA), the William Morris Agency, and International Creative Management (ICM). Agents, particularly those from the largest agencies, are indispensable in cutting deals that lead to new films, sitcoms and drama series.

Packaging is increasingly more important today because motion pictures studios have changed. They are no longer the self-contained, complete production facilities they once were, with their own inhouse staff of producers, writers, directors and actors. Studios now place greater emphasis on financing and distribution and are thus much more interested in buying into as complete a project as possible. For example, studios prefer to buy a polished script as opposed to a story idea that must be developed or adapted into a screenplay.

So if your agent shops your script to a studio, you'll find you're generally in a much stronger position going in with a commitment from a star, a major producer, or an "A" list director. While star power carries a lot of weight in Hollywood, even exceptional packages don't always guarantee a sale, and even when sold they don't always ensure a hit.

The elements may look great but if the script isn't strong enough or is too expensive to shoot, the studios may still pass. Unless the script is as powerful as the attached elements, the studio or network is much more likely to pass on it and instead find a package that doesn't carry such a financial risk.

THE ROLE OF THE AGENT

Agents can represent writers, directors, actors and producers, as well as many small and mid-sized production companies. Of particular concern to you as a writer are literary agents and packaging agents.

The primary function of a literary agent is to represent writers. On a practical basis they also serve as a kind of filter. Due to the sheer number of scripts written and circulated each year, it's impossible for any executive or company to read or even review anything more than a small percentage of what's out there. Consequently, most executives at production companies will only deal with writers who have an agent.

Your agent serves as the studio or development executive's first line of defense against the onslaught of scripts that roll into town each year. By giving a particular writer or script their stamp of approval, agents limit and to some extent control the number and quality of scripts that make it to the studios.

Most studios, production companies, and networks are also frequent targets of lawsuits from individuals claiming their idea or script was stolen. To cut down on these nuisance suits, most companies will only read material from agents. Rarely is material accepted from the outside. A good agent will get you and your script to the right people in town, negotiate a deal for a ten percent commission, and help you to stay continuously employed and creative.

Packaging agents serve a somewhat similar function but operate on a grander scale. They work at the larger agencies that have a sizeable stable of talent—writers, directors, actors and producers—as their clients. They will then try to assemble the key elements for a production and assist in the sale of the entire package to the studios or networks.

HOW PACKAGES GET STARTED

Packaging is really about agents as brokers and matchmakers. Agents have an overview of the industry and an ability to put people together who can effectively combine forces.

The process frequently starts with producer-clients of the agency looking for material or when an agent hears what a studio wants. The agent then starts combining elements in creative ways that are lucrative for the client, for the agency, and, hopefully, for the buyer.

Often a package originates at an agency where a client, such as a producer, comes in for a meeting and says, "I'd like to do a TV movie about the inner city with a really positive message and strong female characters." The agency then canvases its writers and starts researching what scripts might already be available. Maybe it's one of yours. If the agency finds something or someone appropriate, it goes back to the producer with that piece of the puzzle. Then it goes to another client, such as a major star, and adds her into the mix. The goal is to give buyers at the studio or network a reason to say yes, which, as we already noted, is difficult.

If you were a writer at a packaging agency, you could also go to your agent and say you have a wonderful project for a particular star. If the script or concept is worthwhile the agent will try to service your project by attaching that star and then assisting with the final sale.

The larger agencies, with their access to all types of talent usually have an easier time creating packages. Nevertheless, if there is no one within the agency who is right for the package, the agents will look outside their own client base to complete the package.

Agencies will also share a package with other agencies. They never want to be in the position of saying to a client, "No, we absolutely won't do this because it has to be all Agency X elements." If need be they will go to another agency such as William Morris, ICM or CAA and combine forces.

Literary agents from smaller firms will often try to set up packages by teaming with larger firms on an as-needed basis. This is one good reason why you want your agent to have good relationships with other agencies in the industry.

WHAT DOES IT COST?

Big agencies are always looking to create opportunities for as many of their clients as possible. They try for a synergy which creates that "undeniable force." If the package is not viable, regardless of whether there's a studio or a network involved, it will probably fail to sell or be picked up.

In a package situation agents do not commission you, the client, directly. Instead they take a percentage of the overall license fee in TV or the budget in film. This can be significantly more than the individual fees they might have earned. The networks or the studios are responsible for paying that commission for the life of the production. The writer, director or actor linked in that package does not pay a commission fee to the agent.

Packaging fees are negotiable but usually cost upwards of ten percent of the production budget. At William Morris, for example, it's five percent up front and five percent off the back end. Other agencies ask three percent up front, three percent deferred and ten percent of the gross from off-network sales (syndication).

Those fees can be a hefty burden on a long running TV series when the producers are trying to keep the overall costs down. Packages are often criticized in TV because the fees paid add up on a week-by-week basis without seeming to add value to the show. Agencies, however, justify the fees by noting that without the package the show may never have gotten on the air in the first place. It's that simple. The only way agents can collect package fees is by creating something with potential value.

By pushing a movie or TV show into production, the packaging agency guarantees you, the writer, a far bigger payoff, while also giving the agency the inside track on filling many of the secondary roles in the production.

THE GOOD, THE BAD, THE UGLY

Agents often get lambasted for taking something nebulous, creating a package out of it, and then pressuring people to buy it. That does occur on occasion, but packaging works best when it benefits both the client and the buyer. Although Hollywood is rife with stories of abuse, such as on the film *Legal Eagles*, overall, packaging is flourishing. More packages are sold now than ever.

Although packaging can increase the saleability of a project, there are some significant downsides you should know. Buyers at the networks or studios may love your script but abhor the rest of the package. The director may be too inexperienced or the star has flopped his last three times out, or the producer shopping it around may have a horrible reputation. Or, worse yet, the network might love the package but feel your writing is not up to snuff.

For new writers a package may be problematic. Some literary agents try to avoid packages for their clients altogether. Usually one element of the package is often sacrificed to close the deal or to appease a star—and that element is frequently you, the writer, who is considered the most expendable.

Major agents at the large firms cater mainly to their big literary stars, the highly successful writers of TV series, movies of the week, or feature movies. On occasion, even top level writers will be set up in deals below their worth just to service the agency package. But packages are rarely assembled with newer or lower level writers at the agency, because such writers often do not have enough impressive credits to make the deal attractive.

Writers, even successful working ones, often wrestle with the decision to sign with a small agency where they are important and get a lot of attention or with a large agency that can rapidly whip up a package deal. At a small agency, you may benefit from careful handling, but at a big agency you can be the beneficiary of some of their packaging functions. There's no simple answer other than finding an agent you like, who likes your writing, and who will work hard to find you work.

The one thing agencies—especially the big agencies—can't promise you is a job. They can, however, promise you exposure, but your writing is what's really going to sell you.

It is extremely difficult to get signed at a big agency if you have no experience. Agents there get a constant flood of calls and inquiries. They are often very selective because their first obligation is to service the writers already on their rosters. Above all, these agents must make sure their current clients have work before they spend time on a newcomer. Most agents would accept new material if they had the time, but frequently they don't.

Smaller agencies are often more able to devote themselves to newer writers. They may be able to work with you and guide you a lot more. Effective agents call upon studio and network executives as well as show producers to read the work of new writers. The agents literally say, "No no no, you don't understand—you have to read this one script. Please."

An agent can easily read at least 50 or 60 scripts before finding that one marketable script. However, every year most agents will take on some new writers; there are few things more exciting for an agent than finding somebody new and getting them a first job.

You must be persistent. Rejection is not always bad. People like to say, "I went to the top," and that's great, but if you're not accepted at a big agency it's not the end of the world. Keep on writing and try to find the person who loves your work. It's a tough process, even for established agents. They have to get somebody to read a new writer without alienating the producers. They have to be persistent enough to get them to read something they think is wonderful.

FADE IN, FADE OUT

As an artist you have the power to create something of value. If you can write well and write the correct type of script, you, too, can also attract the attention of a packaging agent.

And maybe, just maybe, the next time you settle into that theater seat, the trailer for that great new flick that turns up before the feature attraction will be for your movie.

Script Agents: Nonfee-charging and Fee-charging

A quick test: What do you need to succeed in Hollywood?
   a) Great scripts.
   b) Insecurity.
   c) Confidence.
   d) A good agent.
   e) All of the above.
If you answered "e," you've got a good start.

A good script takes time. It takes time to write. It takes time to rewrite. It takes time to write the four or five scripts that precede the really great one. The learning curve from one script to the next is tremendous and you'll probably have a drawer full of work before you've got a script with which to approach an agent. Your talent has to show on the page, and the page has to excite people.

Once you have a script that says what you want it to say, that is the best idea you've ever had, expressed in the best way you know, put it aside. And get on with the next "best idea you've ever had." Practice and hone your skills until you are ready to enter the race. The more horses you enter, the better your chances to win, place or show.

You'll need both confidence and insecurity at the same time. Confidence to enter the business at all. There are less than 300 television movies and far fewer big screen movies made each year. For a 22-week season, a half-hour sitcom buys two freelance scripts. Every year, thousands of new graduates of film schools and writing programs enter the market. But talent will out. If you're good, and you persevere, you will find work. Believe in yourself and your talent, because if you don't, no one else will either.

Use your insecurity to spur you and your work on to become better. Accept that, at the beginning, you know little. Then go out and learn. Read all the books you can find on scriptwriting, from format to dramatic structure. Learn the formulas, but don't become formulaic. Observe the rules, but don't be predictable. Absorb what you learn and make it your own.

And finally, you'll need a good agent. In this book we call agents handling screenplays or teleplays script agents, but in true West Coast parlance they are literary agents, since they represent writers as opposed to actors or musicians. Most studios, networks and production companies will return unsolicited manuscripts unopened and unread for legal protection. An agent has the entree to get your script in the office and on the desk of a story analyst or development executive.

The ideal agent understands what a writer writes, is able to explain it to others, and has credibility with individuals who are in a position to make decisions. An agent sends out material, advises what direction a career should take and makes the financial arrangements. And how do you get a good agent? By going back to the beginning—great scripts.

THE SPEC SCRIPT

There are two sides to an agent's representation of a scriptwriter: finding work on an existing project and selling original scripts. Most writers break in with scripts written on "spec," that is, on speculation without a specific sale in mind. A spec script is a calling card that demonstrates skills and gets your name and abilities before influential people. Movie spec scripts are always original, not for a sequel. Spec scripts for TV are always based on existing TV shows, not for an original concept.

More often than not, a spec script will not be made. An original movie spec can either be optioned or bought outright, with the intention of making a movie, or it can attract rewrite work on a script for an existing project. For TV, on the basis of the spec script a writer can be invited in to pitch five or six ideas to the producers. If an idea is bought, the writer is paid to flesh out the story to an outline. If that is acceptable, the writer can be commissioned to write the script. At that point the inhouse writing staff comes in, and in a lot of cases, rewrites the script. But it's a sale, and the writer receives the residuals every time that episode is shown anywhere in the world. The goal is to sell enough scripts so that you are invited to join the writing staff.

What makes a good spec script? Good writing for a start. Write every single day. Talk to as many people you can find who are different from you. Take an acting class to help you really hear dialogue. Take a directing class to see how movies are put together.

Learn the correct dramatic structure and internalize those rules. Then throw them away and write intuitively. The three act structure is basic and crucial to any dramatic presentation. Act 1—get your hero up a tree. Act 2—throw rocks at him. Act 3—get him down. Some books will tell you that certain events have to happen by a certain page. What they're describing is not a template, but a rhythm. Good scriptwriting is good storytelling.

Spec Scripts for Movies

If you're writing for movies, explore the different genres until you find one you feel comfortable writing. Read and study scripts for movies you admire to find out what makes them work. Choose a premise for yourself, not "the market." What is it you care most about? What is it you know the most about? Write it. Know your characters and what they want. Know what the movie is about and build a rising level of tension that sucks the reader in and makes her care about what happens.

For feature films, you'll need two or three spec scripts, and perhaps a few long-form scripts (miniseries, movies of the week or episodics) as well. Your scripts should depict a layered story with well-developed characters who feel real, each interaction presenting another facet of their personalities.

Spec Scripts for TV

If you want to write for TV, watch a lot of it. Tape four or five episodes of a show and analyze them. Where do the jokes fall? Where do the beats or plot points come? How is the story laid out? Read scripts of a show to find out what professional writers do that works. (Script City, (800)676-2522, and Book City, (800)4-CINEMA, have thousands of movie and TV scripts for sale.)

Your spec script will demonstrate your knowledge of the format and ability to create believable dialogue. Choosing a show you like with characters you're drawn to is most important. Current hot shows for writers include *NYPD Blue, Law and Order, Boston Common, Frasier, 3rd Rock From The Sun* and *Friends*. Shows that are newer may also be good bets, such as *Spin City* and *Something So Right*. If a show has been on three or more years a lot of story lines have already been done, either on camera or in spec scripts. Your spec should be for today's hits, not yesterday's.

You probably already want to write for a specific program. Paradoxically, to be considered for that show your agent will submit a spec script for a different show, because—to protect themselves from lawsuits—producers do not read scripts written for their characters. So pick a show similar in tone and theme to the show you really want to write for. If you want to write for *Friends*, you'll submit a spec script for *Caroline In The City*. The hour-long dramatic shows are more individual in nature. You practically would have had to attend med school to write for *ER*, but *Homicide*, *Law and Order* and *NYPD Blue* have a number of things in common that would make them good specs for one another. Half-hour shows generally have a writing staff and only occasionally buy freelance scripts. Hour-long shows are more likely to pick up scripts written by freelancers.

In writing a spec script, you're not just writing an episode. You're writing an *Emmy-winning* episode. You'll write for the show as it is—and then better than it ever has been. You are not on staff yet, you have plenty of time. Make this the episode the staff writers wish they had written.

But at the same time, certain conventions must be observed. The regular characters always have the most interesting story line. Involve all the characters in the episode. Don't introduce important new characters.

SELLING YOURSELF TO THE SALESPEOPLE

Scriptwriting is an art and craft. Marketing your work is salesmanship, and it's a very competitive world. Give yourself an edge. Read the trades, attend seminars, stay on top of the news. Make opportunities for yourself.

But at the same time, your writing side has to always be working, producing pages for the selling side to hawk. First you sell yourself to an agent. Then the agent sells herself to you. If you both feel the relationship is mutually beneficial, the agent starts selling you to others.

All agents are open to third party recommendations, referrals from a person whose opinion is trusted. To that end, you can pursue development people, producers' assistants, anyone who will read your script. Mail room employees at the bigger agencies are agents in training. They're looking out for the next great script that will earn them a raise, approval and a promotion to the next rung.

The most common path, however, is through a query letter. In one page you identify yourself, what your script is about and why you're contacting this particular agent. Show that you've done some research and make the agent inclined to read your script. Find a connection to the agent—from "my mother hit your sister's car in the parking lot at the mall," to "we both attended the same college," to recent sales you know through your reading the agent has made. Give a three or four line synopsis of your screenplay, with some specific plot elements, not just a generic premise. You can use comparisons as shorthand. *While You Were Sleeping* could be described as "Sleeping Beauty with a twist" and lets the reader into the story quickly, through something she's familiar with already. Be sure to include your name, return address and telephone number in your letter, as well as a SASE. If the response is positive, the agent probably will want to contact you by phone to let you know of her interest, but she will need the SASE to send you a release form that must accompany your script.

Your query might not be read by the agent, but by an assistant. That's okay. There are few professional secretaries in Hollywood, and assistants are looking for material that will earn them the step up they've been working for.

To be taken seriously, your script must be presented professionally. Few agents have the time to develop talent. A less than professional script will be read only once. If it's not ready to be seen, you may have burned that bridge. Putting the cart before the horse, or the agent before the script, will not get you to where you want to go.

The basics of script presentation are simple. Keep your query letter succinct. Never send a script unless it is requested. Always include a SASE with a query or script. Study the correct format for your type of script. Cole and Haag's *Complete Guide to Standard Script Formats* is a good source for the various formats.

Read everything you can about scriptwriting and the industry. As in all business ventures, you must educate yourself about the market to succeed. There are a vast number of books to read. Samuel French Bookstores [(213)876-0570] offers an extensive catalog of books for scriptwriters. *From Script to Screen*, by Linda Seger, J. Michael Straczynski's *The Complete Book of Scriptwriting* and Richard Walter's *Screenwriting* are highly recommended books on the art of scriptwriting. Newsletters such as *Hollywood Scriptwriter* are good sources of information. Trade publications such as *The Hollywood Reporter*, *Premiere*, *Variety* and *The WGA Journal* are invaluable as well. A number of smaller magazines have sprung up in the last few years, including *Script Magazine* and *New York Screenwriter*. See the Resources section for information.

THE WRITERS GUILD OF AMERICA

Many of the script agents listed in this book are signatories to the Writers Guild of America Artists' Manager Basic Agreement. This means they have paid a membership fee and agreed to abide by a standard code of behavior. Enforcement is uneven, however. Although a signatory can, theoretically, be stripped of its signatory status, this rarely happens. Contact the WGA for more information on specific agencies or to check if an agency is a signatory. Agents who are signatories are not permitted to charge a reading fee to WGA members, but are allowed to do so to nonmembers. Likewise, WGA members are permitted to charge for critiques and other services, but they may not refer you to a particular script doctor.

The WGA also offers a registration service which is available to members and nonmembers alike. It's a good idea to register your script before sending it out. Membership in the WGA is earned through the accumulation of professional credits and carries a number of significant benefits. Write the Guild for more information on script registration as well as membership requirements.

HELP WITH YOUR SEARCH

This section contains agents who sell feature film scripts, teleplays and theatrical stage plays. Many of the agencies in the Literary Agents section also handle scripts, but agencies that primarily handle scripts are listed here.

To help you with your search for an agent, we've included a number of special indexes in the back of the book. The Subject Index is divided into sections for fee-charging and nonfee-charging literary agents and script agents. The script agent index is divided into various subject areas specific to scripts, such as mystery, romantic comedy and teen. Some agencies indicated that they were open to all categories. These have been grouped in the subject heading "open." This year we again index the agents according to script types, such as TV movie of the week (mow), sitcom and episodic drama in the Script Agents Format Index.

We've included an Agents Index as well. Often you will read about an agent who is an employee of a larger agency and may not be able to locate her business phone or address. We asked agencies to list the agents on staff, then listed the names in alphabetical order along with the name of the agency they work for. Find the name of the person you would like to contact and then check the agency listing. You will find the page number for the agency's listing in the Listings Index.

A Geographic Index lists agents state by state for those who are looking for an agent close to home. A Client Acceptance Policies index ranks agencies according to their openness to new clients.

Many script agents are also interested in book manuscripts; many literary agents will also consider scripts. Agents who primarily sell books but also handle at least 10 to 15 percent scripts appear among the listings in this section, with the contact information, breakdown of work currently handled and a note to check the full listing in the literary agents section. Those literary agents who sell mostly books and less than 10 to 15 percent scripts appear in Additional Script Agents at the end of this section. Complete listings for these agents appear in the Literary Agents section.

Before contacting any agency, check the listing to make sure it is open to new clients. Those designated (**V**) are currently not interested in expanding their rosters. Some agents will only accept new clients through referrals. Read the listings carefully.

For more information on approaching script agents in particular, see the various articles at the beginning of this section. For information on agents in general and the specifics of the listings, read How to Use Your Guide to Literary Agents and How to Find (and Keep) The Right Agent.

ABOUT THE LISTINGS

The listings in this section differ slightly from those in the literary agent sections. A breakdown of the types of scripts each agency handles is included in the listing. Nonfee-charging and fee-charging agencies are listed together. If an agency is a WGA signatory, we include this information in the listing. As noted above, WGA signatories are not permitted to charge reading fees to members, but may do so to nonmembers. However, most signatories do not charge a reading fee across the board. Many agencies do charge for other services—critiques, consultations, promotion, marketing, etc. Those agencies who charge some type of fee have been indicated with a box (□) symbol by their name. The heading "Recent Sales" is also slightly different. Reflecting the different ways scriptwriters work, we asked for scripts optioned or sold and scripting assignments procured for clients. We've found the film industry is very secretive about sales, but you may be able to get a list of clients or other references upon request.

We've ranked the agencies listed in this section according to their openness to submissions. Below is our ranking system:

I Newer agency actively seeking clients.

II Agency seeking both new and established writers.

III Agency prefers to work with established writers, mostly obtains new clients through referrals.

IV Agency handling only certain types of work or work by writers under certain circumstances.

V Agency not currently seeking new clients. We have included mention of agencies rated **V** to let you know they are currently not open to new clients. *Unless you have a strong recommendation from someone well respected in the field, our advice is to approach only those agents ranked I-IV.*

ABOVE THE LINE AGENCY, (III), 9200 Sunset Blvd., #401, Los Angeles CA 90069. (310)859-6115. Fax: (310)859-6119. Contact: Bruce Bartlett. Owner: Rima Bauer Greer. Estab. 1994. Signatory of WGA. Represents 14 clients. 5% of clients are new/previously unpublished writers. Currently handles: 2½% juvenile books; 5% novels; 90% movie scripts; 2½% TV scripts.
• Prior to starting her own agency, Ms. Greer served as an agent with Writers & Artists Agency.

Handles: Movie scripts. Query. Reports in 2 weeks on queries.
Recent Sales: *Movie scripts sold*: *Blades*, by David Engelbach (Universal); *Shape Shifter*, by Michael Krohn (Riche/Ludwig, Universal); *Youngsters*, by Roger Soffer and Christian Ford (Orr-Cruick-Shank Rysher Ent.). *Scripting assignments: Rand Robinson*, by Chris Mattheson (Interscops); *Atlantis*, by Greg Taylor and Jim Strain (Fox).
Terms: Agent receives 10% commission on domestic sales; 10% on foreign sales.
Tips: Obtains new clients through referrals.

‡**BRET ADAMS, LTD., (III)**, 448 W. 44th St., New York NY 10036. Contact: Bruce Ostler. Estab. 1974. Member of AAR, signatory of WGA. Represents 35 clients. Specializes in theater, film and TV. Currently handles: 25% movie scripts; 25% TV scripts; 50% stage plays. Member agents: Bret Adams (theater, film and TV); Bruce Ostler (theater, film and TV).
Handles: Movie scripts, TV scripts, stage plays. Query.
Terms: Agent receives 10% commission on domestic sales; 20% on foreign sales. Offers written contract.
Tips: Obtains new clients through recommendations.

AEI/ATCHITY EDITORIAL/ENTERTAINMENT INTERNATIONAL, (I), 9601 Wilshire Blvd., Box 1202, Beverly Hills CA 90210. (213)932-0407. Fax: (213)932-0321. E-mail: aeikja@lainet. com. Website: http://www.lainet.com/~aeikja. Contact: Kenneth Atchity. Estab. 1994. Represents 30 clients. 75% of clients are new/previously unpublished writers. Specializes in novel-film tie-ins. Currently handles: 30% nonfiction books; 5% scholarly books; 30% novels; 25% movie scripts; 10% TV scripts. Member agents: Chi-Li Wong; Andrea McKeown; Monica Faulkner; David Angsten; Sidney Kiwitt (business affairs, NY).
● See the expanded listing for this agency in Literary Agents: Fee-charging.

□**AGAPÉ PRODUCTIONS, (III)**, P.O. Box 147, Flat Rock IN 47234. (812)587-5654. Fax: (812)587-0029. Contact: Sue Green or Steve Barnett. Estab. 1990. Signatory of WGA. Member of Indiana Film Commission. Represents 55 clients. 30% of clients are new/previously unpublished writers. Specializes in movie scripts, TV scripts, packaging deals. Currently handles: 2% juvenile books; 4% novels; 70% movie scripts; 10% TV scripts; 2% stage plays; 6% syndicated material; 4% animation; 2% poetry. Member agent: (Mr.) Terry D. Porter.
Handles: Movie scripts (feature film); TV scripts; stage plays. Considers these script subject areas: action/adventure; biography/autobiography; cartoon/comic; family saga; humor/satire; psychic/supernatural; science fiction; self-help/personal improvement; thriller/espionage; true crime/investigative; westerns/frontier. Query. Send outline/proposal. Reports in 2 weeks on queries; 1 month on mss.
Recent Sales: *TV script sold: Deep Space 9*, by Jeff Morris (Mike Piller).
Also Handles: Novels, syndicated material, animation/cartoon, poetry books.
Terms: Agent receives 10% commission on domestic sales; 15% on foreign sales. Offers written contract, binding for 1 year.
Fees: Charges reading fee: $25 for MP/TV scripts, $50 for novels. "If we represent, half of fee is returned." Offers criticism service at same rates. "Critiques written by agent and professional readers I employ." Charges $75/quarter for all except photocopying. Will provide binders if necessary.
Writers' Conferences: Hollywood Scriptwriters (Universal Studios CA, October); Media Focus (NBC Studios CA, October); Heartland Film Fest (Indianapolis); Austin Film Fest.
Tips: Obtains new clients through solicitation, at conferences. "Mr. Porter has numerous contacts within entertainment industry that allow production companies and film executive (director of development) to review/consider purchasing or optioning material. Publishing company contacts very good."

THE AGENCY, (III), 1800 Avenue of the Stars, Suite 400, Los Angeles CA 90067-4206. (310)551-3000. Fax: (310)551-1424. Estab. 1984. Signatory of WGA. Represents 300 clients. No new/previously unpublished writers. Specializes in TV and motion pictures. Currently handles: 45% movie scripts; 45% TV scripts; 10% syndicated material.
Handles: Movie scripts (feature film, animation); TV scripts (TV mow, miniseries, episodic drama, sitcom, animation). Considers these script subject areas: action/adventure; cartoon/animation; comedy; contemporary issues; detective/police/crime; ethnic; family saga; fantasy; historical; horror; humor; juvenile; mainstream; military/war; mystery/suspense; psychic/supernatural; romantic comedy and

● **A BULLET** introduces comments by the editor of the *Guide* indicating special information about the listing.

drama; science fiction; teen; thriller; westerns/frontier; women's issues.
Query: Reports in 2 weeks.
Terms: Agent receives 10% commission on domestic sales; 10% on foreign sales. Offers written contract, binding for 2 years.
Tips: Obtains new clients through recommendations from others.

AGENCY FOR THE PERFORMING ARTS, (II), 9000 Sunset Blvd., Suite 1200, Los Angeles CA 90069. (310)273-0744. Fax: (310)888-4242. Contact: Lee Dinstman. Estab. 1962. Signatory of WGA. Represents 50 clients. Specializes in film and TV scripts. Member agent: Stuart M. Miller.
Handles: Movie scripts (feature film); TV scripts (mow). Considers all nonfiction and fiction areas. Query must include SASE. Reports in 3 weeks on queries.
Terms: Agent receives 10% commission on domestic sales. Offers written contract.
Tips: Obtains new clients through recommendations from others.

LEE ALLAN AGENCY, (II), P.O. Box 18617, Milwaukee WI 53218-0617. (414)357-7708. Fax: call for number. Contact: Lee Matthias. Estab. 1983. Signatory of WGA. Represents 15 clients. 50% of clients are new/previously unpublished writers. Specializes in suspense fiction. Currently handles: 90% novels; 5% movie scripts; 5% TV scripts. Member agents: Lee A. Matthias (all types of genre fiction and screenplays; Andrea Knickerbocker (fantasy, science fiction, romance); (Mr.) Chris Hill (fantasy).
● This agency reports that it is closed to queries and submissions for books through 6/97. See the expanded listing for this agency in Literary Agents: Nonfee-charging.

ALL-STAR TALENT AGENCY, (I), 7834 Alabama Ave., Canoga Park CA 91304-4905. (818)346-4313. Contact: Robert Allred. Estab. 1991. Signatory of WGA. Represents 8 clients. 100% of clients are new/previously unpublished writers. Specializes in film, TV. Currently handles: movie scripts, TV scripts, 4 books.
Handles: Movie scripts (feature film), TV scripts (TV mow, episodic drama, sitcom). Considers these script subject areas: action/adventure; comedy; detective/police/crime; fantasy; historical; horror; humor; juvenile; mainstream; mystery/suspense; psychic/supernatural; romantic comedy and drama; science fiction; sports; thriller; westerns/frontier; "any mainstream film or TV ideas." Query. Reports in 3 weeks on queries; 2 months on mss.
Also Handles: Nonfiction books, scholarly books, textbooks, juvenile books, novels, short story collections, syndicated material. Considers all fiction and nonfiction areas.
Terms: Agent receives 10% commission on domestic sales; 10% on foreign sales with foreign agent receiving additional 10%. Offers written contract, binding for 1 year. 100% of business derived from commissions on ms.
Tips: Obtains new clients through recommendations and solicitation. "A professional appearance in script format, dark and large type and simple binding go a long way to create good first impressions in this business, as does a professional business manner."

THE ALPERN GROUP, (II), 4400 Coldwater Canyon Ave., Suite 125, Studio City CA 91604. (818)752-1877. Fax: (818)752-1859. Contact: Anita Trissel. Estab. 1994. Signatory of WGA. Represents 25 clients. 10% of clients are new/previously unpublished writers. Currently handles: 30% movie scripts; 60% TV scripts; 10% stage plays. Member agent: Jeff Alpern (owner); Anita Trissel (development, queries).
● Prior to opening his agency, Mr. Alpern served as an agent with William Morris.
Handles: Movie scripts (feature film), TV scripts (TV mow, miniseries, episodic drama). Considers these script areas: action/adventure; contemporary issues; detective/police/crime; ethnic; family saga; fantasy; historical; humor; mainstream; romance; science fiction; thriller/espionage. Query with SASE. Reports in 1 month.
Terms: Agent receives 10% commission on domestic sales. Offers written contract.

MICHAEL AMATO AGENCY (II), 1650 Broadway, Suite 307, New York NY 10019. (212)247-4456 or 4457. Fax: (212)664-0641. Contact: Michael Amato. Estab. 1970. Member of SAG, AFTRA. Represents 6 clients. 2% of clients are new/previously unpublished writers. Specializes in TV. Currently handles nonfiction books; stage plays.
Handles: Novels, movie scripts (feature film, documentary, animation), TV scripts (TV mow, miniseries, episodic drama, animation). Considers action/adventure stories only. Query. Reports within a month on queries. Does not return scripts.
Tips: Obtains new clients through recommendations.

‡AMSEL, EISENSTADT & FRAZIER, INC., (III, IV), 6310 San Vincente Blvd. #401, Los Angeles CA 90048. (213)939-1188. Fax: (213)939-0630. Contact: Mike Eisenstadt. Estab. 1975. Signatory of WGA. Specializes in motion picture and TV rights and full-length screenplays. Member agents:

Sara Margoshes (theatrical and longform screenplays); Andrea Newman (mss for motion picture and TV rights and feature screenplays).
Handles: Movie scripts, novels, novellas and short story collections. Considers these nonfiction areas: biography/autobiography, government/politics/law, history, humor, sports, true crime/investigative. Considers these fiction areas: action/adventure; contemporary issues; detective/police/crime; ethnic; fantasy; historical; horror; humor/satire; literary; mainstream; science fiction; sports; thriller/espionage; westerns/frontier; young adult. Query with SASE or postage-paid postcard.
Terms: Agent receives 10% commission on domestic sales. Offers a written contract, binding for 2 years.
Fees: Charges for photocopying.
Tips: Obtains new clients through referrals and occasionally query letters.

MARCIA AMSTERDAM AGENCY, (II), 41 W. 82nd St., New York NY 10024-5613. (212)873-4945. Contact: Marcia Amsterdam. Estab. 1970. Signatory of WGA. Currently handles: 10% nonfiction books; 75% novels; 10% movie scripts; 5% TV scripts.
• See the expanded listing for this agency in Literary Agents: Nonfee-charging.

‡ANGEL CITY TALENT, (II), 1680 N. Vine St., #716, Hollywood CA 90028. (213)463-1680. Contact: Lori Peters. Estab. 1989. Signatory of WGA. Currently handles: 90% movie scripts; 10% TV scripts.
Handles: Movie scripts; TV scripts. Query. Reports in 2 weeks.
Terms: Agent receives 10% commission on domestic sales; 10% on foreign sales. Offers written contract, binding for 1 year.
Tips: Obtains new clients through queries, synopses, referrals.

APOLLO ENTERTAINMENT, (II), 1646 W Julian, Unit C, Chicago IL 60622. (312)862-7864. Fax: (312)862-7974. Contact: Bruce Harrington. Estab. 1993. Signatory of WGA. Represents 8 clients. 20% of clients are new/previously unpublished writers. Specializes in feature screenplays of unordinary topics. Currently handles: 10% nonfiction books; 80% movie scripts; 10% TV scripts. Member agent: Nancy Lombardo (V.P. of Acquisitions).
Handles: Movie scripts, TV scripts. Considers these script subject areas: action/adventure; contemporary issues; detective/police/crime; family saga; fantasy; feminist; gay; glitz; historical; horror; humor; lesbian; mainstream; psychic/supernatural; romance; science fiction; teen; thriller/espionage. Query. Replies in 2 weeks on queries; 6 weeks on mss hard copy; 1 month if on IBM compatible diskette.
Terms: Agent receives 10% commission on domestic sales. Offers written contract, binding for 6 months, 1 year or for sale only, with 30 day cancellation clause.
Also Handles: Novels.
Tips: Obtains new clients through WGA listing, cold readings, through known sources. "Be patient, know your craft and be true to your talent."

THE ARTISTS AGENCY, (II,IV), 10000 Santa Monica Blvd., Suite 305, Los Angeles, CA 90035. (310)277-7779. Fax: (310)785-9338. Contact: Merrily Kane. Estab. 1974. Signatory of WGA. Represents 80 clients. 20% of clients are new/previously unpublished writers. Obtains new clients through referrals. Currently handles: 50% movie scripts; 50% TV scripts.
Handles: Movie scripts (feature film), TV scripts (TV mow). Considers these script subject areas: action/adventure; comedy; contemporary issues; detective/police/crime; mystery/suspense; romantic comedy and drama; thriller. Query. Reports in 2 weeks on queries.
Terms: Agent receives 10% commission. Offers written contract, binding for 1-2 years, per WGA.
Tips: Obtains new clients through recommendations from others.

THE BENNETT AGENCY, (II, III), 150 S. Barrington Ave., Suite #1, Los Angeles CA 90049. (310)471-2251. Fax: (310)471-2254. Contact: Carole Bennett. Estab. 1984. Signatory of WGA, DGA. Represents 15 clients. 2% of clients are new/previously unpublished writers. Specializes in TV sitcom. Currently handles: 5% movie scripts; 95% TV scripts. Member agents: Carole Bennett (owner); Tanna Herr (features).
Handles: Movie scripts (features); TV scripts (sitcom). Considers these script subject areas: comedy; family saga; mainstream. Query. Reports in 1 month on queries and mss.

---

‡ THE DOUBLE DAGGER before a listing indicates the listing is new in this edition.

Recent Sales: *Scripting assignments:* "Most of our clients are on staff on such half-hour sitcoms as *Grace Under Fire.*
Terms: Agent receives 10% commission on domestic sales. Offers written contract.
Tips: Obtains new clients through recommendations from others.

BERMAN BOALS AND FLYNN, (III), 225 Lafayette S., Suite 1207, New York NY 10012. (212)966-0339. Contact: Judy Boals or Jim Flynn. Assistant: Charles Grayauski. Estab. 1972. Member of AAR, Signatory of WGA. Represents about 25 clients. Specializes in dramatic writing for stage, film, TV.
Handles: Movie scripts, TV scripts, stage plays. Query first.
Terms: Agent receives 10% commission.
Tips: Obtains new clients through recommendations from others.

☐**BETHEL AGENCY, (II)**, 360 W. 53rd St., Suite BA, New York NY 10019. (212)664-0455. Contact: Lewis R. Chambers. Estab. 1967. Represents over 25 clients.
Handles: Movie scripts, TV scripts. Considers these nonfiction areas: agriculture/horticulture; animals; anthropology/archaeology; art/architecure/design; biography/autobiography; business; child guidance/parenting; cooking/food/nutrition; crafts/hobbies; current affairs; ethnic/cultural interests; gay/lesbian issues; government/politics/law; health/medicine; history; interior design/decorating; juvenile nonfiction; language/literature/criticism; military/war; money/finance/economics; music/dance/theater/film; nature/environment; photography; psychology; religious/inspirational; science/technology; self-help/personal improvement; sociology; sports; translations; true crime/investigative; women's issues/women's studies. Considers these fiction areas: action/adventure; comedy; confessional; contemporary issues; detective/police/crime; ethnic; family saga; fantasy; feminist; gay; glitz; historical; juvenile; lesbian; literary; mainstream; mystery/suspense; picture book; psychic/supernatural; regional; religious/inspiration; romance (contemporary, gothic, historical, regency); sports; teen; thriller/espionage; westerns/frontier. Query with outline plus 1 sample chapter and SASE. Reports in 1-2 months on queries.
Recent Sales: *The Viper Quarry*, by Dean Feldmeyer (Pocket Books) (nominated for an Edgar); *Pitchfork Hollow*, by Dean Feldmeyer (Pocket Books); *Hamburger Heaven*, by Jeffrey Tennyson (Hyperion); *Words Can Tell*, by Christina Ashton.
Terms: Agent receives 15% commission on domestic sales; 20% on foreign sales. Offers written contract, binding for 6 months to 1 year.
Fees: Charges reading fee only to unpublished authors; writer will be contacted on fee amount.
Tips: Obtains new clients through recommendations from others. "Never send original material."

‡**J. MICHAEL BLOOM & ASSOCIATES, EAST, (III)**, 233 Park Avenue South, 10th Floor, New York NY 10003. (212)529-6500. Fax: (212)275-6941. Contact: J. Michael Bloom. Estab. 1981. Signatory of WGA. Represents 30 clients.
Handles: Movie scripts, TV scripts. Considers all script subject areas. Query for TV scripts; agency only takes referrals for feature films. Reports in 2 weeks on queries; 1 month on mss.
Terms: Agent receives 10% commission on domestic sales.

‡**J. MICHAEL BLOOM & ASSOCIATES, WEST, (III)**, 9255 Sunset Blvd., Suite 710, Los Angeles CA 90069. (310)275-6800. Fax: (310)275-6941. Contact: Sandra Lucchesi. Signatory of WGA. Represents 30 clients.
Handles: Movie scripts, TV scripts. Considers all script subject areas. Query for TV scripts; agency only takes referrals for feature films. Reports in 2 weeks on queries.
Terms: Agent receives 10% commission on domestic sales.

‡**THE BOHRMAN AGENCY, (III)**, 8489 W. Third St., Los Angeles CA 90048. (213)653-6701. Fax: (213)653-6702. Contact: David Wilcox. Signatory of WGA. Represents 40-45 clients.
Handles: Movie scripts, TV scripts, theatrical stage plays. Considers all script subject areas. Query. If interested, reports in 2 weeks. Does not read unsolicited mss.

‡**THE BRODER KURLAND WEBB UFFNER AGENCY, (II, III)**, 9242 Beverly Blvd., Suite 200, Beverly Hills CA 90210. (310)281-3400. Fax: (310)276-3207. Estab. 1983. Signatory of WGA. Represents 500 clients. 10% of clients are new/previously unpublished writers. Specializes in writers, directors and producers for TV and motion pictures. Currently handles 40% movie scripts, 60% TV scripts.
Handles: Movie scripts, TV scripts. Considers these fiction areas: action/adventure; cartoon/comic; contemporary issues; detective/police/crime; ethnic; experimental; family saga; fantasy; historical; horror; mainstream; mystery/suspense; psychic/supernatural; science fiction; thriller/espionage. Query. "We do not accept unsolicited material."

Terms: Agent receives 10% commission. Offers a written contract, binding for 2 years.
Tips: Obtains new clients through recommendations, query letters, "knowledge of writer's work and solicitation by us."

CURTIS BROWN LTD., (II), 10 Astor Place, New York NY 10003-6935. (212)473-5400. Member of AAR; signatory of WGA. Perry Knowlton, Chairman & CEO. Peter L. Ginsberg, President. Member agents: Laura J. Blake; Ellen Geiger; Emilie Jacobson, Vice President; Virginia Knowlton; Timothy Knowlton, COO (films, screenplays, plays); Marilyn Marlow, Executive Vice President; Jess Taylor (film, screenplays, plays); Maureen Walters. Queries to Laura J. Blake.
   • See the expanded listing for this agency in Literary Agents: Nonfee-charging.

DON BUCHWALD AGENCY, (III), 10 E. 44th St., New York NY 10017. (212)867-1070. Also: 9229 Sunset Blvd., Suite 70, Los Angeles CA 90069. Estab. 1977. Signatory of WGA. Represents 50 literary clients. Talent and literary agency.
Handles: Movie scripts (feature film, documentary, animation); TV scripts (TV mow, miniseries, episodic drama, sitcom, variety show, animation, soap opera); stage play. Query with SASE only.
Tips: Obtains new clients through other authors, agents.

KELVIN C. BULGER AND ASSOCIATES, (I), 123 W. Madison, Suite 905, Chicago IL 60602. (312)280-2403. Fax: (312)922-4221. Contact: Kelvin C. Bulger. Estab. 1992. Signatory of WGA. Represents 25 clients. 90% of clients are new/previously unpublished writers. Currently handles: 75% movie scripts; 25% TV scripts.
Handles: Movie scripts (feature film, documentary), TV scripts (TV mow), syndicated material. Considers these script subject areas: action/adventure; cartoon/animation; contemporary issues; ethnic; family saga; historical; humor; religious/inspirational. Query. Reports in 2 weeks on queries; 2 months on mss. "If material is to be returned, writer must enclose SASE."
Recent Sales: *The Playing Field*, (documentary) by Darryl Pitts (CBS).
Terms: Agent receives 10% commission on domestic sales; 10% on foreign sales. Offers written contract, binding from 6 months-1 year.
Tips: Obtains new clients through solicitations and recommendations. "Proofread before submitting to agent. Only replies to letter of inquiries if SASE is enclosed."

CAMDEN, (II), 2049 Central Park E., Suite 3380, Los Angeles CA 90035. (310)289-2700. Fax; (310)289-2718. Contact: Jeff Ordway. Estab. 1980. Signatory of WGA. Represents 60 clients. 5% of clients are new/previously unpublished writers. Currently handles: 50% movie scripts; 50% TV scripts. Member agents: David Wardlow; Jeff Ordway.
Handles: Movie scripts (feature film); TV scripts (TV mow, miniseries, episodic drama, sitcom). Considers all script subject areas, particularly: action/adventure; contemporary issues; detective/police/crime; family saga; fantasy; gay; horror; humor; mainstream; mystery/suspense; romance; science fiction; thriller; western/frontier. Query with SASE. Reports in 1 month on queries.
Also Handles: CD-ROM.
Terms: Agent receives 10% commission on domestic sales; 10% on foreign sales. Offers written contract, binding for 1 year.
Tips: Obtains new clients through recommendations from others and solicitation.

‡□**SUZANNA CAMEJO & ASSOC., (IV)**, 3000 W. Olympic Blvd., Santa Monica CA 90404. (310)449-4064. Fax: (310)449-4026. Contact: Brian K. Lee. Estab. 1992. Represents 5 clients. 30% of clients are new/previously unpublished writers. Specializes in environmental issues, animal rights, women's stories, art-oriented, children/family; no action/adventure or violence. 80% movie scripts; 5% novels; 10% TV scripts; 5% life stories. Member agents: Suzanna Camejo (issue oriented); Brian K. Lee.
Handles: Movie scripts, novels, TV scripts, life stories. Considers these nonfiction areas: animals; nature/environment; women's issues/women's studies. Considers these fiction areas: ethnic; family saga; romance (comedy); environmental; animal. Send outline/proposal and completed scripts (no treatments). Reports in 1 month on mss.
Recent Sales: *Primal Scream*, by John Shirley (Showtime); *The Christmas Project*, by Joe Hindy (Ganesha Partners).
Terms: Agent receives 10% commission on domestic sales; 10% on foreign sales. Offers written contract, binding for 1 year, with 3 weeks cancellation clause.
Fees: Charges $20 reading fee (per script or ms). Criticism service: $20 (per script or ms). Critiques of storyline, subplot, backstory, pace, characterization, dialogue, marketability, commerciality by professional readers. Charges postage for returned scripts.
Writer's Conferences: Cannes Film Festival (France, May); Telluride Film Festival (Colorado, September); Sundance Film Festival (Utah, January); AFM (Los Angeles, February).

Tips: Obtains new clients "by recommendations from others and by reading their material. If the feature script is well-written (3 acts, backstory, subplot) with good characters and dialogue, the material is moving, funny or deals with important issues and is non-violent (no war stories, please), we will read it and represent it."

☐**THE MARSHALL CAMERON AGENCY, (II)**, Rt. 1 Box 125, Lawtey FL 32058. Phone/fax: (904)964-7013. E-mail: marshall.cameron@juno.com. Contact: Margo Prescott. Estab. 1986. Signatory of WGA. Specializes in feature films and TV scripts and true story presentations for MFTS. Currently handles: 95% movie scripts; 5% TV scripts. Member agents: Margo Prescott; Ashton Prescott.
Handles: Movie scripts (feature film), TV scripts (TV mow). No longer represents books. Considers these script subject areas: action/adventure; comedy; contemporary issues; detective/police/crime; drama (contemporary); juvenile; mainstream; mystery/suspense; romantic comedy and drama; thriller/espionage. Query. Reports in 1 week on queries; 1-2 months on mss.
Recent Sales: *Movie/TV mow in development: Syd & Ollie*, by Margo Prescott (Driskill Entertainment); *The Tribe*, by M. Canales (Driskill Entertainment).
Terms: Agent receives 10% commission on domestic sales; 20% on foreign sales. Offers written contract, binding for 1 year.
Fees: No reading fee for screenplays. Charges $85 to review and research all true story material for TV or film ("maybe higher for extensive material"). Offers criticism service, overall criticism, some on line criticism. "We recommend changes, usually 3-10 pages depending on length of the material (on request only)." Payment of criticism fee does not ensure representation.
Tips: "Often professionals in film and TV will recommend us to clients. We also actively solicit material. Always enclose SASE with your query."

CINEMA TALENT INTERNATIONAL, (II), 8033 Sunset Blvd., Suite 808, West Hollywood CA 90046. (213)656-1937. Contact: Marie Heckler. Estab. 1976. Represents approximately 23 clients. 3% of clients are new/previously unpublished writers. Currently handles: 1% nonfiction books; 1% novels; 95% movie scripts; 3% TV scripts. Member agents: George Kriton; George N. Rumanes; Marie Heckler (motion pictures); Nicholas Athans (motion pictures).
Handles: Movie scripts, TV scripts. Query with outline/proposal plus 2 sample chapters. Reports in 4-5 weeks on queries and mss.
Terms: Agent receives 10% on domestic sales; 20% on foreign sales. Offers written contract, binding for 2 years.
Also Handles: Nonfiction books; novels.
Tips: Obtains new clients through recommendations from others.

CIRCLE OF CONFUSION LTD., (II), 666 Fifth Ave., Suite 303J, New York NY 10103. (212)969-0653. Fax: (212)975-7748. Contact: Rajeev K. Agarwal, Lawrence Mattis. Estab. 1990. Signatory of WGA. Represents 60 clients. 60% of clients are new/previously unpublished writers. Specializes in screenplays for film and TV. Currently handles: 15% novels; 5% novellas; 80% movie scripts. Member agents: Rajeev Agarwal, Lawrence Mattis, Annmarie Negretti.
Handles: Movie scripts (feature film). Considers all script subject areas. Send entire ms. Reports in 1 month on queries; 2 months on mss.
Recent Sales: *Movie/TV mow scripts*: *When Heroes Go Down*, by Chabot/Peterka Ka(Fox); *Bound*, by Wachowski/Wachowski (DDLC); *Dust*, by Somonelli/Frumkes (Brigham Park), *Galileo's Wake*, by Chabot/Peterka (Fox); The Longest Night, by Mayerl Claifin (Fox).
Also Handles: Nonfiction books, novels, novellas, short story collections. Considers all nonfiction and fiction areas.
Terms: Agent receives 10% commission on domestic sales; 10% on foreign sales. Offers written contract, binding for 1 year.
Tips: Obtains new clients through queries, recommendations and writing contests. "We look for screenplays and other material for film and television."

☐**CLIENT FIRST—A/K/A LEO P. HAFFEY AGENCY, (II)**, P.O. Box 795, White House TN 37188. (615)325-4780. Contact: Robin Swensen. Estab. 1990. Signatory of WGA. Represents 21 clients. 60% of clients are new/previously unpublished writers. Specializes in movie scripts and novels

---

AN OPEN BOX indicates script agents who charge fees to writers. WGA signatories are not permitted to charge for reading manuscripts, but may charge for critiques or consultations.

for sale to motion picture industry. Currently handles: 30% novels; 70% movie scripts. Member agent: Leo P. Haffey Jr. (attorney/agent to the motion picture industry).
Handles: Movie scripts. Considers these script subject areas: action/adventure; cartoon; animation; comedy; contemporary issues; detective/police/crime; family saga; historical; mystery/suspense; romance (contemporary, historical); science fiction; sports; thriller/espionage; westerns/frontier. Query. Reports in 1 week on queries; 2 months on mss.
Also Handles: Novels, novellas, short story collections.
Terms: Offers written contract, binding for a negotiable length of time.
Fees: Charges $50 reading fee to non-WGA members.
Tips: Obtains new clients through referrals. "The motion picture business is a numbers game like any other. The more you write the better your chances of success. Please send a SASE along with your query letter."

COAST TO COAST TALENT AND LITERARY, (II), 4942 Vineland Ave., Suite 200, North Hollywood CA 91601. (818)762-6278. Fax: (818)762-7049. Estab. 1986. Signatory of WGA. Represents 25 clients. 35% of clients are new/previously unpublished writers. Specializes in one-hour TV features. Currently handles: 10% nonfiction books; 60% movie scripts; 30% TV scripts.
Handles: Movie scripts (feature film, documentary, animation), TV scripts (TV mow, miniseries, episodic drama, sitcom, variety show, animation, soap opera), syndicated material, true stories, humor books. Considers these script subject areas: action/adventure; detective/police/crime; erotica; humor/satire; literary; mystery/suspense; psychic/supernatural; romance; thriller/espionage; true crime. Query. Reports in 2 months on queries; 6 months on mss.
Also Handles: Nonfiction books, novels, humor books.
Terms: Agent receives 10% commission on domestic sales; 15% on foreign sales. Offers written contract, binding for 1 year.
Tips: Obtains new clients through recommendations, query letter. "Be concise in what you're looking for. Don't go on and on in your query letter, get to the point."

COMMUNICATIONS AND ENTERTAINMENT, INC., (III), 5902 Mount Eagle Dr., #903, Alexandria VA 22303-2518. (703)329-3796. Fax: (301)589-2222. Contact: James L. Bearden. Estab. 1989. Represents 10 clients. 50% of clients are new/previously unpublished writers. Specializes in TV, film and print media. Currently handles: 5% juvenile books; 40% movie scripts; 10% novels; 40% TV scripts. Member agents: James Bearden (TV/film); Roslyn Ray (literary).
● Prior to opening his agency, Mr. Bearden worked as a producer/director and an entertainment attorney.
Handles: Movie scripts, TV scripts, syndicated material. Considers these nonfiction areas: history; music/dance/theater/film. Considers these fiction areas: action/adventure; cartoon/comic; contemporary issues; fantasy; historical; science fiction; thriller/espionage. Query with outline/proposal or send entire ms. Reports in 1 months on queries; 3 months on mss.
Also Handles: Novels and juvenile books. Considers these nonfiction areas: biography/autobiography; ethnic/cultural interests; music/dance/theater/film. Considers these fiction areas: action/adventure; mainstream; mystery/suspense; science fiction.
Terms: Agent receives 10% commission on domestic sales; 5% on foreign sales. Offers written contract, varies with project.
Tips: Obtains new clients through referrals and recommendations. "Be patient."

COMMUNICATIONS MANAGEMENT ASSOCIATES, (II, V), (formerly Part-Time Productions), 1129 Sixth Ave., #1, Rockford IL 61104. (815)964-1335. Fax: (815)964-3061. E-mail: producin g@ptp.com. Contact: Tom Lee. Estab. 1989. Signatory of WGA. Represents several dozen clients. 95% of clients are new/previously unpublished writers. Currently handles: 10% novels; 80% movie scripts; 8% TV scripts; 2% short story collections.
Handles: Movie scripts, novels. Considers these fiction areas: action/adventure; contemporary issues; detective/police/crime; erotica; fantasy; feminist; gay; historical; horror; lesbian; mainstream; psychic/supernatural; science fiction; thriller/espionage. Query with outline/proposal, 3 sample chapters and a release. Reports in 2 months on queries; 4 months on mss.
Recent Sales: *Movie/TV mow optioned*: *Decibel Overload*, by Diana Kemp-Jones (SHORE). *Movie/TV mow in development*: *Hoopla; Broken Silence*. *Scripting assignments*: WWA's Sally Walker.
Also Handles: Novels, short story collections, nonfiction books, juvenile books, scholarly books, novellas, poetry books. Considers these fiction areas: action/adventure; contemporary issues; detective/police/crime; erotica; fantasy; historical; horror; juvenile; mainstream; mystery/suspense; picture book; romance (historical, regency); science fiction; thriller/espionage; westerns/frontier; young adult.
Terms: Agent receives 10% commission on domestic sales; 5% on foreign sales. Offers written contract with 60 day cancellation clause. Sometimes charges for postage and photocopying.

Writers' Conferences: Northern Illinois Writers Conference, ABA.
Tips: Obtains new clients through referrals only. "Be respectful and patient with agents, publishers, and producers. If you are in this for a 'fast and easy buck,' look elsewhere."

‡**CONTEMPORARY ARTISTS, (III)**, 1427 Third St. Promenade, Suite 205, Santa Monica CA 90401. (310)395-1800. Fax: (310)394-3308. Contact: Larry Metzger. Established 1963. Signatory of WGA. Represents 10 clients.
Handles: Movie scripts, TV scripts. Considers all script subject areas. Query. If interested, reports in approximately 1 month.
Terms: Agency receives 10% commission on domestic sales; 10% on foreign sales.

THE COPPAGE COMPANY, (III), 11501 Chandler Blvd., North Hollywood CA 91601. (818)980-1106. Fax: (818)509-1474. Contact: Judy Coppage. Estab. 1985. Signatory of WGA, member of DGA, SAG. Represents 25 clients. Specializes in "writers who also produce, direct and act."
Handles: Movie scripts (feature films), TV scripts (original), stage plays. Considers all script subject areas.
Also Handles: Novels, novellas.
Terms: Agent receives 10% commission on domestic sales; 10% on foreign sales. Offers written contract, binding for 2 years.
Tips: Obtains new clients through recommendation only.

‡**DADE/SCHULTZ ASSOCIATES, (IV)**, 12302 Sarah St., Studio City CA 91604. (818)760-3100. Fax: (818)760-1395. Contact: R. Ernest Dade. Represents 10 clients.
Handles: Movie scripts (feature film only). Considers all script subject areas. Query with brief synopsis. Reports in 1 week if interested.
Terms: Agent receives 10% commissions on domestic sales; 10% on foreign sales.

DOUROUX & CO., (II), 445 S. Beverly Dr., Suite 310, Beverly Hills CA 90212-4401. (310)552-0900. Fax: (310)552-0920. Contact: Michael E. Douroux. Estab. 1985. Signatory of WGA, member of DGA. 20% of clients are new/previously unpublished writers. Currently handles: 50% movie scripts; 50% TV scripts. Member agents: Michael E. Douroux (chairman/CEO); Tara T. Thiesmeyer (assistant).
Handles: Movie scripts (feature film); TV scripts (TV mow, episodic drama, sitcom, animation). Considers these script subject areas: action/adventure; comedy; detective/police/crime; family saga; fantasy; historical; humor/satire; mainstream; mystery/suspense; romantic comedy and drama; science fiction; thriller/espionage; westerns/frontier. Query.
Terms: Agent receives 10% commission. Offers written contract, binding for 2 years. Charges for photocopying only.

DRAMATIC PUBLISHING, (IV), 311 Washington St., Woodstock IL 60098. (815)338-7170. Fax: (815)338-8981. Contact: Linda Habjan. Estab. 1885. Specializes in a full range of stage plays, musicals and instructional books about theater. Currently handles: 2% textbooks; 98% stage plays.
Handles: Stage plays. Reports in 3-9 months.

☐**DYKEMAN ASSOCIATES INC., (III)**, 4115 Rawlins, Dallas TX 75219. (214)528-2991. Fax: (214)528-0241. E-mail: adykeman@airmail.net. Contact: Literary Department. Estab. 1987. 30% of clients are new/previously unpublished writers. Currently handles: 15% novels; 85% screenplays.
Handles: Movie scripts, TV scripts. Considers these script subject areas: action/adventure; comedy; contemporary issues; suspense; thriller. Query with proposal and summary. Reports in 2-3 weeks on queries; 1-2 months on mss.
Also Handles: Fiction books, nonfiction books, juvenile books.
Terms: Agent receives 15% commission on domestic sales; 15% on foreign sales. Offers written contract.
Fees: Charges $250 reading fee for book mss. Consideration of screenplays is gratis. Criticism service included in reading fee. Critiques are written by professional evaluator. Charges for postage, copies, long distance phone calls, faxes. Payment of reading fee does not ensure representation.

☐**EARTH TRACKS AGENCY, (I, II)**, 4809 Avenue N, Suite 286, Brooklyn NY 11234. Contact: David Krinsky. Estab. 1990. Signatory of WGA. Represents 3 clients. 50% of clients are new/previously unpublished writers. Specializes in "movie and TV script sales of original material." Currently handles: 10% novels; 80% movie scripts; 10% TV scripts. Member agents: David Krinsky (movie scripts); Howard Smith.
Handles: Movie scripts (feature film), TV scripts (TV mow, sitcom). Considers these script subject areas: action/adventure; comedy; contemporary issues; police/crime; erotica; experimental; horror; mainstream; teen; thriller. Query with SASE. Reports in 4-6 weeks on queries; 6-8 weeks on mss (only if requested).

Recent Sales: *Movie in development*: *Hot Steaming Coffee.*
Terms: Agent receives 10-12% commission on domestic sales; 10-12% on foreign sales. Offers written contract, binding for 6-24 months.
Fees: "No fee for TV or movie scriptwriters. For books I charge $100 a book, nonrefundable. Criticism service: (if requested), $25 per manuscript submitted. I personally write the critiques. An author *must* provide *proper* postage (SASE) if author wants material returned. If no SASE enclosed, material is not returned. Do not mail queries on books, novels, plays. Mail payment and material for review." 90% of business is derived from commissions on ms sales; 10% is derived from reading fees or criticism service. Payment of criticism fee does not ensure representation.
Tips: Obtains new clients through recommendations and letters of solicitations by mail. "Send a one-page letter describing the material the writer wishes the agency to represent. Do *not* send anything other than query letter with short synopsis and SASE. Unsolicited scripts will not be returned. Do not 'hype' the material—just explain exactly what you are selling. If it is a play, do not state 'screenplay.' If it is a movie script, do not state 'manuscript,' as that implies a book. Be specific, give description (summary) of material. Do not send query letters regarding representing books, plays or novels. They will not be read or returned. No one may submit material of any kind by registered or certified mail. If will be returned. For any script request, author will be asked to sign release form. No screenplays about the mafia. No period pieces (contemporary only). No high-tech, high budget type queries. If you have contacted this agency with no response, do not submit more material."

EPSTEIN-WYCKOFF AND ASSOCIATES, (II), 280 S. Beverly Dr., #400, Beverly Hills CA 90212-3904. (310)278-7222. Fax: (310)278-4640. Contact: Karin Wakefield. Estab. 1990. Signatory of WGA. Represents 20 clients. Specializes in features, TV, books and stage plays. Currently handles: 1% nonfiction books; 1% novels; 60% movie scripts; 40% TV scripts; 2% stage plays.
Handles: Movie scripts (feature film), TV scripts (TV mow, miniseries, episodic drama, sitcom, animation, soap opera), stage plays. Considers these script subject areas: action/adventure; comedy; contemporary issues; detective/police/crime; erotica; family saga; feminist; gay; historical; juvenile; lesbian; mainstream; mystery/suspense; romantic comedy and drama; teen; thriller. Query with SASE. Reports in 1 week on queries; 1 month on mss, if solicited.
Terms: Agent receives 15% commission on domestic sales of books, 10% on scripts; 20% on foreign sales. Offers written contract, binding for 1 year. Charges for photocopying.
Also Handles: Nonfiction books, novels.
Writers' Conferences: ABA.
Tips: Obtains new clients through recommendations, queries.

‡ES TALENT AGENCY, (I), 55 New Montgomery, #511, San Francisco CA 94105. (415)543-6575. Fax: (415)543-6534. Contact: Ed Silver. Estab. 1995. Signatory of WGA. Represents 25 clients. 70% of clients are new/previously unpublished writers. Specializes in theatrical screenplays, mow's and miniseries. Currently handles: 20% nonfiction books; 50% movie scripts; 30% novels. Member agent: Ed Silver.
Handles: Movie scripts, TV scripts. Considers these fiction areas: action/adventure; humor/satire; mainstream; mystery/suspense; thriller/espionage. Query. Reports in 3-4 weeks on queries; 3-4 weeks on mss.
Terms: Agent receives 10% commission on script sales; 15-20% on novels. Offers written contract with 30 day cancellation clause.
Writer's Conferences: Writers Connection: Selling to Hollywood (August).
Tips: Obtains new clients through recommendations and queries from WGA agency list.

☐F.L.A.I.R. or FIRST LITERARY ARTISTS INTERNATIONAL REPRESENTATIVES (II, IV), P.O. Box 666, Coram NY 11727-0666. Fax: (516)331-2438. Contact: Jacqulin Chambers. Estab. 1991. Represents 15 clients. Specializes in screenplays and mows. Member agents: Ruth Schulman (TV mow, screenplays), Jacqulin Chambers (new clientele, screenplays).
Handles: Movie scripts (feature film), TV scripts (TV mow). Considers these script subject areas: action/adventure; archaeology; child guidance/parenting; comedy; contemporary issues; detective/police/crime; erotica; family saga; fantasy; film; health/medicine; inspirational; juvenile; mainstream; money/finance/economics; mystery/suspense; nature/environment; psychology; psychic/supernatural;

ALWAYS INCLUDE a self-addressed, stamped envelope (SASE) for reply or return of your manuscript.

romantic comedy and drama; teen; true crime/investigative; women's issues. Query with synopsis. Reports in 2 weeks on queries; 6 months on mss.

Recent Sales: *Movie sold*: *My Dead Neighbor*, by Danny Brockner (Lock-n-Load Productions); *Sleep in the Dust*, by Andy Froemke (Richard Sears Films). *Movie/TV mow in development*: *Witness to Murder*, by Bill Johnston (Stuart Benjamin Productions).

Terms: Agent receives 10% commission on domestic sales; 15% on foreign sales. Offers written contract, binding for 1 year.

Fees: Edit and critique service: screenplays $250; sitcoms $100. "I give a complete listing of what can be improved within their script, as well as suggested changes. I have compiled an at-home workshop for screen and sitcom writers: screenwriters $50; sitcom writers $20." Charges marketing fee, office expenses, postage, photocopying and phone calls. 70% of business is derived from commissions on ms sales; 30% from reading fees or criticism service. Payment of criticism fee does not ensure representation.

Tips: "Become a member of the Writer's Digest Book Club and you will learn a lot. Learning the format for screenplays and sitcoms is essential. Register all your work with either the copyright office or the WGA. Write from the heart and try and make it commercially viable. You must send a query letter and synopsis of your script with a SASE. Please do not call."

FLORENCE FEILER LITERARY AGENCY, (III), 1524 Sunset Plaza Dr., Los Angeles CA 90069. (213)652-6920. Fax: (213)652-0945. Associate: Joyce Boorn. Estab. 1976. Member of PEN American Center, Women in Film, California Writers Club, MWA. Represents 40 clients. None are unpublished writers. "Quality is the criterion." Specializes in fiction, nonfiction, screenplays, TV. No short stories.
Handles: Movie scripts (feature film); TV scripts (TV mow, episodic drama). Considers these script subject areas: detective/police/crime; family saga; gay; historical; juvenile; lesbian; mystery/suspense; romantic comedy and drama; thriller. Query with outline only. Reports in 2 weeks on queries. "We will not accept simultaneous queries to other agents."
Recent Sales: *A Lantern In Her Hand*, by Bess Streeter Aldrich (Kraft-General Foods); *Cheers For Miss Bishop*, by Bess Streeter Aldrich (Scripps Howard); *The Caryatids* and *The Angelic Avengers*, by Isak Dinesen (Kenneth Madsen).
Terms: Agent receives 10% commission on domestic sales; 10% on dramatic sales; 20% on foreign sales.

☐**FRIEDA FISHBEIN LTD., (II)**, 2556 Hubbard St., Brooklyn NY 11235-6223. (212)247-4398. Contact: Janice Fishbein. Estab. 1928. Represents 32 clients. 50% of clients are new/previously unpublished writers. Currently handles: 10% nonfiction books; 5% young adult; 60% novels; 10% movie scripts; 10% stage plays; 5% TV scripts. Member agents: Heidi Carlson (contemporary and literary); Douglas Michael (play and screenplay scripts).
● See the expanded listing for this agency in Literary Agents: Fee-charging.

B.R. FLEURY AGENCY, (I, II), 1228 E. Colonial Dr., Orlando FL 32803. (407)896-4976. Contact: Blanche or Margaret. Estab. 1994. Signatory of WGA. Currently handles: 50% books; 50% scripts.
Handles: Movie scripts (feature film/documentary). Considers these script subject areas: action/adventure; comedy; detective/police/crime; family saga; historical; horror; mainstream; mystery/suspense; psychic/supernatural; romantic comedy and drama; thriller. Query with SASE or call for information. Reports immediately on queries; 3 months on scripts.
Terms: WGA guidelines.
Also Handles: Nonfiction books, novels. Considers these nonfiction areas: agriculture/horticulture; animals; anthropology/archaeology; art/architecture/design; biography; business; child guidance/parenting; cooking/food/nutrition; education; health/medicine; how-to; humor; interior design/decorating; juvenile; money/finance/economics; film; nature/environment; New Age/metaphysics; photography; psychology; science/technology; self-help/personal improvement; sociology; true crime/investigative. Considers these fiction areas: action; detective/police/crime; ethnic; experimental; family saga; fantasy; historical; horror; humor/satire; literary; mainstream; mystery/suspense; psychic/supernatural; regional; romance (contemporary, gothic, historical, regency); science fiction; sports; thriller/espionage; westerns/frontier; young adult. Call for guidelines.
Terms: Agent receives 15% commission on domestic sales. Offers written contract, binding as per contract.
Tips: Obtains new clients through referrals and listings. "Be creative."

☐**FRAN LITERARY AGENCY, (I, II)**, 7235 Split Creek, San Antonio TX 78238-3627. (210)684-1569. Contact: Fran Rathmann. Estab. 1993. Represents 32 clients. 55% of clients are new/previously unpublished writers. "Very interested in Star Trek novels/screenplays." Currently handles: 15% nonfiction books; 10% juvenile books; 30% novels; 5% novellas; 5% poetry books; 15% movie scripts; 20% TV scripts.
● See the expanded listing for this agency in Literary Agents: Fee-charging.

ROBERT A. FREEDMAN DRAMATIC AGENCY, INC., (II, III), 1501 Broadway, Suite 2310, New York NY 10036. (212)840-5760. President: Robert A. Freedman. Vice President: Selma Luttinger. Estab. 1928. Member of AAR, signatory of WGA. Prefers to work with established authors; works with a small number of new authors. Specializes in plays, movie scripts and TV scripts.

• Robert Freedman has served as vice president of the dramatic division of AAR.

Handles: Movie scripts; TV scripts; stage plays. Query. No unsolicited mss. Usually reports in 2 weeks on queries; 3 months on mss.

Terms: Agent receives 10% on dramatic sales; "and, as is customary, 20% on amateur rights." Charges for photocopying.

Recent Sales: "We will speak directly with any prospective client concerning sales that are relevant to his/her specific script."

SAMUEL FRENCH, INC., (II, III), 45 W. 25th St., New York NY 10010-2751. (212)206-8990. Fax: (212)206-1429. Editors: William Talbot and Lawrence Harbison. Estab. 1830. Member of AAR. Represents plays which it publishes for production rights. Member agents: Pam Newton, Brad Lohrenze.

Handles: Stage plays (theatrical stage play, variety show). Considers these script subject areas: comedy; contemporary issues; detective/police/crime; ethnic; experimental; fantasy; horror; mystery/suspense; religious/inspirational; thriller. Query or send entire ms. Replies "immediately" on queries; decision in 2-8 months regarding publication. "Enclose SASE."

Terms: Agent usually receives 10% professional production royalties; variable amateur production royalties.

‡THE GAGE GROUP, (II), 9255 Sunset Blvd., Suite 515, Los Angeles CA 90069. (310)859-8777. Fax: (310)859-8166. Estab. 1976. Signatory of WGA. Represents 27 clients.

Handles: Movies scripts (feature film), TV scripts, theatrical stage plays. Considers all script subject areas. Query. Reports in 2-4 weeks on queries and mss.

Terms: Agent receives 10% commission on domestic sales; 10% commission on foreign sales.

□THE GARY-PAUL AGENCY, (II), 84 Canaan Court, Suite 17, Stratford CT 06497-4609. Phone/fax: (203)336-0257. E-mail: gcmaynard@aol.com. Contact: Gary Maynard. Estab. 1989. Represents 33 clients. Specializes in client representation and promotion. Most clients are freelance writers. Member agents: Gary Maynard, Paul Carbonaro, Paul Caravatt.

• Prior to opening his agency, Mr. Maynard was a motion picture writer/director.

Handles: Movie scripts; TV scripts; educational and technical publications; films/videos; products. Considers all script subject areas. Query with letter of introduction. Reports in 10 days on requested submissions.

Recent Sales: *Movie/TV mow in development:* A Laying of Hands, by Michele Verhoosky (The Onyx Group); *Ms. Wollstonecraft*, by Joanne Netland (Private Investor). *Movie/TV mow sold: The Waters Edge*, by Gary Maynard/Mark Trumbull (Waters Edge Prods.).

Terms: Agent receives 10% commission.

Fees: No charge for client representation. Charges marketing expenses to circulate ms. Also markets products.

Writers' Conferences: NBC Writers' Workshop (Burbank, CA), Script Festival (Los Angeles, CA), Yale University Writers' Workshop, Media Art Center Writers' Workshop (New Haven, CT), Fairfield University "Industry Profile Symposium" (Fairfield, CT).

Tips: "There is no such thing as a dull story, just dull storytelling. Give us a call."

RICHARD GAUTHREAUX—A LITERARY AGENCY, (II), 2742 Jasper St., Kenner LA 70062. (504)466-6741. Contact: Jay Richards. Estab. 1985. Represents 11 clients. 75% of clients are new/previously unpublished writers. Currently handles: 45% novels; 25% movie scripts; 20% TV scripts; 5% stage plays; 5% short story.

Handles: Movie scripts, TV scripts, stage plays. Considers these nonfiction areas: sports; true crime/investigative. Considers these fiction areas: horror; thriller/espionage. Query. Reports in 2 weeks on queries; 2 months on mss.

Terms: Agent receives 10% commission on domestic sales; 15% on foreign sales. Offers written contract, binding for 6 months.

Also Handles: Novels. Considers these nonfiction areas: sports. Considers these fiction areas: detective/police/crime; horror; thriller/espionage.

Tips: Obtains new listings through guild listing, local referrals.

GEDDES AGENCY, (IV), 1201 Greenacre Ave., Los Angeles CA 90046. (213)878-1155. Contact: Literary Department. Estab. 1983 in L.A., 1967 in Chicago. Signatory of WGA, SAG, AFTRA. Represents 10 clients. 100% of clients are new/previously unpublished writers. "We are mainly representing actors—writers are more 'on the side.' " Currently handles: 100% movie scripts. Member agent: Ann Geddes.
Handles: Movie scripts. Query with synopsis. Reports in 2 months on mss only if interested.
Terms: Agent receives 10% commission on domestic sales. Offers written contract, binding for 1 year. Charges for "handling and postage for a script to be returned—otherwise it is recycled."
Tips: Obtains new clients through recommendations from others and through mailed-in synopses. "Send in query—say how many scripts available for representation. Send synopsis of each one. Mention something about yourself."

THE LAYA GELFF AGENCY, (IV), 16133 Ventura Blvd., Suite 700, Encino CA 91436. (818)713-2610. Estab. 1985. Signatory of WGA. Represents many clients. No new/previously unpublished writers. Specializes in TV and film scripts; WGA members only. Currently handles: 50% movie scripts; 50% TV scripts.
Handles: Movie scripts; TV scripts. Query with SASE. Reports in 2 weeks on queries; 1 month on mss. "Must have SASE for reply."
Terms: Agent receives 10% commission on domestic sales; 10% on foreign sales. Offers standard WGA contract.
Tips: Obtains new clients through recommendations from others.

THE GERSH AGENCY, (II, III), 232 N. Canon Dr., Beverly Hills CA 90210. (310)274-6611. Fax: (310)274-4035. Contact: Laurie Zaifert. Estab. 1962. Less than 10% of clients are new/previously unpublished writers. Special interests: "mainstream—convertible to film and television." Member agent: Ron Bernstein.
Handles: Movie scripts (feature film, animation); TV scripts (TV mow, miniseries, sitcom). Considers all script subject areas. Send query letter with SASE, a brief synopsis and brief personal background. Does not accept any unsolicited material.
Recent Sales: Film rights to *Shot in the Heart*, by Mikal Gilmore; *Pigs in Heaven*, by Barbara Kingsolver.
Terms: Agent receives 10% commission on domestic sales. "We strictly deal in *published* manuscripts in terms of potential film or television sales, on a strictly 10% commission—sometimes split with a New York literary agency or various top agencies."

THE SEBASTIAN GIBSON AGENCY, (I), 125 Tahquitz Canyon Way, Suite 200, Palm Springs CA 92262. (619)322-2200. Fax: (619)322-3857. Contact: Sebastian Gibson. Estab. 1995. Member of the California Bar Association and Desert Bar Association. 100% of clients are new/previously unpublished writers. Specializes in fiction. Currently handles: 100% novels.
• See the expanded listing for this agency in Literary Agents: Nonfee-Charging.

GOLD/MARSHAK & ASSOCIATES, (II), 3500 W. Olive Ave., Suite 1400, Burbank CA 91505. (818)972-4300. Fax: (818)955-6411. Contact: Jenette Jenson, junior agent. Estab. 1993. Signatory of WGA. Represents 43 literary clients. 40% of clients are new/previously unpublished writers. Currently handles: 40% movie scripts; 40% TV scripts; 10% stage plays; 10% syndicated material. Member agent: Mr. Jeff Melnick (mows, features).
• Prior to joining the agency Mr. Melnick was a development executive. He also worked at two other agencies.
Handles: Movie scripts (feature film); TV scripts (TV mows, miniseries, episodic drama, sitcom, soap opera); stage plays; syndicated material. Considers these script subject areas: action/adventure; comedy; contemporary issues; detective/police/crime/family saga; ethnic; family saga; feminist; gay; lesbian; mainstream; mystery/suspense; psychic/supernatural; romantic comedy and drama; science fiction; sports; thriller/espionage; women's issues. Query with outline/proposal. "No unsolicited mss." Reports in 1 week on queries; 1 month on mss.

AGENTS RANKED I AND II are most open to both established and new writers. Agents ranked **III** are open to established writers with publishing-industry references.

Recent Sales: *Movie/TV mow optioned/sold: Down the Road* (HBO); *Independence* (Fox); *The Rose Tattoo* (Showtime); *Into the Light* (Hallmark Presentation).
Terms: Agent receives 10% commission on domestic sales; 10% on foreign sales.
Tips: Obtains new clients through recommendations from others, solicitation and at conferences and film schools.

MICHELLE GORDON & ASSOCIATES, (III), 260 S. Beverly Dr., Suite 308, Beverly Hills CA 90212. (310)246-9930. Contact: Michelle Gordon. Estab. 1993. Signatory of WGA. Represents 4 clients. None are new/previously unpublished writers. Currently handles: 100% movie scripts.
Handles: Movie scripts. Considers these script subject areas: biography/autobiography; contemporary issues; detective/police/crime; feminist; government/politics/law; psychology; true crime/investigative; women's issues/women's studies. Query. Reports in 2 weeks on queries.
Terms: Agent receives 10% commission on domestic sales; 10% on foreign sales. Offers written contract, binding for 1 year.
Tips: Obtains new clients through recommendations and solicitation.

GRAHAM AGENCY, (II), 311 W. 43rd St., New York NY 10036. (212)489-7730. Owner: Earl Graham. Estab. 1971. Represents 40 clients. 30% of clients are new/unproduced writers. Specializes in playwrights and screenwriters only. "We're interested in commercial material of quality." Currently handles: movie scripts, stage plays.
Handles: Stage plays, movie scripts. No one-acts, no material for children. "We consider on the basis of the letters of inquiry." Writers *must* query before sending any material for consideration. Reports in 3 months on queries; 6 weeks on mss.
Terms: Agent receives 10% commission.
Tips: Obtains new clients through queries and referrals. "Contact appropriate agents, not all of them. Write a concise, intelligent letter giving the gist of what you are offering."

ARTHUR B. GREENE, (III), 101 Park Ave., 43rd Floor, New York NY 10178. (212)661-8200. Fax: (212)370-7884. Contact: Arthur Greene. Estab. 1980. Represents 20 clients. 10% of clients are new/previously unpublished writers. Specializes in movies, TV and fiction. Currently handles: 25% novels; 10% novellas; 10% short story collections; 25% movie scripts; 10% TV scripts; 10% stage plays; 10% other.
Handles: Movie scripts (feature film); TV scripts (TV mow); stage play. Considers these script subject areas: action/adventure; detective/police/crime; horror; mystery/suspense. Query. Reports in 2 weeks on queries. No written contract, 30 day cancellation clause. 100% of business is derived from commissions on sales.
Also Handles: Novels. Considers these nonfiction areas: animals; music/dance/theater/film; sports. Considers these fiction areas: action/adventure; detective/police/crime; horror; mystery/suspense; sports; thriller/espionage. Query. Reports in 2 weeks on queries. No written contract, 30 day cancellation clause.
Terms: Agent receives 10% commission on domestic sales; 20% on foreign sales.
Tips: Obtains new clients through recommendations from others.

‡LARRY GROSSMAN & ASSOC., (IV), 211 S. Beverly Dr., Beverly Hills CA 90212. (310)550-8127. Fax: (310)550-8129. Contact: Larry Grossman. Estab. 1975. Signatory of WGA. Specializes in comedy screenplays and TV comedy. Currently handles 50% movie scripts, 50% TV scripts.
Handles: Movie scripts, TV scripts. Considers these fiction areas: detective/police/crime; humor/satire; mainstream; mystery/suspense. Query. Reports in 10 days on queries.
Terms: Agent receives 10% commission on domestic sales. Offers written contract.
Tips: Obtains new clients through recommendations from others, solicitation.

THE SUSAN GURMAN AGENCY, (IV), #15A, 865 West End Ave., New York NY 10025-8403. (212)864-5243. Fax: (212)864-5055. Contact: Susan Gurman. Estab. 1993. Signatory of WGA. 28% of clients are new/previously unpublished writers. Specializes in referred screenwriters and playwrights. Currently handles: 50% movie scripts; 30% stage plays; 20% books. Member agents: Lauren Rott (books).
Handles: Movie scripts; stage plays; nonfiction books; juvenile books; novels; TV scripts. Referral only. Reports in 2 weeks on queries; 2 months on mss. Considers these nonfiction areas: biography/autobiography; true crime/investigative. Considers these fiction areas: detective/police/crime; family saga; history; literary; mainstream; mystery/suspense; thriller/espionage.
Terms: Agent receives 10% commission on domestic sales; 10% on foreign sales.
Tips: Obtains new clients *through referral only*. No letters of inquiry.

‡THE HAEGGSTROM OFFICE, (III), 6404 Wilshire Blvd., Suite 1100, Los Angeles CA 90048. (213)658-9111. Contact: Anita Haeggstrom. Estab. 1989. Member of AEA, AFTRA, DGA, SAG; signatory of WGA. Represents 4 clients.

Handles: Movie scripts (feature film), TV scripts (TV mow, sitcom, soap opera, miniseries, variety show, syndicated material, episodic drama, animation). Query only. No unsolicited material. Reports immediately on queries, but only if interested. Does not respond if not interested.
Terms: Agent receives 10% commission on domestic sales; 10% on foreign sales.

HEACOCK LITERARY AGENCY, INC., (II), 1523 Sixth St., Suite #14, Santa Monica CA 90401-2514. (310)393-6227. Contact: Rosalie Heacock. Estab. 1978. Member of AAR, Author's Guild, ATA, SCBWI; signatory of WGA. Represents 60 clients. 10% of clients are new/previously unpublished writers. Currently handles: 90% nonfiction books; 10% novels. Member agents: Rosalie Heacock (psychology, philosophy, women's studies, alternative health, new technology, futurism, new idea books, art and artists); Ms. Robin Henning (fiction and nonfiction).
- See the expanded listing for this agency in Literary Agents: Nonfee-charging.

‡HEADLINE ARTISTS AGENCY, (II), 16400 Ventura Blvd., Suite 235, Encino CA 91436. (818)986-1730. Fax: (818)995-1115. Contact: Rosanna Kahane. Estab. 1991. Signatory of WGA. Represents 6 clients.
Handles: Screenplays. Considers all script subject areas. Query. Reports in 2 weeks on queries.
Terms: Agent receives 10% commission on domestic sales; 10% on foreign sales.

☐ALICE HILTON LITERARY AGENCY, (II), 13131 Welby Way, North Hollywood CA 91606-1041. (818)982-2546. Fax: (818)765-8207. Contact: Alice Hilton. Estab. 1986. Eager to work with new/unpublished writers. "Interested in any quality material, although agent's personal taste runs in the genre of 'Cheers.' 'L.A. Law,' 'American Playhouse,' 'Masterpiece Theatre' and Woody Allen vintage humor."
- See the expanded listing for this agency in the Literary Agents: Fee-charging.

CAROLYN HODGES AGENCY, (III), 1980 Glenwood Dr., Boulder CO 80304-2329. (303)443-4636. Fax: (303)443-4636. Contact: Carolyn Hodges. Estab. 1989. Signatory of WGA. Represents 18 clients. 90% of clients are new/previously unpublished writers. Represents only screenwriters for film and TV mows. Currently handles: 80% movie scripts; 20% TV scripts.
- Prior to opening her agency, Ms. Hodges was a freelance writer and founded the Writers In The Rockies Screenwriting conference that has been held for the past 13 years.
Handles: Movie scripts (feature film); TV scripts (TV mow). Considers these script subject areas: action/adventure; contemporary issues; detective/police/crime; experimental; feminist; gay; glitz; lesbian; literary; mainstream; mystery/suspense; psychic/supernatural; romance (contemporary). Query with 1 page synopsis. Reports in 1 week on queries; 10 weeks on mss.
Terms: Agent receives 10% on domestic sales; foreign sales "depend on each individual negotiation." Offers written contract, standard WGA. No charge for criticism. "I always try to offer concrete feedback, even when rejecting a piece of material."
Recent Sales: Available upon request.
Writers' Conferences: Director and founder of Writers In The Rockies Film Screenwriting Conference (Boulder CO, August).
Tips: Obtains new clients by referral only. "Become proficient at your craft. Attend all workshops accessible to you. READ all the books applicable to your area of interest. READ as many 'produced' screenplays as possible. Live a full, vital and rewarding life so your writing will have something to say. Get involved in a writer's support group. Network with other writers. Receive 'critiques' from your peers and consider merit of suggestions. Don't be afraid to re-examine your perspective."

BARBARA HOGENSON AGENCY, (III), 19 W. 44th St., Suite 1000, New York NY 10036. (212)730-7306. Fax: (212)730-8970. Contact: Barbara Hogenson. Estab. 1994. Member of AAR, signatory of WGA. Represents 60 clients. 5% of clients are new/previously unpublished writers. Currently handles: 35% nonfiction books; 15% novels; 15% movie scripts; 35% stage plays.
- Ms. Hogenson was with the prestigious Lucy Kroll Agency for ten years before starting her own agency.
Handles: Movie scripts, stage plays. Query with outline and SASE. No unsolicited mss. Reports in 1 month.

☐ **AN OPEN BOX** indicates script agents who charge fees to writers. WGA signatories are not permitted to charge for reading manuscripts, but may charge for critiques or consultations.

Also Handles: Nonfiction books, novels. Considers these fiction areas: art/architecture/design; biography/autobiography; cooking/food/nutrition; history; humor; interior design/decorating; music/dance/theater/film; photography; popular culture. Considers these fiction areas: action/adventure; contemporary issues; detective/police/crime; ethnic; historical; humor/satire; literary; mainstream; mystery/suspense; romance (contemporary); thriller/espionage.

Recent Sales: *Steichen*, by Penelope Niven; *The Artful Table*, by E. Herbert and D. Gorman; *Everyday Things*, by S. Slesin and S. Cliff; and *Grateful Dead Social History*, by Carol Brightman.

Terms: Agent receives 10% on film and TV sales; 15% commission on domestic sales of books; 20% on foreign sales of books. Offers written contract, binding for 2 years with 90 day cancellation clause. 100% of business derived from commissions on sales.

Tips: Obtains new clients strictly by referral.

□**THE EDDY HOWARD AGENCY (III)**, % 37 Bernard St., Eatontown NJ 07724-1906. (908)542-3525. Contact: Eddy Howard Pevovar, N.D., Ph.D. Estab. 1986. Signatory of WGA. Represents 20 clients. 1% of clients are new/previously unpublished writers. Specializes in film, sitcom and literary. Currently handles: 5% nonfiction books; 5% scholarly books; 5% juvenile books; 5% novels; 30% movie scripts; 30% TV scripts; 10% stage plays; 5% short story collections; 1% syndicated material; 4% other. Member agents: Eddy Howard Pevovar, N.D., Ph.D. (agency executive); Francine Gail (director of comedy development).

Handles: Movie scripts (feature film, documentary, animation), TV scripts (TV mows, miniseries, episodic drama, sitcom, variety show, animation, soap opera, educational), stage plays. Considers these script subject areas: action/adventure; cartoon/animation; comedy; erotica; family saga; historical; humor; juvenile; mainstream; romantic comedy; sports; teen; thriller; western/frontier.

Also Handles: Nonfiction books, scholarly books, textbooks, juvenile books, novels, novellas, short story collections, syndicated material. Considers these areas: agriculture/horticulture; animals; anthropology/archaeology; cooking/food/nutrition; crafts/hobbies; education; health/medicine; humor; juvenile nonfiction; music/dance/theater/film; nature/environment; New Age/metaphysics; photography; psychology; science/technology; self-help/personal improvement; sports; translations; women's issues/women's studies. Considers these fiction areas: cartoon/comic; erotica; experimental; fantasy; humor/satire; juvenile; literary; mainstream; picture book; psychic/supernatural; regional; young adult. Query with outline and proposal—include phone number. Reports in 5 days on queries; 2 months on mss.

Terms: Agent receives 10% commission on domestic sales; 15% on foreign sales. Offers written contract.

Fees: No fees. Offers criticism service: corrective—style, grammar, punctuation, spelling, format. Technical critical evaluation with fee (saleability, timeliness, accuracy).

Writers' Conferences: Instructor—Writers Workshops at Brookdale College; Community Education Division.

Tips: Obtains new clients through recommendations from others. "I was rejected 12 times before I ever had my first book published and I was rejected 34 times before my first magazine article was published. Stick to what you believe in . . . Don't give up! Never give up! Take constructive criticism for whatever it's worth and keep yourself focused. Each rejection a beginner receives is one step closer to the grand finale—acceptance. It's sometimes good to get your manuscript peer reviewed. This is one way to obtain objective analysis of your work, and see what others think about it. Remember, if it weren't for new writers . . . there'd be *no* writers."

HUDSON AGENCY, (I, IV), 3 Travis Lane, Montrose NY 10548. (914)737-1475. Fax: (914)736-3064. Contact: Susan or Pat Giordano. Estab. 1994. Signatory of WGA. Represents 12 clients. 80% of clients are new/previously unpublished writers. Specializes in feature film and TV only. Currently handles: 50% movie scripts; 50% TV scripts. Member agents: Sue Giordano, Pat Giordano.

Handles: Movie scripts (feature film, documentary), TV scripts (TV mow, miniseries); PG or PG-13 only. Considers these script subject areas: action/adventure; comedy; contemporary issues; detective/police/crime; ethnic; family saga; fantasy; historical; juvenile; mainstream; mystery/suspense; romantic comedy and drama; science fiction; sports; teen; thriller/espionage; westerns/frontier. Send outline and sample pages. Reports in 1 week on queries; 3 weeks on mss.

Terms: Agent receives 15% commission on domestic sales; 15% on foreign sales "for a first time writer on the first sale."

Tips: Obtains new clients through recommendations from others and listing on WGA agency list. "Yes, we may be small, but we work very hard for our clients. Any script we are representing gets excellent exposure to producers. Our network is over 500 contacts in the business and growing rapidly. We are GOOD salespeople. Ultimately it all depends on the quality of the writing and the market for the subject matter. Do not query unless you have taken at least one screenwriting course and read all of Syd Field's books."

‡□**HWA TALENT REPS., (III)**, 1964 Westwood Blvd., Suite 400, Los Angeles CA 90025. (310)446-1313. Fax: (310)446-1364. Contact: Matt J. Klaar. Estab. 1985. Signatory of WGA. 20% of

clients are new/previously unpublished writers. Currently handles: 10% nonfiction books, 70% movie scripts, 10% novels, 10% TV scripts.

Handles: Nonfiction books, movie scripts, novels, TV scripts. Considers these nonfiction areas: animals; biography/autobiography; business; gay/lesbian issues; language/literature/literature/criticism; military/war; music/dance/theater/film; nature/environment; sports. Considers these fiction areas: action/adventure; cartoon/comic; contemporary issues; detective/police/crime; erotica; ethnic; family saga; fantasy; feminist; gay; horror; humor/satire; literary; mystery/suspense; psychic/supernatural; religious/inspirational; romance (gothic, historical); science fiction; sports; thriller/espionage; westerns/frontier. Send outline/proposal with query. Does not answer queries.

Recent Sales: *Hard Wired*, by Jeff Vintar (Walt Disney); *The Happy Man*, by Eric Higgs (Warners); *Spaceless*, by Jeff Vintar (Fox 2000); *The Forgotten*, by Chris Easton.

Terms: Agent receives 10% commission on domestic sales. Offers written contract, binding for 1 year. WGA rules on termination apply.

Fees: Criticism service: "I give notes for free."

Tips: Obtains new clients through referrals only. "A good query letter is important. Use any relationship you have in the business to get your material read."

INTERNATIONAL CREATIVE MANAGEMENT, (III), 8942 Wilshire Blvd., Beverly Hills CA 90211. (310)550-4000. Fax: (310)550-4100. East Coast office: 40 W. 57th St., New York NY 10019. (212)556-5600. Signatory of WGA, member of AAR. Member agents: *TV*: Scott Arnovitz; Tricia Davey; Paul Haas; Nancy Josephson; Steve Sanford; Jeanne Williams. *Movies*: Barbara Dreyfus; Richard Feldman; Ken Kamins; Steve Rabineau; Jeff Robinov; Jim Rosen; David Wirtschafter.

INTERNATIONAL LEONARDS CORP., (II), 3612 N. Washington Blvd., Indianapolis IN 46205-3534. (317)926-7566. Contact: David Leonards. Estab. 1972. Signatory of WGA. Currently handles: 50% movie scripts; 50% TV scripts.

Handles: Movie scripts (feature film, animation), TV scripts (TV mow, sitcom, variety show). Considers these script subject areas: action/adventure; cartoon/animation; comedy; contemporary issues; detective/police/crime; horror; mystery/suspense; romantic comedy; science fiction; sports; thriller. Query. Reports in 1 month on queries; 6 months on mss.

Terms: Agent receives 10% commission on domestic sales; 10% on foreign sales. Offers written contract, "WGA standard," which "varies."

Tips: Obtains new clients through recommendations and queries.

□**CAROLYN JENKS AGENCY, (II)**, 205 Walden St., Suite 1A, Cambridge MA 02140-3507. Phone/fax: (617)876-6927. Contact: Carolyn Jenks. Estab. 1990. 50% of clients are new/previously unpublished writers. Currently handles: 5% nonfiction books; 75% novels; 5% movie scripts; 10% stage plays; 5% TV scripts.

● See the expanded listing for this agency in Literary Agents: Fee-charging.

LESLIE KALLEN AGENCY, (III), 15303 Ventura Blvd., Sherman Oaks CA 91403. (818)906-2785. Fax: (818)906-8931. Contact: J.R. Gowan. Estab. 1988. Signatory of WGA, DGA. Specializes in feature films and mows.

Handles: Movie scripts (feature film); TV scripts (TV mow). Query. "No phone inquiries for representation."

Terms: Agent receives 10% commission on domestic sales.

Tips: "Write a two- to three-paragraph query that makes an agent excited to read the material."

CHARLENE KAY AGENCY, 901 Beaudry St., Suite 6, St. Jean/Richelieu, Quebec J3A 1C6 Canada. (514)348-5296. Director of Development: Louise Meyers. Estab. 1992. Signatory of WGA; member of BMI. 100% of clients are new/previously unpublished writers. Specializes in teleplays and screenplays. Currently handles: 25% TV scripts; 50% TV spec scripts; 25% movie scripts.

Handles: Movie scripts (feature film), TV scripts (TV mow). Considers these script subject areas: action/adventure; fantasy; psychic/supernatural; science fiction; biography/autobiography; family saga. No thrillers. "Real-life stories and biographical movies or something unique: a story that is out of the ordinary something we don't see too often. A *well-written* and *well-constructed* script." Query with outline/proposal by mail only. Reports in 1 month on queries with SASE (or IRC outside Canada). Reports in 8-10 weeks on mss.

Terms: Agent receives 10% commission on domestic sales; 10% on foreign sales. Offers written contract, binding for 1 year. Returns Canadian scripts if SASE provided; returns scripts from US if 14 IRCs are included on an envelope.

Tips: "My agency is listed on the WGA lists and query letters arrive by the dozens every week. As my present clients understand, success comes with patience. A sale rarely happens overnight, especially when you are dealing with totally unknown writers. We are not impressed by the credentials of a writer, amateur or professional or by his or her pitching techniques, but by his or her story ideas and ability to build a well-crafted script."

KERIN-GOLDBERG ASSOCIATES, (II, IV), (formerly Charles Kerin Associates), 155 E. 55th St., #5D, New York NY 10022. (212)838-7373. Fax: (212)838-0774. Contact: Charles Kerin. Estab. 1984. Signatory of WGA. Represents 29 clients. Specializes in theater plays, screenplays, teleplays. Currently handles: 30% movie scripts; 30% TV scripts; 40% stage plays.
Handles: Movie scripts (feature film); TV scripts (TV mow, miniseries, episodic drama, sitcom, variety show, syndicated material); stage plays. Considers all script subject areas. Query. Reports in 1 month on queries; 2 months on scripts. "Scripts are not returned."
Terms: Agent receives 10% commission on domestic sales; 10% commission on foreign sales. Offers written contract. 100% of business is derived from commissions on sales.
Tips: Obtains new clients through recommendations from others.

‡WILLIAM KERWIN AGENCY, (II), 1605 N. Cahuenga, Suite 202, Hollywood CA 90028. (213)469-5155. Contact: Al Wood and Bill Kerwin. Estab. 1979. Signatory of WGA. Represents 5 clients. Currently handles: 100% movie scripts.
Handles: Considers these fiction areas: mystery/suspense; romance; science fiction; thriller/espionage. Query. Reports in 1 day on queries; 2-4 weeks on mss.
Terms: Agent receives 10% commission on domestic sales; 10% on foreign sales. Offers written contract, binding for 1-2 years, with 30 day cancellation clause.
Fees: Offers free criticism service.
Tips: Obtains new clients through recommendations and solicitation. "Listen. Be nice."

THE JOYCE KETAY AGENCY, (II, III), 1501 Broadway, Suite 1908, New York NY 10036. (212)354-6825. Fax: (212)354-6732. Contact: Joyce Ketay, Carl Mulert. Playwrights and screenwriters only. No novels. Member of AAR. Member agents: Joyce Ketay, Carl Mulert, Wendy Streeter.
Handles: Movie scripts (feature film), TV scripts (TV mow, episodic drama, sitcom). Considers these script subject areas: action/adventure; comedy; contemporary issues; detective/police/crime; ethnic; experimental; family saga; fantasy; feminist; gay; glitz; historical; juvenile; lesbian; mainstream; mystery/suspense; psychic/supernatural; romantic comedy and drama; thriller; westerns/frontier.
Recent Sales: *Angels in America,* by Tony Kushner (Robert Altman and Avenue Pictures).

KICK ENTERTAINMENT, (I), 1934 E. 123rd St., Cleveland OH 44106-1912. Phone/fax: (216)791-2515. Contact: Sam Klein. Estab. 1992. Signatory of WGA. Represents 8 clients. 100% of clients are new/previously unpublished writers. Currently handles: 100% movie scripts. Member agents: Geno Trunzo (director-creative affairs); Fred Landsmann (TV).
Handles: Movie scripts (feature film). Considers these script subject areas: action/adventure; comedy; detective/police/crime; family saga; fantasy; horror; mainstream; military/war; mystery/suspense; psychic/supernatural; romantic comedy and drama; science fiction; thriller/espionage; true crime/investigative; westerns/frontier. Query. Reports in 2 weeks on queries; 6-8 weeks on mss.
Terms: Agent receives 10% commission on domestic sales; 10% on foreign sales. Offers written contract, binding for 1 or 2 years.
Tips: "Always send a query letter first, and enclose a SASE. We now presently represent clients in six states."

PAUL KOHNER, INC., (IV), 9300 Wilshire Blvd., Suite 555, Beverly Hills CA 90212-3211. (310)550-1060. Contact: Gary Salt. Estab. 1938. Member of ATA, signatory of WGA. Represents 150 clients. 10% of clients are new/previously unpublished writers. Specializes in film and TV rights sales and representation of film and TV writers.
Handles: Firm/TV rights to published books; movie scripts (feature film, documentary, animation), TV scripts (TV mow, miniseries, episodic drama, sitcom, variety show, animation; soap opera), stage plays. Considers these script subject areas: action/adventure; comedy; detective/police/crime; ethnic; family saga; feminist; historical; mainstream; mystery/suspense; romantic comedy and drama. Query with SASE. Reports in 3-4 weeks on queries.

AGENTS WHO SPECIALIZE in a specific subject area such as computer books or in handling the work of certain writers such as gay or lesbian writers are ranked **IV**.

Terms: Agent receives 10% commission on domestic sales; 10% on foreign sales. Offers written contract, binding for 1-3 years. "We charge for copying manuscripts or scripts for submission unless a sufficient quantitiy is supplied by the author. All unsolicited material is automatically returned unread."

‡**THE KOPALOFF COMPANY, (III)**, 6440 Olympic Blvd., Los Angeles CA 90048. (213)782-1854. Fax: (213)782-1877. Contact: Don Kopaloff. Estab. 1976. Member of AFF, DGA, signatory of WGA.
Handles: Movie scripts, TV scripts. Considers all script subject areas. Query. Reports in 1 month if interested. After query letter is accepted, writer must sign release. Not accepting unsolicited mss.
Terms: Agent receives 10% commission on domestic sales; 10% commission on foreign sales.

THE CANDACE LAKE AGENCY, (II, IV), 822 S. Robertson Blvd., #200, Los Angeles CA 90035. (310)289-0600. Fax: (310)289-0619. Contact: Elizabeth Thomas. Estab. 1977. Signatory of WGA, member of DGA. 50% of clients are new/previously unpublished writers. Specializes in screenplay and teleplay writers. Currently handles: 20% novels; 40% movie scripts; 40% TV scripts.
Handles: Movie scripts (feature film), TV scripts (TV mow, episodic drama, sitcom). Considers all script subject areas. Query with SASE. Reports in 1 month on queries; 3 months on scripts.
Also Handles: Novels. Considers all fiction types. Query with SASE. Reports in 1 month on queries; 3 months on mss.
Terms: Agent receives 10% commission on domestic sales; 10% on foreign sales. Offers written contract, binding for 2 years. Charges for photocopying. 100% of business is derived from commissions on sales.
Tips: Obtains new clients through referrals.

☐**L. HARRY LEE LITERARY AGENCY, (II)**, Box #203, Rocky Point NY 11778-0203. (516)744-1188. Contact: L. Harry Lee. Estab. 1979, member of Dramatists Guild. Represents 285 clients. 65% of clients are new/previously unpublished writers. Specializes in movie scripts. "Comedy is our strength, both features and sitcoms, also movie of the week, science fiction, novels and TV. We have developed two sitcoms of our own." Currently handles: 30% novels; 50% movie scripts; 5% stage plays; 15% TV scripts. Member agents: Mary Lee Gaylor (episodic TV, feature films); Charles Rothery (feature films, sitcoms, movie of the week); Katie Polk (features, mini-series, children's TV); Patti Roenbeck (science fiction, fantasy, romance, historical romance); Frank Killeen (action, war stories, American historical, westerns); Hollister Barr (mainstream, feature films, romantic comedies); Edwina Berkman (novels, contemporary, romance, mystery); Sal Senese (motion picture screenplays, mows, original TV episodic series, sitcoms); Judith Faria (all romance, fantasy, mainstream); Charis Biggis (plays, historical novels, westerns, action/suspense/thriller films); Stacy Parker (love stories, socially significant stories/films, time travel science fiction); Jane Breoge (sitcoms, after-school specials, mini-series, episodic TV); Cami Callirgos (mainstream/contemporary/humor, mystery/suspense); Vito Brenna (action/adventure, romantic comedy, feature films); Anastassia Evereaux (feature films, romantic comedies).
   ● This agency favors comedy. They're trying to get away from violence, trying to be entertaining instead of thrilling. They don't represent anything in the horror genre.
Handles: Movie scripts (feature film), TV scripts (TV mow, episodic drama, sitcom), stage plays. Considers these script subject areas: action/adventure; comedy; contemporary issues; detective/police/crime; family saga; fantasy; feel good family stories; foreign intrigue; historical; mainstream; mystery/suspense; psychic/supernatural; reality shows; romantic drama (futuristic, contemporary, historical); science fiction; sports; thriller; westerns/frontier; zany comedies. Query "with a short writing or background résumé of the writer. A SASE is a must. No dot matrix, we don't read them." Reports in "return mail" on queries; 1 month on mss. "We notify the writer when to expect a reply."
Recent Sales: *Movie/TV mow optioned/sold*: The City Island Messenger, by James G. Kingston (Lighthorse); Who's the Fox? Who's the Hunter?, by James E. Colaneri (Universal Pictures); How Dare They . . . , by James E. Colaneri (Lighthorse Prods.). *Movie/TV mow in development*: Everybody in This Place is Innocent (sitcom). *Scripting assignments*: Manhunt, by Joe Riccardi (CBS); Terror @ Ten, by Rick Seron (NBC).
Also Handles: Novels. Considers these fiction areas: action/adventure; detective/police/crime; erotica; family saga; fantasy; historical; humor/satire; literary; mainstream; mystery/suspense; romance (contemporary, gothic, historical, regency); science fiction; sports; thriller/espionage; westerns/frontier; young adult.
Books: *Forever*, by Patricia Roenbeck (Zebra); *On A Midnight Road*, by Robert Beine (Freeman Press); *Cutter's Way*, by Ginny Fleming (Simon & Schuster).
Terms: Agent receives 10% on movie/TV scripts and plays; 15% commission on domestic sales; 20% on foreign sales. Offers written contract "by the manuscript which can be broken by mutual consent; the length is as long as the copyright runs."

INSIDER REPORT

Agent as mentor: risk + forbearance = *Turk-182*

Agents acquire writers who prove they can deliver a polished script. Thus most agents need a finished, strong and saleable manuscript in hand before they'll invest time in a writer. But is it possible for an agent who has rejected a writer's submission to spend time on that writer when the writer has nothing close to saleable in sight? It's not likely, but, yes, it does happen.

James Kingston spent most of the 1970s going to school, acquiring advanced degrees, and holding down jobs as hospital administrator, social worker, special education teacher, and even karate instructor. All the while he kept writing fiction, eventually completing two unpublished novels. After he finished his second novel, however, Kingston's novel

James Kingston

writing career crashed. That's because he met agent L. Harry Lee.

"Harry was running some writer's workshops I attended. I gave him my material and he said he'd read it." Read it Lee did, but he wasn't too impressed with the saleability of Kingston's fiction. In fact, Lee was so unwilling to represent either novel that he encouraged Kingston to refrain from trying to improve or rewrite the material—and he told Kingston he didn't want to see another word of his fiction, that Kingston ought to chuck fiction writing altogether.

Sounds like a great way to start an author-agent relationship. Says Kingston, "Harry called and said my novels were written more like screenplays than novels. To him they were just massive treatments, nothing more. He was right, because once he said that I realized I'd always been much more interested in theater and motion pictures than I was in literature, so I guess that showed in my writing."

But Kingston had no experience writing screenplays. "I told Harry I knew nothing about how to write a screenplay. I said, 'if you can show me what to do—how to write a script—I'll do it.' I didn't think he'd respond favorably, but—surprisingly—he didn't turn down my request. He taught me how to write a screenplay."

Germinal to this instruction were Lee's workshops. "It really dawned on me during those seminars that the screenplay format is not material that lends itself to be read by one individual. It has to be a group reading, like a play. You have to hear the lines come back to you from different people. You get to see how someone can unintentionally emphasize what you think is the wrong word and the whole meaning of the dialogue changes, sometimes for the better, sometimes not. But you get to notice how hearing something can totally change the meaning from what you intended when you put it on the page."

By going through these workshops and dedicating himself to writing, Kingston had a few polished scripts he wanted Lee to represent. Lee agreed to represent them but encouraged Kingston not to worry too much about selling the material, to expect many rejection letters at this early stage in his career. After a few years of writing and trying to sell what Kingston now calls "pretty weak scripts," he decided to write a treatment based on his unfortunate experience with a Bronx graffiti artist who had taken the liberty of turning Kingston's van into a spraypainter's canvas. He pitched the treatment at a workshop and took it to Lee as well, who liked the idea. Kingston proceeded to write the screenplay and sent it to Lee. When Lee read it, he immediately called Kingston, saying, "I'm going to send this out and this one is going to sell." Two years and 105 rejection letters later, the script remained unsold. But Lee kept insisting, "Don't worry. I know this story is going to be picked up and made into a picture. We just need to give it more time."

Through a series of freak yet propitious happenings, Kingston's script landed in the hands of Hollywood executive Dyan Cannon. She read the script on a flight from L.A. to New York and fell in love with it. Once in New York, she immediately arranged a meeting with Kingston and after talking with him for three hours she was impressed with him and had her personal manager fly to New York the next day to speak with Kingston. Not surprisingly, Kingston began to suspect the script was going to be turned into a movie. But no. Cannon liked his writing but didn't want his script; she just wanted him to cowrite a movie with her for Interscope. Kingston agreed, of course, and was handsomely paid for his efforts, but this movie—which he spent a year writing with Cannon—was never made. Despite spending an entire year hobnobbing and rubbing elbows with some of Hollywood's major players, Kingston still had no viable motion picture script with his name stamped on it—and Lee, unfortunately, hadn't yet collected any commissions from Kingston's writing.

But all was not in vain. To Kingston's surprise, that project with Cannon prompted Interscope to approach Kingston with an offer for the script of *Turk-182*—two years after they rejected it. As Kingston relates the story: "They came to me and said, 'Now we'd like to make *Turk-182*. We're making *Revenge of the Nerds* and *Three Men and a Baby* and we want to make *Turk-182* also." Kingston received a generous contract; the movie was made, and the ever-patient Harry Lee finally reaped some commission benefits off Kingston's writing.

A happy tale indeed, but two questions remain: Why did Lee opt to invest time in Kingston's career without even seeing a partial script? And why, after so many rejections, would he spend so much time working with Kingston even though he was making not a penny from his work? "He must have seen some possible script potential in those two novels, because I was not a strong writer when Harry took me on," says Kingston. "He must have felt that either he could do something good for me, he could make money off me, or both. Harry's a nice guy, of course, but writers have to face it: An agent is not in it for his health. The agent is there to keep himself in business, and every time he sends out a script he's really putting his own reputation on the line. So, no, it doesn't make business sense for an agent to spend any time on somebody who's not going to be

INSIDER REPORT, *Kingston*

financially beneficial, but his faith in me proved worthwhile. I guess he knew he'd cash in someday."

Although Lee's motive for sticking with Kingston might have been purely financial, for Kingston Lee is much more than an agent who takes 10% of his earnings, negotiates his deals, and safeguards his rights. Lee is Kingston's mentor, a guide who reminds him of his writing abilities and his role in the movie's production.

"Few people think they can be the director, actor or producer, but everybody thinks he can be the writer. Harry, however, has been very insistent on letting me know that I'm the writer and all these other people are not. Keeping that in mind really helps me trust what I want to do with a script," says Kingston. "My feeling is that we have an instructor-student relationship, and I think that becomes ingrained because he keeps steering me in the right directions. He pushes me to take the idea to the page. Then he takes the idea to the studios. And hopefully we then take everything to the big screen."

—*Don Prues*

Fees: Does not charge a reading fee. Criticism service: $215 for screenplays; $165 for mow; $95 for TV sitcom; $215 for a mini-series; $1 per page for one-act plays. "All of the agents and readers write carefully thought-out critiques, five-page checklist, two to four pages of notes, and a manuscript that is written on, plus tip sheets and notes that may prove helpful. It's a thorough service, for which we have received the highest praise." Charges for postage, handling, photocopying per submission, "not a general fee." 90% of business is derived from commissions on ms sales. 10% is derived from criticism services. Payment of a criticism fee does not ensure representation.
Tips: Obtains new clients through recommendations, "but mostly queries. If interested in agency representation, write a good story with interesting characters and that's hard to do. Learn your form and format. Take courses, workshops. Read *Writer's Digest*; it's your best source of great information."

LEGACIES (V), 501 Woodstork Circle, Bradenton FL 34209. Phone/fax: (941)792-9159. Executive Director: Mary Ann Amato. Estab. 1993. Signatory of WGA, member of Florida Motion Picture & Television Association, Board of Talent Agents, Dept. of Professional Regulations License No. TA 0000404. 50% of clients are new/previously unpublished writers. Specializes in screenplays. Currently handles: 10% fiction books; 80% screenplays; 10% stage plays.
Handles: Movie scripts (feature film); TV scripts (TV mow); stage plays. Considers these script subject areas: contemporary issues; ethnic; family saga; feminist; historical; humor/satire. Query, then send entire ms. Enclose SASE. Reports in 2 weeks on queries; 6 weeks on mss.
Recent Sales: *Movie optioned/sold*: *Journey from the Jacarandas*, by Patricia A. Friedberg (Eva Monley, producer of *A Far Away Place*). *Movie in development*: *Progress of the Sun*, by Patricia A. Friedberg. *TV MOW in development*: *Shillings*, by Gail Griffin & Janet Noel Sadler (Karen Kramer, KNK Productions).
Terms: Agent receives 15% commission on domestic sales; 20% on foreign sales (WGA percentages on member sales). Offers written contract.
Tips: "Unfortunately, we are too busy to accept new clients for the 1997 year."

LENHOFF/ROBINSON TALENT AND LITERARY AGENCY, INC., (III), 1728 S. La Cienega Blvd., 2nd Floor, Los Angeles CA 90035. (310)558-4700. Fax: (310)558-4440. Contact: Lloyd Robinson. Estab. 1992. Signatory of WGA, franchised by DGA/SAG. Represents 150 clients. 10% of screenwriting clients are new/previously unpublished writers; all are WGA members. "We represent screenwriters, playwrights, novelists and producers, directors." Currently handles: 15% novels; 40% movie scripts; 40% TV scripts; 5% stage plays. Member agents: Charles Lenhoff; Lloyd Robinson; Frank Balkan; Boyd Hancock; Paul McCrillis.
Handles: Movie scripts (feature film, documentary); TV scripts (TV mow, miniseries, episodic drama, variety show); stage play; CD-ROM. Considers these script subject areas: action/adventure; cartoon/

animation; comedy; contemporary issues; detective/police/crime; erotica; ethnic; experimental; family saga; fantasy; mainstream; mystery/suspense; psychic/supernatural; religious/inspirational; romantic comedy and drama; science fiction; sports; teen; thriller; western/frontier. Send outline/proposal, synopsis or log line.

Recent Sales: *Movie scripts optioned/sold*: *Return of Philo T. McGiffen*, by David Poyer; *The Listener*, by Burt Prelutsky; "Harry Denton Series" of novels, by Steve Womack; "Krista Lied," by Mark Homer. *Scripting assignments*: "Fire on the Mountain," by Steve Womack; "J.A.G.," by R. Scott Gemmill; *Walker Texas Ranger*, by Ron Swanson. "We sell or place most of our writers for staff positions in TV and movies. Scripts are sold to individual producing companies and studios."

Terms: Agent receives 10% commission on domestic sales; 10% on foreign sales. Offers written contract, binding for 2 years minimum. Charges for photocopying/messenger when required.

Tips: Obtains new clients only through referral. "We are a talent agency specializing in the copyright business. Fifty percent of our clients generate copyright—screenwriters, playwrights and novelists. Fifty percent of our clients service copyright—producers, directors and cinematographers. We represent only produced, published and/or WGA writers who are eligible for staff TV positions as well as novelists and playwrights whose works may be adapted for film on television."

LINDSTROM LITERARY GROUP, (I), 871 N. Greenbrier St., Arlington VA 22205-1220. (703)522-4730. Fax: (703)527-7624. E-mail: lindlitgrp@aol.com. Contact: Kristin Lindstrom. Estab. 1994. Represents 22 clients. 40% of clients are new/previously unpublished writers. Currently handles: 20% nonfiction books; 70% novels; 10% movie scripts/TV scripts. Member agent: Perry Lindstrom (nonfiction, film/TV scripts).
   ● See the expanded listing for this agency in Literary Agents: Nonfee-charging.

MAJOR CLIENTS AGENCY, (III), 345 N. Maple Dr., #395, Beverly Hills CA 90210. (310)205-5000. (310)205-5099. Contact: Donna Williams Fontno. Estab. 1985. Signatory of WGA. Represents 200 clients. No clients are new/previously unpublished writers. Specializes in TV writers, creators, directors and film writers/directors. Currently handles: 30% movie scripts; 70% TV scripts.

Handles: Movie scripts (feature films); TV scripts (TV mow, sitcom). Considers these script subject areas: detective/police/crime; erotica; family saga; horror; mainstream; mystery/suspense; sports; thriller/espionage. Send outline/proposal. Reports in 2 weeks on queries; 1 month on scripts.

Terms: Agent receives 10% commission on domestic sales; 10% on foreign sales. Offers written contract.

MANUS & ASSOCIATES LITERARY AGENCY, INC. (II), 417 E. 57th St., Suite 5D, New York NY 10022. (212)644-8020. Fax: (212)644-3374. Contact: Janet Wilkens Manus. Also: 430 Cowper St., Palo Alto CA 94301. (415)617-4556. Fax: (415)617-4546. Contact: Jillian Manus. Estab. 1985. Member of AAR. Represents 75 clients. 15% of clients are new/previously unpublished writers. Specializes in quality fiction, mysteries, thrillers, true crime, health, pop psychology. Currently handles: 60% nonfiction books; 10% juvenile books; 20% novels; 25% film rights, TV and feature films.
   ● See the expanded listing for this agency in Literary Agents: Nonfee-charging.

‡MERIDIAN TALENT, INC., (I, II), 499 N. Canon Dr., Third Floor, Beverly Hills CA 90210. (310)652-7799. Fax: (310)854-3966. Contact: Arthur Braun. Estab. 1995. Represents 2 clients. 100% of clients are new/previously unpublished writers. Specializes in screenplays. Currently handles: 100% movie scripts.

Handles: Nonfiction books, juvenile books, movie scripts, scholarly books, novels, TV scripts, stage plays. Considers these nonfiction areas: business; education; how-to; humor; juvenile nonfiction; music/dance/theater/film; self-help/personal improvement. Considers these fiction areas: horror; picture book; romance. Send entire ms. Reports in 1 week on queries; 1 month on mss.

Terms: Agent receives 10% commission on domestic sales; 15% on foreign sales. Offers negotiable written contract, with a negotiable cancellation clause.

Tips: Obtains new clients through solicitation and recommendations.

METROPOLITAN TALENT AGENCY, (III), 4526 Wilshire Blvd., Los Angeles CA 90010. (213)857-4500. Fax: (213)857-4599. Contact: Andy Howard. Estab. 1990. Signatory of WGA. 20% of clients are new/previously unpublished writers. Specializes in feature film, TV rights, novels, screen-

---

‡   THE DOUBLE DAGGER before a listing indicates the listing is new in
     this edition.

plays, stories for the big screen or TV. Currently handles: 10% nonfiction books; 10% novels; 10% novellas; 50% movie scripts; 10% TV scripts; 10% short story collections.
Handles: Movie scripts (feature film, documentary, animation); TV scripts (TV mow,miniseries, sit-com, animation); theatrical stage plays. Considers these script subject areas: action/adventure; cartoon/animation; comedy; contemporary issues; detective/police/crime; erotica; family saga; fantasy; glitz; horror; juvenile; mainstream; mystery/suspense; psychic/supernatural; religious/inspirational; romantic comedy and drama; science fiction; teen; thriller; western/frontier. Query with outline/proposal. Reports in 3 weeks on queries.
Terms: Agent receives 10% commission on domestic sales; 10% on foreign sales. Offers written contract. 100% of business is derived on commissions on sales.
Also Handles: Nonfiction books, scholarly books, juvenile books, novels, novellas, short story collections. Considers these nonfiction areas: biography/autobiography; current affairs; history; humor; nature/environment; popular culture; true crime/investigative. Considers these fiction areas: action/adventure; cartoon/comic; confessional; contemporary issues; detective/police/crime; family saga; fantasy; glitz; historical; horror; humor/satire; mainstream; mystery/suspense; romance (contemporary, gothic, historical); science fiction; thriller/espionage. Query with outline/proposal.

MONTEIRO ROSE AGENCY, (II), 17514 Ventura Blvd., #205, Encino CA 91316. (818)501-1177. Fax: (818)501-1194. Contact: Milissa Brockish. Estab. 1987. Signatory of WGA. Represents 50 clients. Specializes in scripts for animation, TV, film and interactive. Currently handles: 40% movie scripts; 20% TV scripts; 40% animation. Member agents: Candace Monteiro (literary); Fredda Rose (literary); Milissa Brockish (literary/interactive). Currently handles: movie scripts, TV scripts.
Handles: Movie scripts (feature film, animation), TV scripts (TV mow, episodic drama, animation). Considers these script subjects: action/adventure; cartoon/animation; comedy; contemporary issues; detective/police/crime; ethnic; family saga; fantasy; historical; humor; juvenile; mainstream; mystery/suspense; psychic/supernatural; romantic comedy and drama; science fiction; teen; thriller; western/frontier. Query with SASE. Reports in 1 week on queries; 6 weeks on mss.
Terms: Agent receives 10% commission on domestic sales. Offers standard WGA 2 year contract, with 120 day cancellation clause. Charges for photocopying. 100% of business is derived from commissions.
Tips: Obtains new clients through recommendations from others in the entertainment business and query letters. "It does no good to call and try to speak to an agent before they hae read your material, unless referred by someone we know, and then it's best if the referral calls. The best and only way, if you're a new writer, is to send a query letter with a SASE. If an agent is interested, they will request to read it. Also enclose a SASE with the script if you want it back."

☐**MONTGOMERY LITERARY AGENCY, (II)**, P.O. Box 8822, Silver Spring MD 20907-8822. (301)230-1807. Contact: M.E. Olsen. Estab. 1984. Signatory of WGA. 25% of clients are new/previously unpublished writers. Equal interest in scripts (films, TV and videos) and books—"especially in receiving copies of published mystery, western or action/adventure books to review for possible script use." Currently handles: 12% nonfiction books; 2% poetry; 5% juvenile books; 25% novels; 30% movie scripts; 20% TV scripts; 1% stage plays; 1% short story collections; 2% syndicated material; 2% other (comics, etc.).
Handles: Movie scripts (feature film); TV scripts; stage plays. Considers these script subject areas: action/adventure; comedy; contemporary issues; detective/police/crime; mystery/suspense; romantic comedy; science fiction; western. Send entire script with synopsis. Reports in 1 month on queries; 2 months on mss.
Terms: Agent receives 10% commission on scripts.
Also Handles: Nonfiction books, juvenile books, novels, syndicated material. Considers these nonfiction areas: art/architecture/design; biography; business; child guidance; computers; cooking/food/nutrition; crafts/hobbies; current affairs; education; ethnic/cultural interests; government/politics/law; health; history; how-to; humor; juvenile nonfiction; language/literature/criticism; military/war; money/finance/economics; music/dance/theater/film; nature/environment; New Age; photography; popular culture; psychology; science/technology; self-help/personal improvement; sociology; sports; true crime/investigative. Considers these fiction areas: action/adventure; cartoon/comic; contemporary issues; detective/police/crime; ethnic; historical; horror; humor/satire; juvenile; literary; mainstream; psychic/supernatural; regional; romance (contemporary, historical); science fiction; sports; thriller/espionage; westerns; young adult. Send entire ms with synopsis. For published books, send book or copy of cover with synopsis plus SASE. Reports in 1 month on queries; 2 months on mss.
Terms: Agent receives 15% commission on books and plays.
Fees: No reading fee. Offers criticism service. Offers written contract.

MONTGOMERY-WEST LITERARY AGENCY, (IV), 7450 Butler Hills Dr., Salt Lake City UT 84121-5008. Contact: Carole Western. Estab. 1989. Signatory of WGA. Represents 30 clients. 80% of clients are new/previously unpublished writers. Specializes in movie and TV scripts. Currently handles: 10% novels; 90% movie scripts. Member agents: Carole Western (movie and TV scripts); Nancy Gummery (novel, consultant and editor).

● Prior to opening her agency, Ms. Western was a creative writing teacher, holding a Royal Society Arts degree from London University in English Literature, and interned in two talent literary agencies.

Handles: Movie scripts (feature film), TV scripts (TV mow). Considers these script subject areas: action/adventure; comedy; detective/police/crime; family saga; feminist; glitz; juvenile family; mainstream; mystery/suspense; romantic comedy and drama; science fiction; teen; thriller/espionage. Query with outline, 1st act (approximately 26 pages) and SAE. Reports in 2 months on queries; 10 weeks on mss.

Recent Sales: *Movie sold*: *Spaceless* (20th Century Fox), *Long Hello* (Tonque River), *Hardwired* (Warner Bros.), all by Jeff Vintar. *Scripting assignments*: *The Last Hacker* and *Manplus* (Disney); *Hack*, by Incline Prods; *Joyride* (OPV-Longbow).

Also Handles: Novels.

Recent Sales: *Crystal Pyramid*, *Nightmare Cafe*, and *Winds of Karazan*, *Ancient Circle* and *Fire Goddess*, by Carole Western (Cora Verlag [Germany]).

Terms: Agent receives 10% commission on movie scripts; 15% on foreign sales; 15% on networking sales with other agencies. Charges for telephone, postage and consultations.

Writers' Conferences: Attends 3 workshops a year; WGA west Conference.

Tips: "Send in only the finest product you can and keep synopses and treatments brief and to the point. Have patience and be aware of the enormous competition in the writing field."

DEE MURA ENTERPRISES, INC., (II), 269 West Shore Dr., Massapequa NY 11758-8225. (516)795-1616. Fax: (516)795-8757. E-mail: samurai5@ix.netcom.com. Contact: Dee Mura. Estab. 1987. Signatory of WGA. 50% of clients are new/previously published writers. "We work on everything, but are especially interested in true life stories, true crime and women's stories and issues." Currently handles: 20% nonfiction books; 15% scholarly books; 15% juvenile books; 20% novels; 15% movie scripts; 15% TV scripts.

● See the expanded listing for this agency in Literary Agents: Nonfee-charging.

OTITIS MEDIA, (II), 1926 DuPont Ave. S., Minneapolis MN 55403. (612)377-4918. Fax: (612)377-3096. E-mail: brbotm19@popmail.skypaint.com. Contact: Hannibal Harris. Signatory of WGA. Currently handles: novels; movie scripts; stage plays; TV scripts. Member agents: Hannibal Harris (queries, evaluation of proposals, books) Greg Boylan (screenplays, TV scripts); Ingrid DiLeonardo (script and ms evaluation, story development); B.R. Boylan (novels, nonfiction, screenplays, stage plays).

Handles: Movie scripts (feature film), TV scripts (TV mow), stage plays. Considers these script subject areas: action/adventure; comedy; historical; mystery/suspense; romantic comedy and drama; thriller. Send proposal.

Also Handles: Nonfiction books, novels. Considers these nonfiction areas: anthropology/archaeology; biography/autobiography; health/medicine; history; humor; military/war; music/dance/theater/film; photography; true crime/investigative. Considers these fiction areas: historical; humor/satire; mainstream; thriller/espionage.

Terms: Agent receives 15% on domestic sales; 20% on foreign sales. Offers written contract. "We prefer that the writer supply whatever additional copies we request."

Tips: "Seminars or classes in creative writing alone are insufficient to attract our attention. You should be constantly writing and rewriting before you submit your first work. Correct format, spelling and grammar are essential. We shall respond quickly to a query letter containing a one page outline, a list of your writing credits, and the opening ten pages of only *one* work at a time . . . plus an SASE. (No SASE means we do *not* return anything.) Please, in your query letter, try not to be cute, clever, or hardsell. Save us all the time of having to read about what your relatives, friends, teachers, paid 'editors' or gurus think about your story. Nor do we need a pitch about who will want this book or movie, spend money for it and how much it will earn for writer, editor/producer, and agent. You should, in a few short paragraphs, be able to summarize the work to the point where we'll ask for more. We are appalled to receive works whose cover page is dated and who indicate that this is a first draft. No producer or editor is likely to read a first draft of anything. Please don't call us the day we receive your manuscript, asking us how much we like it. In fact, please don't call us. We'll contact you if we want more."

DOROTHY PALMER, (III), 235 W. 56 St., New York NY 10019. Phone/fax: (212)765-4280. Estab. 1990. Signatory of WGA. Represents 12 clients. 90% of clients are new/previously unpublished writers. Specializes in screenplays, TV. Currently handles: 70% movie scripts, 30% TV scripts.

Handles: Movie scripts (feature film), TV scripts (TV mow, episodic drama, sitcom, soap opera). Considers these script subject areas: comedy; cooking/food/nutrition; current affairs; detective/police/crime; family saga; health/medicine; mainstream; mystery/suspense; romantic comedy; romantic drama; thriller/espionage; true crime/investigative; women's issues/women's studies. Send entire ms with outline/proposal.

Recent Sales: *Movie/TV mow optioned: Love Me or I'll Kill You,* by Anthony King (Maple Hill).

Terms: Agent receives 10% commission on domestic sales; 10% on foreign sales. Offers written contract, binding for 1 year.

Tips: Obtains new clients through recommendations from others. "Do *not* telephone. When I find a script that interests me, I call the writer. Calls to me are a turn-off because it cuts into my reading time."

PANDA TALENT, (II), 3721 Hoen Ave., Santa Rosa CA 95405. (707)576-0711. Fax: (707)544-2765. Contact: Audrey Grace. Estab. 1977. Signatory of WGA, SAG, AFTRA, Equity. Represents 10 clients. 80% of clients are new/previously unpublished writers. Currently handles: 5% novels; 40% TV scripts; 50% movie scripts; 5% stage plays. Story readers: Steven Grace (science fiction/war/action); Vicki Lima (mysterious/romance); Cleo West (western/true stories).

Handles: Movie scripts (feature film); TV scripts (TV mow, episodic drama, sitcom). Handles these script subject areas: action/adventure; animals; comedy; detective/police/crime; ethnic; family saga; military/war; mystery/suspense; romantic comedy and drama; science fiction; true crime/investigative; westerns/frontier. Query with treatment. Reports in 3 weeks on queries; 2 months on mss. Must include SASE.

Terms: Agent receives 10% commission on domestic sales; 10% on foreign sales.

THE PARTOS COMPANY, (II), 6363 Wilshire Blvd., Suite 227, Los Angeles CA 90048. (213)876-5500. Fax: (213)876-7836. Contact: Jim Barquette. Estab. 1991. Signatory of WGA. Represents 20 clients. 50% of clients are new/previously unpublished writers. Specializes in independent features. Currently handles: 90% movie scripts; 10% TV scripts (features only). Member agents: Walter Partos (below the line and literary); Jim Barquette (literary); Cynthia Guber (actors).

Handles: Movie scripts (feature film); TV scripts (TV mow). Considers these script subject areas: action/adventure; comedy; contemporary issues; detective/police/crime; ethnic; experimental; family saga; fantasy; feminist; gay; horror; humor; juvenile; lesbian; mainstream; mystery/suspense; psychic/supernatural; romantic comedy and drama; science fiction; teen; thriller. Query. Reports in 1 month on queries; 3 months on scripts.

Terms: Agent receives 10% commission on domestic sales; 10% on foreign sales. Offers written contract, binding for 1 year plus WGA Rider W. 100% of business is derived from commissions on sales.

PELHAM LITERARY AGENCY, (I), 2290 E. Fremont Ave., Suite C, Littleton CO 80122. (303)347-0623. Contact: Howard Pelham. Estab. 1994. Represents 10 clients. 50% of clients are new/previously unpublished writers. Specializes in genre fiction. Owner has published 15 novels in these categories. Currently handles: 10% nonfiction books; 80% novels; 10% short story collections.

• See the expanded listing for this agency in Literary Agents: Nonfee-charging.

‡BARRY PERELMAN AGENCY, (II), 9200 Sunset Blvd., #1201, Los Angeles CA 90069. (310)274-5999. Fax: (310)274-6445. Contact: Chris Robert. Estab. 1982. Signatory of WGA, DGA. Represents 40 clients. 15% of clients are new/previously unpublished writers. Specializes in motion pictures/packaging. Currently handles: 4% nonfiction books; 60% movie scripts; 10% novels; 25% TV scripts; 1% stage plays. Member agents: Barry Perelman (motion picture/TV/packaging/below-the-line); Chris Robert (motion picture/TV).

Handles: Movie scripts. Considers these nonfiction areas: biography/autobiography; current affairs; government/politics/law; history; military/war; true crime/investigative. Considers these fiction areas: action/adventure; detective/police/crime; historical; horror; mystery/suspense; romance (contemporary); science fiction; thriller/espionage. Send outline/proposal with query. Reports in 1 month.

Terms: Agent receives 10% commission on domestic sales; 10% on foreign sales. Offers written contract, binding for 1-2 years. Charges for postage and photocopying.

Tips: Obtains new clients through recommendations and query letters.

IF YOU'RE LOOKING for a particular agent, check the Agents Index to find at which agency the agent works. Then check the listing for that agency in the appropriate section.

STEPHEN PEVNER, INC., (II), 248 W. 73rd St., 2nd Floor, New York NY 10023. (212)496-0474. Fax: (212)496-0796. E-mail: spevner@aol.com. Contact: Stephen Pevner. Estab. 1991. Member of AAR, signatory of WGA. Represents under 50 clients. 50% of clients are new/previously unpublished writers. Specializes in motion pictures, novels, humor, pop culture, urban fiction, independent filmmakers. Currently handles: 25% nonfiction books; 25% novels; 25% movie scripts; TV scripts; stage plays.
- Mr. Pevner represents a number of substantial independent writer/directors. See the expanded listing for this agency in Literary Agents: Nonfee-charging.

A PICTURE OF YOU, (II), 1176 Elizabeth Dr., Hamilton OH 45013-3507. (513)863-2993. Fax: (513)825-2409. E-mail: apictureofyou@prodigy.com. Contact: Lenny Minelli. Estab. 1993. Signatory of WGA. Represents 25 clients. 60% of clients are new/previously unpublished writers. Specializes in screenplays and TV scripts. Currently handles: 70% movie scripts; 20% TV scripts; 10% syndicated material.
Handles: Movie scripts (feature film), TV scripts (miniseries, episodic drama, soap opera, syndicated material). Considers these script subject areas: action/adventure; comedy; detective/police/crime; erotica; family saga; fantasy; gay; horror; mainstream; mystery/suspense; psychic/supernatural; religious/inspirational; romantic drama; thriller; western/frontier. Query with SASE first. Reports in 3 weeks on queries; 1 month on scripts.
Also Handles: Nonfiction books, novels, novellas, short story collections. Considers these nonfiction areas: gay/lesbian issues; history; juvenile nonfiction; music/dance/theatre/film; religious/inspirational; self-help/personal. Considers these fiction areas: action/adventure; detective/police/crime; erotica; ethnic; family saga; fantasy; gay; glitz; historical; horror; lesbian; literary; mainstream; mystery/suspense; religious; romance (contemporary, gothic, historical); thriller/espionage; westerns/frontier; young adult.
Recent Sales: *Movie/TV mow optioned/in development: Don't Leave*, by Tina Novarro (Randy Neuman); *Satan and the Saint*, by Alex LaPerchia (Lee Thornburg); and *The Golem*, by Scott Wegener (David Garrison).
Terms: Agent receives 10% commission on domestic sales; 15% on foreign sales. Offers written contract, binding for 1 year, with 90 day cancellation clause. Charges for postage/express mail and long distance calls. 100% of business is derived from commissions on sales.
Tips: Obtains new clients through recommendations and queries. "Make sure that the script is the best it can be before seeking an agent."

□PMA LITERARY AND FILM MANAGEMENT, INC., 132 W. 22nd St., 12th Floor, New York NY 10011-1817. (212)929-1222. Fax: (212)206-0238. E-mail: pmalitfilm@aol.com. President: Peter Miller. Member agents: Jennifer Robinson (film and fiction); Yuri Skuins (fiction and nonfiction); Jody Saltzman. Estab. 1975. Represents 80 clients. 50% of clients are new/unpublished writers. Specializes in commercial fiction and nonfiction, thrillers, true crime and "fiction with *real* motion picture and television potential." Currently handles: 50% fiction; 25% nonfiction; 25% screenplays.
- See the expanded listing for this agency in the Literary Agents: Fee-charging.

‡PREMIERE ARTISTS AGENCY, (V), 8899 Beverly Blvd., Suite 510, Los Angeles CA 90048. Fax: (310)205-3981. Estab. 1992. Member of DGA, SAG and AFTRA, signatory of WGA. Represents 200 clients. 10% of clients are new/previously unpublished writers. Specializes in top writers for TV and feature films; top directors for TV/features. Currently handles: 40% movie scripts, 20% novels, 40% TV scripts. Member agents: Susan Sussman (TV/motion picture writers and directors and producers); John Ufland (novels/TV and motion picture writers and directors); Deborah Deuble (TV/motion picture writers, novels); Sheryl Peterson (motion picture writers/directors); Kirk Braufman (motion picture writers/actors); Mike Packennam (actors—talent); Karen Goldberg (actors, talent); Julie Hoxie (actors, talent); Richard Sanke (TV/motion picture writers and directors); Lori Smaller (writers and actors—talent).
Handles: Movie scripts, TV scripts. Considers these nonfiction areas: how-to; humor. Considers these fiction areas: action/adventure; cartoon/comic; contemporary issues; detective/police/crime; erotica; ethnic; experimental; family saga; fantasy; feminist; gay; historical; humor/satire; juvenile; lesbian; mainstream; mystery/suspense; psychic/supernatural; romance (contemporary, gothic, historical, regency); science fiction; sports; thriller/espionage; westerns/frontier. Query. "Unsolicited scripts will be returned unopened." Responds only if interested.
Terms: Agent receives 10% commission on domestic sales; 10% on foreign sales. Offers written contract.
Also Handles: Novels. Considers these fiction areas: action/adventure, cartoon/comic; contemporary issues; detective/police/crime; erotica; ethnic; family saga; fantasy; feminist; gay; glitz; historical; horror; humor/satire; juvenile; lesbian; literary; mainstream; mystery/suspense; psychic/supernatural; romance (contemporary, gothic, historical); science fiction; sports; thriller/espionage; westerns/frontier; young adult. Query with SASE and industry referrals.

Tips: "99% of the time, new clients are obtained from recommendations—primarily from studio executives, producers, lawyers and managers. The best way to find an agent is to obtain an entertainment attorney or manager."

PRODUCERS & CREATIVES GROUP, (II), 7060 Hollywood Blvd., Suite 1025, Los Angeles CA 90028. (213)465-1600. Fax: (213)461-2967. Contact: Sue Waldman. Estab. 1992. Represents 54 clients. 10% of clients are new/previously unpublished writers. Specializes in family entertainment. Currently handles: 50% movie scripts; 40% TV scripts; 10% short story collections. Member agents: George Bailey; Adam Dearden; Sue Waldman; Matt Goldberg (story editor).
Handles: Movie scripts (feature film), TV scripts (TV mow, miniseries episodic drama, sitcom, soap opera). Considers these script subject areas: contemporary issues; detective/police/crime; ethnic; family saga; fantasy; feminist; horror; juvenile; mainstream; mystery/suspense; romantic comedy and drama; psychic/supernatural; teen; thriller. Send outline/proposal with SASE. Reports in 2 weeks on queries; 2 months on mss.
Also Handles: Short story collections. Considers these nonfiction areas: biography/autobiography; juvenile nonfiction; popular culture; true crime/investigative. Considers these fiction areas: detective/police/crime; family saga; fantasy; horror; juvenile; mainstream; picture book; romance (contemporary); science fiction; thriller/espionage. Reports in 5 days on queries; 2 months on mss.
Terms: Agent receives 10% commission on domestic sales; 10% on foreign sales. Offers written contract, binding for 1 year, with 30 day cancellation clause. 100% of business is derived from commissions on sales.
Tips: Obtains new clients through recommendation and references.

‡THE QUILLCO AGENCY, (II), 3104 W. Cumberland Court, Westlake Village CA 91362. (805)495-8436. Fax: (805)297-4469. Contact: Stacy Billings (owner). Estab. 1993. Signatory of WGA. Represents 70 clients.
Handles: Movie scripts (feature film, documentary, animation), TV scripts (TV mow). No Vietnam, Mob, women-bashing, or exploitation films. Query. Reports in 1 month on queries.
Terms: Agent receives 10% commission on domestic sales; 10% on foreign sales.

REDWOOD EMPIRE AGENCY, (II), P.O. Box 1946, Guerneville CA 95446-1146. (707)869-1146. E-mail: redemp@aol.com. Contact: Jim Sorrells or Rodney Shull. Estab. 1992. Represents 6 clients. 90% of clients are new/previously unpublished writers. Specializes in screenplays, big screen or TV. Currently handles: 100% movie scripts.
Handles: Movie scripts (feature film, TV mow). Considers these script subject areas: comedy; contemporary issues; erotica; family saga; fantasy; feminist; gay; historical; juvenile; lesbian; romance (contemporary). Query with 1 page synopsis. Reports in 1 week on queries; 1 month on mss.
Terms: Agent receives 10% commission on domestic sales; 10% on foreign sales. Offers criticism service: structure, characterization, dialogue, format style. No fee. "Writer must supply copies of script as needed. We ship and handle."
Tips: Obtains new clients through word of mouth, letter in *Hollywood Scriptwriter*. "Most interested in ordinary people confronting real-life situations."

RENAISSANCE—H.N. SWANSON, (III), 8523 Sunset Blvd., Los Angeles CA 90069. (310)289-3636. Contact: Joel Gotler. Signatory of WGA. Member of SAG, AFTRA, DGA. Represents over 150 clients. 10% of clients are new/previously unpublished writers. Currently handles: 60% novels; 40% movie and TV scripts. Member agents: Irv Schwartz, partner (TV writers); Allan Nevins, partner (book publishing); Brian Lipson, associate (motion pictures writers); Joel Gotler, partner (film rights); Steven Fisher.
● See the expanded listing for this agency in Literary Agents: Nonfee-charging.

STEPHANIE ROGERS AND ASSOCIATES, (III), 3575 Cahuenga Blvd. West, 2nd Floor, Los Angeles CA 90068. (213)851-5155. Owner: Stephanie Rogers. Estab. 1980. Signatory of WGA. Represents 40 clients. 20% of clients are new/unproduced writers. Prefers that the writer has been produced (movies or TV), his/her properties optioned or has references. Prefers to work with published/established authors. Currently handles: 10% novels; 50% movie scripts; 40% TV scripts.
● Prior to opening her agency, Ms. Rogers served as a development executive at Universal TV and Paramount.
Handles: Movie scripts (feature film), TV scripts (TV mow). Considers these script subject areas: action/adventure; dramas (contemporary); romantic comedies; suspense/thrillers. Must be professional in presentation and not over 125 pages. Query. No unsolicited mss. SASE required.
Recent Sales: *TV mow optioned/sold*: The Lady, by Don Henry (Hearst for Lifetime); *Lifeline*, by Bob Hopkins (Movie Vista Productions USA); *Sweetwater Redemption*, by Jeff Elison (Hearst for CBS); *Movie in development*: Prototype, by Doug Lefler (Island Pictures); *Dr. Dazzle*, by Joel Kauffmann and Don Yost (Jones Entertainment); *Pilot/Movie*: Venice Beach, USA, by Bob Hopkins (Len

Hill Productions); *Scripting assignments*: *October Moon*, by Jeff Elison (Turner Pictures); episodic assignments: *Dr. Quinn, Murder, She Wrote, Hercules, Silk Stalkings*, etc.
Also Handles: Novels (only wishes to see those that have been published and can translate to screen).
Terms: Agent receives 10% commission on domestic sales; 10% on dramatic sales; 20% on foreign sales. Charges for phone, photocopying and messenger expenses.
Tips: "When writing a query letter, you should give a short bio of your background, a thumbnail sketch (no more than a paragraph) of the material you are looking to market and an explanation of how or where (books, classes or workshops) you studied screenwriting." Include SASE for response.

VICTORIA SANDERS LITERARY AGENCY, (II), 241 Avenue of the Americas, New York NY 10014-4822. (212)633-8811. Fax: (212)633-0525. Contact: Victoria Sanders and/or Diane Dickensheid. Estab. 1993. Member of AAR, signatory of WGA. Represents 50 clients. 25% of clients are new/previously unpublished writers. Currently handles: 50% nonfiction books; 50% novels.
• See the expanded listing for this agency in Literary Agents: Nonfee-charging.

JACK SCAGNETTI TALENT & LITERARY AGENCY, (III), 5118 Vineland Ave., #102, North Hollywood CA 91601. (818)762-3871. Contact: Jack Scagnetti. Estab. 1974. Signatory of WGA, member of Academy of Television Arts and Sciences. Represents 40 clients. 50% of clients are new/previously unpublished writers. Specializes in film books with many photographs. Currently handles: 20% nonfiction books; 70% movie scripts; 10% TV scripts. Member agents: Jack Scagnetti (nonfiction and screenplays); Leonard Bloom (men's novels).
• See Mr. Scagnetti's article, What Your Script Demands Before an Agent Sees It, in this edition of the *Guide*.
Handles: Movie scripts (feature film), TV scripts (TV mow, episodic drama). Considers these script subject areas: action/adventure; comedy; detective/police/crime; family saga; historical; horror; mainstream; mystery/suspense; romantic comedy and drama; sports; thriller; westerns/frontier. Query with outline/proposal. Reports in 1 month on queries; 2 months on mss.
Also Handles: Nonfiction, novels. Considers these nonfiction areas: biography/autobiography; cooking/food/nutrition; health; current affairs; how-to; military/war; music/dance/theater/film; self-help/personal; sports; true crime/investigative; women's issues/women's studies. Considers these fiction areas: action/adventure; contemporary issues; detective/police/crime; family saga; historical; mainstream; mystery/suspense; picture book; romance (contemporary); sports; thriller/espionage; westerns/frontier.
Recent Sales: *Scripting assignments*: *Star Trek: Voyager* series. *Movie/TV mow optioned*: *Kastner's Cutthroat* (44 Blue Prods). *Movie/TV mow*: *Pain*, feature film (Concorde-New Horizons).
Terms: Agent receives 10% commission on domestic sales; 15% on foreign sales. Offers written contract, binding for 6 months-1 year. Charges for postage and photocopies.
Tips: Obtains new clients through "referrals by others and query letters sent to us. Write a good synopsis, short and to the point and include marketing data for the book."

SUSAN SCHULMAN, A LITERARY AGENCY, (III), 454 W. 44th St., New York NY 10036-5205. (212)713-1633/4/5. Fax: (212)586-8830. E-mail: schulman@aol.com. President: Susan Schulman. Estab. 1979. Member of AAR, Dramatists Guild, Women's Media Group. 10-15% of clients are new/unpublished writers. Prefers to work with published/established authors; works with a small number of new/unpublished authors. Currently handles: 70% nonfiction books; 20% novels; 10% stage plays. Member agents: Clyde Kuemmerle (theater); Angel Butts (theater); Nicole Rajani (foreign rights).
• See the expanded listing for this agency in Literary Agents: Nonfee-charging.

‡SHAPIRO-LICHTMAN, (III), Shapiro-Lichtman Building, 8827 Beverly Blvd., Los Angeles CA 90048. (310)859-8877. Fax: (310)859-7153. Contact: Martin Shapiro. Estab. 1969. Signatory of WGA. 10% of clients are new/previously unpublished writers.
Handles: Nonfiction books, movie scripts, novels, TV scripts, novellas, stage plays. Considers all nonfiction areas. Considers all fiction areas. Query. Reports in 10 days on queries.
Terms: Agent receives 10% commission on domestic sales; 20% on foreign sales. Offers written contract, binding for 2 years.
Tips: Obtains new clients through recommendations from others.

KEN SHERMAN & ASSOCIATES, (III), 9507 Santa Monica Blvd. Beverly Hills CA 90210. (310)273-3840. Fax: (310)271-2875. Contact: Ken Sherman. Estab. 1989. Member of DGA, BAFTA, PEN Int'l, signatory of WGA. Represents 40 clients. 10% of clients are new/previously unpublished writers. Specializes in solid writers for film, TV, books and rights to books for film and TV. Currently handles: nonfiction books, juvenile books, novels, movie scripts, TV scripts.
• Prior to opening his agency, Mr. Sherman was with the William Morris Agency, The Lantz Office, and Paul Kohner, Inc.

Handles: Nonfiction, novels, movie scripts, TV scripts. Considers all nonfiction and fiction areas. *Contact by referral only please.* Reports in approximately 1 month on mss.

Recent Sales: *Brazil*, by John Updike (film rights to Glaucia Carmagos); *Fifth Sacred Thing*, by Starhawk (Bantam); *Questions From Dad*, by Dwight Twilly (Tuttle); *Snow Falling on Cedars*, by David Guterson (Universal Pictures).

Terms: Agent receives 15% commission on domestic sales. Offers written contract. Charges for office expenses, postage, photocopying, negotiable expenses.

Writers' Conferences: Maui; Squaw Valley; Santa Barbara.

Tips: Obtains new clients through recommendations only.

☐**SILVER SCREEN PLACEMENTS, (II)**, 602 65th St., Downers Grove IL 60516-3020. (630)963-2124. Fax: (630)963-1998. E-mail: levin29@mail.idt.net. Contact: William Levin. Estab. 1991. Signatory of WGA. Represents 6 clients. 100% of clients are new/previously unpublished writers. Currently handles: 10% juvenile books, 10% novels, 80% movie scripts.

Handles: Movie scripts (feature film). Considers these script subject areas: action/adventure; comedy; contemporary issues; detective/police/crime; family saga; fantasy; historical; juvenile; mainstream; mystery/suspense; science fiction; thriller/espionage; young adult. Brief query with outline/proposal and SASE. Reports in 1 week on queries; 6 weeks on mss.

Recent Sales: *TV script optioned/sold: Orphan Train*, by Geier (Noci Productions).

Terms: Agent receives 10% commission on domestic sales; 15% on foreign sales. Offers written contract, binding for 2-4 years.

Also Handles: Juvenile books, novels. Considers these nonfiction areas: education; juvenile nonfiction; language/literature/criticism. Consider these fiction areas: action/adventure; cartoon/comic; contemporary issues; detective/police/crime; family saga; fantasy; historical; humor/satire; juvenile; mainstream; mystery/suspense; science fiction; thriller/espionage; young adult.

Fees: Criticism service: $195 per script or ms. Critiques written by contract writer, and are 5-7 pages plus partial editing of work.

Tips: Obtains new clients through recommendations from other parties, as well as being listed with WGA and *Guide to Literary Agents.* "Advise against 'cutsie' inquiry letters."

SISTER MANIA PRODUCTIONS, INC., (III, V), 916 Penn St., Brackenridge PA 15014. (412)226-2964. E-mail: jims@thebridge.com. Contact: Literary Department. Estab. 1978. Signatory of WGA. Represents 12 clients. 20% of clients are new/previously unpublished writers. "We also package, develop and produce." Currently handles: 80% movie scripts, 10% TV scripts, 10% syndicated material.

Handles: Movie scripts (feature film), TV scripts, syndicated material. Considers these script subject areas: action/adventure; comedy; detective/police/crime; experimental; family saga; horror; language/literature/criticism; money/finance/economics; romance; thriller/espionage; true crime/investigative. Query. Reports up to 1 month on queries; 1-2 months on mss.

Also Handles: Nonfiction books, juvenile books, scholarly books, novels. Considers these nonfiction areas: biography/autobiography; business; computers/electronics; history; humor; juvenile nonfiction; military/war; money/finance/economics; music/dance/theater/film; New Age metaphysics; science/technology; self-help/personal improvement; women's issues/women's studies. Considers these fiction areas: action/adventure; contemporary issues; detective/police/crime; ethnic; family saga; fantasy; historical; horror; humor/satire; juvenile; literary; mainstream; mystery/suspense; picture book; romance (contemporary); science fiction; thriller/espionage.

Recent Sales: *Movie/TV mow screenplays optioned: Steelcode; Blood Sisters; The Wanderer.*

Terms: Offers written contract. Offers criticism service, no fees for clients.

Tips: Usually obtains new clients through "very creative query with project creative and executive appeal in maintaining integrity through quality products."

‡**SUSAN SMITH AND ASSOC., (II)**, 121 N. San Vicente Blvd., Beverly Hills CA 90211. (213)852-9777. Fax: (213)658-7170. Estab. 1969. Signatory of WGA. Represents 120 clients. 20% of clients are new/previously unpublished writers. Specializes in screenplays. Member agents: Wendi Niad (feature films); Deborah Obad (TV); Stephen Gates (features).

☐ **AN OPEN BOX** indicates script agents who charge fees to writers. WGA signatories are not permitted to charge for reading manuscripts, but may charge for critiques or consultations.

Handles: Movie scripts, TV scripts. Query. Reports in 1 month on queries.
Terms: Agent receives 10% commission on domestic sales; 10% on foreign sales. Offers written contract, binding for 1-3 years, with a cancellation clause per WGA.
Tips: Obtains new clients through recommendations from others, solicitation.

‡**LEE SOBEL MGMT. ASSOCIATES (LSMA), (II)**, 123 W. 93 St., Suite 2C, New York NY 10025. Phone/fax: (212)865-8356. E-mail: garagerock@aol.com. Contact: Lee Bennett Sobel. Estab. 1991. Represents 15 clients. 50% of clients are new/previously unpublished writers. Specializes in mystery novels and screenplays. Currently handles: 50% movie scripts; 50% novels. Member agents: Margaret Lancaster (development);
Handles: Nonfiction books, movie scripts, novels. Considers these nonfiction areas: art/architecture/ design; biography/autobiography; music/dance/theater/film. Considers these fiction areas: action/adventure; detective/police/crime; horror; mystery/suspense; science fiction; thriller/espionage. Query.
Recent Sales: *Violent Spring*, by Gary Phillips (Berkley); *Perdition, USA*, by Gary Phillips (Berkley).
Terms: Agent receives 15% commission on domestic sales; 15% on foreign sales.
Tips: "Be patient and never call—simply send a brief synopsis and SASE. We will contact the writer if interested. Do not badger us—simply move on to the next agent if unsatisfied with our response."

‡**CAMILLE SORICE AGENCY (II)**, 9950 Canoga Ave., #A5, Chatsworth CA 91311-6703. Contact: Camille Sorice. Estab. 1988. Signatory of WGA.
Handles: Movie scripts (feature film). Considers these script subject areas: action/adventure; comedy; detective/police/crime; family saga; historical; mystery/suspense; romantic comedy and drama; westerns/frontier. Send query letters. Reports in 6 weeks on mss.
Tips: "No calls. Query letters accepted."

STANTON & ASSOCIATES LITERARY AGENCY (II), 4413 Clemson Dr., Garland TX 75042. (214)276-5427. Fax: (214)276-5426. Contact: Henry Stanton, Harry Preston. Estab. 1990. Signatory of WGA. Represents 36 clients. 90% of clients are new screenwriters. Specializes in screenplays only. Currently handles: 50% movie scripts; 50% TV scripts.
  ● Prior to joining the agency, Mr. Preston was with the MGM script department and an author and screenwriter for 40 years.
Handles: Movie scripts (feature film), TV scripts (TV mow). Query. Reports in 1 week on queries; 1 month on screenplays (review).
Recent Sales: *Inner Secrets* (Clarke Entertainment); *For Love and Money* (NBC); *Crossing the Line* (LaMoth Productions); *Splintered Image* (Hearst Entertainment); *Belle and Her Boys* (Bob Banner Associates); *The Body Shop* and *Sisters Revenge* (Esquivel Entertainment).
Terms: Agent receives 15% commission on domestic sales. Offers written contract, binding for 2 years on individual screenplays. Returns scripts with reader's comments.
Tips: Obtains new clients through WGA listing, *Hollywood Scriptwriter*, word of mouth (in Dallas). "We have writers available to edit or ghostwrite screenplays. Fees vary dependent on the writer. All writers should always please enclose a SASE with any queries."

□**STAR LITERARY SERVICE, (II)**, 1540 N. Louis, Tucson AZ 85712-3830. (520)326-4146. Contact: Marilyn Caponegri. Estab. 1990. Signatory of WGA. Represents 9 clients. 80% of clients are new/previously unpublished writers. Currently handles: 100% movie scripts.
Handles: Movie scripts (feature film); TV scripts (TV mow). Considers these script subject areas: action/adventure; biography/autobiography; detective/police/crime; mystery; psychic/supernatural; romance; thriller/espionage. Query. Reports in 2 weeks on queries; 6 weeks on mss.
Recent Sales: *TV mow optioned: Psychic Evidence* (Breen Productions) and *Over the Edge* (Hill/ Field Entertainment), both by Carol Costa.
Terms: Agent receives 10% commission on domestic sales. Offers written contract, binding for 2 years.
Fees: Criticism service: $100 for a maximum of 150 pages. Agent writes critiques that "point out problems in dialogue, plotting and character development and determines the overall marketability of the project."

THE PUBLISHING FIELD is constantly changing! If you're still using this book and it is 1998 or later, buy the newest edition of *Guide to Literary Agents* at your favorite bookstore or order directly from Writer's Digest Books.

Tips: Obtains new clients through queries. "Stick with popular genres such as mystery, comedy, romance. Always include a SASE."

‡□**STARWATCHER, (IV)**, P.O. Box 17270, Encino CA 91416. (818)343-9922. Fax: (818)996-0943. E-mail: rjmlof@haven.ios.com. Contact: Jean-Marc Lofficier. Estab. 1985. Represents 45 clients. Specializes in selling rights of comic books, children's books properties; and selling artists' services to Hollywood. Currently handles: 100% comic books.
Handles: Comic books. Considers these fiction areas: cartoon/comic; science fiction. Query. Reports in 1 week on queries.
Recent Sales: *Blueberry*, by Giraud/Charlier (Blueturtle); *Rock City*, by Moebius (Eclectic Films).
Terms: Agent receives 10% commission on domestic sales; 10% on foreign sales. Offers written contract, binding for 1 year, with a 30 day cancellation clause.
Fees: Offers criticism service. Verbal critiques.
Writers' Conferences: Comicon International (San Diego, CA, July/August).

‡**STONE MANNERS AGENCY, (III)**, 8091 Selma Ave., Los Angeles CA 90046. (213)654-7575. Contact: Casey Bierer. Estab. 1982. Signatory of WGA. Represents 135 clients.
Handles: Movie scripts, TV scripts. Considers all script subject areas. Query. Reports in 1 month if interested in query. Will contact only if interested. No unsolicited material accepted.
Terms: Agent receives 10% commission on domestic sales; 10% commission on foreign sales.

TALENT SOURCE, 107 E. Hall St., P.O. Box 14120, Savannah GA 31416. (912)232-9390. Fax: (912)232-8213. Contact: Michael L. Shortt. Estab. 1991. Signatory of WGA. 35% of clients are new/previously unpublished writers. Currently handles: 75% movie scripts; 25% TV scripts.
Handles: Movie scripts (feature film), TV scripts. Send outline with character breakdown. Reports in 6 weeks on queries.
Terms: Agent receives 10% commission on domestic sales; 15% on foreign sales. Offers written contract.
Tips: Obtains new clients through word of mouth.

THE TANTLEFF OFFICE, (II), 375 Greenwich St., Suite 700, New York NY 10013. (212)941-3939. Fax: (212)941-3948. President: Jack Tantleff. Estab. 1986. Signatory of WGA, member of AAR. Specializes in theater, film, TV, fiction and nonfiction. Member agents: John Santoianni (theater); Charmaine Ferenczi (theater); Jill Bock (TV and film); Anthony Gardner (fiction, nonfiction books); Alan Willig (talent); Jay Kane (talent); Robyne Kintz (talent).
Handles: Movie scripts, TV scripts, stage plays, musicals, fiction and nonfiction books. Query with outline.
Terms: Agent receives 10% commission on domestic sales; 10% on dramatic sales; 10% on foreign sales: 15% on book sales.

□**A TOTAL ACTING EXPERIENCE, (II)**, Dept. N.W., 20501 Ventura Blvd., Suite 399, Woodland Hills CA 91364-2360. (818)340-9249. Contact: Dan A. Bellacicco. Estab. 1984. Signatory of WGA, SAG, AFTRA. Represents 30 clients. 50% of clients are new/previously unpublished writers. Specializes in "quality instead of quantity." Currently handles: 5% nonfiction books; 5% juvenile books; 10% novels; 5% novellas; 5% short story collections; 50% movie scripts; 5% stage plays; 10% TV scripts; 5% how-to books and videos.
Handles: Movie scripts (feature film, documentary), TV scripts (TV mow, episodic drama, sitcom, variety show, soap opera, animation), stage plays, syndicated material, how-to books, videos. "No heavy drugs." Considers these script subject areas: action/adventure; cartoon/animation; comedy; contemporary issues; detective/police/crime; erotica; ethnic; experimental; family saga; fantasy; historical; horror; juvenile; mainstream; mystery/suspense; psychic/supernatural; religious/inspirational; romantic comedy and drama; science fiction; sports; teen; thriller; westerns/frontier. Query with outline and 3 sample chapters. Reports in 3 months on mss. "We will respond *only* if interested; material will *not* be returned. Please include your e-mail address."
Also Handles: Nonfiction books, textbooks, juvenile books, novels, novellas, short story collections, poetry books. Considers these nonfiction areas: animals; art/architecture/design; biography/autobiography; business; child guidance/parenting; computers/electronics; cooking/food/nutrition; crafts/hobbies; current affairs; education; ethnic/cultural interests; government/politics/law; health/medicine; history; how-to; humor; juvenile nonfiction; language/literature/criticism; military/war; money/finance/economics; music/dance/theater/film; nature/environment; New Age/metaphysics; photography; popular culture; psychology; religious/inspirational; science/technology; self-help/personal improvement; sociology; sports; translations; true crime/investigative; women's issues/women's studies; "any well-written work!" Considers these fiction areas: action/adventure; cartoon/comic; confessional; contemporary issues; detective/police/crime; erotica; ethnic; experimental; family saga; fantasy; glitz; historical; horror; humor/satire; juvenile; literary; mainstream; mystery/suspense; picture book; psychic/supernat-

ural; regional; religious/inspirational; romance (contemporary, gothic, historical, regency); science fiction; sports; thriller/espionage; westerns/frontier; young adult.
Terms: Agent receives 10% on domestic sales; 10% on foreign sales. Offers written contract, binding
for 2 years or more.
Fees: Offers criticism service (for our clients only at no charge.) 60% of business is derived from
commission on ms sales.
Tips: Obtains new clients through mail and conferences. "We seek new sincere, quality writers for
long-term relationships. We would love to see film, television, and stage material that remains relevant
and provocative 20 years from today; dialogue that is fresh and unpredictable; story, and characters
that are enlightening, humorous, witty, creative, inspiring, and, most of all, entertaining. Please keep
in mind quality not quantity. Your characters must be well delineated and fully developed with high
contrast. Respond only if you appreciate our old fashioned agency nurturing, strong guidance, and in
return: your honesty, loyalty and a quality commitment."

THE TURTLE AGENCY, (III), 12456 Ventura Blvd., Suite 1, Studio City CA 91604. (818)506-
6898. Fax: (818)506-1723. Contact: Cindy Turtle, Amy Dresner. Estab. 1985. Signatory of WGA,
member of SAG, AFTRA. Represents 45 clients. Specializes in network TV, features, interactive.
Currently handles: 5% novels; 25% movie scripts; 70% TV scripts.
Handles: Movie scripts (feature film); TV scripts (TV mow). Considers these script subject areas:
action/adventure; detective/police/crime; erotica; fantasy; historical; mainstream; mystery/suspense;
psychic/supernatural; romance; science fiction; thriller/espionage; westerns/frontier; young adult.
Query. Reports in 2 weeks on queries; 1 month on mss. "If writer would like material returned, enclose
SASE."
Terms: Agent receives 10% commission on domestic sales. Offers written contract, binding for 2
years.
Tips: Obtains new clients through recommendations, usually—on *rare* occasions through query let-
ters.

ANNETTE VAN DUREN AGENCY, (III), 925 N. Sweetzer Ave., #12, Los Angeles CA 90069.
(213)650-3643. Fax: (213)654-3893. Contact: Annette Van Duren or Patricia Murphy. Estab. 1985.
Signatory of WGA. Represents 12 clients. No clients are new/previously unpublished writers. Currently
handles: 10% novels; 50% movie scripts; 40% TV scripts.
Handles: Movie scripts (feature film, animation), TV scripts (TV mow, sitcom, animation). Considers
these script subject areas: action/adventure; cartoon/animation; comedy; contemporary issues; juvenile;
mainstream; romantic comedy and drama; science fiction; thriller. Query with SASE. Reports in 2
weeks on queries.
Also Handles: Novels. Considers these nonfiction areas: true crime/investigative. Considers these
fiction areas: action/adventure; cartoon/comic; contemporary issues; detective/police/crime; humor/
satire; juvenile; mainstream; science fiction; thriller/espionage; westerns/frontier; young adult. Query.
Reports in weeks on queries.
Terms: Agent receives 10% commission on domestic sales. Offers written contract, binding for 2
years.
Tips: Obtains new clients only through recommendations from "clients or other business associates."

THE VINES AGENCY, INC, (II), 409 E. Sixth St., #4, New York NY 10009. (212)777-5522. Fax:
(212)777-5978. Contact: Jimmy C. Vines or Gary Neuwirth. Estab. 1995. Represents 52 clients. 2%
of clients are new/previously unpublished writers. Specializes in mystery, suspense, science fiction,
mainstream novels, graphic novels, CD-ROMs, screenplays, teleplays. Currently handles: 10% nonfiction books; 2% scholarly books; 10% juvenile books; 50% novels; 15% movie scripts; 5% TV scripts;
1% stage plays; 5% short story collections; 2% syndicated material.
   ● See the expanded listing for this agency in Literary Agents: Nonfee-charging.

WARDEN, WHITE & KANE, INC., (II, IV), 8444 Wilshire Blvd., 4th Floor, Beverly Hills CA
90211. Estab. 1990. Signatory of WGA, DGA. Represents 100 clients. 10% of clients are new/pre-
viously unpublished writers. Specializes in film. Currently handles: 100% movie scripts. Member
agents: David Warden, Steve White.
Handles: Movie scripts (feature film). Only by referral. Reports in 2 months on queries.
Recent Sales: *Mango*, by Miles Millar (New Line); *Bullet Proof*, by Phoebe Dorin and Christian
Stoianovich (Universal). "Also sold *Sleepless in Seattle* and represents author of *Batman*."
Terms: Agent receives 10% commission on domestic sales; 10% on foreign sales. Offers written
contract, binding for 2 years. Charges for photocopying.
Tips: Obtains new clients only through referrals.

☐**SANDRA WATT & ASSOCIATES, (II)**, 8033 Sunset Blvd., Suite 4053, Hollywood CA 90046-
2427. (213)851-1021. Contact: Davida South. Estab. 1977. Signatory of WGA. Represents 55 clients.

15% of clients are new/previously unpublished writers. Specializes in scripts: film noir; family; romantic comedies; books: women's fiction, mystery, young adult commercial nonfiction. Currently handles: 40% nonfiction books; 35% novels; 25% movie scripts. Member agents: Sandra Watt (scripts, nonfiction, novels); Davida South (scripts).
• See the expanded listing for this agency in Literary Agents: Nonfee-charging.

PEREGRINE WHITTLESEY AGENCY, (II), 345 E. 80 St., New York NY 10021. (212)737-0153. Fax: (212)734-5176. Contact: Peregrine Whittlesey. Estab. 1986. Signatory of WGA. Represents 30 clients. 50% of clients are new/previously unpublished writers. Specializes in playwrights who also write for screen and TV. Currently handles: 20% movie scripts, 80% stage plays.
Handles: Movie scripts, stage plays. Query. Reports in 1 week on queries; 1 month on mss.
Recent Sales: *The Stick Wife* and *0 Pioneers!*, Darrah Cloud (Dramatic Publishing); *Alabama Rain*, by Heather McCutchen (Dramatic Publishing).
Terms: Agent receives 10% commission on domestic sales; 15% on foreign sales. Offers written contract, binding for 2 years.
Tips: Obtains new clients through recommendations from others.

‡WORKING ARTISTS TALENT AGENCY, (III, V), 10914 Rathburn Ave., North Ridge CA 91326-2855. (818)368-8222. Fax: (818)368-7574. Contact: Debora Koslowsky. Estab. 1994. Signatory of WGA. Represents 20 clients.
Handles: Movie scripts (feature film), TV scripts. Considers these script subject areas: romantic, thriller, political action. Not interested in acquiring new clients at this time. Finds new clients through referrals only.

THE WRIGHT CONCEPT, (II), 1811 W. Burbank Blvd., Burbank CA 91506. (818)954-8943. (818)954-9370. Contact: Jason Wright. Estab. 1985. Signatory of WGA, DGA. Specializes in TV comedy writers and feature comedy writers. Currently handles: 50% movie scripts; 50% TV scripts. Member agents: Marcie Wright (TV); Jason Wright (features)
Handles: Movie scripts (feature film, animation); TV scripts (TV mow, episodic drama, sitcom, variety show, animation, syndicated material). Considers these script subject areas: action/adventure; cartoon/animation; comedy; detective/police/crime; ethnic; fantasy; humor; juvenile; mystery/suspense; romantic comedy and drama; thriller; western/frontier. Query with SASE. Reports in 2 weeks.
Recent Sales: *Movie scripts optioned/sold: Black Sheep*, by Fred Wolf (Paramount); *The Cure*, by Robert Kuhn (Universal); *Snow White*, by Tom Szollosi (Interscope). *TV scripts optioned/sold: Pretender, Sherman Oaks, U.S.A. High, Ellen. Scripting assignments: The Crew, Saturday Night Live, Dennis Miller Live, The Simpsons, Bike Patrol, Star Trek Voyager, Sea Quest.*
Terms: Agent receives 10% commission on sales. Offers written contract, binding for 1 year, with 90 day cancellation clause. 100% of business is derived from commissions on sales.
Writers' Conferences: Speaks at UCLA 3-4 times a year.
Tips: Obtains new clients through recommendations and queries.

ANN WRIGHT REPRESENTATIVES, (II), 165 W. 46th St., Suite 1105, New York NY 10036-2501. Dan Wright. Estab. 1961. Signatory of WGA. Represents 45 clients. 40% of clients are new/unpublished writers. Prefers to work with published/established authors; works with a small number of new/unpublished authors. "Eager to work with published/established authors; works with a small number of new/unpublished authors. "Eager to work with any author with material that we can effectively market in the motion picture business worldwide." Specializes in "book or screenplays with strong motion picture potential." Currently handles: 50% novels; 40% movie scripts; 10% TV scripts.
Handles: Movie scripts (feature film); TV scripts (TV mow, episodic drama, sitcom). Considers these script subject areas: action/adventure; comedy; detective/police/crime; gay; historical; horror; humor; lesbian; mainstream; mystery/suspense; psychic/supernatural; romantic comedy and drama; sports; thriller; westerns/frontier. Query with outline and SASE. Does not read unsolicited mss. Reports in 3 weeks on queries; 3 months on mss. "All work must be sent with a SASE to ensure its return."
Recent Sales: *Movie/TV mow scripts optioned/sold: Baubles*, by Brian Neich (Jonathan Demme for Tristar); *Movie/TV MOW in development*: *Ride Home*, by Tom Dempsey; *Scripting assignments*: *The Red Zoltaire* by Alex Stirling (Schulz Film Ltd.)..

● **A BULLET** introduces comments by the editor of the *Guide* indicating special information about the listing.

Also Handles: Novels. Considers these fiction areas: action/adventure; detective/police/crime; family saga; fantasy; feminist; gay; historical; horror; humor/satire; lesbian; literary; mainstream; mystery/suspense; romance (contemporary, historical, regency); sports; thriller/espionage; westerns/frontier; young adult.

Books: *The Bermuda Virus*, by Bob O'Quinn (Bermudiana Publishing); *The Da Vinci Deception*, by Thomas Swan (Bantam Books); *A Wing and A Prayer*, by John Morano (Northwest Publishing); *Vengeance*, by Bob Mendez (Intercontinental).

Terms: Agent receives 10% commission on domestic sales; 10% on dramatic sales; 15-20% on foreign sales; 20% on packaging. Offers written contract, binding for 2 years. Critiques only works of signed clients. Charges for photocopying expenses.

Tips: "Send a letter with SASE. Something about the work, something about the writer."

WRITERS & ARTISTS (III), 19 W. 44th St., Suite 1000, New York NY 10036. (212)391-1112. Fax: (212)398-9877. Contact: William Craver or Peter Hagen. Estab. 1970. Member of AAR, signatory of WGA. Represents 100 clients. West Coast location: Suite 900, 924 Westwood Blvd., Los Angeles CA 90024. (310)824-6300. Fax: (310)824-6343.

Handles: Movie scripts (feature film), TV scripts (TV mow, miniseries, episodic drama), stage plays. Considers all script subject areas. Query with brief description of project, bio and SASE. Reports in 2-4 weeks on queries only when accompanied by SASE. No unsolicited mss accepted.

Recent Sales: *Irreperable Harm*, by Lee Gruenefeld (Warner Books, BOMC alternate, TV rights to Wolper Co. for Warner Bros.); *All Fall Down*, by Lee Gruenfeld (Warner, Books, movie rights to Tristar).

☐**WRITER'S CONSULTING GROUP, (II, III)** P.O. Box 492, Burbank CA 91503-0492. (818)841-9294. Director: Jim Barmeier. Estab. 1983. Represents 10 clients. "We will work with established and unestablished writers. We welcome unsolicited queries." Currently handles: 40% nonfiction books; 20% novels; 40% movie scripts.
● See the expanded listing for this agency in Literary Agents: Fee-charging.

Additional Script Agents

The following agencies have indicated they are *primarily* interested in handling book manuscripts, but also handle less than ten to fifteen percent scripts. After reading the listing (you can find the page number in the Listings Index), send them a query to obtain more information on their needs and manuscript submission policies. Note: Double daggers (‡) preceding titles indicate listings new to this edition.

‡Joseph Anthony Agency
Appleseeds Management
The Author's Agency
Author Aid Associates
Pema Brown
Charisma Communications, Ltd.
‡The Cohen Agency
‡CS International Literary Agency
The Lois de la Haba Agency Inc.
Farber Literary Agency Inc.
‡Fort Ross Inc. Russian-American Publishing Projects
Jay Garon-Brooke Assoc. Inc.
Graham Literary Agency, Inc.

The Charlotte Gusay Literary Agency
‡The Jett Literary Agency
Law Offices of Robert L. Fenton PC
Lawrence Jordan Literary Agency
Lazear Agency Incorporated
Literary and Creative Artists Agency Inc.
The Evan Marshall Agency
Henry Morrison, Inc.
BK Nelson Literary Agency & Lecture Bureau
Fifi Oscard Agency Inc.
Paraview, Inc.
Julie Popkin
Sidney E. Porcelain

The Portman Organization
Puddingstone Literary Agency
Diane Raintree Agency
‡Rhodes Literary Agency
Southern Literary Agency
Gloria Stern Agency (CA)
Marianne Strong Literary Agency
‡Mark Sullivan Associates
Toad Hall, Inc.
Jeanne Toomey Associates
Mary Jack Wald Associates, Inc.
James Warren Literary Agency
Karen Gantz Zahler Literary Agency

Resources

Professional Organizations

ORGANIZATIONS FOR AGENTS

ASSOCIATION OF AUTHORS' REPRESENTATIVES (AAR), 3rd Floor, 10 Astor Place, New York NY 10003. A list of member agents is available for $7 and SAE with 55 cents for postage.

ORGANIZATIONS FOR WRITERS

The following professional organizations publish newsletters and hold conferences and meetings in which they often share information on agents.

AMERICAN SOCIETY OF JOURNALISTS & AUTHORS, 1501 Broadway, Suite 302, New York NY 10036. (212)997-0947.

THE AUTHORS GUILD INC., 330 W. 42nd St., 29th Floor, New York NY 10036. (212)563-5904.

THE AUTHORS LEAGUE OF AMERICA, INC., 330 W. 42nd St., New York NY 10036. (212)564-8350.

CANADIAN AUTHORS ASSOCIATION, Box 419, Campbellsford, Ontario K0L 1L0 Canada. (705)653-0323. Provides a literary agent list to members.

COUNCIL OF WRITERS ORGANIZATIONS, % Michigan Living, 1 Auto Club Dr., Dearborn MI 48126. (313)336-1211.

THE DRAMATISTS GUILD, 1501 Broadway, Suite 701, New York NY 10036. (212)398-9366.

HORROR WRITERS ASSOCIATION, Nancy Etchemendy, treasurer, P.O. Box 50577, Palo Alto CA 94303.

INTERNATIONAL ASSOCIATION OF CRIME WRITERS INC., North American Branch, JAF Box 1500, New York NY 10016. (212)243-8966.

THE INTERNATIONAL WOMEN'S WRITING GUILD, P.O. Box 810, Gracie Station, New York NY 10028. (212)737-7536. Provides a literary agent list to members and holds "Meet the Agents and Editors" in April and October.

MYSTERY WRITERS OF AMERICA (MWA), 17 E. 47th St., 6th Floor, New York NY 10017.

NATIONAL LEAGUE OF AMERICAN PEN WOMEN, 1300 17th St. NW, Washington DC 20036-1973. (202)785-1997.

NATIONAL WRITERS ASSOCIATION, 1450 S. Havana, Suite 424, Aurora CO 80012. (303)751-7844. In addition to agent referrals, also operates an agency for members.

NATIONAL WRITERS UNION, 113 University Place, 6th Floor, New York NY 10003-4527. (212)254-0279. A trade union, this organization has an agent data base available to members.

PEN AMERICAN CENTER, 568 Broadway, New York NY 10012. (212)334-1660.

POETS & WRITERS, 72 Spring St., Room 301, New York NY 10012. (212)226-3586. Operates an information line, taking calls from 11-3 EST Monday through Friday.

ROMANCE WRITERS OF AMERICA, 13700 Veterans Memorial Dr., #315, Houston TX 77014. (713)440-6885. Publishes an annual agent list for members for $10.

SCIENCE FICTION AND FANTASY WRITERS OF AMERICA, 5 Winding Brook Dr., #1B, Guilderland NY 12084.

SOCIETY OF CHILDREN'S BOOK WRITERS & ILLUSTRATORS, 22736 Van Owen St., #106, West Hills CA 91307. (818)888-8760. Provides a literary agents list to members.

VOLUNTEER LAWYERS FOR THE ARTS, One E. 53rd St., 6th Floor, New York NY 10022. (212)319-2787.

WASHINGTON INDEPENDENT WRITERS, 733 15th St. NW, Room 220, Washington DC 20005. (202)347-4973.

WESTERN WRITERS OF AMERICA, 1012 Fair St., Franklin TN 37064. (615)791-1444.

WOMEN IN COMMUNICATIONS, INC., 10605 Judicial Dr., Suite A4, Fairfax VA 22030. (703)359-9000.

WRITERS GUILD OF ALBERTA, 11759 Groat St., Edmonton, Alberta T5M 3K6 Canada. (403)422-8174.

WRITERS GUILD OF AMERICA-EAST, 555 W. 57th St., New York NY 10019. (212)767-7800. Provides list of WGA signatory agents for $1.29.

WRITERS GUILD OF AMERICA-WEST, 8955 Beverly Blvd., West Hollywood CA 90048. (310)550-1000. Provides a list of WGA signatory agents for $2 and SASE sent to Agency Department.

Table of Acronyms

The organizations and their acronyms listed below are frequently referred to in the listings and are widely used in the industries of agenting and writing.

AAP	American Association of Publishers	NASW	National Association of Science Writers
AAR	Association of Authors' Representatives (merger of ILAA and SAR)	NLAPW	National League of American Pen Women
ABA	American Booksellers Association	NWA	National Writers Association
ABWA	Associated Business Writers of America	OWAA	Outdoor Writers Association of America, Inc.
AEB	Association of Editorial Businesses	RWA	Romance Writers of America
AFTRA	American Federation of TV and Radio Artists	SAG	Screen Actor's Guild
AGVA	American Guild of Variety Artists	SAR	Society of Authors' Representatives (see AAR)
AMWA	American Medical Writer's Association	SATW	Society of American Travel Writers
ASJA	American Society of Journalists and Authors	SCBWI	Society of Children's Book Writers & Illustrators
ATA	Association of Talent Agents	SFWA	Science Fiction and Fantasy Writers of America
AWA	Aviation/Space Writers Association	WGA	Writers Guild of America
CAA	Canadian Authors Association	WIA	Women in the Arts Foundation, Inc.
DGA	Director's Guild of America	WIF	Women in Film
GWAA	Garden Writers Association of America	WICI	Women in Communications, Inc.
HWA	Horror Writers of America	WIW	Washington Independent Writers
IACP	International Association of Culinary Professionals	WNBA	Women's National Book Association
ILAA	Independent Literary Agents Association (see AAR)	WRW	Washington Romance Writers (chapter of RWA)
MWA	Mystery Writers of America, Inc.	WWA	Western Writers of America

Recommended Books & Publications

BOOKS OF INTEREST

ADVENTURES IN THE SCREEN TRADE, by William Goldman, published by Warner Books, 1271 Avenue of the Americas, New York NY 10020.

THE ART OF DRAMATIC WRITING, by Lajos Egri, published by Touchstone, a division of Simon & Schuster, 1230 Avenue of the Americas, New York NY 10020.

BE YOUR OWN LITERARY AGENT, by Martin Levin, published by Ten Speed Press, P.O. Box 7123, Berkeley CA 94707.

BUSINESS & LEGAL FORMS FOR AUTHORS AND SELF-PUBLISHERS, by Tad Crawford, published by Allworth Press, c/o Writer's Digest Books, 1507 Dana Ave., Cincinnati OH 45207.

THE CAREER NOVELIST, by Donald Maass, published by Heinemann, 361 Hanover St., Portsmouth NH 03801-3912.

CHILDREN'S WRITER'S & ILLUSTRATOR'S MARKET, edited by Alice P. Buening, published by Writer's Digest Books, 1507 Dana Ave., Cincinnati OH 45207.

THE COMPLETE BOOK OF SCRIPTWRITING, revised edition, by J. Michael Straczynski, published by Writer's Digest Books, 1507 Dana Ave., Cincinnati OH 45207.

THE COMPLETE GUIDE TO STANDARD SCRIPT FORMAT (Parts 1 and 2), by Hillis Cole and Judith Haag, published by CMC Publishing, 11642 Otsego St., N. Hollywood CA 91601.

DRAMATISTS SOURCEBOOK, edited by Kathy Sova, published by Theatre Communications Group, Inc., 355 Lexington Ave., New York NY 10017-0217.

EDITORS ON EDITING: WHAT WRITERS SHOULD KNOW ABOUT WHAT EDITORS DO, edited by Gerald Gross, published by Grove-Atlantic, 841 Broadway, New York NY 10003-4793.

ESSENTIAL SOFTWARE FOR WRITERS, by Hy Bender, published by Writer's Digest Books, 1507 Dana Ave., Cincinnati OH 45207.

FOUR SCREENPLAYS, by Syd Field, published by Dell, 1540 Broadway, New York NY 10036-4094.

FROM SCRIPT TO SCREEN, by Linda Seger and Edward Jay Whetmore, published by Henry Holt & Co., Inc., 115 W. 18th St., New York NY 10011.

GETTING YOUR SCRIPT THROUGH THE HOLLYWOOD MAZE, by Linda Stuart, published by Acrobat Books, P.O. Box 870, Venice CA 90294.

THE GUIDE TO WRITERS CONFERENCES, published by ShawGuides, 10 W. 66th St., Suite 30H, New York NY 10023. (212)799-6464.

HOW TO BE YOUR OWN LITERARY AGENT, by Richard Curtis, published by Houghton Mifflin Company, 222 Berkeley St., Boston MA 02116.

HOW TO FIND AND WORK WITH A LITERARY AGENT audiotape, by Anita Diamant, published by Writer's AudioShop, 204 E. 35th St., Austin TX 78705.

HOW TO PITCH & SELL YOUR TV SCRIPT, by David Silver, published by Writer's Digest Books, 1507 Dana Ave., Cincinnati OH 45207.

HOW TO SELL YOUR IDEA TO HOLLYWOOD, by Robert Kosberg with Mim Eichler, published by HarperCollins, 10 E. 53rd St., New York NY 10022-5299.

HOW TO SELL YOUR SCREENPLAY, by Carl Sautter, published by New Chapter Press, 381 Park Ave. S., Suite 1122, New York NY 10016.

HOW TO WRITE A BOOK PROPOSAL, by Michael Larsen, published by Writer's Digest Books, 1507 Dana Ave., Cincinnati OH 45207.

HOW TO WRITE ATTENTION-GRABBING QUERY & COVER LETTERS, by John Wood, published by Writer's Digest Books, 1507 Dana Ave., Cincinnati OH 45207.

HOW TO WRITE IRRESISTIBLE QUERY LETTERS, by Lisa Collier Cool, published by Writer's Digest Books, 1507 Dana Ave., Cincinnati OH 45207

THE INSIDER'S GUIDE TO BOOK EDITORS, PUBLISHERS & LITERARY AGENTS, by Jeff Herman, published by Prima Communications, Box 1260, Rocklin CA 95677-1260.

LITERARY AGENTS: A WRITER'S GUIDE, by Adam Begley, published by Viking Penguin, 375 Hudson St., New York NY 10014-3657.

LITERARY AGENTS: WHAT THEY DO, HOW THEY DO IT, HOW TO FIND & WORK WITH THE RIGHT ONE FOR YOU, by Michael Larsen, published by John Wiley & Sons, 605 Third Ave., New York NY 10158-0012.

LITERARY MARKET PLACE (LMP), R.R. Bowker Company, 121 Chanlon Road, New Providence NJ 07974.

MAKING A GOOD SCRIPT GREAT, by Dr. Linda Seger, published by Samuel French Trade, 7623 Sunset Blvd., Hollywood CA 90046.

MANUSCRIPT SUBMISSION, by Scott Edelstein, published by Writer's Digest Books, 1507 Dana Ave., Cincinnati OH 45207.

THE NEW SCREENWRITER LOOKS AT THE NEW SCREENWRITER, by William Froug, published by Silman-James Press, 1181 Angelo Dr., Beverly Hills CA 90210.

NOVEL & SHORT STORY WRITER'S MARKET, edited by Barbara A. Kuroff, published by Writer's Digest Books, 1507 Dana Ave., Cincinnati OH 45207.

OPENING THE DOORS TO HOLLYWOOD: HOW TO SELL YOUR IDEA, by Carlos de Abreu & Howard Jay Smith, published by Custos Morum Publishers, 433 N. Camden Dr., Suite 600, Beverly Hills CA 90210.

THE SCREENWRITER'S BIBLE: A COMPLETE GUIDE TO WRITING, FORMATTING & SELLING YOUR SCRIPT, by David Trottier, published by Silman-James Press, 1181 Angelo Dr., Beverly Hills CA 90210.

SCREENWRITERS ON SCREENWRITING: THE BEST IN THE BUSINESS DISCUSS THEIR CRAFT, by Joel Engel, published by Hyperion, 114 Fifth Ave., New York NY 10011.

SCREENWRITER'S SOFTWARE GUIDE, published by Butterworth-Heineman, 313 Washington St., Newton MA 02158.

SCREENWRITING TRICKS OF THE TRADE, by William Froug, published by Silman-James Press, 1181 Angelo Dr., Beverly Hills CA 90210.

SCREENWRITING, by Richard Walter, published by Plume, an imprint of Penguin USA, 375 Hudson St., New York NY 10014-3657.

THE SCRIPT IS FINISHED, NOW WHAT DO I DO?, by K. Callan, published by Sweden Press, Box 1612, Studio City CA 91614.

SELLING YOUR SCREENPLAY, by Cynthia Whitcomb, published by Crown, 201 E. 50th St., New York NY 10022.

SUCCESSFUL SCRIPTWRITING, by Jurgen Wolff and Kerry Cox, published by Writer's Digest Books, 1507 Dana Ave., Cincinnati OH 45207.

THEATRE DIRECTORY, Theatre Communications Group, Inc., 355 Lexington Ave., New York NY 10017-0217.

THE TV SCRIPTWRITER'S HANDBOOK, by Alfred Brenner, published by Silman-James Press, 1181 Angelo Dr., Beverly Hills CA 90210.

WORKING IN HOLLYWOOD, by Alexandra Brouwer and Thomas Lee Wright, published by Avon, 1350 Avenue of the Americas, New York NY 10019.

THE WRITER'S BOOK OF CHECKLISTS, by Scott Edelstein, published by Writer's Digest Books, 1507 Dana Ave., Cincinnati OH 45207.

THE WRITER'S DIGEST GUIDE TO MANUSCRIPT FORMATS, by Dian Dincin Buchman and Seli Groves, published by Writer's Digest Books, 1507 Dana Ave., Cincinnati OH 45207.

WRITER'S ESSENTIAL DESK REFERENCE Second Edition, published by Writer's Digest Books, 1507 Dana Ave., Cincinnati OH 45207.

THE WRITER'S GUIDE TO HOLLYWOOD DIRECTORS, PRODUCERS & SCREEN-WRITER'S AGENTS: WHO THEY ARE! WHAT THEY WANT! & HOW TO WIN THEM OVER!, published by Prima Publishing, 3875 Atherton Rd., Rocklin CA 95765.

THE WRITER'S LEGAL COMPANION, by Brad Bunnin and Peter Beren, published by Addison Wesley, One Jacob Way, Reading MA 01867.

WRITER'S MARKET, edited by Kirsten Holm, published by Writer's Digest Books, 1507 Dana Ave., Cincinnati OH 45207.

WRITING SCREENPLAYS THAT SELL, by Michael Hauge, published by HarperCollins, 10 E. 53rd St., New York NY 10022-5299.

BOOKSTORES AND CATALOGS

BOOK CITY, Dept. 101, 308 N. San Fernando Blvd., Burbank CA 91502, (818)848-4417, and 6627 Hollywood Blvd., Hollywood CA 90028, (800)4-CINEMA. Catalog $2.50.

SAMUEL FRENCH THEATRE & FILM BOOKSHOPS, 7623 Sunset Blvd., Hollywood CA 90046. (213)876-0570.

SCRIPT CITY, 8033 Sunset Blvd., Suite 1500, Hollywood CA 90046. (800)676-2522. Catalog $2.

PUBLICATIONS OF INTEREST

DAILY VARIETY, 5700 Wilshire Blvd., Los Angeles CA 90036.

EDITOR & PUBLISHER, The Editor & Publisher Co., Inc., 11 W. 19th St., New York NY 10011-4234.

HOLLYWOOD AGENTS & MANAGERS DIRECTORY, published by Hollywood Creative Directory, 3000 Olympic Blvd., Suite 2413, Santa Monica CA 90404.

HOLLYWOOD CREATIVE DIRECTORY, published by Hollywood Creative Directory, 3000 Olympic Blvd., Suite 2413, Santa Monica CA 90404.

HOLLYWOOD REPORTER, 5055 Wilshire Blvd., Los Angeles CA 90036-4396.

HOLLYWOOD SCRIPTWRITER, 1626 N. Wilcox, #385, Hollywood CA 90028. E-mail: kerry-cox@aol.com.

NEW YORK SCREENWRITER, published by the New York Screenwriter, 548 8th Ave., Suite 401, New York NY 10018.

POETS & WRITERS, 72 Spring St., New York NY 10012.

PREMIERE MAGAZINE, published by Hachette Filipacchi Magazines, 1633 Broadway, New York NY 10019.

PUBLISHERS WEEKLY, 249 W. 17th St., New York NY 10011.

SCRIPT MAGAZINE, published by Forum, P.O. Box 7, Long Green Pike, Baldwin MD 21013-0007.

THE WRITER, 120 Boylston St., Boston MA 02116-4615.

WRITER'S DIGEST, 1507 Dana Ave., Cincinnati OH 45207.

WRITERS GUILD OF AMERICA, Membership Directory, published by the Writers Guild of America, 8955 Beverly Blvd., West Hollywood CA 90048.

Glossary

Advance. Money that a publisher pays a writer prior to book publication, usually paid in installments, such as one-half upon signing the contract; one-half upon delivery of the complete, satisfactory manuscript. An advance is paid against the royalty money to be earned by the book. Agents take their percentage off the top of the advance as well as from the royalties earned.

Auction. Publishers sometimes bid for the acquisition of a book manuscript with excellent sales prospects. The bids are for the amount of the author's advance, guaranteed dollar amounts, advertising and promotional expenses, royalty percentage, etc.

Backlist. Those books still in print from previous years' publication.

Bio. Brief (usually one page) background information about an artist, writer or photographer. Includes work and educational experience.

Boilerplate. A standardized publishing contract. Most authors and agents make many changes on the boilerplate before accepting the contract.

Category fiction. A term used to include all various types of fiction. See *genre*.

Clips. Writing samples, usually from newspapers or magazines, of your published work.

Concept. A statement that summarizes a screenplay or teleplay—before the treatment is written.

Contributor's copies. Copies of the author's book sent to the author. The number of contributor's copies is often negotiated in the publishing contract.

Copyediting. Editing of a manuscript for writing style, grammar, punctuation and factual accuracy.

Cover letter. A brief descriptive letter sent with a manuscript submitted to an agent or publisher.

Critiquing service. A service offered by some agents in which writers pay a fee for comments on the saleability or other qualities of their manuscript. Sometimes the critique includes suggestions on how to improve the work. Fees vary, as do the quality of the critiques.

Deal memo. The memorandum of agreement between a publisher and author that precedes the actual contract and includes important issues such as royalty, advance, rights, distribution and option clauses.

Editing service. A service offered by some agents in which writers pay a fee—either lump sum or per-page—to have their manuscript edited. The quality and extent of the editing varies from agency to agency.

Electronic rights. Secondary or subsidiary rights dealing with electronic/multimedia formats (e.g., CD-ROMs, electronic magazines).

Elements. Actors, directors and producers attached to a project to make an attractive package.

Episodic drama. Hour-long continuing TV show, often shown at 10 p.m.

Evaluation fees. Fees an agent may charge to evaluate material. The extent and quality of this evaluation varies, but comments usually concern the saleability of the manuscript.

Exclusive. Offering a manuscript, usually for a set period of time, to just one agent and guaranteeing that agent is the only one looking at the manuscript.

Floor bid. If a publisher is very interested in a manuscript he may offer to enter a floor bid when the book goes to auction. The publisher sits out of the auction, but agrees to take the book by topping the highest bid by an agreed-upon percentage (usually 10 percent).

Foreign rights agent. An agent who handles selling the rights to a country other than that of the first book agent. Usually an additional percentage (about 5 percent) will be added on to the first book agent's commission to cover the foreign rights agent.

Genre. Refers to either a general classification of writing such as a novel, poem or short story or to the categories within those classifications, such as problem novels or sonnets. Genre fiction is a term that covers various types of commercial novels such as mystery, romance, western, science fiction or horror.

Ghosting/ghostwriting. A writer puts into literary form the words, ideas or knowledge of another person under that person's name. Some agents offer this service; others pair ghostwriters with celebrities or experts.

High concept. A story idea easily expressed in a quick, one-line description.

Imprint. The name applied to a publisher's specific line of books.

IRC. International Reply Coupon. Buy at a post office to enclose with material sent outside your country to cover the cost of return postage. The recipient turns them in for stamps in their own country.

Log line. A one-line description of a plot as it might appear in *TV Guide*.

Mainstream fiction. Fiction on subjects or trends that transcend popular novel categories such as mystery or romance. Using conventional methods, this kind of fiction tells stories about people and their conflicts.

Marketing fee. Fee charged by some agents to cover marketing expenses. It may be used to cover postage, telephone calls, faxes, photocopying or any other expense incurred in marketing a manuscript.

Mass market paperbacks. Softcover book, usually around 4×7, on a popular subject directed at a general audience and sold in groceries and drugstores as well as bookstores.

MFTS. Made for TV series. A series developed for television also known as episodics.

Midlist. Those titles on a publisher's list expected to have limited sales. Midlist books are mainstream, not literary, scholarly or genre, and are usually written by new or relatively unknown writers.

Miniseries. A limited dramatic series written for television, often based on a popular novel.

MOW. Movie of the week. A movie script written especially for television, usually seven acts with time for commercial breaks. Topics are often contemporary, sometimes controversial, fictional accounts. Also known as a made-for-TV-movie.

Net receipts. One method of royalty payment based on the amount of money a book publisher receives on the sale of the book after the booksellers' discounts, special sales discounts and returned copies.

Novelization. A novel created from the script of a popular movie, usually called a movie "tie-in" and published in paperback.

Novella. A short novel or long short story, usually 7,000 to 15,000 words. Also called a novelette.

Option clause. A contract clause giving a publisher the right to publish an author's next book.

Outline. A summary of a book's contents in 5 to 15 double-spaced pages; often in the form of chapter headings with a descriptive sentence or two under each one to show the scope of the book. A script's outline is a scene-by-scene narrative description of the story (10-15 pages for a ½-hour teleplay; 15-25 pages for 1-hour; 25-40 pages for 90 minutes and 40-60 pages for a 2-hour feature film or teleplay).

Over-the-transom. Slang for the path of an unsolicited manuscript into the slush pile.

Packaging. The process of putting elements together, increasing the chances of a project being made.

Pitch. The process where a writer meets with a producer and briefly outlines ideas that could be developed if the writer is hired to write a script for the project.

Proofreading. Close reading and correction of a manuscript's typographical errors.

Property. Books or scripts forming the basis for a movie or TV project.

Proposal. An offer to an editor or publisher to write a specific work, usually a package consisting of an outline and sample chapters.

Prospectus. A preliminary, written description of a book, usually one page in length.

Query. A letter written to an agent or a potential market, to elicit interest in a writer's work.

Reader. A person employed by an agent or buyer to go through the slush pile of manuscripts and scripts and select those worth considering.

Release. A statement that your idea is original, has never been sold to anyone else and that you are selling negotiated rights to the idea upon payment.

Remainders. Leftover copies of an out-of-print or slow-selling book purchased from the publisher at a reduced rate. Depending on the contract, a reduced royalty or no royalty is paid on remaindered books.

Reporting time. The time it takes the agent to get back to you on your query or submission.

Royalties. A percentage of the retail price paid to the author for each copy of the book that is sold. Agents take their percentage from the royalties earned as well as from the advance.

SASE. Self-addressed, stamped envelope; should be included with all correspondence.

Script. Broad term covering teleplay, screenplay or stage play. Sometimes used as a shortened version of the word "manuscript" when referring to books.

Simultaneous submission. Sending a manuscript to several agents or publishers at the same time. Simultaneous queries are common; simultaneous submissions are unacceptable to many agents or publishers.

Slush pile. A stack of unsolicited submissions in the office of an editor, agent or publisher.

Spec script. A script written on speculation without expectation of a sale.

Standard commission. The commission an agent earns on the sales of a manuscript or script. For literary agents, this commission percentage (usually between 10 and 20 percent) is taken from the advance and royalties paid to the writer. For script agents, the commission is taken from script sales; if handling plays, agents take a percentage from the box office proceeds.

Storyboards. Series of panels which illustrates a progressive sequence or graphics and story copy for a TV commercial, film or filmstrip.

Subagent. An agent handling certain subsidiary rights, usually working in conjunction with the agent who handled the book rights. The percentage paid the book agent is increased to pay the subagent.

Subsidiary. An incorporated branch of a company or conglomerate (e.g., Alfred Knopf, Inc. is a subsidiary of Random House, Inc.).

Subsidiary rights. All rights other than book publishing rights included in a book publishing contract, such as paperback rights, bookclub rights, movie rights. Part of an agent's job is to negotiate those rights and advise you on which to sell and which to keep.

Synopsis. A brief summary of a story, novel or play. As a part of a book proposal, it is a comprehensive summary condensed in a page or page and a half, single-spaced. See also *outline*.

Tearsheet. Published samples of your work, usually pages torn from a magazine.

Trade book. Either a hard cover or soft cover book; subject matter frequently concerns a special interest for a general audience; sold mainly in bookstores.

Treatment. Synopsis of a television or film script (40-60 pages for a 2-hour feature film or teleplay).

Turnaround. When a script has been in development but not made in the time allotted, it can be put back on the market.

Unsolicited manuscript. An unrequested manuscript sent to an editor, agent or publisher.

Young adult. The general classification of books written for readers age 12-18.

Young reader. Books written for readers 5-8 years old, where artwork only supports the text.

Client Acceptance Policies

We've ranked the agencies according to their openness to submissions. Some agencies are listed under more than one category. A double dagger (‡) precedes listings new to this edition.

I—NEWER AGENCIES ACTIVELY SEEKING CLIENTS

Nonfee-charging agents
Author's Agency, The
Becker Literary Agency, The Wendy
‡Bedford Book Works, Inc., The
Behar Literary Agency, Josh
‡Book Deals, Inc.
‡Brock Gannon Literary Agency
DH Literary, Inc.
Dystel Literary Management, Jane
Elliott Agency
Emerald Literary Agency
Fleury Agency, B.R.
Gibson Agency, The Sebastian
Henderson Literary Representation
‡Just Write Agency, Inc.
Lewis & Company, Karen
Lindstrom Literary Group

Michaels Literary Agency, Inc., Doris S.
New Brand Agency Group
New England Publishing Associates, Inc.
Pelham Literary Agency
Rowland Agency, The Damaris
Travis Literary Agency, Susan
Valcourt Agency, Inc., The Richard R.

Fee-charging literary agents
AEI/Atchity Editorial/ Entertainment International
Ahearn Agency, Inc., The
Alp Arts Co.
‡CS International Literary Agency
Fran Literary Agency
Independent Publishing Agency
‡Jett Literary Agency, The
McKinley, Literary Agency, Virginia C.

‡Nordhaus-Wolcott Literary Agency
QCorp Literary Agency
Remington Literary Assoc., Inc.
‡Stadler Literary Agency

Script agents
AEI/Atchity Editorial/ Entertainment International
All-Star Talent Agency
Bulger And Associates, Kelvin C.
Earth Tracks Agency
‡ES Talent Agency
Fleury Agency, B.R.
Fran Literary Agency
Gibson Agency, The Sebastian
Hudson Agency
Kick Entertainment
Lindstrom Literary Group
‡Meridian Talent, Inc.
Pelham Literary Agency

II—AGENCIES SEEKING BOTH NEW AND ESTABLISHED WRITERS

Nonfee-charging agents
Adler & Robin Books Inc.
Agency Chicago
Agents Inc. for Medical and Mental Health Professionals
Ajlouny Agency, The Joseph S.
Allan Agency, Lee
Allen Literary Agency, Linda
Amsterdam Agency, Marcia
Apollo Entertainment
Appleseeds Management
Author's Agency, The
‡Authors Alliance, Inc.
Baldi Literary Agency, Malaga
Barrett Books Inc., Loretta
Bernstein, Pam
Bernstein Literary Agency, Meredith
‡Bial Agency, Daniel

Black Literary Agency, Inc., David
Blassingame Spectrum Corp.
Boates Literary Agency, Reid
Bova Literary Agency, The Barbara
Brandt Agency, The Joan
Brown Associates Inc., Marie
Brown Ltd., Curtis
Browne Ltd., Pema
Buck Agency, Howard
Cantrell-Colas Inc., Literary Agency
Carvainis Agency, Inc., Maria
Castiglia Literary Agency
Charlton Associates, James
Circle of Confusion Ltd.
Ciske & Dietz Literary Agency
Clausen Associates, Connie
Cohen, Inc. Literary Agency, Ruth

Cohen Literary Agency Ltd., Hy
Columbia Literary Associates, Inc.
Coover Agency, The Doe
Cornfield Literary Agency, Robert
Crown International Literature and Arts Agency, Bonnie R.
Cypher, Author's Representative, James R.
Darhansoff & Verrill Literary Agents
Daves Agency, Joan
DH Literary, Inc.
DHS Literary, Inc.
Diamant Literary Agency, The Writer's Workshop, Inc., Anita
Dijkstra Literary Agency, Sandra
Dolger Agency, The Jonathan

Donadio and Ashworth, Inc.
Doyen Literary Services, Inc.
Ducas, Robert
Dupree/Miller and Associates
  Inc. Literary
Dystel Literary Management,
  Jane
Educational Design Services,
  Inc.
Elek Associates, Peter
Ellenberg Literary Agency,
  Ethan
Elliott Agency
Ellison Inc., Nicholas
Emerald Literary Agency
Esq. Literary Productions
Eth Literary Representation,
  Felicia
Farber Literary Agency Inc.
‡Feigen Literary Agency,
  Brenda
First Books, Inc.
Flaherty, Literary Agent, Joyce
  A.
Flaming Star Literary
  Enterprises
Flannery Literary
‡Fleming Associates, Arthur
Fleury Agency, B.R.
Franklin Associates, Ltd., Lynn
  C.
‡Frustrated Writer's Ltd., The
‡Fullerton Associates, Sheryl
  B.
Garon-Brooke Assoc. Inc., Jay
Gartenberg, Literary Agent,
  Max
Gautreaux—A Literary Agency,
  Richard
Goddard Book Group
Goldfarb & Graybill, Attorneys
  at Law
‡Goodman-Andrew-Agency,
  Inc.
Gordon Agency, Charlotte
Graham Literary Agency, Inc.
Greenburger Associates, Inc.,
  Sanford J.
Greene, Literary Agent, Randall
  Elisha
Grimes Literary Agency, Lew
‡Grosvenor Literary Agency,
  Deborah
Hamilburg Agency, The
  Mitchell J.
Hardy Agency, The
‡Harp, Chadwick Allen
Hawkins & Associates, Inc.,
  John
Heacock Literary Agency, Inc.
Henderson Literary
  Representation
Herman Agency, Inc., The Jeff
Herner Rights Agency, Susan
Hill Associates, Frederick
Hull House Literary Agency

IMG Literary
International Publisher
  Associates Inc.
J de S Associates Inc.
Jabberwocky Literary Agency
James Peter Associates, Inc.
Jordan Literary Agency,
  Lawrence
‡Henshaw Group, Richard
Gusay Literary Agency, The
  Charlotte
Kern Literary Agency, Natasha
Ketz Agency, Louise B.
Kirchoff/Wohlberg, Inc.,
  Authors' Representation
  Division
Kouts, Literary Agent, Barbara
  S.
Kroll Literary Agency, Edite
Lake Agency, The Candace
Lampack Agency, Inc., Peter
Lantz-Joy Harris Literary
  Agency Inc., The Robert
Larsen/Elizabeth Pomada
  Literary Agents, Michael
Lasher Agency, The Maureen
Lazear Agency Incorporated
‡Leap First
Lescher & Lescher Ltd.
Levant & Wales, Literary
  Agency, Inc.
Levine Communications, Inc.,
  James
Levine Literary Agency, Inc.,
  Ellen
Lewis & Company, Karen
Lieberman Associates, Robert
Lincoln Literary Agency, Ray
Lipkind Agency, Wendy
Literary Group, The
Lowenstein Associates, Inc.
McBride Literary Agency,
  Margret
Maccoby Literary Agency, Gina
McDonough, Literary Agent,
  Richard P.
Madsen Agency, Robert
Mainhardt Agency, Ricia
Mann Agency, Carol
Manus & Associates Literary
  Agency, Inc.
Marcil Literary Agency, Inc.,
  The Denise
Markowitz Literary Agency,
  Barbara
Markson Literary Agency,
  Elaine
Morrison, Inc., Henry
Mura Enterprises, Inc., Dee
Nathan, Ruth
‡National Writers Literary
  Agency
Nazor Literary Agency, Karen
Nine Muses and Apollo Inc.
Nolan Literary Agency, The
  Betsy

Norma-Lewis Agency, The
Oscard Agency, Inc., Fifi
Otitis Media
Paraview, Inc.
Paton Literary Agency, Kathi J.
Pelter, Rodney
Pevner, Inc., Stephen
Pocono Literary Agency, Inc.
Pom Inc.
Popkin, Julie
Porcelain, Sidney E.
Potomac Literary Agency, The
Priest Literary Agency, Aaron
  M.
Protter Literary Agent, Susan
  Ann
Pryor, Inc., Roberta
Publishing Services
Quicksilver Books-Literary
  Agents
Rees Literary Agency, Helen
Rinaldi Literary Agency, Angela
Robbins Literary Agency, BJ
Robbins Office, Inc., The
Rotrosen Agency, Jane
Rubinstein Literary Agency,
  Inc., Pesha
‡Russell & Volkening
Russell-Simenauer Literary
  Agency Inc.
Sanders Literary Agency,
  Victoria
Sandum & Associates
Schmidt Literary Agency,
  Harold
Schwartz Agency, Laurens R.
Seligman, Literary Agent, Lynn
Seymour Agency, The
Shepard Agency, The
‡Skolnick, Irene
Snell Literary Agency, Michael
Sommer, Inc., Elyse
Spieler, F. Joseph
Stauffer Associates, Nancy
Stern Literary Agency, Gloria
  (TX)
‡Sweeney Literary Agency,
  Emma
Taylor Literary Enterprises,
  Sandra
‡Tenth Avenue Editions, Inc.
2M Communications Ltd.
Urstadt Inc. Agency, Susan P.
Valcourt Agency, Inc., The
  Richard R.
Van Der Leun & Associates
Vines Agency, Inc., The
Ware Literary Agency, John A.
Waterside Productions, Inc.
Watkins Loomis Agency, Inc.
Watt & Associates, Sandra
Wecksler-Incomco
West Coast Literary Associates
Weyr Agency, Rhoda
Witherspoon & Associates, Inc.
Wreschner, Authors'

Representative, Ruth
Writers' Productions
Writers' Representatives, Inc.
‡Young Agency Inc., The Gay
Zeckendorf Assoc. Inc., Susan
‡Zitwer Agency, Barbara J.

Fee-charging agents

‡A.A. Fair Literary Agency
Acacia House Publishing
  Services Ltd.
Alp Arts Co.
‡Anthony Agency, Joseph
Author Aid Associates
‡Author Author Literary
  Agency Ltd.
‡Authors' Marketing Services
  Ltd.
‡Author's Services Literary
  Ageny
Blake Group Literary Agency,
  The
Brinke Literary Agency, The
Brown, Literary Agent,
  Antoinette
Cambridge Literary Associates
Catalog℠ Literary Agency, The
Chadd-Stevens Literary Agency
Coast to Coast Talent and
  Literary
Fishbein Ltd., Frieda
ForthWrite Literary Agency
Fran Literary Agency
Gelles-Cole Literary
  Enterprises
GEM Literary Services
Gislason Agency, The
Gladden Unlimited
Hamilton's Literary Agency,
  Andrew
Hilton Literary Agency, Alice
Hubbs Agency, Yvonne
  Trudeau
Jenks Agency, Carolyn
Kellock & Associates Ltd., J.
Kirkland Literary Agency, The
‡Klausner International
  Literary Agency, Bertha
Law Offices of Robert L. Fenton
  PC
Lawyer's Literary Agency, Inc.
Lee Literary Agency, L. Harry
Literary Group West
Lopopolo Literary Agency, Toni
M.H. International Literary
  Agency

McLean Literary Agency
Mews Books Ltd.
Montgomery Literary Agency
Nelson Literary Agency &
  Lecture Bureau, BK
Northwest Literary Services
Pell Agency, William
Penmarin Books
Puddingstone Literary Agency
Raintree Agency, Diane
Remington Literary Assoc., Inc.
Rhodes Literary Agency
SLC Enterprises
Stern Agency, Gloria (CA)
‡Sullivan Associates, Mark
Taylor Literary Agency,
  Dawson
Toomey Associates, Jeanne
Tornetta Agency, Phyllis
Total Acting Experience, A
Visions Press
Wallerstein Agency, The Gerry
  B.
Warren Literary Agency, James
‡Write Therapist, The Writer's
  Consulting Group

Script agents

Agency for the Performing Arts
Allan Agency, Lee
Alpern Group, The
Amato Agency, Michael
Amsterdam Agency, Marcia
‡Angel City Talent
Apollo Entertainment
Artists Agency, The
Bennett Agency, The
Bethel Agency
‡Broder Kurland Webb Uffner
  Agency, The
Brown Ltd., Curtis
Camden
Cameron Agency, The
  Marshall
Cinema Talent International
Circle of Confusion Ltd.
Client First—A/K/A Leo P.
  Haffey Agency
Coast to Coast Talent and
  Literary
Communications Management
  Associates
Douroux & Co.
Earth Tracks Agency
Epstein-Wyckoff and
  Associates
F.L.A.I.R. or First Literary
  Artists International
  Representatives

Fishbein Ltd., Frieda
Fleury Agency, B.R.
Fran Literary Agency
Freedman Dramatic Agency,
  Inc., Robert A.
French, Inc., Samuel
‡Gage Group, The
Gary-Paul Agency, The
Gauthreaux—A Literary
  Agency, Richard
Gersh Agency, The
Gold/Marshak & Associates
Graham Agency
Heacock Literary Agency, Inc.
‡Headline Artists Agency
Hilton Literary Agency, Alice
International Leonards Corp.
Jenks Agency, Carolyn
Kerin-Goldberg Associates
‡Kerwin Agency, William
Ketay Agency, The Joyce
Lake Agency, The Candace
Lee Literary Agency, L. Harry
Manus & Associates Literary
  Agency, Inc.
‡Meridian Talent, Inc.
Monteiro Rose Agency
Montgomery Literary Agency
Mura Enterprises, Inc., Dee
Otitis Media
Panda Talent
Partos Company, The
‡Perelman Agency, Barry
Pevner, Inc., Stephen
Picture of You, A
Producers & Creatives Group
‡Quillco Agency, The
Redwood Empire Agency
Sanders Literary Agency
Silver Screen Placements
‡Smith and Assoc., Susan
‡Sobel Mgmt. Associates
  (LSMA), Lee
‡Sorice Agency, Camille
Stanton & Associates Literary
  Agency
Star Literary Service
Tantleff Office, The
Total Acting Experience, A
Vines Agency, Inc., The
Warden, White & Kane, Inc.
Watt & Associates, Sandra
Whittlesey Agency, Peregrine
Wright Concept, The
Wright Representatives, Ann
Writer's Consulting Group

There are seven **Writer's Digest School** courses to help you write better and sell more:

Novel Writing Workshop. A professional novelist helps you iron out your plot, develop your main characters, write the background for your novel, and complete the opening scene and a summary of your novel's complete story. You'll even identify potential publishers and write a query letter.

Marketing Your Nonfiction Book. You'll work with your mentor to create a book proposal that you can send directly to a publisher. You'll develop and refine your book idea, write a chapter-by-chapter outline of your subject, line up your sources of information, write sample chapters, and complete your query letter.

Writing & Selling Short Stories. Learn the basics of writing/selling short stories: plotting, characterization, dialogue, theme, conflict, and other elements of a marketable short story. Course includes writing assignments and one complete short story.

Writing & Selling Nonfiction Articles. Master the fundamentals of writing/selling nonfiction articles: finding article ideas, conducting interviews, writing effective query letters and attention-getting leads, targeting your articles to the right publication. Course includes writing assignments and one complete article manuscript (and its revision).

Writing Your Life Stories. With the help of a professional writer you'll chronicle your life or your family's. Learn the important steps to documenting your history including researching and organizing your material, continuity, pacing and more!

Writer's Digest Criticism Service. Have your work evaluated by a professional writer before you submit it for pay. Whether you write books, articles, short stories or poetry, you'll get an objective review plus the specific writing and marketing advice that only a professional can provide.

Secrets of Selling Your Manuscripts. Discover all the best-kept secrets for mailing out strategic, targeted manuscript submissions. Learn how to "slant" your writing so you can publish the same material over and over, which publishing houses are your best bet, and much more.

Mail this card today for **FREE** information!

NO POSTAGE
NECESSARY
IF MAILED
IN THE
UNITED STATES

BUSINESS REPLY MAIL

FIRST-CLASS MAIL   PERMIT NO. 17   CINCINNATI, OHIO

POSTAGE WILL BE PAID BY ADDRESSEE

WRITER'S DIGEST SCHOOL
1507 DANA AVE
CINCINNATI OH 45207-9965

III—AGENCIES PREFERRING TO WORK WITH ESTABLISHED WRITERS, MOSTLY OBTAIN NEW CLIENTS THROUGH REFERRALS

Nonfee-charging agents

Andrews & Associates Inc., Bart
Authors' Literary Agency
Axelrod Agency, The
Balkin Agency, Inc.
‡Bedford Book Works, Inc., The
Borchardt Inc., Georges
‡Brady Literary Management
Brandenburgh & Associates Literary Agency
Brandt & Brandt Literary Agents Inc.
Brown Associates Inc., Marie
Brown Literary Agency, Inc., Andrea
Casselman Literary Agent, Martha
‡Cohen Agency, The
Collin Literary Agent, Frances
Congdon Associates, Inc., Don
Connor Literary Agency
Crawford Literary Agency
Curtis Associates, Inc., Richard
de la Haba Agency Inc., The Lois
Diamond Literary Agency, Inc. (CO)
Elmo Agency Inc., Ann
Feiler Literary Agency, Florence
Flaherty, Literary Agent, Joyce A.
Foley Literary Agency, The
Gartenberg, Literary Agent, Max
‡Goodman Associates
Greene, Arthur B.
‡Gregory Inc., Blanche C.
‡Grosvenor Literary Agency, Deborah
Henshaw Group, Richard
Hochmann Books, John L.
Hoffman Literary Agency, Berenice
Hogenson Agency, Barbara
International Creative Management
‡Jet Literary Associates, Inc.
Kellock Company, Inc., The
Kidde, Hoyt & Picard
Klinger, Inc., Harvey
Lasher Agency, The Maureen
Levine Literary Agency, Inc., Ellen
‡Lichtman, Trister, Singer & Ross
Literary and Creative Artists Agency Inc.

Lord Literistic, Inc., Sterling
Love Literary Agency, Nancy
‡Lukeman Literary Management Ltd.
Maass Literary Agency, Donald
McGrath, Helen
Mann Agency, Carol
March Tenth, Inc.
Martell Agency, The
‡Mendez Inc., Toni
Metropolitan Talent Agency 100
Miller Agency, The
Moran Agency, Maureen
Morris Agency, William
Morrison, Inc., Henry
Multimedia Product Development, Inc.
Naggar Literary Agency, Jean V.
Nazor Literary Agency, Karen
Nugent Literary
Ober Associates, Harold
Palmer & Dodge Agency, The
Paraview, Inc.
Parks Agency, The Richard
Pine Associates, Inc., Arthur
Pom Inc.
Porcelain, Sidney E.
Rees Literary Agency, Helen
Renaissance—H.N. Swanson
Riverside Literary Agency
‡Schlessinger Agency, Blanche
Schulman, A Literary Agency, Susan
Sebastian Literary Agency
Shukat Company Ltd., The
Siegel, International Literary Agency, Inc., Rosalie
Singer Literary Agency Inc., Evelyn
‡Slopen Literary Agency, Beverley
Smith, Literary Agent, Valerie
Spieler, F. Joseph
Spitzer Literary Agency, Philip G.
Stauffer Associates, Nancy
Stern Literary Agency, Gloria (TX)
Targ Literary Agency, Inc., Roslyn
Teal Literary Agency, Patricia
Van Duren Agency, Annette
Wald Associates, Inc., Mary Jack
Wallace Literary Agency, Inc.
Wasserman Literary Agency, Inc., Harriet
Weingel-Fidel Agency, The

Weyr Agency, Rhoda
Wieser & Wieser, Inc.
Wreschner, Authors' Representative, Ruth
Writers House
Zahler Literary Agency, Karen Gantz

Fee-charging agents

Acacia House Publishing Services Ltd.
Blake Group Literary Agency, The
Collier Associates
‡Fort Ross Inc. Russian-American Publishing Projects
Howard Agency, The Eddy
JLM Literary Agents
Marshall Agency, The Evan
Mews Books Ltd.
Nelson Literary Agency & Lecture Bureau, BK
Portman Organization, The
Rogers Literary Representation, Irene
Southern Literary Agency
Steinberg Literary Agency, Michael
Strong Literary Agency, Marianne
Writer's Consulting Group

Script agents

Above The Line Agency
‡Adams, Ltd., Bret
Agapé Productions
Agency, The
‡Amsel, Eisenstadt & Frazier, Inc.
Bennett Agency, The
Berman Boals and Flynn
‡Bloom & Associates, East, J. Michael
‡Bloom & Associates, West, J. Michael
‡Bohrman Agency, The
‡Broder Kurland Webb Uffner Agency, The
Buchwald Agency, Don
Communications and Entertainment, Inc.
‡Contemporary Artists
Coppage Company, The
Dykeman Associates Inc.
Feiler Literary Agency, Florence
Freedman Dramatic Agency, Inc., Robert A.
French, Inc., Samuel

Gersh Agency, The
Gordon & Associates, Michelle
Greene, Arthur B.
‡Haeggstrom Office, The
Hodges Agency, Carolyn
Hogenson Agency, Barbara
Howard Agency, The Eddy
‡HWA Talent Reps.
International Creative
　Management
Kallen Agency, Leslie
Ketay Agency, The Joyce

‡Kopaloff Company, The
Lenhoff/Robinson Talent and
　Literary Agency, Inc.
Major Clients Agency
Metropolitan Talent Agency
Palmer, Dorothy
Renaissance—H.N. Swanson
Rogers and Associates,
　Stephanie
Scagnetti Talent & Literary
　Agency, Jack

Schulman, A Literary Agency,
　Susan
‡Shapiro-Lichtman
Sherman & Associates, Ken
Sister Mania Productions, Inc.
‡Stone Manners Agency
Turtle Agency, The
Van Duren Agency, Annette
‡Working Artists Talent
　Agency
Writers & Artists
Writer's Consulting Group

IV—AGENCIES HANDLING ONLY CERTAIN TYPES OF WORK OR WORK BY WRITERS UNDER CERTAIN CIRCUMSTANCES

Nonfee-charging agents
Brown Literary Agency, Inc.,
　Andrea
Bykofsky Associates, Inc.,
　Sheree
Charisma Communications,
　Ltd.
Columbia Literary Associates,
　Inc.
Connor Literary Agency
DHS Literary, Inc.
Educational Design Services,
　Inc.
Elek Associates, Peter
Fleming Agency, Peter
‡Ghosts & Collaborators
　International
Graham Literary Agency, Inc.
Gusay Literary Agency, The
　Charlotte
Hochmann Books, John L.

Lake Agency, The Candace
Levant & Wales, Literary
　Agency, Inc.
Moore Literary Agency
‡National Writers Literary
　Agency
Paul Literati, The Richard
Perkins Associates
‡Scovil Chichak Galen Literary
　Agency
Stepping Stone
Stern Literary Agency, Gloria
　(TX)
Toad Hall, Inc.
Weiner Literary Agency,
　Cherry

Fee-charging agents
Clark Literary Agency, SJ
Executive Excellence

Script agents
‡Amsel, Eisenstadt & Frazier,
　Inc.
Artists Agency, The
‡Camejo & Assoc., Suzanna
‡Dade/Schultz Associates
Dramatic Publishing
F.L.A.I.R. or First Literary
　Artists International
　Representatives
Geddes Agency
Gelff Agency, The Laya
‡Grossman & Assoc., Larry
Gurman Agency, The Susan
Hudson Agency
Kerin-Goldberg Associates
Kohner, Inc., Paul
Lake Agency, The Candace
Montgomery-West Literary
　Agency
‡Starwatcher
Warden, White & Kane, Inc.

V—AGENCIES NOT CURRENTLY SEEKING NEW CLIENTS

Nonfee-charging agents
‡Gregory Inc., Blanche C.
‡Oasis Literary Agency, The
‡Rittenberg Literary Agency,
　Inc., Ann
‡Schlessinger Agency, Blanche
Weil Agency, Inc., The Wendy
Weiner Literary Agency,
　Cherry

Fee-charging agents
Allegra Literary Agency
‡CDK Technical
　Communications, Inc.
‡Janus Literary Agency

Script agents
Communications Management
　Associates
Legacies
‡Premiere Artists Agency
Sister Mania Productions, Inc.
‡Working Artists Talent
　Agency

Subject Index

The subject index is divided into nonfiction and fiction subject categories for each section—Nonfee-charging Literary Agents, Fee-charging Literary Agents and Script Agents. To find an agent interested in the type of manuscript you've written, see the appropriate sections under subject headings that best describe your work. Check the Listings Index for the page number of the agent's listing. Agents who are open to most fiction or nonfiction subjects appear in the "Open" heading. Note: Double daggers (‡) preceding titles indicate listings new to this edition.

NONFEE-CHARGING AGENTS/FICTION

Action/adventure: Allan Agency, Lee; Allen Literary Agency, Linda; Amsterdam Agency, Marcia; Baldi Literary Agency, Malaga; Barrett Books Inc., Loretta; Behar Literary Agency, Josh; Bernstein, Pam; ‡Bial Agency, Daniel; Bova Literary Agency, The Barbara; Brandt & Brandt Literary Agents Inc.; ‡Brock Gannon Literary Agency; Browne Ltd., Pema; Buck Agency, Howard; Carvainis Agency, Inc., Maria; Circle of Confusion Ltd.; Curtis Associates, Inc., Richard; Cypher, Author's Representative, James R.; DH Literary, Inc.; DHS Literary, Inc.; Diamant Literary Agency, The Writer's Workshop, Inc., Anita; Doyen Literary Services, Inc.; Ducas, Robert; Dupree/Miller and Associates Inc. Literary; Dystel Literary Management, Jane; Elliott Agency; Elmo Agency Inc., Ann; Esq. Literary Productions; Farber Literary Agency Inc.; ‡Feigen Literary Agency, Brenda; Flannery Literary; ‡Fleming Associates, Arthur; Fleury Agency, B.R.; Gibson Agency, The Sebastian; Goldfarb & Graybill, Attorneys at Law; Greenburger Associates, Inc., Sanford J.; Greene, Arthur B.; Greene, Literary Agent, Randall Elisha; ‡Grosvenor Literary Agency, Deborah; Gusay Literary Agency, The Charlotte; Hawkins & Associates, Inc., John; Henshaw Group, Richard; Herner Rights Agency, Susan; Jabberwocky Literary Agency; Klinger, Inc., Harvey; Lampack Agency, Inc., Peter; Lantz-Joy Harris Literary Agency Inc., The Robert; Larsen/Elizabeth Pomada Literary Agents, Michael; Lasher Agency, The Maureen; Lewis & Company, Karen; Lincoln Literary Agency, Ray; Lindstrom Literary Group; Literary Group, The; ‡Lukeman Literary Management Ltd.; McBride Literary Agency, Margret; Mainhardt Agency, Ricia; Manus & Associates Literary Agency, Inc.; Metropolitan Talent Agency; Michaels Literary Agency, Inc., Doris S.; Morrison, Inc., Henry; Mura Enterprises, Inc. Dee; Naggar Literary Agency, Jean V.; ‡National Writers Literary Agency; Nazor Literary Agency, Karen; New Brand Agency Group; Norma-Lewis Agency, The; Otitis Media; Paraview, Inc.; Parks Agency, The Richard; Pelham Literary Agency; Pelter, Rodney; Pevner, Inc., Stephen; Pine Associates, Inc, Arthur; Pom Inc.; Potomac Literary Agency, The; Quicksilver Books-Literary Agents; Renaissance—H.N. Swanson; Rose Agency, Inc.; ‡Russell & Volkening; Sanders Literary Agency, Victoria; Schmidt Literary Agency, Harold; Seymour Agency, The; Travis Literary Agency, Susan; Van Duren Agency, Annette; Vines Agency, Inc., The; Wald Associates, Inc., Mary Jack; Weiner Literary Agency, Cherry; West Coast Literary Associates; Wreschner, Authors' Representative, Ruth; Zeckendorf Assoc. Inc., Susan

Cartoon/comic: Axelrod Agency, The; Baldi Literary Agency, Malaga; Barrett Books Inc., Loretta; ‡Bial Agency, Daniel; Buck Agency, Howard; Circle of Confusion Ltd.; DH Literary, Inc.; Dupree/Miller and Associates Inc. Literary; Gibson Agency, The Sebastian; Gusay Literary Agency, The Charlotte; Hawkins & Associates, Inc., John; Jabberwocky Literary Agency; Lantz-Joy Harris Literary Agency Inc., The Robert; Levant & Wales, Literary Agency, Inc.; Literary Group, The; Metropolitan Talent Agency; Nazor Literary Agency, Karen; Pelter, Rodney; Pevner, Inc., Stephen; Van Duren Agency, Annette; Vines Agency, Inc., The

Confessional: Barrett Books Inc., Loretta; ‡Brock Gannon Literary Agency; Buck Agency, Howard; Circle of Confusion Ltd.; ‡Feigen Literary Agency, Brenda; Gusay Literary Agency, The Charlotte; Lantz-Joy Harris Literary Agency Inc., The Robert; ‡Lukeman Literary Management Ltd.; Manus & Associates Literary Agency, Inc.; March Tenth, Inc.; Metropolitan Talent Agency; Pelter, Rodney

Contemporary issues: Adler & Robin Books Inc.; Agents Inc. for Medical and Mental Health Professionals; Allan Agency, Lee; Allen Literary Agency, Linda; ‡Authors Alliance, Inc.; Baldi Literary Agency, Malaga; Barrett Books Inc., Loretta; ‡Bedford Book Works, Inc., The; Bernstein, Pam; ‡Bial Agency, Daniel; Boates Literary Agency, Reid; ‡Book Deals, Inc.; Bova Literary Agency, The Barbara; Brandt Agency, The Joan; Brandt & Brandt Literary Agents Inc.; ‡Brock Gannon Literary Agency; Brown Associates Inc., Marie; Browne Ltd., Pema; Buck Agency, Howard; Cantrell-Colas Inc., Literary Agency; Castiglia Literary Agency; Charisma Communications, Ltd.; Circle of Confusion Ltd.; ‡Cohen Agency, The; Connor Literary Agency; Cypher, Author's Representative, James R.; de la Haba Agency Inc., The Lois; DH Literary, Inc.; Diamant Literary Agency, The Writer's Workshop, Inc., Anita; Dijkstra Literary Agency, Sandra; Doyen Literary Services, Inc.; Ducas, Robert; Dupree/Miller and Associates Inc. Literary; Dystel Literary Management, Jane; Elliott Agency; Elmo Agency Inc., Ann; Esq. Literary Productions; Farber Literary Agency Inc.; ‡Feigen Literary Agency, Brenda; Feiler Literary Agency, Florence; Flaherty, Literary

Agent, Joyce A.; Flannery Literary; ‡Fleming Associates, Arthur; Garon-Brooke Assoc. Inc., Jay; Gibson Agency, The Sebastian; Goldfarb & Graybill, Attorneys at Law; ‡Goodman-Andrew-Agency, Inc.; Gordon Agency, Charlotte; Greenburger Associates, Inc., Sanford J.; Greene, Literary Agent, Randall Elisha; ‡Grosvenor Literary Agency, Deborah; Gusay Literary Agency, The Charlotte; Hawkins & Associates, Inc., John; Herner Rights Agency, Susan; IMG Literary; Jabberwocky Literary Agency; Kidde, Hoyt & Picard; Kouts, Literary Agent, Barbara S.; Lampack Agency, Inc., Peter; Lantz-Joy Harris Literary Agency Inc., The Robert; Larsen/Elizabeth Pomada Literary Agents, Michael; Lasher Agency, The Maureen; Levine Communications, Inc., James; Lincoln Literary Agency, Ray; Lindstrom Literary Group; Literary Group, The; Lowenstein Associates, Inc.; McGrath, Helen; Mainhardt Agency, Ricia; Manus & Associates Literary Agency, Inc.; Markowitz Literary Agency, Barbara; Metropolitan Talent Agency; Michaels Literary Agency, Inc., Doris S.; Multimedia Product Development, Inc.; Mura Enterprises, Inc., Dee; Naggar Literary Agency, Jean V.; Nazor Literary Agency, Karen; New Brand Agency Group; Norma-Lewis Agency, The; Palmer & Dodge Agency, The; Paraview, Inc.; Parks Agency, The Richard; Paul Literati, The Richard; Pelter, Rodney; Pevner, Inc., Stephen; Pocono Literary Agency, Inc.; Pom Inc.; Potomac Literary Agency, The; Pryor, Inc., Roberta; Publishing Services; Rees Literary Agency, Helen; Renaissance—H.N. Swanson; Rinaldi Literary Agency, Angela; Robbins Literary Agency, BJ; Rose Agency, Inc.; Russell-Simenauer Literary Agency Inc.; Sanders Literary Agency, Victoria; Schmidt Literary Agency, Harold; Schulman, A Literary Agency, Susan; Seligman, Literary Agent, Lynn; Shepard Agency, The; Singer Literary Agency Inc., Evelyn; ‡Skolnick, Irene; Spitzer Literary Agency, Philip G.; Stauffer Associates, Nancy; Stepping Stone; Stern Literary Agency (TX), Gloria; Travis Literary Agency, Susan; Valcourt Agency, Inc., The Richard R.; Van Der Leun & Associates; Van Duren Agency, Annette; Vines Agency, Inc., The; Wald Associates, Inc., Mary Jack; Watkins Loomis Agency, Inc.; Watt & Associates, Sandra; Wecksler-Incomco; Weiner Literary Agency, Cherry; Weingel-Fidel Agency, The; West Coast Literary Associates; Wieser & Wieser, Inc.; Witherspoon & Associates, Inc.; Wreschner, Authors' Representative, Ruth; Zeckendorf Assoc. Inc., Susan

Detective/police/crime: Adler & Robin Books Inc.; Agents Inc. for Medical and Mental Health Professionals; Allan Agency, Lee; Allen Literary Agency, Linda; Amsterdam Agency, Marcia; Appleseeds Management; ‡Authors Alliance, Inc.; ‡Authors' Literary Agency; Axelrod Agency, The; Baldi Literary Agency, Malaga; Barrett Books Inc., Loretta; Behar Literary Agency, Josh; Bernstein, Pam; ‡Bial Agency, Daniel; Boates Literary Agency, Reid; Bova Literary Agency, The Barbara; Brandt Agency, The Joan; Brandt & Brandt Literary Agents Inc.; ‡Brock Gannon Literary Agency; Browne Ltd., Pema; Buck Agency, Howard; Cantrell-Colas Inc., Literary Agency; Carvainis Agency, Inc., Maria; Charisma Communications, Ltd.; Circle of Confusion Ltd.; ‡Cohen Agency, The; Cohen, Inc. Literary Agency, Ruth; Collin Literary Agent, Frances; Connor Literary Agency; Curtis Associates, Inc., Richard; Cypher, Author's Representative, James R.; de la Haba Agency Inc., The Lois; DH Literary, Inc.; DHS Literary, Inc.; Diamant Literary Agency, The Writer's Workshop, Inc., Anita; Diamond Literary Agency, Inc. (CO); Dijkstra Literary Agency, Sandra; Doyen Literary Services, Inc.; Ducas, Robert; Dupree/Miller and Associates Inc. Literary; Dystel Literary Management, Jane; Ellenberg Literary Agency, Ethan; Elliott Agency; Elmo Agency Inc., Ann; Esq. Literary Productions; ‡Feigen Literary Agency, Brenda; Feiler Literary Agency, Florence; Flaherty, Literary Agent, Joyce A.; ‡Fleming Associates, Arthur; Fleury Agency, B.R.; Garon-Brooke Assoc. Inc., Jay; Gibson Agency, The Sebastian; Goldfarb & Graybill, Attorneys at Law; Graham Literary Agency, Inc.; Greenburger Associates, Inc., Sanford J.; Greene, Arthur B.; Greene, Literary Agent, Randall Elisha; ‡Grosvenor Literary Agency, Deborah; Gusay Literary Agency, The Charlotte; Hawkins & Associates, Inc., John; Henshaw Group, Richard; Herner Rights Agency, Susan; Hull House Literary Agency; IMG Literary; J de S Associates Inc.; Jabberwocky Literary Agency; ‡Just Write Agency, Inc.; Kern Literary Agency, Natasha; Kidde, Hoyt & Picard; Klinger, Inc., Harvey; Lampack Agency, Inc., Peter; Lantz-Joy Harris Literary Agency Inc., The Robert; Larsen/Elizabeth Pomada Literary Agents, Michael; Lasher Agency, The Maureen; Lewis & Company, Karen; Lincoln Literary Agency, Ray; Lindstrom Literary Group; Literary Group, The; Love Literary Agency, Nancy; Lowenstein Associates, Inc.; Maass Literary Agency, Donald; McBride Literary Agency, Margret; McGrath, Helen; Mainhardt Agency, Ricia; Manus & Associates Literary Agency, Inc.; Markowitz Literary Agency, Barbara; Metropolitan Talent Agency; Morrison, Inc., Henry; Multimedia Product Development, Inc.; Mura Enterprises, Inc., Dee; Naggar Literary Agency, Jean V.; New Brand Agency Group; Norma-Lewis Agency, The; Parks Agency, The Richard; Pelham Literary Agency; Pelter, Rodney; Perkins Associates; Pevner, Inc., Stephen; Pine Associates, Inc, Arthur; Pocono Literary Agency, Inc.; Pom Inc.; Potomac Literary Agency, The; Protter Literary Agent, Susan Ann; Pryor, Inc., Roberta; Rees Literary Agency, Helen; Renaissance—H.N. Swanson; Rinaldi Literary Agency, Angela; Robbins Literary Agency, BJ; Rowland Agency, The Damaris; Rubinstein Literary Agency, Inc., Pesha; ‡Russell & Volkening; ‡Schlessinger Agency, Blanche; Schmidt Literary Agency, Harold; Schulman, A Literary Agency, Susan; Seligman, Literary Agent, Lynn; Seymour Agency, The; Singer Literary Agency Inc., Evelyn; ‡Slopen Literary Agency, Beverley; Spitzer Literary Agency, Philip G.; Stern Literary Agency (TX), Gloria; Targ Literary Agency, Inc., Roslyn; Van Duren Agency, Annette; Vines Agency, Inc., The; Wald Associates, Inc., Mary Jack; Wallace Literary Agency, Inc.; Ware Literary Agency, John A.; Watkins Loomis Agency, Inc.; Watt & Associates, Sandra; Weiner Literary Agency, Cherry; West Coast Literary Associates; Wieser & Wieser, Inc.; Witherspoon & Associates, Inc.; Wreschner, Authors' Representative, Ruth; Zeckendorf Assoc. Inc., Susan; ‡Zitwer Agency, Barbara J.

Erotica: Allan Agency, Lee; Agency Chicago; ‡Authors Alliance, Inc.; Baldi Literary Agency, Malaga; Barrett Books Inc., Loretta; ‡Bial Agency, Daniel; Brandt & Brandt Literary Agents Inc.; ‡Brock Gannon Literary Agency; Buck Agency, Howard; Circle of Confusion Ltd.; ‡Cohen Agency, The; DHS Literary, Inc.; Gusay Literary Agency, The Charlotte; Lantz-Joy Harris Literary Agency Inc., The Robert; Lewis & Company, Karen; Lowenstein Associates, Inc.; Mainhardt Agency, Ricia; Paraview, Inc.; Paul Literati, The Richard; Pelter, Rodney; Pevner, Inc., Stephen; Pom Inc.; Travis Literary Agency, Susan

Ethnic: Allen Literary Agency, Linda; Apollo Entertainment; Baldi Literary Agency, Malaga; Barrett Books Inc.,

Loretta; Bernstein, Pam; ‡Bial Agency, Daniel; ‡Book Deals, Inc.; Brandt & Brandt Literary Agents Inc.; ‡Brock Gannon Literary Agency; Brown Associates Inc., Marie; Browne Ltd., Pema; Buck Agency, Howard; Cantrell-Colas Inc., Literary Agency; Castiglia Literary Agency; Circle of Confusion Ltd.; ‡Cohen Agency, The; Cohen, Inc. Literary Agency, Ruth; Collin Literary Agent, Frances; Connor Literary Agency; Crown International Literature and Arts Agency, Bonnie R.; Cypher, Author's Representative, James R.; Daves Agency, Joan; de la Haba Agency Inc., The Lois; DH Literary, Inc.; DHS Literary, Inc.; Dijkstra Literary Agency, Sandra; Doyen Literary Services, Inc.; Dupree/Miller and Associates Inc. Literary; Dystel Literary Management, Jane; Elmo Agency Inc., Ann; Eth Literary Representation, Felicia; Flannery Literary; ‡Fleming Associates, Arthur; Fleury Agency, B.R.; Gibson Agency, The Sebastian; Goldfarb & Graybill, Attorneys at Law; ‡Goodman-Andrew-Agency, Inc.; Greenburger Associates, Inc., Sanford J.; ‡Grosvenor Literary Agency, Deborah; Gusay Literary Agency, The Charlotte; Hawkins & Associates, Inc., John; Henshaw Group, Richard; Herner Rights Agency, Susan; Jabberwocky Literary Agency; Kern Literary Agency, Natasha; Lantz-Joy Harris Literary Agency Inc., The Robert; Larsen/Elizabeth Pomada Literary Agents, Michael; Levant & Wales, Literary Agency, Inc.; Lewis & Company, Karen; ‡Lichtman, Trister, Singer & Ross; Lincoln Literary Agency, Ray; Lindstrom Literary Group; Literary Group, The; Love Literary Agency, Nancy; Lowenstein Associates, Inc.; McBride Literary Agency, Margret; Mainhardt Agency, Ricia; Manus & Associates Literary Agency, Inc.; March Tenth, Inc.; Markowitz Literary Agency, Barbara; Multimedia Product Development, Inc.; Mura Enterprises, Inc., Dee; Naggar Literary Agency, Jean V.; Nazor Literary Agency, Karen; Nine Muses and Apollo Inc.; Palmer & Dodge Agency, The; Paraview, Inc.; Parks Agency, The Richard; Paul Literati, The Richard; Pelter, Rodney; Perkins Associates; Pevner, Inc., Stephen; Potomac Literary Agency, The; Publishing Services; Renaissance—H.N. Swanson; Rinaldi Literary Agency, Angela; Robbins Literary Agency, BJ; Rubinstein Literary Agency, Inc., Pesha; ‡Russell & Volkening; Schmidt Literary Agency, Harold; Seligman, Literary Agent, Lynn; Seymour Agency, The; Singer Literary Agency Inc., Evelyn; Spieler, F. Joseph; Stepping Stone; Stern Literary Agency (TX), Gloria; ‡Sweeney Literary Agency, Emma; Travis Literary Agency, Susan; Van Der Leun & Associates; Vines Agency, Inc., The; Wald Associates, Inc., Mary Jack; Watkins Loomis Agency, Inc.; Witherspoon & Associates, Inc.; Wreschner, Authors' Representative, Ruth; ‡Young Agency Inc., The Gay; Zeckendorf Assoc. Inc., Susan; ‡Zitwer Agency, Barbara J.

Experimental: Agency Chicago; Baldi Literary Agency, Malaga; Barrett Books Inc., Loretta; Brandt & Brandt Literary Agents Inc.; Buck Agency, Howard; Cantrell-Colas Inc., Literary Agency; Circle of Confusion Ltd.; Connor Literary Agency; Crown International Literature and Arts Agency, Bonnie R.; Diamant Literary Agency, The Writer's Workshop, Inc., Anita; Dupree/Miller and Associates Inc. Literary; Flannery Literary; Fleury Agency, B.R.; Gusay Literary Agency, The Charlotte; Hawkins & Associates, Inc., John; Lantz-Joy Harris Literary Agency Inc., The Robert; Larsen/Elizabeth Pomada Literary Agents, Michael; Levant & Wales, Literary Agency, Inc.; ‡Lukeman Literary Management Ltd.; Mura Enterprises, Inc., Dee; Paul Literati, The Richard; Pelter, Rodney; Pevner, Inc., Stephen; Potomac Literary Agency, The; Rinaldi Literary Agency, Angela; Stern Literary Agency (TX), Gloria; Wald Associates, Inc., Mary Jack; West Coast Literary Associates

Family saga: Axelrod Agency, The; Barrett Books Inc., Loretta; Boates Literary Agency, Reid; Bova Literary Agency, The Barbara; Brandt & Brandt Literary Agents Inc.; ‡Brock Gannon Literary Agency; Buck Agency, Howard; Cantrell-Colas Inc., Literary Agency; Carvainis Agency, Inc., Maria; Circle of Confusion Ltd.; Collin Literary Agent, Frances; Connor Literary Agency; Crown International Literature and Arts Agency, Bonnie R.; Curtis Associates, Inc., Richard; Cypher, Author's Representative, James R.; Daves Agency, Joan; de la Haba Agency Inc., The Lois; Diamant Literary Agency, The Writer's Workshop, Inc., Anita; Diamond Literary Agency, Inc. (CO); Dijkstra Literary Agency, Sandra; Doyen Literary Services, Inc.; Ducas, Robert; Dupree/Miller and Associates Inc. Literary; Dystel Literary Management, Jane; Ellenberg Literary Agency, Ethan; Elmo Agency Inc., Ann; ‡Feigen Literary Agency, Brenda; Feiler Literary Agency, Florence; Flaherty, Literary Agent, Joyce A.; Flannery Literary; ‡Fleming Associates, Arthur; Fleury Agency, B.R.; Garon-Brooke Assoc. Inc., Jay; Gibson Agency, The Sebastian; Gordon Agency, Charlotte; Greenburger Associates, Inc., Sanford J.; Greene, Literary Agent, Randall Elisha; ‡Grosvenor Literary Agency, Deborah; Gusay Literary Agency, The Charlotte; Hawkins & Associates, Inc., John; Henshaw Group, Richard; Herner Rights Agency, Susan; Jabberwocky Literary Agency; Klinger, Inc., Harvey; Kouts, Literary Agent, Barbara S.; Lampack Agency, Inc., Peter; Lantz-Joy Harris Literary Agency Inc., The Robert; Larsen/Elizabeth Pomada Literary Agents, Michael; Lasher Agency, The Maureen; Lincoln Literary Agency, Ray; Lindstrom Literary Group; Literary Group, The; Maass Literary Agency, Donald; McGrath, Helen; Mainhardt Agency, Ricia; Manus & Associates Literary Agency, Inc.; March Tenth, Inc.; Marcil Literary Agency, Inc., The Denise; Metropolitan Talent Agency; Michaels Literary Agency, Inc., Doris S.; Morrison, Inc., Henry; Multimedia Product Development, Inc.; Mura Enterprises, Inc., Dee; Naggar Literary Agency, Jean V.; Norma-Lewis Agency, The; Paraview, Inc.; Parks Agency, The Richard; Paul Literati, The Richard; Pelter, Rodney; Pine Associates, Inc, Arthur; Pocono Literary Agency, Inc.; Potomac Literary Agency, The; Renaissance—H.N. Swanson; Rinaldi Literary Agency, Angela; Robbins Literary Agency, BJ; Rose Agency, Inc.; Russell-Simenauer Literary Agency Inc.; Sanders Literary Agency, Victoria; Schmidt Literary Agency, Harold; Shepard Agency, The; Spieler, F. Joseph; Stern Literary Agency (TX), Gloria; ‡Sweeney Literary Agency, Emma; Wald Associates, Inc., Mary Jack; Watt & Associates, Sandra; Weiner Literary Agency, Cherry; Witherspoon & Associates, Inc.; Wreschner, Authors' Representative, Ruth; Zeckendorf Assoc. Inc., Susan

Fantasy: Allan Agency, Lee; Apollo Entertainment; Appleseeds Management; ‡Authors Alliance, Inc.; Authors' Literary Agency; Barrett Books Inc., Loretta; Becker Literary Agency, The Wendy; Behar Literary Agency, Josh; ‡Brock Gannon Literary Agency; Carvainis Agency, Inc., Maria; Circle of Confusion Ltd.; ‡Cohen Agency, The; Collin Literary Agent, Frances; Curtis Associates, Inc., Richard; de la Haba Agency Inc., The Lois; Doyen Literary Services, Inc.; Dupree/Miller and Associates Inc. Literary; Ellenberg Literary Agency, Ethan; ‡Fleming Associates, Arthur; Fleury Agency, B.R.; ‡Fullerton Associates, Sheryl B.; Garon-Brooke Assoc. Inc., Jay; Gibson Agency, The

Sebastian; Graham Literary Agency, Inc.; Gusay Literary Agency, The Charlotte; Hawkins & Associates, Inc., John; Henshaw Group, Richard; Herner Rights Agency, Susan; Jabberwocky Literary Agency; Larsen/Elizabeth Pomada Literary Agents, Michael; Lincoln Literary Agency, Ray; Lindstrom Literary Group; Literary Group, The; Maass Literary Agency, Donald; Mainhardt Agency, Ricia; Metropolitan Talent Agency; Mura Enterprises, Inc., Dee; New Brand Agency Group; ‡Oasis Literary Agency, The; Paraview, Inc.; Pelham Literary Agency; Pelter, Rodney; Pom Inc.; Renaissance—H.N. Swanson; Seligman, Literary Agent, Lynn; Smith, Literary Agent, Valerie; Vines Agency, Inc., The; Weiner Literary Agency, Cherry

Feminist: Allan Agency, Lee; Allen Literary Agency, Linda; Baldi Literary Agency, Malaga; Barrett Books Inc., Loretta; ‡Bial Agency, Daniel; Brandt & Brandt Literary Agents Inc.; ‡Brock Gannon Literary Agency; Brown Associates Inc., Marie; Browne Ltd., Pema; Buck Agency, Howard; Cantrell-Colas Inc., Literary Agency; Circle of Confusion Ltd.; ‡Cohen Agency, The; Curtis Associates, Inc., Richard; Cypher, Author's Representative, James R.; de la Haba Agency Inc., The Lois; DH Literary, Inc.; DHS Literary, Inc.; Diamant Literary Agency, The Writer's Workshop, Inc., Anita; Dijkstra Literary Agency, Sandra; Dupree/Miller and Associates Inc. Literary; Eth Literary Representation, Felicia; ‡Feigen Literary Agency, Brenda; Flaherty, Literary Agent, Joyce A.; ‡Fleming Associates, Arthur; Gibson Agency, The Sebastian; Goldfarb & Graybill, Attorneys at Law; Greenburger Associates, Inc., Sanford J.; Gusay Literary Agency, The Charlotte; Hawkins & Associates, Inc., John; Herner Rights Agency, Susan; Kern Literary Agency, Natasha; Kidde, Hoyt & Picard; Kouts, Literary Agent, Barbara S.; Lantz-Joy Harris Literary Agency Inc., The Robert; Larsen/Elizabeth Pomada Literary Agents, Michael; Lasher Agency, The Maureen; ‡Leap First; Levant & Wales, Literary Agency, Inc.; ‡Lichtman, Trister, Singer & Ross; Lincoln Literary Agency, Ray; Literary Group, The; Lowenstein Associates, Inc.; Mainhardt Agency, Ricia; Manus & Associates Literary Agency, Inc.; Michaels Literary Agency, Inc., Doris S.; Mura Enterprises, Inc., Dee; Naggar Literary Agency, Jean V.; Nazor Literary Agency, Karen; Palmer & Dodge Agency, The; Parks Agency, The Richard; Pelter, Rodney; Pom Inc.; Potomac Literary Agency, The; Publishing Services; Rinaldi Literary Agency, Angela; Russell-Simenauer Literary Agency Inc.; Sanders Literary Agency, Victoria; Schmidt Literary Agency, Harold; Seligman, Literary Agent, Lynn; Singer Literary Agency Inc., Evelyn; Spieler, F. Joseph; Stern Literary Agency (TX), Gloria; ‡Sweeney Literary Agency, Emma; Travis Literary Agency, Susan; Vines Agency, Inc., The; Wald Associates, Inc., Mary Jack; Witherspoon & Associates, Inc.; ‡Young Agency Inc., The Gay

Gay: Allen Literary Agency, Linda; Apollo Entertainment; Barrett Books Inc., Loretta; ‡Bial Agency, Daniel; Brandt & Brandt Literary Agents Inc.; ‡Brock Gannon Literary Agency; Brown Associates Inc., Marie; Browne Ltd., Pema; Buck Agency, Howard; Circle of Confusion Ltd.; Cypher, Author's Representative, James R.; Daves Agency, Joan; de la Haba Agency Inc., The Lois; DHS Literary, Inc.; Diamant Literary Agency, The Writer's Workshop, Inc., Anita; Dupree/Miller and Associates Inc. Literary; Dystel Literary Management, Jane; Eth Literary Representation, Felicia; ‡Feigen Literary Agency, Brenda; Feiler Literary Agency, Florence; ‡Fleming Associates, Arthur; ‡Fullerton Associates, Sheryl B.; Garon-Brooke Assoc. Inc., Jay; Goldfarb & Graybill, Attorneys at Law; ‡Goodman-Andrew-Agency, Inc.; Gordon Agency, Charlotte; Greenburger Associates, Inc., Sanford J.; ‡Grosvenor Literary Agency, Deborah; Gusay Literary Agency, The Charlotte; Hawkins & Associates, Inc., John; Jabberwocky Literary Agency; Kidde, Hoyt & Picard; Lantz-Joy Harris Literary Agency Inc., The Robert; Larsen/Elizabeth Pomada Literary Agents, Michael; Levant & Wales, Literary Agency, Inc.; ‡Lichtman, Trister, Singer & Ross; Lincoln Literary Agency, Ray; Literary Group, The; Lowenstein Associates, Inc.; Mura Enterprises, Inc., Dee; Palmer & Dodge Agency, The; Paraview, Inc.; Parks Agency, The Richard; Paul Literati, The Richard; Perkins Associates; Pevner, Inc., Stephen; Potomac Literary Agency, The; Robbins Literary Agency, BJ; Russell-Simenauer Literary Agency Inc.; Sanders Literary Agency, Victoria; Seligman, Literary Agent, Lynn; Spieler, F. Joseph; ‡Sweeney Literary Agency, Emma; Travis Literary Agency, Susan; Wald Associates, Inc., Mary Jack; Watkins Loomis Agency, Inc.; Witherspoon & Associates, Inc.; Wreschner, Authors' Representative, Ruth; ‡Zitwer Agency, Barbara J.

Glitz: Allen Literary Agency, Linda; Amsterdam Agency, Marcia; Authors Alliance, Inc.; Axelrod Agency, The; Barrett Books Inc., Loretta; Bova Literary Agency, The Barbara; Browne Ltd., Pema; Buck Agency, Howard; Carvainis Agency, Inc., Maria; Castiglia Literary Agency; Circle of Confusion Ltd.; Connor Literary Agency; DH Literary, Inc.; Diamond Literary Agency, Inc. (CO); Doyen Literary Services, Inc.; Dupree/Miller and Associates Inc. Literary; Elmo Agency Inc., Ann; Gibson Agency, The Sebastian; Goldfarb & Graybill, Attorneys at Law; Greenburger Associates, Inc., Sanford J.; Gusay Literary Agency, The Charlotte; Hawkins & Associates, Inc., John; Henshaw Group, Richard; Herner Rights Agency, Susan; Jabberwocky Literary Agency; Kidde, Hoyt & Picard; Klinger, Inc., Harvey; Lampack Agency, Inc., Peter; Lantz-Joy Harris Literary Agency Inc., The Robert; Larsen/Elizabeth Pomada Literary Agents, Michael; Mainhardt Agency, Ricia; Metropolitan Talent Agency; Multimedia Product Development, Inc.; Mura Enterprises, Inc., Dee; Parks Agency, The Richard; Pelter, Rodney; Pevner, Inc., Stephen; Pom Inc.; Quicksilver Books-Literary Agents; Rees Literary Agency, Helen; Rinaldi Literary Agency, Angela; Rubinstein Literary Agency, Inc., Pesha; Russell-Simenauer Literary Agency Inc.; ‡Schlessinger Agency, Blanche; Schmidt Literary Agency, Harold; Seymour Agency, The; Teal Literary Agency, Patricia; Wald Associates, Inc., Mary Jack; Weiner Literary Agency, Cherry; Witherspoon & Associates, Inc.; Wreschner, Authors' Representative, Ruth; Zeckendorf Assoc. Inc., Susan; ‡Zitwer Agency, Barbara J.

Historical: Amsterdam Agency, Marcia; Apollo Entertainment; ‡Authors Alliance, Inc.; Authors' Literary Agency; Axelrod Agency, The; Baldi Literary Agency, Malaga; Barrett Books Inc., Loretta; Bernstein, Pam; Blassingame Spectrum Corp.; ‡Book Deals, Inc.; Brandt & Brandt Literary Agents Inc.; ‡Brock Gannon Literary Agency; Brown Associates Inc., Marie; Brown Literary Agency, Inc., Andrea; Browne Ltd., Pema; Buck Agency, Howard; Cantrell-Colas Inc., Literary Agency; Carvainis Agency, Inc., Maria; Circle of Confusion Ltd.; ‡Cohen Agency, The; Cohen, Inc. Literary Agency, Ruth; Collin Literary Agent, Frances; Connor Literary Agency; Crown International Literature and Arts Agency, Bonnie R.; Curtis Associates, Inc., Richard; Cypher, Author's Representative, James R.; de la Haba Agency Inc., The Lois; DH Literary, Inc.; DHS Literary, Inc.; Diamant Literary Agency, The Writer's Workshop, Inc., Anita; Diamond Literary Agency, Inc. (CO); Doyen Literary Services, Inc.; Dupree/Miller and Associates Inc. Literary; Ellenberg Literary Agency, Ethan; Elmo Agency Inc., Ann; Feiler Literary Agency, Florence; Flaherty, Literary Agent, Joyce A.; Flannery Literary; ‡Fleming Associates, Arthur; Fleury Agency, B.R.; Gibson Agency, The Sebastian; Greenburger Associates, Inc., Sanford J.; ‡Grosvenor Literary Agency, Deborah; Gusay Literary Agency, The Charlotte; Hawkins & Associates, Inc., John; Henshaw Group, Richard; Herner Rights Agency, Susan; J de S Associates Inc.; Jabberwocky Literary Agency; ‡Just Write Agency, Inc.; Kern Literary Agency, Natasha; Kidde, Hoyt & Picard; Kouts, Literary Agent, Barbara S.; Lampack Agency, Inc., Peter; Lantz-Joy Harris Literary Agency Inc., The Robert; Larsen/Elizabeth Pomada Literary Agents, Michael; Lasher Agency, The Maureen; Lincoln Literary Agency, Ray; Lindstrom Literary Group; Literary Group, The; Lowenstein Associates, Inc.; Maass Literary Agency, Donald; McBride Literary Agency, Margret; Mainhardt Agency, Ricia; March Tenth, Inc.; Marcil Literary Agency, Inc., The Denise; Metropolitan Talent Agency; Michaels Literary Agency, Inc., Doris S.; Multimedia Product Development, Inc.; Mura Enterprises, Inc., Dee; Naggar Literary Agency, Jean V.; Nathan, Ruth; Norma-Lewis Agency, The; ‡Oasis Literary Agency, The; Otitis Media; Paraview, Inc.; Parks Agency, The Richard; Pelter, Rodney; Pocono Literary Agency, Inc.; Pom Inc.; Potomac Literary Agency, The; Pryor, Inc., Roberta; Publishing Services; Rees Literary Agency, Helen; Renaissance—H.N. Swanson; Rose Agency, Inc.; Rowland Agency, The Damaris; Russell-Simenauer Literary Agency Inc.; Schmidt Literary Agency, Harold; Schulman, A Literary Agency, Susan; Seligman, Literary Agent, Lynn; Seymour Agency, The; Shepard Agency, The; Singer Literary Agency Inc., Evelyn; ‡Skolnick, Irene; Toad Hall, Inc.; Travis Literary Agency, Susan; Valcourt Agency, Inc., The Richard R.; Van Der Leun & Associates; Wald Associates, Inc., Mary Jack; Wecksler-Incomco; Weiner Literary Agency, Cherry; West Coast Literary Associates; Wieser & Wieser, Inc.; Witherspoon & Associates, Inc.; Wreschner, Authors' Representative, Ruth; Zeckendorf Assoc. Inc., Susan

Horror: Allan Agency, Lee; Allen Literary Agency, Linda; Amsterdam Agency, Marcia; Appleseeds Management; Authors' Literary Agency; Barrett Books Inc., Loretta; ‡Brock Gannon Literary Agency; Buck Agency, Howard; Circle of Confusion Ltd.; ‡Cohen Agency, The; Connor Literary Agency; Curtis Associates, Inc., Richard; Cypher, Author's Representative, James R.; DHS Literary, Inc.; Doyen Literary Services, Inc.; Dupree/Miller and Associates Inc. Literary; Elliott Agency; ‡Fleming Associates, Arthur; Fleury Agency, B.R.; Gibson Agency, The Sebastian; Greene, Arthur B.; Henshaw Group, Richard; Herner Rights Agency, Susan; Jabberwocky Literary Agency; Klinger, Inc., Harvey; Larsen/Elizabeth Pomada Literary Agents, Michael; March Tenth, Inc.; ‡Lukeman Literary Management Ltd.; Maass Literary Agency, Donald; Mainhardt Agency, Ricia; March Tenth, Inc.; Metropolitan Talent Agency; New Brand Agency Group; Norma-Lewis Agency, The; Parks Agency, The Richard; Pelham Literary Agency; Perkins Associates; Pevner, Inc., Stephen; Pocono Literary Agency, Inc.; Pom Inc.; Schmidt Literary Agency, Harold; Seligman, Literary Agent, Lynn; Seymour Agency, The; Vines Agency, Inc., The; Wreschner, Authors' Representative, Ruth

Humor/satire: Barrett Books Inc., Loretta; ‡Bial Agency, Daniel; ‡Book Deals, Inc.; ‡Brock Gannon Literary Agency; Cantrell-Colas Inc., Literary Agency; Carvainis Agency, Inc., Maria; ‡Cohen Agency, The; Cypher, Author's Representative, James R.; Elliott Agency; ‡Fleming Associates, Arthur; Fleury Agency, B.R.; Gibson Agency, The Sebastian; Greene, Literary Agent, Randall Elisha; ‡Grosvenor Literary Agency, Deborah; Jabberwocky Literary Agency; Larsen/Elizabeth Pomada Literary Agents, Michael; Lowenstein Associates, Inc.; Mura Enterprises, Inc., Dee; New Brand Agency Group; Paul Literati, The Richard; Pevner, Inc., Stephen; Pocono Literary Agency, Inc.; Pom Inc.; Renaissance—H.N. Swanson; Rose Agency, Inc.; Seligman, Literary Agent, Lynn; Seymour Agency, The; Spieler, F. Joseph; Van Duren Agency, Annette; Vines Agency, Inc., The; Wald Associates, Inc., Mary Jack; ‡Zitwer Agency, Barbara J.

Juvenile: Barrett Books Inc., Loretta; ‡Brock Gannon Literary Agency; Brown Associates Inc., Marie; Brown Literary Agency, Inc., Andrea; Browne Ltd., Pema; Cantrell-Colas Inc., Literary Agency; Carvainis Agency, Inc., Maria; Circle of Confusion Ltd.; Cohen, Inc. Literary Agency, Ruth; de la Haba Agency Inc., The Lois; Diamant Literary Agency, The Writer's Workshop, Inc., Anita; Elek Associates, Peter; Ellenberg Literary Agency, Ethan; Elmo Agency Inc., Ann; Farber Literary Agency Inc.; Feiler Literary Agency, Florence; Flannery Literary; ‡Fleming Associates, Arthur; Fleury Agency, B.R.; Gibson Agency, The Sebastian; Gordon Agency, Charlotte; Greenburger Associates, Inc., Sanford J.; Gusay Literary Agency, The Charlotte; Hawkins & Associates, Inc., John; Henshaw Group, Richard; J de S Associates Inc.; Jabberwocky Literary Agency; Kirchoff/Wohlberg, Inc., Authors' Representation Division; Kouts, Literary Agent, Barbara S.; Kroll Literary Agency, Edite; Lincoln Literary Agency, Ray; Maccoby Literary Agency, Gina; Mainhardt Agency, Ricia; Markowitz Literary Agency, Barbara; Multimedia Product Development, Inc.; Mura Enterprises, Inc., Dee; ‡National Writers Literary Agency; Norma-Lewis Agency, The; Pocono Literary Agency, Inc.; Pryor, Inc., Roberta; Rose Agency, Inc.; Rubinstein Literary Agency, Inc., Pesha; ‡Russell & Volkening; Targ Literary Agency, Inc., Roslyn; Van Duren Agency, Annette; Vines Agency, Inc., The; Wald Associates, Inc., Mary Jack; Wasserman Literary Agency, Inc., Harriet; Wecksler-Incomco; Wreschner, Authors' Representative, Ruth; ‡Young Agency Inc., The Gay

Lesbian: Allen Literary Agency, Linda; Baldi Literary Agency, Malaga; Barrett Books Inc., Loretta; Brandt & Brandt Literary Agents Inc.; ‡Brock Gannon Literary Agency; Browne Ltd., Pema; Buck Agency, Howard; Circle of Confusion Ltd.; Cypher, Author's Representative, James R.; Dupree/Miller and Associates Inc. Literary; Dystel Literary Management, Jane; Eth Literary Representation, Felicia; ‡Feigen Literary Agency, Brenda; Feiler Literary Agency, Florence; ‡Fleming Associates, Arthur; ‡Fullerton Associates, Sheryl B.; ‡Goodman-Andrew-Agency, Inc.; Gordon Agency, Charlotte; Greenburger Associates, Inc., Sanford J.; ‡Grosvenor Literary Agency, Deborah; Gusay Literary Agency, The Charlotte; Hawkins & Associates, Inc., John; Jabberwocky Literary Agency; Kidde, Hoyt &

Picard; Lantz-Joy Harris Literary Agency Inc., The Robert; Larsen/Elizabeth Pomada Literary Agents, Michael; Levant & Wales, Literary Agency, Inc.; Lincoln Literary Agency, Ray; Literary Group, The; Lowenstein Associates, Inc.; Mura Enterprises, Inc. Dee; Parks Agency, The Richard; Paul Literati, The Richard; Pelter, Rodney; Perkins Associates; Pevner, Inc., Stephen; Potomac Literary Agency, The; Robbins Literary Agency, BJ; Sanders Literary Agency, Victoria; Schmidt Literary Agency, Harold; Schulman, A Literary Agency, Susan; Seligman, Literary Agent, Lynn; Spieler, F. Joseph; ‡Sweeney Literary Agency, Emma; Travis Literary Agency, Susan; Witherspoon & Associates, Inc.; Wreschner, Authors' Representative, Ruth

Literary: Adler & Robin Books Inc.; Allen Literary Agency, Linda; ‡Authors Alliance, Inc.; Axelrod Agency, The; Baldi Literary Agency, Malaga; Barrett Books Inc., Loretta; ‡Bedford Book Works, Inc., The; Behar Literary Agency, Josh; ‡Bial Agency, Daniel; Blassingame Spectrum Corp.; ‡Book Deals, Inc.; Borchardt Inc., Georges; Brandt Agency, The Joan; Brandt & Brandt Literary Agents Inc.; ‡Brock Gannon Literary Agency; Brown Associates Inc., Marie; Browne Ltd., Pema; Buck Agency, Howard; Cantrell-Colas Inc., Literary Agency; Carvainis Agency, Inc., Maria; Castiglia Literary Agency; Circle of Confusion Ltd.; ‡Cohen Agency, The; Cohen, Inc. Literary Agency, Ruth; Collin Literary Agent, Frances; Congdon Associates, Inc., Don; Connor Literary Agency; Cornfield Literary Agency, Robert; Crown International Literature and Arts Agency, Bonnie R.; Cypher, Author's Representative, James R.; Darhansoff & Verrill Literary Agents; Daves Agency, Joan; de la Haba Agency Inc., The Lois; DH Literary, Inc.; DHS Literary, Inc.; Diamant Literary Agency, The Writer's Workshop, Inc., Anita; Dijkstra Literary Agency, Sandra; Doyen Literary Services, Inc.; Ducas, Robert; Dupree/Miller and Associates Inc. Literary; Dystel Literary Management, Jane; Ellenberg Literary Agency, Ethan; Elliott Agency; Ellison Inc., Nicholas; Elmo Agency Inc., Ann; Emerald Literary Agency; Eth Literary Representation, Felicia; Farber Literary Agency Inc.; Feiler Literary Agency, Florence; Flaming Star Literary Enterprises; Flannery Literary; Franklin Associates, Ltd., Lynn C.; Garon-Brooke Assoc. Inc., Jay; Gibson Agency, The Sebastian; Goldfarb & Graybill, Attorneys at Law; ‡Goodman-Andrew-Agency, Inc.; Gordon Agency, Charlotte; Greenburger Associates, Inc., Sanford J.; Greene, Literary Agent, Randall Elisha; ‡Grosvenor Literary Agency, Deborah; Gusay Literary Agency, The Charlotte; Hardy Agency, The; Hawkins & Associates, Inc., John; Henshaw Group, Richard; Herner Rights Agency, Susan; Hill Associates, Frederick; Hull House Literary Agency; IMG Literary; J de S Associates Inc.; Jabberwocky Literary Agency; Kidde, Hoyt & Picard; Klinger, Inc., Harvey; Kouts, Literary Agent, Barbara S.; Lampack Agency, Inc., Peter; Lantz-Joy Harris Literary Agency Inc., The Robert; Larsen/Elizabeth Pomada Literary Agents, Michael; Lasher Agency, The Maureen; ‡Leap First; Levant & Wales, Literary Agency, Inc.; Levine Communications, Inc., James; Levine Literary Agency, Inc., Ellen; Lewis & Company, Karen; ‡Lichtman, Trister, Singer & Ross; Lincoln Literary Agency, Ray; Lowenstein Associates, Inc.; ‡Lukeman Literary Management Ltd.; Maass Literary Agency, Donald; McBride Literary Agency, Margret; Maccoby Literary Agency, Gina; McGrath, Helen; Mainhardt Agency, Ricia; Mann Agency, Carol; March Tenth, Inc.; Markson Literary Agency, Elaine; Michaels Literary Agency, Inc., Doris S.; Multimedia Product Development, Inc.; Mura Enterprises, Inc., Dee; Naggar Literary Agency, Jean V.; Nazor Literary Agency, Karen; New Brand Agency Group; Nine Muses and Apollo Inc.; Palmer & Dodge Agency, The; Paraview, Inc.; Parks Agency, The Richard; Paton Literary Agency, Kathi J.; Paul Literati, The Richard; Pelham Literary Agency; Pelter, Rodney; Perkins Associates; Pevner, Inc., Stephen; Pine Associates, Inc, Arthur; Pom Inc.; Popkin, Julie; Potomac Literary Agency, The; Pryor, Inc., Roberta; Publishing Services; Quicksilver Books-Literary Agents; Rees Literary Agency, Helen; Renaissance—H.N. Swanson; Rinaldi Literary Agency, Angela; ‡Rittenberg Literary Agency, Inc., Ann; Robbins Literary Agency, BJ; Rowland Agency, The Damaris; ‡Russell & Volkening; Russell-Simenauer Literary Agency Inc.; Sanders Literary Agency, Victoria; Sandum & Associates; Schmidt Literary Agency, Harold; Schulman, A Literary Agency, Susan; Seligman, Literary Agent, Lynn; Shepard Agency, The; Singer Literary Agency Inc., Evelyn; ‡Skolnick, Irene; ‡Slopen Literary Agency, Beverley; Smith, Literary Agent, Valerie; Spieler, F. Joseph; Spitzer Literary Agency, Philip G.; Stauffer Associates, Nancy; Stepping Stone; Stern Literary Agency (TX), Gloria; ‡Sweeney Literary Agency, Emma; Travis Literary Agency, Susan; Van Der Leun & Associates; Vines Agency, Inc., The; Wald Associates, Inc., Mary Jack; Wallace Literary Agency, Inc.; Watkins Loomis Agency, Inc.; Wecksler-Incomco; Weingel-Fidel Agency, The; West Coast Literary Associates; Wieser & Wieser, Inc.; Witherspoon & Associates, Inc.; Wreschner, Authors' Representative, Ruth; Writers' Productions; Writers' Representatives, Inc.; ‡Young Agency Inc., The Gay; Zeckendorf Assoc. Inc., Susan

Mainstream: Adler & Robin Books Inc.; Allen Literary Agency, Linda; Amsterdam Agency, Marcia; ‡Authors Alliance, Inc.; Axelrod Agency, The; Baldi Literary Agency, Malaga; Barrett Books Inc., Loretta; ‡Bedford Book Works, Inc., The; Bernstein, Pam; Blassingame Spectrum Corp.; Boates Literary Agency, Reid; ‡Book Deals, Inc.; Bova Literary Agency, The Barbara; Brandt Agency, The Joan; Brandt & Brandt Literary Agents Inc.; ‡Brock Gannon Literary Agency; Brown Associates Inc., Marie; Browne Ltd., Pema; Buck Agency, Howard; Cantrell-Colas Inc., Literary Agency; Carvainis Agency, Inc., Maria; Castiglia Literary Agency; Circle of Confusion Ltd.; ‡Cohen Agency, The; Cohen, Inc. Literary Agency, Ruth; Collin Literary Agent, Frances; Columbia Literary Associates, Inc.; Curtis Associates, Inc., Richard; Cypher, Author's Representative, James R.; Daves Agency, Joan; de la Haba Agency Inc., The Lois; DH Literary, Inc.; DHS Literary, Inc.; Diamant Literary Agency, The Writer's Workshop, Inc., Anita; Diamond Literary Agency, Inc. (CO); Dijkstra Literary Agency, Sandra; Doyen Literary Services, Inc.; Ducas, Robert; Dupree/Miller and Associates Inc. Literary; Dystel Literary Management, Jane; Ellenberg Literary Agency, Ethan; Elliott Agency; Ellison Inc., Nicholas; Elmo Agency Inc., Ann; Esq. Literary Productions; Eth Literary Representation, Felicia; Farber Literary Agency Inc.; ‡Feigen Literary Agency, Brenda; Feiler Literary Agency, Florence; Flaherty, Literary Agent, Joyce A.; Flannery Literary; ‡Fleming Associates, Arthur; Fleury Agency, B.R.; Franklin Associates, Ltd., Lynn C.; Garon-Brooke Assoc. Inc., Jay; Gibson Agency, The Sebastian; Goldfarb & Graybill, Attorneys at Law; ‡Goodman-Andrew-Agency, Inc.; Greenburger Associates, Inc., Sanford J.; Greene, Literary Agent, Randall Elisha; ‡Grosvenor Literary Agency, Deborah; Gusay Literary Agency, The Charlotte; Hawkins & Associates, Inc., John; Henshaw Group, Richard; Herner Rights Agency, Susan; Hill Associates, Frederick; Hull House Literary Agency; IMG Literary; International Publisher Associates Inc.; J de S Associates

Inc.; Jabberwocky Literary Agency; Kern Literary Agency, Natasha; Kidde, Hoyt & Picard; Klinger, Inc., Harvey; Kouts, Literary Agent, Barbara S.; Lampack Agency, Inc., Peter; Lantz-Joy Harris Literary Agency Inc., The Robert; Larsen/Elizabeth Pomada Literary Agents, Michael; Lasher Agency, The Maureen; Levant & Wales, Literary Agency, Inc.; Levine Communications, Inc., James; Lewis & Company, Karen; Lincoln Literary Agency, Ray; Lindstrom Literary Group; Lipkind Agency, Wendy; Lord Literistic, Inc., Sterling; Lowenstein Associates, Inc.; ‡Lukeman Literary Management Ltd.; Maass Literary Agency, Donald; McBride Literary Agency, Margret; Maccoby Literary Agency, Gina; McGrath, Helen; Mainhardt Agency, Ricia; Manus & Associates Literary Agency, Inc.; March Tenth, Inc.; Markowitz Literary Agency, Barbara; Markson Literary Agency, Elaine; Metropolitan Talent Agency; Michaels Literary Agency, Inc., Doris S.; Multimedia Product Development, Inc.; Mura Enterprises, Inc., Dee; Naggar Literary Agency, Jean V.; ‡National Writers Literary Agency; New Brand Agency Group; Nine Muses and Apollo Inc.; Norma-Lewis Agency, The; Otitis Media; Palmer & Dodge Agency, The; Paraview, Inc.; Parks Agency, The Richard; Paton Literary Agency, Kathi J.; Paul Literati, The Richard; Pelham Literary Agency; Pelter, Rodney; Perkins Associates; Pevner, Inc., Stephen; Pine Associates, Inc, Arthur; Pocono Literary Agency, Inc.; Pom Inc.; Popkin, Julie; Potomac Literary Agency, The; Pryor, Inc., Roberta; Publishing Services; Quicksilver Books-Literary Agents; Rees Literary Agency, Helen; Renaissance—H.N. Swanson; Rinaldi Literary Agency, Angela; Robbins Literary Agency, BJ; Rose Agency, Inc.; Rowland Agency, The Damaris; Rubinstein Literary Agency, Inc., Pesha; ‡Russell & Volkening; Russell-Simenauer Literary Agency Inc.; Sandum & Associates; ‡Schlessinger Agency, Blanche; Schmidt Literary Agency, Harold; Schulman, A Literary Agency, Susan; Seligman, Literary Agent, Lynn; Seymour Agency, The; Singer Literary Agency Inc., Evelyn; Smith, Literary Agent, Valerie; Spieler, F. Joseph; Spitzer Literary Agency, Philip G.; Stauffer Associates, Nancy; Stepping Stone; Stern Literary Agency (TX), Gloria; Teal Literary Agency, Patricia; Travis Literary Agency, Susan; Van Der Leun & Associates; Van Duren Agency, Annette; Vines Agency, Inc., The; Wald Associates, Inc., Mary Jack; Wallace Literary Agency, Inc.; Ware Literary Agency, John A.; Watkins Loomis Agency, Inc.; Watt & Associates, Sandra; Wecksler-Incomco; Weiner Literary Agency, Cherry; Weingel-Fidel Agency, The; West Coast Literary Associates; Wieser & Wieser, Inc.; Witherspoon & Associates, Inc.; Wreschner, Authors' Representative, Ruth; ‡Young Agency Inc., The Gay; Zeckendorf Assoc. Inc., Susan; ‡Zitwer Agency, Barbara J.

Mystery/suspense: Adler & Robin Books Inc.; Agents Inc. for Medical and Mental Health Professionals; Allan Agency, Lee; Allen Literary Agency, Linda; Amsterdam Agency, Marcia; Appleseeds Management; Authors Alliance, Inc.; ‡Authors' Literary Agency; Axelrod Agency, The; Baldi Literary Agency, Malaga; Barrett Books Inc., Loretta; Becker Literary Agency, The Wendy; ‡Bedford Book Works, Inc., The; Bernstein, Pam; Blassingame Spectrum Corp.; Boates Literary Agency, Reid; Bova Literary Agency, The Barbara; Brandt Agency, The Joan; Brandt & Brandt Literary Agents Inc.; ‡Brock Gannon Literary Agency; Brown Associates Inc., Marie; Browne Ltd., Pema; Buck Agency, Howard; Cantrell-Colas Inc., Literary Agency; Carvainis Agency, Inc., Maria; Castiglia Literary Agency; Charisma Communications, Ltd.; Circle of Confusion Ltd.; Ciske & Dietz Literary Agency; ‡Cohen Agency, The; Cohen, Inc. Literary Agency, Ruth; Collin Literary Agent, Frances; Connor Literary Agency; Curtis Associates, Inc., Richard; Cypher, Author's Representative, James R.; de la Haba Agency Inc., The Lois; DHS Literary, Inc.; Diamant Literary Agency, The Writer's Workshop, Inc., Anita; Diamond Literary Agency, Inc. (CO); Dijkstra Literary Agency, Sandra; Doyen Literary Services, Inc.; Ducas, Robert; Dupree/Miller and Associates Inc. Literary; Ellenberg Literary Agency, Ethan; Elmo Agency Inc., Ann; Esq. Literary Productions; Farber Literary Agency Inc.; ‡Feigen Literary Agency, Brenda; Feiler Literary Agency, Florence; Flaherty, Literary Agent, Joyce A.; Flannery Literary; ‡Fleming Associates, Arthur; Garon-Brooke Assoc. Inc., Jay; Goldfarb & Graybill, Attorneys at Law; Gordon Agency, Charlotte; Graham Literary Agency, Inc.; Greenburger Associates, Inc., Sanford J.; Greene, Arthur B.; ‡Grosvenor Literary Agency, Deborah; Gusay Literary Agency, The Charlotte; Hawkins & Associates, Inc., John; Herner Rights Agency, Susan; Hull House Literary Agency; J de S Associates Inc.; Kern Literary Agency, Natasha; Kidde, Hoyt & Picard; Klinger, Inc., Harvey; Kouts, Literary Agent, Barbara S.; Lampack Agency, Inc., Peter; Lantz-Joy Harris Literary Agency Inc., The Robert; Larsen/Elizabeth Pomada Literary Agents, Michael; Levine Literary Agency, Inc., Ellen; Lewis & Company, Karen; Lincoln Literary Agency, Ray; Literary Group, The; Love Literary Agency, Nancy; Lowenstein Associates, Inc.; Maass Literary Agency, Donald; McBride Literary Agency, Margret; Maccoby Literary Agency, Gina; McGrath, Helen; Manus & Associates Literary Agency, Inc.; Marcil Literary Agency, Inc., The Denise; Markowitz Literary Agency, Barbara; Metropolitan Talent Agency; Multimedia Product Development, Inc.; Mura Enterprises, Inc., Dee; Naggar Literary Agency, Jean V.; New Brand Agency Group; Norma-Lewis Agency, The; ‡Oasis Literary Agency, The; Otitis Media; Parks Agency, The Richard; Pelter, Rodney; Perkins Associates; Pocono Literary Agency, Inc.; Pom Inc.; Popkin, Julie; Porcelain, Sidney E.; Potomac Literary Agency, The; Protter Literary Agent, Susan Ann; Pryor, Inc., Roberta; Quicksilver Books-Literary Agents; Rees Literary Agency, Helen; Renaissance—H.N. Swanson; Robbins Literary Agency, BJ; Rose Agency, Inc.; Rubinstein Literary Agency, Inc., Pesha; ‡Russell & Volkening; Russell-Simenauer Literary Agency Inc.; ‡Schlessinger Agency, Blanche; Schmidt Literary Agency, Harold; Schulman, A Literary Agency, Susan; Seligman, Literary Agent, Lynn; Seymour Agency, The; Singer Literary Agency Inc., Evelyn; ‡Slopen Literary Agency, Beverley; Spitzer Literary Agency, Philip G.; Stepping Stone; Stern Literary Agency (TX), Gloria; Targ Literary Agency, Inc., Roslyn; Teal Literary Agency, Patricia; Toad Hall, Inc.; Travis Literary Agency, Susan; Vines Agency, Inc., The; Wald Associates, Inc., Mary Jack; Wallace Literary Agency, Inc.; Ware Literary Agency, John A.; Watkins Loomis Agency, Inc.; Watt & Associates, Sandra; Weiner Literary Agency, Cherry; West Coast Literary Associates; Wieser & Wieser, Inc.; Witherspoon & Associates, Inc.; Wreschner, Authors' Representative, Ruth; Zeckendorf Assoc. Inc., Susan; ‡Zitwer Agency, Barbara J.

Open to all fiction categories: Author's Agency, The; Bernstein Literary Agency, Meredith; Brown Ltd., Curtis; Bykofsky Associates, Inc., Sheree; Circle of Confusion Ltd.; Cohen Literary Agency Ltd., Hy; Congdon Associates, Inc., Don; ‡Frustrated Writer's Ltd., The; ‡Goodman Associates; Hamilburg Agency, The Mitchell J.; ‡Harp, Chadwick Allen; Hoffman Literary Agency, Berenice; Lazear Agency Incorporated; Madsen Agency, Robert;

Martell Agency, The; Moran Agency, Maureen; Ober Associates, Harold; Writers House; Zahler Literary Agency, Karen Gantz

Picture book: Axelrod Agency, The; Barrett Books Inc., Loretta; Brown Literary Agency, Inc., Andrea; Browne Ltd., Pema; Circle of Confusion Ltd.; Cohen, Inc. Literary Agency, Ruth; Dupree/Miller and Associates Inc. Literary; Elek Associates, Peter; Ellenberg Literary Agency, Ethan; Flannery Literary; ‡Fleming Associates, Arthur; Gibson Agency, The Sebastian; Gusay Literary Agency, The Charlotte; Hawkins & Associates, Inc., John; Heacock Literary Agency, Inc.; Jabberwocky Literary Agency; Kouts, Literary Agent, Barbara S.; Kroll Literary Agency, Edite; Lantz-Joy Harris Literary Agency Inc., The Robert; Mainhardt Agency, Ricia; Multimedia Product Development, Inc.; ‡National Writers Literary Agency; Norma-Lewis Agency, The; Pocono Literary Agency, Inc.; Rubinstein Literary Agency, Inc., Pesha; ‡Russell & Volkening; Vines Agency, Inc., The; Wald Associates, Inc., Mary Jack; Wecksler-Incomco

Psychic/supernatural: Allan Agency, Lee; Allen Literary Agency, Linda; Appleseeds Management; Barrett Books Inc., Loretta; Behar Literary Agency, Josh; Brandt & Brandt Literary Agents Inc.; ‡Brock Gannon Literary Agency; Browne Ltd., Pema; Buck Agency, Howard; Cantrell-Colas Inc., Literary Agency; Circle of Confusion Ltd.; Collin Literary Agent, Frances; DH Literary, Inc.; Diamant Literary Agency, The Writer's Workshop, Inc., Anita; Doyen Literary Services, Inc.; Dupree/Miller and Associates Inc. Literary; Elmo Agency Inc., Ann; ‡Fleming Associates, Arthur; Fleury Agency, B.R.; Gibson Agency, The Sebastian; Greenburger Associates, Inc., Sanford J.; Gusay Literary Agency, The Charlotte; Hawkins & Associates, Inc., John; Henshaw Group, Richard; Jabberwocky Literary Agency; Lantz-Joy Harris Literary Agency Inc., The Robert; Larsen/Elizabeth Pomada Literary Agents, Michael; Lincoln Literary Agency, Ray; Literary Group, The; Maass Literary Agency, Donald; McGrath, Helen; Mainhardt Agency, Ricia; Mura Enterprises, Inc. Dee; Naggar Literary Agency, Jean V.; Paraview, Inc.; Parks Agency, The Richard; Pelter, Rodney; Perkins Associates; Pevner, Inc., Stephen; Pocono Literary Agency, Inc.; Rowland Agency, The Damaris; Rubinstein Literary Agency, Inc., Pesha; Russell-Simenauer Literary Agency Inc.; Schmidt Literary Agency, Harold; Vines Agency, Inc., The; Weiner Literary Agency, Cherry

Regional: Allen Literary Agency, Linda; Baldi Literary Agency, Malaga; Barrett Books Inc., Loretta; Bova Literary Agency, The Barbara; Brandt & Brandt Literary Agents Inc.; ‡Brock Gannon Literary Agency; Buck Agency, Howard; Circle of Confusion Ltd.; ‡Cohen Agency, The; Collin Literary Agent, Frances; Elmo Agency Inc., Ann; Fleury Agency, B.R.; Gibson Agency, The Sebastian; Greenburger Associates, Inc., Sanford J.; Greene, Literary Agent, Randall Elisha; Gusay Literary Agency, The Charlotte; Hawkins & Associates, Inc., John; Jabberwocky Literary Agency; Kidde, Hoyt & Picard; Lantz-Joy Harris Literary Agency Inc., The Robert; Lincoln Literary Agency, Ray; Mura Enterprises, Inc., Dee; Nazor Literary Agency, Karen; Paraview, Inc.; Paul Literati, The Richard; Pelter, Rodney; Shepard Agency, The; Singer Literary Agency Inc., Evelyn; Vines Agency, Inc., The; Watt & Associates, Sandra; West Coast Literary Associates

Religious/inspirational: Barrett Books Inc., Loretta; Brandenburgh & Associates Literary Agency; ‡Brock Gannon Literary Agency; Browne Ltd., Pema; Buck Agency, Howard; Charisma Communications, Ltd.; Circle of Confusion Ltd.; Ciske & Dietz Literary Agency; de la Haba Agency Inc., The Lois; Diamant Literary Agency, The Writer's Workshop, Inc., Anita; Dupree/Miller and Associates Inc. Literary; Feiler Literary Agency, Florence; ‡Fleming Associates, Arthur; Gibson Agency, The Sebastian; Gusay Literary Agency, The Charlotte; Hawkins & Associates, Inc., John; Lantz-Joy Harris Literary Agency Inc., The Robert; Larsen/Elizabeth Pomada Literary Agents, Michael; Multimedia Product Development, Inc.; New Brand Agency Group; ‡Oasis Literary Agency, The; Pelter, Rodney; Rose Agency, Inc.; Seymour Agency, The; Watt & Associates, Sandra

Romance: Allen Literary Agency, Linda; Amsterdam Agency, Marcia; Authors Alliance, Inc.; ‡Authors' Literary Agency; Axelrod Agency, The; Barrett Books Inc., Loretta; Becker Literary Agency, The Wendy; Behar Literary Agency, Josh; Bernstein, Pam; Bova Literary Agency, The Barbara; Brandt & Brandt Literary Agents Inc.; ‡Brock Gannon Literary Agency; Brown Literary Agency, Inc., Andrea; Browne Ltd., Pema; Buck Agency, Howard; Carvainis Agency, Inc., Maria; Circle of Confusion Ltd.; Ciske & Dietz Literary Agency; ‡Cohen Agency, The; Cohen, Inc. Literary Agency, Ruth; Collin Literary Agent, Frances; Columbia Literary Associates, Inc.; Curtis Associates, Inc., Richard; Diamant Literary Agency, The Writer's Workshop, Inc., Anita; Diamond Literary Agency, Inc. (CO); Dupree/Miller and Associates Inc. Literary; Ellenberg Literary Agency, Ethan; Elmo Agency Inc., Ann; Feiler Literary Agency, Florence; Flaherty, Literary Agent, Joyce A.; ‡Fleming Associates, Arthur; Fleury Agency, B.R.; Garon-Brooke Assoc. Inc., Jay; Gibson Agency, The Sebastian; Gordon Agency, Charlotte; Greene, Literary Agent, Randall Elisha; ‡Grosvenor Literary Agency, Deborah; Herner Rights Agency, Susan; Jabberwocky Literary Agency; Kern Literary Agency, Natasha; Kidde, Hoyt & Picard; Klinger, Inc., Harvey; Lantz-Joy Harris Literary Agency Inc., The Robert; Larsen/Elizabeth Pomada Literary Agents, Michael; Lincoln Literary Agency, Ray; Literary Group, The; Lowenstein Associates, Inc.; Maass Literary Agency, Donald; McGrath, Helen; Mainhardt Agency, Ricia; Marcil Literary Agency, Inc., The Denise; Multimedia Product Development, Inc.; Mura Enterprises, Inc., Dee; New Brand Agency Group; Norma-Lewis Agency, The; ‡Oasis Literary Agency, The; Paraview, Inc.; Parks Agency, The Richard; Pelham Literary Agency; Pine Associates, Inc, Arthur; Pocono Literary Agency, Inc.; Rose Agency, Inc.; Rowland Agency, The Damaris; Rubinstein Literary Agency, Inc., Pesha; Russell-Simenauer Literary Agency Inc.; Seymour Agency, The; Teal Literary Agency, Patricia; Toad Hall, Inc.; Travis Literary Agency, Susan; Vines Agency, Inc., The; Weiner Literary Agency, Cherry; West Coast Literary Associates; Wieser & Wieser, Inc.; Witherspoon & Associates, Inc.; Wreschner, Authors' Representative, Ruth

Science fiction: Agents Inc. for Medical and Mental Health Professionals; Allan Agency, Lee; Amsterdam Agency, Marcia; Appleseeds Management; ‡Authors Alliance, Inc.; Authors' Literary Agency; Becker Literary Agency, The Wendy; Behar Literary Agency, Josh; Blassingame Spectrum Corp.; ‡Book Deals, Inc.; Bova Literary

The; McBride Literary Agency, Margret; Mainhardt Agency, Ricia; Multimedia Product Development, Inc.; Mura Enterprises, Inc., Dee; Norma-Lewis Agency, The; Parks Agency, The Richard; Pelham Literary Agency; Pelter, Rodney; Potomac Literary Agency, The; Rose Agency, Inc.; Seymour Agency, The; Targ Literary Agency, Inc., Roslyn; Vines Agency, Inc., The; Wald Associates, Inc., Mary Jack; Weiner Literary Agency, Cherry; West Coast Literary Associates

Young adult: Amsterdam Agency, Marcia; Authors' Literary Agency; Barrett Books Inc., Loretta; Brandt & Brandt Literary Agents Inc.; ‡Brock Gannon Literary Agency; Brown Literary Agency, Inc., Andrea; Browne Ltd., Pema; Cantrell-Colas Inc., Literary Agency; Carvainis Agency, Inc., Maria; Circle of Confusion Ltd.; Cohen, Inc. Literary Agency, Ruth; de la Haba Agency Inc., The Lois; Diamant Literary Agency, The Writer's Workshop, Inc., Anita; Ellenberg Literary Agency, Ethan; Elmo Agency Inc., Ann; Farber Literary Agency Inc.; Feiler Literary Agency, Florence; Flannery Literary; Fleury Agency, B.R.; Gibson Agency, The Sebastian; Gordon Agency, Charlotte; Gusay Literary Agency, The Charlotte; Henshaw Group, Richard; J de S Associates Inc.; Jabberwocky Literary Agency; Kirchoff/Wohlberg, Inc., Authors' Representation Division; Kouts, Literary Agent, Barbara S.; Lantz-Joy Harris Literary Agency Inc., The Robert; Lincoln Literary Agency, Ray; Literary Group, The; Maccoby Literary Agency, Gina; Mainhardt Agency, Ricia; Markowitz Literary Agency, Barbara; Mura Enterprises, Inc., Dee; ‡National Writers Literary Agency; Norma-Lewis Agency, The; Parks Agency, The Richard; Pocono Literary Agency, Inc.; Pryor, Inc., Roberta; Rose Agency, Inc.; ‡Russell & Volkening; Schulman, A Literary Agency, Susan; Smith, Literary Agent, Valerie; Van Duren Agency, Annette; Vines Agency, Inc., The; Wald Associates, Inc., Mary Jack; Wasserman Literary Agency, Inc., Harriet; Watkins Loomis Agency, Inc.; Wreschner, Authors' Representative, Ruth; ‡Young Agency Inc., The Gay

Nonfee-charging agents/Nonfiction

Agriculture/horticulture: Baldi Literary Agency, Malaga; Brandt & Brandt Literary Agents Inc.; Buck Agency, Howard; Casselman Literary Agent, Martha; Clausen Associates, Connie; de la Haba Agency Inc., The Lois; Ellison Inc., Nicholas; ‡Fleming Associates, Arthur; Fleury Agency, B.R.; Gartenberg, Literary Agent, Max; Goddard Book Group; ‡Goodman-Andrew-Agency, Inc.; Greene, Literary Agent, Randall Elisha; Hawkins & Associates, Inc., John; Kern Literary Agency, Natasha; Levant & Wales, Literary Agency, Inc.; Lieberman Associates, Robert; Lincoln Literary Agency, Ray; Mainhardt Agency, Ricia; Multimedia Product Development, Inc.; Mura Enterprises, Inc. Dee; Parks Agency, The Richard; Pocono Literary Agency, Inc.; Shepard Agency, The; ‡Sweeney Literary Agency, Emma; Taylor Literary Enterprises, Sandra; Travis Literary Agency, Susan; Urstadt Inc. Agency, Susan P.; Watt & Associates, Sandra

Animals: Author's Agency, The; Baldi Literary Agency, Malaga; Balkin Agency, Inc.; ‡Bial Agency, Daniel; Boates Literary Agency, Reid; ‡Book Deals, Inc.; Brandt & Brandt Literary Agents Inc.; ‡Brock Gannon Literary Agency; Brown Literary Agency, Inc., Andrea; Buck Agency, Howard; Castiglia Literary Agency; Cornfield Literary Agency, Robert; DH Literary, Inc.; Diamant Literary Agency, The Writer's Workshop, Inc., Anita; Ducas, Robert; Dystel Literary Management, Jane; Ellison Inc., Nicholas; Eth Literary Representation, Felicia; Flaherty, Literary Agent, Joyce A.; ‡Fleming Associates, Arthur; Fleury Agency, B.R.; Gartenberg, Literary Agent, Max; Gibson Agency, The Sebastian; Goddard Book Group; Greene, Arthur B.; ‡Grosvenor Literary Agency, Deborah; Hawkins & Associates, Inc., John; Henshaw Group, Richard; Kern Literary Agency, Natasha; Lasher Agency, The Maureen; Levant & Wales, Literary Agency, Inc.; Levine Communications, Inc., James; Lincoln Literary Agency, Ray; Literary Group, The; Love Literary Agency, Nancy; Lowenstein Associates, Inc.; ‡Lukeman Literary Management Ltd.; Mainhardt Agency, Ricia; Multimedia Product Development, Inc.; Mura Enterprises, Inc., Dee; ‡National Writers Literary Agency; Nine Muses and Apollo Inc.; Parks Agency, The Richard; Pryor, Inc., Roberta; Rowland Agency, The Damaris; Shepard Agency, The; Stauffer Associates, Nancy; Stepping Stone; ‡Sweeney Literary Agency, Emma; Teal Literary Agency, Patricia; Toad Hall, Inc.; Urstadt Inc. Agency, Susan P.; Ware Literary Agency, John A.; Watt & Associates, Sandra; Writers House

Anthropology: Allen Literary Agency, Linda; Author's Agency, The; Baldi Literary Agency, Malaga; Balkin Agency, Inc.; ‡Bial Agency, Daniel; Boates Literary Agency, Reid; Borchardt Inc., Georges; Brandt & Brandt Literary Agents Inc.; ‡Brock Gannon Literary Agency; Brown Literary Agency, Inc., Andrea; Browne Ltd., Pema; Buck Agency, Howard; Cantrell-Colas Inc., Literary Agency; Casselman Literary Agent, Martha; Castiglia Literary Agency; Circle of Confusion Ltd.; Collin Literary Agent, Frances; Coover Agency, The Doe; Cornfield Literary Agency, Robert; Darhansoff & Verrill Literary Agents; de la Haba Agency Inc., The Lois; DH Literary, Inc.; Dijkstra Literary Agency, Sandra; Dystel Literary Management, Jane; Educational Design Services, Inc.; Elek Associates, Peter; Ellison Inc., Nicholas; Elmo Agency Inc., Ann; Eth Literary Representation, Felicia; Fleury Agency, B.R.; ‡Fullerton Associates, Sheryl B.; Gibson Agency, The Sebastian; ‡Goodman-Andrew-Agency, Inc.; Gordon Agency, Charlotte; ‡Grosvenor Literary Agency, Deborah; Hawkins & Associates, Inc., John; Heacock Literary Agency, Inc.; Herner Rights Agency, Susan; Hochmann Books, John L.; Hull House Literary Agency; James Peter Associates, Inc.; Kellock Company, Inc., The; Kern Literary Agency, Natasha; Lampack Agency, Inc., Peter; Larsen/Elizabeth Pomada Literary Agents, Michael; Lasher Agency, The Maureen; Levant & Wales, Literary Agency, Inc.; Levine Literary Agency, Inc., Ellen; ‡Lichtman, Trister, Singer & Ross; Lieberman Associates, Robert; Lincoln Literary Agency, Ray; Literary Group, The; Lowenstein Associates, Inc.; ‡Lukeman Literary Management Ltd.; Mainhardt Agency, Ricia; Mann Agency, Carol; Miller Agency, The; Morrison, Inc., Henry; Multimedia Product Development, Inc.; Mura Enterprises, Inc., Dee; Otitis Media; Palmer & Dodge Agency, The; Parks Agency, The Richard; Pryor, Inc., Roberta; Quicksilver Books-Literary Agents; ‡Russell & Volkening; Schmidt Literary Agency, Harold; Schulman, A Literary Agency, Susan; Seligman, Literary Agent, Lynn; Singer Literary Agency Inc., Evelyn; ‡Slopen Literary Agency, Beverley; Stepping Stone; Stern Literary Agency (TX), Gloria; ‡Sweeney Literary Agency, Emma;

Toad Hall, Inc.; Urstadt Inc. Agency, Susan P.; Wallace Literary Agency, Inc.; Ware Literary Agency, John A.; Watt & Associates, Sandra; Witherspoon & Associates, Inc.

Art/architecture/design: Agency Chicago; Allen Literary Agency, Linda; ‡Authors Alliance, Inc.; Axelrod Agency, The; Baldi Literary Agency, Malaga; Becker Literary Agency, The Wendy; Boates Literary Agency, Reid; ‡Book Deals, Inc.; Brandt & Brandt Literary Agents Inc.; Brown Associates Inc., Marie; Brown Literary Agency, Inc., Andrea; Browne Ltd., Pema; Buck Agency, Howard; Cantrell-Colas Inc., Literary Agency; Cornfield Literary Agency, Robert; de la Haba Agency Inc., The Lois; Diamant Literary Agency, The Writer's Workshop, Inc., Anita; Ellison Inc., Nicholas; Elmo Agency Inc., Ann; ‡Feigen Literary Agency, Brenda; Feiler Literary Agency, Florence; ‡Fleming Associates, Arthur; Fleury Agency, B.R.; Gartenberg, Literary Agent, Max; Gibson Agency, The Sebastian; Goddard Book Group; ‡Goodman-Andrew-Agency, Inc.; ‡Grosvenor Literary Agency, Deborah; Hawkins & Associates, Inc., John; Heacock Literary Agency, Inc.; Henderson Literary Representation; Hochmann Books, John L.; Hull House Literary Agency; James Peter Associates, Inc.; Kellock Company, Inc., The; Kern Literary Agency, Natasha; Kidde, Hoyt & Picard; Lampack Agency, Inc., Peter; Larsen/Elizabeth Pomada Literary Agents, Michael; Lasher Agency, The Maureen; Levant & Wales, Literary Agency, Inc.; Levine Communications, Inc., James; Lieberman Associates, Robert; Lincoln Literary Agency, Ray; Lowenstein Associates, Inc.; ‡Lukeman Literary Management Ltd.; Mann Agency, Carol; Miller Agency, The; Nathan, Ruth; Norma-Lewis Agency, The; Parks Agency, The Richard; Perkins Associates; Pevner, Inc., Stephen; Popkin, Julie; Pryor, Inc., Roberta; ‡Russell & Volkening; Schmidt Literary Agency, Harold; Seligman, Literary Agent, Lynn; Seymour Agency, The; Stepping Stone; Stern Literary Agency (TX), Gloria; ‡Sweeney Literary Agency, Emma; ‡Tenth Avenue Editions, Inc.; Urstadt Inc. Agency, Susan P.; Waterside Productions, Inc.; Watkins Loomis Agency, Inc.; Watt & Associates, Sandra; Wecksler-Incomco; Weingel-Fidel Agency, The; Writers House; Zeckendorf Assoc. Inc., Susan

Biography/autobiography: Adler & Robin Books Inc.; Ajlouny Agency, The Joseph S.; Allen Literary Agency, Linda; Andrews & Associates Inc., Bart; Author's Agency, The; ‡Authors Alliance, Inc.; Baldi Literary Agency, Malaga; Balkin Agency, Inc.; Becker Literary Agency, The Wendy; ‡Bedford Book Works, Inc., The; Behar Literary Agency, Josh; Bernstein, Pam; ‡Bial Agency, Daniel; Boates Literary Agency, Reid; ‡Book Deals, Inc.; Borchardt Inc., Georges; Bova Literary Agency, The Barbara; Brandt & Brandt Literary Agents Inc.; ‡Brock Gannon Literary Agency; Brown Associates Inc., Marie; Brown Literary Agency, Inc., Andrea; Browne Ltd., Pema; Buck Agency, Howard; Bykofsky Associates, Inc., Sheree; Cantrell-Colas Inc., Literary Agency; Carvainis Agency, Inc., Maria; Casselman Literary Agent, Martha; Castiglia Literary Agency; Charisma Communications, Ltd.; Circle of Confusion Ltd.; Clausen Associates, Connie; ‡Cohen Agency, The; Collin Literary Agent, Frances; Cornfield Literary Agency, Robert; Crawford Literary Agency; Curtis Associates, Inc., Richard; Cypher, Author's Representative, James R.; Darhansoff & Verrill Literary Agents; Daves Agency, Joan; de la Haba Agency Inc., The Lois; DH Literary, Inc.; DHS Literary, Inc.; Diamant Literary Agency, The Writer's Workshop, Inc., Anita; Dijkstra Literary Agency, Sandra; Ducas, Robert; Dystel Literary Management, Jane; Ellenberg Literary Agency, Ethan; Elmo Agency Inc., Ann; Emerald Literary Agency; Eth Literary Representation, Felicia; ‡Feigen Literary Agency, Brenda; Flaherty, Literary Agent, Joyce A.; ‡Fleming Associates, Arthur; Fleury Agency, B.R.; Franklin Associates, Ltd., Lynn C.; ‡Fullerton Associates, Sheryl B.; Garon-Brooke Assoc. Inc., Jay; Gartenberg, Literary Agent, Max; Gibson Agency, The Sebastian; Goddard Book Group; ‡Goodman-Andrew-Agency, Inc.; Greene, Literary Agent, Randall Elisha; ‡Grosvenor Literary Agency, Deborah; Hardy Agency, The; Hawkins & Associates, Inc., John; Heacock Literary Agency, Inc.; Henderson Literary Representation; Henshaw Group, Richard; Herner Rights Agency, Susan; Hill Associates, Frederick; Hochmann Books, John L.; Hull House Literary Agency; IMG Literary; J de S Associates Inc.; Jabberwocky Literary Agency; James Peter Associates, Inc.; ‡Janus Literary Agency; Jordan Literary Agency, Lawrence; Kellock Company, Inc., The; Kern Literary Agency, Natasha; Ketz Agency, Louise B.; Kidde, Hoyt & Picard; Klinger, Inc., Harvey; Kouts, Literary Agent, Barbara S.; Lampack Agency, Inc., Peter; Larsen/Elizabeth Pomada Literary Agents, Michael; Lasher Agency, The Maureen; Levant & Wales, Literary Agency, Inc.; Levine Communications, Inc., James; Levine Literary Agency, Inc., Ellen; ‡Lichtman, Trister, Singer & Ross; Lincoln Literary Agency, Ray; Lindstrom Literary Group; Lipkind Agency, Wendy; Literary Group, The; Love Literary Agency, Nancy; Lowenstein Associates, Inc.; ‡Lukeman Literary Management Ltd.; McBride Literary Agency, Margret; Maccoby Literary Agency, Gina; McGrath, Helen; Mainhardt Agency, Ricia; Mann Agency, Carol; Manus & Associates Literary Agency, Inc.; March Tenth, Inc.; Markowitz Literary Agency, Barbara; Metropolitan Talent Agency; Michaels Literary Agency, Inc., Doris S.; Miller Agency, The; Morrison, Inc., Henry; Multimedia Product Development, Inc.; Mura Enterprises, Inc., Dee; Naggar Literary Agency, Jean V.; Nathan, Ruth; ‡National Writers Literary Agency; Nazor Literary Agency, Karen; New Brand Agency Group; New England Publishing Associates, Inc.; Nine Muses and Apollo Inc.; Norma-Lewis Agency, The; Nugent Literary; Otitis Media; Palmer & Dodge Agency, The; Parks Agency, The Richard; Pevner, Inc., Stephen; Pocono Literary Agency, Inc.; Pom Inc.; Potomac Literary Agency, The; Protter Literary Agent, Susan Ann; Pryor, Inc., Roberta; Publishing Services; Quicksilver Books-Literary Agents; Rees Literary Agency, Helen; Renaissance—H.N. Swanson; Rinaldi Literary Agency, Angela; Robbins Literary Agency, BJ; ‡Russell & Volkening; Sanders Literary Agency, Victoria; ‡Schlessinger Agency, Blanche; Schmidt Literary Agency, Harold; Schulman, A Literary Agency, Susan; Sebastian Literary Agency; Seligman, Literary Agent, Lynn; Shepard Agency, The; Singer Literary Agency Inc., Evelyn; ‡Skolnick, Irene; ‡Slopen Literary Agency, Beverley; Spieler, F. Joseph; Spitzer Literary Agency, Philip G.; Stauffer Associates, Nancy; Stepping Stone; Stern Literary Agency (TX), Gloria; ‡Sweeney Literary Agency, Emma; Teal Literary Agency, Patricia; ‡Tenth Avenue Editions, Inc.; Travis Literary Agency, Susan; 2M Communications Ltd.; Urstadt Inc. Agency, Susan P.; Valcourt Agency, Inc., The Richard R.; Wald Associates, Inc., Mary Jack; Wallace Literary Agency, Inc.; Ware Literary Agency, John A.; Waterside Productions, Inc.; Watkins Loomis Agency, Inc.; Wecksler-Incomco; Weingel-Fidel Agency, The; West Coast Literary Associates; Witherspoon & Associates, Inc.; Wreschner, Authors' Representative, Ruth; Writers House; Zeckendorf Assoc. Inc., Susan; ‡Zitwer Agency, Barbara J.

Business: Adler & Robin Books Inc.; Allen Literary Agency, Linda; Appleseeds Management; Author's Agency, The; ‡Authors Alliance, Inc.; Axelrod Agency, The; Baldi Literary Agency, Malaga; Becker Literary Agency, The Wendy; ‡Bedford Book Works, Inc., The; Behar Literary Agency, Josh; ‡Bial Agency, Daniel; Boates Literary Agency, Reid; ‡Book Deals, Inc.; Bova Literary Agency, The Barbara; Brandt & Brandt Literary Agents Inc.; ‡Brock Gannon Literary Agency; Brown Associates Inc., Marie; Browne Ltd., Pema; Buck Agency, Howard; Bykofsky Associates, Inc., Sheree; Carvainis Agency, Inc., Maria; Castiglia Literary Agency; Connor Literary Agency; Coover Agency, The Doe; Crawford Literary Agency; Curtis Associates, Inc., Richard; Cypher, Author's Representative, James R.; de la Haba Agency Inc., The Lois; DH Literary, Inc.; DHS Literary, Inc.; Diamant Literary Agency, The Writer's Workshop, Inc., Anita; Diamond Literary Agency, Inc. (CO); Dijkstra Literary Agency, Sandra; Ducas, Robert; Dystel Literary Management, Jane; Educational Design Services, Inc.; Ellenberg Literary Agency, Ethan; Ellison Inc., Nicholas; Elmo Agency Inc., Ann; Emerald Literary Agency; Eth Literary Representation, Felicia; ‡Fleming Associates, Arthur; Fleury Agency, B.R.; ‡Fullerton Associates, Sheryl B.; Gibson Agency, The Sebastian; Goddard Book Group; ‡Goodman-Andrew-Agency, Inc.; Gordon Agency, Charlotte; Greene, Literary Agent, Randall Elisha; ‡Grosvenor Literary Agency, Deborah; Hawkins & Associates, Inc., John; Heacock Literary Agency, Inc.; Henderson Literary Representation; Henshaw Group, Richard; Herman Agency, Inc., The Jeff; Herner Rights Agency, Susan; Hull House Literary Agency; IMG Literary; J de S Associates Inc.; Jabberwocky Literary Agency; James Peter Associates, Inc.; ‡Janus Literary Agency; Jordan Literary Agency, Lawrence; ‡Just Write Agency, Inc.; Kellock Company, Inc., The; Kern Literary Agency, Natasha; Ketz Agency, Louise B.; Lampack Agency, Inc., Peter; Larsen/Elizabeth Pomada Literary Agents, Michael; Lasher Agency, The Maureen; Levant & Wales, Literary Agency, Inc.; Levine Communications, Inc., James; ‡Lichtman, Trister, Singer & Ross; Lieberman Associates, Robert; Lincoln Literary Agency, Ray; Literary and Creative Artists Agency Inc.; Literary Group, The; Lowenstein Associates, Inc.; ‡Lukeman Literary Management Ltd.; McBride Literary Agency, Margret; McGrath, Helen; Mainhardt Agency, Ricia; Mann Agency, Carol; Manus & Associates Literary Agency, Inc.; Marcil Literary Agency, Inc., The Denise; Michaels Literary Agency, Inc., Doris S.; Miller Agency, The; Multimedia Product Development, Inc.; Mura Enterprises, Inc., Dee; Nazor Literary Agency, Karen; New England Publishing Associates, Inc.; Nine Muses and Apollo Inc.; Palmer & Dodge Agency, The; Parks Agency, The Richard; Paton Literary Agency, Kathi J.; Pevner, Inc., Stephen; Pine Associates, Inc, Arthur; Pocono Literary Agency, Inc.; Pom Inc.; Potomac Literary Agency, The; Quicksilver Books-Literary Agents; Rees Literary Agency, Helen; Rinaldi Literary Agency, Angela; Rose Agency, Inc.; ‡Russell & Volkening; Schmidt Literary Agency, Harold; Schulman, A Literary Agency, Susan; Sebastian Literary Agency; Seligman, Literary Agent, Lynn; Shepard Agency, The; Singer Literary Agency Inc., Evelyn; ‡Slopen Literary Agency, Beverley; Snell Literary Agency, Michael; Spieler, F. Joseph; Spitzer Literary Agency, Philip G.; Stauffer Associates, Nancy; Stepping Stone; Stern Literary Agency (TX), Gloria; ‡Tenth Avenue Editions, Inc.; Toad Hall, Inc.; Travis Literary Agency, Susan; Urstadt Inc. Agency, Susan P.; Valcourt Agency, Inc., The Richard R.; Vines Agency, Inc., The; Waterside Productions, Inc.; Wecksler-Incomco; Wieser & Wieser, Inc.; Witherspoon & Associates, Inc.; Wreschner, Authors' Representative, Ruth; Writers House; ‡Young Agency Inc., The Gay

Child guidance/parenting: Adler & Robin Books Inc.; Allen Literary Agency, Linda; Author's Agency, The; ‡Authors Alliance, Inc.; Becker Literary Agency, The Wendy; Bernstein, Pam; ‡Bial Agency, Daniel; Boates Literary Agency, Reid; Brandt & Brandt Literary Agents Inc.; ‡Brock Gannon Literary Agency; Browne Ltd., Pema; Buck Agency, Howard; Bykofsky Associates, Inc., Sheree; Cantrell-Colas Inc., Literary Agency; Castiglia Literary Agency; Charlton Associates, James; ‡Cohen Agency, The; Connor Literary Agency; Coover Agency, The Doe; Crawford Literary Agency; Curtis Associates, Inc., Richard; DH Literary, Inc.; DHS Literary, Inc.; Diamant Literary Agency, The Writer's Workshop, Inc., Anita; Dijkstra Literary Agency, Sandra; Dystel Literary Management, Jane; Educational Design Services, Inc.; Elek Associates, Peter; Ellenberg Literary Agency, Ethan; Ellison Inc., Nicholas; Elmo Agency Inc., Ann; Eth Literary Representation, Felicia; ‡Feigen Literary Agency, Brenda; Flaherty, Literary Agent Joyce A.; Flannery Literary; ‡Fleming Associates, Arthur; Fleury Agency, B.R.; ‡Frustrated Writer's Ltd., The; Garon-Brooke Assoc. Inc., Jay; Gartenberg, Literary Agent, Max; Goddard Book Group; ‡Goodman-Andrew-Agency, Inc.; ‡Grosvenor Literary Agency, Deborah; Hawkins & Associates, Inc., John; Heacock Literary Agency, Inc.; Henderson Literary Representation; Henshaw Group, Richard; Herner Rights Agency, Susan; James Peter Associates, Inc.; Kellock Company, Inc., The; Kern Literary Agency, Natasha; Kouts, Literary Agent, Barbara S.; Larsen/Elizabeth Pomada Literary Agents, Michael; Lasher Agency, The Maureen; Levant & Wales, Literary Agency, Inc.; Levine Communications, Inc., James; Lincoln Literary Agency, Ray; Literary Group, The; Love Literary Agency, Nancy; Lowenstein Associates, Inc.; ‡Lukeman Literary Management Ltd.; McBride Literary Agency, Margret; Mainhardt Agency, Ricia; Mann Agency, Carol; Manus & Associates Literary Agency, Inc.; Marcil Literary Agency, Inc., The Denise; Miller Agency, The; Multimedia Product Development, Inc.; Mura Enterprises, Inc., Dee; Naggar Literary Agency, Jean V.; ‡National Writers Literary Agency; New England Publishing Associates, Inc.; Norma-Lewis Agency, The; Palmer & Dodge Agency, The; Parks Agency, The Richard; Paton Literary Agency, Kathi J.; Protter Literary Agent, Susan Ann; Publishing Services; Quicksilver Books-Literary Agents; Rinaldi Literary Agency, Angela; Robbins Literary Agency, BJ; Rose Agency, Inc.; Russell-Simenauer Literary Agency Inc.; Schulman, A Literary Agency, Susan; Sebastian Literary Agency; Seligman, Literary Agent, Lynn; Shepard Agency, The; Singer Literary Agency Inc., Evelyn; ‡Slopen Literary Agency, Beverley; Spieler, F. Joseph; Stepping Stone; Stern Literary Agency (TX), Gloria; Teal Literary Agency, Patricia; ‡Tenth Avenue Editions, Inc.; Toad Hall, Inc.; Travis Literary Agency, Susan; 2M Communications Ltd.; Urstadt Inc. Agency, Susan P.; Vines Agency, Inc., The; Waterside Productions, Inc.; Wreschner, Authors' Representative, Ruth; Writers House; Zeckendorf Assoc. Inc., Susan

Computers/electronics: Adler & Robin Books Inc.; Allen Literary Agency, Linda; ‡Authors Alliance, Inc.; Axelrod Agency, The; Baldi Literary Agency, Malaga; Buck Agency, Howard; Cypher, Author's Representative, James R.; DHS Literary, Inc.; Ellison Inc., Nicholas; Elmo Agency Inc., Ann; Fleury Agency, B.R.; Graham Literary

Agency, Inc.; Henderson Literary Representation; Henshaw Group, Richard; Herman Agency, Inc., The Jeff; Jordan Literary Agency, Lawrence; Kellock Company, Inc., The; Levine Communications, Inc., James; Lieberman Associates, Robert; Moore Literary Agency; Mura Enterprises, Inc., Dee; Nazor Literary Agency, Karen; Shepard Agency, The; Waterside Productions, Inc.; ‡Young Agency Inc., The Gay

Cooking/food/nutrition: Adler & Robin Books Inc.; Agents Inc. for Medical and Mental Health Professionals; Ajlouny Agency, The Joseph S.; Author's Agency, The; ‡Authors Alliance, Inc.; Baldi Literary Agency, Malaga; Becker Literary Agency, The Wendy; Bernstein, Pam; ‡Bial Agency, Daniel; ‡Book Deals, Inc.; Bova Literary Agency, The Barbara; Brandt & Brandt Literary Agents Inc.; ‡Brock Gannon Literary Agency; Browne Ltd., Pema; Bykofsky Associates, Inc., Sheree; Cantrell-Colas Inc., Literary Agency; Casselman Literary Agent, Martha; Castiglia Literary Agency; Charlton Associates, James; Ciske & Dietz Literary Agency; Clausen Associates, Connie; Columbia Literary Associates, Inc.; Connor Literary Agency; Coover Agency, The Doe; Cornfield Literary Agency, Robert; Crawford Literary Agency; de la Haba Agency Inc., The Lois; DH Literary, Inc.; DHS Literary, Inc.; Diamant Literary Agency, The Writer's Workshop, Inc., Anita; Dijkstra Literary Agency, Sandra; Dystel Literary Management, Jane; Ellenberg Literary Agency, Ethan; Ellison Inc., Nicholas; Elmo Agency Inc., Ann; Esq. Literary Productions; Farber Literary Agency Inc.; Feiler Literary Agency, Florence; Fleming Associates, Arthur; Fleury Agency, B.R.; Gibson Agency, The Sebastian; Goddard Book Group; ‡Goodman-Andrew-Agency, Inc.; ‡Grosvenor Literary Agency, Deborah; Hawkins & Associates, Inc., John; Heacock Literary Agency, Inc.; Henderson Representation; Henshaw Group, Richard; Herner Rights Agency, Susan; Hochmann Books, John L.; Jabberwocky Literary Agency; Kellock Company, Inc., The; Kern Literary Agency, Natasha; Klinger, Inc., Harvey; Larsen/Elizabeth Pomada Literary Agents, Michael; Lasher Agency, The Maureen; Levine Communications, Inc., James; ‡Lichtman, Trister, Singer & Ross; Lincoln Literary Agency, Ray; Literary and Creative Artists Agency Inc.; Literary Group, The; Love Literary Agency, Nancy; ‡Lukeman Literary Management Ltd.; McBride Literary Agency, Margret; Mainhardt Agency, Ricia; Marcil Literary Agency, Inc., The Denise; Miller Agency, The; Multimedia Product Development, Inc.; Nazor Literary Agency, Karen; Norma-Lewis Agency, The; Parks Agency, The Richard; Pevner, Inc., Stephen; Pocono Literary Agency, Inc.; Pom Inc.; Pryor, Inc., Roberta; Publishing Services; Quicksilver Books-Literary Agents; Rinaldi Literary Agency, Angela; Robbins Literary Agency, BJ; Rowland Agency, The Damaris; ‡Russell & Volkening; Russell-Simenauer Literary Agency Inc.; ‡Schlessinger Agency, Blanche; Seligman, Literary Agent, Lynn; Shepard Agency, The; ‡Slopen Literary Agency, Beverley; Spieler, F. Joseph; Stepping Stone; Stern Literary Agency (TX), Gloria; Taylor Literary Enterprises, Sandra; Toad Hall, Inc.; Travis Literary Agency, Susan; Urstadt Inc. Agency, Susan P.; Watkins Loomis Agency, Inc.; Wieser & Wieser, Inc.; Wreschner, Authors' Representative, Ruth; Writers House; ‡Young Agency Inc., The Gay

Crafts/hobbies: Author's Agency, The; ‡Authors Alliance, Inc.; Becker Literary Agency, The Wendy; Brandt & Brandt Literary Agents Inc.; Buck Agency, Howard; Connor Literary Agency; Diamant Literary Agency, The Writer's Workshop, Inc., Anita; Ellison Inc., Nicholas; Elmo Agency Inc., Ann; Feiler Literary Agency, Florence; Flaherty, Literary Agent, Joyce A.; Fleury Agency, B.R.; Hawkins & Associates, Inc., John; Heacock Literary Agency, Inc.; ‡Janus Literary Agency; Kellock Company, Inc., The; Larsen/Elizabeth Pomada Literary Agents, Michael; Lincoln Literary Agency, Ray; Literary Group, The; Lowenstein Associates, Inc.; Mainhardt Agency, Ricia; Multimedia Product Development, Inc.; Norma-Lewis Agency, The; Parks Agency, The Richard; Shepard Agency, The; Toad Hall, Inc.; Travis Literary Agency, Susan; Urstadt Inc. Agency, Susan P.; Watt & Associates, Sandra; Wreschner, Authors' Representative, Ruth

Current affairs: Adler & Robin Books Inc.; Author's Agency, The; ‡Authors Alliance, Inc.; Baldi Literary Agency, Malaga; Balkin Agency, Inc.; Becker Literary Agency, The Wendy; ‡Bedford Book Works, Inc., The; Bernstein, Pam; ‡Bial Agency, Daniel; Boates Literary Agency, Reid; ‡Book Deals, Inc.; Borchardt Inc., Georges; Brandt & Brandt Literary Agents Inc.; ‡Brock Gannon Literary Agency; Brown Literary Agency, Inc., Andrea; Browne Ltd., Pema; Buck Agency, Howard; Bykofsky Associates, Inc., Sheree; Cantrell-Colas Inc., Literary Agency; Carvainis Agency, Inc., Maria; Castiglia Literary Agency; Charisma Communications, Ltd.; Circle of Confusion Ltd.; Connor Literary Agency; Cypher, Author's Representative, James R.; Darhansoff & Verrill Literary Agents; de la Haba Agency Inc., The Lois; DH Literary, Inc.; DHS Literary, Inc.; Diamant Literary Agency, The Writer's Workshop, Inc., Anita; Dijkstra Literary Agency, Sandra; Ducas, Robert; Dystel Literary Management, Jane; Educational Design Services, Inc.; Ellenberg Literary Agency, Ethan; Ellison Inc., Nicholas; Elmo Agency Inc., Ann; Emerald Literary Agency; Eth Literary Representation, Felicia; Flaming Star Literary Enterprises; Fleury Agency, B.R.; Franklin Associates, Ltd., Lynn C.; ‡Fullerton Associates, Sheryl B.; Gartenberg, Literary Agent, Max; Gibson Agency, The Sebastian; ‡Goodman-Andrew-Agency, Inc.; Greene, Literary Agent, Randall Elisha; ‡Grosvenor Literary Agency, Deborah; Hardy Agency, The; Hawkins & Associates, Inc., John; Henderson Literary Representation; Henshaw Group, Richard; Herner Rights Agency, Susan; Hill Associates, Frederick; Hochmann Books, John L.; Hull House Literary Agency; IMG Literary; J de S Associates Inc.; Jabberwocky Literary Agency; James Peter Associates, Inc.; ‡Janus Literary Agency; Kellock Company, Inc., The; Kern Literary Agency, Natasha; Ketz Agency, Louise B.; Kidde, Hoyt & Picard; Kouts, Literary Agent, Barbara S.; Lampack Agency, Inc., Peter; Larsen/Elizabeth Pomada Literary Agents, Michael; Lasher Agency, The Maureen; Levant & Wales, Literary Agency, Inc.; Levine Literary Agency, Inc., Ellen; Lincoln Literary Agency, Ray; Lindstrom Literary Group; Lipkind Agency, Wendy; Literary Group, The; Love Literary Agency, Nancy; Lowenstein Associates, Inc.; ‡Lukeman Literary Management Ltd.; McBride Literary Agency, Margret; Maccoby Literary Agency, Gina; McGrath, Helen; Mainhardt Agency, Ricia; Mann Agency, Carol; Manus & Associates Literary Agency, Inc.; March Tenth, Inc.; Markowitz Literary Agency, Barbara; Metropolitan Talent Agency; Michaels Literary Agency, Inc., Doris S.; Miller Agency, The; Multimedia Product Development, Inc.; Mura Enterprises, Inc., Dee; Naggar Literary Agency, Jean V.; Nazor Literary Agency, Karen; Nine Muses and Apollo Inc.; Norma-Lewis Agency, The; Palmer & Dodge Agency, The; Parks Agency, The Richard; Perkins Associates; Pevner, Inc., Stephen; Pine Associates, Inc, Arthur; Pocono Literary

Agency, Inc.; Pom Inc.; Potomac Literary Agency, The; Pryor, Inc., Roberta; Quicksilver Books-Literary Agents; Rees Literary Agency, Helen; Rinaldi Literary Agency, Angela; Robbins Literary Agency, BJ; ‡Russell & Volkening; Russell-Simenauer Literary Agency Inc.; Sanders Literary Agency, Victoria; Schmidt Literary Agency, Harold; Schulman, A Literary Agency, Susan; Sebastian Literary Agency; Seligman, Literary Agent, Lynn; Shepard Agency, The; Singer Literary Agency Inc., Evelyn; ‡Skolnick, Irene; ‡Slopen Literary Agency, Beverley; Spieler, F. Joseph; Spitzer Literary Agency, Philip G.; Stauffer Associates, Nancy; Stepping Stone; Stern Literary Agency (TX), Gloria; Urstadt Inc. Agency, Susan P.; Valcourt Agency, Inc., The Richard R.; Wald Associates, Inc., Mary Jack; Wallace Literary Agency, Inc.; Ware Literary Agency, John A.; Watkins Loomis Agency, Inc.; Watt & Associates, Sandra; Wecksler-Incomco; West Coast Literary Associates; Wieser & Wieser, Inc.; Witherspoon & Associates, Inc.; Wreschner, Authors' Representative, Ruth; ‡Young Agency Inc., The Gay; ‡Zitwer Agency, Barbara J.

Education: Author's Agency, The; ‡Authors Alliance, Inc.; Browne Ltd., Pema; Buck Agency, Howard; ‡Cohen Agency, The; DH Literary, Inc.; Dystel Literary Management, Jane; Elmo Agency Inc., Ann; Feiler Literary Agency, Florence; Fleury Agency, B.R.; ‡Fullerton Associates, Sheryl B.; ‡Goodman-Andrew-Agency, Inc.; Henderson Literary Representation; ‡Janus Literary Agency; Kellock Company, Inc., The; Kern Literary Agency, Natasha; Levant & Wales, Literary Agency, Inc.; ‡Lichtman, Trister, Singer & Ross; Lieberman Associates, Robert; Literary Group, The; Lowenstein Associates, Inc.; Mura Enterprises, Inc., Dee; ‡National Writers Literary Agency; New Brand Agency Group; Palmer & Dodge Agency, The; Pocono Literary Agency, Inc.; Publishing Services; Robbins Literary Agency, BJ; Rose Agency, Inc.; ‡Russell & Volkening; Russell-Simenauer Literary Agency Inc.; Schulman, A Literary Agency, Susan; Seligman, Literary Agent, Lynn; Urstadt Inc. Agency, Susan P.; Valcourt Agency, Inc., The Richard R.

Ethnic/cultural interests: Adler & Robin Books Inc.; Allen Literary Agency, Linda; Author's Agency, The; Baldi Literary Agency, Malaga; ‡Bial Agency, Daniel; Boates Literary Agency, Reid; ‡Book Deals, Inc.; Brandt & Brandt Literary Agents Inc.; ‡Brock Gannon Literary Agency; Brown Associates Inc., Marie; Brown Literary Agency, Inc., Andrea; Browne Ltd., Pema; Buck Agency, Howard; Bykofsky Associates, Inc., Sheree; Cantrell-Colas Inc., Literary Agency; Castiglia Literary Agency; Clausen Associates, Connie; ‡Cohen Agency, The; Cohen, Inc. Literary Agency, Ruth; Connor Literary Agency; Coover Agency, The Doe; Crown International Literature and Arts Agency, Bonnie R.; Cypher, Author's Representative, James R.; de la Haba Agency Inc., The Lois; DH Literary, Inc.; DHS Literary, Inc.; Dijkstra Literary Agency, Sandra; Dystel Literary Management, Jane; Educational Design Services, Inc.; Ellison Inc., Nicholas; Eth Literary Representation, Felicia; Fleury Agency, B.R.; ‡Fullerton Associates, Sheryl B.; Gibson Agency, The Sebastian; Goddard Book Group; ‡Goodman-Andrew-Agency, Inc.; Hawkins & Associates, Inc., John; Heacock Literary Agency, Inc.; Henderson Literary Representation; Herner Rights Agency, Susan; Hull House Literary Agency; IMG Literary; J de S Associates Inc.; James Peter Associates, Inc.; Kellock Company, Inc., The; Kern Literary Agency, Natasha; Kidde, Hoyt & Picard; Kouts, Literary Agent, Barbara S.; Larsen/Elizabeth Pomada Literary Agents, Michael; Lasher Agency, The Maureen; ‡Leap First; Levant & Wales, Literary Agency, Inc.; Lewis & Company, Karen; ‡Lichtman, Trister, Singer & Ross; Lincoln Literary Agency, Ray; Lindstrom Literary Group; Literary Group, The; Love Literary Agency, Nancy; Lowenstein Associates, Inc.; McBride Literary Agency, Margret; Maccoby Literary Agency, Gina; Mainhardt Agency, Ricia; Mann Agency, Carol; Manus & Associates Literary Agency, Inc.; Michaels Literary Agency, Inc., Doris S.; Miller Agency, The; Multimedia Product Development, Inc.; Mura Enterprises, Inc., Dee; Nazor Literary Agency, Karen; Nine Muses and Apollo Inc.; Norma-Lewis Agency, The; Palmer & Dodge Agency, The; Parks Agency, The Richard; Perkins Associates; Pevner, Inc., Stephen; Pom Inc.; Potomac Literary Agency, The; Pryor, Inc., Roberta; Publishing Services; Quicksilver Books-Literary Agents; Robbins Literary Agency, BJ; ‡Russell & Volkening; Sanders Literary Agency, Victoria; Schmidt Literary Agency, Harold; Schulman, A Literary Agency, Susan; Sebastian Literary Agency; Seligman, Literary Agent, Lynn; Singer Literary Agency Inc., Evelyn; Spieler, F. Joseph; Spitzer Literary Agency, Philip G.; Stauffer Associates, Nancy; Stepping Stone; Stern Literary Agency (TX), Gloria; ‡Sweeney Literary Agency, Emma; ‡Tenth Avenue Editions, Inc.; Travis Literary Agency, Susan; 2M Communications Ltd.; Urstadt Inc. Agency, Susan P.; Valcourt Agency, Inc., The Richard R.; Wald Associates, Inc., Mary Jack; Waterside Productions, Inc.; Watkins Loomis Agency, Inc.; West Coast Literary Associates; Witherspoon & Associates, Inc.; Wreschner, Authors' Representative, Ruth; ‡Young Agency Inc., The Gay; ‡Zitwer Agency, Barbara J.

Gay/lesbian issues: Adler & Robin Books Inc.; Allen Literary Agency, Linda; Baldi Literary Agency, Malaga; ‡Bial Agency, Daniel; Brandt & Brandt Literary Agents Inc.; ‡Brock Gannon Literary Agency; Brown Associates Inc., Marie; Browne Ltd., Pema; Buck Agency, Howard; Bykofsky Associates, Inc., Sheree; Circle of Confusion Ltd.; Clausen Associates, Connie; Cypher, Author's Representative, James R.; Daves Agency, Joan; de la Haba Agency Inc., The Lois; DH Literary, Inc.; DHS Literary, Inc.; Ducas, Robert; Dystel Literary Management, Jane; Eth Literary Representation, Felicia; Feiler Literary Agency, Florence; ‡Fleming Associates, Arthur; ‡Fullerton Associates, Sheryl B.; Garon-Brooke Assoc. Inc., Jay; ‡Goodman-Andrew-Agency, Inc.; ‡Grosvenor Literary Agency, Deborah; Hawkins & Associates, Inc., John; Henderson Literary Representation; Henshaw Group, Richard; Herner Rights Agency, Susan; Hochmann Books, John L.; IMG Literary; Jabberwocky Literary Agency; James Peter Associates, Inc.; Kern Literary Agency, Natasha; Kidde, Hoyt & Picard; Larsen/Elizabeth Pomada Literary Agents, Michael; Levant & Wales, Literary Agency, Inc.; Levine Communications, Inc., James; Lewis & Company, Karen; ‡Lichtman, Trister, Singer & Ross; Lincoln Literary Agency, Ray; Literary Group, The; Love Literary Agency, Nancy; Lowenstein Associates, Inc.; McBride Literary Agency, Margret; Miller Agency, The; Mura Enterprises, Inc., Dee; Nazor Literary Agency, Karen; Nine Muses and Apollo Inc.; Palmer & Dodge Agency, The; Parks Agency, The Richard; Perkins Associates; Pevner, Inc., Stephen; Potomac Literary Agency, The; Pryor, Inc., Roberta; Robbins Literary Agency, BJ; ‡Russell & Volkening; Sanders Literary Agency, Victoria; Schmidt Literary Agency, Harold; Schulman, A Literary Agency, Susan; Spieler, F. Joseph; Stepping Stone; ‡Sweeney Literary Agency, Emma; Travis Literary Agency, Susan; 2M Communications Ltd.; Ware Literary Agency, John A.; Watkins Loomis Agency,

Inc.; Witherspoon & Associates, Inc.; Wreschner, Authors' Representative, Ruth; ‡Zitwer Agency, Barbara J.

Government/politics/law: Adler & Robin Books Inc.; Allen Literary Agency, Linda; Author's Agency, The; ‡Authors Alliance, Inc.; Axelrod Agency, The; Baldi Literary Agency, Malaga; Becker Literary Agency, The Wendy; Bernstein, Pam; ‡Bial Agency, Daniel; Black Literary Agency, Inc., David; Boates Literary Agency, Reid; ‡Book Deals, Inc.; Brandt & Brandt Literary Agents Inc.; ‡Brock Gannon Literary Agency; Browne Ltd., Pema; Buck Agency, Howard; Cantrell-Colas Inc., Literary Agency; Carvainis Agency, Inc., Maria; Charisma Communications, Ltd.; Circle of Confusion Ltd.; ‡Cohen Agency, The; Connor Literary Agency; Cypher, Author's Representative, James R.; de la Haba Agency Inc., The Lois; DH Literary, Inc.; Diamant Literary Agency, The Writer's Workshop, Inc., Anita; Dijkstra Literary Agency, Sandra; Ducas, Robert; Dystel Literary Management, Jane; Educational Design Services, Inc.; Ellison Inc., Nicholas; Emerald Literary Agency; Eth Literary Representation, Felicia; ‡Feigen Literary Agency, Brenda; Flaming Star Literary Enterprises; Fleury Agency, B.R.; Gibson Agency, The Sebastian; Goddard Book Group; ‡Goodman-Andrew-Agency, Inc.; Graham Literary Agency, Inc.; Greene, Literary Agent, Randall Elisha; ‡Grosvenor Literary Agency, Deborah; Hardy Agency, The; Hawkins & Associates, Inc., John; Henderson Literary Representation; Henshaw Group, Richard; Herman Agency, Inc., The Jeff; Herner Rights Agency, Susan; Hill Associates, Frederick; Hochmann Books, John L.; Hull House Literary Agency; IMG Literary; J de S Associates Inc.; Jabberwocky Literary Agency; James Peter Associates, Inc.; ‡Janus Literary Agency; Kellock Company, Inc., The; Lampack Agency, Inc., Peter; Larsen/Elizabeth Pomada Literary Agents, Michael; Lasher Agency, The Maureen; ‡Lichtman, Trister, Singer & Ross; Lincoln Literary Agency, Ray; Literary and Creative Artists Agency Inc.; Literary Group, The; Love Literary Agency, Nancy; Lowenstein Associates, Inc.; McBride Literary Agency, Margret; Mainhardt Agency, Ricia; Mann Agency, Carol; Morrison, Inc., Henry; Mura Enterprises, Inc., Dee; Naggar Literary Agency, Jean V.; ‡National Writers Literary Agency; Nazor Literary Agency, Karen; New England Publishing Associates, Inc.; Nine Muses and Apollo Inc.; Norma-Lewis Agency, The; Palmer & Dodge Agency, The; Parks Agency, The Richard; Pevner, Inc., Stephen; Pocono Literary Agency, Inc.; Popkin, Julie; Pryor, Inc., Roberta; Rees Literary Agency, Helen; Robbins Literary Agency, BJ; ‡Russell & Volkening; Sanders Literary Agency, Victoria; Schmidt Literary Agency, Harold; Schulman, A Literary Agency, Susan; Sebastian Literary Agency; Seligman, Literary Agent, Lynn; Shepard Agency, The; Singer Literary Agency Inc., Evelyn; Snell Literary Agency, Michael; Spieler, F. Joseph; Spitzer Literary Agency, Philip G.; Stern Literary Agency (TX), Gloria; Valcourt Agency, Inc., The Richard R.; Ware Literary Agency, John A.; West Coast Literary Associates; Witherspoon & Associates, Inc.; Wreschner, Authors' Representative, Ruth; ‡Young Agency Inc., The Gay

Health/medicine: Adler & Robin Books Inc.; Agency Chicago; Appleseeds Management; Author's Agency, The; ‡Authors Alliance, Inc.; Axelrod Agency, The; Baldi Literary Agency, Malaga; Balkin Agency, Inc.; ‡Bedford Book Works, Inc., The; Bernstein, Pam; Boates Literary Agency, Reid; ‡Book Deals, Inc.; Brandt & Brandt Literary Agents Inc.; ‡Brock Gannon Literary Agency; Browne Ltd., Pema; Buck Agency, Howard; Bykofsky Associates, Inc., Sheree; Cantrell-Colas Inc., Literary Agency; Carvainis Agency, Inc., Maria; Casselman Literary Agent, Martha; Castiglia Literary Agency; Charlton Associates, James; Circle of Confusion Ltd.; Clausen Associates, Connie; Collin Literary Agent, Frances; Columbia Literary Associates, Inc.; Connor Literary Agency; Coover Agency, The Doe; Cypher, Author's Representative, James R.; Darhansoff & Verrill Literary Agents; de la Haba Agency Inc., The Lois; DH Literary, Inc.; Diamant Literary Agency, The Writer's Workshop, Inc., Anita; Diamond Literary Agency, Inc. (CO); Dijkstra Literary Agency, Sandra; Ducas, Robert; Dystel Literary Management, Jane; Ellenberg Literary Agency, Ethan; Ellison Inc., Nicholas; Elmo Agency Inc., Ann; Esq. Literary Productions; Eth Literary Representation, Felicia; ‡Feigen Literary Agency, Brenda; Feiler Literary Agency, Florence; Flaherty, Literary Agent, Joyce A.; Flaming Star Literary Enterprises; Fleury Agency, B.R.; Franklin Associates, Ltd., Lynn C.; ‡Fullerton Associates, Sheryl B.; Garon-Brooke Assoc. Inc., Jay; Gartenberg, Literary Agent, Max; Gibson Agency, The Sebastian; Goddard Book Group; ‡Goodman-Andrew-Agency, Inc.; Gordon Agency, Charlotte; ‡Grosvenor Literary Agency, Deborah; Hardy Agency, The; Hawkins & Associates, Inc., John; Heacock Literary Agency, Inc.; Henderson Literary Representation; Henshaw Group, Richard; Herman Agency, Inc., The Jeff; Herner Rights Agency, Susan; Hochmann Books, John L.; J de S Associates Inc.; Jabberwocky Literary Agency; James Peter Associates, Inc.; ‡Janus Literary Agency; Jordan Literary Agency, Lawrence; Kellock Company, Inc., The; Kern Literary Agency, Natasha; Klinger, Inc., Harvey; Kouts, Literary Agent, Barbara S.; Lampack Agency, Inc., Peter; Larsen/Elizabeth Pomada Literary Agents, Michael; Lasher Agency, The Maureen; ‡Leap First; Levant & Wales, Literary Agency, Inc.; Levine Communications, Inc., James; Levine Literary Agency, Inc., Ellen; Lieberman Associates, Robert; Lincoln Literary Agency, Ray; Lipkind Agency, Wendy; Literary and Creative Artists Agency Inc.; Literary Group, The; Love Literary Agency, Nancy; Lowenstein Associates, Inc.; ‡Lukeman Literary Management Ltd.; McBride Literary Agency, Margret; McGrath, Helen; Mainhardt Agency, Ricia; Mann Agency, Carol; Manus & Associates Literary Agency, Inc.; March Tenth, Inc.; Marcil Literary Agency, Inc., The Denise; Michaels Literary Agency, Inc., Doris S.; Miller Agency, The; Multimedia Product Development, Inc.; Mura Enterprises, Inc., Dee; Naggar Literary Agency, Jean V.; New England Publishing Associates, Inc.; Nine Muses and Apollo Inc.; Norma-Lewis Agency, The; Nugent Literary; Otitis Media; Palmer & Dodge Agency, The; Parks Agency, The Richard; Pine Associates, Inc, Arthur; Pocono Literary Agency, Inc.; Pom Inc.; Protter Literary Agent, Susan Ann; Publishing Services; Quicksilver Books-Literary Agents; Rees Literary Agency, Helen; Rinaldi Literary Agency, Angela; Robbins Literary Agency, BJ; Rose Agency, Inc.; Rowland Agency, The Damaris; ‡Russell & Volkening; Russell-Simenauer Literary Agency Inc.; ‡Schlessinger Agency, Blanche; Schmidt Literary Agency, Harold; Schulman, A Literary Agency, Susan; Sebastian Literary Agency; Seligman, Literary Agent, Lynn; Shepard Agency, The; Singer Literary Agency Inc., Evelyn; Snell Literary Agency, Michael; Spitzer Literary Agency, Philip G.; Stepping Stone; Stern Literary Agency (TX), Gloria; Taylor Literary Enterprises, Sandra; Teal Literary Agency, Patricia; Toad Hall, Inc.; Travis Literary Agency, Susan; 2M Communications Ltd.; Urstadt Inc. Agency, Susan P.; Valcourt Agency, Inc., The Richard R.; Waterside Productions, Inc.; Wieser & Wieser, Inc.; Witherspoon & Associates, Inc.; Wreschner, Authors' Representative, Ruth; Writers House; ‡Young Agency Inc., The Gay; Zeckendorf Assoc. Inc., Susan

History: Allan Agency, Lee; Adler & Robin Books Inc.; Ajlouny Agency, The Joseph S.; Allen Literary Agency, Linda; Author's Agency, The; ‡Authors Alliance, Inc.; Axelrod Agency, The; Baldi Literary Agency, Malaga; Balkin Agency, Inc.; Becker Literary Agency, The Wendy; ‡Bedford Book Works, Inc., The; ‡Bial Agency, Daniel; Boates Literary Agency, Reid; ‡Book Deals, Inc.; Borchardt Inc., Georges; Brandt & Brandt Literary Agents Inc.; Brown Associates Inc., Marie; Brown Literary Agency, Inc., Andrea; Buck Agency, Howard; Bykofsky Associates, Inc., Sheree; Cantrell-Colas Inc., Literary Agency; Carvainis Agency, Inc., Maria; Castiglia Literary Agency; Circle of Confusion Ltd.; Collin Literary Agent, Frances; Coover Agency, The Doe; Cornfield Literary Agency, Robert; Curtis Associates, Inc., Richard; Cypher, Author's Representative, James R.; Darhansoff & Verrill Literary Agents; de la Haba Agency Inc., The Lois; DH Literary, Inc.; Diamant Literary Agency, The Writer's Workshop, Inc., Anita; Dijkstra Literary Agency, Sandra; Ducas, Robert; Dystel Literary Management, Jane; Educational Design Services, Inc.; Ellenberg Literary Agency, Ethan; Ellison Inc., Nicholas; Elmo Agency Inc., Ann; Eth Literary Representation, Felicia; Feiler Literary Agency, Florence; Fleury Agency, B.R.; Franklin Associates, Ltd., Lynn C.; Garon-Brooke Assoc. Inc., Jay; Gartenberg, Literary Agent, Max; Gibson Agency, The Sebastian; Goddard Book Group; ‡Goodman-Andrew-Agency, Inc.; Gordon Agency, Charlotte; Greene, Literary Agent, Randall Elisha; ‡Grosvenor Literary Agency, Deborah; Hawkins & Associates, Inc., John; Heacock Literary Agency, Inc.; Henderson Literary Representation; Herman Agency, Inc., The Jeff; Herner Rights Agency, Susan; Hochmann Books, John L.; Hull House Literary Agency; IMG Literary; J de S Associates Inc.; Jabberwocky Literary Agency; James Peter Associates, Inc.; ‡Janus Literary Agency; ‡Just Write Agency, Inc.; Kellock Company, Inc., The; Ketz Agency, Louise B.; Kidde, Hoyt & Picard; Kouts, Literary Agent, Barbara S.; Lampack Agency, Inc., Peter; Larsen/Elizabeth Pomada Literary Agents, Michael; Lasher Agency, The Maureen; ‡Leap First; Lincoln Literary Agency, Ray; Lindstrom Literary Group; Lipkind Agency, Wendy; Literary Group, The; Love Literary Agency, Nancy; Lowenstein Associates, Inc.; McBride Literary Agency, Margret; McGrath, Helen; Mainhardt Agency, Ricia; Mann Agency, Carol; March Tenth, Inc.; Metropolitan Talent Agency; Michaels Literary Agency, Inc., Doris S.; Morrison, Inc., Henry; Mura Enterprises, Inc., Dee; Naggar Literary Agency, Jean V.; Nazor Literary Agency, Karen; New England Publishing Associates, Inc.; Nine Muses and Apollo Inc.; Norma-Lewis Agency, The; Otitis Media; Palmer & Dodge Agency, The; Parks Agency, The Richard; Pevner, Inc., Stephen; Pocono Literary Agency, Inc.; Popkin, Julie; Potomac Literary Agency, The; Pryor, Inc., Roberta; Quicksilver Books-Literary Agents; Rees Literary Agency, Helen; Renaissance—H.N. Swanson; ‡Russell & Volkening; Sanders Literary Agency, Victoria; Schmidt Literary Agency, Harold; Schulman, A Literary Agency, Susan; Seligman, Literary Agent, Lynn; Shepard Agency, The; Spieler, F. Joseph; Spitzer Literary Agency, Philip G.; Stepping Stone; Stern Literary Agency (TX), Gloria; ‡Sweeney Literary Agency, Emma; Urstadt Inc. Agency, Susan P.; Valcourt Agency, Inc., The Richard R.; Wald Associates, Inc., Mary Jack; Wallace Literary Agency, Inc.; Ware Literary Agency, John A.; Watkins Loomis Agency, Inc.; Wecksler-Incomco; West Coast Literary Associates; Wieser & Wieser, Inc.; Witherspoon & Associates, Inc.; Wreschner, Authors' Representative, Ruth; Writers House; ‡Young Agency Inc., The Gay; Zeckendorf Assoc. Inc., Susan

How to: Adler & Robin Books Inc.; Ajlouny Agency, The Joseph S.; Author's Agency, The; ‡Authors Alliance, Inc.; Authors' Literary Agency; Balkin Agency, Inc.; Becker Literary Agency, The Wendy; ‡Bedford Book Works, Inc., The; Bernstein, Pam; ‡Bial Agency, Daniel; Bova Literary Agency, The Barbara; ‡Brock Gannon Literary Agency; Brown Literary Agency, Inc., Andrea; Browne Ltd., Pema; Buck Agency, Howard; Bykofsky Associates, Inc., Sheree; Charlton Associates, James; Clausen Associates, Connie; Connor Literary Agency; Crawford Literary Agency; Cypher, Author's Representative, James R.; DH Literary, Inc.; Elmo Agency Inc., Ann; Feiler Literary Agency, Florence; Flaherty, Literary Agent, Joyce A.; ‡Fleming Associates, Arthur; Fleury Agency, B.R.; ‡Frustrated Writer's Ltd., The; ‡Fullerton Associates, Sheryl B.; ‡Goodman-Andrew-Agency, Inc.; Greene, Literary Agent, Randall Elisha; ‡Grosvenor Literary Agency, Deborah; Heacock Literary Agency, Inc.; Henderson Literary Representation; Henshaw Group, Richard; Herman Agency, Inc., The Jeff; Herner Rights Agency, Susan; ‡Janus Literary Agency; Kellock Company, Inc., The; Kern Literary Agency, Natasha; Larsen/Elizabeth Pomada Literary Agents, Michael; Lasher Agency, The Maureen; Literary Group, The; Love Literary Agency, Nancy; Lowenstein Associates, Inc.; McBride Literary Agency, Margret; McGrath, Helen; Mainhardt Agency, Ricia; Manus & Associates Literary Agency, Inc.; Marcil Literary Agency, Inc., The Denise; Michaels Literary Agency, Inc., Doris S.; Multimedia Product Development, Inc.; Mura Enterprises, Inc., Dee; ‡National Writers Literary Agency; Nazor Literary Agency, Karen; New Brand Agency Group; Parks Agency, The Richard; Quicksilver Books-Literary Agents; Robbins Literary Agency, BJ; Russell-Simenauer Literary Agency Inc.; ‡Schlessinger Agency, Blanche; Schulman, A Literary Agency, Susan; Seligman, Literary Agent, Lynn; Singer Literary Agency Inc., Evelyn; Stern Literary Agency (TX), Gloria; Taylor Literary Enterprises, Sandra; Teal Literary Agency, Patricia; Toad Hall, Inc.; Travis Literary Agency, Susan; Urstadt Inc. Agency, Susan P.; Vines Agency, Inc., The; Watt & Associates, Sandra; Wreschner, Authors' Representative, Ruth

Humor: Ajlouny Agency, The Joseph S.; Author's Agency, The; ‡Authors Alliance, Inc.; Becker Literary Agency, The Wendy; ‡Bedford Book Works, Inc., The; ‡Bial Agency, Daniel; ‡Brock Gannon Literary Agency; Brown Literary Agency, Inc., Andrea; Buck Agency, Howard; Bykofsky Associates, Inc., Sheree; Charlton Associates, James; Circle of Confusion Ltd.; Clausen Associates, Connie; Connor Literary Agency; Cypher, Author's Representative, James R.; DH Literary, Inc.; Dystel Literary Management, Jane; Elliott Agency; ‡Fleming Associates, Arthur; Gibson Agency, The Sebastian; ‡Goodman-Andrew-Agency, Inc.; ‡Grosvenor Literary Agency, Deborah; Henderson Literary Representation; Henshaw Group, Richard; Jabberwocky Literary Agency; Kellock Company, Inc., The; Larsen/Elizabeth Pomada Literary Agents, Michael; ‡Lichtman, Trister, Singer & Ross; Literary Group, The; Lowenstein Associates, Inc.; Mainhardt Agency, Ricia; March Tenth, Inc.; Metropolitan Talent Agency; Multimedia Product Development, Inc.; Mura Enterprises, Inc., Dee; New Brand Agency Group; Nine Muses and Apollo Inc.;

Otitis Media; Parks Agency, The Richard; Pevner, Inc., Stephen; Robbins Literary Agency, BJ; Sanders Literary Agency, Victoria; Seligman, Literary Agent, Lynn; ‡Sweeney Literary Agency, Emma; Vines Agency, Inc., The; Waterside Productions, Inc.; Watt & Associates, Sandra; ‡Young Agency, The Gay; ‡Zitwer Agency, Barbara J.

Interior design/decorating: Author's Agency, The; ‡Authors Alliance, Inc.; Baldi Literary Agency, Malaga; Becker Literary Agency, The Wendy; Brandt & Brandt Literary Agents Inc.; Buck Agency, Howard; Connor Literary Agency; Ellison Inc., Nicholas; Fleury Agency, B.R.; Goddard Book Group; Hawkins & Associates, Inc., John; Henderson Literary Representation; Kellock Company, Inc., The; Larsen/Elizabeth Pomada Literary Agents, Michael; Lincoln Literary Agency, Ray; Mainhardt Agency, Ricia; Mann Agency, Carol; Seligman, Literary Agent, Lynn; Shepard Agency, The; Stepping Stone; ‡Sweeney Literary Agency, Emma; Travis Literary Agency, Susan; Urstadt Inc. Agency, Susan P.; Writers House; Authors Alliance, Inc.; Brandt & Brandt Literary Agents Inc.

Juvenile nonfiction: ‡Brock Gannon Literary Agency; Brown Associates Inc., Marie; Brown Literary Agency, Inc., Andrea; Browne Ltd., Pema; Cantrell-Colas Inc., Literary Agency; Circle of Confusion Ltd.; Cohen, Inc. Literary Agency, Ruth; de la Haba Agency Inc., The Lois; Diamant Literary Agency, The Writer's Workshop, Inc., Anita; Educational Design Services, Inc.; Elek Associates, Peter; Ellenberg Literary Agency, Ethan; Ellison Inc., Nicholas; Elmo Agency Inc., Ann; Feiler Literary Agency, Florence; Flannery Literary; ‡Fleming Associates, Arthur; Fleury Agency, B.R.; ‡Frustrated Writer's Ltd., The; Gordon Agency, Charlotte; Hawkins & Associates, Inc., John; Henderson Literary Representation; Henshaw Group, Richard; Kirchoff/Wohlberg, Inc., Authors' Representation Division; Kouts, Literary Agent, Barbara S.; Lewis & Company, Karen; Lincoln Literary Agency, Ray; Literary Group, The; Maccoby Literary Agency, Gina; Mainhardt Agency, Ricia; Markowitz Literary Agency, Barbara; Morrison, Inc., Henry; Multimedia Product Development, Inc.; Mura Enterprises, Inc., Dee; Naggar Literary Agency, Jean V.; ‡National Writers Literary Agency; Norma-Lewis Agency, The; Pocono Literary Agency, Inc.; Pryor, Inc., Roberta; Rose Agency, Inc.; ‡Russell & Volkening; Schulman, A Literary Agency, Susan; Seymour Agency, The; Shepard Agency, The; Singer Literary Agency Inc., Evelyn; Targ Literary Agency, Inc., Roslyn; ‡Tenth Avenue Editions, Inc.; Urstadt Inc. Agency, Susan P.; Vines Agency, Inc., The; Wald Associates, Inc., Mary Jack; Wasserman Literary Agency, Inc., Harriet; Wreschner, Authors' Representative, Ruth; Writers House; ‡Young Agency Inc., The Gay

Language/literature/criticism: Author's Agency, The; ‡Authors Alliance, Inc.; Baldi Literary Agency, Malaga; Balkin Agency, Inc.; ‡Bial Agency, Daniel; Boates Literary Agency, Reid; Brandt & Brandt Literary Agents Inc.; ‡Brock Gannon Literary Agency; Buck Agency, Howard; Cantrell-Colas Inc., Literary Agency; Castiglia Literary Agency; ‡Cohen Agency, The; Connor Literary Agency; Coover Agency, The Doe; Cornfield Literary Agency, Robert; Cypher, Author's Representative, James R.; Darhansoff & Verrill Literary Agents; DH Literary, Inc.; Dijkstra Literary Agency, Sandra; Educational Design Services, Inc.; Ellison Inc., Nicholas; Emerald Literary Agency; ‡Feigen Literary Agency, Brenda; Fleury Agency, B.R.; ‡Goodman-Andrew-Agency, Inc.; Greene, Literary Agent, Randall Elisha; ‡Grosvenor Literary Agency, Deborah; Hawkins & Associates, Inc., John; Heacock Literary Agency, Inc.; Herner Rights Agency, Susan; Hill Associates, Frederick; Jabberwocky Literary Agency; James Peter Associates, Inc.; Kern Literary Agency, Natasha; Kidde, Hoyt & Picard; Larsen/Elizabeth Pomada Literary Agents, Michael; Levant & Wales, Literary Agency, Inc.; Lincoln Literary Agency, Ray; Literary Group, The; Lowenstein Associates, Inc.; ‡Lukeman Literary Management Ltd.; March Tenth, Inc.; Miller Agency, The; New England Publishing Associates, Inc.; Nine Muses and Apollo Inc.; Palmer & Dodge Agency, The; Parks Agency, The Richard; Pevner, Inc., Stephen; Popkin, Julie; Potomac Literary Agency, The; Quicksilver Books-Literary Agents; ‡Russell & Volkening; Sanders Literary Agency, Victoria; Schmidt Literary Agency, Harold; Seligman, Literary Agent, Lynn; Shepard Agency, The; Spitzer Literary Agency, Philip G.; Stern Literary Agency (TX), Gloria; ‡Sweeney Literary Agency, Emma; ‡Tenth Avenue Editions, Inc.; Valcourt Agency, Inc., The Richard R.; Wald Associates, Inc., Mary Jack; Wallace Literary Agency, Inc.; Ware Literary Agency, John A.; Watt & Associates, Sandra; West Coast Literary Associates; ‡Young Agency Inc., The Gay; ‡Zitwer Agency, Barbara J.

Military/war: Author's Agency, The; ‡Authors Alliance, Inc.; Baldi Literary Agency, Malaga; Becker Literary Agency, The Wendy; ‡Bial Agency, Daniel; Brandt & Brandt Literary Agents Inc.; ‡Brock Gannon Literary Agency; Browne Ltd., Pema; Buck Agency, Howard; Cantrell-Colas Inc., Literary Agency; Carvainis Agency, Inc., Maria; Charisma Communications, Ltd.; Charlton Associates, James; Circle of Confusion Ltd.; Curtis Associates, Inc., Richard; Cypher, Author's Representative, James R.; DH Literary, Inc.; Dijkstra Literary Agency, Sandra; Ducas, Robert; Dystel Literary Management, Jane; Educational Design Services, Inc.; Ellison Inc., Nicholas; Feiler Literary Agency, Florence; ‡Fleming Associates, Arthur; ‡Frustrated Writer's Ltd., The; Garon-Brooke Assoc. Inc., Jay; Gartenberg, Literary Agent, Max; Gibson Agency, The Sebastian; ‡Grosvenor Literary Agency, Deborah; Hawkins & Associates, Inc., John; Henshaw Group, Richard; Hochmann Books, John L.; Hull House Literary Agency; J de S Associates Inc.; Jabberwocky Literary Agency; James Peter Associates, Inc.; Kellock Company, Inc., The; Ketz Agency, Louise B.; Literary Group, The; ‡Lukeman Literary Management Ltd.; McGrath, Helen; Mura Enterprises, Inc. Dee; New Brand Agency Group; New England Publishing Associates, Inc.; Otitis Media; Parks Agency, The Richard; Pocono Literary Agency, Inc.; Potomac Literary Agency, The; Pryor, Inc., Roberta; ‡Russell & Volkening; Schmidt Literary Agency, Harold; Schulman, A Literary Agency, Susan; Spitzer Literary Agency, Philip G.; Urstadt Inc. Agency, Susan P.; Valcourt Agency, Inc., The Richard R.; Wallace Literary Agency, Inc.; Ware Literary Agency, John A.; Writers House

Money/finance/economics: Adler & Robin Books Inc.; Appleseeds Management; Author's Agency, The; ‡Authors Alliance, Inc.; Axelrod Agency, The; Baldi Literary Agency, Malaga; Becker Literary Agency, The Wendy; ‡Bedford Book Works, Inc., The; Behar Literary Agency, Josh; Bial Agency, Daniel; ‡Book Deals, Inc.; Bova Literary Agency, The Barbara; Brandt & Brandt Literary Agents Inc.; ‡Brock Gannon Literary Agency; Brown

Associates Inc., Marie; Browne Ltd., Pema; Buck Agency, Howard; Cantrell-Colas Inc., Literary Agency; Carvainis Agency, Inc., Maria; Castiglia Literary Agency; Clausen Associates, Connie; Connor Literary Agency; Coover Agency, The Doe; Curtis Associates, Inc., Richard; Cypher, Author's Representative, James R.; de la Haba Agency Inc., The Lois; DH Literary, Inc.; Diamant Literary Agency, The Writer's Workshop, Inc., Anita; Diamond Literary Agency, Inc. (CO); Dijkstra Literary Agency, Sandra; Ducas, Robert; Dystel Literary Management, Jane; Educational Design Services, Inc.; Ellison Inc., Nicholas; Elmo Agency Inc., Ann; Emerald Literary Agency; ‡Fleming Associates, Arthur; Fleury Agency, B.R.; ‡Fullerton Associates, Sheryl B.; Gartenberg, Literary Agent, Max; Gibson Agency, The Sebastian; Goddard Book Group; Gordon Agency, Charlotte; ‡Grosvenor Literary Agency, Deborah; Hawkins & Associates, Inc., John; Heacock Literary Agency, Inc.; Henderson Literary Representation; Henshaw Group, Richard; Hull House Literary Agency; IMG Literary; Jabberwocky Literary Agency; James Peter Associates, Inc.; ‡Janus Literary Agency; Kellock Company, Inc., The; Kern Literary Agency, Natasha; Ketz Agency, Louise B.; Lampack Agency, Inc., Peter; Larsen/Elizabeth Pomada Literary Agents, Michael; Levine Communications, Inc., James; ‡Lichtman, Trister, Singer & Ross; Lieberman Associates, Robert; Lincoln Literary Agency, Ray; Literary Group, The; Lowenstein Associates, Inc.; ‡Lukeman Literary Management Ltd.; McBride Literary Agency, Margret; Mainhardt Agency, Ricia; Mann Agency, Carol; Marcil Literary Agency, Inc., The Denise; Michaels Literary Agency, Inc., Doris S.; Multimedia Product Development, Inc.; Mura Enterprises, Inc., Dee; New England Publishing Associates, Inc.; Palmer & Dodge Agency, The; Parks Agency, The Richard; Pevner, Inc., Stephen; Pine Associates, Inc, Arthur; Pocono Literary Agency, Inc.; Pom Inc.; Potomac Literary Agency, The; Rees Literary Agency, Helen; Rinaldi Literary Agency, Angela; ‡Russell & Volkening; Russell-Simenauer Literary Agency Inc.; Schmidt Literary Agency, Harold; Schulman, A Literary Agency, Susan; Sebastian Literary Agency; Seligman, Literary Agent, Lynn; Shepard Agency, The; Singer Literary Agency Inc., Evelyn; Spieler, F. Joseph; Stern Literary Agency (TX), Gloria; Travis Literary Agency, Susan; Urstadt Inc. Agency, Susan P.; Valcourt Agency, Inc., The Richard R.; Vines Agency, Inc., The; Waterside Productions, Inc.; Wieser & Wieser, Inc.; Witherspoon & Associates, Inc.; Wreschner, Authors' Representative, Ruth; Writers House; ‡Young Agency Inc., The Gay

Multimedia: Elek Associates, Peter; Kellock Company, Inc., The; Larsen/Elizabeth Pomada Literary Agents, Michael; Lazear Agency Incorporated; Marcil Literary Agency, Inc., The Denise; Multimedia Product Development, Inc.; Nine Muses and Apollo Inc.; Writers House

Music/dance/theater/film: Allen Literary Agency, Linda; Andrews & Associates Inc., Bart; Appleseeds Management; Author's Agency, The; ‡Authors Alliance, Inc.; Axelrod Agency, The; Baldi Literary Agency, Malaga; Balkin Agency, Inc.; Becker Literary Agency, The Wendy; ‡Bial Agency, Daniel; Brandt & Brandt Literary Agents Inc.; ‡Brock Gannon Literary Agency; Brown Associates Inc., Marie; Buck Agency, Howard; Bykofsky Associates, Inc., Sheree; ‡Cohen Agency, The; Cornfield Literary Agency, Robert; Curtis Associates, Inc., Richard; Cypher, Author's Representative, James R.; de la Haba Agency Inc., The Lois; DH Literary, Inc.; Ellison Inc., Nicholas; Elmo Agency Inc., Ann; Farber Literary Agency Inc.; ‡Feigen Literary Agency, Brenda; Garon-Brooke Assoc. Inc., Jay; Gartenberg, Literary Agent, Max; Gibson Agency, The Sebastian; ‡Goodman-Andrew-Agency, Inc.; Greene, Arthur B.; ‡Grosvenor Literary Agency, Deborah; Hawkins & Associates, Inc., John; Heacock Literary Agency, Inc.; Henderson Literary Representation; Henshaw Group, Richard; Hochmann Books, John L.; Hull House Literary Agency; Jabberwocky Literary Agency; James Peter Associates, Inc.; Kellock Company, Inc., The; Kouts, Literary Agent, Barbara S.; Lampack Agency, Inc., Peter; Larsen/Elizabeth Pomada Literary Agents, Michael; Lieberman Associates, Robert; Lincoln Literary Agency, Ray; Literary Group, The; Lowenstein Associates, Inc.; ‡Lukeman Literary Management Ltd.; McBride Literary Agency, Margret; March Tenth, Inc.; Markowitz Literary Agency, Barbara; Michaels Literary Agency, Inc., Doris S.; Nathan, Ruth; Nazor Literary Agency, Karen; Norma-Lewis Agency, The; Otitis Media; Palmer & Dodge Agency, The; Parks Agency, The Richard; Perkins Associates; Pevner, Inc., Stephen; Pom Inc.; Pryor, Inc., Roberta; Renaissance—H.N. Swanson; Robbins Literary Agency, BJ; ‡Russell & Volkening; Sanders Literary Agency, Victoria; Schmidt Literary Agency, Harold; Schulman, A Literary Agency, Susan; Seligman, Literary Agent, Lynn; Shepard Agency, The; Spitzer Literary Agency, Philip G.; 2M Communications Ltd.; Urstadt Inc. Agency, Susan P.; Vines Agency, Inc., The; Wald Associates, Inc., Mary Jack; Wecksler-Incomco; Weingel-Fidel Agency, The; West Coast Literary Associates; Witherspoon & Associates, Inc.; Writers House; ‡Young Agency Inc., The Gay; Zeckendorf Assoc. Inc., Susan; ‡Zitwer Agency, Barbara J.

Nature/environment:: Adler & Robin Books Inc.; Agency Chicago; Allen Literary Agency, Linda; Author's Agency, The; ‡Authors Alliance, Inc.; Axelrod Agency, The; Baldi Literary Agency, Malaga; Balkin Agency, Inc.; Becker Literary Agency, The Wendy; ‡Bial Agency, Daniel; Boates Literary Agency, Reid; ‡Book Deals, Inc.; Brandt & Brandt Literary Agents Inc.; ‡Brock Gannon Literary Agency; Brown Literary Agency, Inc., Andrea; Browne Ltd., Pema; Buck Agency, Howard; Cantrell-Colas Inc., Literary Agency; Castiglia Literary Agency; Collin Literary Agent, Frances; Coover Agency, The Doe; Crown International Literature and Arts Agency, Bonnie R.; Cypher, Author's Representative, James R.; Darhansoff & Verrill Literary Agents; de la Haba Agency Inc., The Lois; DH Literary, Inc.; Diamant Literary Agency, The Writer's Workshop, Inc., Anita; Dijkstra Literary Agency, Sandra; Ducas, Robert; Elek Associates, Peter; Elliott Agency; Ellison Inc., Nicholas; Eth Literary Representation, Felicia; Flaherty, Literary Agent, Joyce A.; Flaming Star Literary Enterprises; Fleury Agency, B.R.; Gartenberg, Literary Agent, Max; Gibson Agency, The Sebastian; Goddard Book Group; ‡Goodman-Andrew-Agency, Inc.; Gordon Agency, Charlotte; Graham Literary Agency, Inc.; ‡Grosvenor Literary Agency, Deborah; Hawkins & Associates, Inc., John; Heacock Literary Agency, Inc.; Henshaw Group, Richard; Herner Rights Agency, Susan; Jabberwocky Literary Agency; Kellock Company, Inc., The; Kern Literary Agency, Natasha; Kouts, Literary Agent, Barbara S.; Larsen/Elizabeth Pomada Literary Agents, Michael; Lasher Agency, The Maureen; Levant & Wales, Literary Agency, Inc.; Levine Communications, Inc., James; Lichtman, Trister, Singer & Ross; Lieberman Associates, Robert; Lincoln Literary Agency, Ray; Literary Group, The; Love Literary Agency, Nancy; Lowenstein Associates, Inc.; ‡Lukeman Literary Management Ltd.; Mainhardt Agency, Ricia; Manus & Associates Literary Agency,

A Literary Agency, Susan; Seligman, Literary Agent, Lynn; Spitzer Literary Agency, Philip G.; Stauffer Associates, Nancy; ‡Tenth Avenue Editions, Inc.; Toad Hall, Inc.; Travis Literary Agency, Susan; Urstadt Inc. Agency, Susan P.; Vines Agency, Inc., The; Ware Literary Agency, John A.; Waterside Productions, Inc.; Watkins Loomis Agency, Inc.; Watt & Associates, Sandra; Wreschner, Authors' Representative, Ruth; ‡Young Agency Inc., The Gay; ‡Zitwer Agency, Barbara J.

Psychology: Agents Inc. for Medical and Mental Health Professionals; Allen Literary Agency, Linda; Appleseeds Management; Author's Agency, The; ‡Authors Alliance, Inc.; Authors' Literary Agency; Baldi Literary Agency, Malaga; Becker Literary Agency, The Wendy; ‡Bedford Book Works, Inc., The; Bernstein, Pam; ‡Bial Agency, Daniel; Boates Literary Agency, Reid; Brandt & Brandt Literary Agents Inc.; Brown Associates Inc., Marie; Browne Ltd., Pema; Buck Agency, Howard; Bykofsky Associates, Inc., Sheree; Cantrell-Colas Inc., Literary Agency; Carvainis Agency, Inc., Maria; Castiglia Literary Agency; Clausen Associates, Connie; Coover Agency, The Doe; Cypher, Author's Representative, James R.; de la Haba Agency Inc., The Lois; DH Literary, Inc.; Diamant Literary Agency, The Writer's Workshop, Inc., Anita; Diamond Literary Agency, Inc. (CO); Dijkstra Literary Agency, Sandra; Dystel Literary Management, Jane; Ellenberg Literary Agency, Ethan; Ellison Inc., Nicholas; Elmo Agency Inc., Ann; Emerald Literary Agency; Eth Literary Representation, Felicia; Farber Literary Agency Inc.; ‡Feigen Literary Agency, Brenda; Feiler Literary Agency, Florence; Flaherty, Literary Agent, Joyce A.; ‡Fleming Associates, Arthur; Fleury Agency, B.R.; Franklin Associates, Ltd., Lynn C.; ‡Frustrated Writer's Ltd., The; ‡Fullerton Associates, Sheryl B.; Garon-Brooke Assoc. Inc., Jay; Gartenberg, Literary Agent, Max; Gibson Agency, The Sebastian; Goddard Book Group; ‡Goodman-Andrew-Agency, Inc.; Gordon Agency, Charlotte; Greene, Literary Agent, Randall Elisha; ‡Grosvenor Literary Agency, Deborah; Hawkins & Associates, Inc., John; Heacock Literary Agency, Inc.; Henderson Literary Representation; Henshaw Group, Richard; Herman Agency, Inc., The Jeff; Herner Rights Agency, Susan; James Peter Associates, Inc.; Kellock Company, Inc., The; Kern Literary Agency, Natasha; Kidde, Hoyt & Picard; Klinger, Inc., Harvey; Kouts, Literary Agent, Barbara S.; Larsen/Elizabeth Pomada Literary Agents, Michael; Lasher Agency, The Maureen; ‡Leap First; Levant & Wales, Literary Agency, Inc.; Levine Communications, Inc., James; Levine Literary Agency, Inc., Ellen; ‡Lichtman, Trister, Singer & Ross; Lieberman Associates, Robert; Lincoln Literary Agency, Ray; Lindstrom Literary Group; Literary Group, The; Love Literary Agency, Nancy; Lowenstein Associates, Inc.; ‡Lukeman Literary Management Ltd.; McBride Literary Agency, Margret; McGrath, Helen; Mainhardt Agency, Ricia; Mann Agency, Carol; Manus & Associates Literary Agency, Inc.; Marcil Literary Agency, Inc., The Denise; Miller Agency, The; Multimedia Product Development, Inc.; Naggar Literary Agency, Jean V.; New England Publishing Associates, Inc.; Nine Muses and Apollo Inc.; Palmer & Dodge Agency, The; Parks Agency, The Richard; Paton Literary Agency, Kathi J.; Pine Associates, Inc, Arthur; Pocono Literary Agency, Inc.; Potomac Literary Agency, The; Protter Literary Agent, Susan Ann; Quicksilver Books-Literary Agents; Rinaldi Literary Agency, Angela; Robbins Literary Agency, BJ; ‡Russell & Volkening; Russell-Simenauer Literary Agency Inc.; Sanders Literary Agency, Victoria; Schmidt Literary Agency, Harold; Schulman, A Literary Agency, Susan; Sebastian Literary Agency; Seligman, Literary Agent, Lynn; Shepard Agency, The; Singer Literary Agency Inc., Evelyn; ‡Slopen Literary Agency, Beverley; Snell Literary Agency, Michael; Spitzer Literary Agency, Philip G.; Stepping Stone; Stern Literary Agency (TX), Gloria; Teal Literary Agency, Patricia; Travis Literary Agency, Susan; Vines Agency, Inc., The; Ware Literary Agency, John A.; Waterside Productions, Inc.; Watt & Associates, Sandra; Weingel-Fidel Agency, The; West Coast Literary Associates; Wieser & Wieser, Inc.; Wreschner, Authors' Representative, Ruth; Writers House; Zeckendorf Assoc. Inc., Susan; ‡Zitwer Agency, Barbara J.

Religious/inspirational: Author's Agency, The; ‡Authors Alliance, Inc.; Bernstein, Pam; ‡Bial Agency, Daniel; Brandenburgh & Associates Literary Agency; ‡Brock Gannon Literary Agency; Brown Associates Inc., Marie; Browne Ltd., Pema; Buck Agency, Howard; Bykofsky Associates, Inc., Sheree; Castiglia Literary Agency; Ciske & Dietz Literary Agency; Coover Agency, The Doe; de la Haba Agency Inc., The Lois; DH Literary, Inc.; Diamant Literary Agency, The Writer's Workshop, Inc., Anita; Dystel Literary Management, Jane; Ellenberg Literary Agency, Ethan; Ellison Inc., Nicholas; Emerald Literary Agency; Feiler Literary Agency, Florence; ‡Fleming Associates, Arthur; Franklin Associates, Ltd., Lynn C.; ‡Fullerton Associates, Sheryl B.; Gibson Agency, The Sebastian; Greene, Literary Agent, Randall Elisha; ‡Grosvenor Literary Agency, Deborah; Heacock Literary Agency, Inc.; Henderson Literary Representation; Herner Rights Agency, Susan; Jordan Literary Agency, Lawrence; Kellock Company, Inc., The; Larsen/Elizabeth Pomada Literary Agents, Michael; Levine Communications, Inc., James; ‡Lichtman, Trister, Singer & Ross; Literary Group, The; Lowenstein Associates, Inc.; Lukeman Literary Management Ltd.; McBride Literary Agency, Margret; Marcil Literary Agency, Inc., The Denise; Multimedia Product Development, Inc.; Naggar Literary Agency, Jean V.; New Brand Agency Group; Nine Muses and Apollo Inc.; Palmer & Dodge Agency, The; Pevner, Inc., Stephen; Quicksilver Books-Literary Agents; Rose Agency, Inc.; Rowland Agency, The Damaris; Russell-Simenauer Literary Agency Inc.; Schulman, A Literary Agency, Susan; Seymour Agency, The; Shepard Agency, The; Singer Literary Agency Inc., Evelyn; Stepping Stone; Toad Hall, Inc.; Travis Literary Agency, Susan; Watt & Associates, Sandra; Wreschner, Authors' Representative, Ruth

Science/technology: Agents Inc. for Medical and Mental Health Professionals; Author's Agency, The; Axelrod Agency, The; Baldi Literary Agency, Malaga; Balkin Agency, Inc.; Becker Literary Agency, The Wendy; ‡Bedford Book Works, Inc., The; Bernstein, Pam; ‡Bial Agency, Daniel; Boates Literary Agency, Reid; ‡Book Deals, Inc.; Bova Literary Agency, The Barbara; Brandt & Brandt Literary Agents Inc.; Brown Literary Agency, Inc., Andrea; Browne Ltd., Pema; Cantrell-Colas Inc., Literary Agency; Carvainis Agency, Inc., Maria; Castiglia Literary Agency; Coover Agency, The Doe; Curtis Associates, Inc., Richard; Cypher, Author's Representative, James R.; Darhansoff & Verrill Literary Agents; DH Literary, Inc.; Diamant Literary Agency, The Writer's Workshop, Inc., Anita; Dijkstra Literary Agency, Sandra; Ducas, Robert; Dystel Literary Management, Jane; Educational Design Services, Inc.; Elek Associates, Peter; Ellenberg Literary Agency, Ethan; Elliott Agency; Ellison Inc., Nicholas; Eth Literary Representation, Felicia; Flaming Star Literary Enterprises; Fleury Agency, B.R.; Gartenberg, Literary Agent,

Max; Gibson Agency, The Sebastian; Goddard Book Group; Graham Literary Agency, Inc.; ‡Grosvenor Literary Agency, Deborah; Hawkins & Associates, Inc., John; Heacock Literary Agency, Inc.; Henderson Literary Representation; Henshaw Group, Richard; Herner Rights Agency, Susan; Jabberwocky Literary Agency; Jordan Literary Agency, Lawrence; Kellock Company, Inc., The; Kern Literary Agency, Natasha; Ketz Agency, Louise B.; Klinger, Inc., Harvey; Larsen/Elizabeth Pomada Literary Agents, Michael; Lasher Agency, The Maureen; Levant & Wales, Literary Agency, Inc.; Levine Communications, Inc., James; Levine Literary Agency, Inc., Ellen; ‡Lichtman, Trister, Singer & Ross; Lieberman Associates, Robert; Lincoln Literary Agency, Ray; Lindstrom Literary Group; Lipkind Agency, Wendy; Literary Group, The; Love Literary Agency, Nancy; Lowenstein Associates, Inc.; McBride Literary Agency, Margret; Mainhardt Agency, Ricia; Multimedia Product Development, Inc.; Mura Enterprises, Inc., Dee; ‡National Writers Literary Agency; Nazor Literary Agency, Karen; New England Publishing Associates, Inc.; Nine Muses and Apollo Inc.; Palmer & Dodge Agency, The; Parks Agency, The Richard; Perkins Associates; Pevner, Inc., Stephen; Potomac Literary Agency, The; Protter Literary Agent, Susan Ann; Quicksilver Books-Literary Agents; ‡Russell & Volkening; Schmidt Literary Agency, Harold; Seligman, Literary Agent, Lynn; Singer Literary Agency Inc., Evelyn; Snell Literary Agency, Michael; Stern Literary Agency (TX), Gloria; Wallace Literary Agency, Inc.; Ware Literary Agency, John A.; Watkins Loomis Agency, Inc.; Weingel-Fidel Agency, The; Witherspoon & Associates, Inc.; Wreschner, Authors' Representative, Ruth; Writers House; ‡Young Agency Inc., The Gay; Zeckendorf Assoc. Inc., Susan

Self-help/personal improvement: Agents Inc. for Medical and Mental Health Professionals; Appleseeds Management; Author's Agency, The; ‡Authors Alliance, Inc.; Authors' Literary Agency; Baldi Literary Agency, Malaga; Behar Literary Agency, Josh; Bernstein, Pam; ‡Bial Agency, Daniel; Boates Literary Agency, Reid; Bova Literary Agency, The Barbara; Brandt & Brandt Literary Agents Inc.; ‡Brock Gannon Literary Agency; Brown Associates Inc., Marie; Browne Ltd., Pema; Buck Agency, Howard; Bykofsky Associates, Inc., Sheree; Cantrell-Colas Inc., Literary Agency; Castiglia Literary Agency; Charlton Associates, James; Ciske & Dietz Literary Agency; Columbia Literary Associates, Inc.; Connor Literary Agency; Curtis Associates, Inc., Richard; Cypher, Author's Representative, James R.; de la Haba Agency Inc., The Lois; DH Literary, Inc.; Diamant Literary Agency, The Writer's Workshop, Inc., Anita; Diamond Literary Agency, Inc. (CO); Dijkstra Literary Agency, Sandra; Ellenberg Literary Agency, Ethan; Elmo Agency Inc., Ann; Emerald Literary Agency; ‡Feigen Literary Agency, Brenda; Feiler Literary Agency, Florence; Flaherty, Literary Agent, Joyce A.; Flaming Star Literary Enterprises; ‡Fleming Associates, Arthur; Fleury Agency, B.R.; Franklin Associates, Ltd., Lynn C.; ‡Fullerton Associates, Sheryl B.; Garon-Brooke Assoc. Inc., Jay; Gartenberg, Literary Agent, Max; Gibson Agency, The Sebastian; Goddard Book Group; ‡Goodman-Andrew-Agency, Inc.; ‡Grosvenor Literary Agency, Deborah; Hawkins & Associates, Inc., John; Heacock Literary Agency, Inc.; Henderson Literary Representation; Henshaw Group, Richard; Herman Agency, Inc., The Jeff; Herner Rights Agency, Susan; J de S Associates Inc.; James Peter Associates, Inc.; ‡Janus Literary Agency; Jordan Literary Agency, Lawrence; Kellock Company, Inc., The; Kern Literary Agency, Natasha; Kidde, Hoyt & Picard; Klinger, Inc., Harvey; Kouts, Literary Agent, Barbara S.; Larsen/Elizabeth Pomada Literary Agents, Michael; Lasher Agency, The Maureen; Levant & Wales, Literary Agency, Inc.; Levine Communications, Inc., James; Lewis & Company, Karen; ‡Lichtman, Trister, Singer & Ross; Lincoln Literary Agency, Ray; Literary and Creative Artists Agency Inc.; Literary Group, The; Love Literary Agency, Nancy; Lowenstein Associates, Inc.; ‡Lukeman Literary Management Ltd.; McBride Literary Agency, Margret; McGrath, Helen; Mainhardt Agency, Ricia; Mann Agency, Carol; Manus & Associates Literary Agency, Inc.; Marcil Literary Agency, Inc., The Denise; Michaels Literary Agency, Inc., Doris S.; Miller Agency, The; Multimedia Product Development, Inc.; Mura Enterprises, Inc., Dee; Naggar Literary Agency, Jean V.; New England Publishing Associates, Inc.; Norma-Lewis Agency, The; Palmer & Dodge Agency, The; Parks Agency, The Richard; Pine Associates, Inc, Arthur; Pocono Literary Agency, Inc.; Potomac Literary Agency, The; Publishing Services; Quicksilver Books-Literary Agents; Rinaldi Literary Agency, Angela; Robbins Literary Agency, BJ; Rose Agency, Inc.; Russell-Simenauer Literary Agency Inc.; ‡Schlessinger Agency, Blanche; Schmidt Literary Agency, Harold; Schulman, A Literary Agency, Susan; Sebastian Literary Agency; Seligman, Literary Agent, Lynn; Shepard Agency, The; Singer Literary Agency Inc., Evelyn; Stauffer Associates, Nancy; Stepping Stone; Stern Literary Agency (TX), Gloria; Targ Literary Agency, Inc., Roslyn; Teal Literary Agency, Patricia; Toad Hall, Inc.; Travis Literary Agency, Susan; 2M Communications Ltd.; Urstadt Inc. Agency, Susan P.; Watt & Associates, Sandra; Weiner Literary Agency, Cherry; Witherspoon & Associates, Inc.; Wreschner, Authors' Representative, Ruth; Writers House; ‡Zitwer Agency, Barbara J.

Sociology: Agents Inc. for Medical and Mental Health Professionals; Allen Literary Agency, Linda; Author's Agency, The; Baldi Literary Agency, Malaga; Balkin Agency, Inc.; Becker Literary Agency, The Wendy; Bernstein, Pam; ‡Bial Agency, Daniel; Brandt & Brandt Literary Agents Inc.; Brown Associates Inc., Marie; Brown Literary Agency, Inc., Andrea; Buck Agency, Howard; Cantrell-Colas Inc., Literary Agency; Castiglia Literary Agency; Coover Agency, The Doe; Cypher, Author's Representative, James R.; DH Literary, Inc.; Dijkstra Literary Agency, Sandra; Educational Design Services, Inc.; Ellison Inc., Nicholas; Eth Literary Representation, Felicia; Flaherty, Literary Agent, Joyce A.; Fleming Associates, Arthur; Fleury Agency, B.R.; ‡Frustrated Writer's Ltd., The; ‡Fullerton Associates, Sheryl B.; Gibson Agency, The Sebastian; Goddard Book Group; ‡Goodman-Andrew-Agency, Inc.; Gordon Agency, Charlotte; ‡Grosvenor Literary Agency, Deborah; Hawkins & Associates, Inc., John; Heacock Literary Agency, Inc.; Henderson Literary Representation; Henshaw Group, Richard; Herner Rights Agency, Susan; Hochmann Books, John L.; Hull House Literary Agency; J de S Associates Inc.; Jabberwocky Literary Agency; Kellock Company, Inc., The; Kidde, Hoyt & Picard; Larsen/Elizabeth Pomada Literary Agents, Michael; Lasher Agency, The Maureen; ‡Leap First; Levine Communications, Inc., James; ‡Lichtman, Trister, Singer & Ross; Lieberman Associates, Robert; Lincoln Literary Agency, Ray; Lipkind Agency, Wendy; Literary Group, The; Love Literary Agency, Nancy; Lowenstein Associates, Inc.; McBride Literary Agency, Margret; Mainhardt Agency, Ricia; Mann Agency, Carol; Multimedia Product Development, Inc.; Mura Enterprises, Inc., Dee; Naggar Literary Agency, Jean V.; Nazor Literary Agency, Karen; New England Publishing Associates, Inc.; Palmer & Dodge Agency, The;

Parks Agency, The Richard; Paton Literary Agency, Kathi J.; Pevner, Inc., Stephen; Pryor, Inc., Roberta; Quicksilver Books-Literary Agents; Rinaldi Literary Agency, Angela; Robbins Literary Agency, BJ; ‡Russell & Volkening; Schmidt Literary Agency, Harold; Schulman, A Literary Agency, Susan; Sebastian Literary Agency; Seligman, Literary Agent, Lynn; Shepard Agency, The; ‡Slopen Literary Agency, Beverley; Spieler, F. Joseph; Spitzer Literary Agency, Philip G.; Stauffer Associates, Nancy; Stern Literary Agency (TX), Gloria; Valcourt Agency, Inc., The Richard R.; Wald Associates, Inc., Mary Jack; Waterside Productions, Inc.; Weiner Literary Agency, Cherry; Weingel-Fidel Agency, The; Zeckendorf Assoc. Inc., Susan

Sports: Agency Chicago; Agents Inc. for Medical and Mental Health Professionals; Author's Agency, The; ‡Authors Alliance, Inc.; Becker Literary Agency, The Wendy; ‡Bedford Book Works, Inc., The; ‡Bial Agency, Daniel; Black Literary Agency, Inc., David; Boates Literary Agency, Reid; ‡Book Deals, Inc.; Brandt & Brandt Literary Agents Inc.; ‡Brock Gannon Literary Agency; Brown Literary Agency, Inc., Andrea; Browne Ltd., Pema; Buck Agency, Howard; Circle of Confusion Ltd.; Connor Literary Agency; Curtis Associates, Inc., Richard; Cypher, Author's Representative, James R.; DH Literary, Inc.; DHS Literary, Inc.; Diamant Literary Agency, The Writer's Workshop, Inc., Anita; Dijkstra Literary Agency, Sandra; Ducas, Robert; Flaming Star Literary Enterprises; ‡Fleming Associates, Arthur; Fleury Agency, B.R.; ‡Frustrated Writer's Ltd., The; Gartenberg, Literary Agent, Max; Gibson Agency, The Sebastian; ‡Goodman-Andrew-Agency, Inc.; Greene, Arthur B.; ‡Grosvenor Literary Agency, Deborah; Hawkins & Associates, Inc., John; Henderson Literary Representation; Henshaw Group, Richard; IMG Literary; J de S Associates Inc.; Jabberwocky Literary Agency; ‡Janus Literary Agency; Jordan Literary Agency, Lawrence; Kellock Company, Inc., The; Ketz Agency, Louise B.; Klinger, Inc., Harvey; Larsen/Elizabeth Pomada Literary Agents, Michael; Lasher Agency, The Maureen; ‡Leap First; Levant & Wales, Literary Agency, Inc.; Levine Communications, Inc., James; ‡Lichtman, Trister, Singer & Ross; Lincoln Literary Agency, Ray; Literary Group, The; Lowenstein Associates, Inc.; McBride Literary Agency, Margret; McGrath, Helen; Mainhardt Agency, Ricia; Markowitz Literary Agency, Barbara; Michaels Literary Agency, Inc., Doris S.; Miller Agency, The; Multimedia Product Development, Inc.; Mura Enterprises, Inc., Dee; ‡National Writers Literary Agency; Nazor Literary Agency, Karen; New Brand Agency Group; Pocono Literary Agency, Inc.; Pom Inc.; Potomac Literary Agency, The; Quicksilver Books-Literary Agents; Robbins Literary Agency, BJ; ‡Russell & Volkening; Shepard Agency, The; Spitzer Literary Agency, Philip G.; Stern Literary Agency (TX), Gloria; Urstadt Inc. Agency, Susan P.; Ware Literary Agency, John A.; Waterside Productions, Inc.; Watt & Associates, Sandra

Translations: Author's Agency, The; Balkin Agency, Inc.; ‡Book Deals, Inc.; Buck Agency, Howard; Crown International Literature and Arts Agency, Bonnie R.; Daves Agency, Joan; Ellison Inc., Nicholas; Gibson Agency, The Sebastian; ‡Grosvenor Literary Agency, Deborah; J de S Associates Inc.; ‡Lukeman Literary Management Ltd.; Sanders Literary Agency, Victoria; Schmidt Literary Agency, Harold; Schulman, A Literary Agency, Susan; Seligman, Literary Agent, Lynn; Stauffer Associates, Nancy; ‡Sweeney Literary Agency, Emma; Wald Associates, Inc., Mary Jack; Watkins Loomis Agency, Inc.; Wieser & Wieser, Inc.

True crime/investigative: Adler & Robin Books Inc.; Agency Chicago; Allen Literary Agency, Linda; Appleseeds Management; Author's Agency, The; ‡Authors Alliance, Inc.; Authors' Literary Agency; Baldi Literary Agency, Malaga; Balkin Agency, Inc.; Bernstein, Pam; ‡Bial Agency, Daniel; Boates Literary Agency, Reid; Bova Literary Agency, The Barbara; Brandt & Brandt Literary Agents Inc.; ‡Brock Gannon Literary Agency; Browne Ltd., Pema; Buck Agency, Howard; Bykofsky Associates, Inc., Sheree; Cantrell-Colas Inc., Literary Agency; Carvainis Agency, Inc., Maria; Charisma Communications, Ltd.; Circle of Confusion Ltd.; Ciske & Dietz Literary Agency; Clausen Associates, Connie; Collin Literary Agent, Frances; Connor Literary Agency; Coover Agency, The Doe; Crawford Literary Agency; Curtis Associates, Inc., Richard; Cypher, Author's Representative, James R.; DH Literary, Inc.; DHS Literary, Inc.; Diamant Literary Agency, The Writer's Workshop, Inc., Anita; Dijkstra Literary Agency, Sandra; Ducas, Robert; Dystel Literary Management, Jane; Elek Associates, Peter; Ellenberg Literary Agency, Ethan; Elliott Agency; Ellison Inc., Nicholas; Elmo Agency Inc., Ann; Eth Literary Representation, Felicia; Feiler Literary Agency, Florence; Flaherty, Literary Agent, Joyce A.; Fleury Agency, B.R.; ‡Frustrated Writer's Ltd., The; Garon-Brooke Assoc. Inc., Jay; Gartenberg, Literary Agent, Max; Gibson Agency, The Sebastian; ‡Goodman-Andrew-Agency, Inc.; Graham Literary Agency, Inc.; Greene, Literary Agent, Randall Elisha; Hawkins & Associates, Inc., John; Henderson Literary Representation; Henshaw Group, Richard; Herner Rights Agency, Susan; Hull House Literary Agency; IMG Literary; Jabberwocky Literary Agency; ‡Janus Literary Agency; ‡Just Write Agency, Inc.; Kern Literary Agency, Natasha; Klinger, Inc., Harvey; Lampack Agency, Inc., Peter; Larsen/Elizabeth Pomada Literary Agents, Michael; Lasher Agency, The Maureen; ‡Lichtman, Trister, Singer & Ross; Literary Group, The; Love Literary Agency, Nancy; Lowenstein Associates, Inc.; ‡Lukeman Literary Management Ltd.; McBride Literary Agency, Margret; Mainhardt Agency, Ricia; Mann Agency, Carol; Manus & Associates Literary Agency, Inc.; Metropolitan Talent Agency; Multimedia Product Development, Inc.; Mura Enterprises, Inc., Dee; Nathan, Ruth; New England Publishing Associates, Inc.; Norma-Lewis Agency, The; Nugent Literary; Otitis Media; Potomac Literary Agency, The; Pryor, Inc., Roberta; Quicksilver Books-Literary Agents; Renaissance—H.N. Swanson; Rinaldi Literary Agency, Angela; Robbins Literary Agency, BJ; ‡Russell & Volkening; Russell-Simenauer Literary Agency Inc.; ‡Schlessinger Agency, Blanche; Schmidt Literary Agency, Harold; Schulman, A Literary Agency, Susan; Seligman, Literary Agent, Lynn; ‡Slopen Literary Agency, Beverley; Spitzer Literary Agency, Philip G.; Stern Literary Agency (TX), Gloria; Teal Literary Agency, Patricia; Van Duren Agency, Annette; Vines Agency, Inc., The; Wald Associates, Inc., Mary Jack; Wallace Literary Agency, Inc.; Ware Literary Agency, John A.; Waterside Productions, Inc.; Watkins Loomis Agency, Inc.; Watt & Associates, Sandra; Weingel-Fidel Agency, The; West Coast Literary Associates; Wieser & Wieser, Inc.; Witherspoon & Associates, Inc.; Wreschner, Authors' Representative, Ruth; Writers House; Zeckendorf Assoc. Inc., Susan; ‡Zitwer Agency, Barbara J.

Women's issues/women's studies: ‡Fullerton Associates, Sheryl B.; James Peter Associates, Inc.; Adler

& Robin Books Inc.; Allen Literary Agency, Linda; Author's Agency, The; Authors' Literary Agency; Baldi Literary Agency, Malaga; Becker Literary Agency, The Wendy; ‡Bedford Book Works, Inc., The; Behar Literary Agency, Josh; Bernstein, Pam; ‡Bial Agency, Daniel; Boates Literary Agency, Reid; Borchardt Inc., Georges; Bova Literary Agency, The Barbara; Brandt & Brandt Literary Agents Inc.; ‡Brock Gannon Literary Agency; Brown Associates Inc., Marie; Browne Ltd., Pema; Buck Agency, Howard; Bykofsky Associates, Inc., Sheree; Cantrell-Colas Inc., Literary Agency; Carvainis Agency, Inc., Maria; Casselman Literary Agent, Martha; Castiglia Literary Agency; Circle of Confusion Ltd.; Ciske & Dietz Literary Agency; Clausen Associates, Connie; ‡Cohen Agency, The; Cohen, Inc. Literary Agency, Ruth; Connor Literary Agency; Coover Agency, The Doe; Crawford Literary Agency; Crown International Literature and Arts Agency, Bonnie R.; Cypher, Author's Representative, James R.; Daves Agency, Joan; de la Haba Agency Inc., The Lois; DH Literary, Inc.; Diamant Literary Agency, The Writer's Workshop, Inc., Anita; Dijkstra Literary Agency, Sandra; Dystel Literary Management, Jane; Educational Design Services, Inc.; Ellison Inc., Nicholas; Elmo Agency Inc., Ann; Emerald Literary Agency; Eth Literary Representation, Felicia; ‡Feigen Literary Agency, Brenda; Feiler Literary Agency, Florence; Flaherty, Literary Agent, Joyce A.; ‡Fleming Associates, Arthur; Gartenberg, Literary Agent, Max; Gibson Agency, The Sebastian; Goddard Book Group; ‡Goodman-Andrew-Agency, Inc.; Gordon Agency, Charlotte; Hawkins & Associates, Inc., John; Heacock Literary Agency, Inc.; Henderson Literary Representation; Henshaw Group, Richard; Herner Rights Agency, Susan; Hill Associates, Frederick; IMG Literary; Jabberwocky Literary Agency; Kellock Company, Inc., The; Kern Literary Agency, Natasha; Kidde, Hoyt & Picard; Klinger, Inc., Harvey; Kouts, Literary Agent, Barbara S.; Kroll Literary Agency, Edite; Lampack Agency, Inc., Peter; Larsen/Elizabeth Pomada Literary Agents, Michael; Lasher Agency, The Maureen; ‡Leap First; Levant & Wales, Literary Agency, Inc.; Levine Communications, Inc., James; Levine Literary Agency, Inc., Ellen; Lewis & Company, Karen; Lincoln Literary Agency, Ray; Lipkind Agency, Wendy; Literary Group, The; Love Literary Agency, Nancy; Lowenstein Associates, Inc.; ‡Lukeman Literary Management Ltd.; McBride Literary Agency, Margret; Maccoby Literary Agency, Gina; McGrath, Helen; Mainhardt Agency, Ricia; Mann Agency, Carol; Manus & Associates Literary Agency, Inc.; Marcil Literary Agency, Inc., The Denise; Markowitz Literary Agency, Barbara; Michaels Literary Agency, Inc., Doris S.; Miller Agency, The; Multimedia Product Development, Inc.; Mura Enterprises, Inc., Dee; Naggar Literary Agency, Jean V.; Nazor Literary Agency, Karen; New England Publishing Associates, Inc.; Nine Muses and Apollo Inc.; Norma-Lewis Agency, The; Palmer & Dodge Agency, The; Parks Agency, The Richard; Paton Literary Agency, Kathi J.; Pocono Literary Agency, Inc.; Pom Inc.; Popkin, Julie; Pryor, Inc., Roberta; Publishing Services; Quicksilver Books-Literary Agents; Rees Literary Agency, Helen; Rinaldi Literary Agency, Angela; ‡Rittenberg Literary Agency, Inc., Ann; Robbins Literary Agency, BJ; Rowland Agency, The Damaris; ‡Russell & Volkening; Russell-Simenauer Literary Agency Inc.; Sanders Literary Agency, Victoria; Schmidt Literary Agency, Harold; Schulman, A Literary Agency, Susan; Sebastian Literary Agency; Seligman, Literary Agent, Lynn; Shepard Agency, The; Singer Literary Agency Inc., Evelyn; ‡Slopen Literary Agency, Beverley; Snell Literary Agency, Michael; Spieler, F. Joseph; Stepping Stone; Stern Literary Agency (TX), Gloria; ‡Sweeney Literary Agency, Emma; Teal Literary Agency, Patricia; Travis Literary Agency, Susan; 2M Communications Ltd.; Urstadt Inc. Agency, Susan P.; Vines Agency, Inc., The; Ware Literary Agency, John A.; Waterside Productions, Inc.; Watkins Loomis Agency, Inc.; Watt & Associates, Sandra; Weingel-Fidel Agency, The; West Coast Literary Associates; Witherspoon & Associates, Inc.; Wreschner, Authors' Representative, Ruth; Writers House; ‡Young Agency Inc., The Gay; Zeckendorf Assoc. Inc., Susan

FEE-CHARGING LITERARY AGENTS/FICTION

Action/adventure: A.A. Fair Literary Agency; Acacia House Publishing Services Ltd.; AEI/Atchity Editorial/Entertainment International; Ahearn Agency, Inc., The; ‡Anthony Agency, Joseph; Author Aid Associates; Author Author Literary Agency Ltd.; Authors' Marketing Services Ltd.; Author's Services Literary Ageny; Brinke Literary Agency, The; Brown, Literary Agent, Antoinette; Cambridge Literary Associates; Catalog™ Literary Agency, The; Chadd-Stevens Literary Agency; Collier Associates; Fishbein Ltd., Frieda; ‡Fort Ross Inc. Russian-American Publishing Projects; ForthWrite Literary Agency; Fran Literary Agency; GEM Literary Services; Gladden Unlimited; Hamilton's Literary Agency, Andrew; Hilton Literary Agency, Alice; Hubbs Agency, Yvonne Trudeau; Independent Publishing Agency; Jett Literary Agency, The; Kellock & Associates Ltd., J.; Kirkland Literary Agency, The; Law Offices of Robert L. Fenton PC; Lee Literary Agency, L. Harry; Literary Group West; McKinley, Literary Agency, Virginia C.; Marshall Agency, The Evan; Montgomery Literary Agency; Nelson Literary Agency & Lecture Bureau, BK; ‡Nordhaus-Wolcott Literary Agency; Northwest Literary Services; Pell Agency, William; Penmarin Books; PMA Literary and Film Management, Inc.; Portman Organization, The; Puddingstone Literary Agency; QCorp Literary Agency; Remington Literary Assoc., Inc.; Rhodes Literary Agency; Southern Literary Agency; Steinberg Literary Agency, Michael; Stern Agency, Gloria (CA); Strong Literary Agency, Marianne; Wallerstein Agency, The Gerry B.; Writer's Consulting Group

Animation: Fran Literary Agency

Cartoon/comic: Authors' Marketing Services Ltd.; Chadd-Stevens Literary Agency; ‡Fort Ross Inc. Russian-American Publishing Projects; Fran Literary Agency; Howard Agency, The Eddy; Independent Publishing Agency; Jett Literary Agency, The; Montgomery Literary Agency; Nelson Literary Agency & Lecture Bureau, BK; Remington Literary Assoc., Inc.

Comedy: Nelson Literary Agency & Lecture Bureau, BK

Confessional: ‡Anthony Agency, Joseph; Author Aid Associates; Chadd-Stevens Literary Agency; Hamilton's Literary Agency, Andrew; Hilton Literary Agency, Alice; Independent Publishing Agency; Jett Literary Agency,

The; M.H. International Literary Agency; Northwest Literary Services; QCorp Literary Agency; Rhodes Literary Agency; Visions Press

Contemporary issues: AEI/Atchity Editorial/Entertainment International; Ahearn Agency, Inc., The; Author Aid Associates; Author Author Literary Agency Ltd.; Author's Services Literary Ageny; Cambridge Literary Associates; Connor Literary Agency; Fishbein Ltd., Frieda; Fran Literary Agency; Hamilton's Literary Agency, Andrew; Hilton Literary Agency, Alice; Hubbs Agency, Yvonne Trudeau; Independent Publishing Agency; Jenks Agency, Carolyn; Jett Literary Agency, The; Kellock & Associates Ltd., J.; Kirkland Literary Agency, The; Law Offices of Robert L. Fenton PC; Lopopolo Literary Agency, Toni; McKinley, Literary Agency, Virginia C.; Marshall Agency, The Evan; Montgomery Literary Agency; Nelson Literary Agency & Lecture Bureau, BK; Northwest Literary Services; Penmarin Books; PMA Literary and Film Management, Inc.; QCorp Literary Agency; Remington Literary Assoc., Inc.; Rhodes Literary Agency; ‡Stadler Literary Agency; Steinberg Literary Agency, Michael; Stern Agency, Gloria (CA); Strong Literary Agency, Marianne; Tornetta Agency, Phyllis; Visions Press; Wallerstein Agency, The Gerry B.; Writer's Consulting Group

Detective/police/crime: A.A. Fair Literary Agency; Acacia House Publishing Services Ltd.; Ahearn Agency, Inc., The; Allegra Literary Agency; ‡Anthony Agency, Joseph; Author Aid Associates; Author Author Literary Agency Ltd.; Authors' Marketing Services Ltd.; Author's Services Literary Ageny; Cambridge Literary Associates; Chadd-Stevens Literary Agency; Clark Literary Agency, SJ; Collier Associates; Connor Literary Agency; Fishbein Ltd., Frieda; ‡Fort Ross Inc. Russian-American Publishing Projects; Fran Literary Agency; GEM Literary Services; Gladden Unlimited; Hamilton's Literary Agency, Andrew; Hilton Literary Agency, Alice; Independent Publishing Agency; Jett Literary Agency, The; Kellock & Associates Ltd., J.; Kirkland Literary Agency, The; Law Offices of Robert L. Fenton PC; Lee Literary Agency, L. Harry; Literary Group West; Lopopolo Literary Agency, Toni; M.H. International Literary Agency; McKinley, Literary Agency, Virginia C.; Marshall Agency, The Evan; Montgomery Literary Agency; Nelson Literary Agency & Lecture Bureau, BK; ‡Nordhaus-Wolcott Literary Agency; Northwest Literary Services; Pell Agency, William; Penmarin Books; PMA Literary and Film Management, Inc.; Portman Organization, The; Puddingstone Literary Agency; QCorp Literary Agency; Remington Literary Assoc., Inc.; Rhodes Literary Agency; SLC Enterprises; Southern Literary Agency; ‡Stadler Literary Agency; Steinberg Literary Agency, Michael; Stern Agency, Gloria (CA); Strong Literary Agency, Marianne; Taylor Literary Agency, Dawson; Toomey Associates, Jeanne; Wallerstein Agency, The Gerry B.; Writer's Consulting Group

Documentary: Independent Publishing Agency; ‡Nordhaus-Wolcott Literary Agency

Episodic drama: Hilton Literary Agency, Alice; Independent Publishing Agency; Law Offices of Robert L. Fenton PC

Erotica: AEI/Atchity Editorial/Entertainment International; ‡Anthony Agency, Joseph; Author Aid Associates; Author Author Literary Agency Ltd.; Cambridge Literary Associates; Chadd-Stevens Literary Agency; ‡Fort Ross Inc. Russian-American Publishing Projects; Hamilton's Literary Agency, Andrew; Hilton Literary Agency, Alice; Howard Agency, The Eddy; Independent Publishing Agency; Lee Literary Agency, L. Harry; Lopopolo Literary Agency, Toni; Marshall Agency, The Evan; ‡Nordhaus-Wolcott Literary Agency; Northwest Literary Services; QCorp Literary Agency; Remington Literary Assoc., Inc.; Rhodes Literary Agency; Steinberg Literary Agency, Michael; Stern Agency, Gloria (CA); Visions Press

Ethnic: A.A. Fair Literary Agency; Ahearn Agency, Inc., The; Author Aid Associates; Chadd-Stevens Literary Agency; Connor Literary Agency; Fran Literary Agency; Gladden Unlimited; Hilton Literary Agency, Alice; Independent Publishing Agency; Kellock & Associates Ltd., J.; Kirkland Literary Agency, The; Law Offices of Robert L. Fenton PC; Lopopolo Literary Agency, Toni; McKinley, Literary Agency, Virginia C.; Marshall Agency, The Evan; Montgomery Literary Agency; Northwest Literary Services; Penmarin Books; QCorp Literary Agency; Remington Literary Assoc., Inc.; Rhodes Literary Agency; Visions Press

Experimental: Author Aid Associates; Author Author Literary Agency Ltd.; ‡CDK Technical Communications, Inc.; Chadd-Stevens Literary Agency; Connor Literary Agency; Howard Agency, The Eddy; Independent Publishing Agency; Kellock & Associates Ltd., J.; Montgomery Literary Agency; ‡Nordhaus-Wolcott Literary Agency; Northwest Literary Services; Penmarin Books; QCorp Literary Agency; Rhodes Literary Agency

Family saga: A.A. Fair Literary Agency; Ahearn Agency, Inc., The; Author Aid Associates; Author Author Literary Agency Ltd.; Authors' Marketing Services Ltd.; Cambridge Literary Associates; Catalog™ Literary Agency, The; Chadd-Stevens Literary Agency; Connor Literary Agency; Fishbein Ltd., Frieda; ForthWrite Literary Agency; GEM Literary Services; Hamilton's Literary Agency, Andrew; Hubbs Agency, Yvonne Trudeau; Jenks Agency, Carolyn; Jett Literary Agency, The; Kellock & Associates Ltd., J.; Kirkland Literary Agency, The; Lee Literary Agency, L. Harry; Lopopolo Literary Agency, Toni; McKinley, Literary Agency, Virginia C.; Marshall Agency, The Evan; Montgomery Literary Agency; Nelson Literary Agency & Lecture Bureau, BK; Northwest Literary Services; Portman Organization, The; QCorp Literary Agency; Remington Literary Assoc., Inc.; Rhodes Literary Agency; ‡Stadler Literary Agency; Strong Literary Agency, Marianne; Wallerstein Agency, The Gerry B.; Writer's Consulting Group

Fantasy: A.A. Fair Literary Agency; Ahearn Agency, Inc., The; ‡Anthony Agency, Joseph; Author Aid Associates; Author Author Literary Agency Ltd.; Authors' Marketing Services Ltd.; Author's Services Literary Ageny; Brinke Literary Agency, The; Cambridge Literary Associates; Chadd-Stevens Literary Agency; Collier Associates; Fishbein Ltd., Frieda; ‡Fort Ross Inc. Russian-American Publishing Projects; Fran Literary Agency; GEM Literary Services; Gislason Agency, The; Hilton Literary Agency, Alice; Howard Agency, The Eddy; Hubbs Agency, Yvonne

Trudeau; Independent Publishing Agency; Jett Literary Agency, The; Kellock & Associates Ltd., J.; Kirkland Literary Agency, The; Lee Literary Agency, L. Harry; McKinley, Literary Agency, Virginia C.; Montgomery Literary Agency; Nelson Literary Agency & Lecture Bureau, BK; ‡Nordhaus-Wolcott Literary Agency; Northwest Literary Services; QCorp Literary Agency; Remington Literary Assoc., Inc.; Rhodes Literary Agency; Stern Agency, Gloria (CA)

Feature film: Hamilton's Literary Agency, Andrew; Independent Publishing Agency; Law Offices of Robert L. Fenton PC; McKinley, Literary Agency, Virginia C.; McLean Literary Agency; Portman Organization, The; Raintree Agency, Diane; ‡Sullivan Associates, Mark

Feminist: Ahearn Agency, Inc., The; Author Author Literary Agency Ltd.; Author's Services Literary Ageny; Fishbein Ltd., Frieda; GEM Literary Services; Gislason Agency, The; Hubbs Agency, Yvonne Trudeau; Independent Publishing Agency; Jenks Agency, Carolyn; Jett Literary Agency, The; Kellock & Associates Ltd., J.; Lopopolo Literary Agency, Toni; McKinley, Literary Agency, Virginia C.; Nelson Literary Agency & Lecture Bureau, BK; Northwest Literary Services; QCorp Literary Agency; Rhodes Literary Agency; SLC Enterprises; ‡Stadler Literary Agency; Stern Agency, Gloria (CA); Writer's Consulting Group

Gay: Ahearn Agency, Inc., The; Author Author Literary Agency Ltd.; Author's Services Literary Ageny; Chadd-Stevens Literary Agency; QCorp Literary Agency; Rhodes Literary Agency; Visions Press

Glitz: A.A. Fair Literary Agency; Ahearn Agency, Inc., The; Author Aid Associates; Chadd-Stevens Literary Agency; Connor Literary Agency; Gladden Unlimited; Hubbs Agency, Yvonne Trudeau; Jett Literary Agency, The; JLM Literary Agents; Kellock & Associates Ltd., J.; Kirkland Literary Agency, The; Law Offices of Robert L. Fenton PC; Lopopolo Literary Agency, Toni; Marshall Agency, The Evan; Montgomery Literary Agency; Nelson Literary Agency & Lecture Bureau, BK; QCorp Literary Agency; Remington Literary Assoc., Inc.; Rhodes Literary Agency; Stern Agency, Gloria (CA); Strong Literary Agency, Marianne; Wallerstein Agency, The Gerry B.

Historical: A.A. Fair Literary Agency; Acacia House Publishing Services Ltd.; AEI/Atchity Editorial/Entertainment International; Ahearn Agency, Inc., The; Author Aid Associates; Author Author Literary Agency Ltd.; Authors' Marketing Services Ltd.; Author's Services Literary Ageny; Brown, Literary Agent, Antoinette; Cambridge Literary Associates; Chadd-Stevens Literary Agency; Fishbein Ltd., Frieda; Fran Literary Agency; GEM Literary Services; Hilton Literary Agency, Alice; Hubbs Agency, Yvonne Trudeau; Independent Publishing Agency; Jenks Agency, Carolyn; Jett Literary Agency, The; Kellock & Associates Ltd., J.; Kirkland Literary Agency, The; Law Offices of Robert L. Fenton PC; Lee Literary Agency, L. Harry; Literary Group West; Lopopolo Literary Agency, Toni; M.H. International Literary Agency; Marshall Agency, The Evan; Montgomery Literary Agency; Nelson Literary Agency & Lecture Bureau, BK; ‡Nordhaus-Wolcott Literary Agency; Northwest Literary Services; Penmarin Books; Portman Organization, The; QCorp Literary Agency; Remington Literary Assoc., Inc.; Rhodes Literary Agency; SLC Enterprises; Strong Literary Agency, Marianne; Wallerstein Agency, The Gerry B.

Horror: AEI/Atchity Editorial/Entertainment International; Ahearn Agency, Inc., The; Author Aid Associates; Author Author Literary Agency Ltd.; Authors' Marketing Services Ltd.; Author's Services Literary Ageny; Cambridge Literary Associates; Catalog™ Literary Agency, The; Chadd-Stevens Literary Agency; Connor Literary Agency; ‡Fort Ross Inc. Russian-American Publishing Projects; Fran Literary Agency; GEM Literary Services; Gladden Unlimited; Hilton Literary Agency, Alice; Jett Literary Agency, The; Kellock & Associates Ltd., J.; Kirkland Literary Agency, The; Lee Literary Agency, L. Harry; Marshall Agency, The Evan; Montgomery Literary Agency; Nelson Literary Agency & Lecture Bureau, BK; ‡Nordhaus-Wolcott Literary Agency; PMA Literary and Film Management, Inc.; Puddingstone Literary Agency; Remington Literary Assoc., Inc.; Rhodes Literary Agency; Stern Agency, Gloria (CA); Writer's Consulting Group

Humor/satire: A.A. Fair Literary Agency; Author Aid Associates; Author Author Literary Agency Ltd.; Author's Services Literary Ageny; GEM Literary Services; Independent Publishing Agency; Jett Literary Agency, The; Kirkland Literary Agency, The; Law Offices of Robert L. Fenton PC; Lee Literary Agency, L. Harry; McKinley, Literary Agency, Virginia C.; Marshall Agency, The Evan; Montgomery Literary Agency; Pell Agency, William; Remington Literary Assoc., Inc.; Rhodes Literary Agency; ‡Stadler Literary Agency

Juvenile: A.A. Fair Literary Agency; Ahearn Agency, Inc., The; Allegra Literary Agency; Author Aid Associates; Author Author Literary Agency Ltd.; Author's Services Literary Ageny; Cambridge Literary Associates; Catalog™ Literary Agency, The; Chadd-Stevens Literary Agency; Clark Literary Agency, SJ; ForthWrite Literary Agency; Fran Literary Agency; GEM Literary Services; Hamilton's Literary Agency, Andrew; Hilton Literary Agency, Alice; Howard Agency, The Eddy; Independent Publishing Agency; Jett Literary Agency, The; Kellock & Associates Ltd., J.; McKinley, Literary Agency, Virginia C.; Montgomery Literary Agency; Northwest Literary Services; QCorp Literary Agency; Remington Literary Assoc., Inc.; Rhodes Literary Agency; SLC Enterprises; ‡Stadler Literary Agency

Lesbian: Ahearn Agency, Inc., The; Author Aid Associates; Author's Services Literary Ageny; Chadd-Stevens Literary Agency; Hamilton's Literary Agency, Andrew; Jenks Agency, Carolyn; QCorp Literary Agency; Rhodes Literary Agency; Visions Press

Literary: A.A. Fair Literary Agency; Acacia House Publishing Services Ltd.; AEI/Atchity Editorial/Entertainment International; Ahearn Agency, Inc., The; Author Aid Associates; Authors' Marketing Services Ltd.; Cambridge Literary Associates; ‡CDK Technical Communications, Inc.; Chadd-Stevens Literary Agency; Connor Literary Agency; GEM Literary Services; Hilton Literary Agency, Alice; Howard Agency, The Eddy; Independent Publishing Agency; Jenks Agency, Carolyn; Jett Literary Agency, The; Kellock & Associates Ltd., J.; Kirkland Literary Agency, The; Lee Literary Agency, L. Harry; Lopopolo Literary Agency, Toni; McKinley, Literary Agency, Virginia C.;

Marshall Agency, The Evan; Montgomery Literary Agency; Nelson Literary Agency & Lecture Bureau, BK; ‡Nordhaus-Wolcott Literary Agency; Northwest Literary Services; Penmarin Books; PMA Literary and Film Management, Inc.; QCorp Literary Agency; Rhodes Literary Agency; SLC Enterprises; ‡Stadler Literary Agency; Stern Agency, Gloria (CA); Strong Literary Agency, Marianne; Wallerstein Agency, The Gerry B.

Mainstream: A.A. Fair Literary Agency; Acacia House Publishing Services Ltd.; AEI/Atchity Editorial/Entertainment International; Ahearn Agency, Inc., The; Allegra Literary Agency; Author Aid Associates; Authors' Marketing Services Ltd.; Author's Services Literary Ageny; Cambridge Literary Associates; Catalog® Literary Agency, The; ‡CDK Technical Communications, Inc.; Chadd-Stevens Literary Agency; Collier Associates; Fishbein Ltd., Frieda; Fran Literary Agency; GEM Literary Services; Gladden Unlimited; Hilton Literary Agency, Alice; Howard Agency, The Eddy; Hubbs Agency, Yvonne Trudeau; Independent Publishing Agency; Jett Literary Agency, The; Kirkland Literary Agency, The; Law Offices of Robert L. Fenton PC; Lee Literary Agency, L. Harry; Literary Group West; Lopopolo Literary Agency, Toni; Marshall Agency, The Evan; Montgomery Literary Agency; Nelson Literary Agency & Lecture Bureau, BK; ‡Nordhaus-Wolcott Literary Agency; Northwest Literary Services; Penmarin Books; PMA Literary and Film Management, Inc.; QCorp Literary Agency; Remington Literary Assoc., Inc.; Rhodes Literary Agency; Southern Literary Agency; ‡Stadler Literary Agency; Steinberg Literary Agency, Michael; Stern Agency, Gloria (CA); Strong Literary Agency, Marianne; Visions Press; Wallerstein Agency, The Gerry B.; Writer's Consulting Group

Movie of the week: Independent Publishing Agency; Law Offices of Robert L. Fenton PC; McLean Literary Agency; Portman Organization, The; Raintree Agency, Diane

Mystery/suspense: Acacia House Publishing Services Ltd.; AEI/Atchity Editorial/Entertainment International; Ahearn Agency, Inc., The; Allegra Literary Agency; ‡Anthony Agency, Joseph; Author Aid Associates; Author Author Literary Agency Ltd.; Authors' Marketing Services Ltd.; Author's Services Literary Ageny; Brinke Literary Agency, The; Brown, Literary Agent, Antoinette; Cambridge Literary Associates; Chadd-Stevens Literary Agency; Clark Literary Agency, SJ; Collier Associates; Connor Literary Agency; Fishbein Ltd., Frieda; ‡Fort Ross Inc. Russian-American Publishing Projects; Fran Literary Agency; GEM Literary Services; Gislason Agency, The; Hamilton's Literary Agency, Andrew; Hilton Literary Agency, Alice; Hubbs Agency, Yvonne Trudeau; Independent Publishing Agency; Jenks Agency, Carolyn; Jett Literary Agency, The; JLM Literary Agents; Kellock & Associates Ltd., J.; Kirkland Literary Agency, The; Law Offices of Robert L. Fenton PC; Lee Literary Agency, L. Harry; Lopopolo Literary Agency, Toni; M.H. International Literary Agency; McKinley, Literary Agency, Virginia C.; Marshall Agency, The Evan; Nelson Literary Agency & Lecture Bureau, BK; ‡Nordhaus-Wolcott Literary Agency; Northwest Literary Services; Penmarin Books; PMA Literary and Film Management, Inc.; Portman Organization, The; QCorp Literary Agency; Remington Literary Assoc., Inc.; Southern Literary Agency; ‡Stadler Literary Agency; Steinberg Literary Agency, Michael; Taylor Literary Agency, Dawson; Tornetta Agency, Phyllis; Wallerstein Agency, The Gerry B.; Writer's Consulting Group

Open to all fiction categories: Brinke Literary Agency, The; ‡CS International Literary Agency; ‡Klausner International Literary Agency, Bertha; McLean Literary Agency; Raintree Agency, Diane; Rogers Literary Representation, Irene; ‡Sullivan Associates, Mark; Total Acting Experience, A

Picture books: Alp Arts Co.; Author Aid Associates; Author Author Literary Agency Ltd.; Author's Services Literary Ageny; Chadd-Stevens Literary Agency; Clark Literary Agency, SJ; ForthWrite Literary Agency; Fran Literary Agency; GEM Literary Services; Hilton Literary Agency, Alice; Howard Agency, The Eddy; Independent Publishing Agency; Jett Literary Agency, The; Kellock & Associates Ltd., J.; Montgomery Literary Agency; Northwest Literary Services; QCorp Literary Agency; Remington Literary Assoc., Inc.; SLC Enterprises

Psychic/supernatural: Ahearn Agency, Inc., The; ‡Anthony Agency, Joseph; Author Aid Associates; Author Author Literary Agency Ltd.; Authors' Marketing Services Ltd.; Author's Services Literary Ageny; Brinke Literary Agency, The; Chadd-Stevens Literary Agency; Clark Literary Agency, SJ; GEM Literary Services; Hamilton's Literary Agency, Andrew; Hilton Literary Agency, Alice; Howard Agency, The Eddy; Hubbs Agency, Yvonne Trudeau; Independent Publishing Agency; JLM Literary Agents; Kirkland Literary Agency, The; Lopopolo Literary Agency, Toni; Marshall Agency, The Evan; Montgomery Literary Agency; Nelson Literary Agency & Lecture Bureau, BK; ‡Nordhaus-Wolcott Literary Agency; Northwest Literary Services; QCorp Literary Agency; Remington Literary Assoc., Inc.; Rhodes Literary Agency; ‡Stadler Literary Agency; Toomey Associates, Jeanne

Regional: Ahearn Agency, Inc., The; Author Aid Associates; Author Author Literary Agency Ltd.; Cambridge Literary Associates; ‡CDK Technical Communications, Inc.; Chadd-Stevens Literary Agency; Fran Literary Agency; Howard Agency, The Eddy; Jenks Agency, Carolyn; Jett Literary Agency, The; Montgomery Literary Agency; QCorp Literary Agency; Remington Literary Assoc., Inc.; SLC Enterprises

Religious/inspiration: Allegra Literary Agency; Author Aid Associates; Brinke Literary Agency, The; Cambridge Literary Associates; Chadd-Stevens Literary Agency; GEM Literary Services; Hamilton's Literary Agency, Andrew; McKinley, Literary Agency, Virginia C.; Marshall Agency, The Evan; QCorp Literary Agency; Remington Literary Assoc., Inc.; Rhodes Literary Agency; Strong Literary Agency, Marianne

Romance: A.A. Fair Literary Agency; Acacia House Publishing Services Ltd.; Ahearn Agency, Inc., The; Allegra Literary Agency; ‡Anthony Agency, Joseph; Author Aid Associates; Author Author Literary Agency Ltd.; Authors' Marketing Services Ltd.; Author's Services Literary Ageny; Brown, Literary Agent, Antoinette; Cambridge Literary Associates; Catalog® Literary Agency, The; Chadd-Stevens Literary Agency; Collier Associates; Fishbein Ltd., Frieda; ‡Fort Ross Inc. Russian-American Publishing Projects; GEM Literary Services; Gislason Agency, The;

Hamilton's Literary Agency, Andrew; Hilton Literary Agency, Alice; Hubbs Agency, Yvonne Trudeau; Jett Literary Agency, The; JLM Literary Agents; Kellock & Associates Ltd., J.; Kirkland Literary Agency, The; Law Offices of Robert L. Fenton PC; Lee Literary Agency, L. Harry; McKinley, Literary Agency, Virginia C.; Marshall Agency, The Evan; Montgomery Literary Agency; Nelson Literary Agency & Lecture Bureau, BK; ‡Nordhaus-Wolcott Literary Agency; Northwest Literary Services; Portman Organization, The; QCorp Literary Agency; Remington Literary Assoc., Inc.; Rhodes Literary Agency; SLC Enterprises; Stern Agency, Gloria (CA); Strong Literary Agency, Marianne; Tornetta Agency, Phyllis; Visions Press; Wallerstein Agency, The Gerry B.; Warren Literary Agency, James

Romantic comedy: Law Offices of Robert L. Fenton PC; McKinley, Literary Agency, Virginia C.

Romantic drama: Law Offices of Robert L. Fenton PC

Science fiction: A.A. Fair Literary Agency; AEI/Atchity Editorial/Entertainment International; Ahearn Agency, Inc., The; ‡Anthony Agency, Joseph; Author Aid Associates; Author Author Literary Agency Ltd.; Authors' Marketing Services Ltd.; Author's Services Literary Ageny; Brinke Literary Agency, The; Cambridge Literary Associates; Catalog℠ Literary Agency, The; Chadd-Stevens Literary Agency; Collier Associates; Fishbein Ltd., Frieda; ‡Fort Ross Inc. Russian-American Publishing Projects; Fran Literary Agency; GEM Literary Services; Gislason Agency, The; Hilton Literary Agency, Alice; Hubbs Agency, Yvonne Trudeau; Jett Literary Agency, The; Kellock & Associates Ltd., J.; Kirkland Literary Agency, The; Law Offices of Robert L. Fenton PC; Lee Literary Agency, L. Harry; Marshall Agency, The Evan; Montgomery Literary Agency; Nelson Literary Agency & Lecture Bureau, BK; ‡Nordhaus-Wolcott Literary Agency; Northwest Literary Services; Portman Organization, The; Puddingstone Literary Agency; QCorp Literary Agency; Remington Literary Assoc., Inc.; Rhodes Literary Agency; Steinberg Literary Agency, Michael; Stern Agency, Gloria (CA)

Sitcom: Fran Literary Agency; Independent Publishing Agency; Raintree Agency, Diane

Sports: Author Aid Associates; Author Author Literary Agency Ltd.; Cambridge Literary Associates; Chadd-Stevens Literary Agency; Hamilton's Literary Agency, Andrew; Hilton Literary Agency, Alice; Kellock & Associates Ltd., J.; Law Offices of Robert L. Fenton PC; Lee Literary Agency, L. Harry; Montgomery Literary Agency; Nelson Literary Agency & Lecture Bureau, BK; Northwest Literary Services; Portman Organization, The; QCorp Literary Agency; Remington Literary Assoc., Inc.; Rhodes Literary Agency; SLC Enterprises

Thriller/espionage: A.A. Fair Literary Agency; Acacia House Publishing Services Ltd.; AEI/Atchity Editorial/ Entertainment International; Ahearn Agency, Inc., The; ‡Anthony Agency, Joseph; Author Aid Associates; Author Author Literary Agency Ltd.; Authors' Marketing Services Ltd.; Author's Services Literary Ageny; Brinke Literary Agency, The; Brown, Literary Agent, Antoinette; Cambridge Literary Associates; Catalog℠ Literary Agency, The; Chadd-Stevens Literary Agency; Clark Literary Agency, SJ; Collier Associates; Connor Literary Agency; Fishbein Ltd., Frieda; ‡Fort Ross Inc. Russian-American Publishing Projects; Fran Literary Agency; GEM Literary Services; Gladden Unlimited; Hamilton's Literary Agency, Andrew; Hilton Literary Agency, Alice; Hubbs Agency, Yvonne Trudeau; Independent Publishing Agency; Jenks Agency, Carolyn; Jett Literary Agency, The; Kellock & Associates Ltd., J.; Kirkland Literary Agency, The; Law Offices of Robert L. Fenton PC; Lee Literary Agency, L. Harry; Literary Group West; Marshall Agency, The Evan; Montgomery Literary Agency; Nelson Literary Agency & Lecture Bureau, BK; ‡Nordhaus-Wolcott Literary Agency; Northwest Literary Services; Pell Agency, William; Penmarin Books; PMA Literary and Film Management, Inc.; Portman Organization, The; Puddingstone Literary Agency; QCorp Literary Agency; Remington Literary Assoc., Inc.; Rhodes Literary Agency; Southern Literary Agency; ‡Stadler Literary Agency; Steinberg Literary Agency, Michael; Stern Agency, Gloria (CA); Strong Literary Agency, Marianne; Taylor Literary Agency, Dawson; Toomey Associates, Jeanne; Wallerstein Agency, The Gerry B.; Writer's Consulting Group

Westerns/frontier: A.A. Fair Literary Agency; Ahearn Agency, Inc., The; Author Aid Associates; Author Author Literary Agency Ltd.; Author's Services Literary Ageny; Cambridge Literary Associates; Chadd-Stevens Literary Agency; Collier Associates; Fran Literary Agency; GEM Literary Services; Hamilton's Literary Agency, Andrew; Hilton Literary Agency, Alice; Jenks Agency, Carolyn; Jett Literary Agency, The; Kellock & Associates Ltd., J.; Kirkland Literary Agency, The; Law Offices of Robert L. Fenton PC; Lee Literary Agency, L. Harry; Lopopolo Literary Agency, Toni; McKinley, Literary Agency, Virginia C.; Marshall Agency, The Evan; Montgomery Literary Agency; Nelson Literary Agency & Lecture Bureau, BK; ‡Nordhaus-Wolcott Literary Agency; Northwest Literary Services; Portman Organization, The; QCorp Literary Agency; Remington Literary Assoc.; Rhodes Literary Agency; Stern Agency, Gloria (CA); Strong Literary Agency, Marianne; Wallerstein Agency, The Gerry B.

Young adult: Ahearn Agency, Inc., The; Alp Arts Co.; ‡Anthony Agency, Joseph; Author Aid Associates; Author Author Literary Agency Ltd.; Author's Services Literary Ageny; Cambridge Literary Associates; Catalog℠ Literary Agency, The; Chadd-Stevens Literary Agency; Clark Literary Agency, SJ; Fishbein Ltd., Frieda; ‡Fort Ross Inc. Russian-American Publishing Projects; ForthWrite Literary Agency; Fran Literary Agency; GEM Literary Services; Hamilton's Literary Agency, Andrew; Hilton Literary Agency, Alice; Howard Agency, The Eddy; Independent Publishing Agency; Jenks Agency, Carolyn; Jett Literary Agency, The; Kellock & Associates Ltd., J.; Lee Literary Agency, L. Harry; Montgomery Literary Agency; ‡Nordhaus-Wolcott Literary Agency; Northwest Literary Services; PMA Literary and Film Management, Inc.; QCorp Literary Agency; Remington Literary Assoc., Inc.; Rhodes Literary Agency; SLC Enterprises; ‡Stadler Literary Agency; Visions Press; Wallerstein Agency, Gerry B.

FEE-CHARGING LITERARY AGENTS/NONFICTION

Agriculture/horticulture: A.A. Fair Literary Agency; Catalog™ Literary Agency, The; ForthWrite Literary Agency; Fran Literary Agency; Howard Agency, The Eddy; McLean Literary Agency; Montgomery Literary Agency; Nelson Literary Agency & Lecture Bureau, BK; Northwest Literary Services; Remington Literary Assoc., Inc.; Toomey Associates, Jeanne; Wallerstein Agency, The Gerry B.

Animals: A.A. Fair Literary Agency; Acacia House Publishing Services Ltd.; Ahearn Agency, Inc., The; Author Aid Associates; Brinke Literary Agency, The; Catalog™ Literary Agency, The; Fishbein Ltd., Frieda; ForthWrite Literary Agency; Fran Literary Agency; Hamilton's Literary Agency, Andrew; Howard Agency, The Eddy; Jenks Agency, Carolyn; Jett Literary Agency, The; Kellock & Associates Ltd., J.; Lopopolo Literary Agency, Toni; McKinley, Literary Agency, Virginia C.; McLean Literary Agency; Marshall Agency, The Evan; Montgomery Literary Agency; Nelson Literary Agency & Lecture Bureau, BK; Northwest Literary Services; Penmarin Books; Remington Literary Assoc., Inc.; Rhodes Literary Agency; Toomey Associates, Jeanne; Total Acting Experience, A; Wallerstein Agency, The Gerry B.

Anthropology: A.A. Fair Literary Agency; AEI/Atchity Editorial/Entertainment International; Author Aid Associates; Author Author Literary Agency Ltd.; Brinke Literary Agency, The; Catalog™ Literary Agency, The; ForthWrite Literary Agency; Howard Agency, The Eddy; Independent Publishing Agency; Kellock & Associates Ltd., J.; Lopopolo Literary Agency, Toni; Montgomery Literary Agency; Nelson Literary Agency & Lecture Bureau, BK; Penmarin Books; Remington Literary Assoc., Inc.; Rhodes Literary Agency; Southern Literary Agency; ‡Sullivan Associates, Mark; Toomey Associates, Jeanne; Total Acting Experience, A; Wallerstein Agency, The Gerry B.

Art/architecture/design: ForthWrite Literary Agency; Independent Publishing Agency; Kellock & Associates Ltd., J.; Lopopolo Literary Agency, Toni; McLean Literary Agency; Marshall Agency, The Evan; Montgomery Literary Agency; Nelson Literary Agency & Lecture Bureau, BK; Northwest Literary Services; Penmarin Books; Remington Literary Assoc., Inc.; Rhodes Literary Agency; Strong Literary Agency, Marianne; Toomey Associates, Jeanne; Total Acting Experience, A; Wallerstein Agency, The Gerry B.

Biography/autobiography: Acacia House Publishing Services Ltd.; AEI/Atchity Editorial/Entertainment International; Ahearn Agency, Inc., The; Author Aid Associates; Author Author Literary Agency Ltd.; Authors' Marketing Services Ltd.; Brinke Literary Agency, The; Cambridge Literary Associates; Collier Associates; Fishbein Ltd., Frieda; ‡Fort Ross Inc. Russian-American Publishing Projects; ForthWrite Literary Agency; Fran Literary Agency; GEM Literary Services; Gladden Unlimited; Hamilton's Literary Agency, Andrew; Independent Publishing Agency; Janus Literary Agency; Jenks Agency, Carolyn; Jett Literary Agency, The; JLM Literary Agents; Kellock & Associates Ltd., J.; Law Offices of Robert L. Fenton PC; Lawyer's Literary Agency, Inc.; Lopopolo Literary Agency, Toni; McKinley, Literary Agency, Virginia C.; McLean Literary Agency; Marshall Agency, The Evan; Montgomery Literary Agency; Nelson Literary Agency & Lecture Bureau, BK; Northwest Literary Services; Pell Agency, William; Penmarin Books; Portman Organization, The; Remington Literary Assoc., Inc.; Rhodes Literary Agency; SLC Enterprises; Southern Literary Agency; Steinberg Literary Agency, Michael; Stern Agency, Gloria (CA); Strong Literary Agency, Marianne; ‡Sullivan Associates, Mark; Toomey Associates, Jeanne; Total Acting Experience, A; Wallerstein Agency, The Gerry B.; Writer's Consulting Group

Business: AEI/Atchity Editorial/Entertainment International; Ahearn Agency, Inc., The; Author Author Literary Agency Ltd.; Authors' Marketing Services Ltd.; Author's Services Literary Ageny; Brown, Literary Agent, Antoinette; Cambridge Literary Associates; Catalog™ Literary Agency, The; ‡CDK Technical Communications, Inc.; Collier Associates; Connor Literary Agency; Executive Excellence; ForthWrite Literary Agency; Fran Literary Agency; GEM Literary Services; Gladden Unlimited; Hamilton's Literary Agency, Andrew; Independent Publishing Agency; Janus Literary Agency; Jett Literary Agency, The; JLM Literary Agents; Kellock & Associates Ltd., J.; Law Offices of Robert L. Fenton PC; Lopopolo Literary Agency, Toni; McKinley, Literary Agency, Virginia C.; McLean Literary Agency; Marshall Agency, The Evan; Montgomery Literary Agency; Nelson Literary Agency & Lecture Bureau, BK; Penmarin Books; PMA Literary and Film Management, Inc.; Puddingstone Literary Agency; Remington Literary Assoc., Inc.; Rhodes Literary Agency; SLC Enterprises; Southern Literary Agency; Steinberg Literary Agency, Michael; Stern Agency, Gloria (CA); Strong Literary Agency, Marianne; ‡Sullivan Associates, Mark; Total Acting Experience, A; Wallerstein Agency, The Gerry B.; ‡Write Therapist, The; Writer's Consulting Group

Child guidance/parenting: A.A. Fair Literary Agency; AEI/Atchity Editorial/Entertainment International; Ahearn Agency, Inc., The; Author Author Literary Agency Ltd.; Authors' Marketing Services Ltd.; Catalog™ Literary Agency, The; Connor Literary Agency; ForthWrite Literary Agency; Fran Literary Agency; GEM Literary Services; Hamilton's Literary Agency, Andrew; Independent Publishing Agency; Jett Literary Agency, The; Kellock & Associates Ltd., J.; Law Offices of Robert L. Fenton PC; Lopopolo Literary Agency, Toni; McKinley, Literary Agency, Virginia C.; McLean Literary Agency; Marshall Agency, The Evan; Montgomery Literary Agency; Nelson Literary Agency & Lecture Bureau, BK; Northwest Literary Services; Penmarin Books; Remington Literary Assoc., Inc.; Rhodes Literary Agency; Southern Literary Agency; ‡Stadler Literary Agency; Stern Agency, Gloria (CA); Strong Literary Agency, Marianne; Total Acting Experience, A; Wallerstein Agency, The Gerry B.

Computers/electronics: AEI/Atchity Editorial/Entertainment International; Catalog™ Literary Agency, The; ‡CDK Technical Communications, Inc.; Collier Associates; GEM Literary Services; Law Offices of Robert L. Fenton PC; Montgomery Literary Agency; Nelson Literary Agency & Lecture Bureau, BK; Remington Literary Assoc., Inc.; Steinberg Literary Agency, Michael; Stern Agency, Gloria (CA); Total Acting Experience, A

Cooking/food/nutrition: A.A. Fair Literary Agency; Acacia House Publishing Services Ltd.; Author Author Literary Agency Ltd.; Authors' Marketing Services Ltd.; Catalog℠ Literary Agency, The; Collier Associates; Connor Literary Agency; Fishbein Ltd., Frieda; ForthWrite Literary Agency; Fran Literary Agency; GEM Literary Services; Hamilton's Literary Agency, Andrew; Howard Agency, The Eddy; Independent Publishing Agency; Jenks Agency, Carolyn; Jett Literary Agency, The; Kellock & Associates Ltd., J.; Lopopolo Literary Agency, Toni; Marshall Agency, The Evan; Montgomery Literary Agency; Nelson Literary Agency & Lecture Bureau, BK; Northwest Literary Services; Penmarin Books; Remington Literary Assoc., Inc.; Rhodes Literary Agency; SLC Enterprises; Stern Agency, Gloria (CA); Strong Literary Agency, Marianne; ‡Sullivan Associates, Mark; Total Acting Experience, A; Wallerstein Agency, The Gerry B.

Crafts/hobbies: A.A. Fair Literary Agency; Acacia House Publishing Services Ltd.; Author Author Literary Agency Ltd.; Catalog℠ Literary Agency, The; Collier Associates; Connor Literary Agency; ForthWrite Literary Agency; Fran Literary Agency; Howard Agency, The Eddy; Independent Publishing Agency; Janus Literary Agency; Jett Literary Agency, The; McLean Literary Agency; Marshall Agency, The Evan; Montgomery Literary Agency; Nelson Literary Agency & Lecture Bureau, BK; Northwest Literary Services; Penmarin Books; Remington Literary Assoc., Inc.; Rhodes Literary Agency; ‡Sullivan Associates, Mark; Total Acting Experience, A; Wallerstein Agency, The Gerry B.

Current affairs: Acacia House Publishing Services Ltd.; Ahearn Agency, Inc., The; Author Aid Associates; Authors' Marketing Services Ltd.; Author's Services Literary Ageny; Cambridge Literary Associates; Catalog℠ Literary Agency, The; Connor Literary Agency; Fishbein Ltd., Frieda; GEM Literary Services; Hamilton's Literary Agency, Andrew; Hubbs Agency, Yvonne Trudeau; Independent Publishing Agency; Janus Literary Agency; Jett Literary Agency, The; JLM Literary Agents; Kellock & Associates Ltd., J.; Kirkland Literary Agency, The; Law Offices of Robert L. Fenton PC; Literary Group West; McLean Literary Agency; Marshall Agency, The Evan; Montgomery Literary Agency; Nelson Literary Agency & Lecture Bureau, BK; Penmarin Books; Portman Organization, The; Remington Literary Assoc., Inc.; Rhodes Literary Agency; SLC Enterprises; ‡Stadler Literary Agency; Stern Agency, Gloria (CA); Strong Literary Agency, Marianne; ‡Sullivan Associates, Mark; Total Acting Experience, A; Wallerstein Agency, The Gerry B.; Writer's Consulting Group

Education: Author Author Literary Agency Ltd.; Authors' Marketing Services Ltd.; Catalog℠ Literary Agency, The; Howard Agency, The Eddy; Janus Literary Agency; Jett Literary Agency, The; McLean Literary Agency; Montgomery Literary Agency; Nelson Literary Agency & Lecture Bureau, BK; Remington Literary Assoc., Inc.; Rhodes Literary Agency; Stern Agency, Gloria (CA); Strong Literary Agency, Marianne; Total Acting Experience, A; Wallerstein Agency, The Gerry B.; Writer's Consulting Group

Ethnic/cultural interest: A.A. Fair Literary Agency; Ahearn Agency, Inc., The; Author Aid Associates; Author Author Literary Agency Ltd.; Brown, Literary Agent, Antoinette; Catalog℠ Literary Agency, The; Connor Literary Agency; Fran Literary Agency; Hamilton's Literary Agency, Andrew; Independent Publishing Agency; Literary Group West; Lopopolo Literary Agency, Toni; McKinley, Literary Agency, Virginia C.; McLean Literary Agency; Montgomery Literary Agency; Nelson Literary Agency & Lecture Bureau, BK; Northwest Literary Services; Remington Literary Assoc., Inc.; Rhodes Literary Agency; Stern Agency, Gloria (CA); Total Acting Experience, A; Visions Press; Wallerstein Agency, The Gerry B.

Gay/lesbian issues: Ahearn Agency, Inc., The; Author Author Literary Agency Ltd.; Author's Services Literary Ageny; GEM Literary Services; Jenks Agency, Carolyn; Northwest Literary Services; Rhodes Literary Agency; Stern Agency, Gloria (CA); Visions Press; Wallerstein Agency, The Gerry B.

Government/politics/law: AEI/Atchity Editorial/Entertainment International; Author Author Literary Agency Ltd.; Author's Services Literary Ageny; Cambridge Literary Associates; Catalog℠ Literary Agency, The; Connor Literary Agency; GEM Literary Services; Hamilton's Literary Agency, Andrew; Independent Publishing Agency; Janus Literary Agency; Law Offices of Robert L. Fenton PC; Lawyer's Literary Agency, Inc.; McLean Literary Agency; Marshall Agency, The Evan; Montgomery Literary Agency; Nelson Literary Agency & Lecture Bureau, BK; Penmarin Books; Remington Literary Assoc., Inc.; Rhodes Literary Agency; Toomey Associates, Jeanne; Total Acting Experience, A; Wallerstein Agency, The Gerry B.

Health/medicine: Acacia House Publishing Services Ltd.; AEI/Atchity Editorial/Entertainment International; Ahearn Agency, Inc., The; ‡Anthony Agency, Joseph; Author Aid Associates; Author Author Literary Agency Ltd.; Authors' Marketing Services Ltd.; Brown, Literary Agent, Antoinette; Catalog℠ Literary Agency, The; Connor Literary Agency; Executive Excellence; ForthWrite Literary Agency; Fran Literary Agency; Hamilton's Literary Agency, Andrew; Howard Agency, The Eddy; Independent Publishing Agency; Janus Literary Agency; Jenks Agency, Carolyn; Jett Literary Agency, The; Kellock & Associates Ltd., J.; Law Offices of Robert L. Fenton PC; Lopopolo Literary Agency, Toni; McKinley, Literary Agency, Virginia C.; McLean Literary Agency; Marshall Agency, The Evan; Montgomery Literary Agency; Nelson Literary Agency & Lecture Bureau, BK; Northwest Literary Services; Penmarin Books; Remington Literary Assoc., Inc.; Rhodes Literary Agency; Rogers Literary Representation, Irene; Southern Literary Agency; Stern Agency, Gloria (CA); Strong Literary Agency, Marianne; ‡Sullivan Associates, Mark; Total Acting Experience, A; Wallerstein Agency, The Gerry B.; ‡Write Therapist, The; Writer's Consulting Group

History: A.A. Fair Literary Agency; Ahearn Agency, Inc., The; Author Aid Associates; Author Author Literary Agency Ltd.; Authors' Marketing Services Ltd.; Brinke Literary Agency, The; Brown, Literary Agent, Antoinette; Cambridge Literary Associates; Collier Associates; ‡Fort Ross Inc. Russian-American Publishing Projects; ForthWrite Literary Agency; Fran Literary Agency; Hamilton's Literary Agency, Andrew; Hubbs Agency, Yvonne Trudeau; Independent Publishing Agency; Janus Literary Agency; Jenks Agency, Carolyn; Jett Literary Agency, The; Kellock & Associates Ltd., J.; Lee Literary Agency, L. Harry; Lopopolo Literary Agency, Toni; McLean Literary Agency; Marshall Agency, The Evan; Montgomery Literary Agency; Nelson Literary Agency & Lecture Bureau, BK; Northwest Literary Services; Penmarin Books; Portman Organization, The; Remington Literary Assoc., Inc.; Rhodes Literary Agency; SLC Enterprises; Southern Literary Agency; Steinberg Literary Agency, Michael; Strong Literary Agency, Marianne; Toomey Associates, Jeanne; Total Acting Experience, A; Wallerstein Agency, Gerry B.

How-to: A.A. Fair Literary Agency; AEI/Atchity Editorial/Entertainment International; Author Aid Associates; Author Author Literary Agency Ltd.; Authors' Marketing Services Ltd.; Author's Services Literary Ageny; Cambridge Literary Associates; Catalog℠ Literary Agency, The; ‡CDK Technical Communications, Inc.; Collier Associates; Connor Literary Agency; Fran Literary Agency; GEM Literary Services; Gislason Agency, The; Janus Literary Agency; Jett Literary Agency, The; Lopopolo Literary Agency, Toni; McLean Literary Agency; Marshall Agency, The Evan; Montgomery Literary Agency; Nelson Literary Agency & Lecture Bureau, BK; Northwest Literary Services; Penmarin Books; Puddingstone Literary Agency; Remington Literary Assoc., Inc.; Rhodes Literary Agency; Steinberg Literary Agency, Michael; Stern Agency, Gloria (CA); Strong Literary Agency, Marianne; Total Acting Experience, A; Wallerstein Agency, The Gerry B.

Humor: AEI/Atchity Editorial/Entertainment International; Author Aid Associates; Author Author Literary Agency Ltd.; Author's Services Literary Ageny; Cambridge Literary Associates; Coast to Coast Talent and Literary; Connor Literary Agency; Fran Literary Agency; GEM Literary Services; Howard Agency, The Eddy; Jett Literary Agency, The; Kirkland Literary Agency, The; McLean Literary Agency; Marshall Agency, The Evan; Montgomery Literary Agency; ‡Nordhaus-Wolcott Literary Agency; Northwest Literary Services; Remington Literary Assoc., Inc.; Rhodes Literary Agency; ‡Stadler Literary Agency; Total Acting Experience, A; Wallerstein Agency, The Gerry B.

Interior design/decorating: Author Author Literary Agency Ltd.; Connor Literary Agency; ForthWrite Literary Agency; Fran Literary Agency; Jett Literary Agency, The; McLean Literary Agency; Marshall Agency, The Evan; Remington Literary Assoc., Inc.; Strong Literary Agency, Marianne; ‡Sullivan Associates, Mark; Toomey Associates, Jeanne; Total Acting Experience, A; Wallerstein Agency, The Gerry B.

Juvenile nonfiction: A.A. Fair Literary Agency; Ahearn Agency, Inc., The; Alp Arts Co.; Author Aid Associates; Author Author Literary Agency Ltd.; Cambridge Literary Associates; Catalog℠ Literary Agency, The; Fishbein Ltd., Frieda; ForthWrite Literary Agency; Fran Literary Agency; GEM Literary Services; Hamilton's Literary Agency, Andrew; Howard Agency, The Eddy; Independent Publishing Agency; Jett Literary Agency, The; Kellock & Associates Ltd., J.; McKinley, Literary Agency, Virginia C.; McLean Literary Agency; Montgomery Literary Agency; Northwest Literary Services; Remington Literary Assoc., Inc.; Rhodes Literary Agency; ‡Stadler Literary Agency; Strong Literary Agency, Marianne; Total Acting Experience, A

Language/literature/criticism: Acacia House Publishing Services Ltd.; AEI/Atchity Editorial/Entertainment International; Author Aid Associates; Author Author Literary Agency Ltd.; Connor Literary Agency; Independent Publishing Agency; Jett Literary Agency, The; Kellock & Associates Ltd., J.; Lopopolo Literary Agency, Toni; McLean Literary Agency; Marshall Agency, The Evan; Montgomery Literary Agency; Nelson Literary Agency & Lecture Bureau, BK; Northwest Literary Services; Puddingstone Literary Agency; Remington Literary Assoc., Inc.; Rhodes Literary Agency; Stern Agency, Gloria (CA); ‡Sullivan Associates, Mark; Total Acting Experience, A; Wallerstein Agency, The Gerry B.

Military/war: A.A. Fair Literary Agency; Acacia House Publishing Services Ltd.; ‡Anthony Agency, Joseph; Author Aid Associates; Author Author Literary Agency Ltd.; Authors' Marketing Services Ltd.; Author's Services Literary Ageny; Cambridge Literary Associates; Catalog℠ Literary Agency, The; Fishbein Ltd., Frieda; Fran Literary Agency; Independent Publishing Agency; Law Offices of Robert L. Fenton PC; Lee Literary Agency, L. Harry; Literary Group West; McKinley, Literary Agency, Virginia C.; McLean Literary Agency; Marshall Agency, The Evan; Montgomery Literary Agency; Nelson Literary Agency & Lecture Bureau, BK; Portman Organization, The; Puddingstone Literary Agency; Remington Literary Assoc., Inc.; Rhodes Literary Agency; Strong Literary Agency, Marianne; ‡Sullivan Associates, Mark; Taylor Literary Agency, Dawson; Total Acting Experience, A; Wallerstein Agency, The Gerry B.

Money/finance/economics: AEI/Atchity Editorial/Entertainment International; Author Author Literary Agency Ltd.; Authors' Marketing Services Ltd.; Author's Services Literary Ageny; Catalog℠ Literary Agency, The; ‡CDK Technical Communications, Inc.; Connor Literary Agency; ForthWrite Literary Agency; GEM Literary Services; Hamilton's Literary Agency, Andrew; Independent Publishing Agency; Janus Literary Agency; Jett Literary Agency, The; JLM Literary Agents; Law Offices of Robert L. Fenton PC; Lopopolo Literary Agency, Toni; McKinley, Literary Agency, Virginia C.; McLean Literary Agency; Marshall Agency, The Evan; Montgomery Literary Agency; Nelson Literary Agency & Lecture Bureau, BK; Penmarin Books; Remington Literary Assoc., Inc.; Rhodes Literary Agency; Southern Literary Agency; Steinberg Literary Agency, Michael; Stern Agency, Gloria (CA); Strong Literary Agency, Marianne; ‡Sullivan Associates, Mark; Toomey Associates, Jeanne; Total Acting Experience, A; Wallerstein Agency, The Gerry B.; Writer's Consulting Group

Multimedia: ForthWrite Literary Agency; Howard Agency, The Eddy; Jenks Agency, Carolyn; Marshall Agency, The Evan; Mews Books Ltd.; Nelson Literary Agency & Lecture Bureau, BK

Music/dance/theater/film: Acacia House Publishing Services Ltd.; AEI/Atchity Editorial/Entertainment

Order Form

☐ **YES!** Start my subscription to *Writer's Digest*, the magazine thousands of successful writers rely on to hit their target markets. I pay just $19.97 for 12 monthly issues...a savings of more than $15 off the newsstand price.

☐ I'm enclosing payment (or paying by credit card). Add an extra issue to my subscription FREE — 13 in all!

Charge my ☐ Visa ☐ MC

Exp. _____

Signature _____

☐ I prefer to be billed later for 12 issues.

NAME _____

ADDRESS _____

CITY_____ STATE _____ ZIP _____

Outside U.S. add $10 (includes GST in Canada) and remit in U.S. funds. Annual newsstand rate $35.88. Allow 4-6 weeks for first issue delivery.

SAVE MORE THAN $15!

YOUR MONTHLY GUIDE TO GETTING PUBLISHED

TVLM5

Inc.; Rhodes Literary Agency; ‡Sullivan Associates, Mark; Total Acting Experience, A; Wallerstein Agency, The Gerry B.; Writer's Consulting Group

Self-help/personal improvement: A.A. Fair Literary Agency; AEI/Atchity Editorial/Entertainment International; Ahearn Agency, Inc., The; ‡Anthony Agency, Joseph; Author Aid Associates; Author Author Literary Agency Ltd.; Authors' Marketing Services Ltd.; Brinke Literary Agency, The; Brown, Literary Agent, Antoinette; Catalog℠ Literary Agency, The; ‡CDK Technical Communications, Inc.; Coast to Coast Talent and Literary; Collier Associates; Connor Literary Agency; Executive Excellence; Fishbein Ltd., Frieda; ‡Fort Ross Inc. Russian-American Publishing Projects; Fran Literary Agency; GEM Literary Services; Gislason Agency, The; Gladden Unlimited; Hamilton's Literary Agency, Andrew; Howard Agency, The Eddy; Independent Publishing Agency; Janus Literary Agency; Jett Literary Agency, The; JLM Literary Agents; Kellock & Associates Ltd., J.; Kirkland Literary Agency, The; Law Offices of Robert L. Fenton PC; Lopopolo Literary Agency, Toni; McKinley, Literary Agency, Virginia C.; McLean Literary Agency; Marshall Agency, The Evan; Montgomery Literary Agency; Nelson Literary Agency & Lecture Bureau, BK; Northwest Literary Services; Penmarin Books; Remington Literary Assoc., Inc.; Rhodes Literary Agency; Rogers Literary Representation, Irene; Southern Literary Agency; ‡Stadler Literary Agency; Steinberg Literary Agency, Michael; Stern Agency, Gloria (CA); Strong Literary Agency, Marianne; Total Acting Experience, A; Visions Press; Wallerstein Agency, The Gerry B.; ‡Write Therapist, The; Writer's Consulting Group

Sociology: Author Aid Associates; Author Author Literary Agency Ltd.; Brinke Literary Agency, The; Catalog℠ Literary Agency, The; ForthWrite Literary Agency; Hamilton's Literary Agency, Andrew; Independent Publishing Agency; Jett Literary Agency, The; JLM Literary Agents; McKinley, Literary Agency, Virginia C.; McLean Literary Agency; Montgomery Literary Agency; Nelson Literary Agency & Lecture Bureau, BK; Penmarin Books; Remington Literary Assoc., Inc.; Rhodes Literary Agency; ‡Stadler Literary Agency; Stern Agency, Gloria (CA); Total Acting Experience, A; Wallerstein Agency, The Gerry B.

Sports: Author Aid Associates; Author Author Literary Agency Ltd.; Authors' Marketing Services Ltd.; Cambridge Literary Associates; Catalog℠ Literary Agency, The; Connor Literary Agency; Hamilton's Literary Agency, Andrew; Howard Agency, The Eddy; Independent Publishing Agency; Janus Literary Agency; Jett Literary Agency, The; Kellock & Associates Ltd., J.; Law Offices of Robert L. Fenton PC; McKinley, Literary Agency, Virginia C.; Montgomery Literary Agency; Nelson Literary Agency & Lecture Bureau, BK; Northwest Literary Services; Penmarin Books; Portman Organization, The; Remington Literary Assoc., Inc.; Rhodes Literary Agency; SLC Enterprises; ‡Sullivan Associates, Mark; Taylor Literary Agency, Dawson; Total Acting Experience, A; Wallerstein Agency, The Gerry B.

Translations: AEI/Atchity Editorial/Entertainment International; Author Aid Associates; ‡Fort Ross Inc. Russian-American Publishing Projects; Howard Agency, The Eddy; M.H. International Literary Agency; Northwest Literary Services; Rhodes Literary Agency; Total Acting Experience, A

True crime/investigative: A.A. Fair Literary Agency; AEI/Atchity Editorial/Entertainment International; Ahearn Agency, Inc., The; ‡Anthony Agency, Joseph; Author Aid Associates; Author Author Literary Agency Ltd.; Authors' Marketing Services Ltd.; Author's Services Literary Ageny; Cambridge Literary Associates; Clark Literary Agency, SJ; Coast to Coast Talent and Literary; Collier Associates; Connor Literary Agency; Fishbein Ltd., Frieda; ‡Fort Ross Inc. Russian-American Publishing Projects; GEM Literary Services; Gislason Agency, The; Gladden Unlimited; Hamilton's Literary Agency, Andrew; Independent Publishing Agency; Janus Literary Agency; Jett Literary Agency, The; JLM Literary Agents; Kellock & Associates Ltd., J.; Law Offices of Robert L. Fenton PC; Lawyer's Literary Agency, Inc.; Literary Group West; Lopopolo Literary Agency, Toni; McLean Literary Agency; Marshall Agency, The Evan; Montgomery Literary Agency; Nelson Literary Agency & Lecture Bureau, BK; Northwest Literary Services; Penmarin Books; PMA Literary and Film Management, Inc.; Portman Organization, The; Puddingstone Literary Agency; Remington Literary Assoc., Inc.; Rhodes Literary Agency; Stern Agency, Gloria (CA); Strong Literary Agency, Marianne; Toomey Associates, Jeanne; Total Acting Experience, A; Wallerstein Agency, The Gerry B.; Writer's Consulting Group

Women's issues/women's studies: A.A. Fair Literary Agency; AEI/Atchity Editorial/Entertainment International; Ahearn Agency, Inc., The; Author Aid Associates; Author Author Literary Agency Ltd.; Author's Services Literary Ageny; Brown, Literary Agent, Antoinette; Catalog℠ Literary Agency, The; Coast to Coast Talent and Literary; Collier Associates; Connor Literary Agency; Fishbein Ltd., Frieda; ForthWrite Literary Agency; GEM Literary Services; Hamilton's Literary Agency, Andrew; Howard Agency, The Eddy; Hubbs Agency, Yvonne Trudeau; Independent Publishing Agency; Jenks Agency, Carolyn; Jett Literary Agency, The; JLM Literary Agents; Kellock & Associates Ltd., J.; Law Offices of Robert L. Fenton PC; Lopopolo Literary Agency, Toni; McKinley, Literary Agency, Virginia C.; McLean Literary Agency; Marshall Agency, The Evan; Nelson Literary Agency & Lecture Bureau, BK; Northwest Literary Services; PMA Literary and Film Management, Inc.; Portman Organization, The; Remington Literary Assoc., Inc.; Rhodes Literary Agency; SLC Enterprises; ‡Stadler Literary Agency; Stern Agency, Gloria (CA); Strong Literary Agency, Marianne; Total Acting Experience, A; Visions Press; Wallerstein Agency, The Gerry B.

SCRIPT AGENTS/FICTION

Action/adventure: AEI/Atchity Editorial/Entertainment International; Agapé Productions; Agency, The; Alpern Group, The; Amato Agency, Michael; ‡Amsel, Eisenstadt & Frazier, Inc.; Apollo Entertainment; Artists Agency, The; Bethel Agency; ‡Broder Kurland Webb Uffner Agency, The; Brown Ltd., Curtis; Bulger And Associates, Kelvin C.; Cameron Agency, The Marshall; Circle of Confusion Ltd.; Client First—A/K/A Leo P. Haffey Agency;

Coast to Coast Talent and Literary; Communications Management Associates; Douroux & Co.; Dykeman Associates Inc.; Earth Tracks Agency; Epstein-Wyckoff and Associates; ‡ES Talent Agency; F.L.A.I.R. or First Literary Artists International Representatives; Fleury Agency, B.R.; Fran Literary Agency; Gold/Marshak & Associates; Greene, Arthur B.; Heacock Literary Agency, Inc.; Hodges Agency, Carolyn; Hogenson Agency, Barbara; Howard Agency, The Eddy; Hudson Agency; ‡HWA Talent Reps.; International Leonards Corp.; Jenks Agency, Carolyn; Kay Agency, Charlene; Ketay Agency, The Joyce; Kohner, Inc., Paul; Lee Literary Agency, L. Harry; Lenhoff/Robinson Talent and Literary Agency, Inc.; Lindstrom Literary Group; Metropolitan Talent Agency; Monteiro Rose Agency; Montgomery Literary Agency; Montgomery-West Literary Agency; Mura Enterprises, Inc., Dee; Otitis Media; Panda Talent; Partos Company, The; ‡Perelman Agency, Barry; Pevner, Inc., Stephen; Picture Of You, A; PMA Literary and Film Management, Inc.; ‡Premiere Artists Agency; Producers & Creatives Group; Renaissance—H.N. Swanson; Rogers and Associates, Stephanie; Sanders Literary Agency, Victoria; Scagnetti Talent & Literary Agency, Jack; Silver Screen Placements; Sister Mania Productions, Inc.; ‡Sobel Mgmt. Associates (LSMA), Lee; Star Literary Service; Total Acting Experience, A; Turtle Agency, The; Van Duren Agency, Annette; Wright Concept, The; Wright Representatives, Ann; Writer's Consulting Group

Animation: Above The Line Agency; Agency, The; Amato Agency, Michael; Buchwald Agency, Don; Coast to Coast Talent and Literary; Douroux & Co.; Epstein-Wyckoff and Associates; Fran Literary Agency; Gersh Agency, The; ‡Haeggstrom Office, The; Heacock Literary Agency, Inc.; Howard Agency, The Eddy; International Leonards Corp.; Kohner, Inc., Paul; Lenhoff/Robinson Talent and Literary Agency, Inc.; Metropolitan Talent Agency; Monteiro Rose Agency; Mura Enterprises, Inc., Dee; ‡Quillco Agency, The; Renaissance—H.N. Swanson; Total Acting Experience, A; Van Duren Agency, Annette; Wright Concept, The

Cartoon/comic: Agapé Productions; Agency, The; ‡Broder Kurland Webb Uffner Agency, The; Bulger And Associates, Kelvin C.; Circle of Confusion Ltd.; Client First—A/K/A Leo P. Haffey Agency; Fran Literary Agency; Howard Agency, The Eddy; ‡HWA Talent Reps.; International Leonards Corp.; Lenhoff/Robinson Talent and Literary Agency, Inc.; Metropolitan Talent Agency; Monteiro Rose Agency; Mura Enterprises, Inc., Dee; ‡Premiere Artists Agency; Renaissance—H.N. Swanson; ‡Starwatcher; Total Acting Experience, A; Van Duren Agency, Annette; Wright Concept, The

Comedy: AEI/Atchity Editorial/Entertainment International; Agency, The; All-Star Talent Agency; Artists Agency, The; Bennett Agency, The; Brown Ltd., Curtis; Cameron Agency, The Marshall; Circle of Confusion Ltd.; Client First—A/K/A Leo P. Haffey Agency; Douroux & Co.; Dykeman Associates Inc.; Earth Tracks Agency; Epstein-Wyckoff and Associates; F.L.A.I.R. or First Literary Artists International Representatives; Fleury Agency, B.R.; Fran Literary Agency; French, Inc., Samuel; Gold/Marshak & Associates; Heacock Literary Agency, Inc.; Howard Agency, The Eddy; Hudson Agency; International Leonards Corp.; Jenks Agency, Carolyn; Ketay Agency, The Joyce; Kick Entertainment; Kohner, Inc., Paul; Lee Literary Agency, L. Harry; Lenhoff/Robinson Talent and Literary Agency, Inc.; Lindstrom Literary Group; Metropolitan Talent Agency; Monteiro Rose Agency; Montgomery Literary Agency; Montgomery-West Literary Agency; Mura Enterprises, Inc., Dee; Otitis Media; Palmer, Dorothy; Panda Talent; Partos Company, The; Pevner, Inc., Stephen; Picture Of You, A; PMA Literary and Film Management, Inc.; Producers & Creatives Group; Redwood Empire Agency; Renaissance—H.N. Swanson; Sanders Literary Agency, Victoria; Scagnetti Talent & Literary Agency, Jack; Schulman, A Literary Agency, Susan; Silver Screen Placements; Sister Mania Productions, Inc.; Total Acting Experience, A; Van Duren Agency, Annette; Wright Concept, The; Wright Representatives, Ann; Writer's Consulting Group

Confessional: Bethel Agency

Contemporary issues: AEI/Atchity Editorial/Entertainment International; Agency, The; Alpern Group, The; ‡Amsel, Eisenstadt & Frazier, Inc.; Apollo Entertainment; Artists Agency, The; Bethel Agency; ‡Broder Kurland Webb Uffner Agency, The; Bulger And Associates, Kelvin C.; Camden; Cameron Agency, The Marshall; Circle of Confusion Ltd.; Client First—A/K/A Leo P. Haffey Agency; Communications Management Associates; Dykeman Associates Inc.; Earth Tracks Agency; Epstein-Wyckoff and Associates; F.L.A.I.R. or First Literary Artists International Representatives; Fran Literary Agency; French, Inc., Samuel; Gold/Marshak & Associates; Gordon & Associates, Michelle; Heacock Literary Agency, Inc.; Hodges Agency, Carolyn; Hogenson Agency, Barbara; Hudson Agency; ‡HWA Talent Reps.; International Leonards Corp.; Jenks Agency, Carolyn; Ketay Agency, The Joyce; Lee Literary Agency, L. Harry; Legacies; Lenhoff/Robinson Talent and Literary Agency, Inc.; Manus & Associates Literary Agency, Inc.; Metropolitan Talent Agency; Monteiro Rose Agency; Montgomery Literary Agency; Mura Enterprises, Inc., Dee; Partos Company, The; Pevner, Inc., Stephen; PMA Literary and Film Management, Inc.; ‡Premiere Artists Agency; Producers & Creatives Group; Redwood Empire Agency; Renaissance—H.N. Swanson; Rogers and Associates, Stephanie; Sanders Literary Agency, Victoria; Schulman, A Literary Agency, Susan; Silver Screen Placements; Total Acting Experience, A; Van Duren Agency, Annette; Watt & Associates, Sandra; Writer's Consulting Group

Detective/police/crime: AEI/Atchity Editorial/Entertainment International; Agency, The; Alpern Group, The; ‡Amsel, Eisenstadt & Frazier, Inc.; Apollo Entertainment; Artists Agency, The; Bethel Agency; ‡Broder Kurland Webb Uffner Agency, The; Brown Ltd., Curtis; Camden; Cameron Agency, The Marshall; Circle of Confusion Ltd.; Client First—A/K/A Leo P. Haffey Agency; Coast to Coast Talent and Literary; Communications Management Associates; Douroux & Co.; Earth Tracks Agency; Epstein-Wyckoff and Associates; F.L.A.I.R. or First Literary Artists International Representatives; Feiler Literary Agency, Florence; Fleury Agency, B.R.; Fran Literary Agency; French, Inc., Samuel; Gauthreaux—A Literary Agency, Richard; Gold/Marshak & Associates; Gordon & Associates, Michelle; Greene, Arthur B.; ‡Grossman & Assoc., Larry; Gurman Agency, The Susan; Heacock Literary Agency, Inc.; Hodges Agency, Carolyn; Hogenson Agency, Barbara; Hudson Agency; ‡HWA Talent Reps.; International

Leonards Corp.; Ketay Agency, The Joyce; Kohner, Inc., Paul; Lee Literary Agency, L. Harry; Lenhoff/Robinson Talent and Literary Agency, Inc.; Lindstrom Literary Group; Major Clients Agency; Manus & Associates Literary Agency, Inc.; Metropolitan Talent Agency; Monteiro Rose Agency; Montgomery Literary Agency; Montgomery-West Literary Agency; Mura Enterprises, Inc., Dee; Palmer, Dorothy; Panda Talent; Partos Company, The; ‡Perelman Agency, Barry; Pevner, Inc., Stephen; Picture Of You, A; ‡Premiere Artists Agency; Producers & Creatives Group; Renaissance—H.N. Swanson; Scagnetti Talent & Literary Agency, Jack; Schulman, A Literary Agency, Susan; Silver Screen Placements; Sister Mania Productions, Inc.; ‡Sobel Mgmt. Associates (LSMA), Lee; Star Literary Service; Total Acting Experience, A; Turtle Agency, The; Watt & Associates, Sandra; Wright Concept, The; Wright Representatives, Ann; Writer's Consulting Group

Documentary: Amato Agency, Michael; Buchwald Agency, Don; Bulger And Associates, Kelvin C.; Coast to Coast Talent and Literary; Fleury Agency, B.R.; Fran Literary Agency; Heacock Literary Agency, Inc.; Hilton Literary Agency, Alice; Howard Agency, The Eddy; Hudson Agency; Jenks Agency, Carolyn; Kohner, Inc., Paul; Metropolitan Talent Agency; Mura Enterprises, Inc., Dee; ‡Quillco Agency, The; Total Acting Experience, A

Episodic drama: Agency, The; All-Star Talent Agency; Alpern Group, The; Amato Agency, Michael; Buchwald Agency, Don; Camden; Coast to Coast Talent and Literary; Coppage Company, The; Douroux & Co.; Epstein-Wyckoff and Associates; Feiler Literary Agency, Florence; Fran Literary Agency; Gold/Marshak & Associates; ‡Haeggstrom Office, The; Howard Agency, The Eddy; Jenks Agency, Carolyn; Kerin-Goldberg Associates; Ketay Agency, The Joyce; Kohner, Inc., Paul; Lee Literary Agency, L. Harry; Lenhoff/Robinson Talent and Literary Agency, Inc.; Monteiro Rose Agency; Mura Enterprises, Inc., Dee; Palmer, Dorothy; Panda Talent; Picture Of You, A; Producers & Creatives Group; Renaissance—H.N. Swanson; Scagnetti Talent & Literary Agency, Jack; Total Acting Experience, A; Turtle Agency, The; Wright Concept, The; Wright Representatives, Ann; Writers & Artists

Erotica: AEI/Atchity Editorial/Entertainment International; Circle of Confusion Ltd.; Coast to Coast Talent and Literary; Communications Management Associates; Earth Tracks Agency; Epstein-Wyckoff and Associates; F.L.A.I.R. or First Literary Artists International Representatives; Gold/Marshak & Associates; Howard Agency, The Eddy; ‡HWA Talent Reps.; Lenhoff/Robinson Talent and Literary Agency, Inc.; Major Clients Agency; Metropolitan Talent Agency; Picture Of You, A; PMA Literary and Film Management, Inc.; ‡Premiere Artists Agency; Producers & Creatives Group; Redwood Empire Agency; Renaissance—H.N. Swanson; Total Acting Experience, A; Turtle Agency, The

Ethnic: Agency, The; Alpern Group, The; ‡Amsel, Eisenstadt & Frazier, Inc.; Bethel Agency; ‡Broder Kurland Webb Uffner Agency, The; Brown Ltd., Curtis; Bulger And Associates, Kelvin C.; ‡Camejo & Assoc., Suzanna; Circle of Confusion Ltd.; Communications and Entertainment, Inc.; French, Inc., Samuel; Gold/Marshak & Associates; Hogenson Agency, Barbara; Hudson Agency; ‡HWA Talent Reps.; Ketay Agency, The Joyce; Kohner, Inc., Paul; Legacies; Lenhoff/Robinson Talent and Literary Agency, Inc.; Lindstrom Literary Group; Monteiro Rose Agency; Panda Talent; Partos Company, The; Picture Of You, A; PMA Literary and Film Management, Inc.; ‡Premiere Artists Agency; Producers & Creatives Group; Renaissance—H.N. Swanson; Total Acting Experience, A; Wright Concept, The

Experimental: Circle of Confusion Ltd.; Earth Tracks Agency; French, Inc., Samuel; Hodges Agency, Carolyn; Ketay Agency, The Joyce; Lenhoff/Robinson Talent and Literary Agency, Inc.; Partos Company, The; ‡Premiere Artists Agency; Renaissance—H.N. Swanson; Sister Mania Productions, Inc.; Total Acting Experience, A

Family saga: Agapé Productions; Agency, The; Alpern Group, The; ‡Amsel, Eisenstadt & Frazier, Inc.; Apollo Entertainment; Bennett Agency, The; Bethel Agency; ‡Broder Kurland Webb Uffner Agency, The; Bulger And Associates, Kelvin C.; Camden; ‡Camejo & Assoc., Suzanna; Circle of Confusion Ltd.; Client First—A/K/A Leo P. Haffey Agency; Douroux & Co.; Epstein-Wyckoff and Associates; F.L.A.I.R. or First Literary Artists International Representatives; Feiler Literary Agency, Florence; Fleury Agency, B.R.; Fran Literary Agency; Gold/Marshak & Associates; Gurman Agency, The Susan; Heacock Literary Agency, Inc.; Howard Agency, The Eddy; Hudson Agency; ‡HWA Talent Reps.; Jenks Agency, Carolyn; Kay Agency, Charlene; Ketay Agency, The Joyce; Kohner, Inc., Paul; Lee Literary Agency, L. Harry; Legacies; Lenhoff/Robinson Talent and Literary Agency, Inc.; Lindstrom Literary Group; Major Clients Agency; Manus & Associates Literary Agency, Inc.; Metropolitan Talent Agency; Monteiro Rose Agency; Montgomery-West Literary Agency; Mura Enterprises, Inc., Dee; Palmer, Dorothy; Panda Talent; Partos Company, The; Picture Of You, A; ‡Premiere Artists Agency; Producers & Creatives Group; Redwood Empire Agency; Renaissance—H.N. Swanson; Sanders Literary Agency, Victoria; Scagnetti Talent & Literary Agency, Jack; Silver Screen Placements; Sister Mania Productions, Inc.; Total Acting Experience, A; Turtle Agency, The; Watt & Associates, Sandra; Writer's Consulting Group

Fantasy: Agency, The; All-Star Talent Agency; Alpern Group, The; ‡Amsel, Eisenstadt & Frazier, Inc.; Bethel Agency; ‡Broder Kurland Webb Uffner Agency, The; Camden; Circle of Confusion Ltd.; Communications Management Associates; Douroux & Co.; F.L.A.I.R. or First Literary Artists International Representatives; French, Inc., Samuel; ‡HWA Talent Reps.; Kay Agency, Charlene; Ketay Agency, The Joyce; Lee Literary Agency, L. Harry; Lenhoff/Robinson Talent and Literary Agency, Inc.; Metropolitan Talent Agency; Monteiro Rose Agency; Mura Enterprises, Inc., Dee; Partos Company, The; Picture Of You, A; ‡Premiere Artists Agency; Producers & Creatives Group; Redwood Empire Agency; Renaissance—H.N. Swanson; Silver Screen Placements; Total Acting Experience, A; Turtle Agency, The; Wright Concept, The

Feature: Above The Line Agency; AEI/Atchity Editorial/Entertainment International; Agapé Productions; Agency, The; Agency for the Performing Arts; All-Star Talent Agency; Alpern Group, The; Amato Agency, Michael; Artists Agency, The; Buchwald Agency, Don; Bulger and Associates, Kelvin C.; Camden; Cameron Agency, The

Screen Placements; Total Acting Experience, A; Van Duren Agency, Annette; Wright Concept, The

Lesbian: Apollo Entertainment; Bethel Agency; Brown Ltd., Curtis; Circle of Confusion Ltd.; Communications Management Associates; Epstein-Wyckoff and Associates; Feiler Literary Agency, Florence; Gold/Marshak & Associates; Hodges Agency, Carolyn; Ketay Agency, The Joyce; Partos Company, The; Pevner, Inc., Stephen; Picture Of You, A; ‡Premiere Artists Agency; Redwood Empire Agency; Renaissance—H.N. Swanson; Wright Representatives, Ann

Literary: ‡Amsel, Eisenstadt & Frazier, Inc.; Bethel Agency; Coast to Coast Talent and Literary; Gurman Agency, The Susan; Hodges Agency, Carolyn; Hogenson Agency, Barbara; ‡HWA Talent Reps.; Picture Of You, A

Mainstream: AEI/Atchity Editorial/Entertainment International; Agency, The; Alpern Group, The; ‡Amsel, Eisenstadt & Frazier, Inc.; Apollo Entertainment; Bennett Agency, The; Bethel Agency; ‡Broder Kurland Webb Uffner Agency, The; Brown Ltd., Curtis; Camden; Cameron Agency, The Marshall; Circle of Confusion Ltd.; Communications and Entertainment, Inc.; Communications Management Associates; Douroux & Co.; Earth Tracks Agency; Epstein-Wyckoff and Associates; ‡ES Talent Agency; F.L.A.I.R. or First Literary Artists International Representatives; Fleury Agency, B.R.; Fran Literary Agency; ‡Grossman & Assoc., Larry; Gurman Agency, The Susan; Heacock Literary Agency, Inc.; Hodges Agency, Carolyn; Hogenson Agency, Barbara; Howard Agency, The Eddy; Jenks Agency, Carolyn; Ketay Agency, The Joyce; Kick Entertainment; Kohner, Inc., Paul; Lee Literary Agency, L. Harry; Lenhoff/Robinson Talent and Literary Agency, Inc.; Lindstrom Literary Group; Major Clients Agency; Manus & Associates Literary Agency, Inc.; Metropolitan Talent Agency; Monteiro Rose Agency; Montgomery-West Literary Agency; Mura Enterprises, Inc., Dee; Palmer, Dorothy; Partos Company, The; Pevner, Inc., Stephen; Picture Of You, A; PMA Literary and Film Management, Inc.; ‡Premiere Artists Agency; Producers & Creatives Group; Renaissance—H.N. Swanson; Scagnetti Talent & Literary Agency, Jack; Schulman, A Literary Agency, Susan; Silver Screen Placements; Total Acting Experience, A; Turtle Agency, The; Van Duren Agency, Annette; Wright Representatives, Ann; Writer's Consulting Group

Miniseries: Agency, The; Alpern Group, The; Amato Agency, Michael; Buchwald Agency, Don; Camden; Coast to Coast Talent and Literary; Epstein-Wyckoff and Associates; Gersh Agency, The; Gold/Marshak & Associates; ‡Haeggstrom Office, The; Howard Agency, The Eddy; Hudson Agency; Kerin-Goldberg Associates; Kohner, Inc., Paul; Lenhoff/Robinson Talent and Literary Agency, Inc.; Lindstrom Literary Group; Metropolitan Talent Agency; Mura Enterprises, Inc., Dee; Picture Of You, A; PMA Literary and Film Management, Inc.; Producers & Creatives Group; Sanders Literary Agency, Victoria; Writers & Artists

Movie of the week: Above The Line Agency; AEI/Atchity Editorial/Entertainment International; Agency, The; All-Star Talent Agency; Alpern Group, The; Amato Agency, Michael; Artists Agency, The; Buchwald Agency, Don; Bulger And Associates, Kelvin C.; Camden; Cameron Agency, The Marshall; Coast to Coast Talent and Literary; Douroux & Co.; Earth Tracks Agency; Epstein-Wyckoff and Associates; Feiler Literary Agency, Florence; Fishbein Ltd., Frieda; Fran Literary Agency; Gersh Agency, The; Gold/Marshak & Associates; Greene, Arthur B.; ‡Haeggstrom Office, The; Heacock Literary Agency, Inc.; Hilton Literary Agency, Alice; Hodges Agency, Carolyn; Howard Agency, The Eddy; Hudson Agency; International Leonards Corp.; Jenks Agency, Carolyn; Kallen Agency, Leslie; Kay Agency, Charlene; Kerin-Goldberg Associates; Ketay Agency, The Joyce; Kohner, Inc., Paul; Lee Literary Agency, L. Harry; Legacies; Lenhoff/Robinson Talent and Literary Agency, Inc.; Lindstrom Literary Group; Major Clients Agency; Manus & Associates Literary Agency, Inc.; Metropolitan Talent Agency; Monteiro Rose Agency; Montgomery-West Literary Agency; Mura Enterprises, Inc., Dee; Otitis Media; Palmer, Dorothy; Panda Talent; Partos Company, The; Pevner, Inc., Stephen; PMA Literary and Film Management, Inc.; Producers & Creatives Group; ‡Quillco Agency, The; Redwood Empire Agency; Renaissance—H.N. Swanson; Rogers and Associates, Stephanie; Sanders Literary Agency, Victoria; Scagnetti Talent & Literary Agency, Jack; Stanton & Associates Literary Agency; Star Literary Service; Total Acting Experience, A; Turtle Agency, The; Van Duren Agency, Annette; Watt & Associates, Sandra; Wright Concept, The; Wright Representatives, Ann; Writers & Artists; Writer's Consulting Group

Mystery/suspense: AEI/Atchity Editorial/Entertainment International; Agency, The; Artists Agency, The; Bethel Agency; ‡Broder Kurland Webb Uffner Agency, The; Brown Ltd., Curtis; Cameron Agency, The Marshall; Circle of Confusion Ltd.; Client First—A/K/A Leo P. Haffey Agency; Coast to Coast Talent and Literary; Communications and Entertainment, Inc.; Douroux & Co.; Dykeman Associates Inc.; Epstein-Wyckoff and Associates; ‡ES Talent Agency; F.L.A.I.R. or First Literary Artists International Representatives; Feiler Literary Agency, Florence; Fleury Agency, B.R.; Fran Literary Agency; French, Inc., Samuel; Gold/Marshak & Associates; Greene, Arthur B.; ‡Grossman & Assoc., Larry; Gurman Agency, The Susan; Heacock Literary Agency, Inc.; Hodges Agency, Carolyn; Hogenson Agency, Barbara; Hudson Agency; ‡HWA Talent Reps.; International Leonards Corp.; Jenks Agency, Carolyn; ‡Kerwin Agency, William; Ketay Agency, The Joyce; Kohner, Inc., Paul; Lee Literary Agency, L. Harry; Lenhoff/Robinson Talent and Literary Agency, Inc.; Lindstrom Literary Group; Major Clients Agency; Manus & Associates Literary Agency, Inc.; Metropolitan Talent Agency; Monteiro Rose Agency; Montgomery Literary Agency; Montgomery-West Literary Agency; Mura Enterprises, Inc., Dee; Otitis Media; Palmer, Dorothy; Panda Talent; Partos Company, The; ‡Perelman Agency, Barry; Pevner, Inc., Stephen; Picture Of You, A; PMA Literary and Film Management, Inc.; ‡Premiere Artists Agency; Producers & Creatives Group; Renaissance—H.N. Swanson; Scagnetti Talent & Literary Agency, Jack; Schulman, A Literary Agency, Susan; Silver Screen Placements; ‡Sobel Mgmt. Associates (LSMA), Lee; Star Literary Service; Total Acting Experience, A; Turtle Agency, The; Wright Concept, The; Wright Representatives, Ann; Writer's Consulting Group

Open to all fiction categories: Agency for the Performing Arts; All-Star Talent Agency; ‡Bloom &

Associates, East, J. Michael Bloom; ‡Bloom & Associates, West, J. Michael; ‡Bohrman Agency, The; Circle of Confusion Ltd.; ‡Contemporary Artists; Coppage Company, The; ‡Dade/Schultz Associates; ‡Gage Group, The; Gary-Paul Agency, The; Gersh Agency, The; ‡Headline Artists Agency; Hilton Literary Agency, Alice; Hogenson Agency, Barbara; Kerin-Goldberg Associates; ‡Kopaloff Company, The; Lake Agency, The Candace; ‡Shapiro-Lichtman; Sherman & Associates, Ken; ‡Stone Manners Agency; Writers & Artists

Packaging agent: Ketay Agency, The Joyce; Lee Literary Agency, L. Harry; Palmer, Dorothy; Panda Talent

Picture book: Bethel Agency; ‡Meridian Talent, Inc.

Psychic/supernatural: AEI/Atchity Editorial/Entertainment International; Agapé Productions; Agency, The; Apollo Entertainment; Bethel Agency; ‡Broder Kurland Webb Uffner Agency, The; Brown Ltd., Curtis; Circle of Confusion Ltd.; Coast to Coast Talent and Literary; Communications Management Associates; F.L.A.I.R. or First Literary Artists International Representatives; Fleury Agency, B.R.; Gold/Marshak & Associates; Heacock Literary Agency, Inc.; Hodges Agency, Carolyn; ‡HWA Talent Reps.; Kay Agency, Charlene; Ketay Agency, The Joyce; Lee Literary Agency, L. Harry; Lenhoff/Robinson Talent and Literary Agency, Inc.; Metropolitan Talent Agency; Monteiro Rose Agency; Mura Enterprises, Inc., Dee; Partos Company, The; Picture Of You, A; PMA Literary and Film Management, Inc.; ‡Premiere Artists Agency; Producers & Creatives Group; Renaissance—H.N. Swanson; Total Acting Experience, A; Turtle Agency, The; Watt & Associates, Sandra; Wright Representatives, Ann; Writer's Consulting Group

Regional: Bethel Agency; Bulger And Associates, Kelvin C.; Circle of Confusion Ltd.

Religious/inspirational: Agency, The; Bethel Agency; French, Inc., Samuel; Howard Agency, The Eddy; ‡HWA Talent Reps.; Lenhoff/Robinson Talent and Literary Agency, Inc.; Metropolitan Talent Agency; Mura Enterprises, Inc., Dee; Picture Of You, A; Renaissance—H.N. Swanson; Total Acting Experience, A; Watt & Associates, Sandra

Romance: Alpern Group, The; Apollo Entertainment; Bethel Agency; Camden; ‡Camejo & Assoc., Suzanna; Client First—A/K/A Leo P. Haffey Agency; Coast to Coast Talent and Literary; Hodges Agency, Carolyn; Hogenson Agency, Barbara; ‡HWA Talent Reps.; Kay Agency, Charlene; ‡Kerwin Agency, William; Lee Literary Agency, L. Harry; ‡Meridian Talent, Inc.; Montgomery-West Literary Agency; Palmer, Dorothy; ‡Perelman Agency, Barry; ‡Premiere Artists Agency; Redwood Empire Agency; Renaissance—H.N. Swanson; Sister Mania Productions, Inc.; Turtle Agency, The; ‡Working Artists Talent Agency

Romantic comedy: AEI/Atchity Editorial/Entertainment International; Agency, The; All-Star Talent Agency; Artists Agency, The; Brown Ltd., Curtis; Cameron Agency, The Marshall; Circle of Confusion Ltd.; Douroux & Co.; Epstein-Wyckoff and Associates; F.L.A.I.R. or First Literary Artists International Representatives; Feiler Literary Agency, Florence; Fleury Agency, B.R.; Fran Literary Agency; Gold/Marshak & Associates; Howard Agency, The Eddy; Hudson Agency; International Leonards Corp.; Jenks Agency, Carolyn; Ketay Agency, The Joyce; Kick Entertainment; Kohner, Inc., Paul; Lenhoff/Robinson Talent and Literary Agency, Inc.; Lindstrom Literary Group; Manus & Associates Literary Agency, Inc.; Monteiro Rose Agency; Montgomery Literary Agency; Montgomery-West Literary Agency; Mura Enterprises, Inc., Dee; Otitis Media; Palmer, Dorothy; Panda Talent; Partos Company, The; Pevner, Inc., Stephen; PMA Literary and Film Management, Inc.; Producers & Creatives Group; Rogers and Associates, Stephanie; Sanders Literary Agency, Victoria; Scagnetti Talent & Literary Agency, Jack; Total Acting Experience, A; Van Duren Agency, Annette; Watt & Associates, Sandra; Wright Concept, The; Wright Representatives, Ann; Writer's Consulting Group

Romantic drama: AEI/Atchity Editorial/Entertainment International; Agency, The; All-Star Talent Agency; Artists Agency, The; Brown Ltd., Curtis; Cameron Agency, The Marshall; Circle of Confusion Ltd.; Douroux & Co.; Epstein-Wyckoff and Associates; F.L.A.I.R. or First Literary Artists International Representatives; Feiler Literary Agency, Florence; Fleury Agency, B.R.; Fran Literary Agency; Gold/Marshak & Associates; Hudson Agency; Jenks Agency, Carolyn; Ketay Agency, The Joyce; Kick Entertainment; Kohner, Inc., Paul; Lee Literary Agency, L. Harry; Lenhoff/Robinson Talent and Literary Agency, Inc.; Lindstrom Literary Group; Metropolitan Talent Agency; Montgomery-West Literary Agency; Mura Enterprises, Inc., Dee; Otitis Media; Palmer, Dorothy; Panda Talent; Partos Company, The; Pevner, Inc., Stephen; Picture Of You, A; PMA Literary and Film Management, Inc.; Producers & Creatives Group; Sanders Literary Agency, Victoria; Scagnetti Talent & Literary Agency, Jack; Total Acting Experience, A; Van Duren Agency, Annette; Watt & Associates, Sandra; Wright Concept, The; Wright Representatives, Ann; Writer's Consulting Group

Science fiction: AEI/Atchity Editorial/Entertainment International; Agapé Productions; Agency, The; Alpern Group, The; ‡Amsel, Eisenstadt & Frazier, Inc.; Apollo Entertainment; ‡Broder Kurland Webb Uffner Agency, The; Camden; Circle of Confusion Ltd.; Client First—A/K/A Leo P. Haffey Agency; Communications Management Associates; Douroux & Co.; Fran Literary Agency; Gold/Marshak & Associates; Hudson Agency; ‡HWA Talent Reps.; International Leonards Corp.; Kay Agency, Charlene; ‡Kerwin Agency, William; Lee Literary Agency, L. Harry; Lenhoff/Robinson Talent and Literary Agency, Inc.; Metropolitan Talent Agency; Monteiro Rose Agency; Montgomery Literary Agency; Montgomery-West Literary Agency; Mura Enterprises, Inc., Dee; Panda Talent; Partos Company, The; ‡Perelman Agency, Barry; Pevner, Inc., Stephen; PMA Literary and Film Management, Inc.; ‡Premiere Artists Agency; Producers & Creatives Group; Renaissance—H.N. Swanson; Silver Screen Placements; ‡Sobel Mgmt. Associates (LSMA), Lee; ‡Starwatcher; Turtle Agency, The; Van Duren Agency, Annette

Sitcom: Agency, The; Agency for the Performing Arts; All-Star Talent Agency; Buchwald Agency, Don; Camden; Coast to Coast Talent and Literary; Coppage Company, The; Douroux & Co.; Earth Tracks Agency; Epstein-Wyckoff and Associates; Gersh Agency, The; Gold/Marshak & Associates; ‡Haeggstrom Office, The; Hilton Literary Agency, Alice; Howard Agency, The Eddy; International Leonards Corp.; Kerin-Goldberg Associates; Ketay Agency, The Joyce; Kohner, Inc., Paul; Lee Literary Agency, L. Harry; Legacies; Major Clients Agency; Metropolitan Talent Agency; Mura Enterprises, Inc., Dee; Palmer, Dorothy; Panda Talent; Pevner, Inc., Stephen; Producers & Creatives Group; Renaissance—H.N. Swanson; Total Acting Experience, A; Turtle Agency, The; Van Duren Agency, Annette; Wright Concept, The; Wright Representatives, Ann

Soap opera: Buchwald Agency, Don; Coast to Coast Talent and Literary; Epstein-Wyckoff and Associates; Gold/Marshak & Associates; ‡Haeggstrom Office, The; Howard Agency, The Eddy; Kohner, Inc., Paul; Mura Enterprises, Dee; Palmer, Dorothy; Picture Of You, A; Producers & Creatives Group; Total Acting Experience, A

Sports: ‡Amsel, Eisenstadt & Frazier, Inc.; Bethel Agency; Circle of Confusion Ltd.; Client First—A/K/A Leo P. Haffey Agency; Fleury Agency, B.R.; Gold/Marshak & Associates; Heacock Literary Agency, Inc.; Howard Agency, The Eddy; Hudson Agency; ‡HWA Talent Reps.; International Leonards Corp.; Lee Literary Agency, L. Harry; Lenhoff/Robinson Talent and Literary Agency, Inc.; Major Clients Agency; Mura Enterprises, Inc., Dee; ‡Premiere Artists Agency; Renaissance—H.N. Swanson; Scagnetti Talent & Literary Agency, Jack; Total Acting Experience, A; Wright Representatives, Ann

Stage play: Agapé Productions; Buchwald Agency, Don; Dramatic Publishing; Epstein-Wyckoff and Associates; Feiler Literary Agency, Florence; Fishbein Ltd., Frieda; French, Inc., Samuel; Gold/Marshak & Associates; Graham Agency; Greene, Arthur B.; Gurman Agency, The Susan; Howard Agency, The Eddy; Jenks Agency, Carolyn; Kerin-Goldberg Associates; Ketay Agency, The Joyce; Kohner, Inc., Paul; Lee Literary Agency, L. Harry; Legacies; Lenhoff/Robinson Talent and Literary Agency, Inc.; Metropolitan Talent Agency; Montgomery Literary Agency; Otitis Media; Pevner, Inc., Stephen; Total Acting Experience, A; Writers & Artists

Thriller/espionage: AEI/Atchity Editorial/Entertainment International; Agape Productions; Agency, The; Alpern Group, The; ‡Amsel, Eisenstadt & Frazier, Inc.; Apollo Entertainment; Artists Agency, The; Bethel Agency; ‡Broder Kurland Webb Uffner Agency, The; Brown Ltd., Curtis; Camden; Cameron Agency, The Marshall; Circle of Confusion Ltd.; Client First—A/K/A Leo P. Haffey Agency; Coast to Coast Talent and Literary; Communications Management Associates; Douroux & Co.; Dykeman Associates Inc.; Earth Tracks Agency; Epstein-Wyckoff and Associates; ‡ES Talent Agency; F.L.A.I.R. or First Literary Artists International Representatives; Feiler Literary Agency, Florence; Fleury Agency, B.R.; Fran Literary Agency; French, Inc., Samuel; Gauthreaux—A Literary Agency, Richard; Gold/Marshak & Associates; Gurman Agency, The Susan; Heacock Literary Agency, Inc.; Hogenson Agency, Barbara; Howard Agency, The Eddy; Hudson Agency; ‡HWA Talent Reps.; International Leonards Corp.; Jenks Agency, Carolyn; Kay Agency, Charlene; ‡Kerwin Agency, William; Ketay Agency, The Joyce; Lee Literary Agency, L. Harry; Lenhoff/Robinson Talent and Literary Agency, Inc.; Lindstrom Literary Group; Major Clients Agency; Manus & Associates Literary Agency, Inc.; Metropolitan Talent Agency; Monteiro Rose Agency; Montgomery-West Literary Agency; Mura Enterprises, Inc., Dee; Otitis Media; Palmer, Dorothy; Partos Company, The; ‡Perelman Agency, Barry; Pevner, Inc., Stephen; Picture Of You, A; PMA Literary and Film Management, Inc.; ‡Premiere Artists Agency; Producers & Creatives Group; Renaissance—H.N. Swanson; Rogers and Associates, Stephanie; Sanders Literary Agency, Victoria; Scagnetti Talent & Literary Agency, Jack; Silver Screen Placements; Sister Mania Productions, Inc.; ‡Sobel Mgmt. Associates (LSMA), Lee; Star Literary Service; Total Acting Experience, A; Turtle Agency, The; Van Duren Agency, Annette; ‡Working Artists Talent Agency; Wright Concept, The; Wright Representatives, Ann; Writer's Consulting Group

Variety show: Buchwald Agency, Don; Coast to Coast Talent and Literary; French, Inc., Samuel; ‡Haeggstrom Office, The; Howard Agency, The Eddy; International Leonards Corp.; Kerin-Goldberg Associates; Kohner, Inc., Paul; Lenhoff/Robinson Talent and Literary Agency, Inc.; Mura Enterprises, Inc., Dee; Total Acting Experience, A; Wright Concept, The

Westerns/frontier: Agapé Productions; Agency, The; ‡Amsel, Eisenstadt & Frazier, Inc.; Bethel Agency; Brown Ltd., Curtis; Camden; Circle of Confusion Ltd.; Client First—A/K/A Leo P. Haffey Agency; Douroux & Co.; Fran Literary Agency; Howard Agency, The Eddy; Hudson Agency; ‡HWA Talent Reps.; Jenks Agency, Carolyn; Ketay Agency, The Joyce; Lee Literary Agency, L. Harry; Lenhoff/Robinson Talent and Literary Agency, Inc.; Metropolitan Talent Agency; Monteiro Rose Agency; Montgomery Literary Agency; Mura Enterprises, Inc., Dee; Panda Talent; Picture Of You, A; PMA Literary and Film Management, Inc.; ‡Premiere Artists Agency; Renaissance—H.N. Swanson; Scagnetti Talent & Literary Agency, Jack; Total Acting Experience, A; Turtle Agency, The; Wright Concept, The; Wright Representatives, Ann

Young adult: ‡Amsel, Eisenstadt & Frazier, Inc.; Picture Of You, A; Silver Screen Placements; Turtle Agency

SCRIPT AGENTS/NONFICTION

Agriculture/horticulture: Bethel Agency

Animals: Bethel Agency; ‡Camejo & Assoc., Suzanna; ‡HWA Talent Reps.; Panda Talent

Anthropology: Bethel Agency; F.L.A.I.R. or First Literary Artists International Representatives

Art/architecture/design: Bethel Agency; Hogenson Agency, Barbara; ‡Sobel Mgmt. Associates, Lee

Biography/autobiography: Agapé Productions; ‡Amsel, Eisenstadt & Frazier, Inc.; Bethel Agency; Communications and Entertainment, Inc.; Gordon & Associates, Michelle; Gurman Agency, The Susan; Hogenson

Agency, Barbara; ‡HWA Talent Reps.; ‡Perelman Agency, Barry; ‡Sobel Mgmt. Associates (LSMA), Lee; Star Literary Service

Business: Bethel Agency; ‡HWA Talent Reps.; ‡Meridian Talent, Inc.

Child guidance/parenting: Bethel Agency; F.L.A.I.R. or First Literary Artists International Representatives

Cooking/food/nutrition: Bethel Agency; Hogenson Agency, Barbara; Palmer, Dorothy; Scagnetti Talent & Literary Agency, Jack

Crafts/hobbies: Bethel Agency

Current affairs: Bethel Agency; Palmer, Dorothy; ‡Perelman Agency, Barry

Education: ‡Meridian Talent, Inc.

Ethnic/cultural interests: Bethel Agency

Gay/lesbian issues: Bethel Agency; ‡HWA Talent Reps.; Picture Of You, A

Government/politics/law: ‡Amsel, Eisenstadt & Frazier, Inc.; Bethel Agency; Gordon & Associates, Michelle; ‡Perelman Agency, Barry

Health/medicine: Bethel Agency; F.L.A.I.R. or First Literary Artists International Representatives; Palmer, Dorothy; Scagnetti Talent & Literary Agency, Jack

History: ‡Amsel, Eisenstadt & Frazier, Inc.; Bethel Agency; Hogenson Agency, Barbara; Kohner, Inc., Paul; ‡Perelman Agency, Barry; Picture Of You, A; Scagnetti Talent & Literary Agency, Jack

How-to: Hogenson Agency, Barbara; ‡Meridian Talent, Inc.; ‡Premiere Artists Agency

Humor: Agapé Productions; ‡Amsel, Eisenstadt & Frazier, Inc.; Hogenson Agency, Barbara; ‡Meridian Talent, Inc.; ‡Premiere Artists Agency

Interior design/decorating: Bethel Agency; Hogenson Agency, Barbara

Juvenile nonfiction: Bethel Agency; F.L.A.I.R. or First Literary Artists International Representatives; ‡Meridian Talent, Inc.; Picture Of You, A

Language/literature/criticism: Bethel Agency; Hogenson Agency, Barbara; ‡HWA Talent Reps.; Sister Mania Productions, Inc.

Military/war: Agency, The; Bethel Agency; ‡HWA Talent Reps.; Kohner, Inc., Paul; Panda Talent; ‡Perelman Agency, Barry

Money/finance/economics: Bethel Agency; F.L.A.I.R. or First Literary Artists International Representatives; Sister Mania Productions, Inc.

Multimedia: Agency, The; Circle of Confusion Ltd.; Howard Agency, The Eddy; International Leonards Corp.; Jenks Agency, Carolyn; Lenhoff/Robinson Talent and Literary Agency, Inc.; Montgomery Literary Agency; Total Acting Experience, A; Turtle Agency, The

Music/dance/theater/film: Bethel Agency; F.L.A.I.R. or First Literary Artists International Representatives; Hogenson Agency, Barbara; ‡HWA Talent Reps.; Kohner, Inc., Paul; ‡Meridian Talent, Inc.; Picture Of You, A; ‡Sobel Mgmt. Associates (LSMA), Lee

Nature/environment: Bethel Agency; ‡Camejo & Assoc., Suzanna; F.L.A.I.R. or First Literary Artists International Representatives; ‡HWA Talent Reps.

Open to all nonfiction categories: Agency for the Performing Arts; All-Star Talent Agency; Circle of Confusion Ltd.; ‡Shapiro-Lichtman; Sherman & Associates, Ken

Photography: Bethel Agency; Hogenson Agency, Barbara

Popular culture: Hogenson Agency, Barbara

Psychology: Bethel Agency; F.L.A.I.R. or First Literary Artists International Representatives; Gordon & Associates, Michelle

Religious/inspirational: Bethel Agency; Dykeman Associates Inc.; F.L.A.I.R. or First Literary Artists International Representatives; Picture Of You, A

Science/technology: Bethel Agency

Self-help/personal improvement: Agapé Productions; Bethel Agency; F.L.A.I.R. or First Literary Artists International Representatives; ‡Meridian Talent, Inc.; Picture Of You, A; Scagnetti Talent & Literary Agency, Jack

Sociology: Bethel Agency

Sports: ‡Amsel, Eisenstadt & Frazier, Inc.; Bethel Agency; Gauthreaux—A Literary Agency, Richard; ‡HWA Talent Reps.

Teen: AEI/Atchity Editorial/Entertainment International; Agency, The; Apollo Entertainment; Bethel Agency; Circle of Confusion Ltd.; Earth Tracks Agency; Epstein-Wyckoff and Associates; F.L.A.I.R. or First Literary Artists International Representatives; Fleury Agency, B.R.; Howard Agency, The Eddy; Hudson Agency; Lenhoff/Robinson Talent and Literary Agency, Inc.; Metropolitan Talent Agency; Monteiro Rose Agency; Montgomery-West Literary Agency; Mura Enterprises, Inc., Dee; Partos Company, The; Pevner, Inc., Stephen; PMA Literary and Film Management, Inc.; Producers & Creatives Group; Renaissance—H.N. Swanson; Total Acting Experience, A

Translations: Bethel Agency

True crime/investigative: Agape Productions; ‡Amsel, Eisenstadt & Frazier, Inc.; Bethel Agency; F.L.A.I.R. or First Literary Artists International Representatives; Gauthreaux—A Literary Agency, Richard; Gordon & Associates, Michelle; Gurman Agency, The Susan; Hogenson Agency, Barbara; Kohner, Inc., Paul; Manus & Associates Literary Agency, Inc.; Palmer, Dorothy; Panda Talent; ‡Perelman Agency, Barry; Sister Mania Productions, Inc.

Women's issues/women's studies: Agency, The; Bethel Agency; ‡Camejo & Assoc., Suzanna; F.L.A.I.R. or First Literary Artists International Representatives; Gold/Marshak & Associates; Gordon & Associates, Michelle; Palmer, Dorothy; Scagnetti Talent & Literary Agency, Jack

Script Agents/Format Index

This index will help you determine agencies interested in handling scripts for particular types of movies or TV programs. These formats are delineated into ten categories: animation; documentary; episodic drama; feature film; miniseries; movie of the week (mow); sitcom; soap opera; stage play; variety show. Once you find the agency you're interested in, refer to the Listing Index for the page number. Note: Double daggers (‡) preceding titles indicate listings new to this edition.

Animation: Above The Line Agency; Agency, The; Amato Agency, Michael; Buchwald Agency, Don; Coast to Coast Talent and Literary; Douroux & Co.; Epstein-Wyckoff and Associates; Fran Literary Agency; Gersh Agency, The; ‡Haeggstrom Office, The; Heacock Literary Agency, Inc.; Howard Agency, The Eddy; International Leonards Corp.; Kohner, Inc., Paul; Lenhoff/Robinson Talent and Literary Agency, Inc.; Metropolitan Talent Agency; Monteiro Rose Agency; Mura Enterprises, Inc., Dee; ‡Quillco Agency, The; Renaissance—H.N. Swanson; Total Acting Experience, A; Van Duren Agency, Annette; Wright Concept, The

Documentary: Amato Agency, Michael; Buchwald Agency, Don; Bulger And Associates, Kelvin C.; Coast to Coast Talent and Literary; Fleury Agency, B.R.; Fran Literary Agency; Heacock Literary Agency, Inc.; Hilton Literary Agency, Alice; Howard Agency, The Eddy; Hudson Agency; Jenks Agency, Carolyn; Kohner, Inc., Paul; Metropolitan Talent Agency; Mura Enterprises, Inc., Dee; ‡Quillco Agency, The; Total Acting Experience, A

Episodic drama: Agency, The; All-Star Talent Agency; Alpern Group, The; Amato Agency, Michael; Buchwald Agency, Don; Camden; Coast to Coast Talent and Literary; Coppage Company, The; Douroux & Co.; Epstein-Wyckoff and Associates; Feiler Literary Agency, Florence; Fran Literary Agency; Gold/Marshak & Associates; ‡Haeggstrom Office, The; Howard Agency, The Eddy; Jenks Agency, Carolyn; Kerin-Goldberg Associates; Ketay Agency, The Joyce; Kohner, Inc., Paul; Lee Literary Agency, L. Harry; Lenhoff/Robinson Talent and Literary Agency, Inc.; Monteiro Rose Agency; Mura Enterprises, Inc., Dee; Palmer, Dorothy; Panda Talent; Picture Of You, A; Producers & Creatives Group; Renaissance—H.N. Swanson; Scagnetti Talent & Literary Agency, Jack; Total Acting Experience, A; Turtle Agency, The; Wright Concept, The; Wright Representatives, Ann; Writers & Artists

Feature film: Above The Line Agency; AEI/Atchity Editorial/Entertainment International; Agape Productions; Agency, The; Agency for the Performing Arts; All-Star Talent Agency; Alpern Group, The; Amato Agency, Michael; Artists Agency, The; Buchwald Agency, Don; Bulger And Associates, Kelvin C.; Camden; Cameron Agency, The Marshall; Circle of Confusion Ltd.; Coast to Coast Talent and Literary; Coppage Company, The; ‡Dade/Schultz Associates; Douroux & Co.; Earth Tracks Agency; Epstein-Wyckoff and Associates; Feiler Literary Agency, Florence; Fishbein Ltd., Frieda; Fleury Agency, B.R.; Fran Literary Agency; ‡Gage Group, The; Geddes Agency; Gelff Agency, The Laya; Gersh Agency, The; Gold/Marshak & Associates; Gordon & Associates, Michelle; Graham Agency; Greene, Arthur B.; Gurman Agency, The Susan; ‡Haeggstrom Office, The; Heacock Literary Agency, Inc.; Hilton Literary Agency, Alice; Hodges Agency, Carolyn; Howard Agency, The Eddy; Hudson Agency; International Leonards Corp.; Jenks Agency, Carolyn; Kallen Agency, Leslie; Kay Agency, Charlene; Kerin-Goldberg Associates; Ketay Agency, The Joyce; Kick Entertainment; Kohner, Inc., Paul; Lee Literary Agency, L. Harry; Legacies; Lenhoff/Robinson Talent and Literary Agency, Inc.; Lindstrom Literary Group; Major Clients Agency; Manus & Associates Literary Agency, Inc.; Metropolitan Talent Agency; Monteiro Rose Agency; Montgomery Literary Agency; Montgomery-West Literary Agency; Mura Enterprises, Inc., Dee; Otitis Media; Palmer, Dorothy; Panda Talent; Partos Company, The; Pevner, Inc., Stephen; Picture Of You, A; PMA Literary and Film Management, Inc.; Producers & Creatives Group; ‡Quillco Agency, The; Redwood Empire Agency; Renaissance—H.N. Swanson; Rogers and Associates, Stephanie; Sanders Literary Agency, Victoria; Scagnetti Talent & Literary Agency, Jack; Sister Mania Productions, Inc.; ‡Sorice Agency, Camille; Stanton & Associates Literary Agency; Star Literary Service; Talent Source; Total Acting Experience, A; Turtle Agency, The; Van Duren Agency, Annette; Warden, White & Kane, Inc.; Watt & Associates, Sandra; ‡Working Artists Talent Agency; Wright Concept, The; Wright Representatives, Ann; Writers & Artists; Writer's Consulting Group

Miniseries: Agency, The; Alpern Group, The; Amato Agency, Michael; Buchwald Agency, Don; Camden; Coast to Coast Talent and Literary; Epstein-Wyckoff and Associates; Gersh Agency, The; Gold/Marshak & Associates; ‡Haeggstrom Office, The; Howard Agency, The Eddy; Hudson Agency; Kerin-Goldberg Associates; Kohner, Inc., Paul; Lenhoff/Robinson Talent and Literary Agency, Inc.; Lindstrom Literary Group; Metropolitan Talent Agency; Mura Enterprises, Inc., Dee; Picture Of You, A; PMA Literary and Film Management, Inc.; Producers & Creatives Group; Sanders Literary Agency, Victoria; Writers & Artists

Movie of the week: Above The Line Agency; AEI/Atchity Editorial/Entertainment International; Agency, The; All-Star Talent Agency; Alpern Group, The; Amato Agency, Michael; Artists Agency, The; Buchwald Agency,

Don; Bulger And Associates, Kelvin C.; Camden; Cameron Agency, The Marshall; Coast to Coast Talent and Literary; Douroux & Co.; Earth Tracks Agency; Epstein-Wyckoff and Associates; Feiler Literary Agency, Florence; Fishbein Ltd., Frieda; Fran Literary Agency; Gersh Agency, The; Gold/Marshak & Associates; Greene, Arthur B.; ‡Haeggstrom Office, The; Heacock Literary Agency, Inc.; Hilton Literary Agency, Alice; Hodges Agency, Carolyn; Howard Agency, The Eddy; Hudson Agency; International Leonards Corp.; Jenks Agency, Carolyn; Kallen Agency, Leslie; Kay Agency, Charlene; Kerin-Goldberg Associates; Ketay Agency, The Joyce; Kohner, Inc., Paul; Lee Literary Agency, L. Harry; Legacies; Lenhoff/Robinson Talent and Literary Agency, Inc.; Lindstrom Literary Group; Major Clients Agency; Manus & Associates Literary Agency, Inc.; Metropolitan Talent Agency; Monteiro Rose Agency; Montgomery-West Literary Agency; Mura Enterprises, Inc., Dee; Otitis Media; Palmer, Dorothy; Panda Talent; Partos Company, The; Pevner, Inc., Stephen; PMA Literary and Film Management, Inc.; Producers & Creatives Group; ‡Quillco Agency, The; Redwood Empire Agency; Renaissance—H.N. Swanson; Rogers and Associates, Stephanie; Sanders Literary Agency, Victoria; Scagnetti Talent & Literary Agency, Jack; ‡Sorice Agency, Camille; Stanton & Associates Literary Agency; Star Literary Service; Total Acting Experience, A; Turtle Agency, The; Van Duren Agency, Annette; Watt & Associates, Sandra; Wright Concept, The; Wright Representatives, Ann; Writers & Artists; Writer's Consulting Group

Sitcom: Agency, The; Agency for the Performing Arts; All-Star Talent Agency; Buchwald Agency, Don; Camden; Coast to Coast Talent and Literary; Coppage Company, The; Douroux & Co.; Earth Tracks Agency; Epstein-Wyckoff and Associates; Gersh Agency, The; Gold/Marshak & Associates; ‡Haeggstrom Office, The; Hilton Literary Agency, Alice; Howard Agency, The Eddy; International Leonards Corp.; Kerin-Goldberg Associates; Ketay Agency, The Joyce; Kohner, Inc., Paul; Lee Literary Agency, L. Harry; Legacies; Major Clients Agency; Metropolitan Talent Agency; Mura Enterprises, Inc., Dee; Palmer, Dorothy; Panda Talent; Pevner, Inc., Stephen; Producers & Creatives Group; Renaissance—H.N. Swanson; Total Acting Experience, A; Turtle Agency, The; Van Duren Agency, Annette; Wright Concept, The; Wright Representatives, Ann

Soap opera: Buchwald Agency, Don; Coast to Coast Talent and Literary; Epstein-Wyckoff and Associates; Gold/Marshak & Associates; ‡Haeggstrom Office, The; Howard Agency, The Eddy; Kohner, Inc., Paul; Mura Enterprises, Inc., Dee; Palmer, Dorothy; Picture Of You, A; Producers & Creatives Group; Total Acting Experience

Stage play: Agapé Productions; Buchwald Agency, Don; Dramatic Publishing; Epstein-Wyckoff and Associates; Feiler Literary Agency, Florence; Fishbein Ltd., Frieda; French, Inc., Samuel; Gauthreaux—A Literary Agency, Richard; Gold/Marshak & Associates; Graham Agency; Greene, Arthur B.; Gurman Agency, The Susan; Howard Agency, The Eddy; Jenks Agency, Carolyn; Kerin-Goldberg Associates; Ketay Agency, The Joyce; Kohner, Inc., Paul; Lee Literary Agency, L. Harry; Legacies; Lenhoff/Robinson Talent and Literary Agency, Inc.; Metropolitan Talent Agency; Montgomery Literary Agency; Otitis Media; Pevner, Inc., Stephen; Total Acting Experience, A; Writers & Artists

Variety show: Buchwald Agency, Don; Coast to Coast Talent and Literary; French, Inc., Samuel; ‡Haeggstrom Office, The; Howard Agency, The Eddy; International Leonards Corp.; Kerin-Goldberg Associates; Kohner, Inc., Paul; Lenhoff/Robinson Talent and Literary Agency, Inc.; Mura Enterprises, Inc., Dee; Total Acting Experience, A; Wright Concept, The

Geographic Index

Some writers prefer to work with an agent in their vicinity. If you're such a writer, this index offers you the opportunity to easily select agents closest to home. Agencies are separated by state, and this year we've also arranged them according to the sections in which they appear in the book (Nonfee-charging, Fee-charging or Script). Once you find the agency you're interested in, refer to the Listing Index for the page number. Note: Double daggers (‡) preceding titles indicate listings new to this edition.

International Creative
Management
Kallen Agency, Leslie
Kohner, Inc., Paul
‡Kopaloff Company, The
Lenhoff/Robinson Talent and
Literary Agency, Inc.
Major Clients Agency
Manus & Associates Literary
Agency, Inc.
Metropolitan Talent Agency
Monteiro Rose Agency
Panda Talent
Partos Company, The
Producers & Creatives Group
‡Quillco Agency, The
Redwood Empire Agency
Renaissance—H.N. Swanson
Rogers and Associates,
Stephanie
Scagnetti Talent & Literary
Agency, Jack
‡Shapiro-Lichtman
Sherman & Associates, Ken
‡Smith and Assoc., Susan
‡Stone Manners Agency
Total Acting Experience, A
Turtle Agency, The
Van Duren Agency, Annette
Warden, White & Kane, Inc.
Watt & Associates, Sandra
‡Working Artists Talent
Agency
Wright Concept, The
Writer's Consulting Group

COLORADO
Nonfee-charging
Diamond Literary Agency, Inc.
‡National Writers Literary
Agency
Pelham Literary Agency

Fee-charging
Alp Arts Co.

Script
Hodges Agency, Carolyn
Pelham Literary Agency

CONNECTICUT
Nonfee-charging
J de S Associates Inc.
New England Publishing
Associates, Inc.
Urstadt Agency, Susan P.
Van Der Leun & Associates
Writers' Productions

Fee-charging
Independent Publishing
Agency

Mews Books Ltd.
Toomey Associates, Jeanne

Script
Gary-Paul Agency, The

DISTRICT OF COLUMBIA
Nonfee-charging
Adler & Robin Books Inc.
Goldfarb & Graybill, Attorneys
at Law
‡Lichtman, Trister, Singer &
Ross
Literary and Creative Artists
Agency Inc.

FLORIDA
Nonfee-charging
Bova Literary Agency, The
Barbara
‡Brock Gannon Literary
Agency
Elmo Agency Inc., Ann
Fleury Agency, B.R.
International Publisher
Associates Inc.
Kellock Company, Inc., The
Nugent Literary

Fee-charging
Collier Associates
Lawyer's Literary Agency, Inc.
Taylor Literary Agency,
Dawson

Script
Cameron Agency, The
Marshall
Fleury Agency, B.R.
Legacies

GEORGIA
Nonfee-charging
Baldi Literary Agency, Malaga
Brandt Agency, The Joan
Graham Literary Agency, Inc.
Pelter, Rodney
Schmidt Literary Agency,
Harold

Fee-charging
Allegra Literary Agency

Script
Talent Source

HAWAII
Nonfee-charging
‡Sweeney Literary Agency,
Emma

IDAHO
Nonfee-charging
Author's Agency, The

ILLINOIS
Nonfee-charging
Agency Chicago
Apollo Entertainment
‡Book Deals, Inc.
First Books, Inc.
Goddard Book Group
Multimedia Product
Development, Inc.

Fee-charging
Portman Organization, The
SLC Enterprises
Steinberg Literary Agency,
Michael

Script
Apollo Entertainment
Bulger and Associates, Kelvin
Communications Management
Associates
Dramatic Publishing
Silver Screen Placements

INDIANA
Nonfee-charging
Rose Agency, Inc.

Fee-charging
Agapé Productions
International Leonards Corp.

IOWA
Nonfee-charging
Doyen Literary Services, Inc.

KANSAS
Fee-charging
‡Nordhaus-Wolcott Literary
Agency

KENTUCKY
Nonfee-charging
Greene, Literary Agent, Randall
Elisha

LOUISIANA
Nonfee-charging
Gautreaux—A Literary Agency,
Richard

‡Goodman Associates
Gordon Agency, Charlotte
Greenburger Associates, Inc., Sanford J.
Greene, Arthur B.
‡Gregory Inc., Blanche C.
Grimes Literary Agency, Lew
Hawkins & Associates, Inc., John
Henshaw Group, Richard
Herman Agency, Inc., The Jeff
Herner Rights Agency, Susan
Hochmann Books, John L.
Hoffman Literary Agency, Berenice
Hogenson Agency, Barbara
Hull House Literary Agency
IMG Literary
International Creative Management
Jabberwocky Literary Agency
‡Jet Literary Associates, Inc.
Jordan Literary Agency, Lawrence
Ketz Agency, Louise B.
Kidde, Hoyt & Picard
Kirchoff/Wohlberg, Inc., Authors' Representation Division
Klinger, Inc., Harvey
Kouts, Literary Agent, Barbara
Lampack Agency, Inc., Peter
Lantz-Joy Harris Literary Agency Inc., The Robert
‡Leap First
Lescher & Lescher Ltd.
Levine Communications, Inc., James
Levine Literary Agency, Inc., Ellen
Lieberman Associates, Robert
Lipkind Agency, Wendy
Literary Group, The
Lord Literistic, Inc., Sterling
Love Literary Agency, Nancy
Lowenstein Associates, Inc.
Lukeman Literary Management Ltd.
Maass Literary Agency, Donald
Maccoby Literary Agency, Gina
Mainhardt Agency, Ricia
Mann Agency, Carol
Manus & Associates Literary Agency, Inc.
Marcil Literary Agency, Inc., The Denise
Markson Literary Agency, Elaine
Martell Agency, The
‡Mendez Inc., Toni
Michaels Literary Agency, Inc., Doris S.
Miller Agency, The
Moran Agency, Maureen
Morris Agency, William

Morrison, Inc., Henry
Mura Enterprises, Inc., Dee
Naggar Literary Agency, Jean
Nathan, Ruth
Nine Muses and Apollo Inc.
Nolan Literary Agency, The Betsy
Norma-Lewis Agency, The
Ober Associates, Harold
Oscard Agency, Inc., Fifi
Paraview, Inc.
Parks Agency, The Richard
Paton Literary Agency, Kathi J.
Pelter, Rodney
Perkins Associates
Pevner, Inc., Stephen
Pine Associates, Inc., Arthur
Pom Inc.
Priest Literary Agency, Aaron
Protter Literary Agent, Susan Ann
Pryor, Inc., Roberta
Publishing Services
Quicksilver Books-Literary Agents
‡Rittenberg Literary Agency, Inc., Ann
Robbins Office, Inc., The
Rotrosen Agency, Jane
Russell & Volkening
Sanders Literary Agency, Victoria
Sandum & Associates
Schmidt Literary Agency, Harold
Schulman, A Literary Agency, Susan
Schwartz Agency, Laurens R.
‡Scovil Chichak Galen Literary Agency
Seymour Agency, The
Shepard Agency, The
Shukat Company Ltd., The
Singer Literary Agency Inc., Evelyn
‡Skolnick, Irene
Smith, Literary Agent, Valerie
Sommer, Inc., Elyse
Spieler, F. Joseph
Spitzer Literary Agency, Philip
Stepping Stone
‡Sweeney Literary Agency, Emma
Targ Literary Agency, Inc., Roslyn
‡Tenth Avenue Editions, Inc.
2M Communications Ltd.
Valcourt Agency, Inc., The Richard R.
Vines Agency, Inc., The
Wald Associates, Inc., Mary Jack
Wallace Literary Agency, Inc.
Ware Literary Agency, John

Wasserman Literary Agency, Inc., Harriet
Watkins Loomis Agency, Inc.
Wecksler-Incomco
Weingel-Fidel Agency, The
Weyr Agency, Rhoda
Wieser & Wieser, Inc.
Witherspoon & Associates, Inc.
Wreschner, Authors' Representative, Ruth
Writers House
Writers' Representatives, Inc.
‡Young Agency Inc., The Gay
Zahler Literary Agency, Karen Gantz
Zeckendorf Assoc. Inc., Susan
‡Zitwer Agency, Barbara J.

Fee-charging
Author Aid Associates
Connor Literary Agency
‡CS International Literary Agency
Fishbein Ltd., Frieda
Gelles-Cole Literary Enterprises
Lee Literary Agency, L. Harry
Nelson Literary Agency & Lecture Bureau, BK
Pell Agency, William
PMA Literary and Film Management, Inc.
Raintree Agency, Diane
‡Sullivan Associates, Mark
Tornetta Agency, Phyllis

Script
Amato Agency, Michael
Amsterdam Agency, Marcia
Berman Boals and Flynn
Bethel Agency
‡Bloom & Associates, East, J. Michael
Brown Ltd., Curtis
Buchwald Agency, Don
Circle of Confusion Ltd.
Earth Tracks Agency
F.L.A.I.R. or First Literary Artists International Representatives
Fishbein Ltd., Frieda
Freedman Dramatic Agency, Inc., Robert A.
French, Inc., Samuel
Graham Agency
Greene, Arthur B.
Gurman Agency, The Susan
Hogenson Agency, Barbara
Hudson Agency
Kerin-Goldberg Associates
Ketay Agency, The Joyce
Lee Literary Agency, L. Harry
Manus & Associates Literary Agency, Inc.

Mura Enterprises, Inc., Dee
Palmer, Dorothy
Pevner, Inc., Stephen
PMA Literary and Film
 Management, Inc.
Sanders Literary Agency,
 Victoria
Schulman, A Literary Agency,
 Susan
Tantleff Office, The
Vines Agency, Inc., The
Whittlesey Agency, Peregrine
Wright Representatives, Ann
Writers & Artists

OHIO
Fee-charging
GEM Literary Services
Hamilton's Literary Agency,
 Andrew

Script
Kick Entertainment
Picture Of You, A

OREGON
Nonfee-charging
Kern Literary Agency, Natasha

Fee-charging
QCorp Literary Agency

PENNSYLVANIA
Nonfee-charging
Collin Literary Agent, Frances
‡Harp, Chadwick Allen
Lincoln Literary Agency, Ray
Pocono Literary Agency, Inc.
Porcelain, Sidney E.
Schlessinger Agency, Blanche

Toad Hall, Inc.

Fee-charging
Wallerstein Agency, The Gerry

Script
Sister Mania Productions, Inc.

TENNESSEE
Script
Client First—A/K/A Leo P.
 Haffey Agency

TEXAS
Fee-charging
Blake Group Literary Agency,
 The
Chadd-Stevens Literary Agency
Fran Literary Agency
Kirkland Literary Agency, The
Southern Literary Agency

Script
Dykeman Associates Inc.
Fran Literary Agency
Stanton & Associates Literary
 Agency

UTAH
Fee-charging
Executive Excellence

Script
Montgomery-West Literary
 Agency

VERMONT
Nonfee-charging
‡Brady Literary Management
Rowland Agency, The Damaris

VIRGINIA
Fee-charging
Brown, Literary Agent,
 Antoinette

Script
Communications and
 Entertainment, Inc.
Lindstrom Literary Group

WASHINGTON
Nonfee-charging
‡Goodman-Andrew-Agency,
 Inc.
Levant & Wales, Literary
 Agency, Inc.

Fee-charging
Catalog™ Literary Agency, The
McLean Literary Agency

WISCONSIN
Fee-charging
McKinley, Literary Agency,
 Virginia C.

CANADA
Fee-charging
Acacia House Publishing
 Services Ltd.
Author Author Literary Agency
 Ltd.
Authors' Marketing Services
 Ltd.
Kellock & Associates Ltd., J.
Northwest Literary Services

Script
Kay Agency, Charlene

Agents Index

This index of agent names was created to help you locate agents you may have read or heard about even when you do not know which agency they work for. Agent names are listed with their agencies' names. Check the Listing Index for the page number of the agency.

A

Abecassis, A.L. (Ann Elmo Agency)
Adams, Bret (Bret Adams, Ltd.)
Adams, Deborah (The Jeff Herman Agency Inc.)
Adams, Denise (Alice Hilton Literary Agency)
Adler, Bill (Adler & Robin Books)
Agarwal, Rajeev K. (Circle of Confusion Ltd.)
Agyeman, Janell Walden (Marie Brown Associates Inc.)
Ahearn, Pamela G. (The Ahearn Agency, Inc.)
Ajlouny, Joseph S. (The Joseph S. Ajlouny Agency)
Ali, Geisel (BK Nelson Literary Agency & Lecture Bureau)
Allen, Linda (Linda Allen Literary Agency)
Allred, Robert (All-Star Talent Agency)
Aloia, Jr., Richard (The Richard Paul Literati)
Alpern, Jeff (The Alpern Group)
Alterman, Eric (New Brand Agency Group)
Amato, Mary Ann (Legacies)
Amato, Michael (Michael Amato Group)
Amparan, Joann (Wecksler-Incomco)
Amsterdam, Marcia (Marcia Amsterdam Agency)
Anderson, Jeff (M.H. International Literary Agency)
Andiman, Lori (Arthur Pine Associates, Inc.)
Andrew, David M. (Goodman-Andrew-Agency, Inc.)
Andrews, Bart (Bart Andrews & Associates Inc.)
Angsten, David (AEI/Atchity Editorial/Entertainment International)
Anthony, Joseph (Joseph Anthony Agency)

Aragi, Nicole (Watkins Loomis Agency, Inc.)
Armenta, Judith (Martha Casselman Literary Agent)
Arnovitz, Scott (International Creative Management)
Atchity, Kenneth (AEI/Atchity Editorial/Entertainment International)
Axelrod, Steve (The Damaris Rowland Agency)
Axelrod, Steven (The Axelrod Agency)

B

Bach, Julian (IMG Literary)
Bailey, George (Producers & Creatives Group)
Baldi, Malaga (Malaga Baldi Literary Agency)
Balkan, Frank (Lenhoff/Robinson Talent and Literary Agency)
Balkin, Rick (Balkin Agency)
Bankoff, Lisa (International Creative Management)
Banks, Darrell Jerome (Just Write Agency, Inc.)
Barmeier, Jim (Writer's Consulting Group)
Barnett, Steve (Agapé Productions)
Barquette, Jim (The Partos Co.)
Barr, Hollister (L. Harry Lee Literary Agency)
Barrett, Loretta A. (Loretta Barrett Books Inc.)
Bartlett, Bruce (Above the Line Agency)
Barvin, Jude (The Brinke Literary Agency)
Bearden, James L. (Communications and Entertainment, Inc.)
Behar, Josh (Josh Behar Literary Agency)
Bellacicco, Dan A. (A Total Acting Experience)
Belzer, Leonard (Paraview, Inc.)
Bennett, Carole (The Bennett Agency)
Benson, John (BK Nelson Literary Agency & Lecture Bureau)
Benson, JW (BK Nelson Literary Agency & Lecture Bureau)
Bent, Jenny (Goldfarb & Graybill, Attorneys at Law)
Berkman, Edwina (Author's Services Literary Agent)
Berkman, Edwina (L. Harry Lee Literary Agency)
Berkower, Amy (Writers House)
Bernard, Alec (Puddingstone Literary Agency)
Bernstein, Meredith (Meredith Bernstein Literary Agency)
Bernstein, Ron (The Gersh Agency)
Berry, Henry (Independent Publishing Agency)
Bial, Daniel (Daniel Bial Agency)
Bierer, Casey (Stone Manners Agency)
Biggis, Charis (L. Harry Lee Literary Agency)
Billings, Stacy (The Quillco Agency)
Bilmes, Joshua (Jabberwocky Literary Agency)
Bitterman, Annette (Author Aid Associates)
Black, David (David Black Literary Agency, Inc.)
Blake, Laura J. (Curtis Brown)
Blankson, Joanna (Marie Brown Associates Inc.)
Blanton, Sandra (Peter Lampack Agency, Inc.)
Blick, Carolyn Hopwood (Pocono Literary Agency, Inc.)
Bloch, Emily (F. Joseph Spieler)
Bloom, J. Michael (J. Michael Bloom & Associates, East)
Bloom, Leonard (Jack Scagnetti Talent & Literary)
Boals, Judy (Berman, Boals and Flynn)
Boates, Reid (Reid Boates Literary Agency)
Bock, Jill (The Tantleff Office)

Dearden, Adam (Producers & Creatives Group)

deBrandt, Nan (McLean Literary Agency)

Delduca, Rema (Charisma Communications, Ltd.)

Deuble, Deborah (Premiere Artists Agency)

Dever, Donna (Pam Bernstein)

DeWinter, Sharon (Authors' Marketing Services Ltd.)

Dickensheid, Diane (Victoria Sanders Literary Agency)

Dietz, Patricia (Ciske & Dietz Literary Agency)

Dijkstra, Sandra (Sandra Dijkstra Literary Agency)

DiLeonardo, Ingrid (Otitis Media)

Dinstman, Lee (Agency for the Performing Arts)

Diver, Lucienne (Blassingame Spectrum Corp.)

Dixon, Esq., Sherrie (Esq. Literary Productions)

Dolger, Jonathan (The Jonathan Dolger Agency)

Donnelly, Dave (BK Nelson Literary Agency & Lecture Bureau)

Doran, Michael (Southern Literary Agency)

Douglas, Mitch (International Creative Management)

Douroux, Michael E. (Douroux & Co.)

Doyen, B.J. (Doyen Literary Services, Inc.)

Dreyfus, Barbara (International Creative Management)

Dresner, Amy (The Turtle Agency)

Duane, Dick (Jay Garon-Brooke Assoc. Inc.)

Dubovik, Svetlana (Fort Ross Inc. Russian-American Publishing Projects)

Dudin, Ludmiller (The Portman Organization)

Dunham, Jennie (Russell & Volkening)

Dunow, Henry (Harold Ober Associates)

E

Eagle, Theodora (John L. Hochman Books)

Eckstut, Daniel (James Levine Communications, Inc.)

Edelstein, Anne (Harold Ober Associates)

Egan-Miller, Danielle, (Multimedia Product Development)

Eisenstadt, Mike (Amsel, Eisenstadt & Frazier, Inc.)

Ellenberg, Ethan (Ethan Ellenberg Literary Agency)

Elliott, Elaine (Elliott Agency)

Elwell, Jake (Wieser & Wieser)

Emerman, Phyllis A. (The Portman Organization)

Engel, Anne (Jean V. Naggar Literary Agency)

Engel, Roger (The Brinke Literary Agency)

Epley, Thomas (The Potomac Literary Agency)

Esersky, Gareth (Carol Mann Agency)

Eth, Felicia (Felicia Eth Literary Representation)

Etling, H. Allen (Lawyer's Literary Agency, Inc.)

Evereaux, Anastassia (L. Harry Lee Literary Agency)

F

Farber, Ann (Farber Literary Agency Inc.)

Faria, Judith (L. Harry Lee Literary Agency)

Faulkner, Monica (AEI/Atchity Editorial/Entertainment International)

Feder, Josh (Peter Elek Assoc.)

Feigen, Brenda (Brenda Feigen Literary Agency)

Feldman, Leigh (Darhansoff & Verrill Literary Agents)

Feldman, Richard (International Creative Management)

Fenton, Robert L. (Law Offices of Robert L. Fenton PC)

Ferenczi, Charmaine (The Tantleff Office)

Fernandez, Justin E. (Paraview)

Fidel, Loretta (The Weingel-Fidel Agency)

Finch, Diana (Ellen Levine Literary Agency, Inc.)

Fisher, Steven (Renaissance—H.N. Swanson)

Fishman, Joel E. (The Bedford Book Works, Inc.)

Flaherty, John (Joyce A. Flaherty, Literary Agent)

Flaherty, Joyce A. (Joyce A. Flaherty, Literary Agent)

Flanagan, Cecilia (Sandra Watt & Associates)

Flannery, Jennifer (Flannery Literary)

Fleming, Arthur (Arthur Fleming Associates)

Fleming, Peter (Peter Fleming Agency)

Flynn, Jim (Berman, Boals and Flynn)

Foiles, S. James (Appleseeds Management)

Foley, Joan (The Foley Literary Agency)

Foley, Joseph (The Foley Literary Agency)

Fontenot, Mickey (The Frustrated Writer's Ltd.)

Fontenot, Wayne (The Frustrated Writer's Ltd.)

Fontno, Donna Williams (Major Client Agency)

Forbes, Jamie (The Jeff Herman Agency Inc.)

Fortunato, Lee (Joseph Anthony Agency)

Foss, Gwen (The Joseph S. Ajlouny Agency)

Frazier, Warren (John Hawkins & Associates, Inc.)

Free, Jean (Jay Garon-Brooke Assoc. Inc.)

Freedman, Robert A. (Robert A. Freedman Dramatic Agency, Inc.)

Freymann, Sarah Jane (Stepping Stone)

Friedman, Lisa (James Charlton Associates)

Friedrich, Molly (Aaron M. Priest Literary Agency)

Frisk, Mark (Howard Buck Agency)

Fugate, David (Waterside Productions, Inc.)

Fuller, Sandy Ferguson (ALP Arts Co.)

G

Galen, Russell (Scovil Chichak Galen Literary Agency)

Gardner, Anthony (The Tantleff Office)

Gartenberg, Max (Max Gartenberg, Literary Agent)

Gates, Stephen (Susan Smith and Assoc.)

Gaylor, Mary Lee (L. Harry Lee Literary Agency)

Geddes, Ann (Geddes Agency)

Geiger, Ellen (Curtis Brown Ltd.)

Gelles-Cole, Sandi (Gelles-Cole Literary Enterprises)

Geminder, Michele (Witherspoon & Associates, Inc.)

Gerwin-Stoopack, Karen (Loretta Barrett Books Inc.)

Gibson, Sebastian (The Sebastian Gibson Agency)

Ginsberg, Debra (Sandra Dijkstra Literary Agency)

Ginsberg, Peter L. (Curtis Brown)

Ginsberg, Susan (Writers House)

Giordano, Pat (Hudson Agency)

Giordano, Susan (Hudson Agency)

Trunzo, Geno (Kick Entertainment)

Trupin, Jim (Jet Literary Associates, Inc.)

Tsai, Linda (Mark Sullivan Associates)

Tucker, Laura (Richard Curtis Associates Inc.)

Tufts, Ellen Shaw (Lawyer's Literary Agency, Inc.)

Turtle, Cindy (The Turtle Agency)

U

Ufland, John (Premiere Artists Agency)

Urban, Amanda (International Creative Management)

Urdiales, Tony (The Frustrated Writer's Ltd.)

Urstadt, Susan P. (Susan P. Urstadt Inc. Agency)

V

Vadino, Diane (Mark Sullivan Associates)

Valcourt, Richard R. (The Richard R. Valcourt Agency, Inc.)

Valentine, Wendy (The Gislason Agency)

Valentino, Michael (Cambridge Literary Associates)

Valentino, Ralph (Cambridge Literary Associates)

Vallely, Janis C. (Flaming Star Literary Enterprises)

Vallely, Joseph B. (Flaming Star Literary Enterprises)

Van Buren, Chris (Waterside Productions, Inc.)

Van Der Beets, Richard (West Coast Literary Associates)

Van Duren, Annette (Annette Van Duren Agency)

Van der Leun, Patricia (Van der Leun & Associates)

Van Nguyen, Kim (Robert Madsen Agency)

Vance, Lisa Erbach (Aaron M. Priest Literary Agency)

Verrill, Charles (Darhansoff & Verrill Literary Agents)

Vesel, Beth (Sanford J. Greenburger Associates Inc.)

Vesneske, Jr., Ed (Nine Muses and Apollo Inc.)

Vidor, Michael (The Hardy Agency)

Vines, James C. (The Vines Agency, Inc.)

W

Wagner, Matthew (Waterside Productions, Inc.)

Wakefield, Karin (Epstein-Wyckoff and Associates)

Waldman, Sue (Producers & Creatives Group)

Wales, Elizabeth (Levant & Wales, Literary Agency, Inc.)

Wallace, Lois (Wallace Literary Agency, Inc.)

Wallace, Thomas C. (Wallace Literary Agency, Inc.)

Wallerstein, Gerry B. (The Gerry B. Wallerstein Agency)

Walter, Maureen (Curtis Brown)

Warden, David (Warden, White & Kane, Inc.)

Wardlow, David (Camden)

Ware, John A. (John A. Ware Literary Agency)

Wasserman, Harriet (Harriet Wasserman Literary Agency)

Watt, Sandra (Sandra Watt & Associates)

Wax, Eva (Janus Literary Agency)

Waxman, Scott (The Literary Group)

Wecksler, Sally (Wecksler-Incomco)

Weimann, Frank (The Literary Group)

Weiner, Cherry (Cherry Weiner Literary Agency)

West, Cleo (Panda Talent)

Westberg, Phyllis (Harold Ober Associates)

Western, Carole (Montgomery-West Literary Agency)

Whelchel III, Andrew J. (National Writers Literary Agency)

Whelchel, Sandy (National Writers Literary Agency)

White, Steve (Warden, White & Kane, Inc.)

Whitman, John R. (Kirchoff/Wohlberg, Inc., Authors' Representation Division)

Whittlesey, Peregrine (Peregrine Whittlesey Agency)

Wieser, George (Wieser & Wieser, Inc.)

Wieser, Olga (Wieser & Wieser, Inc.)

Wilcox, David (The Bohrman Agency)

Wilkens, Janet (Manus & Associates Literary)

Williams, Jeanne (International Creative Management)

Williams, John Taylor (Ike) (The Palmer & Dodge Agency)

Williamson, Stephen (The Martell Agency)

Willig, Alan (The Tantleff Office)

Winchell, R.J. (The Author's Agency)

Wirtschafter, David (International Creative Management)

Wofford-Girand, Sally (Elaine Markson Literary Agency)

Wolcott, Chris (Nordhaus-Wolcott Literary Agency)

Wong, Chi-Li (AEI/Atchity Editorial/Entertainment International)

Wood, Al (William Kerwin Agency)

Wood, Eleanor (Blassingame Spectrum Corp.)

Wreschner, Ruth (Ruth Wreschner, Authors' Representative)

Wright, Dan (Ann Wright Representatives)

Wright, Jason (The Wright Concept)

Wright, Marcie (The Wright Concept)

Y

Yoon, Howard (Lichtman, Trister, Singer, & Ross)

Yost, Nancy (Lowenstein Associates, Inc.)

Young, Gay (The Gay Young Agency, Inc.)

Yuen, Sue (Susan Herner Rights Agency)

Z

Zahler, Karen Gantz (Karen Gantz Zahler Literary Agency)

Zaifert, Laurie (The Gersh Agency)

Zanders, Richard (Connor Literary Agency)

Zeckendorf, Susan (Susan Zeckendorf Assoc. Inc.)

Ziemska, Elizabeth (Nicholas Ellison, Inc.)

Zuckerman, Albert (Writers House)

Listing Index

A double-dagger (‡) precedes listings new to this edition. Agencies that appeared in the *1996 Guide to Literary Agents* but are not included this year are identified by a two-letter code explaining why the agency is not listed: (**ED**)—Editorial Decision, (**NS**)—Not Accepting Submissions/Too Many Queries, (**NR**)—No (or Late) Response to Listing Request, (**OB**)—Out of Business, (**RR**)—Removed by the Agency's Request, (**UF**)—Uncertain Future.